W9-ACJ-983

THE BASIC WRITINGS OF BERTRAND RUSSELL

Russell at Routledge

The following books by Bertrand Russell are available from Routledge in paperback:

ABC Relativity
Analysis of Matter
Analysis of Mind
Authority and the Individual
Basic Writings of Bertrand Russell
Bertrand Russell's Best
Common Sense and Nuclear Warfare
Conquest of Happiness
Education and the Social Order
Fact and Fiction
Foundations of Geometry
Freedom and Organization, 1814–1914
A History of Western Philosophy
Human Knowledge[
Human Society in Ethics and Politics
Impact of Science on Society
In Praise of Idleness
An Inquiry into Meaning and Truth
Introduction to Mathematical Philosophy
Logic and Knowledge
Marriage and Morals
Mortals and Others, volume 1
Mortals and Others, volume 2
My Philosophical Development
Mysticism and Logic
On Education
Our Knowledge of the External World
An Outline of Philosophy
Philosophical Essays
The Philosophy of Leibniz
Political Ideals
Power
Principles of Mathematics
Principles of Social Reconstruction
Prospects of Industrial Civilization
Roads to Freedom
Sceptical Essays
The Scientific Outlook
Theory of Knowledge
Unpopular Essays
Why I am Not a Christian

The Basic Writings of Bertrand Russell

1903–1959

BERTRAND RUSSELL

EDITED BY

ROBERT E. EGNER

AND

LESTER E. DENONN

with a new Introduction by John G. Slater

Routledge
Taylor & Francis Group

LONDON AND NEW YORK

First published in 1961

Paperback edition first published in 1992
by Routledge
2 Park Square, Milton Park, Abingdon, Oxon, OX14 4RN

Simultaneously published in the USA and Canada
by Routledge
270 Madison Ave, New York, NY 10016

Reprinted 1999, 2001, 2003, 2006 (twice)

Routledge is an imprint of the Taylor & Francis Group, an informa business

© 1961 George Allen & Unwin Ltd
New introduction © 1992 John G. Slater

Printed in Great Britain by
TJ International Ltd, Padstow, Cornwall

All rights reserved. No part of this book may be reprinted or
reproduced or utilized in any form or by any electronic,
mechanical, or other means, now known or hereafter
invented, including photocopying and recording, or in any
information storage or retrieval system, without permission in
writing from the publishers.

British Library Cataloguing in Publication Data
A catalogue record for this book is
available from the British Library.

Library of Congress Cataloging in Publication Data
A catalog record for this book has been requested.

ISBN 10: 0–415–08301–X
ISBN 13: 978–0–415–08301-0

INTRODUCTION

The Basic Writings of Bertrand Russell was first published in 1961. Although Russell wrote a preface for it, he had no hand in selecting its contents; that daunting task fell to its editors, Robert Egner and Lester Denonn. The importance of the book lies in the picture it gives of Russell's broad and diverse interests. If any twentieth-century author is a polymath, then Russell is one. Just about the only traditional branch of philosophy he did not write on is aesthetics. In a letter to Lucy Donnelly, written on 19 October 1913, he told her that the pupil she had sent him from Bryn Mawr had turned up and wanted to study aesthetics. Unfortunately, Cambridge had no one who could help her with aesthetics. 'I feel sure learned aesthetics is rubbish,' he wrote, 'and that it ought to be a matter of literature and taste rather than science. But I don't know whether to tell her so.' Little wonder, then, that he never wrote on the subject.

Russell's wide interests developed gradually over the years. From his grandmother he acquired a love of history and an interest in politics in all of its forms. A Russell was expected to take an interest in political matters and to make his opinion known. Russell wrote on a bewildering variety of public controversies, beginning with free trade and women's suffrage and ending with the Kennedy assassination and the Vietnam war. None of these writings was philosophical, although he often used philosophical techniques to demolish an opponent's argument. In his studies at Cambridge he developed his talents in mathematics, philosophy, and economics. His first degree was in mathematics, which he capped with a year's study of philosophy. Undecided whether to pursue philosophy or economics as a career, he finally picked the former and wrote a successful Fellowship dissertation for Trinity College on non-Euclidean geometry, which made use of both of his undergraduate subjects. But he continued to read economics books, which helped him in his researches on German social democracy, the topic of his first book; after that, economics tends to fade from the picture. While a fellow at Cambridge he wondered whether he had any talent for experimental science, so he arranged to spend some time working in the Cavendish Laboratory, but he quickly discovered that he had no such talent. He did, however, keep abreast with the new physics as it developed, at least until the early 1930s. After that there is no evidence that he continued to read original articles as they came out, although right through the 1950s he continued to read books on physics. His interest in science was not confined to physics; he studied it widely enough to be comfortable generalizing about its method; he adopted a version of the scientific method as his guide to philosophizing.

One question to which he applied his scientific method concerned the nature of mind. To prepare himself to analyse mental concepts he read very widely in the psychological literature of his day, especially the writings of the behaviourists. At about the same time, he was becoming increasingly interested in the philosophy of education. This interest arose from the need to provide an education for his own children. None of the available schools seemed suitable, so he and his second wife decided to open their own school. Running a school proved a formidable task. Russell tried to give guidance to his teachers and others by writing on education; his books and articles defend what is called the progressive view of education.

His school made a heavy drain on his resources, which he had to make up by writing and lecturing for payment. During the 1920s he regularly made lecture tours of the United States, where he was paid much better than elsewhere. And he accepted nearly every offer to write for cash. For a long period, to cite one remarkable example, he wrote a short article every week for the Hearst newspapers. These little pieces usually took some catchy topic – 'Who May Use Lipstick?' or 'Do Dogs Think?' – and discussed it wittily. In a few of them there is quite serious philosophical argument, but mostly they are just fun. As the examples suggest, they range widely, and accordingly add greatly to the sweep of Russell's writings. What is really impressive about them is their erudition; Russell, it seems, never forgot a word he had read.

History, as already mentioned, was another subject for which Russell had a lifetime fascination. Very early in the century he wrote an essay, 'On History', reprinted in this book, which he opened with this ringing declaration: 'Of all the studies by which men acquire citizenship of the intellectual commonwealth, no single one is so indispensable as the study of the past.' He goes on to argue that history is important for two reasons: first, because it is true; and, second, because it enlarges the imagination and suggests feelings and courses of action that may otherwise never fall within the reader's experience. On later occasions he wrote further on the nature of history and its role in human life. *The Problem of China* (1922) was his first historical study and one fruit of the year he spent in China. In 1934 he published a political history of the hundred years preceding the outbreak of the First World War; he called it *Freedom and Organization, 1814–1914*. And later in the decade he undertook a practical history project, the editing for publication of the papers of his parents, Lord and Lady Amberley. *The Amberley Papers* was published in 1937 in two large volumes. For an understanding of his family background it is an indispensable document. During the war, when he was stranded in the United States, he wrote *A History of Western Philosophy* (1945). It is not as reliable a history as some of the more standard efforts, but it is a stimulating book to read, because Russell brings his formidable critical skills to bear on the views and arguments of his predecessors.

Russell is perhaps best known to the general public for his views on religion, a topic which engaged his attention from boyhood onward. Reading John Stuart Mill's *Autobiography* led him to lose his belief in God. Before reading Mill he thought the first-cause argument proved God's existence, but Mill wrote that his father had taught him that to say that God caused the world immediately raised the question what caused God, because if everything requires a cause then God does too. Newly bereft of religious belief, Russell went up to Cambridge where, to his surprise and delight, he found the majority shared his view. For a time, when his love for Lady Ottoline Morrell was in full bloom, he professed to share her interest in mystical religion. 'The Essence of Religion', included here, is a fruit of that period. After this detour, he returned to his usual agnosticism. In 1927 he delivered his famous lecture, 'Why I Am Not a Christian', which shocked the theologians and T. S. Eliot. It too is reprinted here. Delighted that he had touched a raw nerve, he followed it with a number of other essays critical of established religion. Most of these have been collected together, by Paul Edwards, in *Why I Am Not a Christian and Other Essays on Religion and Related Subjects* (1957). Edwards includes a valuable appendix detailing the way in which Russell was prevented in 1940 from taking up a professorship in philosophy at the College of the City of New York. Since the fight was led by high-ranking clerics, it seems more than likely that it was his anti-religious writings and not his views on premarital sexual relations in *Marriage and Morals* (1929) that stirred their ire.

It is nearly impossible to indicate all of the areas of human concern to which Russell contributed his views. But the new reader should be warned that Russell himself did not regard these popular writings as philosophical. Indeed, he did not even think that his books on political theory were philosophical. In the course of replying to his critics in *The Philosophy of Bertrand Russell* (1944), edited by Paul Arthur Schilpp, he made the point that none of these popular pieces was to be judged by philosophical standards. 'I did not write *Principles of Social Reconstruction* in my capacity as a "philosopher"; I wrote it as a human being who suffered from the state of the world, wished to find some way of improving it, and was anxious to speak in plain terms to others who had similar feelings. If I had never written technical books, this would be obvious to everybody; and if the book is to be understood, my technical activities must be forgotten.' Philosophy proper was concerned with problems of logical analysis; therefore much that was traditionally regarded as philosophical turns out, on his conception, not to be so. Even ethics, which he did write upon, was largely excluded; he did allow that some ethical sentences present certain logical problems and to that extent ethics was philosophical, but most of it was not. Happily for the reader, Russell did not refrain from writing on topics he thought unphilosophical, otherwise this book would be much thinner, and much less fun to read, than it is.

Perhaps it would be fitting if I were to conclude this introduction with a brief tribute to Lester E. Denonn (1901-1985), one of the book's editors, whose name has been associated with that of Russell for the last fifty years. Denonn was a New York attorney who specialized in tax law, but his principal love was philosophy and especially the life and work of Russell. Before taking his law degree he had studied philosophy, earning an MA degree, with a thesis on the philosophical significance of Plato's myths, from Cornell University in 1924. After I got to know him, he told me how it happened that he came to collect Russell's writings. His love of books led him to frequent the secondhand stores in New York. One day a bookdealer told him that he should use his time in bookstores more wisely and collect books, not just amass them. Denonn was taken by this remark and asked for suggestions as to what he might collect, mentioning that his resources were very limited. The dealer suggested the works of Russell, then in his prime as a writer. When Denonn indicated interest, the dealer told him that he had just acquired a scrapbook into which a previous owner had mounted a number of Russell's published articles. If Denonn were to buy it, he would have a decent start on a collection, since ephemeral items are always the most difficult to find. Denonn took the bait, bought and read the articles, and was hooked on Russell for life. From then on he never passed up the opportunity to visit secondhand bookstores. Throughout the great depression he bought books, circling a page number to indicate the price he paid for the book. Although he accumulated a mass of material by and about Russell, he was never a systematic collector. Once he had a copy of some publication, say, a paperback copy of *Why Men Fight* (the American title of *Principles of Social Reconstruction*), he would pass up copies of both the British and American first editions. He also had the disconcerting habit, typical of his generation, of throwing away dustwrappers as soon as he got a book home. In Russell's case this was especially serious, since he nearly always wrote his own dustwrapper blurbs. Despite his lack of system he did acquire many items of great scarcity, mostly ephemeral items published only in the United States. After his death his collection was purchased by McMaster University for the Bertrand Russell Archives. It is now being used by Kenneth Blackwell, the archivist, in the preparation of a bibliography of Russell's writings, to be published within the next few years.

Denonn's interest in Russell extended beyond collecting his writings. In the 1940s he met Russell for the first of several times and wrote an article reporting their conversation. His interest in Russell's writings came to the attention of Paul Arthur Schilpp, who was editing a volume on Russell for The Library of Living Philosophers; Schilpp asked Denonn to prepare the bibliography for the book. This bibliography, which was corrected and expanded in later editions, served for decades as the major source for information on Russell's output. Even in its latest version, it lists only a fraction of his writings, concentrating, as it might be expected to do in such a volume, on his philosophical writings. In 1951 Denonn published *The Wit and Wisdom of Bertrand Russell*, a collection of short excerpts from his works; and the following year he brought out another such collection, *Bertrand Russell's Dictionary of Mind, Matter and Morals*, which, as its title suggests, is organized according to concepts. These books, especially the second which had a very wide sale, served to introduce Russell to a new set of readers. So when he joined forces with Robert E. Egner to select the material for this book, he had been thoroughly over the ground to be covered and had definite ideas of what should be included. Egner, a professional philosopher, had edited another book of Russellian excerpts, *Bertrand Russell's Best*, first published in 1958. Sixteen books and eight articles are quoted in it, so he too had devoted much time to studying Russell's writings. At the time this book was prepared for publication, therefore, it would not have been possible to find two editors better prepared for their task than these two men.

John G. Slater
University of Toronto

PREFACE

by Bertrand Russell

Professor Egner and Mr Denonn deserve my very sincere gratitude for the labour and judgment with which they have selected the following items from my writings, which, in the course of a long life, have become so numerous that they must at times have induced a feeling of despair in the editors. The persistence of personal identity which is assumed by the criminal law, and also in the converse process of awarding honours, becomes to one who has reached my age almost a not readily credible paradox. There are things in the following collection which I wrote as long as fifty-seven years ago and which read to me now almost like the work of another person. On a very great many matters my views since I began to write on philosophy have undergone repeated changes. In philosophy, though not in science, there are those who make such changes a matter of reproach. This, I think, results from the tradition which assimilates philosophy with theology rather than with science. For my part, I should regard an unchanging system of philosophical doctrines as proof of intellectual stagnation. A prudent man imbued with the scientific spirit will not claim that his present beliefs are wholly true, though he may console himself with the thought that his earlier beliefs were perhaps not wholly false. Philosophical progress seems to me analogous to the gradually increasing clarity of outline of a mountain approached through mist, which is vaguely visible at first, but even at last remains in some degree indistinct. What I have never been able to accept is that the mist itself conveys valuable elements of truth. There are those who think that clarity, because it is difficult and rare, should be suspect. The rejection of this view has been the deepest impulse in all my philosophical work.

I am glad that Professor Egner and Mr Denonn have not confined themselves in their work of selection to what can be strictly called philosophy. The world in which I have lived has been a very rapidly changing world. The changes have been in part such as I could welcome, but in part such as I could only assimilate in terms borrowed from tragic drama. I could not welcome whole-heartedly any presentation of my activities as a writer which made it seem as though I had been indifferent to the very remarkable transformations which it has been my good or ill fortune to experience.

I should not wish to be thought in earnest only when I am solemn. There are many things that seem to me important to be said, but not best said in a portentous tone of voice. Indeed, it has become increasingly evident to me that portentousness is often, though not always, a device for warding off too close scrutiny. I cannot believe in 'sacred' truths. Whatever one may believe to be true, one ought to be able to convey without any apparatus of Sunday sanctification. For this reason, I am glad that the editors have included some things which might seem lacking in what is called 'high seriousness'.

In conclusion, I should wish to thank the editors once again for having brought together in one volume so just an epitome of my perhaps unduly multifarious writings.

BERTRAND RUSSELL

INTRODUCTION

Lord Russell has never particularly relished being anatomized although he readily consented to each of us attempting it by selections previously published. We have joined in this volume, again with his kind sanction, to present what we trust will be generally accepted as a useful, definitive sampling of complete essays and chapters indicative of the man and his work over more than sixty years of astounding productivity.

When we have been queried on frequent occasions as to the reason for our own continued absorbing interest in the myriads of words that have flowed from his fertile mind, we have uniformly responded that we deliberately chose his works as we know of no one comparable through whose eyes one can survey the status and progress of contemporary thought in its many variegations. It was that idea which prompted our selection from various fields, in many of which Lord Russell pioneered and advanced human thought and in all of which he spoke with distinction.

Few philosophers have had a more profound influence on the course of modern philosophy than Bertrand Russell. Perhaps no technical philosopher has been more widely read, discussed and misunderstood. This volume is an attempt to present within one cover the more definitive essays by Russell from 1903, when he wrote his celebrated essay, 'A Free Man's Worship', to 1959, when he wrote the frequently cited 'The Expanding Mental Universe'.

The essays were chosen for their contribution to thinking *at the time they were written*. As Russell himself says, 'I am in no degree ashamed of having changed my opinions. What physicist who was active in 1900 would dream of boasting that his opinions had not changed?'

There is no adequate substitute for first-hand contact with original thought; nor is there any substitute for reading the definitive works of any great thinker in their entirety. Russell anthologies and collections have appeared which show only one period in his thought. Some, for example, reveal the views he held for a limited time (*Mysticism and Logic*, 1903–1917), while others have been concerned with emphasizing his views on particular subjects (*Why I am not a Christian*, 1957). It was not our purpose to add still another to their number.

Our aim has been to present a wide portrait of the views of one of the few seminal thinkers of the twentieth century. There will no doubt be readers who would have wished that we had made different selections from Russell's works, but this problem confronts any anthologist.

The editors of any volume on a twentieth-century philosopher are faced with a peculiar dilemma. The recency of the period and the strong emotional attitudes about any major figure make it almost impossible to be objective. The historian of an earlier period need only retouch the portraits presented to him by tradition, however distorted they may be, but the anthologist of a contemporary must write under the scrutiny of living admirers and detractors. We venture to submit our selections and to let Russell and his works speak for themselves.

Before letting the reader loose upon the pages that follow, we pause to immortalize a London cabbie who drove one of us from a pleasant visit with Sir Stanley Unwin to a London hotel. It was the day the Wood biography of Russell appeared and the driver noticed a copy being admiringly thumbed.

'Is that the new Russell biography I have been reading about?'

'Yes, and I look forward to reading it.'

'So do I. Wonderful mechanism, isn't he?'

And so we invite you to the pages evidencing this wonderful mechanism.

ROBERT E. EGNER

LESTER E. DENONN

CONTENTS

PART I
Autobiographical Asides

PART II
The Nobel Prize Winning Man of Letters
(Essayist and Short Story Writer)

PART III
The Philosopher of Language

PART IV
The Logician and Philosopher of Mathematics

PART V

The Epistemologist

PART VI

The Metaphysician

PART VII

Historian of Philosophy

PART VIII

The Psychologist

PART IX

The Moral Philosopher

PART X

The Philosopher of Education

PART XI

The Philosopher of Politics

PART XII

The Philosopher in the Field of Economics

PART XIII

The Philosopher of History

PART XIV

The Philosopher of Culture: East and West

PART XV

The Philosopher of Religion

PART XVI

The Philosopher and Expositor of Science

PART XVII

The Analyst of International Affairs

EPIGRAMMATIC INSIGHTS FROM THE PEN
OF RUSSELL

His life, for all its waywardness, had a certain consistency, reminiscent of that of the aristocratic rebels of the early nineteenth century. *His Own Obituary.*

I had a letter from an Anglican bishop not long ago in which he said that *all* my opinions on *everything* were inspired by sexual lust, and that the opinions I expressed were among the causes of the Second World War. BBC Interview with John Freeman. *The Listener*, March 19, 1959.

Boredom as a factor in human behaviour has received, in my opinion, far less attention than it deserves. *The Conquest of Happiness.*

Every man would like to be God, if it were possible; some few find it difficult to admit the impossibility. *Power: A New Social Analysis.*

In spite of the fundamental importance of economic facts in determining politics and beliefs of an age or nation, I do not think that non-economic factors can be neglected without risks of error which may be fatal in practice. *The Practice and Theory of Bolshevism.*

The scepticism that I advocate amounts only to this (1) that when the experts are agreed, the opposite opinion cannot be held to be certain; (2) that when they are not agreed, no opinion can be regarded as certain by a non-expert; and (3) that when they all hold that no sufficient grounds for a positive opinion exist, the ordinary man would do well to suspend his judgment. *Sceptical Essays.*

I should make it my object to teach thinking, not orthodoxy, or even heterodoxy. And I should absolutely never sacrifice intellect to the fancied interest of morals. *On Education Especially in Early Childhood.*

I mean by wisdom a right conception of the ends of life. This is something which science in itself does not provide. Increase of science by itself, therefore, is not enough to guarantee any genuine progress, though it provides one of the ingredients which progress requires. *The Scientific Outlook.*

Rational apprehension of dangers is necessary; fear is not. *On Education Especially in Early Childhood.*

The main things which seem to me important on their own account, and not merely as means to other things, are knowledge, art, instinctive happiness, and relations of friendship or affection. *The Problem of China.*

Instinct, mind and spirit are all essential to a full life; each has its own excellence and its own corruption. *The Analysis of Mind.*

We have, in fact, two kinds of morality side by side: one which we preach but do not practise, and another which we practise but seldom preach. *Sceptical Essays.*

No nation was ever so virtuous as each believes itself, and none was ever so wicked as each believes the other. *Justice in War-Time.*

But if human conceit was staggered for a moment by its kinship with the ape, it soon found a way to reassert itself and that way is the 'philosophy' of evolution. A process which led from the amoeba to man appeared to the philosophers to be obviously a progress—though whether the amoeba would agree with this opinion is not known. *Our Knowledge of the External World.*

Philosophy should be piecemeal and provisional like science; final truth belongs to heaven, not to this world. *An Outline of Philosophy.*

The opinions that are held with passion are always those for which no good ground exists; indeed the passion is the measure of the holder's lack of rational conviction. *Sceptical Essays.*

To save the world requires faith and courage: faith in reason, and courage to proclaim what reason shows to be true. *The Prospects of Industrial Civilization.*

If it is the devil that tempts the young to enjoy themselves, is it not the same personage that persuades the old to condemn their enjoyment? And is not condemnation perhaps merely a form of excitement appropriate to old age? (Nobel Prize Acceptance Speech) *Human Society in Ethics and Politics.*

There is something feeble and a little contemptible about a man who cannot face the perils of life without the help of comfortable myths. *Human Society in Ethics and Politics.*

There are infinite possibilities of error, and more cranks take up unfashionable errors than unfashionable truths. *Unpopular Essays.*

. . . the Crotonians burnt the Pythagorean school. But burning schools, or men for that matter, has always proved singularly unhelpful in stamping out unorthodoxy. *Wisdom of the West.*

CHRONOLOGICAL LIST OF RUSSELL'S PRINCIPAL WORKS

1896 German Social Democracy. (A chapter by Alys Russell.)

1897 An Essay on the Foundations of Geometry.

1900 A Critical Exposition of the Philosophy of Leibniz.

1903 The Principles of Mathematics.

1910 Principia Mathematica—Vol. I. (With A. N. Whitehead.)

1910 Philosophical Essays.

1912 Principia Mathematica—Vol. II. (With A. N. Whitehead.)

1912 The Problems of Philosophy.

1913 Principia Mathematica—Vol. III. (With A. N. Whitehead.)

1914 Our Knowledge of the External World as a Field for Scientific Method in Philosophy.

1914 Scientific Method in Philosophy.

1914 The Philosophy of Bergson. (Controversy with H. W. Carr.)

1915 War, the Offspring of Fear.

1916 Principles of Social Reconstruction. (Why Men Fight: A Method of Abolishing the International Duel.)

1916 Policy of the Entente, 1904–1914. (Part of: Justice in War-Time.)

1916 Justice in War-Time.

1917 Political Ideals.

1918 Mysticism and Logic and Other Essays.

1918 Roads to Freedom: Socialism, Anarchism and Syndicalism. (Proposed Roads to Freedom: Socialism, Anarchism and Syndicalism.)

1919 An Introduction to Mathematical Philosophy.

1920 The Practice and Theory of Bolshevism. (Bolshevism in Theory and Practice.)

1921 The Analysis of Mind.

1922 The Problem of China.

1922 Free Thought and Official Propaganda.

1923 The Prospects of Industrial Civilization. (With Dora Russell.)

1923 The ABC of Atoms.

1924 Bolshevism and the West. (Debate with Scott Nearing.)

1924 Icarus or the Future of Science.

1924 How to be Free and Happy.

1924 Logical Atomism.

1925 The ABC of Relativity.

1925 What I Believe.

1926 On Education Especially in Early Childhood. (Education and the Good Life.)

1927 Why I am not a Christian.

1927 The Analysis of Matter.

1927 An Outline of Philosophy. (Philosophy.)

1928 Sceptical Essays.

1929 Marriage and Morals.

1930 The Conquest of Happiness.

1930 Has Religion Made Useful Contributions to Civilization?

1931 The Scientific Outlook.

1932 Education and the Social Order. (Education and the Modern World.)

1934 Freedom and Organization 1814–1914. (Freedom versus Organization 1814–1914.)

1935 In Praise of Idleness and Other Essays.

1935 Religion and Science.

1936 Which Way to Peace?

1936 Determinism and Physics.

1937 The Amberley Papers. The Letters and Diaries of Bertrand Russell's Parents. (With Patricia Russell.)

1938 Power: A New Social Analysis.

1940 An Inquiry into Meaning and Truth.

1945 A History of Western Philosophy.

1948 Human Knowledge: Its Scope and Limits.

1949 Authority and the Individual.

1950 Unpopular Essays.

CHRONOLOGY OF THE LIFE OF
BERTRAND RUSSELL

1872 MAY 18. Born at Ravenscroft near Trelleck, Monmouthshire, England.

1874 Death of Lady Amberley, mother of Bertrand Russell.

1876 JANUARY. Death of Lord Amberley, father of Bertrand Russell, followed by litigation over the will of his father. The designation of freethinkers as guardians disaffirmed. His grandmother, Lady Russell and Rollo Russell designated as his guardians. At Pembroke Lodge.

1883 First lessons in Euclid from his brother, Frank. Studied under private tutors.

1883 Began his philosophical speculations, particularly on religious problems. Penned his thoughts surreptitiously in a journal.

1890 Entered Trinity College, Cambridge.

1894 Took Moral Science Tripos. Fellowship dissertation on The Foundations of Geometry. Honorary British Attaché in Paris. Marriage to Alys Smith.

1895 Visit to Germany. Study at the University of Berlin. Lectured to the London School of Economics and Political Science on German Social Democracy. Elected Fellow of Trinity College.

1896 Visit to America with Alys Russell. Lectured at Johns Hopkins and Bryn Mawr.

1898 Lectured at Cambridge on Leibniz. With G. E. Moore in rebellion against Kant and Hegel.

1900 Attended the International Congress of Philosophy in Paris.

1905 First success with the Theory of Descriptions.

1907 Stood unsuccessfully for Parliament.

1908 Made a Fellow of the Royal Society.

1910 Entire decade devoted to collaboration with A. N. Whitehead on *Principia Mathematica*. First volume published this year. Failed of nomination for Parliament by the Liberal Party because of agnostic views. Lecturer in Mathematical Logic at Trinity College, Cambridge.

1911 President of The Aristotelian Society. Separation from Alys Russell.

1913 Lecture at École des Hautes Sociales on The Philosophical Importance of Mathematical Logic. Addressed the Heretics at Trinity College on The Philosophy of Bergson.

1914 Gave the Herbert Spencer Lecture in Philosophy at Oxford on Scientific Method in Philosophy. Lectured on Our Knowledge of the External World as Lowell Lecturer in Boston. Public speaker and pamphleteer against World War I.

1915 Address to the Philosophical Society of Manchester on The Ultimate Constituents of Matter.

1916 Fined £100 in the Everett Case because of a pamphlet criticizing a two-year sentence of a conscientious objector. His library sold when the fine was not paid. Bought by his friends. Loss of his lectureship at Trinity College.

1918 Gave a course of eight lectures in London describing his Logical Atomism in which he acknowledges the influence of Wittgenstein over the past four years. Sentenced to six months in Brixton Prison because of an article in which he quoted the report of a Congressional investigation into the use of American troops against strikers. Second Division sentence changed to First Division. Wrote *Introduction to Mathematical Philosophy* while in prison.

1920 Visit to Russia.

1921 Divorce from Alys Russell. Marriage to Dora Black. Visit to China and Japan. Lectured on The Analysis of Mind in London and Pekin. Birth of John, Lord Amberley.

1922 Labour Candidate for Parliament. Gave the Moncure D. Conway Memorial Lecture on Free Thought and Official Propaganda.

1923 Labour Candidate for Parliament. Birth of Kate.

1924 Lecture tour in the United States. Debate with Scott Nearing before the League for Public Discussion on Bolshevism and the West. Lecture to the Free Youth at Cooper Union, New York, on How to be Free and Happy.

1925 Tarner Lectures at Trinity College on The Analysis of Matter.

1927 Lecture tour in the United States. Started a school at Beacon Hill near Petersfield. Became headmaster with Dora Russell as headmistress. Lecture at Battersea Town Hall before the South London Branch of the National Secular Society on Why I am not a Christian.

1929 Lecture tour in the United States. Talk to the Contemporary Thought Class at Northwestern University, Evanston, Illinois, on Three Ways to the World.

1930 Debate with John Cowper Powys in New York on Is Modern Marriage a Failure?

1931 Lecture tour in the United States. Debate with Sherwood Anderson on Shall the Home be Abolished? Became Third Earl Russell on the death of his brother, Frank.

1935 Divorce from Dora Russell. Withdraws from the school.

1936 Gave the Earl Grey Memorial Lecture at Armstrong College, Newcastle upon Tyne, on Determinism and Physics. Marriage to Helen Patricia Spence.

1937 Birth of Conrad.

1938 Lectures at Oxford on Language and Fact. To the United States where he remained until 1944. Radio Discussion with T. V. Smith and Paul Douglas on Taming Economic Power. Visiting Professor at The University of Chicago until 1939.

1939 Radio Discussion on University of Chicago Round Table on Is Security Increasing? Addressed the Sociology Club of The University of Chicago on The Role of the Intellectual in the Modern World. Lectures at The University of California in Los Angeles until 1940.

1940 The William James Lectures at Harvard on An Inquiry into Meaning and Truth. The Bertrand Russell Case involving the loss of his appointment to the College of the City of New York.

1941 Lecturer at The Barnes Foundation in Merion, Pennsylvania, on The History of Philosophy. Spoke over CBS on the Invitation to Learning programme with Huntington Cairns, Allan Tate and Mark Van Doren on Hegel's Philosophy of History. Radio talk over Station WEAF with Rex Stout, entitled Speaking of Liberty.

1942 Spoke over CBS on the Invitation to Learning programme with Jacques Barzun on Descartes's *Discourse on Method* and with Scott Buchanan and Mark Van Doren on Spinoza's *Ethics*. Later with Katherine Ann Porter on Carroll's *Alice in Wonderland*. Spoke on The American Forum of the Air on What About India?

1943 Termination of the Barnes contract. Successful suit for breach of five-year contract.

1944 Speaks at the Rand School, New York, over Station WEVD on Co-operate with Russia. Returns to England. Elected to Fellowship at Trinity College, Cambridge, for a second time. The topic of his annual course: Non-Demonstrative Inference.

1947 Addressed the National Book League at Friends House on Philosophy and Politics.

1948 Accident on flight to Norway en route to Trondheim where he was to lecture on The Prevention of War. Saved himself by swimming in a heavy overcoat for ten minutes. Gave the first Reith Lectures over BBC on Authority and the Individual.

1949 Awarded the Order of Merit. Addressed the Westminster School on Atomic Energy and the Problems of Europe.

1950 Awarded the Nobel Prize for Literature 'in recognition of his many-sided and important work in which he has constantly stood forth as a champion of humanity and freedom of thought'. Visit to Australia.

1951 Gave the Matchette Foundation Lectures at Columbia University in New York on The Impact of Science on Society. Contributed to the BBC Third Programme talks on The Political and Cultural Influence (of America), The Nature and Origin of Scientific Method and Scepticism and Tolerance. Death of Alys Russell.

1952 Divorce from Patricia Russell. Marriage to Edith Finch.

1955 Awarded the Silver Pears Trophy for work on behalf of World Peace.

ACKNOWLEDGEMENTS

We, the editors, are especially grateful to Lord Russell for his kindness and help as this project grew. Editors of anthologies from the works of eminent thinkers are not often so fortunate as to have their work approved by the man himself.

We are also grateful to the following for their generous help and valuable assistance: Karen Bents, Sarah Merrill, Lonna Johnson and Morton White; our wives for their indulgence, encouragement and keen editorial appraisal; and the staffs of our publishers for their full co-operation.

We add one rather unusual acknowledgement. We bow to each other at a distance of almost two thousand miles. Our most enjoyable collaboration in an equal distribution of labour has been done entirely by correspondence by two editors who have never met. All has been jointly done so that we jointly face and share the charge of errors of omission and commission which is usually the reward of any anthologist.

We thank the following publishers and journals for permission to include the selections that have been reprinted in this work:

Messrs George Allen & Unwin Ltd.
Messrs Appleton-Century-Crofts, Inc.
Messrs Albert & Charles Boni Inc.
Cambridge University Press
Columbia University Press
Dover Publications, Inc.
Messrs E. P. Dutton & Co., Inc.
Haldeman-Julius Publications
Harper's Magazine
Messrs William Heinemann & Co., Ltd.
The Hibbert Journal
Messrs Henry Holt & Company
The Humanities Press
The Independent Review
Messrs Alfred A. Knopf, Inc.

Messrs John Lane The Bodley Head
The Library of Living Philosophers
Look Magazine
Liveright Publishing Corporation
Messrs Lund Humphries, Ltd.
Messrs MacGibbon & Kee, Ltd.
The Macmillan Company
The New Statesman
New York Times Magazine
Messrs W. W. Norton & Co., Inc.
Oxford University Press
Messrs Routledge & Kegan Paul, Ltd.
St Louis Post Dispatch
Messrs Simon & Schuster, Inc.
Messrs C. A. Watts & Co., Ltd.

Full details of the source from which each selection has been made are given at the end of each item.

ROBERT E. EGNER
LESTER E. DENONN

SOME THOUGHTS ABOUT
BERTRAND RUSSELL

I owe innumerable happy hours to the reading of Russell's works, something which I cannot say of any other contemporary scientific writer, with the exception of Thorstein Veblen. ALBERT EINSTEIN in *The Philosophy of Bertrand Russell—*The Library of Living Philosophers.

He constitutes a fortunate example showing that a philosopher may owe his success to clarity and cogency, to painstaking analysis and the renunciation of the mysterious language of oracles. HANS REICHENBACH, *ibid.*

The flourishing condition of present-day 'semiotic' is a sufficient testimony to the fertility of Russell's ideas. MAX BLACK, *ibid.*

Leibniz acquired his title to nobility by flattering powerful princes and church officials and by defending their feudal privileges; whereas Russell, though born an aristocrat, has always defended the democratic tradition and courageously opposed political and church authoritarianism at the cost of the very type of worldly success which was so dear to Leibniz. PHILIP P. WIENER, *ibid.*

Russell has not said the last word on these matters [philosophy of science]; but he has certainly inspired a great multitude of students to try to say a better one. If the example of his own splendid devotion to independent thinking counts for anything, it is safe to believe that he would not prefer to have a different estimate placed upon his efforts. ERNEST NAGEL, *ibid.*

Bertrand Russell's philosophical writings are delightful reading. Whatever may be Russell's place in philosophy, his literary writings certainly deserve a place in any anthology of English prose. By this statement I do not mean to belittle Russell's contribution to philosophy. No contemporary writer has done more to stimulate interest in philosophy than Russell and we are all indebted to him. His contribution to logic, perhaps, overshadows his contributions to other branches of philosophy because of its massiveness. But he has enriched brilliantly and suggestively every branch of philosophy. JOHN ELOF BOODIN, *ibid.*

I believe there is little of importance in present-day philosophizing which is not derived from him. The post-Russellians are all propter-Russellians. ALAN WOOD in *Russell's Philosophy: A Study of Its Development.*

His writings combine profundity with wit, trenchant thinking with literary excellence, honesty and clarity with kindliness and wisdom. JAMES R. NEWMAN in *The World of Mathematics*—George Allen & Unwin, London. Simon and Schuster, New York.

Russell is without question one of the most productive and most brilliant thinkers of our age, mathematical logician, philosopher, journalist and libertarian, in some ways reminiscent of his early idol, Mill, and in others of Voltaire because of his brilliance, his scope, and his iconoclasm. MORTON WHITE in *The Age of Analysis: Twentieth Century Philosophers*—Houghton Mifflin Co.

But by far the most devastating use of the sceptical weapon has come in our own time from Bertrand Russell, who turns the Cartesian doubt against the Cartesian ego itself. LESLIE PAUL in *The English Philosophers*—London, Faber & Faber.

For while Russell is often in error on positions he assumes, and while he has engaged in stormy and obdurate controversies with the passion of a political rebel, he has managed always to remind men of those traditions of civility and justice that distinguish the liberal spirit in Western civilization from the times of Pericles to our own day. ADRIENNE KOCH in *Philosophy for a Time of Crisis: An Interpretation with Key Writings by Fifteen Great Modern Thinkers*—New York, E. P. Dutton & Co., Inc., 1959.

> O science metaphysical,
> And very, very quizzical,
> You only make this maze of life the mazier;
> For boasting to illuminate
> Such riddles as Will and Fate
> You muddle them to hazier and hazier.
>
> The cause of every action
> You expound with satisfaction.
> Through the mind in all its corners and recesses
> You say that you have travelled
> And every thread unravelled
> And axioms you call your learned guesses.
>
> Right and wrong you've so dissected
> And their fragments so connected,
> That which we follow doesn't seem to matter,
> But the cobwebs you have wrought,
> And the silly flies they have caught
> It needs no broom miraculous to shatter.
>
> You know no more than I
> What is laughter, tear or sigh,
> Or love, or hate, or anger or compassion;
> Metaphysics then adieu,
> Without you, I can do
> And I think you'll very soon be out of fashion.

Written in 1897 by Lady Russell, grandmother and guardian of Bertrand Russell, as quoted in Earl Russell's (Bertrand Russell's elder brother, Frank) *My Life and Adventure*—London, Cassell & Co., Ltd., 1923.

PART I

Autobiographical Asides

The clarity and succinctness one expects from the works of Russell are well illustrated by his own reference to his attempt to advance the demonstrative methods of mathematics and science into regions conventionally assigned to vague speculation. As Russell says by way of characteristic autobiographical aside: 'I like precision. I like sharp outlines. I hate misty vagueness.'

He reveals that even at the age of eleven he refused to accept what tradition had made appear as indestructible as granite. His brother consented to teach him geometry which, Russell had heard, 'proved things'. When his brother told him that Euclidian axioms *cannot be proved*, his hopes to find some certain knowledge all but vanished.

The selections that follow whet the appetite for the complete autobiography, the publication of which Russell has understandably deferred.

1

MY RELIGIOUS REMINISCENCES

M Y parents, Lord and Lady Amberley, were considered shocking in their day on account of their advanced opinions in politics, theology, and morals. When my mother died in 1874 she was buried without any religious ceremony in the grounds of their house in the Wye Valley. My father intended to be buried there also, but when he died in 1876 his wishes were disregarded, and both were removed to the family vault at Chenies. By my father's will my brother and I were to have been in the guardianship of two friends of his who shared his opinions, but the will was set aside and we were placed by the Court of Chancery in the care of my grandparents. My grandfather, the statesman, died in 1878, and it was his widow who decided the manner of my education. She was a Scotch Presbyterian, who gradually became a Unitarian. I was taken on alternate Sundays to the Parish Church and to the Presbyterian Church, while at home I was taught the tenets of Unitarianism. Eternal punishment and the literal truth of the Bible were not inculcated, and there was no Sabbatarianism beyond a suggestion of avoiding cards on Sunday for fear of shocking the servants. But in other respects morals were austere, and it was held to be certain that conscience, which is the voice of God, is an infallible guide in all practical perplexities.

My childhood was solitary, as my brother was seven years older than I was, and I was not sent to school. Consequently I had abundant leisure for reflection, and when I was about fourteen my thoughts turned to theology. During the four following years I rejected, successively, free will, immortality, and belief in God, and believed that I suffered much pain in the process, though when it was completed I found myself far happier than I had been while I remained in doubt. I think, in retrospect, that loneliness had much more to do with my unhappiness than theological difficulties, for throughout the whole time I never said a word about religion to anyone, with the brief exception of an Agnostic tutor, who was soon sent away, presumably because he did not discourage my unorthodoxy.

What kept me silent was mainly the fear of ridicule. At the age of fourteen I became convinced that the fundamental principle of ethics should be the promotion of human happiness, and at first this appeared to me so self-evident that I supposed it must be the universal opinion. Then I discovered, to my surprise, that it was a view regarded as unorthodox, and called Utilitarianism. I announced, no doubt with a certain pleasure in the long word, that I was a Utilitarian; but the announcement was received with derision. My grandmother for a long time missed no opportunity of ironically submitting ethical conundrums to me, and challenging me to solve them on Utilitarian principles. To my surprise I discovered, in preparing the Amberley Papers, that she had subjected an uncle of mine, in his youth, to the same treatment on the same topic. The result in my case was a determination to keep my thoughts to myself; no doubt in his it was similar. Ridicule, nominally amusing but really an expression of hostility, was the favourite weapon—the worst possible, short of actual cruelty, in dealing with young people. When I became interested in philosophy—a subject which, for some reason, was anathema—I was told that the whole subject could be summed up in the saying: 'What is mind?—No matter. What is matter?—Never mind.' At the fifteenth or sixteenth repetition of this remark it ceased to be amusing.

Nevertheless on most topics the atmosphere was liberal. For instance, Darwinism was accepted as a matter of course. I had at one time, when I was thirteen, a very orthodox Swiss tutor, who, in consequence of something I had said, stated with great earnestness: 'If you are a Darwinian I pity you, for one cannot be a Darwinian and a Christian at the same time.' I did not then believe in the incompatibility, but I was already clear that, if I had to choose, I would choose Darwin.

Until I went to Cambridge I was almost wholly unaware of contemporary movements of thought. I was influenced by Darwin, and then by John Stuart Mill, but more than either by the study of dynamics; my outlook, in fact, was more appropriate to a seventeenth- or eighteenth-century Cartesian than to a post-Darwinian. It seemed to me that all the motions of matter were determined by physical laws, and that in all likelihood this was true of the human body as well as of other matter. Being passionately interested in religion and unable to speak about it, I wrote down my thoughts in Greek letters in a book which I headed 'Greek Exercises', in which, to make concealment more complete, I adopted an original system of phonetic spelling. In this book, when I was fifteen, I wrote: 'Taking free will first to consider, there is no clear dividing line between man and the protozoon. Therefore, if we give free will to man we must give it also to the protozoon. This is rather hard to do. Therefore, unless we are willing to give free will to the protozoon we must not give it to man. This, however, is possible, but it is difficult to imagine. If, as seems to me probable, protoplasm only came together in the ordinary course of nature without any special Providence from God, then we and all animals are simply kept going by chemical forces and are nothing more wonderful than a tree (which no one pretends has free will), and if we had a good enough knowledge of the forces acting on any one at any time, the motives pro and con, the constitution of his brain at any time, then we could tell exactly what he would do.'

Until the age of eighteen I continued to believe in a Deist's God, because the First-Cause argument seemed to me irrefutable. Then in John Stuart Mill's *Autobiography* I found that James Mill had taught him the refutation of that argument—namely, that it gives no answer to the question 'Who made God?' It is curious that Mill should have had so much influence on me, for he was my father's and mother's close friend and the source of many of their opinions, but I did not know this until a much later date. Without being aware that I was following in my father's footsteps, I read, before I went to Cambridge, Mill's *Logic* and *Political Economy*, and made elaborate notes in which I practised the art of expressing the gist of each paragraph in a single sentence. I was already interested in the principles of mathematics, and was profoundly dissatisfied with his assimilation of pure mathematics to empirical science— a view which is now universally abandoned.

Throughout adolescence I read widely, but as I depended mainly on my grandfather's library few of the books I read belonged to my own time. They were a curious collection. I remember, as having been important to me, Milman's *History of Christianity*, Gibbon, Comte, Dante, Machiavelli, Swift, and Carlyle; but above all Shelley—whom, however, though born in the same month as my grandfather, I did not find on his shelves.

It was only at Cambridge that I became aware of the modern world— I mean the world that was modern in the early 'nineties: Ibsen and Shaw, Flaubert and Pater, Walt Whitman, Nietzsche, etc. But I do not think any of these men had much influence on me, with the possible exception of Ibsen. The men who changed my opinions at that time were two: first McTaggart in one direction, and then, after I had become a Fellow, G. E. Moore in the opposite direction. McTaggart made me a Hegelian, and Moore caused me to revert to the opinions I had had before I went to Cambridge. Most of what I learnt at Cambridge had to be painfully unlearnt later; on the whole, what I had learnt for myself from being left alone in an old library had proved more solid.

The influence of German idealism in England has never gone much beyond the universities, but in them, when I was young, it was almost completely dominant. Green and Caird converted Oxford, and Bradley and Bosanquet—the leading British philosophers in the 'nineties—were more in agreement with Hegel than with anyone else, though, for some reason unknown to me, they hardly ever mentioned him. In Cambridge Henry Sidgwick still represented the Benthamite tradition, and James

Ward was a Kantian; but the younger men—Stout, Mackenzie, and McTaggart—were, in varying degrees, Hegelians.

Very different attitudes towards Christian dogma were compatible with acceptance of Hegel. In his philosophy nothing is held to be quite true, and nothing quite false; what can be uttered has only a limited truth, and, since men must talk, we cannot blame them for not speaking the whole truth and nothing but the truth. The best we can do, according to Bradley, is to say things that are 'not intellectually corrigible'—further progress is only possible through a synthesis of thought and feeling, which, when achieved, will lead to our saying nothing. Ideas have degrees of truth, greater or less according to the stage at which they come in the dialectic. God has a good deal of truth, since He comes rather late in the dialectic; but He has not complete truth, since He is swallowed up in the Absolute Idea. The right wing among Hegelians emphasized the truth in the concept of God, the left wing the falsehood, and each wing was true to the Master. A German Hegelian, if he was taking orders, remembered how much truer the concept of God is than, e.g. that of gods; if he was becoming a civil servant, he remembered the even greater truth of the Absolute Idea, whose earthly copy was the Prussian State.

In England teachers of philosophy who were Hegelians almost all belonged to the left wing. 'Religion', says Bradley, 'is practical, and therefore still is dominated by the idea of the Good; and in the essence of this idea is contained an unsolved contradiction. Religion is still forced to maintain unreduced aspects, which, as such, cannot be united; and it exists, in short, by a kind of perpetual oscillation and compromise.' Neither Bradley nor Bosanquet believed in personal immortality. Mackenzie, while I was reading philosophy, stated in a paper which I heard that 'a personal God is, in a sense, a contradiction in terms': he was subsequently one of my examiners. The attitude of these men to religion was thus not one of which the orthodox could approve, but it was by no means one of hostility: they held religion to be an essential ingredient in the truth, and defective only when taken as the whole truth. The sort of view that I had previously held, 'either there is a God or there is not, and probably the latter', seemed to them very crude; the correct opinion, they would say, was that from one point of view there is a God and from another there is not, but from the highest point of view there neither is nor is not. Being myself naturally 'crude', I never succeeded in reaching this pitch of mellowness.

McTaggart, who dominated the philosophical outlook of my generation at Cambridge, was peculiar among Hegelians in various ways. He was more faithful than the others to the dialectic method, and would defend even its details. Unlike some of the school, he was definite in asserting certain things and denying others; he called himself an Atheist, but firmly believed in personal immortality, of which he was convinced that he possessed a logical demonstration. He was four years senior to me, and in my first term was President of the Union. He and I were both so shy that when, about a fortnight after I came up, he called on me, he had not the courage to come in and I had not the courage to ask him in, so that he remained in the doorway about five minutes. Soon, however, the conversation got on to philosophy, and his shyness ceased. I found that all I had thought about ethics and logic and metaphysics was considered to be refuted by an abstruse technique that completely baffled me; and by this same technique it was to be proved that I should live for ever. I found that the old thought this nonsense, but the young thought it good sense, so I determined to study it sympathetically, and for a time I more or less believed it. So, for a short time, did G. E. Moore. But he found the Hegelian philosophy inapplicable to chairs and tables, and I found it inapplicable to mathematics; so with his help I climbed out of it, and back to common sense tempered by mathematical logic.

The intellectual temper of the 'nineties was very different from that of my father's youth: in some ways better, but in many ways worse. There was no longer, among the abler young men, any preoccupation with the details of the Christian faith; they were almost all Agnostics, and not interested in discussions as to the divinity of Christ, or in the details of Biblical criticism. I remember a feeling of contempt when I learned that Henry Sidgwick as a young man, being desirous of knowing whether God exists, thought it necessary, as a first step, to learn Semitic languages, which seemed to me to show an insufficient sense of logical relevance. But I was willing, as were most of my friends, to listen to a metaphysical argument for or against God or immortality or free will; and it was only after acquiring a new logic that I ceased to think such arguments worth examining.

The non-academic heroes of the 'nineties—Ibsen, Strindberg, Nietzsche, and (for a time) Oscar Wilde—differed very greatly from those of the previous generation. The great men of the 'sixties were all 'good' men: they were patient, painstaking, in favour of change only when a detailed and careful investigation had persuaded them that it was necessary in some particular respect. They advocated reforms, and in general their advocacy was successful, so that the world improved very fast; but their temper was not that of rebels. I do not mean that no great rebels existed; Marx and Dostoievsky, to mention only two, did most of their best work in the 'sixties. But these men were almost unknown among cultured people in their own day, and their influence belongs to a much later date. The men who commanded respect in England in the 'sixties—Darwin, Huxley, Newman, the authors of *Essays and Reviews*, etc.—were not fundamentally at war with society; they could meet, as they did in the 'Metaphysical Society', to discuss urbanely whether there is a God. At the end they divided; and Sir Mountstuart Grant Duff, on being asked afterwards whether there is a God, replied: 'Yes, we had a very good majority.' In those days democracy ruled even over Heaven.

But in the 'nineties young men desired something more sweeping and passionate, more bold and less bland. The impulse towards destruction and violence which has swept over the world began in the sphere of literature. Ibsen, Strindberg, and Nietzsche were angry men—not primarily angry about this or that, but just angry. And so they each found an outlook on life that justified anger. The young admired their passion, and found in it an outlet for their own feelings of revolt against parental authority. The assertion of freedom seemed sufficiently noble to justify violence; the violence duly ensued, but freedom was lost in the process.

(*The Rationalist Annual*, 1938, published by C. A. Watts & Co., Ltd.)

2

MY MENTAL DEVELOPMENT

M Y mother having died when I was two years old, and my father when I was three, I was brought up in the house of my grandfather, Lord John Russell, afterwards Earl Russell. Of my parents, Lord and Lady Amberley, I was told almost nothing—so little that I vaguely sensed a dark mystery. It was not until I was twenty-one that I came to know the main outlines of my parents' lives and opinions. I then found, with a sense of bewilderment, that I had gone through almost exactly the same mental and emotional development as my father had.

It was expected of my father that he should take to a political career, which was traditional in the Russell family. He was willing, and was for a short time in Parliament (1867–68); but he had not the temperament or the opinions that would have made political success possible. At the age of twenty-one he decided that he was not a Christian, and refused to go to church on Christmas Day. He became a disciple, and afterwards a friend, of John Stuart Mill, who, as I discovered some years ago, was (so far as is possible in a non-religious sense) my godfather. My parents accepted Mill's opinions, not only such as were comparatively popular, but also those that still shocked public sentiment, such as women's suffrage and birth control. During the general election of 1868, at which my father was a candidate, it was discovered that, at a private meeting of a small society, he had said that birth control was a matter for the medical profession to consider. This let loose a campaign of vilification and slander. A Catholic bishop declared that he advocated infanticide; he was called in print a 'filthy foul-mouthed rake'; on election day, cartoons were exhibited accusing him of immorality, altering his name to 'Vice-count Amberley', and accusing him of advocating 'The French and American system'.[1] By these means he was defeated. The student of comparative sociology may be interested in the similarities between rural England in 1868 and urban New York in 1940. The available documents are collected in *The Amberley Papers*, by my wife and myself. As the

[1] My parents, when in America, had studied such experiments as the Oneida community. They were therefore accused of attempting to corrupt the purity of English family life by introducing un-English transatlantic vices.

reader of this book will see, my father was shy, studious, and ultra-conscientious—perhaps a prig, but the very opposite of a rake.

My father did not give up hope of returning to politics, but never obtained another constituency, and devoted himself to writing a big book, *Analysis of Religious Belief*, which was published after his death. He could not, in any case, have succeeded in politics, because of his very exceptional intellectual integrity; he was always willing to admit the weak points on his own side and the strong points on that of his opponents. Moreover his health was always bad, and he suffered from a consequent lack of physical vigour.

My mother shared my father's opinions, and shocked the 'sixties by addressing meetings in favour of equality for women. She refused to use the phrase 'women's rights', because, as a good Utilitarian, she rejected the doctrine of natural rights.

My father wished my brother and me to be brought up as free-thinkers, and appointed two free-thinkers as our guardians. The Court of Chancery, however, at the request of my grandparents, set aside the will, and I enjoyed the benefits of a Christian upbringing.

In 1876, when after my father's death I was brought to the house of my grandparents, my grandfather was eighty-three and had become very feeble. I remember him sometimes being wheeled about out-of-doors in a bath-chair, sometimes in his room reading Hansard (the official report of debates in Parliament). He was invariably kind to me, and seemed never to object to childish noise. But he was too old to influence me directly. He died in 1878, and my knowledge of him came through his widow, my grandmother, who revered his memory. She was a more powerful influence upon my general outlook than anyone else, although, from adolescence onward, I disagreed with very many of her opinions.

My grandmother was a Scotch Presbyterian, of the border family of the Elliots. Her maternal grandfather suffered obloquy for declaring, on the basis of the thickness of the lava on the slopes of Etna, that the world must have been created before 4004 B.C. One of her great-grandfathers was Robertson, the historian of Charles V.

She was a Puritan, with the moral rigidity of the Covenanters, despising comfort, indifferent to food, hating wine, and regarding tobacco as sinful. Although she had lived her whole life in the great world until my grandfather's retirement in 1866, she was completely unworldly. She had that indifference to money which is only possible to those who have always had enough of it. She wished her children and grandchildren to live useful and virtuous lives, but had no desire that they should achieve what others would regard as success, or that they should marry 'well'. She had the Protestant belief in private judgement and the supremacy of the individual conscience. On my twelfth birthday she gave me a Bible (which I still possess), and wrote her favourite texts on the fly-leaf. One of them was

'Thou shalt not follow a multitude to do evil'; another, 'Be strong, and of a good courage; be not afraid, neither be thou dismayed; for the Lord thy God is with thee whithersoever thou goest'. These texts have profoundly influenced my life, and still seemed to retain some meaning after I had ceased to believe in God.

At the age of seventy, my grandmother became a Unitarian; at the same time, she supported Home Rule for Ireland, and made friends with Irish Members of Parliament, who were being publicly accused of complicity in murder. This shocked people more than now seems imaginable. She was passionately opposed to imperialism, and taught me to think ill of the Afghan and Zulu wars, which occurred when I was about seven. Concerning the occupation of Egypt, however, she said little, as it was due to Mr Gladstone, whom she admired. I remember an argument I had with my German governess, who said that the English, having once gone into Egypt, would never come out, whatever they might promise, whereas I maintained, with much patriotic passion, that the English never broke promises. That was sixty years ago, and they are there still.

My grandfather, seen through the eyes of his widow, made it seem imperative and natural to do something important for the good of mankind. I was told of his introducing the Reform Bill in 1832. Shortly before he died, a delegation of eminent Nonconformists assembled to cheer him and I was told that fifty years earlier he had been one of the leaders in removing their political disabilities. In his sitting-room there was a statue from Italy, presented to my grandfather by the Italian Government, with an inscription: 'A Lord John Russell, L'Italia Riconoscente'; I naturally wished to know what this meant, and learnt, in consequence, the whole saga of Garibaldi and Italian unity. Such things stimulated my ambition to live to some purpose.

My grandfather's library, which became my schoolroom, stimulated me in a different way. There were books of history, some of them very old; I remember in particular a sixteenth-century Guicciardini. There were three huge folio volumes called *L'Art de vérifier les dates*. They were too heavy for me to move, and I speculated as to their contents; I imagined something like the tables for finding Easter in the Prayer Book. At last I became old enough to lift one of the volumes out of the shelf, and I found, to my disgust, that the only 'art' involved was that of looking up the date in the book. Then there were *The Annals of Ireland* by the Four Masters, in which I read about the men who went to Ireland before the Flood and were drowned in it; I wondered how the Four Masters knew about them, and read no further. There were also more ordinary books, such as Machiavelli and Gibbon and Swift, and a book in four volumes that I never opened: *The Works of Andrew Marvell Esq. M.P.* It was not till I grew up that I discovered Marvell was a poet rather than a politician. I was not supposed to read any of these books; otherwise I should probably not have read any of them. The net result of them was to stimulate my interest in history. No doubt my interest was increased by the fact that my family had been prominent in English history since the early sixteenth century. I was taught English history as the record of a struggle against the King for constitutional liberty. William Lord Russell, who was executed under Charles II, was held up for special admiration, and the inference was encouraged that rebellion is often praiseworthy.

A great event in my life, at the age of eleven, was the beginning of Euclid, which was still the accepted textbook of geometry. When I had got over my disappointment in finding that he began with axioms, which had to be accepted without proof, I found great delight in him. Throughout the rest of my boyhood, mathematics absorbed a very large part of my interest. This interest was complex: partly mere pleasure in discovering that I possessed a certain kind of skill, partly delight in the power of deductive reasoning, partly the restfulness of mathematical certainty; but more than any of these (while I was still a boy) the belief that nature operates according to mathematical laws, and that human actions, like planetary motions, could be calculated if we had sufficient skill. By the time I was fifteen, I had arrived at a theory very similar to that of the Cartesians. The movements of living bodies, I felt convinced, were wholly regulated by the laws of dynamics; therefore free will must be an illusion. But, since I accepted consciousness as an indubitable datum, I could not accept materialism, though I had a certain hankering after it on account of its intellectual simplicity and its rejection of 'nonsense'. I still believed in God, because the First-Cause argument seemed irrefutable.

Until I went to Cambridge at the age of eighteen, my life was a very solitary one. I was brought up at home, by German nurses, German and Swiss governesses, and finally by English tutors; I saw little of other children, and when I did they were not important to me. At fourteen or fifteen I became passionately interested in religion, and set to work to examine successively the arguments for free will, immortality, and God. For a few months I had an Agnostic tutor with whom I could talk about these problems, but he was sent away, presumably because he was thought to be undermining my faith. Except during these months, I kept my thoughts to myself, writing them out in a journal in Greek letters to prevent others from reading them. I was suffering the unhappiness natural to lonely adolescence, and I attributed my unhappiness to loss of religious belief. For three years I thought about religion, with a determination not to let my thoughts be influenced by my desires. I discarded first free will, then immortality; I believed in God until I was just eighteen, when I found in Mill's *Autobiography* the sentence: 'My father taught me that the question "Who made me?" cannot be answered, since it immediately suggests the further question "Who made God?" ' In that moment I decided that the First-Cause argument is fallacious.

During these years I read widely, but as my reading was not directed, much of it was futile. I read much bad poetry, especially Tennyson and Byron; at last, at the age of seventeen, I came upon Shelley, whom no one had told me about. He remained for many years the man I loved most among great men of the past. I read a great deal of Carlyle, and admired *Past and Present*, but not *Sartor Resartus*. 'The Everlasting Yea' seemed to me sentimental nonsense. The man with whom I most nearly agreed was Mill. His *Political Economy*, *Liberty*, and *Subjection of Women* influenced me profoundly. I made elaborate notes on the whole of his *Logic*, but could not accept his theory that mathematical propositions are empirical generalizations, though I did not know what else they could be.

All this was before I went to Cambridge. Except during the three months when I had the Agnostic tutor mentioned above, I found no one to speak to about my thoughts. At home I concealed my religious doubts. Once I said that I was a Utilitarian, but was met with such a blast of ridicule that I never again spoke of my opinions at home.

Cambridge opened to me a new world of infinite delight. For the first time I found that, when I uttered my thoughts, they seemed to be accepted as worth considering. Whitehead, who had examined me for entrance scholarships, had mentioned me to various people a year or two senior to me, with the result that within a week I met a number who became my life-long friends. Whitehead, who was already a Fellow and Lecturer, was amazingly kind, but was too much my senior to be a close personal friend until some years later. I found a group of contemporaries, who were able, rather earnest, hard-working, but interested in many things outside their academic work—poetry, philosophy, politics, ethics, indeed the whole world of mental adventure. We used to stay up discussing till very late on Saturday nights, meet for a late breakfast on Sunday, and then go for an all-day walk. Able young men had not yet adopted the pose of cynical superiority which came in some years later, and was first made fashionable in Cambridge by Lytton Strachey. The world seemed hopeful and solid; we all felt convinced that nineteenth-century progress would continue, and that we ourselves should be able to contribute something of value. For those who have been young since 1914 it must be difficult to imagine the happiness of those days.

Among my friends at Cambridge were McTaggart, the Hegelian philosopher; Lowes Dickinson, whose gentle charm made him loved by all who knew him; Charles Sanger, a brilliant mathematician at college, afterwards a barrister, known in legal circles as the editor of Jarman on Wills; two brothers, Crompton and Theodore Llewelyn Davies, sons of a Broad Church clergyman most widely known as one of 'Davies and Vaughan', who translated Plato's *Republic*. These two brothers were the youngest and ablest of a family of seven, all remarkably able; they had also a quite unusual capacity for friendship, a deep desire to be of use to the world, and unrivalled wit. Theodore, the younger of the two, was still in the earlier stages of a brilliant career in the government service when he was drowned in a bathing accident. I have never known any two men so deeply loved by so many friends. Among those of whom I saw most were the three brothers Trevelyan, great-nephews of Macaulay. Of these the oldest became a Labour politician and resigned from the Labour Government because it was not sufficiently socialistic; the second became a poet and published, among other things, an admirable translation of Lucretius; the third, George, achieved fame as an historian. Somewhat junior to me was G. E. Moore, who later had a great influence upon my philosophy.

The set in which I lived was very much influenced by McTaggart, whose wit recommended his Hegelian philosophy. He taught me to consider British empiricism 'crude', and I was willing to believe that Hegel (and in a lesser degree Kant) had a profundity not to be found in Locke, Berkeley, and Hume, or in my former pope, Mill. My first three years at Cambridge, I was too busy with mathematics to read Kant or Hegel, but in my fourth year I concentrated on philosophy. My teachers were Henry Sidgwick, James Ward, and G. F. Stout. Sidgwick represented the British point of view, which I believed myself to have seen through; I therefore thought less of him at that time than I did later. Ward, for whom I had a very great personal affection, set forth a Kantian system, and introduced me to Lotze and Sigwart. Stout, at that time, thought very highly of Bradley; when *Appearance and Reality* was published, he said it had done as much as is humanly possible in ontology. He and McTaggart between them caused me to become a Hegelian; I remember the precise moment, one day in 1894, as I was walking along Trinity Lane, when I saw in a flash (or thought I saw) that the ontological argument is valid. I had gone out to buy a tin of tobacco; on my way back, I suddenly threw it up in the air, and exclaimed as I caught it: 'Great Scott, the ontological argument is sound.' I read Bradley at this time with avidity, and admired him more than any other recent philosopher.

After leaving Cambridge in 1894, I spent a good deal of time in foreign countries. For some months in 1894, I was honorary attaché at the British Embassy in Paris, where I had to copy out long dispatches attempting to persuade the French Government that a lobster is not a fish, to which the French Government would reply that it was a fish in 1713, at the time of the Treaty of Utrecht. I had no desire for a diplomatic career, and left the Embassy in December 1894. I then married, and spent most of 1895 in Berlin, studying economics and German Social Democracy. The Ambassador's wife being a cousin of mine, my wife and I were invited to dinner at the Embassy; but she mentioned that we had gone to a Socialist meeting, and after this the Embassy closed its doors to us. My wife was a Philadelphia Quaker, and in 1896 we spent three months in America. The first place we visited was Walt Whitman's house in Camden, N.J.; she had known him'well, and I greatly admired him. These travels were useful in curing me of a certain Cambridge provincialism; in particular, I came to know the work of Weierstrass, whom my Cambridge teachers had never mentioned. After these travels, we settled down in a workman's cottage in Sussex, to which we added a fairly large workroom. I had at that time enough money to live simply without earning, and I was therefore able to devote all my time to philosophy and mathematics, except the evenings, when we read history aloud.

In the years from 1894 to 1898, I believed in the possibility of proving by metaphysics various things about the universe that religious feeling made me think important. I decided that, if I had sufficient ability, I would devote my life to philosophy. My fellowship dissertation, on the foundations of geometry, was praised by Ward and Whitehead; if it had not been, I should have taken up economics, at which I had been working in Berlin. I remember a spring morning when I walked in the Tiergarten, and planned to write a series of books in the philosophy of the sciences, growing gradually more concrete as I passed from mathematics to biology; I thought I would also write a series of books on social and political questions, growing gradually more abstract. At last I would achieve a Hegelian synthesis in an encyclopaedic work dealing equally with theory and practice. The scheme was inspired by Hegel, and yet something of it survived the change in my philosophy. The moment had had a certain importance: I can still, in memory, feel the squelching of melting snow beneath my feet, and smell the damp earth that promised the end of winter.

During 1898, various things caused me to abandon both Kant and Hegel. I read Hegel's *Greater Logic*, and thought, as I still do, that all he says about mathematics is muddle-headed nonsense. I came to disbelieve Bradley's arguments against relations, and to distrust the logical bases of monism. I disliked the subjectivity of the 'Transcendental Aesthetic'. But these motives would have operated more slowly than they did, but for the influence of G. E. Moore. He also had had a Hegelian period, but it was briefer than mine. He took the lead in rebellion, and I followed, with a sense of emancipation. Bradley argued that everything common sense believes in is mere appearance; we reverted to the opposite extreme, and thought that *everything* is real that common sense, uninfluenced by philosophy or theology, supposes real. With a sense of escaping from prison, we allowed ourselves to think that grass is green, that the sun and stars would exist if no one was aware of them, and also that there is a pluralistic timeless world of Platonic ideas. The world, which had been thin and logical, suddenly became rich and varied and solid. Mathematics could be *quite* true, and not merely a stage in dialectic. Something of this point of view appeared in my *Philosophy of Leibniz*. This book owed its origin to chance. McTaggart, who would, in the normal course, have lectured on Leibniz at Cambridge in 1898, wished to visit his family in New Zealand, and I was asked to take his place for this course. For me, the accident was a fortunate one.

The most important year in my intellectual life was the year 1900, and the most important event in this year was my visit to the International Congress of Philosophy in Paris. Ever since I had begun Euclid at the age of eleven, I had been troubled about the foundations of mathematics; when, later, I came to read philosophy, I found Kant and the empiricists equally unsatisfactory. I did not like the synthetic *a priori*, but yet arithmetic did not seem to consist of empirical generalizations. In Paris in 1900, I was impressed by the fact that, in all discussions, Peano and his pupils had a precision which was not possessed by others. I therefore asked him to give me his works, which he did. As soon as I had mastered his notation, I saw that it extended the region of mathematical precision backwards towards regions which had been given over to philosophical vagueness. Basing myself on him, I invented a notation for relations. Whitehead, fortunately, agreed as to the importance of the method, and in a very short time we worked out together such matters as the definitions of series, cardinals, and ordinals, and the reduction of arithmetic to logic. For nearly a year, we had a rapid series of quick successes. Much of the work had already been done by Frege, but at first we did not know this. The work that ultimately became my contribution to *Principia Mathematica* presented itself to me, at first, as a parenthesis in the refutation of Kant.

In June 1901, this period of honeymoon delight came to an end. Cantor had a proof that there is no greatest cardinal; in applying this proof to the universal class, I was led to the contradiction about classes that are not members of themselves. It soon became clear that this is only one of an infinite class of contradictions. I wrote to Frege, who replied with the utmost gravity that '*die Arithmetik ist ins Schwanken geraten*'. At first, I hoped the matter was trivial and could be easily cleared up; but early hopes were succeeded by something very near to despair. Throughout 1903 and 1904, I pursued will-o'-the-wisps and made no progress. At last, in the spring of 1905, a different problem, which proved soluble, gave the first glimmer of hope. The problem was that of descriptions, and its solution suggested a new technique.

Scholastic realism was a metaphysical theory, but every metaphysical theory has a technical counterpart. I had been a realist in the scholastic or Platonic sense; I had thought that cardinal integers, for instance, have a timeless being. When integers were reduced to classes of classes, this being was transferred to classes. Meinong, whose work interested me, applied the arguments of realism to descriptive phrases. Everyone agrees that 'the golden mountain does not exist' is a true proposition. But it has, apparently, a subject, 'the golden mountain', and if this subject did not designate some object, the proposition would seem to be meaningless. Meinong inferred that there is a golden mountain, which is golden and a mountain, but does not exist. He even thought that the existent golden mountain is existent, but does not exist. This did not satisfy me, and the desire to avoid Meinong's unduly populous realm of being led me to the theory of descriptions. What was of importance in this theory was the discovery that, in analysing a significant sentence, one must not assume that each separate word or phrase has significance on its own account. 'The golden mountain' can be part of a significant sentence, but is not significant in isolation. It soon appeared that class-symbols could be treated like descriptions, i.e. as non-significant parts of significant sentences. This made it possible to see, in a general way, how a solution of the contradictions might be possible. The particular solution offered in *Principia Mathematica* had various defects, but at any rate it showed that the logician is not presented with a complete impasse.

The theory of descriptions, and the attempt to solve the contradictions, had led me to pay attention to the problem of meaning and significance. The definition of 'meaning' as applied to words and 'significance' as applied to sentences is a complex problem, which I tried to deal with in *The Analysis of Mind* (1921) and *An Inquiry into Meaning and Truth* (1940). It is a problem that takes one into psychology and even physiology. The more I have thought about it, the less convinced I have become of the complete independence of logic. Seeing that logic is a much more advanced and exact science than psychology, it is clearly desirable, as far as possible, to delimit the problems that can be dealt with by logical methods. It is here that I have found Occam's razor useful.

Occam's razor, in its original form, was metaphysical: it was a principle of parsimony as regards 'entities'. I still thought of it in this way while *Principia Mathematica* was being written. In Plato, cardinal integers are timeless entities; they are equally so in Frege's *Grundgesetze der Arithmetik*. The definition of cardinals as classes of classes, and the discovery that class-symbols could be 'incomplete symbols', persuaded me that cardinals as entities are unnecessary. But what had really been demonstrated was something quite independent of metaphysics, which is best stated in terms of 'minimum vocabularies'. I mean by a 'minimum vocabulary' one in which no word can be defined in terms of the others. All definitions are theoretically superfluous, and therefore the whole of any science can be expressed by means of a minimum vocabulary for that science. Peano reduced the special vocabulary of arithmetic to three terms; Frege and *Principia Mathematica* maintained that even these are unnecessary, and that a minimum vocabulary for mathematics is the same as for logic. This problem is a purely technical one, and is capable of a precise solution.

There is need, however, of great caution in drawing inferences from minimum vocabularies. In the first place, there are usually, if not always, a number of different minimum vocabularies for a given subject-matter; for example, in the theory of truth-functions we may take 'not-p or not-q' or 'not-p and not-q' as undefined, and there is no reason to prefer one choice to the other. Then again there is often a question as to whether what seems to be a definition is not really an empirical proposition. Suppose, for instance, I define 'red' as 'those visual sensations which are caused by wave lengths of such and such a range of frequencies'. If we take this as what the word 'red' means, no proposition containing the word can have been known before the undulatory theory of light was known and wave lengths could be measured; and yet the word 'red' was used before these discoveries had been made. This makes it clear that in all everyday statements containing the word 'red' this word does not have the meaning assigned to it in the above definition. Consider the question: 'Can everything that we know about colours be known to a blind man?' With the above definition, the answer is yes; with a definition derived from everyday experience, the answer is no. This problem shows how the new logic, like the Aristotelian, can lead to a narrow scholasticism.

Nevertheless, there is one kind of inference which, I think, can be drawn from the study of minimum vocabularies. Take, as one of the most important examples, the traditional problem of universals. It seems fairly certain that no vocabulary can dispense wholly with words that are more or less of the sort called 'universals'. These words, it is true, need never occur as nouns; they may occur only as adjectives or verbs. Probably we could be content with one such word, the word 'similar', and we should never need the word 'similarity'. But the fact that we need the word 'similar' indicates some fact about the world, and not only about language. What fact it indicates about the world, I do not know.

Another illustration of the uses of minimum vocabularies is as regards historical events. To express history, we must have a means of speaking of something which has only happened once, like the death of Caesar. An undue absorption in logic, which is not concerned with history, may cause this need to be overlooked. Spatio-temporal relativity has made it more difficult to satisfy this need than it was in a Newtonian universe, where points and instants supplied particularity.

Thus, broadly speaking, minimum vocabularies are more instructive when they show a certain kind of term to be indispensable than when they show the opposite.

In some respects, my published work, outside mathematical logic, does not at all completely represent my beliefs or my general outlook. Theory of knowledge, with which I have been largely concerned, has a certain essential subjectivity; it asks 'how do *I* know what I know?' and starts inevitably from personal experience. Its data are egocentric, and so are the earlier stages of its argumentation. I have not, so far, got beyond the earlier stages, and have therefore seemed more subjective in outlook than in fact I am. I am not a solipsist, nor an idealist; I believe (though without good grounds) in the world of physics as well as in the world of psychology. But it seems clear that whatever is not experienced must, if known, be known by inference. I find that the fear of solipsism has prevented philosophers from facing this problem, and that either the necessary principles of inference have been left vague, or else the distinction between what is known by experience and what is known by inference has been denied. If I ever have the leisure to undertake another serious investigation of a philosophical problem, I shall attempt to analyse the inferences from experience to the world of physics, assuming them capable of validity, and seeking to discover what principles of inference, if true, would make them valid. Whether these principles, when discovered, are accepted as true, is a matter of temperament; what should not be a matter of temperament should be the proof that acceptance of them is necessary if solipsism is to be rejected.

I come now to what I have attempted to do in connection with social questions. I grew up in an atmosphere of politics, and was expected by my elders to take up a political career. Philosophy, however, interested me more than politics, and when it appeared that I had some aptitude for it, I decided to make it my main work. This pained my grandmother, who alluded to my investigation of the foundations of geometry as 'the life you have been leading', and said in shocked tones: 'O Bertie, I hear you are writing *another* book.' My political interests, though secondary, nevertheless remained very strong. In 1895, when in Berlin, I made a study of German Social Democracy, which I liked as being opposed to the Kaiser, and disliked as (at that time) embodying Marxist orthodoxy. For a time, under the influence of Sidney Webb, I became an imperialist, and even supported the Boer War. This point of view, however, I abandoned completely in 1901; from that time onwards, I felt an intense dislike of the use of force in human relations, though I always admitted that it is sometimes necessary. When Joseph Chamberlain, in 1903, turned against free trade, I wrote and spoke against him, my objections to his proposals being those of an internationalist. I took an active part in the agitation for Women's Suffrage. In 1910, *Principia Mathematica* being practically finished, I wished to stand for Parliament, and should have done so if the Selection Committee had not been shocked to discover that I was a free-thinker.

The First World War gave a new direction to my interests. The war, and the problem of preventing future wars, absorbed me, and the books that I wrote on this and cognate subjects caused me to become known to a wider public. During the war I had hoped that the peace would embody a rational determination to avoid future great wars; this hope was destroyed by the Versailles Treaty. Many of my friends saw hope in Soviet Russia, but when I went there in 1920 I found nothing that I could like or admire. I was then invited to China, where I spent nearly a year. I loved the Chinese, but it was obvious that the resistance to hostile militarisms must destroy much of what was best in their civilization. They seemed to have no alternative except to be conquered or to adopt many of the vices of their enemies. But China did one thing for me that the East is apt to do for Europeans who study it with sensitive sympathy: it taught me to think in long stretches of time, and not to be reduced to despair by the badness of the present. Throughout the increasing gloom of the past twenty years, this habit has helped to make the world less unendurable than it would otherwise have been.

In the years after my return from China, the birth of my two older children caused me to become interested in early education, to which, for some time, I devoted most of my energy. I have been supposed to be an advocate of complete liberty in schools, but this, like the view that I am an anarchist, is a mistake. I think a certain amount of force is indispensable, in education as in government; but I also think that methods can be found which will greatly diminish the necessary amount of force. This problem has both political and private aspects. As a rule, children or adults who are happy are likely to have fewer destructive passions, and therefore to need less restraint, than those who are unhappy. But I do not think that children can be made happy by being deprived of guidance, nor do I think that a sense of social obligation can be fostered if complete idleness is permitted. The question of discipline in childhood, like all other practical questions, is one of degree. Profound unhappiness and instinctive frustration is apt to produce a deep grudge against the world, issuing, sometimes by a very roundabout road, in cruelty and violence. The psychological and social problems involved first occupied my attention during the war of 1914–18; I was especially struck by the fact that, at first, most people seemed to enjoy the war. Clearly this was due to a variety of social ills, some of which were educational. But while individual parents can do much for their individual children, large-scale educational reform must depend upon the state, and therefore upon prior political and economic reforms. The world, however, was moving more and more in the direction of war and dictatorship, and I saw nothing useful that I could do in practical matters. I therefore increasingly reverted to philosophy, and to history in relation to ideas.

History has always interested me more than anything else except philosophy and mathematics. I have never been able to accept any general *schema* of historical development, such as that of Hegel or that of Marx. Nevertheless, general trends can be studied, and the study is profitable in relation to the present. I found much help in understanding the nineteenth century from studying the effect of liberal ideas in the period from 1814 to 1914.[1] The two types of liberalism, the rational and the romantic, represented by Bentham and Rousseau respectively, have continued, ever since, their relations of alternate alliance and conflict.

The relation of philosophy to social conditions has usually been ignored by professional philosophers. Marxists are interested in philosophy as an *effect*, but do not recognize it as a *cause*. Yet plainly every important philosophy is both. Plato is in part an effect of the victory of Sparta in the Peloponnesian war, and is also in part among the causes of Christian theology. To treat him only in the former aspect is to make the growth of the medieval church inexplicable. I am at present writing a history of western philosophy from Thales to the present day, in which every important system is treated equally as an effect and as a cause of social conditions.

My intellectual journeys have been, in some respects, disappointing. When I was young I hoped to find religious satisfaction in philosophy; even after I had abandoned Hegel, the eternal Platonic world gave me something non-human to admire. I thought of mathematics with reverence, and suffered when Wittgenstein led me to regard it as nothing but tautologies. I have always ardently desired to find some justification for the emotions inspired by certain things that seemed to stand outside human life and to deserve feelings of awe. I am thinking in part of very obvious things, such as the starry heavens and a stormy sea on a rocky coast; in part of the vastness of the scientific universe, both in space and time, as compared to the life of mankind; in part of the edifice of impersonal truth, especially truth which, like that of mathematics, does not merely describe the world that happens to exist. Those who attempt to make a religion of humanism, which recognizes nothing greater than man, do not satisfy my emotions. And yet I am unable to believe that, in the world as known, there is anything that I can value outside human beings, and, to a much lesser extent, animals. Not the starry heavens, but their effects on human percipients, have excellence; to admire the universe for its size is slavish and absurd; impersonal non-human truth appears to be a delusion. And so my intellect goes with the humanists, though my emotions violently rebel. In this respect, the 'consolations of philosophy' are not for me.

In more purely intellectual ways, on the contrary, I have found as much satisfaction in philosophy as anyone could reasonably have expected. Many matters which, when I was young, baffled me by the vagueness of all that had been said about them, are now amenable to an exact technique, which makes possible the kind of progress that is customary in science. Where definite knowledge is unattainable, it is sometimes possible to

[1] *Freedom and Organization*, 1814–1914 (1934).

prove that it is unattainable, and it is usually possible to formulate a variety of exact hypotheses, all compatible with the existing evidence. Those philosophers who have adopted the methods derived from logical analysis can argue with each other, not in the old aimless way, but co-operatively, so that both sides can concur as to the outcome. All this is new during my lifetime; the pioneer was Frege, but he remained solitary until his old age. This extension of the sphere of reason to new provinces is something that I value very highly. Philosophic rationality may be choked in the shocks of war and the welter of new persecuting superstitions, but one may hope that it will not be lost utterly or for more than a few centuries. In this respect, my philosophic life has been a happy one.

> (*The Philosophy of Bertrand Russell*, ed. Paul Arthur Schilpp, Library of Living Philosophers, New York: Tudor Publishing Co., 1951.)

3

ADAPTATION:
AN AUTOBIOGRAPHICAL EPITOME

FOR those who are too young to remember the world before 1914, it must be difficult to imagine the contrast for a man of my age between childhood memories and the world of the present day. I try, though with indifferent success, to accustom myself to a world of crumbling empires, Communism, atom bombs, Asian self-assertion, and aristocratic downfall. In this strange insecure world where no one knows whether he will be alive tomorrow, and where ancient states vanish like morning mists, it is not easy for those who, in youth, were accustomed to ancient solidities to believe that what they are now experiencing is a reality and not a transient nightmare. Very little remains of institutions and ways of life that when I was a child appeared as indestructible as granite. I grew up in an atmosphere impregnated with tradition. My parents died before I can remember, and I was brought up by my grandparents. My grandfather was born in the early days of the French Revolution and was in Parliament while Napoleon was still Emperor. As a Whig who followed Fox, he thought the English hostility to the French Revolution and Napoleon excessive, and he visited the exiled Emperor in Elba. It was he who, in 1832, introduced the Reform Bill which started England on the road towards democracy. He was Prime Minister during the Mexican War and during the revolutions of 1848. In common with the whole Russell family, he inherited the peculiar brand of aristocratic liberalism which characterized the Revolution of 1688 in which his ancestor played an important part. I was taught a kind of theoretic republicanism which was prepared to tolerate a monarch so long as he recognized that he was an employee of the people and subject to dismissal if he proved unsatisfactory. My grandfather, who was no respecter of persons, used to explain this point of view to Queen Victoria, and she was not altogether sympathetic. She did, however, give him the house in Richmond Park in which I spent all my youth. I imbibed certain political principles and expectations, and have on the whole retained the former in spite of being compelled to reject the latter. There was to be ordered progress throughout the world, no revolutions, a gradual cessation of war, and an extension of parliamentary government to all those unfortunate regions which did not yet enjoy it. My grandmother used to laugh about a conversation she had had with the Russian Ambassador: she said to him, 'Perhaps some day you will have a parliament in Russia', and he replied, 'God forbid, my dear Lady John.' The Russian Ambassador of today might give the same answer if he changed the first word. The hopes of that period seem now a little absurd. There was to be democracy, but it was assumed that the people would always be ready to follow the advice of wise and experienced aristocrats. There was to be a disappearance of imperialism, but the subject races in Asia and Africa, whom the British would volun- tarily cease to govern, would have learnt the advantage of a bi-cameral legislature composed of Whigs and Tories in about equal numbers, and would reproduce in torrid zones the parliamentary duels of Disraeli and Gladstone which were at their most brilliant at the time when I imbibed my dominant political prejudices. The idea of any insecurity to British power never entered anybody's head. Britannia ruled the waves, and that was that. There was, it is true, Bismarck, whom I was taught to consider a rascal; but it was thought that the civilizing influences of Goethe and Schiller would prevent the Germans from being permanently led into wrong paths by this uncivilized farmer. It was true also that there had been violence in the not-so-distant past. The French in their Revolution had committed excesses which one must deplore, while urging, at the same time, that reactionaries had grossly exaggerated them and that they would not have occurred at all but for the foolish hostility of the rest of Europe to progressive opinions in France. It might perhaps be admitted also that Cromwell had gone too far in cutting off the king's head but, broadly speaking, anything done against kings was to be applauded— unless, indeed, it were done by priests, like Becket, in which case one sided with the king. The atmosphere in the house was one of puritan piety and austerity. There were family prayers at eight o'clock every morning. Although there were eight servants, food was always of Spartan simplicity, and even what there was, if it was at all nice, was considered too good for children. For instance, if there was apple tart and rice pudding, I was only allowed the rice pudding. Cold baths all the year round were insisted upon, and I had to practise the piano from seven- thirty to eight every morning although the fires were not yet lit. My grandmother never allowed herself to sit in an armchair until the evening. Alcohol and tobacco were viewed with disfavour although stern convention compelled them to serve a little wine to guests. Only virtue was prized, virtue at the expense of intellect, health, happiness, and every mundane good.

I rebelled against this atmosphere first in the name of intellect. I was a solitary, shy, priggish youth. I had no experience of the social pleasures of boyhood and did not miss them. But I liked mathematics, and mathematics was suspect because it has no ethical content. I came also to disagree with the theological opinions of my family, and as I grew up I became increasingly interested in philosophy, of which they profoundly disapproved. Every time the subject came up they repeated with unfailing regularity, 'What is mind? No matter. What is matter? Never mind.' After some fifty or sixty repetitions, this remark ceased to amuse me.

When at the age of eighteen I went up to Cambridge, I found myself suddenly and almost bewilderingly among people who spoke the sort of language that was natural to me. If I said anything that I really thought they neither stared at me as if I were a lunatic nor denounced me as if I were a criminal. I had been compelled to live in a morbid atmosphere where an unwholesome kind of morality was encouraged to such an extent as to paralyse intelligence. And to find myself in a world where intelligence was valued and clear thinking was thought to be a good thing caused me an intoxicating delight. It is sometimes said that those who have had an unconventional education will find a difficulty in adjusting themselves to the world. I had no such experience. The environment in which I found myself at Cambridge fitted me like a glove. In the course of my first term I made lifelong friends and I never again had to endure the almost unbearable loneliness of my adolescent years. My first three years at Cambridge were given to mathematics and my fourth year to philosophy. I came in time to think ill of the philosophy that I had been taught, but the learning of it was a delight and it opened to me new and fascinating problems which I hoped to be able to solve. I was especially attracted to problems concerning the foundations of mathematics. I wished to believe that some knowledge is certain and I thought that the best hope of finding certain knowledge was in mathematics. At the same time it was obvious to me that the proofs of mathematical propositions which my teachers had offered me were fallacious. I hoped that better proofs were forthcoming. Subsequent study showed me that my hopes were partly justified. But it took me nearly twenty years to find all the justification that seemed possible and even that fell far short of my youthful hopes.

When I had finished my student years at Cambridge, I had to decide whether to devote my life to philosophy or to politics. Politics had been the habitual pursuit of my family since the sixteenth century, and to think of anything else was viewed as a kind of treachery to my ancestors. Everything was done to show that my path would be smooth if I chose politics. John Morley, who was Irish Secretary, offered me a post. Lord Dufferin, who was British Ambassador in Paris, gave me a job at our Embassy there. My family brought pressure to bear upon me in every way they could think of. For a time I hesitated, but in the end the lure of philosophy proved irresistible. This was my first experience of conflict, and I found it painful. I have since had so much conflict that many people have supposed that I must like it. I should, however, have much preferred to live at peace with everybody. But over and over again profound convictions have forced me into disagreements, even where I least desired them. After I had decided on philosophy, however, everything went smoothly for a long time. I lived mainly in an academic atmosphere where the pursuit of philosophy was not regarded as an eccentric folly. All went well until 1914. But when the First World War broke out, I thought it was a folly and a crime on the part of every one of the Powers involved on both sides. I hoped that England might remain neutral and, when this did not happen, I continued to protest. I found myself isolated from most of my former friends and, what I minded even more, estranged from the current of the national life. I had to fall back upon sources of strength that I hardly knew myself to possess. But something that if I had been religious I should have called the Voice of God, compelled me to persist. Neither then nor later did I think *all* war wrong. It was *that* war, not all war, that I condemned. The Second World War I thought necessary, not because I had changed my opinions on war, but because the circumstances were different. In fact all that made the second war necessary was an outcome of the first war. We owe to the first war and its aftermath Russian Communism, Italian Fascism and German Nazism. We owe to the first war the creation of a chaotic unstable world where there is every reason to fear that the Second World War was not the last, where there is the vast horror of Russian Communism to be combated, where Germany, France and what used to be the Austro-Hungarian Empire have all fallen lower in the scale of civilization, where there is every prospect of chaos in Asia and Africa, where the prospect of vast and horrible carnage inspires daily and hourly terror. All these evils have sprung with the inevitability of Greek tragedy out of the First World War. Consider by way of contrast what would have happened if Britain had remained neutral in that war. The war would have been short. It would have ended in victory for Germany. America would not have been dragged in. Britain would have remained strong and prosperous. Germany would not have been driven into Nazism, Russia, though it would have had a revolution, would in all likelihood have not had the Communist Revolution, since it could not in a short war have been reduced to the condition of utter chaos which prevailed in 1917. The Kaiser's Germany, although war propaganda on our side represented it as atrocious, was in fact only swashbuckling and a little absurd. I had lived in the Kaiser's Germany and I knew that progressive forces in that country were very strong and had every prospect of ultimate success. There was more freedom in the Kaiser's Germany than there is now in any country outside Britain and Scandinavia. We were told at the time that it was a war for freedom, a war for democracy and a war against militarism. As a result of that war freedom has vastly diminished and militarism has vastly increased. As for democracy, its future is still in doubt. I cannot think that the world would now be in anything like the bad state in which it is if English neutrality in the first war had allowed a quick victory to Germany. On these grounds I have never thought that I was mistaken in the line that I took at that time. I also do not regret having attempted throughout the war years to persuade people that the Germans were less wicked than official propaganda represented them as being, for a great deal of the subsequent evil resulted from the severity of the Treaty of Versailles and this severity would not have been possible but for the moral horror with which Germany was viewed. The Second World War was a totally different matter. Very largely as a result of our follies, Nazi Germany had to be fought if human life was to remain tolerable. If the Russians seek world dominion it is to be feared that war with them will be supposed equally necessary. But all this dreadful sequence is an outcome of the mistakes of 1914 and would not have occurred if those mistakes had been avoided.

(*Portraits from Memory*, London: Allen & Unwin; New York: Simon & Schuster, 1956.)

4

WHY I TOOK TO PHILOSOPHY

THE motives which have led men to become philosophers have been of various kinds. The most respectable motive was the desire to understand the world. In early days, while philosophy and science were indistinguishable, this motive predominated. Another motive which was a potent incentive in early times was the illusoriness of the senses. Such questions as: where is the rainbow? Are things really what they seem to be in sunshine or in moonlight? In more modern forms of the same problem—are things really what they look like to the naked eye or what they look like through a microscope? Such puzzles, however, very soon came to be supplemented by a larger problem. When the Greeks began to be doubtful about the Gods of Olympus, some of them sought in philosophy a substitute for traditional beliefs. Through the combination of these two motives there arose a twofold movement in philosophy: on the one hand, it was thought to show that much which passes for knowledge in everyday life is not real knowledge; and on the other hand, that there is a deeper philosophical truth which, according to most philosophers, is more consonant than our everyday beliefs with what we should wish the universe to be. In almost all philosophy doubt has been the goad and certainty has been the goal. There has been doubt about the senses, doubt about science, and doubt about theology. In some philosophers one of these has been more prominent, in others another. Philosophers have also differed widely as to the answers they have suggested to these doubts and even as to whether any answers are possible.

All the traditional motives combined to lead me to philosophy, but there were two that specially influenced me. The one which operated first and continued longest was the desire to find some knowledge that could be accepted as certainly true. The other motive was the desire to find some satisfaction for religious impulses.

I think the first thing that led me towards philosophy (though at that time the word 'philosophy' was still unknown to me) occurred at the age of eleven. My childhood was mainly solitary as my only brother was seven years older than I was. No doubt as a result of much solitude I became rather solemn, with a great deal of time for thinking but not much knowledge for my thoughtfulness to exercise itself upon. I had, though I was not yet aware of it, the pleasure in demonstrations which is typical of the mathematical mind. After I grew up I found others who felt as I did on this matter. My friend G. H. Hardy, who was professor of pure mathematics, enjoyed this pleasure in a very high degree. He told me once that if he could find a proof that I was going to die in five minutes he would of course be sorry to lose me, but this sorrow would be quite outweighed by pleasure in the proof. I entirely sympathized with him and was not at all offended. Before I began the study of geometry somebody had told me that it proved things and this caused me to feel delight when my brother said he would teach it to me. Geometry in those days was still 'Euclid'. My brother began at the beginning with the definitions. These I accepted readily enough. But he came next to the axioms. 'These', he said, 'can't be proved, but they have to be assumed before the rest can be proved.' At these words my hopes crumbled. I had thought it would be wonderful to find something that one could PROVE, and then it turned out that this could only be done by means of assumptions of which there was no proof. I looked at my brother with a sort of indignation and said: 'But why should I admit these things if they can't be proved?' He replied: 'Well, if you won't, we can't go on.' I thought it might be worth while to learn the rest of the story, so I agreed to admit the axioms for the time being. But I remained full of doubt and perplexity as regards a region in which I had hoped to find indisputable clarity. In spite of these doubts, which at most times I forgot, and which I usually supposed capable of some answer not yet known to me, I found great delight in mathematics—much more delight, in fact, than in any other study. I liked to think of the applications of mathematics to the physical world, and I hoped that in time there would be a mathematics of human behaviour as precise as the mathematics of machines. I hoped this because I liked demonstrations, and at most times this motive outweighed the desire, which I also felt, to believe in free will. Nevertheless I never quite overcame my fundamental doubts as to the validity of mathematics.

When I began to learn higher mathematics, fresh difficulties assailed me. My teachers offered me proofs which I felt to be fallacious and which, as I learnt later, had been recognized as fallacious. I did not know then, or for some time after I had left Cambridge, that better proofs had been found by German mathematicians. I therefore remained in a receptive mood for the heroic measures of Kant's philosophy. This suggested a large new survey from which such difficulties as had troubled me looked niggling and unimportant. All this I came later on to think wholly fallacious, but that was only after I had allowed myself to sink deep in the mire of metaphysical muddles. I was encouraged in my transition to philosophy by a certain disgust with mathematics, resulting from too much concentration and too much absorption in the sort of skill that is needed in examinations. The attempt to acquire examination technique had led me to think of mathematics as consisting of artful dodges and ingenious devices and as altogether too much like a cross-word puzzle. When, at the end of my first three years at Cambridge, I emerged from my last mathematical examination I swore that I would never look at mathematics again and sold all my mathematical books. In this mood the survey of philosophy gave me all the delight of a new landscape on emerging from a valley.

It had not been only in mathematics that I sought certainty. Like Descartes (whose work was still unknown to me) I thought that my own existence was, to me, indubitable. Like him, I felt it possible to suppose that the outer world is nothing but a dream. But even if it be, it is a dream that is really dreamt, and the fact that I experience it remains unshakably certain. This line of thought occurred to me first when I was sixteen, and I was glad when I learnt later that Descartes had made it the basis of his philosophy.

At Cambridge my interest in philosophy received a stimulus from another motive. The scepticism which had led me to doubt even mathematics had also led me to question the fundamental dogmas of religion, but I ardently desired to find a way of preserving at least something that could be called religious belief. From the age of fifteen to the age of eighteen I spent a great deal of time and thought on religious belief. I examined fundamental dogmas one by one, hoping with all my heart to find some reason for accepting them. I wrote my thoughts in a notebook which I still possess. They were, of course, crude and youthful, but for the moment I saw no answer to the Agnosticism which they suggested. At Cambridge I was made aware of whole systems of thought of which I had previously been ignorant and I abandoned for a time the ideas which I had worked out in solitude. At Cambridge I was introduced to the philosophy of Hegel who, in the course of nineteen abstruse volumes, professed to have proved something which would do quite well as an emended and sophisticated version of traditional beliefs. Hegel thought of the universe as a closely knit unity. His universe was like a jelly in the fact that, if you touched any one part of it, the whole quivered; but it was unlike a jelly in the fact that it could not really be cut up into parts. The appearance of consisting of parts, according to him, was a delusion. The only reality was the Absolute, which was his name for God. In this philosophy I found comfort for a time. As presented to me by its adherents, especially McTaggart, who was then an intimate friend of mine, Hegel's philosophy had seemed both charming and demonstrable. McTaggart was a philosopher some six years senior to me and throughout his life an ardent disciple of Hegel. He influenced his contemporaries very considerably, and I for a time fell under his sway. There was a curious pleasure in making oneself believe that time and space are unreal, that matter is an illusion, and that the world really consists of nothing but mind. In a rash moment, however, I turned from the disciples to the Master and found in Hegel himself a farrago of confusions and what seemed to me little better than puns. I therefore abandoned his philosophy.

For a time I found satisfaction in a doctrine derived, with modification, from Plato. According to Plato's doctrine, which I accepted only in a watered-down form, there is an unchanging timeless world of ideas of which the world presented to our senses is an imperfect copy. Mathematics, according to this doctrine, deals with the world of ideas and has in consequence an exactness and perfection which is absent from the everyday world. This kind of mathematical mysticism, which Plato derived from Pythagoras, appealed to me. But in the end I found myself obliged to abandon this doctrine also, and I have never since found religious satisfaction in any philosophical doctrine that I could accept.

(*Portraits from Memory*, London: Allen & Unwin; New York: Simon & Schuster, 1956.)

PART II

The Nobel Prize Winning Man of Letters
(Essayist and Short Story Writer)

Few Nobel Prize winners in literature have set forth so revealing an account of how they write as we have here. Russell ever displays a mastery of detail and a precision of presentation that leaves no doubt of his position whether one agrees or disagrees. The clarity of thinking of an ever lucubrating mind is apparent in all he has done. The characteristic style follows naturally. Recognition through the Nobel Prize thus came as no surprise.

While Russell asserts that he no longer thinks well of his most popular essay, 'A Free Man's Worship', no Russell anthology would be complete without it and an anthology of the best twentieth-century prose would be hard put to justify its exclusion. We also sample some of his other essays and two of his short stories. It was late in his life that he caught all unawares by their publication.

5

HOW I WRITE

I CANNOT pretend to know how writing ought to be done, or what a wise critic would advise me to do with a view to improving my own writing. The most that I can do is to relate some things about my own attempts.

Until I was twenty-one, I wished to write more or less in the style of John Stuart Mill. I liked the structure of his sentences and his manner of developing a subject. I had, however, already a different ideal, derived, I suppose, from mathematics. I wished to say everything in the smallest number of words in which it could be said clearly. Perhaps, I thought, one should imitate Baedeker rather than any more literary model. I would spend hours trying to find the shortest way of saying something without ambiguity, and to this aim I was willing to sacrifice all attempts at aesthetic excellence.

At the age of twenty-one, however, I came under a new influence, that of my future brother-in-law, Logan Pearsall Smith. He was at that time exclusively interested in style as opposed to matter. His gods were Flaubert and Walter Pater, and I was quite ready to believe that the way to learn how to write was to copy their technique. He gave me various simple rules, of which I remember only two: 'Put a comma every four words', and 'never use "and" except at the beginning of a sentence.' His most emphatic advice was that one must always re-write. I conscientiously tried this, but found that my first draft was almost always better than my second. This discovery has saved me an immense amount of time. I do not, of course, apply it to the substance, but only to the form. When I discover an error of an important kind, I re-write the whole. What I do not find is that I can improve a sentence when I am satisfied with what it means.

Very gradually I have discovered ways of writing with a minimum of worry and anxiety. When I was young each fresh piece of serious work used to seem to me for a time—perhaps a long time—to be beyond my powers. I would fret myself into a nervous state from fear that it was never going to come right. I would make one unsatisfying attempt after another, and in the end have to discard them all. At last I found that such fumbling attempts were a waste of time. It appeared that after first contemplating a book on some subject, and after giving serious preliminary attention to it, I needed a period of subconscious incubation which could not be hurried and was, if anything, impeded by deliberate thinking. Sometimes I would find, after a time, that I had made a mistake, and that I could not write the book I had had in mind. But often I was more fortunate. Having, by a time of very intense concentration, planted the problem in my subconsciousness, it would germinate underground until, suddenly, the solution emerged with blinding clarity, so that it only remained to write down what had appeared as if in a revelation.

The most curious example of this process, and the one which led me subsequently to rely upon it, occurred at the beginning of 1914. I had undertaken to give the Lowell Lectures at Boston, and had chosen as my subject 'Our Knowledge of the External World'. Throughout 1913 I thought about this topic. In term time in my rooms at Cambridge, in vacations in a quiet inn on the upper reaches of the Thames, I concentrated with such intensity that I sometimes forgot to breathe and emerged panting as from a trance. But all to no avail. To every theory that I could think of I could perceive fatal objections. At last, in despair, I went off to Rome for Christmas, hoping that a holiday would revive my flagging energy. I got back to Cambridge on the last day of 1913, and although my difficulties were still completely unresolved I arranged, because the remaining time was short, to dictate as best as I could to a stenographer. Next morning, as she came in at the door, I suddenly saw exactly what I had to say, and proceeded to dictate the whole book without a moment's hesitation.

I do not want to convey an exaggerated impression. The book was very imperfect, and I now think that it contains serious errors. But it was the best that I could have done at that time, and a more leisurely method (within the time at my disposal) would almost certainly have produced something worse. Whatever may be true of other people, this is the right method for me. Flaubert and Pater, I have found, are best forgotten so far as I am concerned.

Although what I now think about how to write is not so very different from what I thought at the age of eighteen, my development has not been by any means rectilinear. There was a time, in the first years of this century, when I had more florid and rhetorical ambitions. This was the time when I wrote *A Free Man's Worship*, a work of which I do not now think well. At that time I was steeped in Milton's prose, and his rolling periods reverberated through the caverns of my mind. I cannot say that I no longer admire them, but for me to imitate them involves a certain insincerity. In fact, all imitation is dangerous. Nothing could be better in style than the Prayer Book and the Authorized Version of the Bible, but they express a way of thinking and feeling which is different from that of our time. A style is not good unless it is an intimate and almost involuntary expression of the personality of the writer, and then only if the writer's personality is worth expressing. But although direct imitation is always to be deprecated, there is much to be gained by familiarity with good prose, especially in cultivating a sense for prose rhythm.

There are some simple maxims—not perhaps quite so simple as those which my brother-in-law Logan Pearsall Smith offered me—which I think might be commended to writers of expository prose. First: never use a long word if a short word will do. Second: if you want to make a statement with a great many qualifications, put some of the qualifications in separate sentences. Third: do not let the beginning of your sentence lead the reader to an expectation which is contradicted by the end. Take, say, such a sentence as the following, which might occur in a work on sociology: 'Human beings are completely exempt from undesirable behaviour-patterns only when certain prerequisites, not satisfied except in a small percentage of actual cases, have, through some fortuitous concourse of favourable circumstances, whether congenital or environmental, chanced to combine in producing an individual in whom many factors deviate from the norm in a socially advantageous manner.' Let us see if we can translate this sentence into English. I suggest the following: 'All men are scoundrels, or at any rate almost all. The men who are not must have had unusual luck, both in their birth and in their upbringing.' This is shorter and more intelligible, and says just the same thing. But I am afraid any professor who used the second sentence instead of the first would get the sack.

This suggests a word of advice to such of my hearers as may happen to be professors. I am allowed to use plain English because everybody knows that I could use mathematical logic if I chose. Take the statement: 'Some people marry their deceased wives' sisters.' I can express this in language which only becomes intelligible after years of study, and this gives me freedom. I suggest to young professors that their first work should be written in a jargon only to be understood by the erudite few. With that behind them, they can ever after say what they have to say in a language 'understanded of the people'. In these days, when our very lives are at the mercy of the professors, I cannot but think that they would deserve our gratitude if they adopted my advice.

(*Portraits from Memory*, London: Allen & Unwin; New York: Simon & Schuster, 1956.)

6

A FREE MAN'S WORSHIP

To Dr Faustus in his study Mephistophelis told the history of the Creation, saying:

'The endless praises of the choirs of angels had begun to grow wearisome; for, after all, did he not deserve their praise? Had he not given them endless joy? Would it not be more amusing to obtain undeserved praise, to be worshipped by beings whom he tortured? He smiled inwardly, and resolved that the great drama should be performed.

'For countless ages the hot nebula whirled aimlessly through space. At length it began to take shape, the central mass threw off planets, the planets cooled, boiling seas and burning mountains heaved and tossed, from black masses of cloud hot sheets of rain deluged the barely solid crust. And now the first germ of life grew in the depths of the ocean, and developed rapidly in the fructifying warmth into vast forest trees, huge ferns springing from the damp mould, sea monsters breeding, fighting, devouring, and passing away. And from the monsters, as the play unfolded itself, Man was born, with the power of thought, the knowledge of good and evil, and the cruel thirst for worship. And Man saw that all is passing in this mad, monstrous world, that all is struggling to snatch, at any cost, a few brief moments of life before Death's inexorable decree. And Man said: "There is a hidden purpose, could we but fathom it, and the purpose is good; for we must reverence something, and in the visible world there is nothing worthy of reverence." And Man stood aside from the struggle, resolving that God intended harmony to come out of chaos by human efforts. And when he followed the instincts which God had transmitted to him from his ancestry of beasts of prey, he called it Sin, and asked God to forgive him. But he doubted whether he could be justly forgiven, until he invented a divine Plan by which God's wrath was to have been appeased. And seeing the present was bad, he made it yet worse, that thereby the future might be better. And he gave God thanks for the strength that enabled him to forgo even the joys that were possible. And God smiled; and when he saw that Man had become perfect in renunciation and worship, he sent another sun through the sky, which crashed into Man's sun; and all returned again to nebula.

' "Yes," he murmured, "it was a good play; I will have it performed again." '

Such, in outline, but even more purposeless, more void of meaning, is the world which Science presents for our belief. Amid such a world, if anywhere, our ideals henceforward must find a home. That Man is the product of causes which had no prevision of the end they were achieving; that his origin, his growth, his hopes and fears, his loves and his beliefs, are but the outcome of accidental collocations of atoms; that no fire, no heroism, no intensity of thought and feeling, can preserve an individual life beyond the grave; that all the labours of the ages, all the devotion, all the inspiration, all the noonday brightness of human genius, are destined to extinction in the vast death of the solar system, and that the whole temple of Man's achievement must inevitably be buried beneath the debris of a universe in ruins—all these things, if not quite beyond dispute, are yet so nearly certain, that no philosophy which rejects them can hope to stand. Only within the scaffolding of these truths, only on the firm foundation of unyielding despair, can the soul's habitation henceforth be safely built.

How, in such an alien and inhuman world, can so powerless a creature as Man preserve his aspirations untarnished? A strange mystery it is that Nature, omnipotent but blind, in the revolutions of her secular hurryings through the abysses of space, has brought forth at last a child, subject still to her power, but gifted with sight, with knowledge of good and evil, with the capacity of judging all the works of his unthinking Mother. In spite of Death, the mark and seal of the parental control, Man is yet free, during his brief years, to examine, to criticize, to know, and in imagination to create. To him alone, in the world with which he is acquainted, this freedom belongs; and in this lies his superiority to the resistless forces that control his outward life.

The savage, like ourselves, feels the oppression of his impotence before the powers of Nature; but having in himself nothing that he respects more than Power, he is willing to prostrate himself before his gods, without inquiring whether they are worthy of his worship. Pathetic and very terrible is the long history of cruelty and torture, of degradation and human sacrifice, endured in the hope of placating the jealous gods: surely, the trembling believer thinks, when what is most precious has been freely given, their lust for blood must be appeased, and more will not be required. The religion of Moloch—as such creeds may be generically called—is in essence the cringing submission of the slave, who dare not, even in his heart, allow the thought that his master deserves no adulation. Since the independence of ideals is not yet acknowledged, Power may be freely worshipped, and receive an unlimited respect, despite its wanton infliction of pain.

But gradually, as morality grows bolder, the claim of the ideal world begins to be felt; and worship, if it is not to cease, must be given to gods of another kind than those created by the savage. Some, though they feel the demands of the ideal, will still consciously reject them, still urging that naked Power is worthy of worship. Such is the attitude inculcated in God's answer to Job out of the whirlwind: the divine power and knowledge are paraded, but of the divine goodness there is no hint. Such also is the attitude of those who, in our own day, base their morality upon the struggle for survival, maintaining that the survivors are necessarily the fittest. But others, not content with an answer so repugnant to the moral sense, will adopt the position which we have become accustomed to regard as specially religious, maintaining that, in some hidden manner, the world of fact is really harmonious with the world of ideals. Thus Man creates God, all-powerful and all-good, the mystic unity of what is and what should be.

But the world of fact, after all, is not good; and, in submitting our judgement to it, there is an element of slavishness from which our thoughts must be purged. For in all things it is well to exalt the dignity of Man, by freeing him as far as possible from the tyranny of non-human Power. When we have realized that Power is largely bad, that Man, with his knowledge of good and evil, is but a helpless atom in a world which has no such knowledge, the choice is again presented to us: Shall we worship Force, or shall we worship Goodness? Shall our God exist and be evil, or shall he be recognized as the creation of our own conscience?

The answer to this question is very momentous, and affects profoundly our whole morality. The worship of Force, to which Carlyle and Nietzsche and the creed of Militarism have accustomed us, is the result of failure to maintain our own ideals against a hostile universe: it is itself a prostrate submission to evil, a sacrifice of our best to Moloch. If strength indeed is to be respected, let us respect rather the strength of those who refuse that false 'recognition of facts' which fails to recognize that facts are often bad. Let us admit that, in the world we know, there are many things that would be better otherwise, and that the ideals to which we do and must adhere are not realized in the realm of matter. Let us preserve our respect for truth, for beauty, for the ideal of perfection which life does not permit us to attain, though none of these things meet with the approval of the unconscious universe. If Power is bad, as it seems to be, let us reject it from our hearts. In this lies Man's true freedom: in determination to worship only the God created by our own love of the good, to respect only the heaven which inspires the insight of our best moments. In action, in desire, we must submit perpetually to the tyranny of outside forces; but in thought, in aspiration, we are free, free from our fellow men, free from the petty planet on which our bodies impotently crawl, free even, while we live, from the tyranny of death. Let us learn, then, that energy of faith which enables us to live constantly in the vision of the good;

and let us descend, in action, into the world of fact, with that vision always before us.

When first the opposition of fact and ideal grows fully visible, a spirit of fiery revolt, of fierce hatred of the gods, seems necessary to the assertion of freedom. To defy with Promethean constancy a hostile universe, to keep its evil always in view, always actively hated, to refuse no pain that the malice of Power can invent, appears to be the duty of all who will not bow before the inevitable. But indignation is still a bondage, for it compels our thoughts to be occupied with an evil world; and in the fierceness of desire from which rebellion springs there is a kind of self-assertion which it is necessary for the wise to overcome. Indignation is a submission of our thoughts, but not of our desires; the Stoic freedom in which wisdom consists is found in the submission of our desires, but not of our thoughts. From the submission of our desires springs the virtue of resignation; from the freedom of our thoughts springs the whole world of art and philosophy, and the vision of beauty by which, at last, we half reconquer the reluctant world. But the vision of beauty is possible only to unfettered contemplation, to thoughts not weighted by the load of eager wishes; and thus Freedom comes only to those who no longer ask of life that it shall yield them any of those personal goods that are subject to the mutations of Time.

Although the necessity of renunciation is evidence of the existence of evil, yet Christianity, in preaching it, has shown a wisdom exceeding that of the Promethean philosophy of rebellion. It must be admitted that, of the things we desire, some, though they prove impossible, are yet real goods; others, however, as ardently longed for, do not form part of a fully purified ideal. The belief that what must be renounced is bad, though sometimes false, is far less often false than untamed passion supposes; and the creed of religion, by providing a reason for proving that it is never false, has been the means of purifying our hopes by the discovery of many austere truths.

But there is in resignation a further good element: even real goods, when they are unattainable, ought not to be fretfully desired. To every man comes, sooner or later, the great renunciation. For the young, there is nothing unattainable; a good thing desired with the whole force of a passionate will, and yet impossible, is to them not credible. Yet, by death, by illness, by poverty, or by the voice of duty, we must learn, each one of us, that the world was not made for us, and that, however beautiful may be the things we crave, Fate may nevertheless forbid them. It is the part of courage, when misfortune comes, to bear without repining the ruin of our hopes, to turn away our thoughts from vain regrets. This degree of submission to Power is not only just and right: it is the very gate of wisdom.

But passive renunciation is not the whole of wisdom; for not by renunciation alone can we build a temple for the worship of our own ideals. Haunting foreshadowings of the temple appear in the realm of imagination, in music, in architecture, in the untroubled kingdom of reason, and in the golden sunset magic of lyrics, where beauty shines and glows, remote from the touch of sorrow, remote from the fear of change, remote from the failures and disenchantments of the world of fact. In the contemplation of these things the vision of heaven will shape itself in our hearts, giving at once a touchstone to judge the world about us, and an inspiration by which to fashion to our needs whatever is not incapable of serving as a stone in the sacred temple.

Except for those rare spirits that are born without sin, there is a cavern of darkness to be traversed before that temple can be entered. The gate of the cavern is despair, and its floor is paved with the gravestones of abandoned hopes. There Self must die; there the eagerness, the greed of untamed desire must be slain, for only so can the soul be free from the empire of Fate. But out of the cavern the Gate of Renunciation leads again to the daylight of wisdom, by whose radiance a new insight, a new joy, a new tenderness, shine forth to gladden the pilgrim's heart.

When, without the bitterness of impotent rebellion, we have learnt both to resign ourselves to the outward rule of Fate and to recognize that the non-human world is unworthy of our worship, it becomes possible at last so to transform and refashion the unconscious universe, so to transmute it in the crucible of imagination, that a new image of shining gold replaces the old idol of clay. In all the multiform facts of the world— in the visual shapes of trees and mountains and clouds, in the events of the life of Man, even in the very omnipotence of Death—the insight of creative idealism can find the reflection of a beauty which its own thoughts first made. In this way mind asserts its subtle mastery over the thoughtless forces of Nature. The more evil the material with which it deals, the more thwarting to untrained desire, the greater is its achievement in inducing the reluctant rock to yield up its hidden treasures, the prouder its victory in compelling the opposing forces to swell the pageant of its triumph. Of all the arts, Tragedy is the proudest, the most triumphant; for it builds its shining citadel in the very centre of the enemy's country, on the very summit of his highest mountain; from its impregnable watch-towers, his camps and arsenals, his columns and forts, are all revealed; within its walls the free life continues, while the legions of Death and Pain and Despair, and all the servile captains of tyrant Fate, afford the burghers of that dauntless city new spectacles of beauty. Happy those sacred ramparts, thrice happy the dwellers on that all-seeing eminence. Honour to those brave warriors who, through countless ages of warfare, have preserved for us the priceless heritage of liberty, and have kept undefiled by sacrilegious invaders the home of the unsubdued.

But the beauty of Tragedy does but make visible a quality which, in more or less obvious shapes, is present always and everywhere in life. In the spectacle of Death, in the endurance of intolerable pain, and in the irrevocableness of a vanished past, there is a sacredness, an overpowering awe, a feeling of the vastness, the depth, the inexhaustible mystery of existence, in which, as by some strange marriage of pain, the sufferer is bound to the world by bonds of sorrow. In these moments of insight, we lose all eagerness of temporary desire, all struggling and striving for petty ends, all care for the little trivial things that, to a superficial view, make up the common life of day by day; we see, surrounding the narrow raft illumined by the flickering light of human comradeship, the dark ocean on whose rolling waves we toss for a brief hour; from the great night without, a chill blast breaks in upon our refuge; all the loneliness of humanity amid hostile forces is concentrated upon the individual soul, which must struggle alone, with what of courage it can command, against the whole weight of a universe that cares nothing for its hopes and fears. Victory, in this struggle with the powers of darkness, is the true baptism into the glorious company of heroes, the true initiation into the over-mastering beauty of human existence. From that awful encounter of the soul with the outer world, renunciation, wisdom, and charity are born; and with their birth a new life begins. To take into the inmost shrine of the soul the irresistible forces whose puppets we seem to be—Death and change, the irrevocableness of the past, and the powerlessness of Man before the blind hurry of the universe from vanity to vanity—to feel these things and know them is to conquer them.

This is the reason why the Past has such magical power. The beauty of its motionless and silent pictures is like the enchanted purity of late autumn, when the leaves, though one breath would make them fall, still glow against the sky in golden glory. The Past does not change or strive; like Duncan, after life's fitful fever it sleeps well; what was eager and grasping, what was petty and transitory, has faded away, the things that were beautiful and eternal shine out of it like stars in the night. Its beauty, to a soul not worthy of it, is unendurable; but to a soul which has conquered Fate it is the key of religion.

The life of Man, viewed outwardly, is but a small thing in comparison with the forces of Nature. The slave is doomed to worship Time and Fate and Death, because they are greater than anything he finds in himself, and because all his thoughts are of things which they devour. But, great as they are, to think of them greatly, to feel their passionless splendour, is greater still. And such thought makes us free men; we no longer bow before the inevitable in Oriental subjection, but we absorb it, and make it a part of ourselves. To abandon the struggle for private happiness, to expel all eagerness of temporary desire, to burn with passion for eternal things—this is emancipation, and this is the free man's worship. And this liberation is effected by a contemplation of Fate; for Fate itself is subdued by the mind which leaves nothing to be purged by the purifying fire of Time.

United with his fellow men by the strongest of all ties, the tie of a common doom, the free man finds that a new vision is with him always, shedding over every daily task the light of love. The life of Man is a long march through the night, surrounded by invisible foes, tortured by weariness and pain, towards a goal that few can hope to reach, and where none may tarry long. One by one, as they march, our comrades vanish from our sight, seized by the silent orders of omnipotent Death. Very brief is the time in which we can help them, in which their happiness or misery is decided. Be it ours to shed sunshine on their path, to lighten their sorrows by the balm of sympathy, to give them the pure joy of a never-tiring affection, to strengthen failing courage, to instil faith in hours of despair. Let us not weigh in grudging scales their merits and demerits, but let us think only of their need—of the sorrows, the difficulties, perhaps the blindnesses, that make the misery of their lives; let us remember that they are fellow-sufferers in the same darkness, actors in the same tragedy with ourselves. And so, when their day is over, when their good and their evil have become eternal by the immortality of the past, be it ours to feel that, where they suffered, where they failed, no deed of ours was the cause; but wherever a spark of the divine fire kindled in their hearts, we were ready with encouragement, with sympathy, with brave words in which high courage glowed.

Brief and powerless is Man's life; on him and all his race the slow, sure doom falls pitiless and dark. Blind to good and evil, reckless of destruction, omnipotent matter rolls on its relentless way; for Man, condemned today to lose his dearest, tomorrow himself to pass through the gate of darkness, it remains only to cherish, ere yet the blow fall, the lofty thoughts that ennoble his little day; disdaining the coward terrors of the slave of Fate, to worship at the shrine that his own hands have built; undismayed by the empire of chance, to preserve a mind free from the wanton tyranny that rules his outward life; proudly defiant of the irresistible forces that tolerate, for a moment, his knowledge and his condemnation, to sustain alone, a weary but unyielding Atlas, the world that his own ideals have fashioned despite the trampling march of unconscious power.

(*The Independent Review*, December 1903, subsequently reprinted in *Mysticism and Logic*, London: Allen & Unwin, 1917; New York: Simon & Schuster, 1929.)

7

AN OUTLINE OF INTELLECTUAL RUBBISH

MAN is a rational animal—so at least I have been told. Throughout a long life, I have looked diligently for evidence in favour of this statement, but so far I have not had the good fortune to come across it, though I have searched in many countries spread over three continents. On the contrary, I have seen the world plunging continually further into madness. I have seen great nations, formerly leaders of civilization, led astray by preachers of bombastic nonsense. I have seen cruelty, persecution, and superstition increasing by leaps and bounds, until we have almost reached the point where praise of rationality is held to mark a man as an old fogy regrettably surviving from a bygone age. All this is depressing, but gloom is a useless emotion. In order to escape from it, I have been driven to study the past with more attention than I had formerly given to it, and have found, as Erasmus found, that folly is perennial and yet the human race has survived. The follies of our own times are easier to bear when they are seen against the background of past follies. In what follows I shall mix the sillinesses of our day with those of former centuries. Perhaps the result may help in seeing our own times in perspective, and as not much worse than other ages that our ancestors lived through without ultimate disaster.

Aristotle, so far as I know, was the first man to proclaim explicitly that man is a rational animal. His reason for this view was one which does not now seem very impressive; it was, that some people can do sums. He thought that there are three kinds of soul: the vegetable soul, possessed by all living things, both plants and animals, and concerned only with nourishment and growth; the animal soul, concerned with locomotion, and shared by man with the lower animals; and finally the rational soul, or intellect, which is the Divine mind, but in which men participate to a greater or less degree in proportion to their wisdom. It is in virtue of the intellect that man is a rational animal. The intellect is shown in various ways, but most emphatically by mastery of arithmetic. The Greek system of numerals was very bad, so that the multiplication table was quite difficult, and complicated calculations could only be made by very clever people. Nowadays, however, calculating machines do sums better than even the cleverest people, yet no one contends that these useful instruments are immortal, or work by divine inspiration. As arithmetic has grown easier, it has come to be less respected. The consequence is that, though many philosophers continue to tell us what fine fellows we are, it is no longer on account of our arithmetical skill that they praise us.

Since the fashion of the age no longer allows us to point to calculating boys as evidence that man is rational and the soul, at least in part, immortal, let us look elsewhere. Where shall we look first? Shall we look among eminent statesmen, who have so triumphantly guided the world into its present condition? Or shall we choose the men of letters? Or the philosophers? All these have their claims, but I think we should begin with those whom all right-thinking people acknowledge to be the wisest as well as the best of men, namely the clergy. If *they* fail to be rational, what hope is there for us lesser mortals? And alas—though I say it with all due respect—there have been times when their wisdom has not been very obvious, and, strange to say, these were especially the times when the power of the clergy was greatest.

The Ages of Faith, which are praised by our neoscholastics, were the time when the clergy had things all their own way. Daily life was full of miracles wrought by saints and wizardry perpetrated by devils and necromancers. Many thousands of witches were burnt at the stake. Men's sins were punished by pestilence and famine, by earthquake, flood, and fire. And yet, strange to say, they were even more sinful than they are nowadays. Very little was known scientifically about the world. A few learned men remembered Greek proofs that the earth is round, but most people made fun of the notion that there are antipodes. To suppose that there are human beings at the antipodes was heresy. It was generally held (though modern Catholics take a milder view) that the immense majority of mankind are damned. Dangers were held to lurk at every turn. Devils would settle on the food that monks were about to eat, and would take possession of the bodies of incautious feeders who omitted to make the sign of the Cross before each mouthful. Old-fashioned people still say 'bless you' when one sneezes, but they have forgotten the reason for the custom. The reason was that people were thought to sneeze out their souls, and before their souls could get back lurking demons were apt to enter the un-souled body; but if any one said 'God bless you', the demons were frightened off.

Throughout the last four hundred years, during which the growth of science has gradually shown men how to acquire knowledge of the ways of nature and mastery over natural forces, the clergy have fought a losing battle against science, in astronomy and geology, in anatomy and physiology, in biology and psychology and sociology. Ousted from one position, they have taken up another. After being worsted in astronomy, they did their best to prevent the rise of geology; they fought against Darwin in biology, and at the present time they fight against scientific theories of psychology and education. At each stage, they try to make the public forget their earlier obscurantism, in order that their present obscurantism may not be recognized for what it is. Let us note a few instances of irrationality among the clergy since the rise of science, and then inquire whether the rest of mankind are any better.

When Benjamin Franklin invented the lightning-rod, the clergy, both in England and America, with the enthusiastic support of George III, condemned it as an impious attempt to defeat the will of God. For, as all right-thinking people were aware, lightning is sent by God to punish impiety or some other grave sin—the virtuous are never struck by lightning. Therefore if God wants to strike anyone, Benjamin Franklin ought not to defeat His design; indeed, to do so is helping criminals to escape. But God was equal to the occasion, if we are to believe the eminent Dr Price, one of the leading divines of Boston. Lightning having been rendered ineffectual by the 'iron points invented by the sagacious Dr Franklin', Massachusetts was shaken by earthquakes, which Dr Price perceived to be due to God's wrath at the 'iron points'. In a sermon on the subject he said: 'In Boston are more erected than elsewhere in New England, and Boston seems to be more dreadfully shaken. Oh! there is no getting out of the mighty hand of God.' Apparently, however, Providence gave up all hope of curing Boston of its wickedness, for, though lightning-rods became more and more common, earthquakes in Massachusetts have remained rare. Nevertheless, Dr Price's point of view, or something very like it, was still held by one of the most influential men of recent times. When, at one time, there were several bad earthquakes in India, Mahatma Gandhi solemnly warned his compatriots that these disasters had been sent as a punishment for their sins.

Even in my own native island this point of view still exists. During the 1914–18 war, the British Government did much to stimulate the production of food at home. In 1916, when things were not going well, a Scottish clergyman wrote to the newspapers to say that military failure was due to the fact that, with government sanction, potatoes had been planted on the Sabbath. However, disaster was averted, owing to the fact that the Germans disobeyed *all* the Ten Commandments, and not only one of them.

Sometimes, if pious men are to be believed, God's mercies are curiously selective. Toplady, the author of *Rock of Ages*, moved from one vicarage to another; a week after the move, the vicarage he had formerly occupied burnt down, with great loss to the new vicar. Thereupon Toplady thanked God; but what the new vicar did is not known. Borrow, in his *Bible in Spain*, records how without mishap he crossed a mountain pass infested by bandits. The next party to cross, however, were set upon, robbed, and some of them murdered; when Borrow heard of this, he, like Toplady, thanked God.

Although we are taught the Copernican astronomy in our textbooks, it has not yet penetrated to our religion or our morals, and has not even succeeded in destroying belief in astrology. People still think that the Divine Plan has special reference to human beings, and that a special Providence not only looks after the good, but also punishes the wicked. I am sometimes shocked by the blasphemies of those who think themselves pious—for instance, the nuns who never take a bath without wearing a bathrobe all the time. When asked why, since no man can see them, they reply 'Oh, but you forget the good God.' Apparently they conceive of the Deity as a Peeping Tom, whose omnipotence enables Him to see through bathroom walls, but who is foiled by bathrobes. This view strikes me as curious.

The whole conception of 'sin' is one which I find very puzzling, doubtless owing to my sinful nature. If 'sin' consisted in causing needless suffering, I could understand; but on the contrary, sin often consists in avoiding needless suffering. Some years ago, in the English House of Lords, a Bill was introduced to legalize euthanasia in cases of painful and incurable disease. The patient's consent was to be necessary, as well as several medical certificates. To me, in my simplicity, it would seem natural to require the patient's consent, but the late Archbishop of Canterbury, the English official expert on sin, explained the erroneousness of such a view. The patient's consent turns euthanasia into suicide, and suicide is sin. Their Lordships listened to the voice of authority, and rejected the Bill. Consequently, to please the Archbishop—and his God, if he reports truly—victims of cancer still have to endure months of wholly useless agony, unless their doctors or nurses are sufficiently humane to risk a charge of murder. I find difficulty in the conception of a God who gets pleasure from contemplating such tortures; and if there were a God capable of such wanton cruelty, I should certainly not think Him worthy of worship. But that only proves how sunk I am in moral depravity.

I am equally puzzled by the things that are sin and by the things that are not. When the Society for the Prevention of Cruelty to Animals asked the Pope for his support, he refused it, on the ground that human beings owe no duty to the lower animals, and that ill-treating animals is not sinful. This is because animals have no souls. On the other hand, it is wicked to marry your deceased wife's sister—so at least the Church teaches—however much you and she may wish to marry. This is not because of any unhappiness that might result, but because of certain texts in the Bible.

The resurrection of the body, which is an article of the Apostles' Creed, is a dogma which has various curious consequences. There was an author not very many years ago, who had an ingenious method of calculating the date of the end of the world. He argued that there must be enough of the necessary ingredients of a human body to provide everybody with the requisites at the Last Day. By carefully calculating the available raw material, he decided that it would all have been used up by a certain date. When that date comes, the world must end, since otherwise the resurrection of the body would become impossible. Unfortunately, I have forgotten what the date was, but I believe it is not very distant.

St Thomas Aquinas, the official philosopher of the Catholic Church, discussed lengthily and seriously a very grave problem, which, I fear, modern theologians unduly neglect. He imagines a cannibal who has never eaten anything but human flesh, and whose father and mother before him had like propensities. Every particle of his body belongs rightfully to someone else. We cannot suppose that those who have been eaten by cannibals are to go short through all eternity. But, if not, what is left for the cannibal? How is he to be properly roasted in hell, if all his body is restored to its original owners? This is a puzzling question, as the Saint rightly perceives.

In this connection the orthodox have a curious objection to cremation, which seems to show an insufficient realization of God's omnipotence. It is thought that a body which has been burnt will be more difficult for Him to collect together again than one which has been put underground and transformed into worms. No doubt collecting the particles from the air and undoing the chemical work of combustion would be somewhat laborious, but it is surely blasphemous to suppose such a work impossible for the Deity. I conclude that the objection to cremation implies grave heresy. But I doubt whether my opinion will carry much weight with the orthodox.

It was only very slowly and reluctantly that the Church sanctioned the dissection of corpses in connection with the study of medicine. The pioneer in dissection was Vesalius, who was Court physician to the Emperor Charles V. His medical skill led the Emperor to protect him, but after the Emperor was dead he got into trouble. A corpse which he was dissecting was said to have shown signs of life under the knife, and he was accused of murder. The Inquisition was induced by King Philip II to take a lenient view, and only sentenced him to a pilgrimage to the Holy Land. On the way home he was shipwrecked and died of exhaustion. For centuries after this time, medical students at the Papal University in Rome were only allowed to operate on lay figures, from which the sexual parts were omitted.

The sacredness of corpses is a widespread belief. It was carried furthest by the Egyptians, among whom it led to the practice of mummification. It still exists in full force in China. A French surgeon who was employed by the Chinese to teach Western medicine, relates that his demand for corpses to dissect was received with horror, but he was assured that he could have instead an unlimited supply of live criminals. His objection to this alternative was totally unintelligible to his Chinese employers.

Although there are many kinds of sin, seven of which are deadly, the most fruitful field for Satan's wiles is sex. The orthodox Catholic doctrine on this subject is to be found in St Paul, St Augustine, and St Thomas Aquinas. It is best to be celibate, but those who have not the gift of continence may marry. Intercourse in marriage is not sin, provided it is motivated by desire for offspring. All intercourse outside marriage is sin, and so is intercourse within marriage if any measures are adopted to prevent conception. Interruption of pregnancy is sin, even if, in medical opinion, it is the only way of saving the mother's life; for medical opinion is fallible, and God can always save a life by miracle if He sees fit. (This view is embodied in the law of Connecticut.) Venereal disease is God's punishment for sin. It is true that, through a guilty husband, this punishment may fall on an innocent woman and her children, but this is a mysterious dispensation of Providence which it would be impious to question. We must also not inquire why venereal disease was not divinely instituted until the time of Columbus. Since it is the appointed penalty for sin, all measures for its avoidance are also sin—except, of course, a virtuous life. Marriage is nominally indissoluble, but many people who seem to be married are not. In the case of influential Catholics, some ground for nullity can often be found, but for the poor there is no such outlet, except perhaps in cases of impotence. Persons who divorce and remarry are guilty of adultery in the sight of God.

The phrase 'in the sight of God' puzzles me. One would suppose that God sees everything, but apparently this is a mistake. He does not see Reno, for you cannot be divorced in the sight of God. Register offices are a doubtful point. I notice that respectable people, who would not call on anybody who lives in open sin, are quite willing to call on people who have had only a civil marriage; so apparently God does see register offices.

Some eminent men think even the doctrine of the Catholic Church deplorably lax where sex is concerned. Tolstoy and Mahatma Gandhi, in their old age, laid it down that *all* sexual intercourse is wicked, even in marriage and with a view to offspring. The Manicheans thought likewise, relying upon men's native sinfulness to supply them with a continually fresh crop of disciples. This doctrine, however, is heretical, though it is equally heretical to maintain that marriage is as praiseworthy as celibacy. Tolstoy thinks tobacco almost as bad as sex; in one of his novels, a man who is contemplating murder smokes a cigarette first in order to generate the necessary homicidal fury. Tobacco, however, is not prohibited in the Scriptures, though, as Samuel Butler points out, St Paul would no doubt have denounced it if he had known of it.

It is odd that neither the Church nor modern public opinion condemns petting, provided it stops short at a certain point. At what point sin begins is a matter as to which casuists differ. One eminently orthodox Catholic divine laid it down that a confessor may fondle a nun's breasts, provided he does it without evil intent. But I doubt whether modern authorities would agree with him on this point.

Modern morals are a mixture of two elements: on the one hand, rational precepts as to how to live together peaceably in a society, and on the other hand traditional taboos derived originally from some ancient superstition, but proximately from sacred books, Christian, Mohammedan, Hindu, or Buddhist. To some extent the two agree; the prohibition of murder and theft, for instance, is supported both by human reason and by Divine command. But the prohibition of pork or beef has only scriptural authority, and that only in certain religions. It is odd that modern men, who are aware of what science has done in the way of bringing new knowledge and altering the conditions of social life, should still be willing to accept the authority of texts embodying the outlook of very ancient and very ignorant pastoral or agricultural tribes. It is discouraging that many of the precepts whose sacred character is thus uncritically acknowledged should be such as to inflict much wholly unnecessary misery. If men's kindly impulses were stronger, they would find some way of explaining that these precepts are not to be taken literally, any more than the command to 'sell all that thou hast and give to the poor'.

There are logical difficulties in the notion of sin. We are told that sin consists in disobedience to God's commands, but we are also told that God is omnipotent. If He is, nothing contrary to His will can occur; therefore when the sinner disobeys His commands, He must have intended this to happen. St Augustine boldly accepts this view, and asserts that men are led to sin by a blindness with which God afflicts them. But most theologians, in modern times, have felt that, if God causes men to sin, it is not fair to send them to hell for what they cannot help. We are told that sin consists in acting contrary to God's will. This, however, does not get rid of the difficulty. Those who, like Spinoza, take God's omnipotence seriously, deduce that there can be no such thing as sin. This leads to frightful results. What! said Spinoza's contemporaries, was it not wicked of Nero to murder his mother? Was it not wicked of Adam to eat the apple? Is one action just as good as another? Spinoza wriggles, but does not find any satisfactory answer. *If* everything happens in accordance with God's will, God must have wanted Nero to murder his mother; therefore, since God is good, the murder must have been a good thing. From this argument there is no escape.

On the other hand, those who are in earnest in thinking that sin is disobedience to God are compelled to say that God is not omnipotent.

This gets out of all the logical puzzles, and is the view adopted by a certain school of liberal theologians. It has, however, its own difficulties. How are we to know what really is God's will? If the forces of evil have a certain share of power, they may deceive us into accepting as Scripture what is really their work. This was the view of the Gnostics, who thought that the Old Testament was the work of an evil spirit.

As soon as we abandon our own reason, and are content to rely upon authority, there is no end to our troubles. Whose authority? The Old Testament? The New Testament? The Koran? In practice, people choose the book considered sacred by the community in which they are born, and out of that book they choose the parts they like, ignoring the others. At one time, the most influential text in the Bible was: 'Thou shalt not suffer a witch to live.' Nowadays, people pass over this text, in silence if possible; if not, with an apology. And so, even when we have a sacred book, we still choose as truth whatever suits our own prejudices. No Catholic, for instance, takes seriously the text which says that a bishop should be the husband of one wife.

People's beliefs have various causes. One is that there is some evidence for the belief in question. We apply this to matters of fact, such as 'what is so-and-so's telephone number?' or 'who won the World Series?' But as soon as it comes to anything more debatable, the causes of belief become less defensible. We believe, first and foremost, what makes us feel that we are fine fellows. Mr Homo, if he has a good digestion and a sound income, thinks to himself how much more sensible he is than his neighbour so-and-so, who married a flighty wife and is always losing money. He thinks how superior his city is to the one fifty miles away: it has a bigger Chamber of Commerce and a more enterprising Rotary Club, and its mayor has never been in prison. He thinks how immeasurably his country surpasses all others. If he is an Englishman, he thinks of Shakespeare and Milton, or of Newton and Darwin, or of Nelson and Wellington, according to his temperament. If he is a Frenchman, he congratulates himself on the fact that for centuries France has led the world in culture, fashions, and cookery. If he is a Russian, he reflects that he belongs to the only nation which is truly international. If he is a Yugoslav, he boasts of his nation's pigs; if a native of the Principality of Monaco, he boasts of leading the world in the matter of gambling.

But these are not the only matters on which he has to congratulate himself. For is he not an individual of the species *homo sapiens*? Alone among animals he has an immortal soul, and is rational; he knows the difference between good and evil, and has learnt the multiplication table. Did not God make him in His own image? And was not everything created for man's convenience? The sun was made to light the day, and the moon to light the night—though the moon, by some oversight, only shines during half the nocturnal hours. The raw fruits of the earth were made for human sustenance. Even the white tails of rabbits, according to some theologians, have a purpose, namely to make it easier for sportsmen to shoot them. There are, it is true, some inconveniences: lions and tigers are too fierce, the summer is too hot, and the winter too cold. But these things only began after Adam ate the apple; before that, all animals were vegetarians, and the season was always spring. If only Adam had been content with peaches and nectarines, grapes and pears and pineapples, these blessings would still be ours.

Self-importance, individual or generic, is the source of most of our religious beliefs. Even sin is a conception derived from self-importance. Borrow relates how he met a Welsh preacher who was always melancholy. By sympathetic questioning he was brought to confess the source of his sorrow: that at the age of seven he had committed the sin against the Holy Ghost. 'My dear fellow,' said Borrow, 'don't let that trouble you; I know dozens of people in like case. Do not imagine yourself cut off from the rest of mankind by this occurrence; if you inquire, you will find multitudes who suffer from the same misfortune.' From that moment, the man was cured. He had enjoyed feeling singular, but there was no pleasure in being one of a herd of sinners. Most sinners are rather less egotistical; but theologians undoubtedly enjoy the feeling that Man is the special object of God's wrath, as well as of His love. After the Fall, so Milton assures us—

> The Sun
> Had first his precept so to move, so shine,
> As might affect the Earth with cold and heat
> Scarce tolerable, and from the North to call
> Decrepit Winter, from the South to bring
> Solstitial summer's heat.

However disagreeable the results may have been, Adam could hardly help feeling flattered that such vast astronomical phenomena should be brought about to teach *him* a lesson. The whole of theology, in regard to hell no less than to heaven, takes it for granted that Man is what is of most importance in the universe of created beings. Since all theologians are men, this postulate has met with little opposition.

Since evolution became fashionable, the glorification of Man has taken a new form. We are told that evolution has been guided by one great Purpose: through the millions of years when there were only slime, or trilobites, throughout the ages of dinosaurs and giant ferns, of bees and wild flowers, God was preparing the Great Climax. At last, in the fullness of time, He produced Man, including such specimens as Nero and Caligula, Hitler and Mussolini, whose transcendent glory justified the long painful process. For my part, I find even eternal damnation less incredible, and certainly less ridiculous, than this lame and impotent conclusion which we are asked to admire as the supreme effort of Omnipotence. And if God is indeed omnipotent, why could He not have produced the glorious result without such a long and tedious prologue?

Apart from the question whether Man is really so glorious as the theologians of evolution say he is, there is the further difficulty that life on this planet is almost certainly temporary. The earth will grow cold, or the atmosphere will gradually fly off, or there will be an insufficiency of water, or, as Sir James Jeans genially prophesies, the sun will burst and all the planets will be turned into gas. Which of those will happen first, no one knows; but in any case the human race will ultimately die out. Of course, such an event is of little importance from the point of view of orthodox theology, since men are immortal, and will continue to exist in heaven and hell when none are left on earth. But in that case why bother about terrestrial developments? Those who lay stress on the gradual progress from the primitive slime to Man attach an importance to this mundane sphere which should make them shrink from the conclusion that all life on earth is only a brief interlude between the nebula and the eternal frost, or perhaps between one nebula and another. The importance of Man, which is the one indispensable dogma of the theologians, receives no support from a scientific view of the future of the solar system.

There are many other sources of false belief besides self-importance. One of these is love of the marvellous. I knew at one time a scientifically minded conjurer, who used to perform his tricks before a small audience, and then get them, each separately, to write down what they had seen happen. Almost always they wrote down something much more astonishing than the reality, and usually something which no conjurer could have achieved; yet they all thought they were reporting truly what they had seen with their own eyes. This sort of falsification is still more true of rumours. A tells B that last night he saw Mr ———, the eminent prohibitionist, slightly the worse for liquor; B tells C that A saw the good man reeling drunk, C tells D that he was picked up unconscious in the ditch, D tells E that he is well known to pass out every evening. Here, it is true, another motive comes in, namely malice. We like to think ill of our neighbours, and are prepared to believe the worst on very little evidence. But even where there is no such motive, what is marvellous is readily believed unless it goes against some strong prejudice. All history until the eighteenth century is full of prodigies and wonders which modern historians ignore, not because they are less well attested than facts which the historians accept, but because modern taste among the learned prefers what science regards as probable. Shakespeare relates how on the night before Caesar was killed,

A common slave—you know him well by sight—
Held up his left hand, which did flame and burn
Like twenty torches join'd; and yet his hand,
Not sensible of fire, remain'd unscorch'd.
Besides—I have not since put up my sword—
Against the Capitol I met a lion,
Who glar'd upon me, and went surly by,
Without annoying me; and there were drawn
Upon a heap a hundred ghastly women,
Transformed with their fear, who swore they saw
Men all in fire walk up and down the streets.

Shakespeare did not invent these marvels; he found them in reputable historians, who are among those upon whom we depend for our knowledge concerning Julius Caesar. This sort of thing always used to happen at the death of a great man or the beginning of an important war. Even so recently as 1914 the 'angels of Mons' encouraged the British troops. The evidence for such events is very seldom first-hand, and modern historians refuse to accept it—except, of course, where the event is one that has religious importance.

Every powerful emotion has its own myth-making tendency. When the emotion is peculiar to an individual, he is considered more or less mad if he gives credence to such myths as he has invented. But when an emotion is collective, as in war, there is no one to correct the myths that naturally arise. Consequently in all times of great collective excitement unfounded rumours obtain wide credence. In September 1914 almost everybody in England believed that Russian troops had passed through England on the way to the Western Front. Everybody knew someone who had seen them, though no one had seen them himself.

This myth-making faculty is often allied with cruelty. Ever since the Middle Ages, the Jews have been accused of practising ritual murder. There is not an iota of evidence for this accusation, and no sane person who has examined it believes it. Nevertheless it persists. I have met White Russians who were convinced of its truth, and among many Nazis it was accepted without question. Such myths give an excuse for the infliction of torture, and the unfounded belief in them is evidence of the unconscious desire to find some victim to persecute.

There was, until the end of the eighteenth century, a theory that insanity is due to possession by devils. It was inferred that any pain suffered by the patient is also suffered by the devils, so that the best cure is to make the patient suffer so much that the devils will decide to abandon him. The insane, in accordance with this theory, were savagely beaten. This treatment was tried on King George III when he was mad, but without success. It is a curious and painful fact that almost all the completely futile treatments that have been believed in during the long history of medical folly have been such as caused acute suffering to the patient. When anaesthetics were discovered pious people considered them an attempt to evade the will of God. It was pointed out, however, that when God extracted Adam's rib He put him into a deep sleep. This proved that anaesthetics are all right for *men*; women, however, ought to suffer, because of the curse of Eve. In the West votes for women proved this doctrine mistaken, but in Japan, to this day, women in childbirth are not allowed any alleviation through anaesthetics. As the Japanese do not believe in Genesis, this piece of sadism must have some other justification.

The fallacies about 'race' and 'blood', which have always been popular, and which the Nazis embodied in their official creed, have no objective justification; they are believed solely because they minister to self-esteem and to the impulse towards cruelty. In one form or another, these beliefs are as old as civilization; their forms change, but their essence remains. Herodotus tells how Cyrus was brought up by peasants, in complete ignorance of his royal blood; at the age of twelve, his kingly bearing towards other peasant boys revealed the truth. This is a variant of an old story which is found in all Indo-European countries. Even quite modern people say that 'blood will tell'. It is no use for scientific physiologists to assure the world that there is no difference between the blood of a Negro and the blood of a white man. The American Red Cross, in obedience to popular prejudice, at first, when America became involved in the last war, decreed that no Negro blood should be used for blood transfusion. As a result of an agitation, it was conceded that Negro blood might be used, but only for Negro patients. Similarly, in Germany, the Aryan soldier who needed blood transfusion was carefully protected from the contamination of Jewish blood.

In the matter of race, there are different beliefs in different societies. Where monarchy is firmly established, kings are of a higher race than their subjects. Until very recently, it was universally believed that men are congenitally more intelligent than women; even so enlightened a man as Spinoza decides against votes for women on this ground. Among white men, it is held that white men are by nature superior to men of other colours, and especially to black men; in Japan, on the contrary, it is thought that yellow is the best colour. In Haiti, when they make statues of Christ and Satan, they make Christ black and Satan white. Aristotle and Plato considered Greeks so innately superior to barbarians that slavery is justified so long as the master is Greek and the slave barbarian. The American legislators who made the immigration laws consider the Nordics superior to Slavs or Latins or any other white men. But the Nazis, under the stress of war, were led to the conclusion that there are hardly any true Nordics outside Germany; the Norwegians, except Quisling and his few followers, had been corrupted by intermixture with

Finns and Lapps and such. Thus politics are a clue to descent. The biologically pure Nordic love Hitler, and if you did not love Hitler, that was proof of tainted blood.

All this is, of course, pure nonsense, known to be such by everyone who has studied the subject. In schools in America, children of the most diverse origins are subjected to the same educational system, and those whose business it is to measure intelligence quotients and otherwise estimate the native ability of students are unable to make any such racial distinctions as are postulated by the theorists of race. In every national or racial group there are clever children and stupid children. It is not likely that, in the United States, coloured children will develop as success-fully as white children, because of the stigma of social inferiority; but in so far as congenital ability can be detached from environmental influence, there is no clear distinction among different groups. The whole con-ception of superior races is merely a myth generated by the overweening self-esteem of the holders of power. It may be that, some day, better evidence will be forthcoming; perhaps, in time, educators will be able to prove (say) that Jews are on the average more intelligent than Gentiles. But as yet no such evidence exists, and all talk of superior races must be dismissed as nonsense.

There is a special absurdity in applying racial theories to the various populations of Europe. There is not in Europe any such thing as a pure race. Russians have an admixture of Tartar blood, Germans are largely Slavonic, France is a mixture of Celts, Germans, and people of Mediter-ranean race, Italy the same with the addition of the descendants of slaves imported by the Romans. The English are perhaps the most mixed of all. There is no evidence that there is any advantage in belonging to a pure race. The purest races now in existence are the Pygmies, the Hottentots, and the Australian aborigines; the Tasmanians, who were probably even purer, are extinct. They were not the bearers of a brilliant culture. The ancient Greeks, on the other hand, emerged from an amalgamation of northern barbarians and an indigenous population; the Athenians and Ionians, who were the most civilized, were also the most mixed. The supposed merits of racial purity are, it would seem, wholly imaginary.

Superstitions about blood have many forms that have nothing to do with race. The objection to homicide seems to have been, originally, based on the ritual pollution caused by the blood of the victim. God said to Cain: 'The voice of thy brother's blood crieth unto me from the ground.' According to some anthropologists, the mark of Cain was a disguise to prevent Abel's blood from finding him; this appears also to be the original reason for wearing mourning. In many ancient com-munities no difference was made between murder and accidental homi-cide; in either case equally ritual ablution was necessary. The feeling that blood defiles still lingers, for example in the Churching of Women and in taboos connected with menstruation. The idea that a child is of his father's 'blood' has the same superstitious origin. So far as actual blood is concerned, the mother's enters into the child, but not the father's. If blood were as important as is supposed, matriarchy would be the only proper way of tracing descent.

In Russia, where, under the influence of Karl Marx, people since the revolution have been classified by their economic origin, difficulties have arisen not unlike those of German race theorists over the Scandinavian Nordics. There were two theories that had to be reconciled: on the one hand, proletarians were good and other people were bad; on the other hand, Communists were good and other people were bad. The only way of effecting a reconciliation was to alter the meaning of words. A 'proletarian' came to mean a supporter of the government; Lenin, though born a noble, was reckoned a member of the proletariat. On the other hand, the word 'kulak', which was supposed to mean a rich peasant, came to mean any peasant who opposed collectivization. This sort of absurdity always arises when one group of human beings is supposed to be inherently better than another. In America, the highest praise that can be bestowed on an eminent coloured man after he is safely dead is to say 'he was a *white* man'. A courageous woman is called 'masculine'; Macbeth, praising his wife's courage, says:

> Bring forth men children only,
> For thy undaunted mettle should compose
> Nothing but males.

All these ways of speaking come of unwillingness to abandon foolish generalizations.

In the economic sphere there are many widespread superstitions.

Why do people value gold and precious stones? Not simply because of their rarity: there are a number of elements called 'rare earths' which are much rarer than gold, but no one will give a penny for them except a few men of science. There is a theory, for which there is much to be said, that gold and gems were valued originally on account of their supposed magical properties. The mistakes of governments in modern times seem to show that this belief still exists among the sort of men who are called 'practical'. At the end of the 1914–18 war, it was agreed that Germany should pay vast sums to England and France, and they in turn should pay vast sums to the United States. Everyone wanted to be paid in money rather than goods; the 'practical' men failed to notice that there is not that amount of money in the world. They also failed to notice that money is no use unless it is used to buy goods. As they would not use it in this way, it did no good to anyone. There was supposed to be some mystic virtue about gold that made it worth while to dig it up in the

Transvaal and put it underground again in bank vaults in America. In the end, of course, the debtor countries had no more money, and, since they were not allowed to pay in goods, they went bankrupt. The great depression was the direct result of the surviving belief in the magical properties of gold. This superstition now seems dead, but no doubt others will replace it.

Politics is largely governed by sententious platitudes which are devoid of truth.

One of the most widespread popular maxims is, 'human nature cannot be changed'. No one can say whether this is true or not without first defining 'human nature'. But as used it is certainly false. When Mr A utters the maxim, with an air of portentous and conclusive wisdom, what he means is that all men everywhere will always continue to behave as they do in his own home town. A little anthropology will dispel this belief. Among the Tibetans, one wife has many husbands, because men are too poor to support a whole wife; yet family life, according to travellers, is no more unhappy than elsewhere. The practice of lending one's wife to a guest is very common among uncivilized tribes. The Australian aborigines, at puberty, undergo a very painful operation which, throughout the rest of their lives, greatly diminishes sexual potency. Infanticide, which might seem contrary to human nature, was almost universal before the rise of Christianity, and is recommended by Plato to prevent over-population. Private property is not recognized among some savage tribes. Even among highly civilized people, economic considerations will override what is called 'human nature'. In Moscow, where there is an acute housing shortage, when an unmarried woman is pregnant, it often happens that a number of men contend for the legal right to be considered the father of the prospective child, because whoever is judged to be the father acquires the right to share the woman's room, and half a room is better than no roof.

In fact, adult 'human nature' is extremely variable, according to the circumstances of education. Food and sex are very general requirements, but the hermits of the Thebaid eschewed sex altogether and reduced food to the lowest point compatible with survival. By diet and training, people can be made ferocious or meek, masterful or slavish, as may suit the educator. There is no nonsense so arrant that it cannot be made the creed of the vast majority by adequate governmental action. Plato intended his Republic to be founded on a myth which he admitted to be absurd, but he was rightly confident that the populace could be induced to believe it. Hobbes, who thought it important that people should reverence the government, however unworthy it might be, meets the argument that it might be difficult to obtain general assent to anything so irrational by pointing out that people have been brought to believe in the Christian religion, and, in particular, in the dogma of transubstantiation. If he had been alive in 1940, he would have found ample confirmation of his contention in the devotion of German youth to the Nazis.

The power of governments over men's beliefs has been very great ever since the rise of large States. The great majority of Romans became Christian after the Roman Emperors had been converted. In the parts of the Roman Empire that were conquered by the Arabs, most people abandoned Christianity for Islam. The division of Western Europe into Protestant and Catholic regions was determined by the attitude of governments in the sixteenth century. But the power of governments over belief in the present day is vastly greater than at any earlier time. A belief, however untrue, is important when it dominates the actions of large masses of men. In this sense, the beliefs inculcated before the last war by the Japanese, Russian, and German governments were important. Since they were completely divergent, they could not all be true, though they could well all be false. Unfortunately, they were such as to inspire men with an ardent desire to kill one another, even to the point of almost completely inhibiting the impulse of self-preservation. No one can deny, in face of the evidence, that it is easy, given military power, to produce a population of fanatical lunatics. It would be equally easy to produce a population of sane and reasonable people, but many governments do not wish to do so, since such people would fail to admire the politicians who are at the head of these governments.

There is one peculiarly pernicious application of the doctrine that human nature cannot be changed. This is the dogmatic assertion that there will always be wars, because we are so constituted that we feel a need of them. What is true is that a man who has had the kind of diet and education that most men have will wish to fight when provoked. But he will not actually fight unless he has a chance of victory. It is very annoying to be stopped by a policeman, but we do not fight him because we know that he has the overwhelming forces of the State at his back. People who have no occasion for war do not make any impression of being psychologically thwarted. Sweden has had no war since 1814, but the Swedes are one of the happiest and most contented nations in the world. The only cloud upon their national happiness is fear of being involved in the next war. If political organization were such as to make war obviously unprofitable, there is nothing in human nature that would compel its occurrence, or make average people unhappy because of its not occurring. Exactly the same arguments that are now used about the impossibility of preventing war were formerly used in defence of duelling, yet few of us feel thwarted because we are not allowed to fight duels.

I am persuaded that there is absolutely no limit to the absurdities that can, by government action, come to be generally believed. Give me an adequate army, with power to provide it with more pay and better food than falls to the lot of the average man, and I will undertake, within thirty years, to make the majority of the population believe that two and two are three, that water freezes when it gets hot and boils when it gets cold, or any other nonsense that might seem to serve the interest of the State. Of course, even when these beliefs had been generated, people would not put the kettle in the refrigerator when they wanted it to boil. That cold makes water boil would be a Sunday truth, sacred and mystical, to be professed in awed tones, but not to be acted on in daily life. What would happen would be that any verbal denial of the mystic doctrine would be made illegal, and obstinate heretics would be 'frozen' at the stake. No person who did not enthusiastically accept the official doctrine would be allowed to teach or to have any position of power. Only the very highest officials, in their cups, would whisper to each other what rubbish it all is; then they would laugh and drink again. This is hardly a caricature of what happens under some modern governments.

The discovery that man can be scientifically manipulated, and that governments can turn large masses this way or that as they choose, is one of the causes of our misfortunes. There is as much difference between a collection of mentally free citizens and a community moulded by modern methods of propaganda as there is between a heap of raw materials and a battleship. Education, which was at first made universal in order that all might be able to read and write, has been found capable of serving quite other purposes. By instilling nonsense it unifies populations and generates collective enthusiasm. If all governments taught the same nonsense, the harm would not be so great. Unfortunately each has its own brand, and the diversity serves to produce hostility between the devotees of different creeds. If there is ever to be peace in the world, governments will have to agree either to inculcate no dogmas, or all to inculcate the same. The former, I fear, is a Utopian ideal, but perhaps they could agree to teach collectively that all public men, everywhere, are completely virtuous and perfectly wise. Perhaps, after the next war, the surviving politicians may find it prudent to combine on some such programme.

But if conformity has its dangers, so has nonconformity.

Some 'advanced thinkers' are of opinion that any one who differs from the conventional opinion must be in the right. This is a delusion; if it were not, truth would be easier to come by than it is. There are infinite possibilities of error, and more cranks take up unfashionable errors than unfashionable truths. I met once an electrical engineer whose first words to me were: 'How do you do. There are two methods of faith-healing, the one practised by Christ and the one practised by most Christian Scientists. I practise the method practised by Christ.' Shortly afterwards, he was sent to prison for making out fraudulent balance-sheets. The law does not look kindly on the intrusion of faith into this region. I knew also an eminent lunacy doctor who took to philosophy, and taught a new logic which, as he frankly confessed, he had learnt from his lunatics. When he died he left a will founding a professorship for the teaching of his new scientific methods, but unfortunately he left no assets. Arithmetic proved recalcitrant to lunatic logic. On one occasion a man came to ask me to recommend some of my books, as he was interested in philosophy. I did so, but he returned next day saying that he had been reading one of them, and had found only one statement he could understand, and that one seemed to him false. I asked him what it was, and he said it was the statement that Julius Caesar is dead. When I asked him why he did not agree, he drew himself up and said: 'Because I am Julius Caesar.' These examples may suffice to show that you cannot make sure of being right by being eccentric.

Science, which has always had to fight its way against popular beliefs, now has one of its most difficult battles in the sphere of psychology.

People who think they know all about human nature are always hopelessly at sea when they have to do with any abnormality. Some boys never learn to be what, in animals, is called 'house-trained'. The sort of person who won't stand any nonsense deals with such cases by punishment; the boy is beaten, and when he repeats the offence he is beaten worse. All medical men who have studied the matter know that punishment only aggravates the trouble. Sometimes the cause is physical, but usually it is psychological, and only curable by removing some deep-seated and probably unconscious grievance. But most people enjoy punishing anyone who irritates them, and so the medical view is rejected as fancy nonsense. The same sort of thing applies to men who are exhibitionists; they are sent to prison over and over again, but as soon as they come out they repeat the offence. A medical man who specialized in such ailments assured me that the exhibitionist can be cured by the simple device of having trousers that button up the back instead of the front. But this method is not tried because it does not satisfy people's vindictive impulses.

Broadly speaking, punishment is likely to prevent crimes that are sane in origin, but not those that spring from some psychological abnormality. This is now partially recognized; we distinguish between plain theft, which springs from what may be called rational self-interest, and kleptomania, which is a mark of something queer. And homicidal maniacs are not treated like ordinary murderers. But sexual aberrations rouse so much disgust that it is still impossible to have them treated medically rather than punitively. Indignation, though on the whole a useful social force, becomes harmful when it is directed against the victims of maladies that only medical skill can cure.

The same sort of thing happens as regards whole nations. During the 1914–18 war, very naturally, people's vindictive feelings were aroused against the Germans, who were severely punished after their defeat.

During the Second World War it was argued that the Versailles Treaty was ridiculously mild, since it failed to teach a lesson; this time, we were told, there must be *real* severity. To my mind, we should have been more likely to prevent a repetition of German aggression if we had regarded the rank and file of the Nazis as we regard lunatics than by thinking of them as merely and simply criminals. Lunatics, of course, have to be restrained. But lunatics are restrained from prudence, not as a punishment, and so far as prudence permits we try to make them happy. Everybody recognizes that a homicidal maniac will only become more homicidal if he is made miserable. There were, of course, many men among the Nazis who were plain criminals, but there must also have been many who were more or less mad. If Germany is to be successfully incorporated in Western Europe, there must be a complete abandonment of all attempt to instil a feeling of special guilt. Those who are being punished seldom learn to feel kindly towards the men who punish them. And so long as the Germans hate the rest of mankind peace will be precarious.

When one reads of the beliefs of savages, or of the ancient Babylonians and Egyptians, they seem surprising by their capricious absurdity. But beliefs that are just as absurd are still entertained by the uneducated even in the most modern and civilized societies. I have been gravely assured, in America, that people born in March are unlucky and people born in May are peculiarly liable to corns. I do not know the history of these superstitions, but probably they are derived from Babylonian or Egyptian priestly lore. Beliefs begin in the higher social strata, and then, like mud in a river, sink gradually downwards in the educational scale; they may take 3,000 or 4,000 years to sink all the way. In America you may find your coloured maid making some remark that comes straight out of Plato—not the parts of Plato that scholars quote, but the parts where he utters obvious nonsense, such as that men who do not pursue wisdom in this life will be born again as women. Commentators on great philosophers always politely ignore their silly remarks.

Aristotle, in spite of his reputation, is full of absurdities. He says that children should be conceived in the winter, when the wind is in the north, and that if people marry too young the children will be female. He tells us that the blood of females is blacker than that of males; that the pig is the only animal liable to measles; that an elephant suffering from insomnia should have its shoulders rubbed with salt, olive-oil, and warm water; that women have fewer teeth than men, and so on. Nevertheless, he is considered by the great majority of philosophers a paragon of wisdom.

Superstitions about lucky and unlucky days are almost universal. In ancient times they governed the actions of generals. Among ourselves the prejudice against Friday and the number 13 is very active, sailors do not like to sail on a Friday, and many hotels have no 13th floor. The superstitions about Friday and 13 were once believed by those reputed wise; now such men regard them as harmless follies. But probably 2,000 years hence many beliefs of the wise of our day will have come to seem equally foolish. Man is a credulous animal, and must believe *something*; in the absence of good grounds for belief, he will be satisfied with bad ones.

Belief in 'nature' and what is 'natural' is a source of many errors. It used to be, and to some extent still is, powerfully operative in medicine. The human body, left to itself, has a certain power of curing itself; small cuts usually heal, colds pass off, and even serious diseases sometimes disappear without medical treatment. But aids to nature are very desirable, even in these cases. Cuts may turn septic if not disinfected, colds may turn to pneumonia, and serious diseases are only left without treatment by explorers and travellers in remote regions, who have no option. Many practices which have come to seem 'natural' were originally 'unnatural', for instance clothing and washing. Before men adopted clothing they must have found it impossible to live in cold climates. Where there is not a modicum of cleanliness, populations suffer from various diseases, such as typhus, from which Western nations have become exempt. Vaccination was (and by some still is) objected to as 'unnatural'. But there is no consistency in such objections, for no one supposes that a broken bone can be mended by 'natural' behaviour. Eating cooked food is 'unnatural'; so is heating our houses. The Chinese philosopher Lao-tse, whose traditional date is about 600 B.C., objected to roads and bridges and boats as 'unnatural', and in his disgust at such mechanistic devices left China and went to live among the Western barbarians. Every advance in civilization has been denounced as unnatural while it was recent.

The commonest objection to birth control is that it is against 'nature'. (For some reason we are not allowed to say that celibacy is against nature; the only reason I can think of is that it is not new.) Malthus saw only three ways of keeping down the population: moral restraint, vice, and misery. Moral restraint, he admitted, was not likely to be practised on a large scale. 'Vice', i.e. birth control, he, as a clergyman, viewed with abhorrence. There remained misery. In his comfortable parsonage, he contemplated the misery of the great majority of mankind with equanimity, and pointed out the fallacies of the reformers who hoped to alleviate it. Modern theological opponents of birth control are less honest. They pretend to think that God will provide, however many mouths there may be to feed. They ignore the fact that He has never done so hitherto, but has left mankind exposed to periodical famines in which millions died of hunger. They must be deemed to hold—if they are saying what they believe—that from this moment onwards God will work a continual miracle of loaves and fishes which He has hitherto thought unnecessary. Or perhaps they will say that suffering here below is of no importance;

what matters is the hereafter. By their own theology, most of the children whom their opposition to birth control will cause to exist will go to hell. We must suppose, therefore, that they oppose the amelioration of life on earth because they think it a good thing that many millions should suffer eternal torment. By comparison with them, Malthus appears merciful.

Women, as the object of our strongest love and aversion, rouse complex emotions which are embodied in proverbial 'wisdom'.

Almost everybody allows himself or herself some entirely unjustifiable generalization on the subject of Woman. Married men, when they generalize on that subject, judge by their wives; women judge by themselves. It would be amusing to write a history of men's views on women. In antiquity, when male supremacy was unquestioned and Christian ethics were still unknown, women were harmless but rather silly, and a man who took them seriously was somewhat despised. Plato thinks it a grave objection to the drama that the playwright has to imitate women in creating his female roles. With the coming of Christianity woman took on a new part, that of the temptress; but at the same time she was also found capable of being a saint. In Victorian days the saint was much more emphasized than the temptress; Victorian men could not admit themselves susceptible to temptation. The superior virtue of women was made a reason for keeping them out of politics, where, it was held, a lofty virtue is impossible. But the early feminists turned the argument round, and contended that the participation of women would ennoble politics. Since this has turned out to be an illusion, there has been less talk of women's superior virtue, but there are still a number of men who adhere to the monkish view of woman as the temptress. Women themselves, for the most part, think of themselves as the sensible sex, whose business it is to undo the harm that comes of men's impetuous follies. For my part I distrust *all* generalizations about women, favourable and unfavourable, masculine and feminine, ancient and modern; all alike, I should say, result from paucity of experience.

The deeply irrational attitude of each sex towards women may be seen in novels, particularly in bad novels. In bad novels by men, there is the woman with whom the author is in love, who usually possesses every charm, but is somewhat helpless, and requires male protection; sometimes, however, like Shakespeare's Cleopatra, she is an object of exasperated hatred, and is thought to be deeply and desperately wicked. In portraying the heroine, the male author does not write from observation, but merely objectifies his own emotions. In regard to his other female characters, he is more objective, and may even depend upon his notebook; but when he is in love, his passion makes a mist between him and the object of his devotion. Women novelists, also, have two kinds of women in their books. One is themselves, glamorous and kind, an object of lust to the wicked and of love to the good, sensitive, high-souled, and constantly misjudged. The other kind is represented by all other women, and is usually portrayed as petty, spiteful, cruel, and deceitful. It would seem that to judge women without bias is not easy either for men or for women.

Generalizations about national characteristics are just as common and just as unwarranted as generalizations about women. Until 1870, the Germans were thought of as a nation of spectacled professors, evolving everything out of their inner consciousness, and scarcely aware of the outer world, but since 1870 this conception has had to be very sharply revised. Frenchmen seem to be thought of by most Americans as perpetually engaged in amorous intrigue; Walt Whitman, in one of his catalogues, speaks of 'the adulterous French couple on the sly settee'. Americans who go to live in France are astonished, and perhaps disappointed, by the intensity of family life. Before the Russian Revolution, the Russians were credited with a mystical Slav soul, which, while it incapacitated them for ordinary sensible behaviour, gave them a kind of deep wisdom to which more practical nations could not hope to attain. Suddenly everything was changed: mysticism was taboo, and only the most earthly ideals were tolerated. The truth is that what appears to one nation as the national character of another depends upon a few prominent individuals, or upon the class that happens to have power. For this reason, all generalizations on this subject are liable to be completely upset by any important political change.

To avoid the various foolish opinions to which mankind are prone, no superhuman genius is required. A few simple rules will keep you, not from *all* error, but from silly error.

If the matter is one that can be settled by observation, make the observation yourself. Aristotle could have avoided the mistake of thinking that women have fewer teeth than men by the simple device of asking Mrs Aristotle to keep her mouth open while he counted. He did not do so because he thought he knew. Thinking that you know when in fact you don't is a fatal mistake, to which we are all prone. I believe myself that hedgehogs eat black beetles, because I have been told that they do; but if I were writing a book on the habits of hedgehogs, I should not commit myself until I had seen one enjoying this unappetizing diet. Aristotle, however, was less cautious. Ancient and medieval authors knew all about unicorns and salamanders; not one of them thought it necessary to avoid dogmatic statements about them because he had never seen one of them.

Many matters, however, are less easily brought to the test of experience. If, like most of mankind, you have passionate convictions on many such matters, there are ways in which you can make yourself aware of your own bias. If an opinion contrary to your own makes you angry, that is a sign that you are subconsciously aware of having no good reason for thinking as you do. If someone maintains that two and two are five, or that Iceland is on the equator, you feel pity rather than anger, unless you know so little of arithmetic or geography that his opinion shakes your own contrary conviction. The most savage controversies are those about matters as to which there is no good evidence either way. Persecution is used in theology, not in arithmetic, because in arithmetic there is knowledge, but in theology there is only opinion. So whenever you find yourself getting angry about a difference of opinion, be on your guard; you will probably find, on examination, that your belief is going beyond what the evidence warrants.

A good way of ridding yourself of certain kinds of dogmatism is to become aware of opinions held in social circles different from your own. When I was young, I lived much outside my own country—in France, Germany, Italy, and the United States. I found this very profitable in diminishing the intensity of insular prejudice. If you cannot travel, seek out people with whom you disagree, and read a newspaper belonging to a party that is not yours. If the people and the newspaper seem mad, perverse, and wicked, remind yourself that you seem so to them. In this opinion both parties may be right, but they cannot both be wrong. This reflection should generate a certain caution.

Becoming aware of foreign customs, however, does not always have a beneficial effect. In the seventeenth century, when the Manchus conquered China, it was the custom among the Chinese for the women to have small feet, and among the Manchus for the men to wear pigtails. Instead of each dropping their own foolish custom, they each adopted the foolish custom of the other, and the Chinese continued to wear pigtails until they shook off the dominion of the Manchus in the revolution of 1911.

For those who have enough psychological imagination, it is a good plan to imagine an argument with a person having a different bias. This has one advantage, and only one, as compared with actual conversation with opponents; this one advantage is that the method is not subject to the same limitations of time and space. Mahatma Gandhi deplored railways and steamboats and machinery; he would have liked to undo the whole of the industrial revolution. You may never have an opportunity of actually meeting anyone who holds this opinion, because in Western countries most people take the advantage of modern technique for granted. But if you want to make sure that you are right in agreeing with the prevailing opinion, you will find it a good plan to test the arguments that occur to you by considering what Gandhi might have said in refutation of them. I have sometimes been led actually to change my mind as a result of this kind of imaginary dialogue, and, short of this, I have frequently found myself growing less dogmatic and cocksure through realizing the possible reasonableness of a hypothetical opponent.

Be very wary of opinions that flatter your self-esteem. Both men and women, nine times out of ten, are firmly convinced of the superior excellence of their own sex. There is abundant evidence on both sides. If you are a man, you can point out that most poets and men of science are male; if you are a woman, you can retort that so are most criminals. The question is inherently insoluble, but self-esteem conceals this from most people. We are all, whatever part of the world we come from, persuaded that our own nation is superior to all others. Seeing that each nation has its characteristic merits and demerits, we adjust our standard of values so as to make out that the merits possessed by our nation are the really important ones, while its demerits are comparatively trivial. Here, again, the rational man will admit that the question is one to which there is no demonstrably right answer. It is more difficult to deal with the self-esteem of man as man, because we cannot argue out the matter with some non-human mind. The only way I know of dealing with this general human conceit is to remind ourselves that man is a brief episode in the life of a small planet in a little corner of the universe, and that, for aught we know, other parts of the cosmos may contain beings as superior to ourselves as we are to jelly-fish.

Other passions besides self-esteem are common sources of error; of these perhaps the most important is fear. Fear sometimes operates directly, by inventing rumours of disaster in war-time, or by imagining objects of terror, such as ghosts; sometimes it operates indirectly, by creating belief in something comforting, such as the elixir of life, or heaven for ourselves and hell for our enemies. Fear has many forms—fear of death, fear of the dark, fear of the unknown, fear of the herd, and that vague generalized fear that comes to those who conceal from themselves their more specific terrors. Until you have admitted your own fears to yourself, and have guarded yourself by a difficult effort of will against their myth-making power, you cannot hope to think truly about many matters of great importance, especially those with which religious beliefs are concerned. Fear is the main source of superstition, and one of the main sources of cruelty. To conquer fear is the beginning of wisdom, in the pursuit of truth as in the endeavour after a worthy manner of life.

There are two ways of avoiding fear: one is by persuading ourselves that we are immune from disaster, and the other is by the practice of sheer courage. The latter is difficult, and to everybody becomes impossible at a certain point. The former has therefore always been more popular. Primitive magic has the purpose of securing safety, either by injuring enemies, or by protecting oneself by talismans, spells, or incantations. Without any essential change, belief in such ways of avoiding danger survived throughout the many centuries of Babylonian civilization, spread from Babylon throughout the Empire of Alexander, and was acquired by the Romans in the course of their absorption of Hellenistic culture. From the Romans it descended to medieval Christendom and Islam. Science has now lessened the belief in magic, but many people place more faith in mascots than they are willing to avow, and sorcery, while condemned by the Church, is still officially a *possible* sin.

Magic, however, was a crude way of avoiding terrors, and, moreover, not a very effective way, for wicked magicians might always prove stronger than good ones. In the fifteenth, sixteenth and seventeenth centuries, dread of witches and sorcerers led to the burning of hundreds of thousands convicted of these crimes. But newer beliefs, particularly as to the future life, sought more effective ways of combating fear. Socrates on the day of his death (if Plato is to be believed) expressed the conviction that in the next world he would live in the company of the gods and heroes, and surrounded by just spirits who would never object to his endless argumentation. Plato, in his *Republic*, laid it down that cheerful views of the next world must be enforced by the State, not because they were true, but to make soldiers more willing to die in battle. He would have none of the traditional myths about Hades, because they represented the spirits of the dead as unhappy.

Orthodox Christianity, in the Ages of Faith, laid down very definite rules for salvation. First, you must be baptized; then, you must avoid all theological error; last, you must, before dying, repent of your sins and receive absolution. All this would not save you from purgatory, but it would ensure your ultimate arrival in heaven. It was not necessary to *know* theology. An eminent cardinal stated authoritatively that the requirements of orthodoxy would be satisfied if you murmured on your death-bed: 'I believe all·that the Church believes; the Church believes all that I believe.' These very definite directions ought to have made Catholics sure of finding the way to heaven. Nevertheless, the dread of hell persisted, and has caused, in recent times, a great softening of the dogmas as to who will be damned. The doctrine, professed by many modern Christians, that everybody will go to heaven, ought to do away with the fear of death, but in fact this fear is too instinctive to be easily vanquished. F. W. H. Myers, whom spiritualism had converted to belief in a future life, questioned a woman who had lately lost her daughter as to what she supposed had become of her soul. The mother replied: 'Oh well, I suppose she is enjoying eternal bliss, but I wish you wouldn't talk about such unpleasant subjects.' In spite of all that theology can do, heaven remains, to most people, an 'unpleasant subject'.

The most refined religions, such as those of Marcus Aurelius and Spinoza, are still concerned with the conquest of fear. The Stoic doctrine was simple: it maintained that the only true good is virtue, of which no enemy can deprive me; consequently, there is no need to fear enemies. The difficulty was that no one could really believe virtue to be the only good, not even Marcus Aurelius, who, as Emperor, sought not only to make his subjects virtuous, but to protect them against barbarians, pestilences, and famines. Spinoza taught a somewhat similar doctrine. According to him, our true good consists in indifference to our mundane fortunes. Both these men sought to escape from fear by pretending that such things as physical suffering are not really evil. This is a noble way of escaping from fear, but is still based upon false belief. And if genuinely accepted, it would have the bad effect of making men indifferent, not only to their own sufferings, but also to those of others.

Under the influence of great fear, almost everybody becomes superstitious. The sailors who threw Jonah overboard imagined his presence to be the cause of the storm which threatened to wreck their ship. In a similar spirit the Japanese, at the time of the Tokyo earthquake, took to massacring Koreans and Liberals. When the Romans won victories in the Punic wars, the Carthaginians became persuaded that their misfortunes were due to a certain laxity which had crept into the worship of Moloch. Moloch liked having children sacrificed to him, and preferred them aristocratic; but the noble families of Carthage had adopted the practice of surreptitiously substituting plebeian children for their own offspring. This, it was thought, had displeased the god, and at the worst moments even the most aristocratic children were duly consumed in the fire. Strange to say, the Romans were victorious in spite of this democratic reform on the part of their enemies.

Collective fear stimulates herd instinct, and tends to produce ferocity towards those who are not regarded as members of the herd. So it was in the French Revolution, when dread of foreign armies produced the reign of terror. The Soviet Government would· have been less fierce if it had met with less hostility in its first years. Fear generates impulses of cruelty, and therefore promotes such superstitious beliefs as seem to justify cruelty. Neither a man nor a crowd nor a nation can be trusted to act humanely or to think sanely under the influence of a great fear. And for this reason poltroons are more prone to cruelty than brave men, and are also more prone to superstition. When I say this, I am thinking of men who are brave in all respects, not only in facing death. Many a man will have the courage to die gallantly, but will not have the courage to say, or even to think, that the cause for which he is asked to die is an unworthy one. Obloquy is, to most men, more painful than death; that is one reason why, in times of collective excitement, so few men venture to dissent from the prevailing opinion. No Carthaginian denied Moloch, because to do so would have required more courage than was required to face death in battle.

But we have been getting too solemn. Superstitions are not always dark and cruel; often they add to the gaiety of life. I received once a communication from the god Osiris, giving me his telephone number; he lived, at that time, in a suburb of Boston. Although I did not enrol myself among his worshippers, his letter gave me pleasure. I have frequently received letters from men announcing themselves as the Messiah, and urging me not to omit to mention this important fact in my lectures. During prohibition in America, there was a sect which maintained that the communion service ought to be celebrated in whisky, not in wine; this tenet gave them a legal right to a supply of hard liquor, and the sect grew rapidly. There is in England a sect which maintains that the English are the lost ten tribes; there is a stricter sect, which maintains that they are only the tribes of Ephraim and Manasseh. Whenever I encounter a member of either of these sects, I profess myself an adherent of the other, and much pleasant argumentation results. I like also the men who study the Great Pyramid, with a view to deciphering its mystical lore. Many great books have been written on this subject, some of which have been presented to me by their authors. It is a singular fact that the Great Pyramid always predicts the history of the world accurately up to the date of publication of the book in question, but after that date it becomes less reliable. Generally the author expects, very soon, wars in Egypt, followed by Armageddon and the coming of Antichrist, but by this time so many people have been recognized as Antichrist that the reader is reluctantly driven to scepticism.

I admire especially a certain prophetess who lived beside a lake in northern New York State about the year 1820. She announced to her numerous followers that she possessed the power of walking on water, and that she proposed to do so at 11 o'clock on a certain morning. At the stated time, the faithful assembled in their thousands beside the lake. She spoke to them saying: 'Are you all entirely persuaded that I can walk on water?' With one voice they replied: 'We are.' 'In that case', she announced, 'there is no need for me to do so.' And they all went home much edified.

Perhaps the world would lose some of its interest and variety if such beliefs were wholly replaced by cold science. Perhaps we may allow ourselves to be glad of the Abecedarians, who were so called because, having rejected all profane learning, they thought it wicked to learn the ABC. And we may enjoy the perplexity of the South American Jesuit who wondered how the sloth could have travelled, since the Flood, all the way from Mount Ararat to Peru—a journey which its extreme tardiness of locomotion rendered almost incredible. A wise man will enjoy the goods of which there is a plentiful supply, and of intellectual rubbish he will find an abundant diet, in our own age as in every other.

(Haldeman-Julius Publications, Kansas, 1943, subsequently reprinted in *Unpopular Essays*. London: Allen & Unwin; New York: Simon & Schuster, 1950.)

8

THE METAPHYSICIAN'S NIGHTMARE

Retro Me Satanas

MY poor friend Andrei Bumblowski, formerly Professor of Philosophy in a now extinct university of Central Europe, appeared to me to suffer from a harmless kind of lunacy. I am myself a person of robust common sense; I hold that the intellect must not be taken as a guide in life, but only as affording pleasant argumentative games and ways of annoying less agile opponents. Bumblowski, however, did not take this view; he allowed his intellect to lead him whither it would, and the results were odd. He seldom argued, and to most of his friends the grounds of his opinions remained obscure. What was known was that he consistently avoided the word 'not' and all its synonyms. He would not say 'this egg is not fresh', but 'chemical changes have occurred in this egg since it was laid'. He would not say 'I cannot find that book', but 'the books I have found are other than that book'. He would not say 'thou shalt not kill', but 'thou shalt cherish life'. His life was unpractical, but innocent, and I felt for him a considerable affection. It was doubtless this affection which at last unlocked his lips, and led him to relate to me the following very remarkable experience, which I give in his own words:

*   *   *

I had at one time a very bad fever of which I almost died. In my fever I had a long consistent delirium. I dreamt that I was in Hell, and that Hell is a place full of all those happenings that are improbable but not impossible. The effects of this are curious. Some of the damned, when they first arrive below, imagine that they will beguile the tedium of eternity by games of cards. But they find this impossible, because, whenever a pack is shuffled, it comes out in perfect order, beginning with the Ace of Spades and ending with the King of Hearts. There is a special department of Hell for students of probability. In this department there are many typewriters and many monkeys. Every time that a monkey walks on a typewriter, it types by chance one of Shakespeare's sonnets. There is another place of torment for physicists. In this there are kettles and fires, but when the kettles are put on the fires, the water in them freezes. There are also stuffy rooms. But experience has taught the physicists never to open a window because, when they do, all the air rushes out and leaves the room a vacuum. There is another region for gourmets. These men are allowed the most exquisite materials and the most skilful chefs. But when a beefsteak is served up to them, and they take a confident mouthful, they find that it tastes like a rotten egg; whereas, when they try to eat an egg, it tastes like a bad potato.

There is a peculiarly painful chamber inhabited solely by philosophers who have refuted Hume. These philosophers, though in Hell, have not learned wisdom. They continue to be governed by their animal propensity towards induction. But every time that they have made an induction, the next instance falsifies it. This, however, happens only during the first hundred years of their damnation. After that, they learn to expect that an induction will be falsified, and therefore it is not falsified until another century of logical torment has altered their expectation. Throughout all eternity surprise continues, but each time at a higher logical level.

Then there is the Inferno of the orators who have been accustomed while they lived to sway great multitudes by their eloquence. Their eloquence is undimmed and the multitudes are provided, but strange winds blow the sounds about so that the sounds heard by the multitudes, instead of being those uttered by the orators, are only dull and heavy platitudes.

At the very centre of the infernal kingdom is Satan, to whose presence only the more distinguished among the damned are admitted. The improbabilities become greater and greater as Satan is approached, and He Himself is the most complete improbability imaginable. He is pure Nothing, total non-existence, and yet continually changing.

I, because of my philosophical eminence, was early given audience with the Prince of Darkness. I had read of Satan as *der Geist der stets verneint*, the Spirit of Negation. But on entering the Presence I realized with a shock that Satan has a negative body as well as a negative mind. Satan's body is, in fact, a pure and complete vacuum, empty not only of particles of matter but also of particles of light. His prolonged emptiness is secured by a climax of improbability: whenever a particle approaches His outer surface, it happens by chance to collide with another particle which stops it from penetrating the empty region. The empty region, since no light ever penetrates it, is absolutely black—not more or less black, like the things to which we loosely ascribe this word, but utterly, completely and infinitely black. It has a shape, and the shape is that which we are accustomed to ascribe to Satan: horns, hooves, tail and all. All the rest of Hell is filled with murky flame, and against this background Satan stands out in awful majesty. He is not immobile. On the contrary, the emptiness of which He is constituted is in perpetual motion. When anything annoys Him, He swinges the horror of His folded tail like an angry cat. Some-times He goes forth to conquer new realms. Before going forth, He clothes Himself in shining white armour, which completely conceals the nothing-ness within. Only His eyes remain unclothed, and from His eyes piercing rays of nothingness shoot forth seeking what they may conquer. Wherever they find negation, wherever they find prohibition, wherever they find a cult of not-doing, there they enter into the inmost substance of those who are prepared to receive Him. Every negation emanates from Him and returns with a harvest of captured frustrations. The captured frustrations become part of Him, and swell His bulk until He threatens to fill all space. Every moralist whose morality consists of 'don'ts', every timid man who 'lets I dare not wait upon I would', every tyrant who compels his subjects to live in fear, becomes in time a part of Satan.

He is surrounded by a chorus of sycophantic philosophers who have substituted pandiabolism for pantheism. These men maintain that exis-tence is only apparent; non-existence is the only true reality. They hope in time to make the non-existence of appearance appear, for in that moment what we now take to be existence will be seen to be in truth only an outlying portion of the diabolic essence. Although these metaphysicians showed much subtlety, I could not agree with them. I had been accus-tomed while on earth to oppose tyrannous authority, and this habit remained with me in Hell. I began to argue with the metaphysical sycophants:

'What you say is absurd,' I expostulated. 'You proclaim that non-existence is the only reality. You pretend that this black hole which you worship exists. You are trying to persuade me that the non-existent exists. But this is a contradiction: and, however hot the flames of Hell may become, I will never so degrade my logical being as to accept a contradiction.'

At this point the President of the sycophants took up the argument: 'You go too fast, my friend,' he said. 'You deny that the non-existent exists? But what is this to which you deny existence? If the non-existent is nothing, any statement about it is nonsense. And so is your statement that it does not exist. I am afraid you have paid too little attention to the logical analysis of sentences, which ought to have been taught you when you were a boy. Do you not know that every sentence has a subject, and that, if the subject were nothing, the sentence would be nonsense? So, when you proclaim, with virtuous heat, that Satan—who is the non-existent—does not exist, you are plainly contradicting yourself.'

'You', I replied, 'have no doubt been here for some time and continue to embrace somewhat antiquated doctrines. You prate of sentences having subjects, but all that sort of talk is out of date. When I say that Satan, who is the non-existent, does not exist, I mention neither Satan nor the non-existent, but only the word "Satan" and the word "non-existent".

Your fallacies have revealed to me a great truth. The great truth is that the word "not" is superfluous. Henceforth I will not use the word "not".'

At this all the assembled metaphysicians burst into a shout of laughter. 'Hark how the fellow contradicts himself,' they said when the paroxysm of merriment had subsided. 'Hark at his great commandment which is to avoid negation. He will NOT use the word "not", forsooth!'

Though I was nettled, I kept my temper. I had in my pocket a dictionary. I scratched out all the words expressing negation and said: 'My speech shall be composed entirely of the words that remain in this dictionary. By the help of these words that remain, I shall be able to describe everything in the universe. My descriptions will be many, but they will all be of things other than Satan. Satan has reigned too long in this infernal realm. His shining armour was real and inspired terror, but underneath the armour there was only a bad linguistic habit. Avoid the word "not", and His empire is at an end.'

Satan, as the argument proceeded, lashed His tail with ever-increasing fury, and savage rays of darkness shot from His cavernous eyes. But at the last, when I denounced Him as a bad linguistic habit, there was a vast explosion, the air rushed in from all sides, and the horrid shape vanished. The murky air of Hell, which had been due to inspissated rays of nothingness, cleared as if by magic. What had seemed to be monkeys at the typewriters were suddenly seen to be literary critics. The kettles boiled, the cards were jumbled, a fresh breeze blew in at the windows, and the beefsteaks tasted like beefsteaks. With a sense of exquisite liberation, I awoke. I saw that there had been wisdom in my dream, however it might have worn the guise of delirium. From that moment the fever abated, but the delirium—as you may think it—has remained.

(*Nightmares of Eminent Persons*, London: John Lane, The Bodley Head, 1954, Allen & Unwin, 1960; New York: Simon & Schuster, 1955.)

PART III

The Philosopher of Language

Closely related to the advances made in contemporary thought in the fields of logic and mathematical philosophy are the increasingly important strides made in semantics and the philosophy of language. Russell has played a prominent and pivotal part in this advance, although he is not in accord with some of the lengths to which the analytic philosophers have gone. He has stressed the importance of recognizing language relations other than merely that of subject-predicate and the sharp distinction between the 'is' of predication and the 'is' of identity. He has been a pioneer in analysing the meaning of meaning. As such whatever he has added to the philosophy of language has been of great moment.

9

LANGUAGE

THE subject of language is one which has not been studied with sufficient care in traditional philosophy. It was taken for granted that words exist to express 'thoughts', and generally also that 'thoughts' have 'objects' which are what the words 'mean'. It was thought that, by means of language, we could deal directly with what it 'means', and that we need not analyse with any care either of the two supposed properties of words, namely that of 'expressing' thoughts and that of 'meaning' things. Often when philosophers intended to be considering the objects meant by words they were in fact considering only the words, and when they were considering words they made the mistake of supposing, more or less unconsciously, that a word is a single entity, not, as it really is, a set of more or less similar events. The failure to consider language explicitly has been a cause of much that was bad in traditional philosophy. I think myself that 'meaning' can only be understood if we treat language as a bodily habit, which is learnt just as we learn football or bicycling. The only satisfactory way to treat language, to my mind, is to treat it in this way, as Dr Watson does. Indeed, I should regard the theory of language as one of the strongest points in favour of behaviourism.

Man has various advantages over the beasts, for example, fire, clothing, agriculture, and tools—not the possession of domestic animals, for ants have them. But more important than any of these is language. It is not known how or when language arose, nor why chimpanzees do not speak. I doubt if it is even known whether writing or speech is the older form of language. The pictures made in caves by the Cro-Magnon men may have been intended to convey a meaning, and may have been a form of writing. It is known that writing developed out of pictures, for that happened in historical times; but it is not known to what extent pictures had been used in prehistoric times as a means of giving information or commands. As for spoken language, it differs from the cries of animals in being not merely an expression of emotion. Animals have cries of fear, cries expressing pleasure in the discovery of food, and so on, and by means of these cries they influence each other's actions. But they do not appear to have any means of expressing anything except emotions, and then only emotions which they are actually feeling. There is no evidence that they possess anything analogous to narrative. We may say, therefore, without exaggeration, that language is a human prerogative, and probably the chief habit in which we are superior to the 'dumb' animals.

There are three matters to be considered in beginning the study of language. First: what words are, regarded as physical occurrences; secondly, what are the circumstances that lead us to use a given word; thirdly, what are the effects of our hearing or seeing a given word. But as regards the second and third of these questions, we shall find ourselves led on from words to sentences and thus confronted with fresh problems, perhaps demanding rather the methods of *Gestaltpsychologie*.

Ordinary words are of four kinds: spoken, heard, written, and read. It is of course largely a matter of convention that we do not use words of other kinds. There is the deaf-and-dumb language; a Frenchman's shrug of the shoulders is a word; in fact, any kind of externally perceptible bodily movement may become a word, if social usage so ordains. But the convention which has given the supremacy to speaking is one which has a good ground, since there is no other way of producing a number of perceptibly different bodily movements so quickly or with so little muscular effort. Public speaking would be very tedious if statesmen had to use the deaf-and-dumb language, and very exhausting if all words involved as much muscular effort as a shrug of the shoulders. I shall ignore all forms of language except speaking, hearing, writing, and reading, since the others are relatively unimportant and raise no special psychological problems.

A spoken word consists of a series of movements in the larynx and the mouth, combined with breath. Two closely similar series of such movements may be instances of the same word, though they may also not be, since two words with different meanings may sound alike; but two such series which are not closely similar cannot be instances of the same word. (I am confining myself to one language.) Thus a single spoken word, say 'dog', is a certain set of closely similar series of bodily movements, the set having as many members as there are occasions when the word 'dog' is pronounced. The degree of similarity required in order that the occurrence should be an instance of the word 'dog' cannot be specified exactly. Some people say 'dawg', and this must certainly be admitted. A German might say 'tok', and then we should begin to be doubtful. In marginal cases, we cannot be sure whether a word has been pronounced or not. A spoken word is a form of bodily behaviour without sharp boundaries, like jumping or hopping or running. Is a man running or walking? In a walking-race the umpire may have great difficulty in deciding. Similarly there may be cases where it cannot be decided whether a man has said 'dog' or 'dock'. A spoken word is thus at once general and somewhat vague.

We usually take for granted the relation between a word spoken and a word heard. 'Can you hear what I say?' we ask, and the person addressed says 'yes'. This is of course a delusion, a part of the naïve realism of our unreflective outlook on the world. We never hear what is said; we hear something having a complicated causal connection with what is said. There is first the purely physical process of sound-waves from the mouth of the speaker to the ear of the hearer, then a complicated process in the ear and nerves, and then an event in the brain, which is related to our hearing of the sound in a manner to be investigated later, but is at any rate simultaneous with our hearing of the sound. This gives the physical causal connection between the word spoken and the word heard. There is, however, also another connection of a more psychological sort. When a man utters a word, he also hears it himself, so that the word spoken and the word heard become intimately associated for anyone who knows how to speak. And a man who knows how to speak can also utter any word he hears in his own language, so that the association works equally well both ways. It is because of the intimacy of this association that the plain man identifies the word spoken with the word heard, although in fact the two are separated by a wide gulf.

In order that speech may serve its purpose, it is not necessary, as it is not possible, that heard and spoken words should be identical, but it is necessary that when a man utters different words the heard words should be different, and when he utters the same word on two occasions the heard word should be approximately the same on the two occasions. The first of these depends upon the sensitiveness of the ear and its distance from the speaker; we cannot distinguish between two rather similar words if we are too far off from the man who utters them. The second condition depends upon uniformity in the physical conditions, and is realized in all ordinary circumstances. But if the speaker were surrounded by instruments which were resonant to certain notes but not to certain others, some tones of voice might carry and others might be lost. In that case, if he uttered the same word with two different intonations, the hearer might be quite unable to recognize the sameness. Thus the efficacy of speech depends upon a number of physical conditions. These, however, we will take for granted, in order to come as soon as possible to the more psychological parts of our topic.

Written words differ from spoken words in being material structures. A spoken word is a process in the physical world, having an essential time-order; a written word is a series of pieces of matter, having an essential space-order. As to what we mean by 'matter', that is a question with which we shall have to deal at length at a later stage. For the present it is enough to observe that the material structures which constitute written words, unlike the processes that constitute spoken words, are capable of enduring for a long time—sometimes for thousands of years. Moreover, they are not confined to one neighbourhood, but can be made to travel about the world. These are the two great advantages of writing over speech. This, at least, has been the case until recently. But with the coming of radio writing has begun to lose its pre-eminence: one man can now speak to multitudes spread over a whole country. Even in the matter of permanence, speech may become the equal of writing. Perhaps, instead of legal documents, we shall have gramophone records, with voice signatures by the parties to the contract. Perhaps, as in Wells's *When the Sleeper Awakes*, books will no longer be printed but merely arranged for the gramophone. In that case the need for writing may almost cease to exist. However, let us return from these speculations to the world of the present day.

The word read, as opposed to the written or printed word, is just as evanescent as the word spoken or heard. Whenever a written word, exposed to light, is in a suitable spatial relation to a normal eye, it produces a certain complicated effect upon the eye; the part of this process which occurs outside the eye is investigated by the science of light, whereas the part that occurs in the eye belongs to physiological optics. There is then a further process, first in the optic nerve and afterwards in the brain; the process in the brain is simultaneous with vision. What further relation it has to vision is a question as to which there has been much philosophical controversy; we shall return to it at a later stage. The essence of the matter, as regards the causal efficacy of writing, is that the act of writing produces quasi-permanent material structures which, throughout the whole of their duration, produce closely similar results upon all suitably placed normal eyes; and as in the case of speaking, different written words lead to different read words, and the same word written twice leads to the same read word—again with obvious limitations.

So much for the physical side of language, which is often unduly neglected. I come now to the psychological side, which is what really concerns us in this chapter.

The two questions we have to answer, apart from the problems raised by sentences as opposed to words, are: First, what sort of behaviour is stimulated by hearing a word? And secondly, what sort of occasion stimulates us to the behaviour that consists in pronouncing a word? I put the questions in this order because children learn to react to the words of others before they learn to use words themselves. It might be objected that, in the history of the race, the first spoken word must have preceded the first heard word, at least by a fraction of a second. But this is not very relevant, nor is it certainly true. A noise may have meaning to the hearer, but not to the utterer; in that case it is a heard word but not a spoken word. (I shall explain what I mean by 'meaning' shortly.) Friday's footprint had 'meaning' for Robinson Crusoe but not for Friday. However that may be, we shall do better to avoid the very hypothetical parts of anthropology that would be involved, and take up the learning of language as it can be observed in the human infant of the present day. And in the human infant as we know him, definite reactions to the words of others come much earlier than the power of uttering words himself.

A child learns to understand words exactly as he learns any other process of bodily association. If you always say 'bottle' when you give a child his bottle, he presently reacts to the word 'bottle', within limits, as he formerly reacted to the bottle. This is merely an example of the law of association. When the association has been established, parents say that the child 'understands' the word 'bottle', or knows what the word 'means'. Of course the word does not have *all* the effects that the actual bottle has. It does not exert gravitation, it does not nourish, it cannot bump on to the child's head. The effects which are shared by the word and the thing are those which depend upon the law of association or 'conditioned reflexes' or 'learned reactions'. These may be called 'associative' effects or 'mnemic' effects—the latter name being derived from Semon's book *Mneme*,[1] in which he traces all phenomena analogous to memory to a law which is, in effect, not very different from the law of association or 'conditioned reflexes'.

It is possible to be a little more precise as to the class of effects concerned. A physical object is a centre from which a variety of causal chains emanate. If the object is visible to John Smith, one of the causal chains emanating from it consists first of light-waves (or light-quanta) which travel from the object to John Smith's eye, then of events in his eye and optic nerve, then of events in his brain, and then (perhaps) of a reaction on his part. Now mnemic effects belong only to events in living tissue; therefore only those effects of the bottle which happen either inside John Smith's body, or as a result of his reaction to the bottle, can become associated with his hearing the word 'bottle'. And even then only certain events can be associated: nourishment happens in the body, yet the word 'bottle' cannot nourish. The law of conditioned reflexes is subject to ascertainable limitations, but within its limits it supplies what is wanted to explain the understanding of words. The child becomes excited when he sees the bottle; this is already a conditioned reflex, due to experience that this sight precedes a meal. One further stage in conditioning makes the child grow excited when he hears the word 'bottle'. He is then said to 'understand' the word.

We may say, then, that a person understands a word which he hears if, so far as the law of conditioned reflexes is applicable, the effects of the word are the same as those of what it is said to 'mean'. This of course only applies to words like 'bottle', which denote some concrete object or some class of concrete objects. To understand a word such as 'reciprocity' or 'republicanism' is a more complicated matter, and cannot be considered until we have dealt with sentences. But before considering sentences we

[1] London: George Allen & Unwin, Ltd.

have to examine the circumstances which make us use a word, as opposed to the consequences of hearing it used.

Saying a word is more difficult than understanding it, except in the case of a few simple sounds which infants make before they know that they are words, such as 'ma-ma' and 'da-da'. These two are among the many random sounds that all babies make. When a child says 'ma-ma' in the presence of his mother by chance she thinks he knows what this noise means, and she shows pleasure in ways that are agreeable to the infant. Gradually, in accordance with Thorndike's law of effect, he acquires the habit of making this noise in the presence of his mother, because in these circumstances the consequences are pleasant. But it is only a very small number of words that are acquired in this way. The great majority of words are acquired by imitation, combined with the association between thing and word which the parents deliberately establish in the early stages (after the very first stage). It is obvious that using words oneself involves something over and above the association between the *sound* of the word and its meaning. Dogs understand many words, and infants understand far more than they can say. The infant has to discover that it is possible and profitable to make noises like those which he hears. (This statement must not be taken quite literally, or it would be too intellectualistic.) He would never discover this if he did not make noises at random, without the intention of talking. He then gradually finds that he can make noises like those which he hears, and in general the consequences of doing so are pleasant. Parents are pleased, desired objects can be obtained, and—perhaps most important of all—there is a sense of power in making intended instead of accidental noises. But in this whole process there is nothing essentially different from the learning of mazes by rats. It resembles this form of learning, rather than that of Köhler's apes, because no amount of intelligence could enable the child to find out the names of things—as in the case of the mazes, experience is the only possible guide.

When a person knows how to speak, the conditioning proceeds in the opposite direction to that which operates in understanding what others say. The reaction of a person who knows how to speak, when he notices a cat, is naturally to utter the word 'cat'; he may not actually do so, but he will have a reaction leading towards this act, even if for some reason the overt act does not take place. It is true that he may utter the word 'cat' because he is 'thinking' about a cat, not actually seeing one. This, however, as we shall see in a moment, is merely one further stage in the process of conditioning. The use of single words, as opposed to sentences, is wholly explicable, so far as I can see, by the principles which apply to animals in mazes.

Certain philosophers who have a prejudice against analysis contend that the sentence comes first and the single word later. In this connection they always allude to the language of the Patagonians, which their oppo-

nents, of course, do not know. We are given to understand that a Pata-
gonian can understand you if you say 'I am going to fish in the lake behind
the western hill', but that he cannot understand the word 'fish' by itself.
(This instance is imaginary, but it represents the sort of thing that is
asserted.) Now it may be that Patagonians are peculiar—indeed they must
be, or they would not choose to live in Patagonia. But certainly infants in
civilized countries do not behave in this way, with the exception of
Thomas Carlyle and Lord Macaulay. The former never spoke before the
age of three, when, hearing his younger brother cry, he said, 'What ails
wee Jock?' Lord Macaulay 'learned in suffering what he taught in song',
for, having spilt a cup of hot tea over himself at a party, he began his
career as a talker by saying to his hostess, after a time, 'Thank you,
Madam, the agony is abated'. These, however, are facts about biographers,
not about the beginnings of speech in infancy. In all children that have
been carefully observed, sentences come much later than single words.

Children, at first, are limited as to their power of producing sounds, and
also by the paucity of their learned associations. I am sure the reason why
'ma-ma' and 'da-da' have the meaning they have is that they are sounds
which infants make spontaneously at an early age, and are therefore
convenient as sounds to which the elders can attach meaning. In the very
beginning of speech there is not imitation of grown-ups, but the discovery
that sounds made spontaneously have agreeable results. Imitation comes
later, after the child has discovered that sounds can have this quality of
'meaning'. The type of skill involved is throughout exactly similar to that
involved in learning to play a game or ride a bicycle.

We may sum up this theory of meaning in a simple formula. When
through the law of conditioned reflexes, A has come to be a cause of C, we
will call A an 'associative' cause of C, and C an 'associative' effect of A.
We shall say that, to a given person, the word A, when he hears it, 'means'
C, if the associative effects of A are closely similar to those of C; and we
shall say that the word A, when he utters it, 'means' C, if the utterance
of A is an associative effect of C, or of something previously associated
with C. To put the matter more concretely, the word 'Peter' means a
certain person if the associative effects of hearing the word 'Peter' are
closely similar to those of seeing Peter, and the associative causes of
uttering the word 'Peter' are occurrences previously associated with Peter.
Of course as our experience increases in complexity this simple *schema*
becomes obscured and overlaid, but I think it remains fundamentally true.

There is an interesting and valuable book by Messrs C. K. Ogden and
I. A. Richards, called *The Meaning of Meaning*. This book, owing to the
fact that it concentrates on the causes of uttering words, not on the effects
of hearing them, gives only half the above theory, and that in a somewhat
incomplete form. It says that a word and its meaning have the same
causes. I should distinguish between *active* meaning, that of the man

uttering the word, and *passive* meaning, that of the man hearing the word. In active meaning the word is associatively caused by what it means or something associated with this; in passive meaning, the associative effects of the word are approximately the same as those of what it means.

On behaviourist lines, there is no important difference between proper names and what are called 'abstract' or 'generic' words. A child learns to use the word 'cat', which is general, just as he learns to use the word 'Peter', which is a proper name. But in actual fact 'Peter' really covers a number of different occurrences, and is in a sense general. Peter may be near or far, walking or standing or sitting, laughing or frowning. All these produce different stimuli, but the stimuli have enough in common to produce the reaction consisting of the word 'Peter'. Thus there is no essential difference, from a behaviourist point of view, between 'Peter' and 'man'. There are more resemblances between the various stimuli to the word 'Peter' than between those to the word 'man', but this is only a difference of degree. We have no names for the fleeting particular occurrences which make up the several appearances of Peter, because they are not of much practical importance; their importance, in fact, is purely theoretic and philosophical. As such, we shall have a good deal to say about them at a later stage. For the present, we notice that there are many occurrences of Peter, and many occurrences of the word 'Peter'; each, to the man who sees Peter, is a set of events having certain similarities. More exactly, the occurrences of Peter are *causally* connected, whereas the occurrences of the word 'Peter' are connected by similarity. But this is a distinction which need not concern us yet.

General words such as 'man' or 'cat' or 'triangle' are said to denote 'universals', concerning which, from the time of Plato to the present day, philosophers have never ceased to debate. Whether there are universals, and, if so, in what sense, is a metaphysical question, which need not be raised in connection with the use of language. The only point about universals that needs to be raised at this stage is that the correct use of general words is no evidence that a man can think about universals. It has often been supposed that, because we can use a word like 'man' correctly, we must be capable of a corresponding 'abstract idea' of man, but this is quite a mistake. Some reactions are appropriate to one man, some to another, but all have certain elements in common. If the word 'man' produces in us the reactions which are common but no others, we may be said to understand the word 'man'. In learning geometry, one acquires the habit of avoiding special interpretations of such a word as 'triangle'. We know that, when we have a proposition about triangles in general, we must not think specially of a right-angled triangle or any one kind of triangle. This is essentially the process of learning to associate with the word what is associated with *all* triangles; when we have learnt this, we understand the word 'triangle'. Consequently there is no need to suppose that we ever apprehend universals, although we use general words correctly.

Hitherto we have spoken of single words, and among these we have considered only those that can naturally be employed singly. A child uses single words of a certain kind before constructing sentences; but some words presuppose sentences. No one would use the word 'paternity' until after using such sentences as 'John is the father of James'; no one would use the word 'causality' until after using such sentences as 'the fire makes me warm'. Sentences introduce new considerations, and are not quite so easily explained on behaviourist lines. Philosophy, however, imperatively demands an understanding of sentences, and we must therefore consider them.

As we found earlier, all infants outside Patagonia begin with single words, and only achieve sentences later. But they differ enormously in the speed with which they advance from the one to the other. My own two children adopted entirely different methods. My son first practised single letters, then single words, and only achieved correct sentences of more than three or four words at the age of two years and three months. My daughter, on the contrary, advanced very quickly to sentences, in which there was hardly ever an error. At the age of eighteen months, when supposed to be sleeping, she was overhead saying to herself: 'Last year I used to dive off the diving-board, I *did*.' Of course 'last year' was merely a phrase repeated without understanding. And no doubt the first sentences used by children are always repetitions, unchanged, of sentences they have heard used by others. Such cases raise no new principle not involved in the learning of words. What does raise a new principle is the power of putting together known words into a sentence which has never been heard, but which expresses correctly what the infant wishes to convey. This involves the power to manipulate form and structure. It does not, of course, involve the apprehension of form or structure in the abstract, any more than the use of the word 'man' involves apprehension of a universal. But it does involve a causal connection between the form of the stimulus and the form of the reaction. An infant very soon learns to be differently affected by the statement 'cats eat mice' from the way he would be affected by the statement 'mice eat cats'; and not much later he learns to make one of these statements rather than the other. In such a case, the cause (in hearing) or the effect (in speaking) is a whole sentence. It may be that one part of the environment is sufficient to cause one word, while another is sufficient to cause another, but it is only the two parts in their relation that can cause the whole sentence. Thus wherever sentences come in we have a causal relation between two complex facts, namely the fact asserted and the sentence asserting it; the facts as wholes enter into the cause-and-effect relation, which cannot be explained wholly as compounded of relations between their parts. Moreover, as soon as the child has learned to use correctly relational words, such as 'eat', he has become capable of being causally affected by a relational feature of the environment, which involves a new degree of complexity not required for the use of ordinary nouns.

Thus the correct use of relational words, i.e. of sentences, involves what may be correctly termed 'perception of form', i.e. it involves a definite reaction to a stimulus which is a form. Suppose, for example, that a child has learnt to say that one thing is 'above' another when this is in fact the case. The stimulus to the use of the word 'above' is a relational feature of the environment, and we may say that this feature is 'perceived' since it produces a definite reaction. It may be said that the relation *above* is not very like the word 'above'. That is true; but the same is true of ordinary physical objects. A stone, according to the physicists, is not at all like what we see when we look at it, and yet we may be correctly said to 'perceive' it. This, however, is to anticipate. The definite point which has emerged is that, when a person can use sentences correctly, that is a proof of sensitiveness to formal or relational stimuli.

The structure of a sentence asserting some relational fact, such as 'this is above that', or 'Brutus killed Caesar', differs in an important respect from the structure of the fact which it asserts. *Above* is a relation which holds between the two terms 'this' and 'that'; but the *word* 'above' is not a relation. In the sentence the relation is the temporal order of the words (or the spatial order, if they are written), but the word for the relation is itself as substantial as the other words. In inflected languages, such as Latin, the order of the words is not necessary to show the 'sense' of the relation; but in uninflected languages this is the only way of distinguishing between 'Brutus killed Caesar' and 'Caesar killed Brutus'. Words are physical phenomena, having spatial and temporal relations; we make use of these relations in our verbal symbolization of other relations, chiefly to show the 'sense' of the relation, i.e. whether it goes from A to B or from B to A.

A great deal of the confusion about relations which has prevailed in practically all philosophies comes from the fact, which we noticed just now, that relations are indicated, not by other relations, but by words which, in themselves, are just like other words. Consequently, in thinking about relations, we constantly hover between the unsubstantiality of the relation itself and the substantiality of the word. Take, say, the fact that lightning precedes thunder. If we were to express this by a language closely reproducing the structure of the fact, we should have to say simply: 'lightning, thunder', where the fact that the first word precedes the second means that what the first word means precedes what the second word means. But even if we adopted this method for temporal order, we should still need words for all other relations, because we could not without intolerable ambiguity symbolize them also by the order of our words. All this will be important to remember when we come to consider the structure of the world, since nothing but a preliminary study of language will preserve us from being misled by language in our metaphysical speculations.

Throughout this chapter I have said nothing about the narrative and imaginative uses of words; I have dealt with words in connection with an immediate sensible stimulus closely connected with what they mean. The other uses of words are difficult to discuss until we have considered memory and imagination. In the present chapter I have confined myself to a behaviouristic explanation of the effects of words heard as stimuli, and the causes of words spoken when the words apply to something sensibly present. I think we shall find that other uses of words, such as the narrative and imaginative, involve only new applications of the law of association. But we cannot develop this theme until we have discussed several further psychological questions.

(*An Outline of Philosophy*, London: Allen & Unwin, 1927; *Philosophy*, New York: Simon & Schuster, 1927.)

10

SENTENCES, SYNTAX, AND PARTS OF SPEECH

SENTENCES may be interrogative, optative, exclamatory, or imperative; they may also be indicative. Throughout most of the remainder of our discussions, we may confine ourselves to indicative sentences, since these alone are true or false. In addition to being true or false, indicative sentences have two other properties which are of interest to us, and which they share with other sentences. The first of these is that they are composed of words, and have a meaning derivative from that of the words that they contain; the second is that they have a certain kind of unity, in virtue of which they are capable of properties not possessed by their constituent words.

Each of these three properties needs investigation. Let us begin with the unity of a sentence.

A single grammatical sentence may not be logically single. 'I went out and found it was raining' is logically indistinguishable from the two sentences: 'I went out', 'I found it was raining'. But the sentence 'when I went out I found it was raining' is logically single: it asserts that two occurrences were simultaneous. 'Caesar and Pompey were great generals' is logically two sentences, but 'Caesar and Pompey were alike in being great generals' is logically one. For our purposes, it will be convenient to exclude sentences which are not logically single, but consist of two assertions joined by 'and' or 'but' or 'although' or some such conjunction. A single sentence, for our purposes, must be one which says something that cannot be said in two separate simpler sentences.

Consider next such a sentence as 'I should be sorry if you fell ill'. This cannot be divided into 'I shall be sorry' and 'you will fall ill'; it has the kind of unity that we are demanding of a sentence. But it has a complexity which some sentences do not have; neglecting tense, it states a relation between 'I am sorry' and 'you are ill'. We may interpret it as asserting that at any time when the second of these sentences is true, the first is also true. Such sentences may be called 'molecular' in relation to their constituent sentences, which, in the same relation, may be called 'atomic'. Whether any sentences are 'atomic' in a non-relative sense, may, for the present, be left an open question; but whenever we find a sentence to be molecular, we shall do well, while we are considering what makes the unity of sentences, to transfer our attention, in the first place, to its atoms. Roughly, an atomic sentence is one containing only one verb; but this would only be accurate in a strictly logical language.

This matter is by no means simple. Suppose I say first 'A' and then 'B'; you may judge: 'the sound "A" preceded the sound "B" '. But this implies 'the sound "A" occurred' and 'the sound "B" occurred', and adds that one occurrence was earlier than the other. Your statement, therefore, is really analogous to such a statement as 'after I went out I got wet'. It is a molecular statement whose atoms are 'A occurred' and 'B occurred'. Now what do we mean by 'A occurred'? We mean that there was a noise of a certain class, the class called 'A'. Thus when we say 'A preceded B' our statement has a concealed logical form, which is the same as that of the statement: 'first there was the bark of a dog, and then the neigh of a horse'.

Let us pursue this a little further. I say 'A'. Then I say 'what did I say?' Then you reply 'you said "A" '. Now the noise you make when saying 'A' in this reply is different from the noise I originally made; therefore, if 'A' were the name of a particular noise, your statement would be false. It is only because 'A' is the name of a *class* of noises that your statement is true; your statement classifies the noise I made, just as truly as if you had said 'you barked like a dog'. This shows how language forces us into generality even when we most wish to avoid it. If we want to speak about the particular noise that I made, we shall have to give it a proper name, say 'Tom'; and the noise that you made when you said 'A' we will call 'Dick'. Then we can say 'Tom and Dick are A's'. We can say 'I said Tom' but not 'I said "Tom" '. Strictly, we ought not to say 'I said "A" '; we ought to say 'I said an "A" '. All this illustrates a general principle, that when we use a general term, such as 'A' or 'man', we are not having in our minds a universal, but an instance to which the present instance is similar. When we say 'I said "A" ', what we really mean is 'I made a noise closely similar to the noise I am now about to make: "A" .' This, however, is a digression.

We will revert to the supposition that I say first 'A' and then 'B'. We will call the particular occurrence which was my first utterance 'Tom' and that which was my second utterance 'Harry'. Then we can say 'Tom preceded Harry'. This was what we really meant to say when we said 'the sound "A" preceded the sound "B" '; and now, at last, we seem to have reached an atomic sentence which does not merely classify.

It might be objected that, when I say 'Tom preceded Harry', this implies 'Tom occurred' and 'Harry occurred', just as when I said 'the sound "A" preceded the sound "B" ', that implied ' "A" occurred' and ' "B" occurred'. This, I think, would be a logical error. When I say that an unspecified member of a class occurred, my statement is significant provided I know what class is meant; but in the case of a true proper name, the name is meaningless unless it names something, and if it names something, that something must occur. This may seem reminiscent of the ontological argument, but it is really only part of the definition of 'name'. A proper name names something of which there are not a plurality of instances, and names it by a convention *ad hoc*, not by a description composed of words with previously assigned meanings. Unless, therefore, the name names something, it is an empty noise, not a word. And when we say 'Tom preceded Harry', where 'Tom' and 'Harry' are names of particular noises, we do not presuppose 'Tom occurred' and 'Harry occurred', which are both strictly meaningless.

In practice, proper names are not given to single brief occurrences, because most of them are not sufficiently interesting. When we have occasion to mention them, we do so by means of descriptions such as 'the death of Caesar' or 'the birth of Christ'. To speak for the moment in terms of physics, we give proper names to certain continuous stretches of space-time, such as Socrates, France, or the moon. In former days, it would have been said that we give a proper name to a substance or collection of substances, but now we have to find a different phrase to express the object of a proper name.

A proper name, in practice, always embraces many occurrences, but not as a class-name does: the separate occurrences are *parts* of what the name means, not *instances* of it. Consider, say, 'Caesar died'. 'Death' is a generic word for a number of occurrences having certain resemblances to each other, but not necessarily any spatio-temporal interconnection; each of these is *a* death. 'Caesar', on the contrary, stands for a series of occurrences, collectively, not severally. When we say 'Caesar died', we say that one of the series of occurrences which was Caesar was a member of the class of deaths; this occurrence is called 'Caesar's death'.

From a logical point of view, a proper name may be assigned to any continuous portion of space-time. (Macroscopic continuity suffices.) Two parts of one man's life may have different names; for instance, Abram and Abraham, or Octavianus and Augustus. 'The universe' may be regarded as a proper name for the whole of space-time. We *can* give a proper name to very small portions of space-time, provided they are large enough to be noticed. If I say 'A' once at 6 p.m. on a given date, we can give a proper name to this noise, or, to be still more particular, to the auditory sensation that some one person present has in hearing me. But even when we have arrived at this degree of minuteness, we cannot say that we have named something destitute of structure. It may therefore be assumed, at least for the present, that every proper name is the name of a structure, not of something destitute of parts. But this is an empirical fact, not a logical necessity.

If we are to avoid entanglement in questions that are not linguistic, we must distinguish sentences, not by the complexity which they may happen to have, but by that implied in their form. 'Alexander preceded Caesar' is complex owing to the complexity of Alexander and Caesar; but 'x preceded y' does not, by its form, imply that x and y are complex. In fact, since Alexander died before Caesar was born, every constituent of Alexander preceded every constituent of Caesar. We may thus accept 'x precedes y' as an atomic *form* of proposition, even if we cannot actually mention an x and a y which give an atomic proposition. We shall say, then, that a *form* of proposition is atomic if the fact that a proposition is of this form does not logically imply that it is a structure composed of subordinate propositions. And we shall add that it is not logically necessary that a proper name should name a structure which has parts.

The above discussion is a necessary preliminary to the attempt to discover what constitutes the essential unity of a sentence; for this unity, whatever its nature may be, obviously exists in a sentence of atomic form, and should be first investigated in such sentences.

In every significant sentence, some connection is essential between what the several words mean—omitting words which merely serve to indicate syntactical structure. We saw that 'Caesar died' asserts the existence of a common member of two classes, the class of events which was Caesar and the class of events which are deaths. This is only one of the relations that sentences can assert; syntax shows, in each case, what relation is asserted. Some cases are simpler than 'Caesar died', others are more complex. Suppose I point to a daffodil and say 'this is yellow'; here 'this' may be taken as the proper name of a part of my present visual field, and 'yellow' may be taken as a class-name. This proposition, so interpreted, is simpler than 'Caesar died', since it classifies a given object; it is logically analogous to 'this is a death'. We have to be able to know such propositions before we can know that two classes have a common member, which is what is asserted by 'Caesar died'. But 'this is yellow' is not so simple as it looks. When a child learns the meaning of the word 'yellow', there is first an object (or rather a set of objects) which is yellow by definition, and then a perception that other objects are similar in colour. Thus when we say to a child 'this is yellow', what (with luck) we convey to him is: 'this resembles in colour the object which is yellow by definition'. Thus classificatory propositions, or such as assign predicates, would seem to be really propositions asserting similarity. If so, the simplest propositions are relational.

There is, however, a difference between relations that are symmetrical and those that are asymmetrical. A relation is symmetrical when, if it holds between x and y, it also holds between y and x; it is asymmetrical if, when it holds between x and y, it cannot hold between y and x. Thus similarity is symmetrical, and so is dissimilarity; but 'before', 'greater', 'to the right of', and so on, are asymmetrical. There are also relations which are neither symmetrical nor asymmetrical; 'brother' is an example, since, if x is the brother of y, y may be the sister of x. These and asymmetrical relations are called non-symmetrical. Non-symmetrical relations are of the utmost importance, and many famous philosophies are refuted by their existence.

Let us try to state what exactly are the linguistic facts about non-symmetrical relations. The two sentences 'Brutus killed Caesar' and 'Caesar killed Brutus' consist of the same words, arranged, in each case, by the relation of temporal sequence. Nevertheless, one of them is true and the other false. The use of order for this purpose is, of course, not essential; Latin uses inflexions instead. But if you had been a Roman schoolmaster teaching the difference between nominative and accusative, you would have been compelled, at some point, to bring in non-symmetrical relations, and you would have found it natural to explain them by means of spatial or temporal order. Consider for a moment what happened when Brutus killed Caesar: a dagger moved swiftly from Brutus into Caesar. The abstract scheme is 'A moved from B to C', and the fact with which we are concerned is that this is different from 'A moved from C to B'. There were two events, one A-being-at-B, the other A-being-at-C, which we will name x and y respectively. If A moved from B to C, x preceded y; if A moved from C to B, y preceded x. Thus the ultimate source of the difference between 'Brutus killed Caesar' and 'Caesar killed Brutus' is the difference between 'x precedes y' and 'y precedes x', where x and y are events. Similarly in the visual field there are the spatial relations above-and-below, right-and-left, which have the same property of asymmetry. 'Brighter', 'louder', and comparatives generally, are also asymmetrical.

The unity of the sentence is peculiarly obvious in the case of asymmetrical relations: 'x precedes y' and 'y precedes x' consist of the same words, arranged by the same relation of temporal succession; there is nothing whatever in their ingredients to distinguish the one from the other. The sentences differ as wholes, but not in their parts; it is this that I mean when I speak of a sentence as a unity.

At this point, if confusions are to be avoided, it is important to remember that words are universals.[1] In the two sentential utterances 'x precedes y' and 'y precedes x', the two symbols 'x' are not identical, no more are the two symbols 'y'. Let S_1 and S_2 be proper names of these two sentential utterances; let X_1 and X_2 be proper names of the two utterances of 'x', Y_1 and Y_2 of those of 'y', and P_1 and P_2 of those of 'precedes'. Then S_1 consists of the three utterances X_1, P_1, Y_1 in that order, and S_2 consists

---

[1] This does not imply that there are universals. It only asserts that the status of a word, as opposed to its instances, is the same as that of Dog as opposed to various particular dogs.

of the three utterances Y_2, P_2, X_2 in that order. The order in each case is a fact of history, as definite and unalterable as the fact that Alexander preceded Caesar. When we observe that the order of words can be changed, and that we can say 'Caesar killed Brutus' just as easily as 'Brutus killed Caesar', we are apt to think that the words are definite things which are capable of different arrangements. This is a mistake: the words are abstractions, and the verbal utterances can only have whichever order they do have. Though their life is short, they live and die, and they are incapable of resurrection. Everything has the arrangement it has, and is incapable of rearrangement.

I do not wish to be thought needlessly pedantic, and I will therefore point out that clarity on this matter is necessary for the understanding of *possibility*. We say it is *possible* to say either 'Brutus killed Caesar' or 'Caesar killed Brutus', and we do not realize that this is precisely analogous to the fact that it is possible for a man to be to the left of a woman on one occasion, and for another man to be to the right of another woman on another occasion. For: let β be the class of verbal utterances which is the spoken word 'Brutus'; let κ be the class of verbal utterances which is the spoken word 'killed'; and let γ be the class of verbal utterances which is the spoken word 'Caesar'. Then to say that we can say either 'Brutus killed Caesar' or 'Caesar killed Brutus' is to say that (1) there are occurrences x, P, y, such that x is a member of β, P is a member of κ, y is a member of γ, x is just before P and P is just before y; (2) there are occurrences x', P', y' fulfilling the above conditions as to membership of β, κ, γ but such that y' is just before P' and P' just before x'. I maintain that in all cases of possibility, there is a subject which is a variable, defined as satisfying some condition which many values of the variable satisfy, and that of these values some satisfy a further condition while others do not; we then say it is 'possible' that the subject may satisfy this further condition. Symbolically, if 'ϕx and ψx' and 'ϕx and not ψx' are each true for suitable values of x, then, given ϕx, ψx is possible but not necessary. (One must distinguish empirical and logical necessity; but I do not wish to go into this question.)

Another point is to be noted. When we say that the sentences 'x P y' and 'y P x' (where P is an asymmetrical relation) are incompatible, the symbols 'x' and 'y' are universals, since, in our statement, there are two instances of each; but they must be names of particulars. 'Day precedes night' and 'night precedes day' are both true. There is thus, in such cases, an absence of logical homogeneity between the symbol and its meaning: the symbol is a universal while the meaning is particular. This kind of logical heterogeneity is very liable to lead to confusions. All symbols are of the same logical type: they are classes of similar utterances, or similar noises, or similar shapes, but their meanings may be of any type, or of ambiguous type, like the meaning of the word 'type' itself. The relation of a symbol to its meaning necessarily varies according to the type of the meaning, and this fact is important in the theory of symbolism.

Having now dealt with the possible confusions that may arise through saying that the same word can occur in two different sentences, we can henceforth freely use this expression, just as we can say 'the giraffe is to be found in Africa and in the Zoo', without being misled into the belief that this is true of any particular giraffe.

In a language like English, in which the order of the words is essential to the meaning of the sentence, we can put the matter of non-symmetrical relations as follows: given a set of words which is capable of forming a sentence, it often happens that it is capable of forming two or more sentences of which one is true while the others are false, these sentences differing as to the order of the words. Thus the meaning of a sentence, at any rate in some cases, is determined by the *series* of words, not by the *class*. In such cases, the meaning of the sentence is not obtainable as an aggregate of the meanings of the several words. When a person knows who Brutus was, who Caesar was, and what killing is, he still does not know who killed whom when he hears the sentence 'Brutus killed Caesar'; to know this, he requires syntax as well as vocabulary, since the form of the sentence as a whole contributes to the meaning.[1]

To avoid unnecessary lengthiness, let us assume, for the moment, that there is only spoken speech. Then all words *have* a time order, and some words *assert* a time order. We know that, if 'x' and 'y' are names of particular events, then if 'x precedes y' is a true sentence, 'y precedes x' is a false sentence. My present problem is this: can we state anything equivalent to the above in terms which are not concerned with language, but with events? It would seem that we are concerned with a characteristic of temporal relations, and yet, when we try to state what this characteristic is, we appear to be driven to stating a characteristic of sentences about temporal relations. And what applies to temporal relations applies equally to all other asymmetrical relations.

When I hear the sentence 'Brutus killed Caesar', I perceive the time-order of the words; if I did not, I could not know that I had heard that sentence and not 'Caesar killed Brutus'. If I proceed to assert the time-order by the sentences ' "Brutus" preceded "killed" ' and ' "killed" preceded "Caesar" ', I must again be aware of the time-order of the words in these sentences. We must, therefore, be aware of the time-order of events in cases in which we do not assert that they have that time-order, for otherwise we should fall into an endless regress. What is it that we are aware of in such a case?

The following is a theory which might be suggested: when we hear the word 'Brutus', there is an experience analogous to that of the gradually fading tone of a bell; if the word was heard a moment ago, there is still

[1] Sometimes there is ambiguity: cf. 'The muse herself that Orpheus bore'.

now an akoluthic sensation, analogous to that of a moment ago, but fainter. Thus when we have just finished hearing the sentence 'Brutus killed Caesar', we are still having an auditory sensation which might be represented by

Brutus KILLED CAESAR;

whereas when we have just finished hearing 'Caesar killed Brutus', our sensation may be represented by

Caesar KILLED BRUTUS.

These are different sensations, and it is this difference—so it may be contended—that enables us to recognize order in time. According to this theory, when we distinguish between 'Brutus killed Caesar' and 'Caesar killed Brutus', we are distinguishing, not between two wholes composed of exactly similar parts which are successive, but between two wholes composed of somewhat dissimilar parts which are simultaneous. Each of these wholes is characterized by its constituents, and does not need the further mention of an arrangement.

In this theory there is, no doubt, an element of truth. It seems clear, as a matter of psychology, that there are occurrences, which may be classed as sensations, in which a present sound is combined with the fading ghost of a sound heard a moment ago. But if there were no more than this, we should not know that past events have occurred. Assuming that there are akoluthic sensations, how do we know their likeness to and difference from sensations in their first vigour? If we only knew present occurrences which are in fact related to past occurrences, we should never know of this relationship. Clearly we do sometimes, in some sense, know the past, not by inference from the present, but in the same direct way in which we know the present. For if this were not the case, nothing in the present could lead us to suppose that there was a past, or even to understand the supposition.

Let us revert to the proposition: 'if x precedes y, y does not precede x'. It *seems* clear that we do not know this empirically, but it does not *seem* to be a proposition of logic.[1] Yet I do not see how we can say that it is a linguistic convention. The proposition 'x precedes y' can be asserted on the basis of experience. We are saying that, if this experience occurs, no experience will occur such as would lead to 'y precedes x'. It is obvious that, however we re-state the matter, there must always be a negation somewhere in our statement; and I think it is also fairly obvious that negation brings us into the realm of language. When we say 'y does not precede x', it might seem that we can only mean: 'the sentence "y precedes x" is false'. For if we adopt any other interpretation, we shall have to

---

[1] To decide this question, we need a discussion of proper names, to which we shall come later.

admit that we can perceive negative facts, which *seems* preposterous, but perhaps is not, for reasons to be given later. I think something similar may be said about 'if': where this word occurs, it must apply to a sentence. Thus it seems that the proposition we are investigating should be stated: 'at least one of the sentences "x precedes y" and "y precedes x" is false, if x and y are proper names of events'. To carry the matter further demands a definition of falsehood. We will therefore postpone this question until we have reached the discussion of truth and falsehood.

Parts of speech, as they appear in grammar, have no very intimate relation to logical syntax. 'Before' is a preposition and 'precedes' is a verb, but they mean the same thing. The verb, which might seem essential to a sentence, may be absent in many languages, and even in English in such a phrase as 'more haste, less speed'. It is possible, however, to compose a logical language with a logical syntax, and to find, when it has been constructed, certain suggestions in ordinary language which lead up to it.

The most complete part of logic is the theory of conjunctions. These, as they occur in logic, come only between whole sentences; they give rise to molecular sentences, of which the atoms are separated by the conjunctions. This part of the subject is so fully worked out that we need waste no time on it. Moreover, all the earlier problems with which we are concerned arise in regard to sentences of atomic form.

Let us consider a few sentences: (1) this is yellow; (2) this is before that; (3) A gives a book to B.

(1) In 'this is yellow', the word 'this' is a proper name. It is true that, on other occasions, other objects are called 'this', but that is equally true of 'John': when we say 'here's John', we do not mean 'here is some member of the class of people called "John"'; we regard the name as belonging to only one person. Exactly the same is true of 'this'. The word 'men' is applicable to all the objects called severally 'a man', but the word 'these' is not applicable to all the objects severally called 'this' on different occasions.

The word 'yellow' is more difficult. It seems to mean, as suggested above, 'similar in colour to a certain object', this object being yellow by definition. Strictly, of course, since there are many shades of yellow, we need many objects which are yellow by definition: but one may ignore this complication. But since we can distinguish similarity in colour from similarity in other respects (e.g. shape), we do not avoid the necessity of a certain degree of abstraction in arriving at what is meant by 'yellow'.[1] We cannot see colour without shape, or shape without colour; but we can perceive the difference between the similarity of a yellow circle to a yellow triangle and the similarity of a yellow circle to a red circle. It

[1] But consider Carnap's *Logischer Aufbau*; yellow = (by definition) a group all similar to this and each other, and not all similar to anything outside the group.

would seem, therefore, that sensible predicates, such as 'yellow', 'red', 'loud', 'hard', are derived from the perception of kinds of similarity. This applies also to very general predicates such as 'visual', 'audible', 'tactile'. Thus to come back to 'this is yellow', the meaning seems to be 'this has colour-similarity to that', where 'this' and 'that' are proper names, the object called 'that' is yellow by definition, and colour-similarity is a dual relation which can be perceived. It will be observed that colour-similarity is a symmetrical relation. That is the reason which makes it possible to treat 'yellow' as a predicate, and to ignore comparison. Perhaps, indeed, what has been said about the comparison applies only to the *learning* of the word 'yellow'; it may be that, when learnt, it is truly a predicate.[1]

(2) 'This is before that' has already been discussed. Since the relation 'before' is asymmetrical, we cannot regard the proposition as assigning a common predicate to this and that. And if we regard it as assigning different predicates (e.g. dates) to this and that, these predicates themselves will have to have an asymmetrical relation corresponding to 'before'. We may, formally, treat the proposition as meaning 'the date of this is earlier than the date of that', but 'earlier' is an asymmetrical relation just as 'before' was. It is not easy to find a logical method of manufacturing asymmetry out of symmetrical data.[2]

The word 'before', like the word 'yellow', may be derived from comparison. We may start from some very emphatic case of sequence, such as a clock striking twelve, and, by taking other cases of sequence which have no other obvious resemblance to the striking clock, gradually lead to a concentration of attention on sequence. It seems clear, however— whatever may be the case in regard to 'yellow'—that in regard to 'before' this only applies to the learning of the word. The meaning of such words as 'before' or 'colour-similarity' cannot always be derived from comparison, since this would lead to an endless regress. Comparison is a necessary stimulus to abstraction, but abstraction must be possible, at least as regards similarity. And if possible in regard to similarity, it seems pointless to deny it elsewhere.

To say that we understand the word 'before' is to say that, when we perceive two events A and B in a time-sequence, we know whether to say 'A is before B' or 'B is before A', and concerning one of these we know that it describes what we perceive.

(3) 'A gives a book to B.' This means: 'there is an x such that A gives x to B and x is bookish'—using 'bookish', for the moment, to mean the defining quality of books. Let us concentrate on 'A gives C to B', where

---

[1] This question has no substance. The object is to construct a minimum vocabulary, and in this respect it can be done in two ways.

[2] As to this, Dr Sheffer has a way of distinguishing between the couple x-followed-by-y and the couple y-followed-by-x which shows that it is technically possible to construct asymmetry out of symmetrical materials. But it can hardly be maintained that it is more than a technical device.

A, B, C are proper names. (The questions raised by 'there is an x such that' we will consider presently.) I want to consider what sort of occurrence gives us evidence of the truth of this statement. If we are to know its truth, not by hearsay, but by the evidence of our own senses, we must see A and B, and see A holding C, moving C towards B, and finally giving C into B's hands. (I am assuming that C is some small object such as a book, not an estate or a copyright or anything else of which possession is a complicated legal abstraction.) This is logically analogous to 'Brutus killed Caesar with a dagger'. What is essential is that A, B and C should all be sensibly present throughout a finite period of time, during which the spatial relations of C to A and B change. Schematically, the geometrical minimum is as follows: first we see three shapes A_1, B_1, C_1, of which C_1 is close to A_1; then we see three very similar shapes A_2, B_2, C_2, of which C_2 is close to B_2. (I am omitting a number of niceties.) Neither of these two facts alone is sufficient; it is their occurrence in quick succession that is asserted. Even this is not really sufficient: we have to believe that A_1 and A_2, B_1 and B_2, C_1 and C_2 are respectively appearances of the same material objects, however these may be defined. I will ignore the fact that 'giving' involves intention; but even so the complications are alarming. At first sight, it would seem that the minimum assertion involved must be something like this: 'A_1, B_1, C_1 are appearances of three material objects at one time; A_2, B_2, C_2 are appearances of the "same" objects at a slightly later time; C_1 touches A_1 but not B_1; C_2 touches B_2 but not A_2.' I do not go into the evidence required to show that two appearances at different times are appearances of the 'same' object; this is ultimately a question for physics, but in practice and the law-courts grosser methods are tolerated. The important point, for us, is that we have apparently been led to an atomic form involving six terms, namely: 'the proximity of C_1 to A_1 and its comparative remoteness from B_1 is an occurrence slightly anterior to the proximity of C_2 to B_2 and its comparative remoteness from A_2'. We are tempted to conclude that we cannot avoid an atomic form of this degree of complexity if we are to have sensible evidence of such a matter as one person handing an object to another person.

But perhaps this is a mistake. Consider the propositions: C_1 is near A_1, C_1 is far from B_1, A_1 is simultaneous with B_1, B_1 is simultaneous with C_1, A_1 is slightly anterior to A_2, A_2 is simultaneous with B_2, B_2 is simultaneous with C_2, C_2 is near B_2, C_2 is far from A_2. This set of nine propositions is logically equivalent to the one proposition involving A_1, B_1, C_1, A_2, B_2, C_2. The one proposition, therefore, can be an inference, not a datum. There is still a difficulty: 'near' and 'far' are relative terms; in astronomy, Venus is near the earth, but not from the point of view of a person handing something to another person. We can, however, avoid this. We can substitute 'C_1 touches A_1' for 'C_1 is near A_1', and 'something is between C_1 and B_1' for 'C_1 is far from B_1'. Here 'touching' and 'between' are to be visual data. Thus the three-term relation 'between' seems the most complex datum required.

The importance of atomic forms and their contradictories is that—as we shall see—all propositions, or at least all non-psychological propositions justified by observation without inference are of these forms. That is to say, if due care is taken, all the sentences which embody empirical physical data will assert or deny propositions of atomic form. All other physical sentences can theoretically be either proved or disproved (as the case may be), or rendered probable or improbable, by sentences of these forms; and we ought not to include as a datum anything capable of logical proof or disproof by means of other data. But this is merely by way of anticipation.

In a sentence of atomic form, expressed in a strictly logical language, there are a finite number of proper names (any finite number from one upwards), and there is one word which is not a proper name. Examples are: 'x is yellow', 'x is earlier than y', 'x is between y and z', and so on. We can distinguish proper names from other words by the fact that a proper name can occur in every form of atomic sentence, whereas a word which is not a proper name can only occur in an atomic sentence which has the appropriate number of proper names. Thus 'yellow' demands one proper name, 'earlier' demands two, and 'between' demands three. Such terms are called predicates, dyadic relations, triadic relations, etc. Sometimes, for the sake of uniformity, predicates are called monadic relations.

I come now to the parts of speech, other than conjunctions, that cannot occur in atomic forms. Such are 'a', 'the', 'all', 'some', 'many', 'none'. To these, I think, 'not' should be added; but this is analogous to conjunctions. Let us start with 'a'. Suppose you say (truly) 'I saw a man'. It is obvious that 'a man' is not the sort of thing one can see; it is a logical abstraction. What you saw was some particular shape, to which we will give the proper name A; and you judged 'A is human'. The two sentences 'I saw A' and 'A is human' enable you to deduce 'I saw a man', but this latter sentence does not imply that you saw A, or that A is human. When you tell me that you saw a man, I cannot tell whether you saw A or B or C or any other of the men that exist. What is known is the truth of some proposition of the form:

$$\text{'I saw } x \text{ and } x \text{ is human.'}$$

This form is not atomic, being compounded of 'I saw x' and 'x is human'. It can be deduced from 'I saw A and A is human'; thus it can be proved by empirical data, although it is not the sort of sentence that expresses a perceptual datum, since such a sentence would have to mention A or B or C or whoever it was that you saw. *Per contra*, no perceptual data can *disprove* the sentence 'I saw a man'.

Propositions containing 'all' or 'none' can be disproved by empirical data, but not proved except in logic and mathematics. We can prove 'all primes except 2 are odd', because this follows from definitions; but we cannot prove 'all men are mortal', because we cannot prove that we have overlooked no one. In fact, 'all men are mortal' is a statement about everything, not only about all men; it states, concerning every x, that x is either mortal or not human. Until we have examined everything, we cannot be sure but that something unexamined is human but immortal. Since we cannot examine everything, we cannot *know* general propositions empirically.

No proposition containing *the* (in the singular) can be strictly proved by empirical evidence. We do not know that Scott was *the* author of *Waverley*; what we know is that he was *an* author of *Waverley*. For aught we know, somebody in Mars may have also written *Waverley*. To prove that Scott was *the* author, we should have to survey the universe and find that everything in it either did not write *Waverley* or was Scott. This is beyond our powers.

Empirical evidence can prove propositions containing 'a' or 'some', and can disprove propositions containing 'the', 'all', or 'none'. It cannot disprove propositions containing 'a' or 'some', and cannot prove propositions containing 'the', 'all', or 'none'. If empirical evidence is to lead us to disbelieve propositions about 'some' or to believe propositions about 'all', it must be in virtue of some principle of inference other than strict deduction—unless, indeed, there should be propositions containing the word 'all' among our basic propositions.

(*An Inquiry into Meaning and Truth*, London: Allen & Unwin; New York: W. W. Norton, 1940.)

11

THE USES OF LANGUAGE

Language, like other things of mysterious importance, such as breath, blood, sex and lightning, has been viewed superstitiously ever since men were capable of recording their thoughts. Savages fear to disclose their true name to an enemy, lest he should work evil magic by means of it. Origen assures us that pagan sorcerers could achieve more by using the sacred name Jehovah than by means of the names Zeus, Osiris or Brahma. Familiarity makes us blind to the linguistic emphasis in the Commandment: 'Thou shalt not take the *name* of the Lord in vain.' The habit of viewing language superstitiously is not yet extinct. 'In the beginning was the Word', says our version of St John's Gospel, and in reading some logical positivists I am tempted to think that their view is represented by this mistranslated text.

Philosophers, being bookish and theoretical folk, have been interested in language chiefly as a means of making statements and conveying information, but this is only one of its purposes, and perhaps not the most primitive. What is the purpose of language to a sergeant-major? On the one hand there is the language of words of command, designed to cause identical simultaneous bodily movements in a number of hearers; on the other hand there is bad language, designed to cause humility in those in whom the expected bodily movements have not been caused. In neither case are words used, except incidentally, to state facts or convey information.

Language can be used to express emotions, or to influence the behaviour of others. Each of these functions can be performed, though with less adequacy, by pre-linguistic methods. Animals emit shrieks of pain, and infants, before they can speak, can express rage, discomfort, desire, delight, and a whole gamut of feelings, by cries and gurgles of different kinds. A sheep dog emits imperatives to his flock by means hardly distinguishable from those that the shepherd employs towards him. Between such noises and speech no sharp line can be drawn. When the dentist hurts you, you may emit an involuntary groan; this does not count as speech. But if he says 'let me know if I hurt you', and you then make the very same sound, it has become speech, and moreover speech of the sort intended to convey information. This example illustrates the fact that, in the matter of language as in other respects, there is a continuous gradation from animal behaviour to that of the most precise man of science, and from pre-linguistic noises to the polished diction of the lexicographer.

A sound expressive of emotion I shall call an 'interjection'. Imperatives and interjections can already be distinguished in the noises emitted by animals. When a hen clucks at her brood of chickens, she is uttering imperatives, but when she squawks in terror she is expressing emotion. But as appears from your groan at the dentist's, an interjection may convey information, and the outside observer cannot tell whether or not it is intended to do so. Gregarious animals emit distinctive noises when they find food, and other members of the herd are attracted when they hear these noises, but we cannot know whether the noises merely express pleasure or are also intended to state 'food here'.

Whenever an animal is so constructed that a certain kind of circumstance causes a certain kind of emotion, and a certain kind of emotion causes a certain kind of noise, the noise conveys to a suitable observer two pieces of information, first, that the animal has a certain kind of feeling, and second, that a certain kind of circumstance is present. The sound that the animal emits is public, and the circumstance may be public—e.g. the presence of a shoal of fish if the animal is a sea-gull. The animal's cry may act directly on the other members of its species, and *we* shall then say that they 'understand' its cry. But this is to suppose a 'mental' intermediary between the hearing of the cry and the bodily reaction to the sound, and there is no real reason to suppose any such intermediary except when the response is delayed. Much of the importance of language is connected with delayed responses, but I will not yet deal with this topic.

Language has two primary purposes, expression and communication. In its most primitive forms it differs little from some other forms of behaviour. A man may express sorrow by sighing, or by saying 'alas!' or 'woe is me!' He may communicate by pointing or by saying 'look'. Expression and communication are not necessarily separated; if you say 'look' because you see a ghost, you may say it in a tone that expresses horror. This applies not only to elementary forms of language; in poetry, and especially in songs, emotion and information are conveyed by the same means. Music may be considered as a form of language in which emotion is divorced from information, while the telephone book gives information without emotion. But in ordinary speech both elements are usually present.

Communication does not consist only of giving information; commands and questions must be included. Sometimes the two are scarcely separable: if you are walking with a child, and you say 'there's a puddle there', the command 'don't step in it' is implicit. Giving information may be due solely to the fact that the information interests you, or may be designed to influence behaviour. If you have just seen a street accident, you will wish to tell your friends about it because your mind is full of it; but if you tell a child that six times seven is forty-two you do so merely in the hope of influencing his (verbal) behaviour.

Language has two interconnected merits: first, that it is social, and second that it supplies public expression for 'thoughts' which would otherwise remain private. Without language, or some pre-linguistic analogue, our knowledge of the environment is confined to what our own senses have shown us, together with such inferences as our congenital constitution may prompt; but by the help of speech we are able to know what others can relate, and to relate what is no longer sensibly present but only remembered. When we see or hear something which a companion is not seeing or hearing, we can often make him aware of it by the one word 'look' or 'listen', or even by gestures. But if half an hour ago we saw a fox, it is not possible to make another person aware of this fact without language. This depends upon the fact that the word 'fox' applies equally to a fox seen or a fox remembered, so that our memories, which in themselves are private, are represented to others by uttered sounds, which are public. Without language, only that part of our life which consists of public sensations would be communicable, and that only to those so situated as to be able to share the sensations in question.

It will be seen that the utility of language depends upon the distinction between public and private experiences, which is important in considering the empirical basis of physics. This distinction, in turn, depends partly on physiology, partly on the persistence of sound-waves and light-quanta, which makes possible the two forms of language, speech and writing. Thus language depends upon physics, and could not exist without the approximately separable causal chains which, as we shall see, make physical knowledge possible, and since the publicity of sensible objects is only approximate, language applying to them, considered socially, must have a certain lack of precision. I need hardly say that I am *not* asserting that the existence of language requires a *knowledge* of physics. What I am saying is that language would be impossible if the physical world did not in fact have certain characteristics, and that the *theory* of language is at certain points dependent upon a knowledge of the physical world. Language is a means of externalizing and publicizing our own experiences. A dog cannot relate his autobiography; however eloquently he may bark, he cannot tell you that his parents were honest though poor. A man can do this, and he does it by correlating 'thoughts' with public sensations.

Language serves not only to express thoughts, but to make possible thoughts which could not exist without it. It is sometimes maintained that there can be no thought without language, but to this view I cannot assent: I hold that there can be thought, and even true and false belief, without language. But however that may be, it cannot be denied that all fairly elaborate thoughts require words. I can know, in a sense, that I have five fingers, without knowing the word 'five', but I cannot know that the population of London is about eight millions unless I have acquired the language of arithmetic, nor can I have any thought at all closely corresponding to what is asserted in the sentence: 'the ratio of the circumference of a circle to the diameter is approximately $3 \cdot 14159$'. Language, once evolved, acquires a kind of autonomy: we can know, especially in mathematics, that a sentence asserts something true, although what it asserts is too complex to be apprehended even by the best minds. Let us consider for a moment what happens psychologically in such cases.

In mathematics, we start from rather simple sentences which we believe ourselves capable of understanding, and proceed, by rules of inference which we also believe ourselves to understand, to build up more and more complicated symbolic statements, which, if our initial assumptions are true, must be true whatever they may mean. As a rule it is unnecessary to know what they 'mean', if their 'meaning' is taken to be a thought which might occur in the mind of a superhuman mathematical genius. But there is another kind of 'meaning', which gives occasion for pragmatism and instrumentalism. According to those who adopt this view of 'meaning', what a complicated mathematical sentence does is to give a rule for practical procedure in certain kinds of cases. Take, for instance, the above statement about the ratio of the circumference of a circle to the diameter. Suppose you are a brewer, and you desire hoops of a given diameter for your beer barrels, then the sentence gives you a rule by which you can find out how much material you will need. This rule may consist of a fresh sentence for each decimal point, and there is therefore no need ever to grasp its significance as a whole. The autonomy of language enables you to forgo this tedious process of interpretation except at crucial moments.

There are two other uses of language that are of great importance; it enables us to conduct our transactions with the outer world by means of symbols that have (1) a certain degree of permanence in time, (2) a considerable degree of discreteness in space. Each of these merits is more marked in writing than in speech, but is by no means wholly absent in speech. Suppose you have a friend called Mr Jones. As a physical object his boundaries are somewhat vague, both because he is continually losing and acquiring electrons, and because an electron, being a distribution of energy, does not cease abruptly at a certain distance from its centre. The surface of Mr. Jones, therefore, has a certain ghostly impalpable quality, which you do not like to associate with your solid-seeming friend. It is not necessary to go into the niceties of theoretical physics in order to show that Mr Jones is sadly indeterminate. When he is cutting his toe nails, there is a finite time, though a short one, during which it is doubtful whether the parings are still part of him or not. When he eats a mutton chop, at what moment does it become part of him? When he breathes out carbon dioxide, is the carbon part of him until it passes his nostrils? Even if we answer in the affirmative, there is a finite time during which it is questionable whether certain molecules have or have not passed beyond his nostrils. In these and other ways, it is doubtful what is part of Mr Jones and what is not. So much for spatial vagueness.

There is the same problem as regards time. To the question 'what are you looking at?' you may answer 'Mr Jones', although at one time you see him full-face, at another in profile, and at another from behind, and although at one time he may be running a race and at another time dozing in an arm-chair. There is another question, namely, 'what are you thinking of?' to which you may also answer 'Mr Jones', though what is actually in your mind may be very different on different occasions: it may be Mr Jones as a baby, or Mr Jones being cross because his breakfast is late, or Mr Jones receiving the news that he is to be knighted. What you are experiencing is very different on these various occasions, but for many practical purposes it is convenient to regard them as all having a common object, which we suppose to be the meaning of the name 'Mr Jones'. This name, especially when printed, though it cannot wholly escape the indefiniteness and transience of all physical objects, has much less of both than Mr Jones has. Two instances of the printed words 'Mr Jones' are much more alike than (for instance) the spectacle of Mr Jones running and the memory of Mr Jones as a baby. And each instance, if printed, changes much more slowly than Mr Jones does: it does not eat or breathe or cut its toe nails. The name, accordingly, makes it much easier than it would otherwise be to think of Mr Jones as a single quasi-permanent entity, which, though untrue, is convenient in daily life.

Language, as appears from the above discussion of Mr Jones, though a useful and even indispensable tool, is a dangerous one, since it begins by suggesting a definiteness, discreteness, and quasi-permanence in objects which physics seems to show that they do not possess. The philosopher, therefore, is faced with the difficult task of using language to undo the false beliefs that it suggests. Some philosophers, who shrink from the problems and uncertainties and complications involved in such a task, prefer to treat language as autonomous, and try to forget that it is intended to have a relation to fact and to facilitate dealings with the environment. Up to a point, such a treatment has great advantages: logic and mathematics would not have prospered as they have done if logicians and mathematicians had continually remembered that symbols should mean something. 'Art for art's sake' is a maxim which has a legitimate sphere in logic as in painting (though in neither case does it give the whole truth). It may be that singing began as an incident in courtship, and that its biological purpose was to promote sexual intercourse; but this fact (if it be a fact) will not help a composer to produce good music. Language is useful when you wish to order a meal in a restaurant, but this fact, similarly, is of no importance to the pure mathematician.

The philosopher, however, must pursue truth even at the expense of beauty, and in studying language he must not let himself be seduced by the siren songs of mathematics. Language, in its beginnings, is pedestrian and practical, using rough and ready approximations which have at first no beauty and only a very limited degree of truth. Subsequent refinements have too often had aesthetic rather than scientific motives, but from the inquiry upon which we are about to embark aesthetic motives must, however reluctantly, be relentlessly banished.

(*Human Knowledge: Its Scope and Limits*, London: Allen & Unwin; New York: Simon & Schuster, 1948.)

12

THE CULT OF 'COMMON USAGE'

THE most influential school of philosophy in Britain at the present day maintains a certain linguistic doctrine to which I am unable to subscribe. I do not wish to misrepresent this school, but I suppose any opponent of any doctrine is thought to misrepresent it by those who hold it. The doctrine, as I understand it, consists in maintaining that the language of daily life, with words used in their ordinary meanings, suffices for philosophy, which has no need of technical terms or of changes in the signification of common terms. I find myself totally unable to accept this view. I object to it:

(1) Because it is insincere;

(2) Because it is capable of excusing ignorance of mathematics, physics, and neurology in those who have had only a classical education;

(3) Because it is advanced by some in a tone of unctuous rectitude, as if opposition to it were a sin against democracy;

(4) Because it makes philosophy trivial;

(5) Because it makes almost inevitable the perpetuation among philosophers of the muddle-headedness they have taken over from common sense.

(1) *Insincerity*. I will illustrate this by a fable. The Professor of Mental Philosophy, when called by his bedmaker one morning, developed a dangerous frenzy, and had to be taken away by the police in an ambulance. I heard a colleague, a believer in 'common usage', asking the poor philosopher's doctor about the occurrence. The doctor replied that the professor had had an attack of temporary psychotic instability, which had subsided after an hour. The believer in 'common usage', so far from objecting to the doctor's language, repeated it to other inquirers. But it happened that I, who live on the professor's staircase, overheard the following dialogue between the bedmaker and the policeman:

Policeman. 'Ere, I want a word with yer.

Bedmaker. What do you mean—'A word'? I ain't done nothing.

Policeman. Ah, that's just it. Yer ought to 'ave done something. Couldn't yer see the pore gentleman was mental?

Bedmaker. That I could. For an 'ole *h*our 'e went on something chronic. But when they're mental you can't make them understand.

In this little dialogue, 'word', 'mean', 'mental', and 'chronic' are all used in accordance with common usage. They are not so used in the pages of *Mind* by those who pretend that common usage is what they believe in. What in fact they believe in is not common usage, as determined by mass observation, statistics, medians, standard deviations, and the rest of the apparatus. What they believe in is the usage of persons who have their amount of education, neither more nor less. Less is illiteracy, more is pedantry—so we are given to understand.

(2) *An excuse for ignorance.* Every motorist is accustomed to speedometers and accelerators, but unless he has learnt mathematics he attaches no precise significance to 'speed' or 'acceleration'. If he does attach a precise significance to these words, he will know that his speed and his acceleration are at every moment unknowable, and that, if he is fined for speeding, the conviction must be based on insufficient evidence if the time when he is supposed to have speeded is mentioned. On these grounds I will agree with the advocate of common usage that such a word as 'speed', if used in daily life, must be used as in daily life, and not as in mathematics. But then it should be realized that 'speed' is a vague notion, and that equal truth may attach to all three of the statements in the conjugation of the following irregular verb:

'I was at rest' (motorist).

'You were moving at 20 miles an hour' (a friend).

'He was travelling at 60 miles an hour' (the police).

It is because this state of affairs is puzzling to magistrates that mathematicians have abandoned common usage.

(3) Those who advocate common usage in philosophy sometimes speak in a manner that suggests the *mystique* of the 'common man'. They may admit that in organic chemistry there is need of long words, and that quantum physics requires formulae that are difficult to translate into ordinary English, but philosophy (they think) is different. It is not the function of philosophy—so they maintain—to teach something that uneducated people do not know; on the contrary, its function is to teach superior persons that they are not as superior as they thought they were, and that those who are *really* superior can show their skill by making sense of common sense.

It is, of course, a dreadful thing in these days to lay claim to any kind of superiority except in athletics, movies, and moneymaking. Nevertheless I will venture to say that in former centuries common sense made what we now think mistakes. It used to be thought that there could not be people at the antipodes, because they would fall off, or, if they avoided that, they would grow dizzy from standing on their heads. It used to be thought absurd to say that the earth rotates, because everybody can see that it doesn't. When it was first suggested that the sun may be as large as the Peloponnesus, common sense was outraged. But all this was long ago. I do not know at what date common sense became all-wise. Perhaps it was in 1776; perhaps in 1848; or perhaps with the passing of the Education Act in 1870. Or perhaps it was only when physiologists such as Adrian and Sherrington began to make scientific inroads on philosophers' ideas about perception.

(4) Philosophy, as conceived by the school I am discussing, seems to me a trivial and uninteresting pursuit. To discuss endlessly what silly people mean when they say silly things may be amusing but can hardly be important. Does the full moon look as large as a half-crown or as large as a soup plate? Either answer can be proved correct by experiment. It follows that there is an ambiguity in the question. A modern philosopher will clear up the ambiguity for you with meticulous care.

But let us take an example which is less unfair, say the question of immortality. Orthodox Christianity asserts that we survive death. What does it mean by this assertion? And in what sense, if any, is the assertion true? The philosophers with whom I am concerned will consider the first of these questions, but will say that the second is none of their business. I agree entirely that, in this case, a discussion as to what is meant is important and highly necessary as a preliminary to a consideration of the substantial question, but if nothing can be said on the substantial question it seems a waste of time to discuss what it means. These philosophers remind me of the shopkeeper of whom I once asked the shortest way to Winchester. He called to a man in the back premises:

'Gentleman wants to know the shortest way to Winchester.'

'Winchester?' an unseen voice replied.

'Aye.'

'Way to Winchester?'

'Aye.'

'Shortest way?'

'Aye.'

'Dunno.'

He wanted to get the nature of the question clear, but took no interest in answering it. This is exactly what modern philosophy does for the earnest seeker after truth. Is it surprising that young people turn to other studies?

(5) Common sense, though all very well for everyday purposes, is easily confused, even by such simple questions as 'Where is the rainbow?' When you hear a voice on a gramophone record, are you hearing the man who spoke or a reproduction? When you feel a pain in a leg that has been amputated, where is the pain? If you say it is in your head, would it be in your head if the leg had not been amputated? If you say yes, then what reason have you ever for thinking you have a leg? And so on.

No one wants to alter the language of common sense, any more than we wish to give up talking of the sun rising and setting. But astronomers find a different language better, and I contend that a different language is better in philosophy.

Let us take an example. A philosophy containing such a large linguistic element cannot object to the question: What is meant by the word 'word'? But I do not see how this is to be answered within the vocabulary of common sense. Let us take the word 'cat', and for the sake of definiteness let us take the written word. Clearly there are many instances of the word, no one of which *is* the word. If I say 'Let us discuss the word "cat" ', the word 'cat' does not occur in what I say, but only an instance of the word. The word itself is no part of the sensible world; if it is anything, it is an eternal super-sensible entity in a Platonic heaven. The word, we may say, is a class of similar shapes, and, like all classes, is a logical fiction.

But our difficulties are not at an end. Similarity is neither necessary nor sufficient to make a shape a member of the class which is the word 'cat'. The word may be written in capitals or in small letters, legibly or illegibly, in black on a white ground or in white on a blackboard. If I write the word 'catastrophe', the first three letters do not constitute an instance of the word 'cat'. The most necessary thing in an instance of the word is *intention*. If a piece of marble happened to have a vein making the shape 'cat' we should not think this an instance of the word.

It thus appears that we cannot define the word 'word' without (*a*) a logical theory of classes, and (*b*) a psychological understanding of intention. These are difficult matters. I conclude that common sense, whether correct or incorrect in the use of words, does not know in the least what words are—I wish I could believe that this conclusion would render it speechless.

Let us take another problem, that of perception. There is here an admixture of philosophical and scientific questions, but this admixture is inevitable in many questions, or, if not inevitable, can only be avoided by confining ourselves to comparatively unimportant aspects of the matter in hand.

Here is a series of questions and answers.

Q. When I see a table, will what I see be still there if I shut my eyes?

A. That depends upon the sense in which you use the word 'see'.

Q. What is still there when I shut my eyes?

A. This is an empirical question. Don't bother me with it, but ask the physicists.

Q. What exists when my eyes are open, but not when they are shut?

A. This again is empirical, but in deference to previous philosophers I will answer you: coloured surfaces.

Q. May I infer that there are two senses of 'see'? In the first, when I 'see' a table, I 'see' something conjectural about which physics has vague notions that are probably wrong. In the second, I 'see' coloured surfaces which cease to exist when I shut my eyes.

A. That is correct if you want to think clearly, but our philosophy makes clear thinking unnecessary. By oscillating between the two meanings, we avoid paradox and shock, which is more than most philosophers do.

(*Portraits from Memory*, London: Allen & Unwin;
New York: Simon & Schuster, 1956.)

PART IV

The Logician and Philosopher of Mathematics

The impact of *Principia Mathematica* on twentieth-century mathematics, logic, and philosophy was both enormous and paradoxical. On the one hand, this ten-year co-operative labour, in its aim to codify relational inferences, is viewed as one of the world's greatest contributions to knowledge and, on the other hand, there are few, outside of professional specialists, who have read, much less *understood*, particularly the latter parts of this work. At Russell's own suggestion, we include here none of the symbolic expositions, but merely introductory sections which are explanatory of the scope and aim of the work.

The reduction of mathematics to logic and the critical view of traditional logic are the theme of Russell's other important works in the field as illustrated here. We have also given one side of one of the most provocative running debates in contemporary philosophic literature, that between Russell and John Dewey.

13

SYMBOLIC LOGIC

11. SYMBOLIC or formal logic—I shall use these terms as synonyms— is the study of the various general types of deduction. The word *symbolic* designates the subject by an accidental characteristic, for the employment of mathematical symbols, here as elsewhere, is merely a theoretically irrelevant convenience. The syllogism in all its figures belongs to symbolic logic, and would be the whole subject if all deduction were syllogistic, as the scholastic tradition supposed. It is from the recognition of asyllogistic inferences that modern symbolic logic, from Leibniz onward, has derived the motive to progress. Since the publication of Boole's *Laws of Thought* (1854), the subject has been pursued with a certain vigour, and has attained to a very considerable technical development.[1] Nevertheless, the subject achieved almost nothing of utility either to philosophy or to other branches of mathematics, until it was transformed by the new methods of Professor Peano.[2] Symbolic logic has now become not only absolutely essential to every philosophical logician, but also necessary for the comprehension of mathematics generally, and even for the successful practice of certain branches of mathematics. How useful it is in practice can only be judged by those who have experienced the increase of power derived from acquiring it; its theoretical functions must be briefly set forth in the present chapter.[3]

12. Symbolic logic is essentially concerned with inference in general,[4] and is distinguished from various special branches of mathematics mainly by its generality. Neither mathematics nor symbolic logic will study such

---

[1] By far the most complete account of the non-Peanesque methods will be found in the three volumes of Schröder, *Vorlesungen über die Algebra der Logik*, Leipzig, 1890, 1891, 1895.

[2] See *Formulaire de Mathématiques*, Turin, 1895, with subsequent editions in later years; also *Revue de Mathématiques*, Vol. VII, No. 1 (1900). The editions of the *Formulaire* will be quoted as *F.* 1895 and so on. The *Revue de Mathématiques*, which was originally the *Rivista di Matematica*, will be referred to as *R. d. M.*

[3] In what follows the main outlines are due to Professor Peano, except as regards relations; even in those cases where I depart from his views, the problems considered have been suggested to me by his works.

[4] I may as well say at once that I do not distinguish between inference and deduction. What is called induction appears to me to be either disguised deduction or a mere method of making plausible guesses.

special relations as (say) temporal priority, but mathematics will deal explicitly with the class of relations possessing the formal properties of temporal priority—properties which are summed up in the notion of continuity. And the formal properties of a relation may be defined as those that can be expressed in terms of logical constants, or again as those which, while they are preserved, permit our relation to be varied without invalidating any inference in which the said relation is regarded in the light of a variable. But symbolic logic, in the narrower sense which is convenient, will not investigate what inferences are possible in respect of continuous relations (i.e. relations generating continuous series); this investigation belongs to mathematics, but is still too special for symbolic logic. What symbolic logic does investigate is the general rules by which inferences are made, and it requires a classification of relations or propositions only in so far as these general rules introduce particular notions. The particular notions which appear in the propositions of symbolic logic, and all others definable in terms of these notions, are the logical constants. The number of indefinable logical constants is not great: it appears, in fact, to be eight or nine. These notions alone form the subject-matter of the whole of mathematics: no others, except such as are definable in terms of the original eight or nine, occur anywhere in arithmetic, geometry, or rational dynamics. For the technical study of symbolic logic, it is convenient to take as a single indefinable the notion of a formal implication, i.e. of such propositions as 'x is a man implies x is a mortal, for all values of x'—propositions whose general type is: '$\phi(x)$ implies $\psi(x)$ for all values of x', where $\phi(x)$, $\psi(x)$, for all values of x, are propositions. The analysis of this notion of formal implication belongs to the principles of the subject, but is not required for its formal development. In addition to this notion, we require as indefinables the following: Implication between propositions not containing variables, the relation of a term to a class of which it is a member, the notion of *such that*, the notion of relation, and truth. By means of these notions, all the propositions of symbolic logic can be stated.

13. The subject of symbolic logic consists of three parts, the calculus of propositions, the calculus of classes, and the calculus of relations. Between the first two, there is, within limits, a certain parallelism, which arises as follows: In any symbolic expression, the letters may be interpreted as classes or as propositions, and the relation of inclusion in the one case may be replaced by that of formal implication in the other. Thus, for example, in the principle of the syllogism, if a, b, c be classes, and a is contained in b, b in c, then a is contained in c; but if a, b, c be propositions, and a implies b, b implies c, then a implies c. A great deal has been made of this duality, and in the later editions of the *Formulaire*, Peano appears to have sacrificed logical precision to its preservation.[1]

---

[1] On the points where the duality breaks down, cf. Schröder, *op. cit.*, Vol. II, Lecture 21.

But, as a matter of fact, there are many ways in which the calculus of propositions differs from that of classes. Consider, for example, the following: 'If p, q, r are propositions, and p implies q or r, then p implies q or p implies r.' This proposition is true; but its correlative is false, namely: 'If a, b, c are classes, and a is contained in b or c, then a is contained in b or a is contained in c.' For example, English people are all either men or women, but are not all men nor yet all women. The fact is that the duality holds for propositions asserting of a variable term that it belongs to a class, i.e. such propositions as 'x is a man', provided that the implication involved be formal, i.e. one which holds for all values of x. But 'x is a man' is itself not a proposition at all, being neither true nor false; and it is not with such entities that we are concerned in the propositional calculus, but with genuine propositions. To continue the above illustration: It is true that, for all values of x, 'x is a man or a woman' either implies 'x is a man' or implies 'x is a woman'. But it is false that 'x is a man or woman' either implies 'x is a man' for all values of x, or implies 'x is a woman' for all values of x. Thus the implication involved, which is always one of the two, is not formal, since it does not hold for all values of x, being not always the same one of the two. The symbolic affinity of the propositional and the class logic is, in fact, something of a snare, and we have to decide which of the two we are to make fundamental. Mr McColl, in an important series of papers,[1] has contended for the view that implication and propositions are more fundamental than inclusion and classes; and in this opinion I agree with him. But he does not appear to me to realize adequately the distinction between genuine propositions and such as contain a real variable: thus he is led to speak of propositions as sometimes true and sometimes false, which of course is impossible with a genuine proposition. As the distinction involved is of very great importance, I shall dwell on it before proceeding further. A proposition, we may say, is anything that is true or that is false. An expression such as 'x is a man' is therefore not a proposition, for it is neither true nor false. If we give to x any constant value whatever, the expression becomes a proposition: it is thus as it were a schematic form standing for any one of a whole class of propositions. And when we say 'x is a man implies x is a mortal for all values of x', we are not asserting a single implication, but a class of implications; we have now a genuine proposition, in which, though the letter x appears, there is no real variable: the variable is absorbed in the same kind of way as the x under the integral sign in a definite integral, so that the result is no longer a function of x. Peano distinguishes a variable which appears in this way as *apparent*,

[1] Cf. 'The Calculus of Equivalent Statements', *Proceedings of the London Mathematical Society*, Vol. IX and subsequent volumes; 'Symbolic Reasoning', *Mind*, January 1880, October 1897, and January 1900; 'La Logique Symbolique et ses Applications', *Bibliothèque du Congrès International de Philosophie*, Vol. III (Paris, 1901). I shall in future quote the proceedings of the above Congress by the title *Congrès*.

since the proposition does not depend upon the variable; whereas in '*x* is a man' there are different propositions for different values of the variable, and the variable is what Peano calls *real*.[1] I shall speak of propositions exclusively where there is no real variable: where there are one or more real variables, and for all values of the variables the expression involved is a proposition, I shall call the expression a *propositional function*. The study of genuine propositions is, in my opinion, more fundamental than that of classes; but the study of propositional functions appears to be strictly on a par with that of classes, and indeed scarcely distinguishable therefrom. Peano, like McColl, at first regarded propositions as more fundamental than classes, but he, even more definitely, considered propositional functions rather than propositions. From this criticism, Schröder is exempt: his second volume deals with genuine propositions, and points out their formal differences from classes.

(*The Principles of Mathematics*, London: Allen & Unwin, 2nd ed., 1950.)

[1] *F.* 1901, p. 2.

14

ON INDUCTION

W E have been concerned in the attempt to get clear as to our data in the way of knowledge of existence. What things are there in the universe whose existence is known to us owing to our being acquainted with them? So far, our answer has been that we are acquainted with our sense-data, and, probably, with ourselves. These we know to exist. And past sense-data which are remembered are known to have existed in the past. This knowledge supplies our data.

But if we are to be able to draw inferences from these data—if we are to know of the existence of matter, of other people, of the past before our individual memory begins, or of the future, we must know general principles of some kind by means of which such inferences can be drawn. It must be known to us that the existence of some one sort of thing, A, is a sign of the existence of some other sort of thing, B, either at the same time as A or at some earlier or later time, as, for example, thunder is a sign of the earlier existence of lightning. If this were not known to us, we could never extend our knowledge beyond the sphere of our private experience; and this sphere, as we have seen, is exceedingly limited. The question we have now to consider is whether such an extension is possible, and if so, how it is effected.

Let us take as an illustration a matter about which none of us, in fact, feels the slightest doubt. We are all convinced that the sun will rise tomorrow. Why? Is this belief a mere blind outcome of past experience, or can it be justified as a reasonable belief? It is not easy to find a test by which to judge whether a belief of this kind is reasonable or not, but we can at least ascertain what sort of general beliefs would suffice, if true, to justify the judgment that the sun will rise tomorrow, and the many other similar judgments upon which our actions are based.

It is obvious that if we are asked why we believe that the sun will rise tomorrow, we shall naturally answer: 'Because it always has risen every day.' We have a firm belief that it will rise in the future, because it has risen in the past. If we are challenged as to why we believe that it will continue to **rise** as heretofore, we may appeal to the laws of motion: the earth, we shall say, is a freely rotating body, and such bodies do not cease to rotate unless something interferes from outside, and there is nothing outside to interfere with the earth between now and tomorrow. Of course it might be doubted whether we are quite certain that there is nothing outside to interfere, but this is not the interesting doubt. The interesting doubt is as to whether the laws of motion will remain in operation until tomorrow. If this doubt is raised, we find ourselves in the same position as when the doubt about the sunrise was first raised.

The *only* reason for believing that the laws of motion will remain in operation is that they have operated hitherto, so far as our knowledge of the past enables us to judge. It is true that we have a greater body of evidence from the past in favour of the laws of motion than we have in favour of the sunrise, because the sunrise is merely a particular case of fulfilment of the laws of motion, and there are countless other particular cases. But the real question is: Do *any* number of cases of a law being fulfilled in the past afford evidence that it will be fulfilled in the future? If not, it becomes plain that we have no ground whatever for expecting the sun to rise tomorrow, or for expecting the bread we shall eat at our next meal not to poison us, or for any of the other scarcely conscious expectations that control our daily lives. It is to be observed that all such expectations are only *probable*; thus we have not to seek for a proof that they *must* be fulfilled, but only for some reason in favour of the view that they are *likely* to be fulfilled.

Now in dealing with this question we must, to begin with, make an important distinction, without which we should soon become involved in hopeless confusions. Experience has shown us that, hitherto, the frequent repetition of some uniform succession or coexistence has been a *cause* of our expecting the same succession or coexistence on the next occasion. Food that has a certain appearance generally has a certain taste, and it is a severe shock to our expectations when the familiar appearance is found to be associated with an unusual taste. Things which we see become associated, by habit, with certain tactile sensations which we expect if we touch them; one of the horrors of a ghost (in many ghost-stories) is that it fails to give us any sensations of touch. Uneducated people who go abroad for the first time are so surprised as to be incredulous when they find their native language not understood.

And this kind of association is not confined to men; in animals also it is very strong. A horse which has been often driven along a certain road resists the attempt to drive him in a different direction. Domestic animals expect food when they see the person who usually feeds them. We know that all these rather crude expectations of uniformity are liable to be misleading. The man who has fed the chicken every day throughout its life at last wrings its neck instead, showing that more refined views as to the uniformity of nature would have been useful to the chicken.

But in spite of the misleadingness of such expectations, they nevertheless exist. The mere fact that something has happened a certain number of times causes animals and men to expect that it will happen again. Thus our instincts certainly cause us to believe that the sun will rise tomorrow, but we may be in no better a position than the chicken which unexpectedly has its neck wrung. We have therefore to distinguish the fact that past uniformities *cause* expectations as to the future, from the question whether there is any reasonable ground for giving weight to such expectations after the question of their validity has been raised.

The problem we have to discuss is whether there is any reason for believing in what is called 'the uniformity of nature'. The belief in the uniformity of nature is the belief that everything that has happened or will happen is an instance of some general law to which there are *no* exceptions. The crude expectations which we have been considering are all subject to exceptions, and therefore liable to disappoint those who entertain them. But science habitually assumes, at least as a working hypothesis, that general rules which have exceptions can be replaced by general rules which have no exceptions. 'Unsupported bodies in air fall' is a general rule to which balloons and aeroplanes are exceptions. But the laws of motion and the law of gravitation, which account for the fact that most bodies fall, also account for the fact that balloons and aeroplanes can rise; thus the laws of motion and the law of gravitation are not subject to these exceptions.

The belief that the sun will rise tomorrow might be falsified if the earth came suddenly into contact with a large body which destroyed its rotation; but the laws of motion and the law of gravitation would not be infringed by such an event. The business of science is to find uniformities, such as the laws of motion and the law of gravitation, to which, so far as our experience extends, there are no exceptions. In this search science has been remarkably successful, and it may be conceded that such uniformities have held hitherto. This brings us back to the question: Have we any reason, assuming that they have always held in the past, to suppose that they will hold in the future?

It has been argued that we have reason to know that the future will resemble the past, because what was the future has constantly become the past, and has always been found to resemble the past, so that we really have experience of the future, namely of times which were formerly future, which we may call past futures. But such an argument really begs the very question at issue. We have experience of past futures, but not of future futures, and the question is: Will future futures resemble past futures? This question is not to be answered by an argument which starts from past futures alone. We have therefore still to seek for some principle which shall enable us to know that the future will follow the same laws as the past.

The reference to the future in this question is not essential. The same question arises when we apply the laws that work in our experience to past things of which we have no experience—as, for example, in geology, or in theories as to the origin of the Solar System. The question we really have to ask is: 'When two things have been found to be often associated, and no instance is known of the one occurring without the other, does the occurrence of one of the two, in a fresh instance, give any good ground for expecting the other?' On our answer to this question must depend the validity of the whole of our expectations as to the future, the whole of the results obtained by induction, and in fact practically all the beliefs upon which our daily life is based.

It must be conceded, to begin with, that the fact that two things have been found often together and never apart does not, by itself, suffice to *prove* demonstratively that they will be found together in the next case we examine. The most we can hope is that the oftener things are found together, the more probable it becomes that they will be found together another time, and that, if they have been found together often enough, the probability will amount *almost* to certainty. It can never quite reach certainty, because we know that in spite of frequent repetitions there sometimes is a failure at the last, as in the case of the chicken whose neck is wrung. Thus probability is all we ought to seek.

It might be urged, as against the view we are advocating, that we know all natural phenomena to be subject to the reign of law, and that sometimes, on the basis of observation, we can see that only one law can possibly fit the facts of the case. Now to this view there are two answers. The first is that, even if *some* law which has no exceptions applies to our case, we can never, in practice, be sure that we have discovered that law and not one to which there are exceptions. The second is that the reign of law would seem to be itself only probable, and that our belief that it will hold in the future, or in unexamined cases in the past, is itself based upon the very principle we are examining.

The principle we are examining may be called the *principle of induction*, and its two parts may be stated as follows:

(a) When a thing of a certain sort A has been found to be associated with a thing of a certain other sort B, and has never been found dissociated from a thing of the sort B, the greater the number of cases in which A and B have been associated, the greater is the probability that they will be associated in a fresh case in which one of them is known to be present;

(b) Under the same circumstances, a sufficient number of cases of association will make the probability of a fresh association nearly a certainty, and will make it approach certainty without limit.

As just stated, the principle applies only to the verification of our expectation in a single fresh instance. But we want also to know that there is a probability in favour of the general law that things of the sort A are *always* associated with things of the sort B, provided a sufficient number of cases of association are known, and no cases of failure of association are known. The probability of the general law is obviously less than the probability of the particular case, since if the general law is true, the particular case must also be true, whereas the particular case may be true without the general law being true. Nevertheless the probability of the general law is increased by repetitions, just as the probability of the particular case is. We may therefore repeat the two parts of our principle as regards the general law, thus:

(*a*) The greater the number of cases in which a thing of the sort A has been found associated with a thing of the sort B, the more probable it is (if no cases of failure of association are known) that A is always associated with B;

(*b*) Under the same circumstances, a sufficient number of cases of the association of A with B will make it nearly certain that A is always associated with B, and will make this general law approach certainty without limit.

It should be noted that probability is always relative to certain data. In our case, the data are merely the known cases of coexistence of A and B. There may be other data, which *might* be taken into account, which would gravely alter the probability. For example, a man who had seen a great many white swans might argue, by our principle, that on the data it was *probable* that all swans were white, and this might be a perfectly sound argument. The argument is not disproved by the fact that some swans are black, because a thing may very well happen in spite of the fact that some data render it improbable. In the case of the swans, a man might know that colour is a very variable characteristic in many species of animals, and that, therefore, an induction as to colour is peculiarly liable to error. But this knowledge would be a fresh datum, by no means proving that the probability relatively to our previous data had been wrongly estimated. The fact, therefore, that things often fail to fulfil our expectations is no evidence that our expectations will not *probably* be fulfilled in a given case or a given class of cases. Thus our inductive principle is at any rate not capable of being *disproved* by an appeal to experience.

The inductive principle, however, is equally incapable of being *proved* by an appeal to experience. Experience might conceivably confirm the inductive principle as regards the cases that have been already examined; but as regards unexamined cases, it is the inductive principle alone that can justify any inference from what has been examined to what has not been examined. All arguments which, on the basis of experience, argue as to the future or the unexperienced parts of the past or present, assume the inductive principle; hence we can never use experience to prove the inductive principle without begging the question. Thus we must either accept the inductive principle on the ground of its intrinsic evidence, or forgo all justification of our expectations about the future. If the principle is unsound, we have no reason to expect the sun to rise tomorrow, to expect bread to be more nourishing than a stone, or to expect that if we throw ourselves off the roof we shall fall. When we see what looks like our best friend approaching us, we shall have no reason to suppose that his body is not inhabited by the mind of our worst enemy or of some total stranger. All our conduct is based upon associations which have worked in the past, and which we therefore regard as likely to work in the future; and this likelihood is dependent for its validity upon the inductive principle.

The general principles of science, such as the belief in the reign of law, and the belief that every event must have a cause, are as completely dependent upon the inductive principle as are the beliefs of daily life. All such general principles are believed because mankind have found innumerable instances of their truth, and no instances of their falsehood. But this affords no evidence for their truth in the future, unless the inductive principle is assumed.

Thus all knowledge which, on a basis of experience, tells us something about what is not experienced, is based upon a belief which experience can neither confirm nor confute, yet which, at least in its more concrete applications, appears to be as firmly rooted in us as many of the facts of experience. The existence and justification of such beliefs raises some of the most difficult and most debated problems of philosophy.

> (*The Problems of Philosophy*, The Home University Library, London: Oxford University Press; New York: Henry Holt, 1912.)

NOTE ON NON-DEMONSTRATIVE INFERENCE AND INDUCTION

My beliefs about induction underwent important modifications in the year 1944, chiefly owing to the discovery that induction used without common sense leads more often to false conclusions than to true ones. Put briefly, my views since 1944 have been:

Non-demonstrative inference plays a larger part than is usually realized both in science and in common sense. Most of us do not remember anything that happened to us before the age of two, but none of us doubt that we existed before that age. If you walk in the evening with the sun behind you, a shadow marches in front of you and you do not for a moment doubt that it has a causal connection with your own body. It has been usual to suppose that non-demonstrative inferences depend upon induction. This, however, is not true except in a carefully limited sense. The inductions that scientists are inclined to accept are such as commend themselves to what may be called scientific common sense. If common sense is ignored, induction is much more likely to lead to false conclusions than to true ones. Crude induction argues that, if all known instances of A are also instances of B, it is probable, if the instances are sufficiently numerous, that all A's are B's. As a general statement, this is obviously false. Given two classes, A and B, which have a certain number of members in common, there will be infinitely more classes B to which not all A's belong than classes B to which all A's belong. Induction as a general principle is, therefore, demonstrably false, and if it is to be used, it must be used with stated limitations. Take, for instance, the following illustration: You have, let us suppose, a growing boy whose height you measure on the first of every month. You may find that, for a certain period, his rate of growth is constant. If you knew nothing about human growth, you might infer by induction that he would continue to grow at this rate until his head strikes the stars. There are, in fact, an infinite number of formulae which will fit any finite set of facts as to your boy's growth. Pure induction, if valid, would lead you to regard all these formulae as probable, although they contradict each other. Keynes, in his *Treatise on Probability*, shows that under certain circumstances an induction is valid if the generalization in question has a finite probability before any instances of its correctness are known. Accepting this view, I conclude that induction, in so far as it can be validly employed, is not an indemonstrable premiss, but that other indemonstrable premisses are necessary in order to give the necessary finite probability to inductions which we wish to test. The conclusion is that scientific inference demands certain extra-logical postulates of which induction is not one. What seem to me sufficient postulates for the purpose are given in Part VI, Chapter IX, of my *Human Knowledge*. These postulates should, in my opinion, replace induction as what is needed in non-demonstrative inference.

PLAS PENRHYN, PENRHYNDRAETH,   BERTRAND RUSSELL
MERIONETHSHIRE.
March 20, 1959

15

PREFACE TO *PRINCIPIA MATHEMATICA*

THE mathematical treatment of the principles of mathematics, which is the subject of the present work, has arisen from the conjunction of two different studies, both in the main very modern. On the one hand we have the work of analysts and geometers, in the way of formulating and systematizing their axioms, and the work of Cantor and others on such matters as the theory of aggregates. On the other hand we have symbolic logic, which, after a necessary period of growth, has now, thanks to Peano and his followers, acquired the technical adaptability and the logical comprehensiveness that are essential to a mathematical instrument for dealing with what have hitherto been the beginnings of mathematics. From the combination of these two studies two results emerge, namely (1) that what were formerly taken, tacitly or explicitly, as axioms, are either unnecessary or demonstrable; (2) that the same methods by which supposed axioms are demonstrated will give valuable results in regions, such as infinite number, which had formerly been regarded as inaccessible to human knowledge. Hence the scope of mathematics is enlarged both by the addition of new subjects and by a backward extension into provinces hitherto abandoned to philosophy.

The present work was originally intended by us to be comprised in a second volume of *The Principles of Mathematics*. With that object in view, the writing of it was begun in 1900. But as we advanced, it became increasingly evident that the subject is a very much larger one than we had supposed; moreover on many fundamental questions which had been left obscure and doubtful in the former work, we have now arrived at what we believe to be satisfactory solutions. It therefore became necessary to make our book independent of *The Principles of Mathematics*. We have, however, avoided both controversy and general philosophy, and made our statements dogmatic in form. The justification for this is that the chief reason in favour of any theory on the principles of mathematics must always be inductive, i.e. it must lie in the fact that the theory in question enables us to deduce ordinary mathematics. In mathematics, the greatest degree of self-evidence is usually not to be found quite at the beginning, but at some later point; hence the early deductions, until they reach this point, give reasons rather for believing the premisses because true consequences follow from them, than for believing the consequences because they follow from the premisses.

In constructing a deductive system such as that contained in the present work, there are two opposite tasks which have to be concurrently performed. On the one hand, we have to analyse existing mathematics, with a view to discovering what premisses are employed, whether these premisses are mutually consistent, and whether they are capable of reduction to more fundamental premisses. On the other hand, when we have decided upon our premisses, we have to build up again as much as may seem necessary of the data previously analysed, and as many other consequences of our premisses as are of sufficient general interest to deserve statement. The preliminary labour of analysis does not appear in the final presentation, which merely sets forth the outcome of the analysis in certain undefined ideas and undemonstrated propositions. It is not claimed that the analysis could not have been carried farther: we have no reason to suppose that it is impossible to find simpler ideas and axioms by means of which those with which we start could be defined and demonstrated. All that is affirmed is that the ideas and axioms with which we start are sufficient, not that they are necessary.

In making deductions from our premisses, we have considered it essential to carry them up to the point where we have proved as much as is true in whatever would ordinarily be taken for granted. But we have not thought it desirable to limit ourselves too strictly to this task. It is customary to consider only particular cases, even when, with our apparatus, it is just as easy to deal with the general case. For example, cardinal arithmetic is usually conceived in connection with *finite* numbers, but its general laws hold equally for infinite numbers, and are most easily proved without any mention of the distinction between finite and infinite. Again, many of the properties commonly associated with series hold of arrangements which are not strictly serial, but have only some of the distinguishing properties of serial arrangements. In such cases, it is a defect in logical style to prove for a particular class of arrangements what might just as well have been proved more generally. An analogous process of generalization is involved, to a greater or less degree, in all our work. We have sought always the most general reasonably simple hypothesis from which any given conclusion could be reached. For this reason, especially in the later parts of the book, the importance of a proposition usually lies in its hypothesis. The conclusion will often be something which, in a certain class of cases, is familiar, but the hypothesis will, whenever possible, be wide enough to admit many cases besides those in which the conclusion is familiar.

We have found it necessary to give very full proofs, because otherwise it is scarcely possible to see what hypotheses are really required, or whether our results follow from our explicit premises. (It must be remembered that we are not affirming merely that such and such propositions are true, but also that the axioms stated by us are sufficient to prove them.) At the same time, though full proofs are necessary for the avoidance of errors, and for convincing those who may feel doubtful as to our correctness, yet the proofs of propositions may usually be omitted by a reader who is not specially interested in that part of the subject concerned, and who feels no doubt of our substantial accuracy on the matter in hand. The reader who is specially interested in some particular portion of the book will probably find it sufficient, as regards earlier portions, to read the summaries of previous parts, sections, and numbers, since these give explanations of the ideas involved and statements of the principal propositions proved. The proofs in Part I, Section A, however, are necessary, since in the course of them the manner of stating proofs is explained. The proofs of the earliest propositions are given without the omission of any step, but as the work proceeds the proofs are gradually compressed, retaining however sufficient detail to enable the reader by the help of the references to reconstruct proofs in which no step is omitted.

The order adopted is to some extent optional. For example, we have treated cardinal arithmetic and relation-arithmetic before series, but we might have treated series first. To a great extent, however, the order is determined by logical necessities.

A very large part of the labour involved in writing the present work has been expended on the contradictions and paradoxes which have infected logic and the theory of aggregates. We have examined a great number of hypotheses for dealing with these contradictions; many such hypotheses have been advanced by others, and about as many have been invented by ourselves. Sometimes it has cost us several months' work to convince ourselves that a hypothesis was untenable. In the course of such a prolonged study, we have been led, as was to be expected, to modify our views from time to time; but it gradually became evident to us that some form of the doctrine of types must be adopted if the contradictions were to be avoided. The particular form of the doctrine of types advocated in the present work is not logically indispensable, and there are various other forms equally compatible with the truth of our deductions. We have particularized, both because the form of the doctrine which we advocate appears to us the most probable, and because it was necessary to give at least one perfectly definite theory which avoids the contradictions. But hardly anything in our book would be changed by the adoption of a different form of the doctrine of types. In fact, we may go farther, and say that, supposing some other way of avoiding the contradictions to exist, not very much of our book, except what explicitly deals with types, is dependent upon the adoption of the doctrine of types in any form, so soon as it has been shown (as we claim that we have shown) that it is *possible* to construct a mathematical logic which does not lead to contradictions. It should be observed that the whole effect of the doctrine of types is negative: it forbids certain inferences which would otherwise be valid, but does not permit any which would otherwise be invalid. Hence we may reasonably expect that the inferences which the doctrine of types permits would remain valid even if the doctrine should be found to be invalid.

Our logical system is wholly contained in the numbered propositions, which are independent of the Introduction and the Summaries. The Introduction and the Summaries are wholly explanatory, and form no part of the chain of deductions. The explanation of the hierarchy of types in the Introduction differs slightly from that given in *12 of the body of the work. The latter explanation is stricter and is that which is assumed throughout the rest of the book.

The symbolic form of the work has been forced upon us by necessity: without its help we should have been unable to perform the requisite reasoning. It has been developed as the result of actual practice, and is not an excrescence introduced for the mere purpose of exposition. The general method which guides our handling of logical symbols is due to Peano. His great merit consists not so much in his definite logical discoveries nor in the details of his notations (excellent as both are), as in the fact that he first showed how symbolic logic was to be freed from its undue obsession with the forms of ordinary algebra, and thereby made it a suitable instrument for research. Guided by our study of his methods, we have used great freedom in constructing, or reconstructing, a symbolism which shall be adequate to deal with all parts of the subject. No symbol has been introduced except on the ground of its practical utility for the immediate purposes of our reasoning.

A certain number of forward references will be found in the notes and explanations. Although we have taken every reasonable precaution to secure the accuracy of these forward references, we cannot of course guarantee their accuracy with the same confidence as is possible in the case of backward references.

Detailed acknowledgements of obligations to previous writers have not very often been possible, as we have had to transform whatever we have borrowed, in order to adapt it to our system and our notation. Our chief obligations will be obvious to every reader who is familiar with the literature of the subject. In the matter of notation, we have as far as possible followed Peano, supplementing his notation, when necessary, by that of Frege or by that of Schröder. A great deal of the symbolism, however, has had to be new, not so much through dissatisfaction with the symbolism of others, as through the fact that we deal with ideas not previously symbolized. In all questions of logical analysis, our chief debt is to Frege. Where we differ from him, it is largely because the contradictions showed that he, in common with all other logicians ancient and modern, had allowed some error to creep into his premisses; but apart from the contradictions, it would have been almost impossible to detect this error. In arithmetic and the theory of series, our whole work is based on that of Georg Cantor. In geometry we have had continually before us the writings of v. Staudt, Pasch, Peano, Pieri, and Veblen.

We have derived assistance at various stages from the criticisms of friends, notably Mr G. G. Berry of the Bodleian Library and Mr R. G. Hawtrey.

We have to thank the Council of the Royal Society for a grant towards the expenses of printing of £200 from the Government Publication Fund, and also the Syndics of the University Press who have liberally undertaken the greater portion of the expense incurred in the production of the work. The technical excellence, in all departments, of the University Press, and the zeal and courtesy of its officials, have materially lightened the task of proof-correction.

The second volume is already in the press, and both it and the third will appear as soon as the printing can be completed.

A. N. W.
B. R.

CAMBRIDGE,
November, 1910.

(*Principia Mathematica*, Vol. I, in collaboration with Alfred North Whitehead, Cambridge University Press, 1910.)

16

INTRODUCTION TO *PRINCIPIA MATHEMATICA*

THE mathematical logic which occupies Part I of the present work has been constructed under the guidance of three different purposes. In the first place, it aims at effecting the greatest possible analysis of the ideas with which it deals and of the processes by which it conducts demonstrations, and at diminishing to the utmost the number of the undefined ideas and undemonstrated propositions (called respectively *primitive* ideas and *primitive* propositions) from which it starts. In the second place, it is framed with a view to the perfectly precise expression, in its symbols, of mathematical propositions: to secure such expression, and to secure it in the simplest and most convenient notation possible, is the chief motive in the choice of topics. In the third place, the system is specially framed to solve the paradoxes which, in recent years, have troubled students of symbolic logic and the theory of aggregates; it is believed that the theory of types, as set forth in what follows, leads both to the avoidance of contradictions, and to the detection of the precise fallacy which has given rise to them.

Of the above three purposes, the first and third often compel us to adopt methods, definitions, and notations which are more complicated or more difficult than they would be if we had the second object alone in view. This applies especially to the theory of descriptive expressions (∗14 and ∗30) and to the theory of classes and relations (∗20 and ∗21). On these two points, and to a lesser degree on others, it has been found necessary to make some sacrifice of lucidity to correctness. The sacrifice is, however, in the main only temporary: in each case, the notation ultimately adopted, though its real meaning is very complicated, has an apparently simple meaning which, except at certain crucial points, can without danger be substituted in thought for the real meaning. It is therefore convenient, in a preliminary explanation of the notation, to treat these apparently simple meanings as primitive ideas, i.e. as ideas introduced without definition. When the notation has grown more or less familiar, it is easier to follow the more complicated explanations which we believe to be more correct. In the body of the work, where it is necessary to adhere rigidly to the strict logical order, the easier order of development could not be adopted; it is therefore given in the Introduction. The explanations given in Chapter I of the Introduction are such as place lucidity before correctness; the full explanations are partly supplied in succeeding chapters of the Introduction, partly given in the body of the work.

The use of a symbolism, other than that of words, in all parts of the book which aim at embodying strictly accurate demonstrative reasoning, has been forced on us by the consistent pursuit of the above three purposes. The reasons for this extension of symbolism beyond the familiar regions of number and allied ideas are many:

(1) The ideas here employed are more abstract than those familiarly considered in language. Accordingly there are no words which are used mainly in the exact consistent senses which are required here. Any use of words would require unnatural limitations to their ordinary meanings, which would be in fact more difficult to remember consistently than are the definitions of entirely new symbols.

(2) The grammatical structure of language is adapted to a wide variety of usages. Thus it possesses no unique simplicity in representing the few simple, though highly abstract, processes and ideas arising in the deductive trains of reasoning employed here. In fact the very abstract simplicity of the ideas of this work defeats language. Language can represent complex ideas more easily. The proposition 'a whale is big' represents language at its best, giving terse expression to a complicated fact; while the true analysis of 'one is a number' leads, in language, to an intolerable prolixity. Accordingly terseness is gained by using a symbolism especially designed to represent the ideas and processes of deduction which occur in this work.

(3) The adaptation of the rules of the symbolism to the processes of deduction aids the intuition in regions too abstract for the imagination readily to present to the mind the true relation between the ideas employed. For various collocations of symbols become familiar as representing important collocations of ideas; and in turn the possible relations—according to the rules of the symbolism—between these collocations of symbols become familiar, and these further collocations represent still more complicated relations between the abstract ideas. And thus the mind is finally led to construct trains of reasoning in regions of thought in which the imagination would be entirely unable to sustain itself without symbolic help. Ordinary language yields no such help. Its grammatical structure does not represent uniquely the relations between the ideas involved. Thus, 'a whale is big' and 'one is a number' both look alike, so that the eye gives no help to the imagination.

(4) The terseness of the symbolism enables a whole proposition to be represented to the eyesight as one whole, or at most in two or three parts divided where the natural breaks, represented in the symbolism, occur.

This is a humble property, but is in fact very important in connection with the advantages enumerated under the heading (3).

(5) The attainment of the first-mentioned object of this work, namely the complete enumeration of all the ideas and steps in reasoning employed in mathematics, necessitates both terseness and the presentation of each proposition with the maximum of formality in a form as characteristic of itself as possible.

Further light on the methods and symbolism of this book is thrown by a slight consideration of the limits to their useful employment:

(α) Most mathematical investigation is concerned not with the analysis of the complete process of reasoning, but with the presentation of such an abstract of the proof as is sufficient to convince a properly instructed mind. For such investigations the detailed presentation of the steps in reasoning is of course unnecessary, provided that the detail is carried far enough to guard against error. In this connection it may be remembered that the investigations of Weierstrass and others of the same school have shown that, even in the common topics of mathematical thought, much more detail is necessary than previous generations of mathematicians had anticipated.

(β) In proportion as the imagination works easily in any region of thought, symbolism (except for the express purpose of analysis) becomes only necessary as a convenient shorthand writing to register results obtained without its help. It is a subsidiary object of this work to show that, with the aid of symbolism, deductive reasoning can be extended to regions of thought not usually supposed amenable to mathematical treatment. And until the ideas of such branches of knowledge have become more familiar, the detailed type of reasoning, which is also required for the analysis of the steps, is appropriate to the investigation of the general truths concerning these subjects.

(*Principia Mathematica*, Vol. I, in collaboration with Alfred North Whitehead, Cambridge University Press, 1910.)

SUMMARY OF PART III

PRINCIPIA MATHEMATICA

I N this Part we shall be concerned, first, with the definition and general logical properties of cardinal numbers (Section A); then with the operations of addition, multiplication and exponentiation, of which the definitions and formal laws do not require any restriction to finite numbers (Section B); then with the theory of finite and infinite, which is rendered somewhat complicated by the fact that there are two different senses of 'finite', which cannot (so far as is known) be identified without assuming the multiplicative axiom. The theory of finite and infinite will be resumed, in connection with series, in Part V, Section E.

It is in this Part that the theory of types first becomes practically relevant. It will be found that contradictions concerning the maximum cardinal are solved by this theory. We have therefore devoted our first section in this Part (with the exception of two numbers giving the most elementary properties of cardinals in general, and of o and 1 and 2, respectively) to the application of types to cardinals. Every cardinal is typically ambiguous, and we confer typical definiteness by the notations of *63, *64, and *65. It is especially where existence-theorems are concerned that the theory of types is essential. The chief importance of the propositions of the present Part lies, not only, as throughout the book, in the hypotheses necessary to secure the conclusions, but also in the typical ambiguity which can be allowed to the symbols consistently with the truth of the propositions in all the cases thereby included.

(*Principia Mathematica*, Vol. II, in collaboration with Alfred North Whitehead, Cambridge University Press, 1912.)

SUMMARY OF PART IV

PRINCIPIA MATHEMATICA

THE subject to be treated in this Part is a general kind of arithmetic of which ordinal arithmetic is a particular application. The form of arithmetic to be treated in this Part is applicable to all relations, though its chief importance is in regard to such relations as generate series. The analogy with cardinal arithmetic is very close, and the reader will find that what follows is much facilitated by bearing the analogy in mind.

The outlines of relation-arithmetic are as follows. We first define a relation between relations, which we shall call *ordinal similarity* or *likeness*, and which plays the same part for relations as similarity plays for classes. Likeness between P and Q is constituted by the fact that the fields of P and Q can be so correlated by a one-one relation that if any two terms have the relation P, their correlates have the relation Q, and vice versa. If P and Q generate series, we may express this by saying that P and Q are like if their fields can be correlated without change of order. Having defined likeness, our next step is to define the *relation-number* of a relation P as the class of relations which are like P, just as the cardinal number of a class α is the class of classes which are similar to α. We then proceed to addition. The ordinal sum of two relations P and Q is defined as the relation which holds between x and y when x and y have the relation P or the relation Q, or when x is a member of $C'P$ and y is a member of $C'Q$. If P and Q generate series, it will be seen that this defines the sum of P and Q as the series resulting from adding the Q-series after the end of the P-series. The sum is thus not commutative. The sum of the relation-numbers of P and Q is of course the relation-number of their sum, provided $C'P$ and $C'Q$ have no common terms.

The ordinal product of two relations P and Q is the relation between two couples $z \downarrow x$, $w \downarrow y$, when x, y belong to $C'P$ and z, w belong to $C'Q$ and either xPy or $x = y . zQw$. Thus, for example, if the field of P consists of $1_P, 2_P, 3_P,$ and the field of Q consists of $1_Q, 2_Q$, the relation $P \times Q$ will hold from any earlier to any later term of the following series:

$$1_Q \downarrow 1_P, \ 2_Q \downarrow 1_P, \ 1_Q \downarrow 2_P, \ 2_Q \downarrow 2_P, \ 1_Q \downarrow 3_P, \ 2_Q \downarrow 3_P.$$

It is plain that, denoting the ordinal product of P and Q by $P \times Q$, we have

$$C``(P \times Q) = C`P \times C`Q,$$

where the second '$\times$' as standing between classes has the meaning defined in *113·01.

Infinite ordinal sums and products will also be defined, but the definitions are somewhat complicated.

The arithmetic which results from the above definitions satisfies all those of the formal laws which are satisfied in ordinal arithmetic, when this is not confined to finite ordinals; that is to say, relation-numbers satisfy the associative law for addition and for multiplication,[1] they satisfy the distributive law in the shape (where the $+$ and $\times$ are those appropriate to relation-numbers)

$$(\beta + \gamma) \times \alpha = (\beta \times \alpha) + (\gamma \times \alpha),$$

and they satisy the exponential laws

$$\alpha^\beta \times \alpha^\gamma = \alpha^{\beta+\gamma},$$
$$(\alpha^\beta)^\gamma = \alpha^{\beta \times \gamma}.$$

They do not in general satisfy the commutative law either in addition or in multiplication, nor do they satisfy the distributive law in the form

$$\alpha \times (\beta + \gamma) = (\alpha \times \beta) + (\alpha \times \gamma),$$

nor the exponential law

$$\alpha^\gamma \times \beta^\gamma = (\alpha \times \beta)^\gamma.$$

But in the particular case in which the relations concerned are finite serial relations, the corresponding relation-numbers do satisfy these additional formal laws; hence the arithmetic of *finite* ordinals is exactly analogous to that of inductive cardinals (cf. Part V, Section E).

If the relations concerned are limited to well-ordered relations, relation-arithmetic becomes ordinal arithmetic as developed by Cantor; but many of Cantor's propositions, as we shall see in this part, do not require the limitation to well-ordered relations.

> (*Principia Mathematica*, Vol. II, in collaboration with Alfred North Whitehead, Cambridge University Press, 1912.)

---

[1] For the associative law of multiplication, a hypothesis is required as to the kind of relation concerned. Cf. *174.241.25.

19

SUMMARY OF PART V

PRINCIPIA MATHEMATICA

A RELATION is said to be *serial*, or to generate a series, when it possesses three different properties, namely (1) being contained in diversity, (2) transitiveness, (3) connexity, i.e. the property that the relation or its converse holds between any two different members of its field. Thus P is a serial relation if

(1) $P \subset J$, (2) $P^2 \subset P$, (3) $x, y \in C'P \,.\, x \neq y \,.\, \supset_{x,y}: xPy \,.\, \vee \,.\, yPx$.

The third characteristic, that of connexity, may be written more shortly

$$x \in C'P \,.\, \supset_x \,.\, \overrightarrow{P'}x \cup \iota'x \cup \overleftarrow{P'}x = C'P,$$

i.e. $$x \in C'P \,.\, \supset_x \,.\, \overleftrightarrow{P'}x = C'P,$$

using the notation of $*97$; and this, in virtue of $*97 \cdot 23$, is equivalent to

$$\overleftrightarrow{P}{}''C'P \in 0 \cup 1.$$

In virtue of $*50 \cdot 47$, the first two characteristics are equivalent to

$$P \mathbin{\dot\cap} \breve{P} = {}^{\iota\iota}\dot\Lambda \,.\, P^2 \subset P.$$

When $P \mathbin{\dot\cap} \breve{P} = \dot\Lambda$, we say that P is 'asymmetrical'. Thus serial relations are such as are asymmetrical, transitive, and connected.

It might be thought that a serial relation need not be contained in diversity, since we commonly speak of series in which there are repetitions, i.e. in which an earlier term is identical with a later term. Thus, e.g.

$$a, b, c, a, e, f, b, g, h$$

would be called a series of letters, although the letters a and b recur. But in all such cases, there is some means (in the above case, position in space) by which one *occurrence* of a given term is distinguished from another occurrence, and this will be found to mean that there is some other series (in the above case, the series of positions in a line) free from repetitions, with which our pseudo-series has a one-many correlation. Thus, in the above instance, we have a series of nine positions, which we may call

$$1, 2, 3, 4, 5, 6, 7, 8, 9,$$

which form a true series without repetitions; we have a one-many relation, that of *occupying* these positions, by means of which we distinguish occurrences of a, the first occurrence being a as the correlate of 1, the second being a as the correlate of 4. All series in which there are repetitions (which we may call pseudo-series) are thus obtained by correlation with true series, i.e. with series in which there is no repetition. That is to say, a pseudo-series has as its generating relation a relation of the form $S; P$, where P is a serial relation, and S is a one-many relation whose converse domain contains the field of P. Thus what we may call self-subsistent series must be series without repetitions, i.e. series whose generating relations are contained in diversity.

For our purposes, there is no use in distinguishing a series from its generating relation. A series is not a class, since it has a definite order, while a class has no order, but is capable of many orders (unless it contains only one term or none). The generating relation determines the order, and also the class of terms ordered, since this class is the field of the generating relation. Hence the generating relation completely determines the series, and may, for all mathematical purposes, be taken to *be* the series.

When P is transitive, we have

$$P_{po} = P \cdot P_* = P \cup I \upharpoonright C'P.$$

Hence all the propositions of Part II, Section E become greatly simplified when applied to series.

Also, since the field of a connected relation consists of a single family, a series has one first term or none, and one last term or none.

In the case of a serial relation P, the relation P_1 (defined in $*121 \cdot 02$) becomes $P \doteq P^2$, i.e. the relation 'immediately preceding'. In a *discrete* series, the terms in general immediately precede other terms. A *compact* series, on the contrary, is defined as one in which there are terms between any two: in such a series, $P_1 = \dot{\Lambda}$.

It very frequently occurs that we wish to consider the relations of various series which are all contained in some one series; for example, we may wish to consider various series of real numbers, all arranged in order of magnitude. In such a case, if P is the series in which all the others are contained, and α, β, γ, . . . are the fields of the contained series, the contained series themselves are $P \upharpoonright \alpha$, $P \upharpoonright \beta$, $P \upharpoonright \gamma$, . . . Thus when series are given as contained in a given series, they are completely determined by their fields.

In what follows, Section A deals with the elementary properties of series, including maximum and minimum points, sequent points and limits.

Section B will deal with the theory of segments and kindred topics; in this section we shall define 'Dedekindian' series, and shall prove the important proposition that the series of segments of a series is always Dedekindian, i.e. that every class of segments has either a maximum or a limit.

Section C, which stands outside the main developments of the book, is concerned with convergence and the limits of functions and the definition of a continuous function. Its purpose is to show how these notions can be expressed, and many of their properties established, in a much more general way than is usually done, and without assuming that the arguments or values of the functions concerned are either numerical or numerically measurable.

Section D will deal with 'well-ordered' series, i.e. series in which every class containing members of the field has a first term. The properties of well-ordered series are many and important; most of them depend upon the fact that an extended variety of mathematical induction is possible in dealing with well-ordered series. The term 'ordinal number' is confined by usage to the relation-number of a well-ordered series; ordinal numbers will also be considered in our fourth section.

Section E will deal with finite and infinite. We shall show that the distinction between 'inductive' and 'non-reflexive' does not arise in well-ordered series.

Section F will deal with 'compact' series, i.e. series in which there is a term between any two, i.e. in which $P^2 = P$. In particular we shall consider 'rational' series (i.e. series like the series of rationals in order of magnitude) and continuous series (i.e. series like the series of real numbers in order of magnitude). Our treatment of this subject will follow Cantor closely.

(Principia Mathematica, Vol. II, in collaboration with Alfred North Whitehead, Cambridge University Press, 1912.)

20

SUMMARY OF PART VI

PRINCIPIA MATHEMATICA

THE purpose of this Part is to explain the kinds of applications of numbers which may be called *measurement*. For this purpose, we have first to consider generalizations of number. The numbers dealt with hitherto have been only integers (cardinal or ordinal); accordingly, in Section A, we consider positive and negative integers, ratios, and real numbers. (Complex numbers are dealt with later, under geometry, because they do not form a one-dimensional series.)

In Section B, we deal with what may be called 'kinds' of quantity: thus e.g. masses, spatial distances, velocities, each form one kind of quantity. We consider each kind of quantity as what may be called a 'vector-family', i.e. a class of one-one relations all having the same converse domain, and all having their domain contained in their converse domain. In such a case as spatial distances, the applicability of this view is obvious; in such a case as masses, the view becomes applicable by considering e.g. one gramme as + one gramme, i.e. as the relation of a mass m to a mass m' when m exceeds m' by one gramme. What is commonly called simply one gramme will then be the mass which has the relation + one gramme to the zero of mass. The reasons for treating quantities as vectors will be explained in Section B. Various different kinds of vector-families will be considered, the object being to obtain families whose members are capable of measurement either by means of ratios or by means of real numbers.

Section C is concerned with measurement, i.e. with the discovery of ratios, or of the relations expressed by real numbers, between the members of a vector-family. A family of vectors is measurable if it contains a member T (the unit) such that any other member S has to T a relation which is either a ratio or a real number. It will be shown that certain sorts of vector-families are in this sense measurable, and that measurement so defined has the mathematical properties which we expect it to possess.

Section D deals with *cyclic* families of vectors, such as angles or elliptic straight lines. The theory of measurement as applied to such families presents peculiar features, owing to the fact that any number of complete revolutions may be added to a vector without altering it. Thus there is not a single ratio of two vectors, but many ratios, of which we select one as the *principal* ratio.

(*Principia Mathematica*, in collaboration with Alfred North Whitehead, Cambridge University Press, 1913.)

21

INTRODUCTION TO THE SECOND EDITION[1]

PRINCIPIA MATHEMATICA

IN preparing this new edition of *Principia Mathematica*, the authors have thought it best to leave the text unchanged, except as regards misprints and minor errors,[2] even where they were aware of possible improvements. The chief reason for this decision is that any alteration of the propositions would have entailed alteration of the references, which would have meant a very great labour. It seemed preferable, therefore, to state in an introduction the main improvements which appear desirable. Some of these are scarcely open to question; others are, as yet, a matter of opinion.

The most definite improvement resulting from work in mathematical logic during the past fourteen years is the substitution, in Part I, Section A, of the one indefinable '*p* and *q* are incompatible' (or, alternatively, '*p* and *q* are both false') for the two indefinables 'not-*p*' and '*p* or *q*'. This is due to Dr H. M. Sheffer.[3] Consequentially, M. Jean Nicod[4] showed that one primitive proposition could replace the five primitive propositions $*1 \cdot 2 \cdot 3 \cdot 4 \cdot 5 \cdot 6$.

From this there follows a great simplification in the building up of molecular propositions and matrices; $*9$ is replaced by a new chapter, $*8$, given in Appendix A to this volume.

Another point about which there can be no doubt is that there is no need of the distinction between real and apparent variables, nor of the primitive idea 'assertion of a propositional function'. On all occasions where, in *Principia Mathematica*, we have an asserted proposition of the form '$\vdash . fx$' or '$\vdash . fp$', this is to be taken as meaning '$\vdash . (x) . fx$' or '$\vdash . (p) . fp$'. Consequently the primitive proposition $*1 \cdot 11$ is no longer

---

[1] In this introduction, as well as in the Appendices, the authors are under great obligations to Mr F. P. Ramsey of King's College, Cambridge, who has read the whole in MS. and contributed valuable criticisms and suggestions.

[2] In regard to these we are indebted to many readers, but especially to Drs Behmann and Boscovitch, of Göttingen.   [3] *Trans. Amer. Math. Soc.*, Vol. XIV, pp. 481–8.

[4] 'A reduction in the number of the primitive propositions of logic', *Proc. Camb. Phil. Soc.*, Vol. XIX.

required. All that is necessary, in order to adapt the propositions as printed to this change, is the convention that, when the scope of an apparent variable is the whole of the asserted proposition in which it occurs, this fact will not be explicitly indicated unless 'some' is involved instead of 'all'. That is to say, '$\vdash . \phi x$' is to mean '$\vdash . (x) . \phi x$'; but in '$\vdash . (\exists x) . \phi x$' it is still necessary to indicate explicitly the fact that 'some' x (not 'all' x's) is involved.

It is possible to indicate more clearly than was done formerly what are the novelties introduced in Part I, Section B as compared with Section A. They are three in number, two being essential logical novelties, and the third merely notational.

(1) For the 'p' of Section A, we substitute 'ϕx', so that in place of '$\vdash . (p) . fp$' we have '$\vdash . (\phi, x) . f(\phi x)$'. Also, if we have '$\vdash . f(p, q, r, \ldots)$,' we may substitute ϕx, ϕy, ϕz, $\ldots$ for p, q, r, $\ldots$ or ϕx, ϕy for p, q and ψz, $\ldots$ for r, $\ldots$, and so on. We thus obtain a number of new general propositions different from those of Section A.

(2) We introduce in Section B the new primitive idea '$(\exists x) . \phi x$', i.e. existence-propositions, which do not occur in Section A. In virtue of the abolition of the real variable, general propositions of the form '$(p) . fp$' do occur in Section A, but '$(\exists p) . fp$' does not occur.

(3) By means of definitions, we introduce in Section B general propositions which are molecular constituents of other propositions; thus '$(x) . \phi x . \vee . p$' is to mean '$(x) . \phi x \vee p$'.

It is these three novelties which distinguish Section B from Section A.

One point in regard to which improvement is obviously desirable is the axiom of reducibility ($*12 \cdot 1 \cdot 11$). This axiom has a purely pragmatic justification: it leads to the desired results, and to no others. But clearly it is not the sort of axiom with which we can rest content. On this subject, however, it cannot be said that a satisfactory solution is as yet obtainable. Dr Leon Chwistek[1] took the heroic course of dispensing with the axiom without adopting any substitute; from his work, it is clear that this course compels us to sacrifice a great deal of ordinary mathematics. There is another course, recommended by Wittgenstein[2] for philosophical reasons. This is to assume that functions of propositions are always truth-functions, and that a function can only occur in a proposition through its values. There are difficulties in the way of this view, but perhaps they are not insurmountable.[3] It involves the consequence that all functions of functions are extensional. It requires us to maintain that 'A believes p' is not a function of p. How this is possible is shown in *Tractatus Logico-Philosophicus* (*loc. cit.* and pp. 19–21). We are not prepared to assert that this theory is certainly right, but it has seemed worth while to work out its consequences in the following pages. It appears that everything

---

[1] In his 'Theory of Constructive Types'.
[2] *Tractatus Logico-Philosophicus*, *5·54 ff.
[3] See Appendix C.

in Vol. I remains true (though often new proofs are required); the theory of inductive cardinals and ordinals survives; but it seems that the theory of infinite Dedekindian and well-ordered series largely collapses, so that irrationals, and real numbers generally, can no longer be adequately dealt with. Also Cantor's proof that $2^n > n$ breaks down unless n is finite. Perhaps some further axiom, less objectionable than the axiom of reducibility, might give these results, but we have not succeeded in finding such an axiom.

It should be stated that a new and very powerful method in mathematical logic has been invented by Dr H. M. Sheffer. This method, however, would demand a complete re-writing of *Principia Mathematica*. We recommend this task to Dr Sheffer, since what has so far been published by him is scarcely sufficient to enable others to undertake the necessary reconstruction.

> (*Principia Mathematica*, in collaboration with Alfred North Whitehead, Cambridge University Press, 1925.)

22

MATHEMATICS AND LOGIC

MATHEMATICS and logic, historically speaking, have been entirely distinct studies. Mathematics has been connected with science, logic with Greek. But both have developed in modern times: logic has become more mathematical and mathematics has become more logical. The consequence is that it has now become wholly impossible to draw a line between the two; in fact, the two are one. They differ as boy and man: logic is the youth of mathematics and mathematics is the manhood of logic. This view is resented by logicians who, having spent their time in the study of classical texts, are incapable of following a piece of symbolic reasoning, and by mathematicians who have learnt a technique without troubling to inquire into its meaning or justification. Both types are now fortunately growing rarer. So much of modern mathematical work is obviously on the border-line of logic, so much of modern logic is symbolic and formal, that the very close relationship of logic and mathematics has become obvious to every instructed student. The proof of their identity is, of course, a matter of detail: starting with premises which would be universally admitted to belong to logic, and arriving by deduction at results which as obviously belong to mathematics, we find that there is no point at which a sharp line can be drawn, with logic to the left and mathematics to the right. If there are still those who do not admit the identity of logic and mathematics, we may challenge them to indicate at what point, in the successive definitions and deductions of *Principia Mathematica*, they consider that logic ends and mathematics begins. It will then be obvious that any answer must be quite arbitrary.

Starting from the natural numbers, we define 'cardinal number' and show how to generalize the conception of number, and then analyse the conceptions involved in the definition, until we find ourselves dealing with the fundamentals of logic. In a synthetic, deductive treatment these fundamentals come first, and the natural numbers are only reached after a long journey. Such treatment, though formally more correct than that which we adopt, is more difficult for the reader, because the ultimate logical concepts and propositions with which it starts are remote and unfamiliar as compared with the natural numbers. Also they represent the present frontier of knowledge, beyond which is the still unknown; and the dominion of knowledge over them is not as yet very secure.

It used to be said that mathematics is the science of 'quantity'. 'Quantity' is a vague word, but for the sake of argument we may replace it by the word 'number'. The statement that mathematics is the science of number would be untrue in two different ways. On the one hand, there are recognized branches of mathematics which have nothing to do with number—all geometry that does not use co-ordinates or measurement, for example: projective and descriptive geometry, down to the point at which co-ordinates are introduced, does not have to do with number, or even with quantity in the sense of *greater* and *less*. On the other hand, through the definition of cardinals, through the theory of induction and ancestral relations, through the general theory of series, and through the definitions of the arithmetical operations, it has become possible to generalize much that used to be proved only in connection with numbers. The result is that what was formerly the single study of arithmetic has now become divided into numbers of separate studies, no one of which is specially concerned with numbers. The most elementary properties of numbers are concerned with one-one relations, and similarity between classes. Addition is concerned with the construction of mutually exclusive classes respectively similar to a set of classes which are not known to be mutually exclusive. Multiplication is merged in the theory of 'selections', i.e. of a certain kind of one-many relations. Finitude is merged in the general study of ancestral relations, which yields the whole theory of mathematical induction. The ordinal properties of the various kinds of numbers-series, and the elements of the theory of continuity of functions and the limits of functions, can be generalized so as no longer to involve any essential reference to numbers. It is a principle, in all formal reasoning, to generalize to the utmost, since we thereby secure that a given process of deduction shall have more widely applicable results; we are, therefore, in thus generalizing the reasoning of arithmetic, merely following a precept which is universally admitted in mathematics. And in thus generalizing we have, in effect, created a set of new deductive systems, in which traditional arithmetic is at once dissolved and enlarged; but whether any one of these new deductive systems—for example, the theory of selections—is to be said to belong to logic or to arithmetic is entirely arbitrary, and incapable of being decided rationally.

We are thus brought face to face with the question: What is this subject, which may be called indifferently either mathematics or logic? Is there any way in which we can define it?

Certain characteristics of the subject are clear. To begin with, we do not, in this subject, deal with particular things or particular properties: we deal formally with what can be said about *any* thing or *any* property. We are prepared to say that one and one are two, but not that Socrates and Plato are two, because, in our capacity of logicians or pure mathematicians, we have never heard of Socrates and Plato. A world in which there were no such individuals would still be a world in which one and one are two. It is not open to us, as pure mathematicians or logicians, to mention anything at all, because, if we do so, we introduce something irrelevant and not formal. We may make this clear by applying it to the case of the syllogism. Traditional logic says: 'All men are mortal, Socrates is a man, therefore Socrates is mortal.' Now it is clear that what we *mean* to assert, to begin with, is only that the premisses imply the conclusion, not that premisses and conclusion are actually true; even the most traditional logic points out that the actual truth of the premisses is irrelevant to logic. Thus the first change to be made in the above traditional syllogism is to state it in the form: 'If all men are mortal and Socrates is a man, then Socrates is mortal.' We may now observe that it is intended to convey that this argument is valid in virtue of its *form*, not in virtue of the particular terms occurring in it. If we had omitted 'Socrates is a man' from our premisses, we should have had a non-formal argument, only admissible because Socrates is in fact a man; in that case we could not have generalized the argument. But when, as above, the argument is *formal*, nothing depends upon the terms that occur in it. Thus we may substitute α for *men*, β for *mortals*, and x for Socrates, where α and β are any classes whatever, and x is any individual. We then arrive at the statement: 'No matter what possible values x and α and β may have, if all α's are β's and x is an α, then x is a β'; in other words, 'the propositional function "if all α's are β's and x is an α, then x is a β" is always true.' Here at last we have a proposition of logic—the one which is only *suggested* by the traditional statement about Socrates and men and mortals.

It is clear that, if *formal* reasoning is what we are aiming at, we shall always arrive ultimately at statements like the above, in which no actual things or properties are mentioned; this will happen through the mere desire not to waste our time proving in a particular case what can be proved generally. It would be ridiculous to go through a long argument about Socrates, and then go through precisely the same argument again about Plato. If our argument is one (say) which holds of all men, we shall prove it concerning 'x', with the hypothesis 'if x is a man'. With this hypothesis, the argument will retain its hypothetical validity even when x is not a man. But now we shall find that our argument would still be valid if, instead of supposing x to be a man, we were to suppose him to be a monkey or a goose or a Prime Minister. We shall therefore not waste our time taking as our premiss 'x is a man' but shall take 'x is an α', where α is any class of individuals, or 'ϕx' where ϕ is any propositional function of some assigned type. Thus the absence of all mention of particular things or properties in logic or pure mathematics is a necessary result of the fact that this study is, as we say, 'purely formal'.

At this point we find ourselves faced with a problem which is easier to state than to solve. The problem is: 'What are the constituents of a logical proposition?' I do not know the answer, but I propose to explain how the problem arises.

Take (say) the proposition 'Socrates was before Aristotle'. Here it seems obvious that we have a relation between two terms, and that the constituents of the proposition (as well as of the corresponding fact) are simply the two terms and the relation, i.e. Socrates, Aristotle, and *before*. (I ignore the fact that Socrates and Aristotle are not simple; also the fact that what appear to be their names are really truncated descriptions. Neither of these facts is relevant to the present issue.) We may represent the general form of such propositions by '$x \, R \, y$', which may be read 'x has the relation R to y'. This general form may occur in logical propositions, but no particular instance of it can occur. Are we to infer that the general form itself is a constituent of such logical propositions?

Given a proposition, such as 'Socrates is before Aristotle', we have certain constituents and also a certain form. But the form is not itself a new constituent; if it were, we should need a new form to embrace both it and the other constituents. We can, in fact, turn *all* the constituents of a proposition into variables, while keeping the form unchanged. This is what we do when we use such a *schema* as '$x \, R \, y$', which stands for any one of a certain class of propositions, namely, those asserting relations between two terms. We can proceed to general assertions, such as '$x \, R \, y$ is sometimes true'—i.e. there are cases where dual relations hold. This assertion will belong to logic (or mathematics) in the sense in which we are using the word. But in this assertion we do not mention any particular things or particular relations; no particular things or relations can ever enter into a proposition of pure logic. We are left with pure *forms* as the only possible constituents of logical propositions.

I do not wish to assert positively that pure forms—e.g. the form '$x \, R \, y$' —do actually enter into propositions of the kind we are considering. The question of the analysis of such propositions is a difficult one, with con- flicting considerations on the one side and on the other. We cannot embark upon this question now, but we may accept, as a first approxima- tion, the view that *forms* are what enter into logical propositions as their constituents. And we may explain (though not formally define) what we mean by the 'form' of a proposition as follows:—

The 'form' of a proposition is that, in it, that remains unchanged when every constituent of the proposition is replaced by another.

Thus 'Socrates is earlier than Aristotle' has the same form as 'Napoleon is greater than Wellington', though every constituent of the two proposi- tions is different.

We may thus lay down, as a necessary (though not sufficient) character- istic of logical or mathematical propositions, that they are to be such as can be obtained from a proposition containing no variables (i.e. no such words as *all, some, a, the,* etc.) by turning every constituent into a variable and asserting that the result is always true or sometimes true, or that it is always true in respect of some of the variables that the result is sometimes true in respect of the others, or any variant of these forms. And another way of stating the same thing is to say that logic (or mathematics) is concerned only with *forms,* and is concerned with them only in the way of stating that they are always or sometimes true—with all the permutations of 'always' and 'sometimes' that may occur.

There are in every language some words whose sole function is to indicate form. These words, broadly speaking, are commonest in languages having fewest inflections. Take 'Socrates is human'. Here 'is' is not a constituent of the proposition, but merely indicates the subject-predicate form. Similarly in 'Socrates is earlier than Aristotle', 'is' and 'than' merely indicate form; the proposition is the same as 'Socrates precedes Aristotle', in which these words have disappeared and the form is otherwise indicated. Form, as a rule, *can* be indicated otherwise than by specific words: the order of the words can do most of what is wanted. But this principle must not be pressed. For example, it is difficult to see how we could conveniently express molecular forms of propositions (i.e. what we call 'truth-functions') without any word at all. One word or symbol is enough for this purpose, namely, a word or symbol expressing *incompatibility.* But without even one we should find ourselves in difficulties. This, however, is not the point that is important for our present purpose. What is important for us is to observe that form may be the one concern of a general proposition, even when no word or symbol in that proposition designates the form. If we wish to speak about the form itself, we must have a word for it; but if, as in mathematics, we wish to speak about all propositions that have the form, a word for the form will usually be found not indispensable; probably in theory it is *never* indispensable.

Assuming—as I think we may—that the forms of propositions *can* be represented by the forms of the propositions in which they are expressed without any special word for forms, we should arrive at a language in which everything formal belonged to syntax and not to vocabulary. In such a language we could express *all* the propositions of mathematics even if we did not know one single word of the language. The language of mathematical logic, if it were perfected, would be such a language. We should have symbols for variables, such as 'x' and 'R' and 'y', arranged in various ways; and the way of arrangement would indicate that something was being said to be true of all values or some values of the variables. We should not need to know any words, because they would only be needed for giving values to the variables, which is the business of the applied mathematician, not of the pure mathematician or logician. It is one of the marks of a proposition of logic that, given a suitable language, such a proposition can be asserted in such a language by a person who knows the syntax without knowing a single word of the vocabulary.

But, after all, there are words that express form, such as 'is' and 'than'. And in every symbolism hitherto invented for mathematical logic there are symbols having constant formal meanings. We may take as an example the symbol for incompatibility which is employed in building up truth-functions. Such words or symbols may occur in logic. The question is: How are we to define them?

Such words or symbols express what are called 'logical constants'. Logical constants may be defined exactly as we defined forms; in fact, they are in essence the same thing. A fundamental logical constant will be that which is in common among a number of propositions, any one of which can result from any other by substitution of terms one for another. For example, 'Napoleon is greater than Wellington' results from 'Socrates is earlier than Aristotle' by the substitution of 'Napoleon' for 'Socrates', 'Wellington' for 'Aristotle', and 'greater' for 'earlier'. Some propositions can be obtained in this way from the prototype 'Socrates is earlier than Aristotle' and some cannot; those that can are those that are of the form 'x R y', i.e. express dual relations. We cannot obtain from the above prototype by term-for-term substitution such propositions as 'Socrates is human' or 'the Athenians gave the hemlock to Socrates', because the first is of the subject-predicate form and the second expresses a three-term relation. If we are to have any words in our pure logical language, they must be such as express 'logical constants', and 'logical constants' will always either be, or be derived from, what is in common among a group of propositions derivable from each other, in the above manner, by term-for-term substitution. And this which is in common is what we call 'form'.

In this sense all the 'constants' that occur in pure mathematics are logical constants. The number 1, for example, is derivative from propositions of the form: 'There is a term c such that ϕx is true when, and only when, x is c'. This is a function of ϕ, and various different propositions result from giving different values to ϕ. We may (with a little omission of intermediate steps not relevant to our present purpose) take the above function of ϕ as what is meant by 'the class determined by ϕ is a unit class' or 'the class determined by ϕ is a member of 1' (1 being a class of classes). In this way, propositions in which 1 occurs acquire a meaning which is derived from a certain constant logical form. And the same will be found to be the case with all mathematical constants: all are logical constants, or symbolic abbreviations whose full use in a proper context is defined by means of logical constants.

But although all logical (or mathematical) propositions can be expressed wholly in terms of logical constants together with variables, it is not the case that, conversely, all propositions that can be expressed in this way are logical. We have found so far a necessary but not a sufficient criterion of mathematical propositions. We have sufficiently defined the character of the primitive *ideas* in terms of which all the ideas of mathematics can be *defined*, but not of the primitive *propositions* from which all the propositions of mathematics can be *deduced*. This is a more difficult matter, as to which it is not yet known what the full answer is.

We may take the axiom of infinity as an example of a proposition which, though it can be enunciated in logical terms, cannot be asserted by logic to be true. All the propositions of logic have a characteristic which used to be expressed by saying that they were analytic, or that their contradictories were self-contradictory. This mode of statement, however, is not satisfactory. The law of contradiction is merely one among logical propositions; it has no special pre-eminence; and the proof that the contradictory of some proposition is self-contradictory is likely to require other principles of deduction besides the law of contradiction. Nevertheless, the characteristic of logical propositions that we are in search of is the one which was felt, and intended to be defined, by those who said that it consisted in deducibility from the law of contradiction. This characteristic, which, for the moment, we may call *tautology*, obviously does not belong to the assertion that the number of individuals in the universe is n, whatever number n may be. But for the diversity of types, it would be possible to prove logically that there are classes of n terms, where n is any finite integer; or even that there are classes of $\aleph_0$ terms. But, owing to types, such proofs, as we saw in Chapter XIII, are fallacious. We are left to empirical observation to determine whether there are as many as n individuals in the world. Among 'possible' worlds, in the Leibnizian sense, there will be worlds having one, two, three, . . . individuals. There does not even seem any logical necessity why there should be even one individual[1]—why, in fact, there should be any world at all. The ontological proof of the existence of God, if it were valid, would establish the logical necessity of at least one individual. But it is generally recognized as invalid, and in fact rests upon a mistaken view of existence— i.e. it fails to realize that existence can only be asserted of something described, not of something named, so that it is meaningless to argue from 'this is the so-and-so' and 'the so-and-so exists' to 'this exists'. If we reject the ontological argument, we seem driven to conclude that the existence of a world is an accident—i.e. it is not logically necessary. If that be so, no principle of logic can assert 'existence' except under a hypothesis, i.e. none can be of the form 'the propositional function so-and-so is sometimes true'. Propositions of this form, when they occur in logic, will have to occur as hypotheses or consequences of hypotheses, not as complete asserted propositions. The complete asserted propositions of

---

[1] The primitive propositions in *Principia Mathematica* are such as to allow the inference that at least one individual exists. But I now view this as a defect in logical purity.

logic will all be such as affirm that some propositional function is *always* true. For example, it is always true that if p implies q and q implies r then p implies r, or that, if all α's are β's and x is an α then x is a β. Such propositions may occur in logic, and their truth is independent of the existence of the universe. We may lay it down that, if there were no universe, *all* general propositions would be true; for the contradictory of a general proposition is a proposition asserting existence, and would therefore always be false if no universe existed.

Logical propositions are such as can be known *a priori*, without study of the actual world. We only know from a study of empirical facts that Socrates is a man, but we know the correctness of the syllogism in its abstract form (i.e. when it is stated in terms of variables) without needing any appeal to experience. This is a characteristic, not of logical propositions in themselves, but of the way in which we know them. It has, however, a bearing upon the question what their nature may be, since there are some kinds of propositions which it would be very difficult to suppose we could know without experience.

It is clear that the definition of 'logic' or 'mathematics' must be sought by trying to give a new definition of the old notion of 'analytic' propositions. Although we can no longer be satisfied to define logical propositions as those that follow from the law of contradiction, we can and must still admit that they are a wholly different class of propositions from those that we come to know empirically. They all have the characteristic which, a moment ago, we agreed to call 'tautology'. This, combined with the fact that they can be expressed wholly in terms of variables and logical constants (a logical constant being something which remains constant in a proposition even when *all* its constituents are changed)—will give the definition of logic or pure mathematics. For the moment, I do not know how to define 'tautology'.[1] It would be easy to offer a definition which might seem satisfactory for a while; but I know of none that I feel to be satisfactory, in spite of feeling thoroughly familiar with the characteristic of which a definition is wanted. At this point, therefore, for the moment, we reach the frontier of knowledge on our backward journey into the logical foundations of mathematics.

We have now come to an end of our somewhat summary introduction to mathematical philosophy. It is impossible to convey adequately the ideas that are concerned in this subject so long as we abstain from the use of logical symbols. Since ordinary language has no words that naturally express exactly what we wish to express, it is necessary, so long as we adhere to ordinary language, to strain words into unusual meanings; and the reader is sure, after a time if not at first, to lapse into attaching

[1] The importance of 'tautology' for a definition of mathematics was pointed out to me by my former pupil Ludwig Wittgenstein, who was working on the problem. I do not know whether he has solved it, or even whether he is alive or dead.

the usual meanings to words, thus arriving at wrong notions as to what is intended to be said. Moreover, ordinary grammar and syntax is extraordinarily misleading. This is the case, e.g. as regards numbers; 'ten men' is grammatically the same form as 'white men', so that 10 might be thought to be an adjective qualifying 'men'. It is the case, again, wherever propositional functions are involved, and in particular as regards existence and descriptions. Because language is misleading, as well as because it is diffuse and inexact when applied to logic (for which it was never intended), logical symbolism is absolutely necessary to any exact or thorough treatment of our subject. Those readers, therefore, who wish to acquire a mastery of the principles of mathematics will, it is to be hoped, not shrink from the labour of mastering the symbols—a labour which is, in fact, much less than might be thought. As the above hasty survey must have made evident, there are innumerable unsolved problems in the subject, and much work needs to be done. If any student is led into a serious study of mathematical logic by this little book, it will have served the chief purpose for which it has been written.

> (*Introduction to Mathematical Philosophy*, London: Allen and Unwin; New York: The Macmillan Co., 1919.)

23

THE VALIDITY OF INFERENCE

IT is customary in science to regard certain facts as 'data', from which laws and also other facts are 'inferred'. The *practice* of inference is much wider than the theories of any logician would justify, and it is nothing other than the law of association or of 'learned reactions'. In the present chapter, I wish to consider what the logicians have evolved from this primitive form of inference, and what grounds we have, as rational beings, for continuing to infer. But let us first get as clear a notion as we can of what should be meant by a 'datum'.

The conception of a 'datum' cannot be made absolute. Theoretically, it should mean something that we know without inference. But before this has any definite meaning, we must define both 'knowledge' and 'inference'. For our present purpose it will simplify matters to take account only of such knowledge as is expressed in words: for present purposes, therefore, we may say that 'knowledge' means 'the assertion of a true form of words'. This definition is not quite adequate, since a man may be right by chance; but we may ignore this complication. We may then define a 'datum' as follows: a 'datum' is a form of words which a man utters as the result of a stimulus, with no intermediary of any learned reaction beyond what is involved in knowing how to speak. We must, however, permit such learned reactions as consist in adjustments of the sense-organs or in mere increase of sensitivity. These merely improve the receptivity to data, and do not involve anything that can be called inference.

If the above definition is accepted, all our data for knowledge of the external world must be of the nature of percepts. The belief in external objects is a learned reaction acquired in the first months of life, and it is the duty of the philosopher to treat it as an inference whose validity must be tested. A very little consideration shows that, logically, the inference cannot be demonstrative, but must be at best probable. It is not logically *impossible* that my life may be one long dream, in which I merely imagine all the objects that I believe to be external to me. If we are to reject this view, we must do so on the basis of an inductive or analogical argument, which cannot give complete certainty. We perceive other people behaving in a manner analogous to that in which we behave, and we assume that they have had similar stimuli. We may hear a whole crowd say 'Oh' at the moment when we see a rocket burst, and it is natural to suppose that the crowd saw it too. Nor are such arguments confined to living organisms. We can talk to a dictaphone and have it afterwards repeat what we said; this is most easily explained by the hypothesis that at the surface of the dictaphone events happened, while I was speaking, which were closely analogous to those that were happening just outside my ears. It remains *possible* that there is no dictaphone and I have no ears and there is no crowd watching the rocket; my percepts *may* be all that is happening in such cases. But, if so, it is difficult to arrive at any causal laws, and arguments from analogy are more misleading than we are inclined to think them. As a matter of fact, the whole structure of science, as well as the world of common sense, demands the use of induction and analogy if it is to be believed. These forms of inference, therefore, rather than deduction, are those that must be examined if we are to accept the world of science or any world outside our own dreams.

Let us take a simple example of an induction which we have all performed in practice. If we are hungry, we eat certain things we see and not others—it may be said that we infer edibility inductively from a certain visual and olfactory appearance. The history of this process is that children a few months old put everything into their mouths unless they are stopped; sometimes the result is pleasant, sometimes unpleasant; they repeat the former rather than the latter. That is to say: given that an object having a certain visual and olfactory appearance has been found pleasant to eat, an object having a very similar appearance will be eaten; but when a certain appearance has been found connected with unpleasant consequences when eaten, a similar appearance does not lead to eating next time. The question is: what logical justification is there for our behaviour? Given all our past experience, are we more likely to be nourished by bread than by a stone? It is easy to see why we think so, but can we, as philosophers, justify this way of thinking?

It is, of course, obvious that unless one thing can be a sign of another both science and daily life would be impossible. More particularly, reading involves this principle. One accepts printed words as signs, but this is only justifiable by means of induction. I do not mean that induction is necessary to establish the existence of other people, though that also, as we have seen, is true. I mean something simpler. Suppose you want your hair cut, and as you walk along the street you see a notice 'haircutting, first floor'. It is only by means of induction that you can *establish* that this notice makes it in some degree probable that there is a haircutter's establishment on the first floor. I do not mean that you employ the principle of induction; I mean that you act in accordance with it, and that you would have to appeal to it if you were accompanied by a

long-haired sceptical philosopher who refused to go upstairs till he was
persuaded there was some point in doing so.

The principle of induction, *prima facie*, is as follows: Let there be two
kinds of events, A and B (e.g. lightning and thunder), and let many
instances be known in which an event of the kind A has been quickly
followed by one of the kind B, and no instances of the contrary. Then
either a sufficient number of instances of this sequence, or instances of
suitable kinds, will make it increasingly probable that A is always followed
by B, and in time the probability can be made to approach certainty without limit provided the right kind and number of instances can be found.
This is the principle we have to examine. Scientific theories of induction
generally try to substitute well-chosen instances for numerous instances,
and represent number of instances as belonging to crude popular induction.
But in fact popular induction depends upon the emotional interest of the
instances, not upon their number. A child which has burnt its hand *once*
in a candle-flame establishes an induction, but words take longer, because
at first they are not emotionally interesting. The principle used in
primitive practice is: Whatever, on a given occasion, immediately precedes
something very painful or pleasant, is a sign of that interesting event.
Number plays a secondary part as compared with emotional interest.
That is one reason why rational thought is so difficult.

The logical problem of induction is to show that the proposition 'A is
always accompanied (or followed) by B' can be rendered probable by
knowledge of instances in which this happens, provided the instances
are suitably chosen or very numerous. Far the best examination of induction is contained in Mr Keynes's *Treatise on Probability*. There is a valuable
doctor's thesis by the late Jean Nicod, *Le Problème logique de l'induction*,
which is very ably reviewed by R. B. Braithwaite in *Mind*, October 1925.
A man who reads these three will know most of what is known about
induction. The subject is technical and difficult, involving a good deal of
mathematics, but I will attempt to give the gist of the results.

We will begin with the condition in which the problem had been left
by J. S. Mill. He had four canons of induction, by means of which, given
suitable examples, it could be demonstrated that A and B were causally
connected, if the law of causation could be assumed. That is to say, given
the law of causation, the scientific use of induction could be reduced to
deduction. Roughly the method is this: We know that B must have a
cause; the cause cannot be C or D or E or etc., because we find by experiment or observation that these may be present without producing B.
On the other hand, we never succeed in finding A without its being
accompanied (or followed) by B. If A and B are both capable of quantity,
we may find further that the more there is of A the more there is of B.
By such methods we eliminate all possible causes except A; therefore,
since B must have a cause, that cause must be A. All this is not really

induction at all; true induction only comes in in proving the law of causation. This law Mill regards as proved by mere enumeration of instances: we know vast numbers of events which have causes, and no events which can be shown to be uncaused; therefore, it is highly probable that all events have causes. Leaving out of account the fact that the law of causality cannot have quite the form that Mill supposed, we are left with the problem: Does mere number of instances afford a basis for induction? If not, is there any other basis? This is the problem to which Mr Keynes addresses himself.

Mr Keynes holds that an induction may be rendered more probable by number of instances, not because of their mere number, but because of the probability, if the instances are very numerous, that they will have nothing in common except the characteristics in question. We want, let us suppose, to find out whether some quality A is always associated with some quality B. We find instances in which this is the case; but it may happen that in all our instances some quality C is also present, and that it is C that is associated with B. If we can so choose our instances that they have nothing in common except the qualities A and B, then we have better grounds for holding that A is always associated with B. If our instances are very numerous, then, even if we do not *know* that they have no other common quality, it may become quite likely that this is the case. This, according to Mr Keynes, is the sole value of many instances.

A few technical terms are useful. Suppose we want to establish inductively that there is some probability in favour of the generalization: 'Everything that has the property *F* also has the property *f*.' We will call this generalization *g*. Suppose we have observed a number of instances in which *F* and *f* go together, and no instances to the contrary. These instances may have other common properties as well; the sum-total of their common properties is called the *total positive analogy*, and the sum-total of their *known* common properties is called the *known positive analogy*. The properties belonging to some but not to all of the instances in question are called the *negative analogy*: all of them constitute the *total negative analogy*, all those that are known constitute the *known negative analogy*. To strengthen an induction, we want to diminish the positive analogy to the utmost possible extent; this, according to Mr Keynes, is why numerous instances are useful.

On 'pure' induction, where we rely solely upon number of instances, without *knowing* how they affect the analogy, Mr Keynes concludes (p. 236):

'We have shown that if each of the instances necessarily follows from the generalisation, then each additional instance increases the probability of the generalisation, so long as the new instance could not have been predicted with certainty from a knowledge of the former instances. . . . The common notion, that each successive verification of a doubtful principle strengthens it, is formally proved, therefore without any appeal to conceptions of law or of causality. *But we have not proved* that this probability approaches certainty as a limit, or even that our conclusion becomes more likely than not, as the number of verifications or instances is indefinitely increased.'

It is obvious that induction is not much use unless, with suitable care, its conclusions can be rendered more likely to be true than false. This problem therefore necessarily occupies Mr Keynes.

It is found that an induction will approach certainty as a limit if two conditions are fulfilled:

(1) If the generalization is false, the probability of its being true in a new instance when it has been found to be true in a certain number of instances, however great that number may be, falls short of certainty by a finite amount.

(2) There is a finite *a priori* probability in favour of our generalization.

Mr Keynes uses 'finite' here in a special sense. He holds that not all probabilities are numerically measurable; a 'finite' probability is one which exceeds some numerically measurable probability however small. E.g. our generalization has a finite *a priori* probability if it is less unlikely than throwing heads a billion times running.

The difficulty is, however, that there is no easily discoverable way of estimating the *a priori* probability of a generalization. In examining this question, Mr Keynes is led to a very interesting postulate which, if true, will, he thinks, give the required finite *a priori* probability. His postulate as he gives it is not quite correct, but I shall give his form first, and then the necessary modification.

Mr Keynes supposes that the qualities of objects cohere in groups, so that the number of *independent* qualities is much less than the total number of qualities. We may conceive this after the analogy of biological species: a cat has a number of distinctive qualities which are found in all cats, a dog has a number of other distinctive qualities which are found in all dogs. The method of induction can, he says, be justified if we assume 'that the objects in the field, over which our generalisations extend, do not have an infinite number of independent qualities; that, in other words, their characteristics, however numerous, cohere together in groups of invariable connection, which are finite in number' (p. 256). Again (p. 258): 'As a logical foundation for Analogy, therefore, we seem to need some such assumption as that the amount of variety in the universe is limited in such a way that there is no one object so complex that its qualities fall into an infinite number of independent groups . . . or rather that none of the objects about which we generalise are as complex as this; or at least that, though some objects may be infinitely complex, we sometimes have a finite probability that an object about which we seek to generalise is not infinitely complex.'

This postulate is called the 'principle of limitation of variety'. Mr Keynes again finds that it is needed in attempts to establish laws by statistics; if he is right, it is needed for all our scientific knowledge outside pure mathematics. Jean Nicod pointed out that it is not quite sufficiently stringent. We need, according to Mr Keynes, a finite probability that the object in question has only a finite number of independent qualities; but what we really need is a finite probability that the number of its independent qualities is less than some assigned finite number. This is a very different thing, as may be seen by the following illustration. Suppose there is some number of which we know only that it is finite; it is infinitely improbable that it will be less than a million, or a billion, or any other assigned finite number, because, whatever such number we take, the number of smaller numbers is finite and the number of greater numbers is infinite. Nicod requires us to assume that there is a finite number n such that there is a finite probability that the number of independent qualities of our object is less than n. This is a much stronger assumption than Mr Keynes's, which is merely that the number of independent qualities is finite. It is the stronger assumption which is needed to justify induction.

This result is very interesting and very important. It is remarkable that it is in line with the trend of modern science. Eddington has pointed out that there is a certain finite number which is fundamental in the universe, namely the number of electrons. According to the quantum theory, it would seem that the number of possible arrangements of electrons may well also be finite, since they cannot move in all possible orbits, but only in such as make the action in one complete revolution conform to the quantum principle. If all this is true, the principle of limitation of variety may well also be true. We cannot, however, arrive at a proof of our principle in this way, because physics uses induction, and is therefore presumably invalid unless the principle is true. What we can say, in a general way, is that the principle does not refute itself, but, on the contrary, leads to results which confirm it. To this extent, the trend of modern science may be regarded as increasing the plausibility of the principle.

It is important to realize the fundamental position of probability in science. At the very best, induction and analogy only give probability. Every inference worthy of the name is inductive, therefore all inferred knowledge is at best probable. As to what is meant by probability, opinions differ. Mr Keynes takes it as a fundamental logical category: certain premisses may make a conclusion more or less probable, without making it certain. For him, probability is a relation between a premiss and a conclusion. A proposition does not have a definite probability on its own account; in itself, it is merely true or false. But it has probabilities of different amounts in regard to different premisses. When we speak, elliptically, of *the* probability of a proposition, we mean its probability in relation to all our relevant knowledge. A proposition in probability cannot be refuted by mere observation: improbable things may happen and probable things may fail to happen. Nor is an estimate of probability relevant to given evidence proved wrong when further evidence alters the probability.

For this reason the inductive principle cannot be proved or disproved by experience. We might prove validly that such and such a conclusion was enormously probable, and yet it might not happen. We might prove invalidly that it was probable, and yet it might happen. What happens affects the probability of a proposition, since it is relevant evidence; but it never alters the probability relative to the previously available evidence. The whole subject of probability, therefore, on Mr Keynes's theory, is strictly *a priori* and independent of experience.

There is, however, another theory, called the 'frequency theory', which would make probability not indefinable, and would allow empirical evidence to affect our estimates of probability relative to given premises. According to this theory in its crude form, the probability that an object having the property F will have the property f is simply the proportion of the objects having both properties to all those having the property F. For example, in a monogamous country the probability of a married person being male is exactly a half. Mr Keynes advances strong arguments against all forms of this theory that existed when his book was written. There is, however, an article by R. H. Nisbet on 'The Foundations of Probability' in *Mind* for January 1926, which undertakes to rehabilitate the frequency theory. His arguments are interesting, and suffice to show that the controversy is still an open one, but they do not, in my opinion, amount to decisive proof. It is to be observed, however, that the frequency theory, if it could be maintained, would be preferable to Mr Keynes's, because it would get rid of the necessity for treating probability as indefinable, and would bring probability into much closer touch with what actually occurs. Mr Keynes leaves an uncomfortable gap between probability and fact, so that it is far from clear why a rational man will act upon a probability. Nevertheless, the difficulties of the frequency theory are so considerable that I cannot venture to advocate it definitely. Meanwhile, the details of the discussion are unaffected by the view we may take on this fundamental philosophical question. And on either view the principle of limitation of variety will be equally necessary to give validity to the inferences by induction and analogy upon which science and daily life depend.

(*An Outline of Philosophy*, London: Allen & Unwin
Philosophy, New York: W. W. Norton, 1927.)

24

DEWEY'S NEW *LOGIC*

D R DEWEY is the foremost representative of a philosophy which, whether one accepts or rejects it, must undoubtedly be judged to have great importance as a social phenomenon. Unlike most academic professors, Dr Dewey is interested in this aspect of a philosophy. He accounts for much in Greek theory, and more particularly in Aristotelian logic, by the social system of that age. The persistence, among the learned, of elements derived from the Hellenic tradition is one of the reasons for the divorce between university philosophy and practical affairs which is characteristic of our time. Dr Dewey has an outlook which, where it is distinctive, is in harmony with the age of industrialism and collective enterprise. It is natural that his strongest appeal should be to Americans, and also that he should be almost equally appreciated by the progressive elements in countries like China and Mexico, which are endeavouring to pass with great rapidity from medievalism to all that is most modern. His fame, though not his doctrine, is analogous to that enjoyed by Jeremy Bentham in his own day—except that Bentham was more respected abroad than by his compatriots.

In what follows, I shall not be concerned with these general matters, but only with one book: *Logic: The Theory of Inquiry*. This book is very rich and varied in its contents; it contains highly interesting criticisms of past philosophers, very able analyses of the prejudices inspiring traditional formal logic, and an intimate awareness of the realities of scientific investigation. All this makes the book far more concrete than most books called 'Logic'. Since, however, a review should be shorter than the work reviewed, I shall ignore everything that occurs by way of illustration or history, and consider only those positive doctrines which seem to me most characteristic.

In every writer on philosophy there is a concealed metaphysic, usually unconscious; even if his subject is metaphysics, he is almost certain to have an uncritically believed system which underlies his explicit arguments. Reading Dr Dewey makes me aware of my own unconscious metaphysic as well as of his. Where they differ, I find it hard to imagine

any arguments on either side which do not beg the question; on fundamental issues perhaps this is unavoidable.

One of the chief sources of difference between philosophers is a temperamental bias towards synthesis or analysis. Traditionally, British philosophy
was analytic, Continental philosophy synthetic. On this point, I find
myself in the British tradition, while Dr Dewey belongs with the Germans,
and more particularly with Hegel. Instrumentalism, his most characteristic
and important doctrine, is, I think, compatible with an analytic bias, but
in him it takes a form associated with what General Smuts calls 'holism'.
I propose to consider first the 'holistic' aspect of Dr Dewey's logic, and
then the instrumentalist doctrine as he sets it forth.

Dr Dewey himself has told of his debt to Hegel in the article which he
contributed to *Contemporary American Philosophy* (1930). Hegel's thought,
he says,

Supplied a demand for unification that was doubtless an intense emotional
craving, and yet was a hunger that only an intellectualized subject-matter
could satisfy....The sense of divisions and separations that were, I suppose,
borne in upon me as a consequence of a heritage of New England culture,
divisions by way of isolation of self from the world, of soul from body,
of nature from God, brought a painful oppression—or rather, they were
an inward laceration. . . . Hegel's synthesis of subject and object, matter
and spirit, the divine and the human, was, however, no mere intellectual
formula; it operated as an immense release, a liberation. Hegel's treatment of human culture, of institutions and the arts, involved the same
dissolution of hard-and-fast dividing walls, and had a special attraction
for me. (19)

He adds, a page or two later: 'I should never think of ignoring, much less
denying, what an astute critic occasionally refers to as a novel discovery—
that acquaintance with Hegel has left a permanent deposit in my
thinking.' (21)

Data, in the sense in which many empiricists believe in them, are
rejected by Dr Dewey as the starting point of knowledge. There is a process of 'inquiry' (to be considered presently), in the course of which both
subject and object change. The process is, in some degree, continuous
throughout life, and even throughout the history of a cultural community.
Nevertheless, in regard to any one problem, there is a beginning, and this
beginning is called a 'situation'. A situation, we are told, is a 'qualified
existential whole which is unique'.[1] Again: 'Every situation, when it is
analysed, is extensive, containing within itself diverse distinctions and
relations which, in spite of their diversity, form a unified qualitative

[1] This and all further quotations in this essay are from Dewey's *Logic: The Theory of
Inquiry*, unless stated otherwise.

whole.' 'Singular objects exist and singular events occur within a field or situation.' We point *out* rather than point *at*. There is no such thing as passive receptivity; what is *called* the given is selected, and is taken rather than given.

There are a few further statements about what the world is apart from the effects which inquiry has upon it. For instance: 'There is, of course, a natural world that exists independently of the organism, but this world is *environment* only as it enters directly and indirectly into life-functions.' (The words 'of course', here may be taken as indicating an underlying metaphysic.) Again: 'Existence in general must be such as to be *capable* of taking on logical forms.' We are told very little about the nature of things before they are inquired into; we know, however, that, like dishonest politicians, things behave differently when observed from the way in which they behave when no one is paying attention to them.

The question arises: How large is a 'situation'? In connection with historical knowledge, Dr Dewey speaks of the 'temporal continuity of past-present-future'. It is obvious that, in an inquiry into the tides, the sun and moon must be included in the 'situation'. Although this question is nowhere explicitly discussed, I do not see how, on Dr Dewey's principles, a 'situation' can embrace less than the whole universe; this is an inevitable consequence of the insistence upon continuity. It would seem to follow that all inquiry, strictly interpreted, is an attempt to analyse the universe. We shall thus be led to Bradley's view that every judgement qualifies Reality as a whole. Dr Dewey eschews these speculations because his purpose is practical. But if they are to be invalid, it will be necessary (so at least it seems to me) to give more place to logically separable particulars than he seems willing to concede.

The relation of perception to empirical knowledge is not, so far as I have been able to discover, made very clear in this book, what is said on the subject being chiefly negative. We are told that sense-data are not objects of knowledge, and have no objective existential reference. (The word 'existential' occurs frequently in the book, but its meaning is assumed to be known. Here, again, we find evidence of the underlying metaphysic.) When it is said that sense-data have no objective existential reference, what is meant, no doubt, is that sensation is not a relational occurrence in which a subject cognizes something. To this I should entirely assent. Again we are told that there are three common errors to be avoided: (1) that the common-sense world is perceptual; (2) that perception is a mode of cognition; (3) that what is perceived is cognitive in status. Here, again, I agree. But since, clearly, perception is in some way related to empirical knowledge, a problem remains as to what this relation is.

The question of the relation of perception to knowledge is important in connection with 'holism'. For it seems clear that we perceive some things and not others, that percepts are links in causal chains which are to some extent separable from other causal chains, and that some degree of mutual independence in causal chains is essential to all empirical knowledge. Let us examine this question in connection with perception.

Dr Dewey denies 'immediate' knowledge and its supposed indispensability for mediated knowledge. But he admits something which he calls 'apprehension', which has, for him, functions very similar to those usually assigned to 'immediate knowledge'. On this subject he says:

A certain ambiguity in words has played a very considerable role in fostering the doctrine of immediate knowledge. Knowledge in its strictest and most honorific sense is identical with warranted assertion. But 'knowledge' also means understanding, and an object, or an act (and its object) that may be—and has been —called *apprehension*. ... Just as, after considerable experience, we understand meanings directly, as when we hear conversation on a familiar subject or read a book, so because of experience we come to recognize objects on sight. I see or note directly that *this* is a typewriter, *that* is a book, the other thing is a radiator, etc. This kind of direct 'knowledge' I shall call *apprehension*; it is seizing or grasping, intellectually, without questioning. But it is a product, mediated through certain organic mechanisms of retention and habit, and it presupposes prior experiences and mediated conclusions drawn from them. (143)

I still have no criticism to make, except that the 'organic mechanisms of retention and habit' and the 'prior experiences and mediated conclusions' deserve more attention than they receive in this volume. Consider the habit of saying 'book' on certain occasions. We may use this word, as a parrot might, merely because we hear someone else use it. We may use it because we 'think of' a book—whatever may be the correct analysis of this phrase. Or we may use it because we see a book. We cannot do this last unless we have frequently heard the word 'book' at a time when we saw a book. (I am assuming that the word had for us originally an ostensive definition, not a definition derived from the dictionary.) Thus the use of the word 'book' presupposes frequent simultaneity of books and instances of the word 'book' as perceived objects, and the causal law according to which such frequent simultaneity generates a habit. When the habit in question has been formed, it is not the whole environment that causes us to use the word 'book', but only one feature of it; and the effect is only one feature of what is happening in us at the time. Without such separable causal chains the use of language is inexplicable.

Let us pursue a little further this question of 'apprehension'. The common-sense belief 'there is a book', or (what comes to much the same thing) the impulse to use the word 'book' demonstratively, arises as the result of a stimulus of a certain kind. The immediate stimulus is in the brain; before that, there is a stimulus in the optic nerve; before that, at the eye; and, when the common-sense belief is justified, there are light-waves travelling from the book to the eye. We have thus, when the common-sense belief is justified, a rather elaborate causal chain: book, light-waves, eye, optic nerve, brain, utterance of the word 'book'. If any intermediate link in this causal chain can be produced without the usual predecessors, all the subsequent links will be produced just as they would be if the causation had been of the normal sort. Now unusual causes are possible at each stage: physical, by means of mirrors; optical, by defects in the eye; nervous, by suitable stimulation of the optic nerve; cerebral, by the kind of disturbance that produces a hallucination. Consequently, while it is true that the common-sense judgment expressed in the utterance of the word 'book' is not perceptual, it is also true that the common-sense judgment may be erroneous, and the only warranted assertion is: 'A bookish percept is occurring.' It is such considerations that lead me to stress percepts as opposed to common-sense judgments.

Consider, from a purely physical point of view, what is involved in our seeing various objects simultaneously. If the common-sense point of view is to be in any degree justifiable in ordinary circumstances, we must suppose that each visible object is the starting-point of a causal chain which remains, at least in some respects, independent of all the other simultaneous causal chains that lead to our seeing the other objects. We must therefore suppose that natural processes have the character attributed to them by the analyst, rather than the holistic character which the enemies of analysis take for granted. I do not contend that the holistic world is logically impossible, but I do contend that it could not give rise to science or to any empirical knowledge.

The same conclusion may be reached through consideration of language. Words are discrete and separable occurrences; if the world had as much unity as some philosophers contend, it would be impossible to use words to describe it. Perhaps it is impossible; but in that case there can be no excuse for writing books on philosophy.

Dr Dewey would reply that it is not the purpose of such books to *describe* the world, but to *change* it. This brings us to what is perhaps the most important aspect of his philosophy.

I come now to what is most distinctive in Dr Dewey's logic, namely the emphasis upon inquiry as opposed to truth or knowledge. Inquiry is not for him, as for most philosophers, a search for truth; it is an independent activity, defined as follows: 'Inquiry is the controlled or directed transformation of an indeterminate situation into one that is so determinate in its constituent distinctions and relations as to convert the elements of the original situation into a unified whole.' (104) I cannot but think that this definition does not adequately express Dr Dewey's meaning, since it would apply, for instance, to the operations of a drill-sergeant in transforming a collection of raw recruits into a regiment, or of a bricklayer transforming a heap of bricks into a house, and yet it would be impossible to say that the drill-sergeant is 'inquiring' into the recruits, or the brick-layer into the bricks. It is admitted that inquiry alters the object as well as the subject: 'Inquiry is concerned with objective transformations of objective subject-matter.' Propositions are merely tools in effecting these transformations; they are differentiated as means, not as 'true' or 'false'. (287)

Before examining this doctrine, it may be worth while to repeat, what I have pointed out elsewhere,[1] its close similarity to that of another ex-Hegelian, Karl Marx, as stated in his *Theses on Feuerbach* (1845), and afterwards embodied in the theory of dialectical materialism (which Engels never understood).

The chief defect of all previous materialism [says Marx] is that the object, the reality, sensibility, is only apprehended under the form of the object or of contemplation, but not as human sensible activity or practice, not subjectively. Hence it came about that the active side was developed by idealism in opposition to materialism. The question whether objective truth belongs to human thinking is not a question of theory, but a practical question. The truth, i.e. the reality and power, of thought must be demon-strated in practice. Philosophers have only *interpreted* the world in various ways, but the real task is to *alter* it.

Allowing for a certain difference of phraseology, this doctrine is essentially indistinguishable from instrumentalism.

One of the chief difficulties in this point of view—so, at least, it seems to me—consists in distinguishing inquiry from other kinds of practical activity such as drilling recruits or building houses. Inquiry, it is evident, is some kind of interaction between two things, one of which is called the object and the other the subject. There seems to be an assumption that this process is more or less in the nature of an oscillation of which the amplitude gradually grows less, leaving it possible to guess at an ultimate position of equilibrium, in which, when reached, the subject would be said to 'know' the object, or to have arrived at 'truth' concerning it. 'Truth' is not an important concept in Dr Dewey's logic. I looked up 'truth' in the index, and found only the following: 'Defined, 345n. See Assertibility, Warranted.' The note, in its entirety, is as follows:

The best definition of *truth* from the logical standpoint which is known to me is that of Peirce: 'The opinion which is fated to be ultimately agreed to by all who investigate is what we mean by the truth, and the object represented by this opinion is the real.' *Op. cit.*, Vol. V, p. 268 (*Collected Papers of Charles Sanders Peirce*). A more complete (and more

---

[1] *Freedom Versus Organization* (New York, 1934), p. 221.

suggestive) statement is the following: 'Truth is that concordance of an abstract statement with the ideal limit towards which endless investigation would tend to bring scientific belief, which concordance the abstract statement may possess by virtue of the confession of its inaccuracy and one-sidedness, and this confession is an essential ingredient of truth.' (*Ibid.*, 394-5.)[1]

Although these two definitions of 'truth' are Peirce's, not Dr Dewey's, the fact that Dr Dewey accepts them makes it necessary to discuss them as if they were his own. The discussion is required in spite of the unimportance of 'truth' to Dr Dewey, for those of us who make it fundamental are concerned to examine the consequences of giving it such a humble and derivative position.

The acceptance of such a definition as Peirce's makes it natural to mention 'truth' only once, and that in a footnote; for if 'truth' is to be so defined, it is obviously of no philosophical importance. The two definitions are not in complete agreement. According to the first, when we say that a proposition is 'true' we are making a sociological prophecy. If the definition is interpreted strictly, every proposition which is investigated by no one is 'true', but I think Peirce means to include only such propositions as someone investigates. The word 'fated' seems merely rhetorical, and I shall assume that it is not intended seriously. But the word 'ultimately' is much more difficult. As the second definition makes plain, the word is intended in a mathematical rather than a chronological sense. If it were intended chronologically it would make 'truth' depend upon the opinions of the last man left alive as the earth becomes too cold to support life. As he will presumably be entirely occupied in keeping warm and getting nourishment, it is doubtful whether his opinions will be any wiser than ours. But obviously this is not what Peirce has in mind. He imagines a series of opinions, analogous to a series of numbers such as $\frac{1}{2}, \frac{3}{4}, \frac{7}{8} \ldots$ tending to a limit, and each differing less from its predecessor than any earlier member of the series does. This is quite clear in the second definition, where Peirce speaks of 'the ideal limit towards which endless investigation would tend to bring scientific belief'.

I find this definition exceedingly puzzling. To begin with a minor point: what is meant by 'the confession of its inaccuracy'? This seems to imply a standard of accuracy other than that indicated in the definition. Or is 'accuracy' a notion wholly divorced from 'truth'? If Peirce is to be interpreted strictly, he must mean that a statement is 'true' because it says it is inaccurate. This would enthrone Epimenides as the only sage. I think that Peirce, when he says 'inaccurate', means 'unprecise'. The statement that Mr A is about 6 feet tall may be perfectly accurate, but it is not precise. I think it is such statements that Peirce has in mind.

[1] *Logic*, 345*n*.

The main question is: why does Peirce think that there is an 'ideal limit towards which endless investigation would tend to bring scientific belief'? Is this an empirical generalization from the history of research? Or is it an optimistic belief in the perfectibility of man? Does it contain any element of prophecy, or is it a merely hypothetical statement of what would happen if men of science grew continually cleverer? Whatever interpretation we adopt, we seem committed to some very rash assertion. I do not see how we can guess either what will be believed, or what would be believed by men much cleverer than we are. Whether the theory of relativity will be believed twenty years hence depends mainly upon whether Germany wins the next war. Whether it would be believed by people cleverer than we are we cannot tell without being cleverer than we are. Moreover the definition is inapplicable to all the things that are most certain. During breakfast, I may have a well-grounded conviction that I am eating eggs and bacon. I doubt whether scientists 2,000 years hence will investigate whether this was the case, and if they did their opinions would be worth less than mine.

'Truth', therefore, as Peirce defines the term, is a vague concept involving much disputable sociology. Let us see what Dr Dewey has to say about 'assertibility warranted', to which he refers us. We must remember that Dr Dewey's *Logic* has as its sub-title 'The Theory of Inquiry'. 'Inquiry' might, from other points of view, be defined as 'the attempt to discover truth', but for Dr Dewey inquiry is what is primitive, and truth or rather 'warranted assertibility', is derivative. He says (7):

'If inquiry begins in doubt, it terminates in the institution of conditions which remove need for doubt. The latter state of affairs may be designated by the words *belief* and *knowledge*. For reasons that I shall state later I prefer the words "warranted assertibility".'

Again Dr Dewey says:

Were it not that knowledge is related to inquiry as a product to the operations by which it is produced, no distinctions requiring special differentiating designations would exist. Material would merely be a matter of knowledge or of ignorance and error; that would be all that could be said. The content of any given proposition would have the values 'true' and 'false' as final and exclusive attributes. But if knowledge is related to inquiry as its warrantably assertible product, and if inquiry is progressive and temporal, then the material inquired into reveals distinctive properties which need to be designated by distinctive names. As *undergoing* inquiry, the material has a different logical import from that which it has as the *outcome* of inquiry. (118–119)

Again: 'An inferential function is involved in all warranted assertion. The position here defended runs counter to the belief that there is such a

thing as immediate knowledge, and that such knowledge is an indispensable precondition of all mediated knowledge.' (139.)

Let us try to re-state Dr Dewey's theory in other language. I will
begin with what would certainly be a misinterpretation, though one for
which his words would seem to afford some justification. The position
seems to be that there is a certain activity called 'inquiry', as recognizable
as the activities of eating or drinking; like all activity, it is stimulated by
discomfort, and the particular discomfort concerned is called 'doubt',
just as hunger is the discomfort that stimulates eating, and thirst is the
discomfort that stimulates drinking. And as hunger may lead you to kill
an animal, skin it, and cook it, so that though you have been concerned
with the same animal throughout, it is very different when it becomes
food from what it was to begin with, so inquiry manipulates and alters its
subject-matter until it becomes logically assimilable and intellectually
appetizing. Then doubt is allayed, at least for the time. But the subject-
matter of inquiry, like the wild boar of Valhalla, is perpetually re-born,
and the operation of logical cooking has to be more and more delicately
performed as the intellectual palate grows more refined. There is therefore
no end to the process of inquiry, and no dish that can be called 'absolute
truth'.

I do not think that Dr Dewey would accept what has just been said as
an adequate account of his theory. He would, I am convinced, maintain
that inquiry serves a purpose over and above the allaying of doubt. And
he would object that the revival of an inquiry after doubt has been temporarily quieted is not merely a question of refinement of the intellectual
palate, but has some more objective basis. He says (to repeat a quotation
already given): 'If inquiry begins in doubt, it terminates in the institution
of conditions which remove *need* for doubt' (my italics). I do not know
what he means by 'need for doubt,' but I think he means something more
than 'cause of doubt'. If I doubt whether I am a fine fellow, I can cure
the doubt by a suitable dose of alcohol, but this would not be viewed by
him as 'the institution of conditions which remove the *need* for doubt'.
Nor would he reckon suicide a suitable method, although it would be
eminently effective in removing doubt. We must therefore ask ourselves
what he can mean by 'need for doubt'.

For those who make 'truth' fundamental, the difficulty in question
does not arise. There is need for doubt so long as there is an appreciable
likelihood of a mistake. If you add up your accounts twice over, and get
different results, there is 'need for doubt'; but that is because you are
persuaded that there is an objectively right result. If there is not, if all that
is concerned is the psychological fact of inquiry as an activity stimulated
by doubt, we cannot lay down rules as to what *ought* to remove the need
for doubt: we can only observe what does in fact remove doubt. Inquiry
can no longer be regulated by canons. To say that one man is a better

inquirer than another can only mean that he allays more doubts, even if he does so by a brass band and ingenious spot-lighting. All this is not what Dr Dewey means; but if it is not to follow from what he says, inquiry will have to have some goal other than the removal of doubt.

I ask again, therefore: what can he mean by 'the need for doubt'?

The word 'pragmatism' is not mentioned in the index to Dr Dewey's *Logic*, but the preface contains the following passage:

The word 'Pragmatism' does not, I think, occur in the text. Perhaps the word lends itself to misconception. At all events, so much misunderstanding and relatively futile controversy have gathered about the word that it seemed advisable to avoid its use. But in the proper interpretation of 'pragmatic', namely the function of consequences as necessary tests of the validity of propositions, *provided* these consequences are operationally instituted and are such as to resolve the specific problem evoking the operations, the text that follows is thoroughly pragmatic. (iii–iv)

Perhaps, in view of this passage, we may say that there is 'need for doubt' so long as the opinion at which we have arrived does not enable us to secure desired results, although we feel that a different opinion would do so. When our car breaks down, we try various hypotheses as to what is wrong, and there is 'need for doubt' until it goes again. This suggests a way out of our difficulty, which I will try to state in quite general terms.

Beliefs, we are now supposing, may be tested by their consequences, and may be considered to possess 'warranted assertibility' when their consequences are of certain kinds. The consequences to be considered relevant may be logical consequences only, or may be widened to embrace all kinds of effects; and between these two extremes any number of intermediate positions are possible. In the case of the car that won't go, you think it may be this, or it may be that, or it may be the other; if it is *this* and I do so-and-so, the car will go; I do so-and-so and the car does not go; therefore it was not *this*. But when I apply the same experimental procedure to the hypothesis that it was *that*, the car does go; therefore the belief that it was *that* has 'warranted assertibility'. So far, we have only the ordinary procedure of induction: 'If p, then q; now q is true; therefore p is true.' E.g. 'If pigs have wings, then some winged animals are good to eat; now some winged animals are good to eat; therefore pigs have wings.' This form of inference is called 'scientific method'.

Pragmatism, however, involves something more than induction. In induction, we have two premises, namely 'if p, then q', and 'q'. Each of these has to be true in the ordinary sense if they are to confer inductive probability upon 'p'. In order to enable pragmatism to dispense with 'truth' in its ordinary sense, we need some further steps. It will be remembered that Dr Dewey distinguishes 'knowledge' from what he calls 'apprehension', which contains such statements as 'this is a typewriter'. In dealing with the car, we shall, in Dr Dewey's terminology, 'apprehend' that it is going or that it is not going; this sort of thing, which I should take as the quintessential form of knowledge, is no longer to count as such. 'If p, then q' may be a mere bodily habit: I think 'perhaps there is no petrol' and I pour some in, without further thought. I hope to apprehend q, viz. 'the car goes', but I do not. So I try something else. My behaviour is just like that of an animal trying to get out of a cage, and may have just as little intellectual content.

We may, eliminating the intellectual element as far as possible, schematize our behaviour as follows: we desire a certain change C (in our illustration, the change from rest to motion on the part of the car); in our past experience, various acts A_1, A_2, A_3 . . . have been followed by this change; consequently there exists an impulse to perform some one of these acts, and, if it fails to be followed by C, some other of them, until at last, with luck, C takes place. Suppose the act A_n is followed by C; then A_n is appropriate to the situation. So far, everything that I have been describing could be done by an animal and is done by animals that are actuated by strong desires which they cannot immediately gratify. But when we come to human beings, with their linguistic proclivities, the matter becomes somewhat different. The acts A_1, A_2, A_3 . . . may all be sentences: 'Perhaps it is this', 'Perhaps it is that', 'Perhaps it is the other.' . . . Each of these sentences causes certain further acts, which, in turn, set up a chain of effects. One of the sentences causes a chain of effects which includes the desired change C. If this sentence is A_n, we say that A_n is 'true' or has 'warranted assertibility'.

This suggestion needs a good deal of clarification before it becomes a possible hypothesis. As it stands, it is as follows: A hypothesis is called 'true' when it leads the person entertaining it to acts which have effects that he desires. This obviously is too wide. Acts have many consequences, of which some may be pleasant and others unpleasant. In the case of the car, it may, when it finally moves, move so suddenly that it causes you serious bodily injury; this does not show that you were mistaken as to what was the matter with it. Or take another illustration: In a school, a prize is offered for the child that shows most general intelligence; on class-work, four are selected, and the final test is by a *viva voce*; the *viva* consists of one question, 'who is the greatest man now living?' One child says Roosevelt, one says Stalin, one says Hitler, and one says Mussolini. One of them gets the prize, and has therefore, by definition, answered truly. If you know which gets the prize, you know in what country the test was made. It follows that truth is geographical. But this consequence, for some reason, pragmatists would be unwilling to admit.

The first limitation is that we must not take account of *all* the consequences of a hypothesis, but only of those that are relevant to a certain specified desire. You desire the car to move, but not to move into the ditch. If you are only thinking of getting it to move, the truth of your hypothesis is only to be judged by whether it moves, not by whether it moves along the road or into the ditch.

There is another more difficult limitation. The consequences of which account is to be taken must be only such as are considered 'scientific'. The pleasant consequences to the successful schoolchild depend upon the psychology of the teacher, which is considered logically irrelevant. I am not clear what this means, except that the same experiment in a different environment would give different results. It is difficult to imagine any experiment of which the result *cannot* be affected by the environment, but this is a matter of difference of degree. If all *usual* environments give the same results, the environment is irrelevant except on rare occasions.

We may say, therefore: A hypothesis H is to be called 'true' if, in all normal environments, there is a kind of event C such that a man who desires C and entertains the hypothesis H will secure C, while a man who desires C but does not entertain this hypothesis will not secure C.

Thus before we can know H we must have observed large numbers of instances, in many different environments, in which people entertained H, desired C, and secured C. After we have made all these observations, we 'know' H. We did not 'know' that H was entertained, that C was desired, or that C was secured, in any of the many instances; for to 'know' these things, we should have had to apply the pragmatic tests to them. To 'know' that A entertains the hypothesis H, we shall have to find many instances of people who suppose that he does and consequently achieve their desires; similarly to 'know' that A desires C or achieves C. All these things, in Dr Dewey's phrase, will have to be 'apprehended', not 'known'. We cannot possibly 'apprehend' the whole multiplicity of instances at once; therefore the generalization must be not a belief, but a bodily habit, which is the pre-intellectual ancestor of belief in a general proposition.

Even so, there are still difficulties. Dr Dewey and I were once in the town of Changsha during an eclipse of the moon; following immemorial custom, blind men were beating gongs to frighten the heavenly dog, whose attempt to swallow the moon is the cause of eclipses. Throughout thousands of years, this practice of beating gongs has never failed to be successful: every eclipse has come to an end after a sufficient prolongation of the din. This illustration shows that our generalization must not use merely the method of agreement, but also the method of difference. As all this is to be done by the body before knowledge begins, we must suppose the body better versed in Mill's Canons of Induction than any mind except that of a logician. I find this a somewhat difficult hypothesis.

Leaving these questions of detailed definition, let us consider the general problem of the relation of knowledge to the biological aspects of life. It is of course obvious that knowledge, broadly speaking, is one of the means to biological success; it is tempting to say, generally, that knowledge leads to success and error leads to failure; going a step further, the pragmatist may say that 'knowledge' means 'belief leading to success' and 'error' means 'belief leading to failure'. To this view, however, there are many objections, both logical and sociological.

First, we must define 'success' and 'failure'. If we wish to remain in the sphere of biology, we must define 'success' as 'leaving many descendants'. In that sense, as everyone knows, the most civilized are the least successful, and therefore, by definition, the most ignorant. Again: the man who, wishing to commit suicide, takes salt under the impression that it is arsenic, may afterwards beget ten children; in that case, the belief which saved his life was 'true' in the biological sense. This consequence is absurd, and shows that the biological definition is inadequate.

Instead of the objective biological test of success, we must adopt a subjective test: 'success' means 'achieving desired ends'. But this change in the definition of 'success' weakens the position. When you see a man eating salt, you cannot tell whether he is acting on knowledge or error until you have ascertained whether he wishes to commit suicide. To ascertain this, you must discover whether the belief that he wishes to commit suicide will lead to your own success. This involves an endless regress.

Again: if A and B have conflicting desires, A's success may involve B's failure, so that truth for A may be falsehood for B. Suppose, for example, that A desires B's death but does not wish to be morally responsible for it; and suppose B has no wish to commit suicide. If B eats arsenic thinking it is salt, and A sees him doing so, also thinking it is salt, A achieves his desire and B does not; therefore A's belief that the arsenic was salt is 'true' while B's identical belief is 'false'.

The pragmatist may say, in reply, that the success which is a test of truth is social, not individual: a belief is 'true' when the success of the human race is helped by the existence of the belief. This, however, is hopelessly vague. What is 'the success of the human race?' It is a concept for the politician, not for the logician. Moreover, mankind may profit by the errors of the wicked. We must say, therefore: 'A belief is "true" if the consequences of its being believed by all whose acts are affected by it are better, for mankind as a whole, than the consequences of its being disbelieved.' Or, what comes to much the same thing: 'A belief is "true" if an ideally virtuous man will act on it.' Any such view presupposes that we can know ethics before we know anything, and is therefore logically absurd.

Some beliefs which we should all hold to be false have greatly helped success; for example, the Mohammedan belief that the faithful who die in battle go straight to Paradise. When we reject this belief, do we mean merely that it proved an obstacle to science, and therefore to war-technique, and so led ultimately to the subjugation of the Mohammedans by the Christians? Surely not. The question whether you will go to Paradise when you die is as definite as the question whether you will go to New York tomorrow. You would not decide this latter question by investigating whether those who believe they will go to New York tomorrow are on the whole more successful than those who do not. The test of success is only brought in where the usual tests fail. But *if* the Mohammedan belief was true, those who entertained it have long since had empirical evidence of its truth. *Such* evidence is convincing, but the argument from success is not.

The pragmatist's position, if I am not mistaken, is a product of a limited scepticism supplemented by a surprising dogmatism. Our beliefs are obviously not always right, and often call for emendation rather than total rejection. Many questions of the highest emotional interest cannot be answered by means of any of the old conceptions of 'truth', while many of the questions that can be answered, such as 'is this red?' are so uninteresting that the pragmatist ignores them. But in spite of his scepticism, he is confident that he can know whether the consequences of entertaining a belief are such as to satisfy desire. This knowledge is surely far more difficult to secure than the knowledge that the pragmatist begins by questioning, and will have to be obtained, if at all, not by the pragmatist's method, which would lead to an endless regress, but by that very method of observation which, in simpler cases, he has rejected as inadequate.

There are certain general problems connected with such a theory as Dr Dewey's, which perhaps deserve consideration although he does not discuss them. Inquiry, in his system, operates upon a raw material, which it gradually transforms; it is only the final product that can be known. The raw material remains an Unknowable. That being the case, it is not quite clear why it is supposed to exist. A process, not unlike the Hegelian dialectic apart from the triadic form, starts from Pure Being and ends with—what? Presumably a world in which everything can be successfully manipulated owing to the progress of scientific technique. Just as, in Hegel, the earlier categories are not quite real, so, in Dr Dewey's system, nothing can be fully known except the ultimate result of 'inquiry'.

I find this view difficult, not only theoretically, but in view of the actual history of scientific knowledge. The first science to be developed was astronomy, yet it can hardly be supposed that the sun and the planets are much altered by the observations of the astronomers. Telescopes, it is true, alter the sense-data by means of which we know about the heavenly bodies, but sense-data, according to Dr Dewey, are not the subject-matter of knowledge.

'Knowledge' as traditionally conceived is, no doubt, something of a false abstraction. Human beings find themselves in an environment to which they react in various ways; some of these reactions may be regarded as showing 'knowledge' and others as showing 'error'. In the older philosophies, knowledge was conceived too passively, as though it consisted merely in receiving an imprint from the object. I think, however, that, with modern terminology, something not wholly unlike this passive conception of knowledge may still be justified. The circumstances in which we most naturally speak of 'knowledge' are those in which there is a delayed reaction. For instance, I know Mr A's address, but this only leads to action on certain occasions. The reason for isolating knowledge is that what we know not only gives a possibility of successful action, but is in the meantime a part of our constitution. When we consider this aspect of it, we are led to regard it as something not essentially concerned with action, and, owing its capacity for promoting success, as a relation to the object, which can be studied and defined without bringing in the relation to action.

Perhaps the objections which I feel to the instrumentalist logic are merely emotional, and have no logical justification, although I am totally unable to believe that this is the case. Knowledge, if Dr Dewey is right, cannot be any part of the ends of life; it is merely a means to other satisfactions. This view, to those who have been much engaged in the pursuit of knowledge, is distasteful. Dr Dewey himself confesses to having felt this, and resisted it as a temptation. The emphasis upon the practical in his later writings, he says, 'was a reaction against what was more natural, and it served as a protest and a protection against something in myself which, in the pressure of the weight of actual experience, I knew to be a weakness'. Even those who doubt whether such asceticism is necessary either practically or theoretically, cannot but feel the highest respect for the moral force required to practise it consistently throughout a long span of years.

For my part, I believe that too great emphasis upon the practical robs practice itself of its *raison d'être*. We act, in so far as we are not blindly driven by instinct, in order to achieve ends which are not merely further actions, but have in them some element, however precarious and however transient, of rest and peace—not the rest and peace of mere quiescence, but the kind that, in the most intense form, becomes ecstasy. When what passes for knowledge is considered to be no more than a momentary halting-place in a process of inquiry which has no goal outside itself, inquiry can no longer provide intellectual joys, but becomes merely a means to better dinners and more rapid locomotion. Activity can supply only one half of wisdom; the other half depends upon a receptive passivity. Ultimately, the controversy between those who base logic upon 'truth' and those who base it upon 'inquiry' arises from a difference of values, and cannot be argued without, at some point, begging the question. I cannot hope, therefore, that anything in the above pages has validity except for those whose bias resembles my own, while those whose bias resembles Dr Dewey's will find in his book just such an exposition as the subject seems to them to require.

> (*The Philosophy of John Dewey*, ed. Paul Arthur Schilpp. Library of Living Philosophers, New York: Tudor Publishing Co., Inc. 1939.)

25

JOHN DEWEY

JOHN DEWEY, who was born in 1859, is generally admitted to be the leading living philosopher of America. In this estimate I entirely concur. He has had a profound influence, not only among philosophers, but on students of education, aesthetics, and political theory. He is a man of the highest character, liberal in outlook, generous and kind in personal relations, indefatigable in work. With many of his opinions I am in almost complete agreement. Owing to my respect and admiration for him, as well as to personal experience of his kindness, I should wish to agree completely, but to my regret I am compelled to dissent from his most distinctive philosophical doctrine, namely the substitution of 'inquiry' for 'truth' as the fundamental concept of logic and theory of knowledge.

Like William James, Dewey is a New Englander, and carries on the tradition of New England liberalism, which has been abandoned by some of the descendants of the great New Englanders of a hundred years ago. He has never been what might be called a 'mere' philosopher. Education, especially, has been in the forefront of his interests, and his influence on American education has been profound. I, in my lesser way, have tried to have an influence on education very similar to his. Perhaps he, like me, has not always been satisfied with the practice of those who professed to follow his teaching, but any new doctrine, in practice, is bound to be subject to some extravagance and excess. This, however, does not matter so much as might be thought, because the faults of what is new are so much more easily seen than those of what is traditional.

When Dewey became professor of philosophy at Chicago in 1894, pedagogy was included among his subjects. He founded a progressive school, and wrote much about education. What he wrote at this time was summed up in his book *The School and Society* (1899), which is considered the most influential of all his writings. He has continued to write on education throughout his life, almost as much as on philosophy.

Other social and political questions have also had a large share of his thought. Like myself, he was much influenced by visits to Russia and China, negatively in the first case, positively in the second. He was reluctantly a supporter of the First World War. He had an important part in the inquiry as to Trotsky's alleged guilt, and, while he was convinced that the charges were unfounded, he did not think that the Soviet régime would have been satisfactory if Trotsky instead of Stalin had been Lenin's successor. He became persuaded that violent revolution leading to dictatorship is not the way to achieve a good society. Although very liberal in all economic questions, he has never been a Marxist. I heard him say once that, having emancipated himself with some difficulty from the traditional orthodox theology, he was not going to shackle himself with another. In all this his point of view is almost identical with my own.

From the strictly philosophical point of view, the chief importance of Dewey's work lies in his criticism of the traditional notion of 'truth', which is embodied in the theory that he calls 'instrumentalism'. Truth, as conceived by most professional philosophers, is static and final, perfect and eternal; in religious terminology, it may be identified with God's thoughts, and with those thoughts which, as rational beings, we share with God. The perfect model of truth is the multiplication table, which is precise and certain and free from all temporal dross. Since Pythagoras, and still more since Plato, mathematics has been linked with theology, and has profoundly influenced the theory of knowledge of most professional philosophers. Dewey's interests are biological rather than mathematical, and he conceives thought as an evolutionary process. The traditional view would, of course, admit that men gradually come to know more, but each piece of knowledge, when achieved, is regarded as something final. Hegel, it is true, does not regard human knowledge in this way. He conceives human knowledge as an organic whole, gradually growing in every part, and not perfect in any part until the whole is perfect. But although the Hegelian philosophy influenced Dewey in his youth, it still has its Absolute and its eternal world which is more real than the temporal process. These can have no place in Dewey's thought, for which all reality is temporal, and process, though evolutionary, is not, as for Hegel, the unfolding of an eternal Idea.

So far, I am in agreement with Dewey. Nor is this the end of my agreement. Before embarking upon discussion of the points as to which I differ, I will say a few words as to my own view of 'truth'.

The first question is: What sort of thing is 'true' or 'false'? The simplest answer would be: a sentence. 'Columbus crossed the ocean in 1492' is true; 'Columbus crossed the ocean in 1776' is false. This answer is correct, but incomplete. Sentences are true or false, as the case may be, because they are 'significant', and their significance depends upon the language used. If you were translating an account of Columbus into Arabic, you would have to alter '1492' into the corresponding year of the Mohammedan era. Sentences in different languages may have the same significance, and it is the significance, not the words, that determines whether the sentence is 'true' or 'false'. When you assert a sentence, you express a 'belief', which may be equally well expressed in a different language. The 'belief', whatever it may be, is what is 'true' or 'false' or 'more or less true'. Thus we are driven to the investigation of 'belief'.

Now a belief, provided it is sufficiently simple, may exist without being expressed in words. It would be difficult, without using words, to believe that the ratio of the circumference of a circle to the diameter is approximately 3·14159, or that Caesar, when he decided to cross the Rubicon, sealed the fate of the Roman republican constitution. But in simple cases unverbalized beliefs are common. Suppose, for instance, in descending a staircase, you make a mistake as to when you have got to the bottom: you take a step suitable for level ground, and come down with a bump. The result is a violent shock of surprise. You would naturally say, 'I thought I was at the bottom', but in fact you were not thinking about the stairs, or you would not have made the mistake. Your muscles were adjusted in a way suitable to the bottom, when in fact you were not yet there. It was your body rather than your mind that made the mistake— at least that would be a natural way to express what happened. But in fact the distinction between mind and body is a dubious one. It will be better to speak of an 'organism', leaving the division of its activities between the mind and the body undetermined. One can say, then: your organism was adjusted in a manner which would have been suitable if you had been at the bottom, but in fact was not suitable. This failure of adjustment constituted error, and one may say that you were entertaining a false belief.

The *test* of error in the above illustration is *surprise*. I think this is true generally of beliefs that can be tested. A *false* belief is one which, in suitable circumstances, will cause the person entertaining it to experience surprise, while a *true* belief will not have this effect. But although surprise is a good criterion when it is applicable, it does not give the *meaning* of the words 'true' and 'false', and is not always applicable. Suppose you are walking in a thunderstorm, and you say to yourself, 'I am not at all likely to be struck by lightning'. The next moment you are struck, but you experience no surprise, because you are dead. If one day the sun explodes, as Sir James Jeans seems to expect, we shall all perish instantly, and therefore not be surprised, but unless we expect the catastrophe we shall all have been mistaken. Such illustrations suggest objectivity in truth and falsehood: what is true (or false) is a state of the organism, but it is true (or false), in general, in virtue of occurrences outside the organism. Sometimes experimental tests are possible to determine truth and falsehood, but sometimes they are not; when they are not, the alternative nevertheless remains, and is significant.

I will not further develop my view of truth and falsehood, but will proceed to the examination of Dewey's doctrine.

Dewey does not aim at judgments that shall be absolutely 'true', or condemn their contradictories as absolutely 'false'. In his opinion there is a process called 'inquiry', which is one form of mutual adjustment between an organism and its environment. If I wished, from my point of view, to go as far as possible towards agreeing with Dewey, I should begin by an analysis of 'meaning' or 'significance'. Suppose, for example, you are at the Zoo, and you hear a voice through a megaphone saying: 'A lion has just escaped.' You will, in that case, act as you would if you saw the lion—that is to say, you will get away as quickly as possible. The sentence 'a lion has escaped' *means* a certain occurrence, in the sense that it promotes the same behaviour as the occurrence would if you saw it. Broadly: a sentence S 'means' an event E if it promotes behaviour which E would have promoted. If there has in fact been no such occurrence, the sentence is false. Just the same applies to a belief which is not expressed in words. One may say: a belief is a state of an organism promoting behaviour such as a certain occurrence would promote if sensibly present; the occurrence which would promote this behaviour is the 'significance' of the belief. This statement is unduly simplified, but it may serve to indicate the theory I am advocating. So far, I do not think that Dewey and I would disagree very much. But with his further developments I find myself in very definite disagreement.

Dewey makes *inquiry* the essence of logic, not truth or knowledge. He defines inquiry as follows: 'Inquiry is the controlled or directed transformation of an indeterminate situation into one that is so determinate in its constituent distinctions and relations as to convert the elements of the original situation into a unified whole.' He adds that 'inquiry is concerned with objective transformations of objective subject-matter'. This definition is plainly inadequate. Take, for instance, the dealings of a drill-sergeant with a crowd of recruits, or of a bricklayer with a heap of bricks; these exactly fulfil Dewey's definition of 'inquiry'. Since he clearly would not include them, there must be an element in his notion of 'inquiry' which he has forgotten to mention in his definition. What this element is, I shall attempt to determine in a moment. But let us first consider what emerges from the definition as it stands.

It is clear that 'inquiry', as conceived by Dewey, is part of the general process of attempting to make the world more organic. 'Unified wholes' are to be the outcome of inquiries. Dewey's love of what is organic is due partly to biology, partly to the lingering influence of Hegel. Unless on the basis of an unconscious Hegelian metaphysic, I do not see why inquiry should be expected to result in 'unified wholes'. If I am given a pack of cards in disorder, and asked to inquire into their sequence, I shall, if I follow Dewey's prescription, first arrange them in order, and then say that this was the order resulting from inquiry. There will be, it is true, an 'objective transformation of objective subject-matter' while

I am arranging the cards, but the definition allows for this. If, at the end, I am told: 'We wanted to know the sequence of the cards when they were given to you, not after you had rearranged them', I shall, if I am a disciple of Dewey, reply: 'Your ideas are altogether too static. I am a dynamic person, and when I inquire into any subject-matter I first alter it in such a way as to make the inquiry easy.' The notion that such a procedure is legitimate can only be justified by a Hegelian distinction of appearance and reality: the appearance may be confused and fragmentary, but the reality is always orderly and organic. Therefore when I arrange the cards I am only revealing their true eternal nature. But this part of the doctrine is never made explicit. The metaphysic of organism underlies Dewey's theories, but I do not know how far he is aware of this fact.

Let us now try to find the supplement to Dewey's definition which is required in order to distinguish inquiry from other kinds of organizing activity, such as those of the drill-sergeant and the bricklayer. Formerly it would have been said that inquiry is distinguished by its purpose, which is to ascertain some truth. But for Dewey 'truth' is to be defined in terms of 'inquiry', not *vice versa*; he quotes with approval Peirce's definition: 'Truth' is 'the opinion which is fated to be ultimately agreed to by all who investigate'. This leaves us completely in the dark as to what the investigators are doing, for we cannot, without circularity, say that they are endeavouring to ascertain the truth.

I think Dr Dewey's theory might be stated as follows. The relations of an organism to its environment are sometimes satisfactory to the organism, sometimes unsatisfactory. When they are unsatisfactory, the situation may be improved by mutual adjustment. When the alterations by means of which the situation is improved are mainly on the side of the organism—they are never *wholly* on either side—the process involved is called 'inquiry'. For example: during a battle you are mainly concerned to alter the environment, i.e. the enemy; but during the preceding period of reconnaissance you are mainly concerned to adapt your own forces to his dispositions. This earlier period is one of 'inquiry'.

The difficulty of this theory, to my mind, lies in the severing of the relation between a belief and the fact or facts which would commonly be said to 'verify' it. Let us continue to consider the example of a general planning a battle. His reconnaissance planes report to him certain enemy preparations, and he, in consequence, makes certain counter-preparations. Common sense would say that the reports upon which he acts are 'true' if, in fact, the enemy have made the moves which they are said to have made, and that, in that case, the reports remain true even if the general subsequently loses the battle. This view is rejected by Dr Dewey. He does not divide beliefs into 'true' and 'false', but he still has two kinds of beliefs, which we will call 'satisfactory' if the general wins, and 'unsatisfactory' if he is defeated. Until the battle has taken place, he cannot tell what to think about the reports of his scouts.

Generalizing, we may say that Dr Dewey, like everyone else, divides beliefs into two classes, of which one is good and the other bad. He holds, however, that a belief may be good at one time and bad at another; this happens with imperfect theories which are better than their predecessors but worse than their successors. Whether a belief is good or bad depends upon whether the activities which it inspires in the organism entertaining the belief have consequences which are satisfactory or unsatisfactory to it. Thus a belief about some event in the past is to be classified as 'good' or 'bad', not according to whether the event really took place, but according to the future effects of the belief. The results are curious. Suppose somebody says to me: 'Did you have coffee with your breakfast this morning?' If I am an ordinary person, I shall try to remember. But if I am a disciple of Dr Dewey I shall say: 'Wait a while; I must try two experiments before I can tell you.' I shall then first make myself believe that I had coffee, and observe the consequences, if any; I shall then make myself believe that I did not have coffee, and again observe the consequences, if any. I shall then compare the two sets of consequences, to see which I found the more satisfactory. If there is a balance on one side I shall decide for that answer. If there is not, I shall have to confess that I cannot answer the question.

But this is not the end of our troubles. How am I to know the consequences of believing that I had coffee for breakfast? If I say 'the consequences are such-and-such', this in turn will have to be tested by its consequences before I can know whether what I have said was a 'good' or a 'bad' statement. And even if this difficulty were overcome, how am I to judge which set of consequences is the more satisfactory? One decision as to whether I had coffee may fill me with contentment, the other with determination to further the war effort. Each of these may be considered good, but until I have decided which is better I cannot tell whether I had coffee for breakfast. Surely this is absurd.

Dewey's divergence from what has hitherto been regarded as common sense is due to his refusal to admit 'facts' into his metaphysic, in the sense in which 'facts' are stubborn and cannot be manipulated. In this it may be that common sense is changing, and that his view will not seem contrary to what common sense is becoming.

The main difference between Dr Dewey and me is that he judges a belief by its effects, whereas I judge it by its causes where a past occurrence is concerned. I consider such a belief 'true', or as nearly 'true' as we can make it, if it has a certain kind of relation (sometimes very complicated) to its causes. Dr Dewey holds that it has 'warranted assertibility'—which he substitutes for 'truth'—if it has certain kinds of effects. This divergence is connected with a difference of outlook on the world. The past cannot be affected by what we do, and therefore, if truth is determined by what has happened, it is independent of present or future volitions; it represents, in logical form, the limitations on human power. But if truth, or rather 'warranted assertibility', depends upon the future, then, in so far as it is in our power to alter the future, it is in our power to alter what should be asserted. This enlarges the sense of human power, and freedom. Did Caesar cross the Rubicon? I should regard an affirmative answer as unalterably necessitated by a past event. Dr Dewey would decide whether to say yes or no by an appraisal of future events, and there is no reason why these future events could not be arranged by human power so as to make a negative answer the more satisfactory. If I find the belief that Caesar crossed the Rubicon very distasteful, I need not sit down in dull despair; I can, if I have enough skill and power, arrange a social environment in which the statement that he did not cross the Rubicon will have 'warranted assertibility'.

Throughout this book I have sought, where possible, to connect philosophies with the social environment of the philosophers concerned. It has seemed to me that the belief in human power, and the unwillingness to admit 'stubborn facts', were connected with the hopefulness engendered by machine production and the scientific manipulation of our physical environment. This view is shared by many of Dr Dewey's supporters. Thus George Raymond Geiger, in a laudatory essay, says that Dr Dewey's method 'would mean a revolution in thought just as middle-class and unspectacular, but just as stupendous, as the revolution in industry of a century ago'. It seemed to me that I was saying the same thing when I wrote 'Dr Dewey has an outlook which, where it is distinctive, is in harmony with the age of industrialism and collective enterprise. It is natural that his strongest appeal should be to Americans, and also that he should be almost equally appreciated by the progressive elements in countries like China and Mexico.'

To my regret and surprise, this statement, which I had supposed completely innocuous, vexed Dr Dewey, who replied: 'Mr Russell's confirmed habit of connecting the pragmatic theory of knowing with obnoxious aspects of American industrialism . . . is much as if I were to link his philosophy to the interests of the English landed aristocracy.'

For my part, I am accustomed to having my opinions explained (especially by Communists) as due to my connection with the British aristocracy, and I am quite willing to suppose that my views, like other men's, are influenced by social environment. But if, in regard to Dr Dewey, I am mistaken as to the social influences concerned, I regret the mistake. I find, however, that I am not alone in having made it. Santayana, for instance, says: 'In Dewey, as in current science and ethics, there is a pervasive quasi-Hegelian tendency to dissolve the individual into his social functions, as well as everything substantial and actual into something relative and transitional.'

Dr Dewey's world, it seems to me, is one in which human beings occupy the imagination; the cosmos of astronomy, though, of course, acknowledged to exist, is at most times ignored. His philosophy is a power philosophy, though not, like Nietzsche's, a philosophy of individual power; it is the power of the community that is felt to be valuable. It is this element of social power that seems to me to make the philosophy of instrumentalism attractive to those who are more impressed by our new control over natural forces than by the limitations to which that control is still subject.

The attitude of man towards the non-human environment has differed profoundly at different times. The Greeks, with their dread of hubris and their belief in a Necessity or Fate superior even to Zeus, carefully avoided what would have seemed to them insolence towards the universe. The Middle Ages carried submission much further: humility towards God was a Christian's first duty. Initiative was cramped by this attitude, and great originality was scarcely possible. The Renaissance restored human pride, but carried it to the point where it led to anarchy and disaster. Its work was largely undone by the Reformation and the counter-reformation. But modern technique, while not altogether favourable to the lordly individual of the Renaissance, has revived the sense of the collective power of human communities. Man, formerly too humble, begins to think of himself as almost a god. The Italian pragmatist Papini urges us to substitute the 'Imitation of God' for the 'Imitation of Christ'.

In all this I feel a grave danger, the danger of what might be called cosmic impiety. The concept of 'truth' as something dependent upon facts largely outside human control has been one of the ways in which philosophy hitherto has inculcated the necessary element of humility. When this check upon pride is removed, a further step is taken on the road towards a certain kind of madness—the intoxication of power which invaded philosophy with Fichte, and to which modern men, whether philosophers or not, are prone. I am persuaded that this intoxication is the greatest danger of our time, and that any philosophy which, however unintentionally, contributes to it is increasing the danger of vast social disaster.

> (*A History of Western Philosophy*, London: Allen & Unwin; New York: Simon & Schuster, 1946.)

PART V

The Epistemologist

Since ancient Greece, theories of knowledge have run the gamut between the crudely simple and the ultra imaginative. Before the nineteenth century, the attempt to humanize the cosmos had been the preoccupation of almost every major philosopher. The impact of science has changed this view. Modern theories of knowledge are no longer concerned with inventing comforting answers but rather with the problem of gaining new insights.

A study of Russell's theories in the field of epistemology reveals an important aspect of his philosophic contributions. His concern in this area is indicative of his continued interest in the variety of views presented in this century as is evidenced by the three contributions which follow, taken from works spanning over forty years. They also show once more the dynamics of continued reflection as opposed to static adherence to a view originally advanced.

26

KNOWLEDGE BY ACQUAINTANCE AND
KNOWLEDGE BY DESCRIPTION

THERE are two sorts of knowledge: knowledge of things, and knowledge of truths. We shall be concerned exclusively with knowledge of things, of which in turn we shall have to distinguish two kinds. Knowledge of things, when it is of the kind we call knowledge by *acquaintance*, is essentially simpler than any knowledge of truths, and logically independent of knowledge of truths, though it would be rash to assume that human beings ever, in fact, have acquaintance with things without at the same time knowing some truth about them. Knowledge of things by *description*, on the contrary, always involves, as we shall find in the course of the present chapter, some knowledge of truths as its source and ground. But first of all we must make clear what we mean by 'acquaintance' and what we mean by 'description'.

We shall say that we have *acquaintance* with anything of which we are directly aware, without the intermediary of any process of inference or any knowledge of truths. Thus in the presence of my table I am acquainted with the sense-data that make up the appearance of my table—its colour, shape, hardness, smoothness, etc.; all these are things of which I am immediately conscious when I am seeing and touching my table. The particular shade of colour that I am seeing may have many things said about it—I may say that it is brown, that it is rather dark, and so on. But such statements, though they make me know truths *about* the colour, do not make me know the colour itself any better than I did before: so far as concerns knowledge of the colour itself, as opposed to knowledge of truths about it, I know the colour perfectly and completely when I see it, and no further knowledge of it itself is even theoretically possible. Thus the sense-data which make up the appearance of my table are things with which I have acquaintance, things immediately known to me just as they are.

My knowledge of the table as a physical object, on the contrary, is not direct knowledge. Such as it is, it is obtained through acquaintance with the sense-data that make up the appearance of the table. We have seen that it is possible, without absurdity, to doubt whether there is a table at all, whereas it is not possible to doubt the sense-data. My knowledge of the table is of the kind which we shall call 'knowledge by description'. The table is 'the physical object which causes such-and-such sense-data'. This *describes* the table by means of the sense-data. In order to know anything at all about the table, we must know truths connecting it with things with which we have acquaintance: we must know that 'such-and-such sense-data are caused by a physical object'. There is no state of mind in which we are directly aware of the table; all our knowledge of the table is really knowledge of *truths*, and the actual thing which is the table is not, strictly speaking, known to us at all. We know a description, and we know that there is just one object to which this description applies, though the object itself is not directly known to us. In such a case, we say that our knowledge of the object is knowledge by description.

All our knowledge, both knowledge of things and knowledge of truths, rests upon acquaintance as its foundation. It is therefore important to consider what kinds of things there are with which we have acquaintance.

Sense-data, as we have already seen, are among the things with which we are acquainted; in fact, they supply the most obvious and striking example of knowledge by acquaintance. But if they were the sole example, our knowledge would be very much more restricted than it is. We should only know what is now present to our senses: we could not know anything about the past—not even that there was a past—nor could we know any truths about our sense-data, for all knowledge of truths, as we shall show, demands acquaintance with things which are of an essentially different character from sense-data, the things which are sometimes called 'abstract ideas', but which we shall call 'universals'. We have therefore to consider acquaintance with other things besides sense-data if we are to obtain any tolerably adequate analysis of our knowledge.

The first extension beyond sense-data to be considered is acquaintance by *memory*. It is obvious that we often remember what we have seen or heard or had otherwise present to our senses, and that in such cases we are still immediately aware of what we remember, in spite of the fact that it appears as past and not as present. This immediate knowledge by memory is the source of all our knowledge concerning the past: without it, there could be no knowledge of the past by inference, since we should never know that there was anything past to be inferred.

The next extension to be considered is acquaintance by *introspection*. We are not only aware of things, but we are often aware of being aware of them. When I see the sun, I am often aware of my seeing the sun; thus 'my seeing the sun' is an object with which I have acquaintance. When I desire food, I may be aware of my desire for food; thus 'my desiring food' is an object with which I am acquainted. Similarly we may be aware of our feeling pleasure or pain, and generally of the events which happen in our minds. This kind of acquaintance, which may be called self-consciousness, is the source of all our knowledge of mental things. It is obvious that it is only what goes on in our own minds that can be thus known immediately. What goes on in the minds of others is known to us through our perception of their bodies, that is, through the sense-data in us which are associated with their bodies. But for our acquaintance with the contents of our own minds, we should be unable to imagine the minds of others, and therefore we could never arrive at the knowledge that they have minds. It seems natural to suppose that self-consciousness is one of the things that distinguish men from animals: animals, we may suppose, though they have acquaintance with sense-data, never become aware of this acquaintance, and thus never know of their own existence. I do not mean that they *doubt* whether they exist, but that they have never become conscious of the fact that they have sensations and feelings, nor therefore of the fact that they, the subjects of their sensations and feelings, exist.

We have spoken of acquaintance with the contents of our minds as *self*-consciousness, but it is not, of course, consciousness of our *self*: it is consciousness of particular thoughts and feelings. The question whether we are also acquainted with our bare selves, as opposed to particular thoughts and feelings, is a very difficult one, upon which it would be rash to speak positively. When we try to look into ourselves we always seem to come upon some particular thought or feeling, and not upon the 'I' which has the thought or feeling. Nevertheless there are some reasons for thinking that we are acquainted with the 'I', though the acquaintance is hard to disentangle from other things. To make clear what sort of reason there is, let us consider for a moment what our acquaintance with particular thoughts really involves.

When I am acquainted with 'my seeing the sun', it seems plain that I am acquainted with two different things in relation to each other. On the one hand there is the sense-datum which represents the sun to me, on the other hand there is that which sees this sense-datum. All acquaintance, such as my acquaintance with the sense-datum which represents the sun, seems obviously a relation between the person acquainted and the object with which the person is acquainted. When a case of acquaintance is one with which I can be acquainted (as I am acquainted with my acquaintance with the sense-datum representing the sun), it is plain that the person acquainted is myself. Thus, when I am acquainted with my seeing the sun, the whole fact with which I am acquainted is 'Self-acquainted-with-sense-datum'.

Further, we know the truth 'I am acquainted with this sense-datum'. It is hard to see how we could know this truth, or even understand what is meant by it, unless we were acquainted with something which we call 'I'. It does not seem necessary to suppose that we are acquainted with a more or less permanent person, the same today as yesterday, but it does seem as though we must be acquainted with that thing, whatever its nature, which sees the sun and has acquaintance with sense-data. Thus, in some sense it would seem we must be acquainted with our Selves as opposed to our particular experiences. But the question is difficult, and complicated arguments can be adduced on either side. Hence, although acquaintance with ourselves seems *probably* to occur, it is not wise to assert that it undoubtedly does occur.

We may therefore sum up as follows what has been said concerning acquaintance with things that exist. We have acquaintance in sensation with the data of the outer senses, and in introspection with the data of what may be called the inner sense—thoughts, feelings, desires, etc.; we have acquaintance in memory with things which have been data either of the outer senses or of the inner sense. Further, it is probable, though not certain, that we have acquaintance with Self, as that which is aware of things or has desires towards things.

In addition to our acquaintance with particular existing things, we also have acquaintance with what we shall call *universals*, that is to say, general ideas, such as *whiteness, diversity, brotherhood*, and so on. Every complete sentence must contain at least one word which stands for a universal, since all verbs have a meaning which is universal. For the present, it is only necessary to guard against the supposition that whatever we can be acquainted with must be something particular and existent. Awareness of universals is called *conceiving*, and a universal of which we are aware is called a *concept*.

It will be seen that among the objects with which we are acquainted are not included physical objects (as opposed to sense-data), nor other people's minds. These things are known to us by what I call 'knowledge by description', which we must now consider.

By a 'description' I mean any phrase of the form 'a so-and-so' or 'the so-and-so'. A phrase of the form 'a so-and-so' I shall call an 'ambiguous' description; a phrase of the form 'the so-and-so' (in the singular) I shall call a 'definite' description. Thus 'a man' is an ambiguous description, and 'the man with the iron mask' is a definite description. There are various problems connected with ambiguous descriptions, but I pass them by, since they do not directly concern the matter we are discussing, which is the nature of our knowledge concerning objects in cases where we know that there is an object answering to a definite description, though we are not *acquainted* with any such object. This is a matter which is concerned exclusively with *definite* descriptions. I shall therefore, in the sequel, speak simply of 'descriptions' when I mean 'definite descriptions'. Thus a description will mean any phrase of the form 'the so-and-so' in the singular.

We shall say that an object is 'known by description' when we know that it is '*the* so-and-so', i.e. when we know that there is one object, and no more, having a certain property; and it will generally be implied that we do not have knowledge of the same object by acquaintance. We know that the man with the iron mask existed, and many propositions are known about him; but we do not know who he was. We know that the candidate who gets the most votes will be elected, and in this case we are very likely also acquainted (in the only sense in which one can be acquainted with someone else) with the man who is, in fact, the candidate who will get most votes; but we do not know which of the candidates he is, i.e. we do not know any proposition of the form 'A is the candidate who will get most votes' where A is one of the candidates by name. We shall say that we have 'merely descriptive knowledge' of the so-and-so when, although we know that the so-and-so exists, and although we may possibly be acquainted with the object which is, in fact, the so-and-so, yet we do not know any proposition 'a is the so-and-so', where a is something with which we are acquainted.

When we say 'the so-and-so exists', we mean that there is just one object which is the so-and-so. The proposition 'a is the so-and-so' means that a has the property so-and-so, and nothing else has. 'Mr A. is the Unionist candidate for this constituency' means 'Mr A. is a Unionist candidate for this constituency, and no one else is'. 'The Unionist candidate for this constituency exists' means 'someone is a Unionist candidate for this constituency, and no one else is'. Thus, when we are acquainted with an object which is the so-and-so, we know that the so-and-so exists; but we may know that the so-and-so exists when we are not acquainted with any object which we know to be the so-and-so, and even when we are not acquainted with any object which, in fact, is the so-and-so.

Common words, even proper names, are usually really descriptions. That is to say, the thought in the mind of a person using a proper name correctly can generally only be expressed explicitly if we replace the proper name by a description. Moreover, the description required to express the thought will vary for different people, or for the same person at different times. The only thing constant (so long as the name is rightly used) is the object to which the name applies. But so long as this remains constant, the particular description involved usually makes no difference to the truth or falsehood of the proposition in which the name appears.

Let us take some illustrations. Suppose some statement made about Bismarck. Assuming that there is such a thing as direct acquaintance with oneself, Bismarck himself might have used his name directly to designate the particular person with whom he was acquainted. In this case, if he made a judgment about himself, he himself might be a constituent of the judgment. Here the proper name has the direct use which it always wishes to have, as simply standing for a certain object, and not for a description of the object. But if a person who knew Bismarck made a judgment about him, the case is different. What this person was acquainted with were certain sense-data which he connected (rightly, we will suppose) with Bismarck's body. His body, as a physical object, and still more his mind, were only known as the body and the mind connected with these sense-data. That is, they were known by description. It is, of course, very much a matter of chance which characteristics of a man's appearance will come into a friend's mind when he thinks of him; thus the description actually in the friend's mind is accidental. The essential point is that he knows that the various descriptions all apply to the same entity, in spite of not being acquainted with the entity in question.

When we, who did not know Bismarck, make a judgment about him, the description in our minds will probably be some more or less vague mass of historical knowledge—far more, in most cases, than is required to identify him. But, for the sake of illustration, let us assume that we think of him as 'the first Chancellor of the German Empire'. Here all the words are abstract except 'German'. The word 'German' will, again, have different meanings for different people. To some it will recall travels in Germany, to some the look of Germany on the map, and so on. But if we are to obtain a description which we know to be applicable, we shall be compelled, at some point, to bring in a reference to a particular with which we are acquainted. Such reference is involved in any mention of past, present, and future (as opposed to definite dates), or of here and there, or of what others have told us. Thus it would seem that, in some way or other, a description known to be applicable to a particular must involve some reference to a particular with which we are acquainted, if our knowledge about the thing described is not to be merely what follows *logically* from the description. For example, 'the most long-lived of men' is a description involving only universals, which must apply to some man, but we can make no judgments concerning this man which involve knowledge about him beyond what the description gives. If, however, we say, 'The first Chancellor of the German Empire was an astute diplomatist', we can only be assured of the truth of our judgment in virtue of something with which we are acquainted—usually a testimony heard or read. Apart from the information we convey to others, apart from the fact about the actual Bismarck, which gives importance to our judgment, the thought we really have contains the one or more particulars involved, and otherwise consists wholly of concepts.

All names of places—London, England, Europe, the Earth, the Solar System—similarly involve, when used, descriptions which start from some one or more particulars with which we are acquainted. I suspect that even the Universe, as considered by metaphysics, involves such a connection with particulars. In logic, on the contrary, where we are concerned not merely with what does exist, but with whatever might or could exist or be, no reference to actual particulars is involved.

It would seem that, when we make a statement about something only known by description, we often *intend* to make our statement, not in the form involving the description, but about the actual thing described. That is to say, when we say anything about Bismarck, we should like, if we could, to make the judgment which Bismarck alone can make, namely, the judgment of which he himself is a constituent. In this we are necessarily defeated, since the actual Bismarck is unknown to us. But we know that there is an object B, called Bismarck, and that B was an astute diplomatist. We can thus *describe* the proposition we should like to affirm, namely, 'B was an astute diplomatist', where B is the object which was Bismarck. If we are describing Bismarck as 'the first Chancellor of the German Empire', the proposition we should like to affirm may be described as 'the proposition asserting, concerning the actual object which was the first Chancellor of the German Empire, that this object was an astute diplomatist'. What enables us to communicate in spite of the varying descriptions we employ is that we know there is a true proposition concerning the actual Bismarck, and that however we may vary the description (so long as the description is correct) the proposition described is still the same. This proposition, which is described and is known to be true, is what interests us; but we are not acquainted with the proposition itself, and do not know *it*, though we know it is true.

It will be seen that there are various stages in the removal from acquaintance with particulars: there is Bismarck to people who knew him, Bismarck to those who only know of him through history, the man with the iron mask, the longest-lived of men. These are progressively further removed from acquaintance with particulars; the first comes as near to acquaintance as is possible in regard to another person; in the second, we shall still be said to know 'who Bismarck was'; in the third, we do not know who was the man with the iron mask, though we can know many propositions about him which are not logically deducible from the fact that he wore an iron mask; in the fourth, finally, we know nothing beyond what is logically deducible from the definition of the man. There is a similar hierarchy in the region of universals. Many universals, like many particulars, are only known to us by description. But here, as in the case of particulars, knowledge concerning what is known by description is ultimately reducible to knowledge concerning what is known by acquaintance.

The fundamental principle in the analysis of propositions containing descriptions is this: *Every proposition which we can understand must be composed wholly of constituents with which we are acquainted.*

We shall not at this stage attempt to answer all the objections which may be urged against this fundamental principle. For the present, we shall merely point out that, in some way or other, it must be possible to meet these objections, for it is scarcely conceivable that we can make a judgment or entertain a supposition without knowing what it is that we are judging or supposing about. We must attach *some* meaning to the words we use, if we are to speak significantly and not utter mere noise; and the meaning we attach to our words must be something with which we are acquainted. Thus when, for example, we make a statement about Julius Caesar, it is plain that Julias Caesar himself is not before our minds, since we are not acquainted with him. We have in mind some *description* of Julius Caesar: 'the man who was assassinated on the Ides of March', 'the founder of the Roman Empire', or, perhaps, merely 'the man whose name was *Julius Caesar*'. (In this last description, *Julius Caesar* is a noise or shape with which we are acquainted.) Thus our statement does not mean quite what it seems to mean, but means something involving, instead of Julius Caesar, some description of him which is composed wholly of particulars and universals with which we are acquainted.

The chief importance of knowledge by description is that it enables us to pass beyond the limits of our private experience. In spite of the fact that we can only know truths which are wholly composed of terms which we have experienced in acquaintance, we can yet have knowledge by description of things which we have never experienced. In view of the very narrow range of our immediate experience, this result is vital, and until it is understood, much of our knowledge must remain mysterious and therefore doubtful.

(*The Problems of Philosophy*, The Home University Library. London: Oxford University Press; New York: Henry Holt & Co., Inc., 1912.)

27

THEORY OF KNOWLEDGE

FROM August 1914 until the end of 1917 I was wholly occupied with matters arising out of my opposition to the war, but by the beginning of 1918 I had become persuaded that there was no further pacifist work that I could usefully do. I wrote as quickly as I could a book, which I had contracted to produce, called *Roads to Freedom*, but when that was out of the way I began again to work at philosophical subjects. In prison, I wrote first a polemical criticism of Dewey and then the *Introduction to Mathematical Philosophy*. After this I found my thoughts turning to theory of knowledge and to those parts of psychology and of linguistics which seemed relevant to that subject. This was a more or less permanent change in my philosophical interests. The outcome, so far as my own thinking was concerned, is embodied in three books: *The Analysis of Mind* (1921); *An Inquiry into Meaning and Truth* (1940); *Human Knowledge: Its Scope and Limits* (1948).

At the beginning of this work I had no fixed convictions, but only a certain store of maxims and prejudices. I read widely and found, in the end, as I had with the reading that preceded the *Principles of Mathematics*, that a great part of what I had read was irrelevant to my purposes.

Among the prejudices with which I had started, I should enumerate six as specially important:

First. It seemed to me desirable to emphasize the continuity between animal and human minds. I found it common to protest against intellectualist interpretations of animal behaviour, and with these protests I was in broad agreement, but I thought that the methods adopted in interpreting animal behaviour have much more scope than is usually admitted in interpreting what in human beings would be regarded as 'thought' or 'knowledge' or 'inference'. This preconception led me to read a great deal of animal psychology. I found, somewhat to my amusement, that there were two schools in this field, of whom the most important representatives were Thorndike, in America, and Köhler in Germany. It seemed that animals always behave in a manner showing the rightness of the philosophy entertained by the man who observes them. This devastating discovery holds over a wider field. In the seventeenth century, animals were ferocious, but under the influence of Rousseau they began to exemplify the cult of the Noble Savage which Peacock makes fun of in Sir Oran Haut-ton. Throughout the reign of Queen Victoria all apes were virtuous monogamists, but during the dissolute 'twenties their morals underwent a disastrous deterioration. This aspect of animal behaviour, however, did not concern me. What concerned me were the observations on how animals learn. Animals observed by Americans rush about frantically until they hit upon the solution by chance. Animals observed by Germans sit still and scratch their heads until they evolve the solution out of their inner consciousness. I believe both sets of observations to be entirely reliable, and that what an animal will do depends upon the kind of problem that you set before it. The net result of my reading in this subject was to make me very wary of extending any theory beyond the region within which observation had confirmed it.

There was one region where there was a very considerable body of precise experimental knowledge. It was the region of Pavlov's observations on conditioned reflexes in dogs. These experiments led to a philosophy called Behaviourism which had a considerable vogue. The gist of this philosophy is that in psychology we are to rely wholly upon external observations and never to accept data for which the evidence is entirely derived from introspection. As a philosophy, I never felt any inclination to accept this view, but, as a method to be pursued as far as possible, I thought it valuable. I determined in advance that I would push it as far as possible while remaining persuaded that it had very definite limits.

Second. Along with the prejudice in favour of behaviourist methods there went another prejudice in favour of explanations in terms of physics wherever possible. I have always been deeply persuaded that, from a cosmic point of view, life and experience are causally of little importance. The world of astronomy dominates my imagination and I am very conscious of the minuteness of our planet in comparison with the systems of galaxies. I found in Ramsey's *Foundations of Mathematics* a passage expressing what I do *not* feel:

'Where I seem to differ from some of my friends is in attaching little importance to physical size. I don't feel the least humble before the vastness of the heavens. The stars may be large, but they cannot think or love; and these are qualities which impress me far more than size does. I take no credit for weighing nearly seventeen stone.

'My picture of the world is drawn in perspective, and not like a model to scale. The foreground is occupied by human beings and the stars are all as small as threepenny bits. I don't really believe in astronomy, except as a complicated description of part of the course of human and possibly animal sensation. I apply my perspective not merely to space but also to time. In time the world will cool and everything will die; but that is a long time off still, and its present value at compound discount is almost nothing. Nor is the present less valuable because the future will be blank. Humanity, which fills the foreground of my picture, I find interesting and on the whole admirable.'

There is no arguing about feelings, and I do not pretend for a moment that my way of feeling is better than Ramsey's, but it is vastly different. I find little satisfaction in contemplating the human race and its follies. I am happier thinking about the nebula in Andromeda than thinking about Genghis Khan. I cannot, like Kant, put the moral law on the same plane as the starry heavens. The attempt to humanize the cosmos, which underlies the philosophy that calls itself 'Idealism', is displeasing to me quite independently of the question whether it is true or false. I have no wish to think that the world results from the lucubrations of Hegel or even of his Celestial Prototype. In any empirical subject-matter I expect, though without complete confidence, that a thorough understanding will reduce the more important causal laws to those of physics, but where the matter is very complex, I doubt the practical feasibility of the reduction.

Third. I feel that the concept of 'experience' has been very much over-emphasized, especially in the Idealist philosophy, but also in many forms of empiricism. I found, when I began to think about theory of knowledge, that none of the philosophers who emphasize 'experience' tells us what they mean by the word. They seem willing to accept it as an indefinable of which the significance should be obvious. They tend to think that only what is experienced can be known to exist and that it is meaningless to assert that some things exist although we do not know them to exist. I think that this sort of view gives much too much importance to knowledge, or at any rate to something analogous to knowledge. I think also that those who profess such views have not realized all their implications. Few philosophers seem to understand that one may know a proposition of the form 'All A is B' or 'There are A's' without knowing any single A individually. If you are on a pebbly beach you may be quite sure that there are pebbles on the beach that you have not seen or touched. Everybody, in fact, accepts innumerable propositions about things not experienced, but when people begin to philosophize they seem to think it necessary to make themselves artificially stupid. I will admit at once that there are difficulties in explaining how we acquire knowledge that transcends experience, but I think the view that we have no such knowledge is utterly untenable.

Fourth. I had, and have, another prejudice which works in the opposite direction from the one we have just been considering. I think that all knowledge as to what there is in the world, if it does not directly report facts known through perception or memory, must be inferred from premises of which one, at least, is known by perception or memory. I do not think that there is any wholly *a priori* method of proving the existence of anything, but I do think that there are forms of probable inference which must be accepted although they cannot be *proved* by experience.

Fifth. One of the things that I realized in 1918 was that I had not paid enough attention to 'meaning' and to linguistic problems generally. It was then that I began to be aware of the many problems concerned with the relation between words and things. There is first the classification of single words: proper names, adjectives, relation words, conjunctions and such words as 'all' and 'some'. Then there is the question of the significance of sentences and how it comes about that they have the duality of truth and falsehood. I found that, just as there are formalists in arithmetic, who are content to lay down rules for doing sums without reflecting that numbers have to be used in counting, so there are formalists in the wider field of language in general who think that truth is a matter of following certain rules and not of correspondence with fact. Many philosophers speak critically of the 'correspondence theory' of truth, but it always seemed to me that, except in logic and mathematics, no other theory had any chance of being right.

I thought, also, as a consequence of my desire to preserve continuity with animal intelligence, that the importance of language, great as it is, has been over-emphasized. It seemed to me that belief and knowledge have pre-verbal forms, and that they cannot be rightly analysed if this is not realized.

When I first became interested in linguistic problems, I did not at all apprehend their difficulty and complexity. I had only the feeling that they were important, without at first knowing quite what they were. I do not pretend to have arrived at any completeness of knowledge in this sphere, but at any rate my thinking has gradually become more articulated, more definite, and more conscious of the problems involved.

Sixth. This brings me to the last of my initial prejudices, which has been perhaps the most important in all my thinking. This is concerned with method. My method invariably is to start from something vague but puzzling, something which seems indubitable but which I cannot express with any precision. I go through a process which is like that of first seeing something with the naked eye and then examining it through a microscope. I find that by fixity of attention divisions and distinctions appear where none at first was visible, just as through a microscope you can see the bacilli in impure water which without the microscope are not discernible. There are many who decry analysis, but it has seemed to me evident, as in the case of the impure water, that analysis gives new knowledge without destroying any of the previously existing knowledge. This applies not only to the structure of physical things, but quite as much to concepts. 'Knowledge', for example, as commonly used is a very imprecise term covering a number of different things and a number of stages from certainty to slight probability.

It seems to me that philosophical investigation, as far as I have experience of it, starts from that curious and unsatisfactory state of mind in which one feels complete certainty without being able to say what one is certain of. The process that results from prolonged attention is just like that of watching an object approaching through a thick fog: at first it is only a vague darkness, but as it approaches articulations appear and one discovers that it is a man or a woman, or a horse or a cow or what not. It seems to me that those who object to analysis would wish us to be content with the initial dark blur. Belief in the above process is my strongest and most unshakable prejudice as regards the methods of philosophical investigation.

(*My Philosophical Development*, London: Allen & Unwin; New York: Simon & Schuster, 1959.)

28

EPISTEMOLOGICAL PREMISSES

THEORY of knowledge is rendered difficult by the fact that it involves psychology, logic, and the physical sciences, with the result that confusions between different points of view are a constant danger. This danger is particularly acute in connection with the problem of our present chapter, which is that of determining the premisses of our knowledge from an epistemological point of view. And there is a further source of confusion in the fact that, as already noted, theory of knowledge itself may be conceived in two different ways. On the one hand, accepting as knowledge whatever science recognizes as such, we may ask: how have we acquired this knowledge, and how best can we analyse it into premisses and inferences? On the other hand, we may adopt the Cartesian standpoint, and seek to divide what passes for knowledge into more certain and less certain portions. These two inquiries are not so distinct as they might seem, for, since the forms of inference involved are not demonstrative, our premisses will have more certainty than our conclusions. But this fact only makes it the more difficult to avoid confusion between the two inquiries.

An epistemological premiss, which we shall now seek to define, must have three characteristics. It must be (*a*) a logical premiss, (*b*) a psychological premiss, and (*c*) true so far as we can ascertain. Concerning each of these something must be said.

(*a*) Given any systematic body of propositions, such as is contained in some science in which there are general laws, it is possible, usually in an indefinite number of ways, to pick out certain of the propositions as premisses, and deduce the remainder. In the Newtonian theory of the solar system, for example, we can take as premisses the law of gravitation together with the positions and velocities of the planets at a given moment. Any moment will do, and for the law of gravitation we can substitute Kepler's three laws. In conducting such analyses, the logician, as such, is indifferent to the truth or falsehood of the body of propositions concerned, provided they are mutually consistent (if they are not, he will have nothing to do with them). He will, for example, just as willingly consider an imaginary planetary system and a gravitational law other than that of the inverse square. Nor does he pretend that his premisses give the grounds for believing in their consequences, even when both are true. When we are considering grounds of belief, the law of gravitation is an inference, not a premiss.

The logician, in his search for premisses, has one purpose which is emphatically not shared by the epistemologist, namely, that he seeks a *minimum* set of premisses. A set of premisses is a minimum set, in relation to a given body of propositions, if from the whole set, but not from any part of the set, all the given body of propositions can be deduced. Usually many minimum sets exist; the logician prefers those that are shortest, and, among two equally short, the one that is simplest. But these preferences are merely aesthetic.

(*b*) A psychological premiss may be defined as a belief which is not caused by any other belief or beliefs. Psychologically, any belief may be considered to be inferred when it is caused by other beliefs, however invalid the inference may be for logic. The most obvious class of beliefs not caused by other beliefs are those that result directly from perception. These, however, are not the only beliefs that are psychological premisses. Others are required to produce our faith in deductive arguments. Perhaps induction also is based, psychologically, upon primitive beliefs. What others there may be I shall not at the moment inquire.

(*c*) Since we are concerned with theory of *knowledge*, not merely of *belief*, we cannot accept all psychological premisses as epistemological premisses, for two psychological premisses may contradict each other, and therefore not all are true. For example I may think 'there is a man coming downstairs', and the next moment I may realize that it is a reflection of myself in a mirror. For such reasons, psychological premisses must be subjected to analysis before being accepted as premisses for theory of knowledge. In this analysis we are as little sceptical as possible. We assume that perception *can* cause knowledge, although it *may* cause error if we are logically careless. Without this fundamental assumption, we should be reduced to complete scepticism as regards the empirical world. No arguments are logically possible either for or against complete scepticism, which must be admitted to be one among possible philosophies. It is, however, too short and simple to be interesting. I shall, therefore, without more ado, develop the opposite hypothesis, according to which beliefs caused by perception are to be accepted unless there are positive grounds for rejecting them.

Since we can never be completely certain that any given proposition is true, we can never be completely certain that it is an epistemological premiss, even when it possesses the other two defining properties and seems to us to be true. We shall attach different 'weights' (to use a term employed by Professor Reichenbach) to different propositions which we believe and which, if true, are epistemological premisses:

the greatest weight will be given to those of which we are most certain, and the least to those of which we are least certain. Where there is a logical conflict we shall sacrifice the less certain, unless a large number of these are opposed to a very small number of the more certain.

Owing to the absence of certainty, we shall not seek, like the logician, to reduce our premisses to a minimum. On the contrary, we shall be glad when a number of propositions which support one another can all be accepted as epistemological premisses, since this increases the probability of all of them. (I am not thinking of logical deducibility, but of inductive compatibility.)

Epistemological premisses are different according as they are momentary, individual, or social. Let us illustrate. I believe that $16^2 = 256$; at the moment, I believe this on grounds of memory, but probably at some time I did the sum, and I have convinced myself that the received rules of multiplication follow from the premisses of logic. Therefore taking my life as a whole, $16^2 = 256$ is inferred, not from memory, but from logic. In this case, if my logic is correct, there is no difference between the individual and the social premisses.

But now let us take the existence of the Straits of Magellan. Again, my momentary epistemological premiss is memory. But I have had, at various times, better reasons: maps, books of travel, etc. *My* reasons have been the assertions of others, whom I believed to be well-informed and honest. *Their* reasons, traced back, lead to percepts: Magellan, and others who have been in the region concerned when it was not foggy, saw what they took to be land and sea, and by dint of systematized inferences made maps. Treating the knowledge of mankind as one whole, it is the percepts of Magellan and other travellers that provide the epistemological premisses for belief in the Straits of Magellan. Writers who are interested in knowledge as a social phenomenon are apt to concentrate upon social epistemological premisses. For certain purposes this is legitimate, for others not. Social epistemological premisses are relevant in deciding whether to spend public money on a new telescope or an investigation of the Trobriand Islanders. Laboratory experiments aim at establishing new factual premisses which can be incorporated in the accepted system of human knowledge. But for the philosopher there are two prior questions: what reason (if any) have I for believing in the existence of other people? And what reason (if any) have I now for believing that I existed at certain past times, or, more generally, that my present beliefs concerning past times are more or less correct? For me now, only my momentary epistemological premisses are really premisses; the rest must be in some sense inferred. For me as opposed to others, my individual premisses are premisses, but the percepts of others are not. Only those who regard mankind as in some mystical sense a single entity possessed of a single persistent mind have a right to confine their epistemology to the consideration of *social* epistemological premisses.

In the light of these distinctions, let us consider possible definitions of empiricism. I think that the great majority of empiricists are *social* empiricists, a few are *individual* empiricists, and hardly any are *momentary* empiricists. What all empiricists have in common is emphasis upon *perceptive premisses*. We shall seek a definition of this term presently; for the moment I shall say only a few preliminary words.

Speaking psychologically, a 'perceptive premiss' may be defined as a belief caused, as immediately as possible, by a percept. If I believe there *will be* an eclipse because the astronomers say so, my belief is not a perceptive premiss; if I believe there *is* an eclipse because I see it, that is a perceptive premiss. But immediately difficulties arise. What astronomers call an eclipse is a public event, whereas what I am seeing may be due to a defect in my eye or my telescope. While, therefore, the belief 'there is an eclipse' may arise in me without conscious inference, this belief goes beyond the mere expression of what I see. Thus we are driven, in epistemology, to define 'perceptive premiss' more narrowly than would be necessary in psychology. We are driven to this because we want a 'perceptive premiss' to be something which there is never good reason to think false, or, what comes to the same thing, something so defined that two perceptive premisses cannot contradict each other.

Assuming 'perceptive premisses' to have been adequately defined, let us return to the definition of 'empiricism'. My momentary knowledge consists largely of memory, and my individual knowledge consists largely of testimony. But memory, when it is veridical, is related to a previous perceptive premiss, and testimony, when it is veridical, is related to someone else's perceptive premiss. Social empiricism takes these perceptive premisses of other times or other persons as *the* empirical premisses for what is now accepted, and thus evades the problems connected with memory and testimony. This is plainly illegitimate, since there is reason to believe that both memory and testimony sometimes deceive. I, now, can only arrive at the perceptive premisses of other times and other persons by an inference from memory and testimony. If I, now, am to have any reason to believe what I read yesterday in the Encyclopaedia, I must, now, find reason to trust my memory, and to believe, in suitable circumstances, what comes to me in the form of testimony. I must, that is to say, start from *momentary* epistemological premisses. To do anything else is to evade problems which it is part of the business of epistemology to consider.

It follows from the above considerations that epistemology cannot say: 'knowledge is wholly derivable from perceptive premisses together with the principles of demonstrative and probable inference'. Memory premisses, at least, must be added to perceptive premisses. What premisses, if any, must be added in order to make testimony admissible (with common-sense limitations), is a difficult question, which must be borne in mind, but need not be discussed at the moment. The paramount importance of perception, in any tenable form of empiricism, is causal. Memory, when veridical, is causally dependent upon a previous perception; testimony, when veridical, is causally dependent upon someone else's perception. We may say, therefore: 'all human knowledge of matters of fact is in part *caused* by perception'. But a principle of this sort is clearly one which can only be known by inference, if at all; it cannot be a premiss in epistemology. It is fairly clear that part of the *cause* of my believing in the Straits of Magellan is that certain people have seen them, but this is not the *ground* of my belief, since it has to be proved to me (or rather made probable) that such people have had such percepts. To me, their percepts are inferences, not premisses.

(*An Inquiry into Meaning and Truth*. London : Allen & Unwin; New York: W. W. Norton, 1940.)

PART VI

The Metaphysician

Since the beginning of Western Civilization philosophers have been vitally concerned with the enormous questions raised by metaphysics.

Few philosophers have, however, supplied even a brief glimpse of the vast problems to be explored. Perhaps Russell's most distinctive contribution to metaphysics is his novel view of 'Atomism'. While critics have taken him to task for his refusal to abandon this view, none has yet succeeded in finding convincing arguments against his logical atomism. The last of the three selections which follow is particularly searching and revelatory of Russell's fundamental approach.

29

MATERIALISM, PAST AND PRESENT

MATERIALISM as a theory of the nature of the world has had a curious history. Arising almost at the beginning of Greek philosophy, it has persisted down to our own time, in spite of the fact that very few eminent philosophers have advocated it. It has been associated with many scientific advances, and has seemed, in certain epochs, almost synonymous with a scientific outlook. Accusations of materialism have always been brought by the orthodox against their opponents, with the result that the less discriminating opponents have adopted materialism because they believed it to be an essential part of their opposition. At the present moment, the official creed of one of the largest States in the world is materialism, although hardly anyone in the learned world explicitly adheres to this theory. A system of thought which has such persistent vitality must be worth studying, in spite of the professional contempt which is poured on it by most professors of metaphysics.

Lange's *History of Materialism*, here re-issued in 'The International Library of Psychology, Philosophy, and Scientific Method', is a monumental work, of the highest value to all who wish to know what has been said by advocates of materialism, and why philosophers have in the main remained unconvinced. The first edition appeared in 1865, at the height of the period often described as 'The materialistic 'sixties'. The preface to the second edition is dated June 1873. The author died in 1875, before the reaction against materialism had made itself felt. Lange, while very sympathetic to materialism in its struggles with older dogmatic systems, was himself by no means a materialist. He is described by Professor Cohen, in the Preface to the Ninth Edition (1921), as an 'apostle of the Kantian view of the world', to which Professor Cohen himself adheres. The description is quite correct. Lange considers that materialism is unable to explain consciousness, and is refuted, on scientific grounds, by the psychology and physiology of sensation, which shows that the world studied by physics is a world dependent on our modes of perception, not a world existing independently on its own account.

It is a commonplace to object to materialism on ethical grounds, since it is supposed to have a deleterious effect on conduct. While energetically repelling many forms of this criticism, Lange nevertheless upholds it in the end, since he regards the economics of the Manchester school and the ruthlessness of modern competition as attributable to a materialistic outlook. This is perhaps the weakest part of his book, in spite of the fact that, unlike most German learned men, he had considerable experience of practical life. In 1861, at the age of 33, he resigned his position as a teacher, and became secretary of the Duisburg Chamber of Commerce. But his position became difficult owing to his radical opinions, which found vent in various directions. He edited a newspaper called *The Rhine and Ruhr Gazette*, and he wrote a book called *Die Arbeiterfrage in ihrer Bedeutung für Gegenwart und Zukunft*, which appeared in the same year as his *History of Materialism*. His industry was little short of miraculous, for in this same year he published yet another book, *Die Grundlegung der mathematischen Psychologie*—and all this without neglecting the newspaper or the Chamber of Commerce.

In the following year (1866) he went to Switzerland, where he again took up academic work, becoming Professor at Zurich in 1870, and returning to Germany in 1872 as Professor at Marburg. But his experiences in the world of industry and commerce undoubtedly helped to widen his outlook, and to give him an understanding, not always possessed by the learned, of the operation of theories when they pass out into the marketplace. He remarks that, in England, philosophers are often statesmen, and, what is still more extraordinary, statesmen are sometimes philosophers. He does not point out how often the mixture is damaging to both, making the statesman too theoretical and the philosopher too practical.

Lange's book is divided into two parts, one dealing with the times before Kant, the other with Kant and his successors. This division shows the very great importance which he attaches to the philosopher of Königsberg —an importance which, perhaps, may seem less as time goes on. Kant's system is intimately bound up with the state of the exact sciences in his day: Euclidean geometry gives the foundation of the transcendental aesthetic, and the Aristotelian syllogism gives the ground for the deduction of the categories. Now that geometry has become non-Euclidean and logic non-Aristotelian, Kant's arguments require restatement; to what extent this is possible, is still a moot question. To the present writer, the first half of Lange's book appears considerably better than the second, because it is less affected by the author's views on matters which are still undecided. In the periods before Kant, his critical judgment is extraordinarily sound. The account of Greek atomism, the analysis of Plato's influence for good and evil, are admirable. The combination of scientific materialism with theological orthodoxy in seventeenth-century England, and its contrast with the revolutionary materialism of eighteenth-century France, are set forth with a nice historical sense. But it is always a very difficult task to see one's own time in historical perspective. Apart from philosophical predilections, there is difficulty in disentangling what is important and permanent in the purely scientific work of one's own generation. The problems which occupied the men of science sixty years ago were very different from those of the present day, and it was impossible to know which of them would prove to be historically important.

On the question: what is true and what false in materialism? it is possible to speak with more learning and more complication than in former days, but it may be doubted whether any substantially new arguments have been invented since Greek times. Nevertheless, it may be profitable to attempt a survey of the position as it appears in the light of modern science.

The theory of Democritus was intelligible and simple. The world consisted of hard round atoms of various sizes, all falling, but the heavier atoms falling faster, so that they would occasionally impinge upon the lighter atoms. If the impact was not exactly in the line of centres, there would be a resultant sideways motion, which accounts for the fact that bodies do not move only in one direction. This view, of course, had to be modified for purely physical reasons, but the modifications were not important until we come to Descartes with his plenum and his doctrine of vortices. This showed that atomism is not an essential part of materialistic physics. Newton's followers introduced another modification, namely, action at a distance (which Newton himself still regarded as impossible). To this day the oscillation continues between atoms with action at a distance and a continuous medium (the aether) with continuous transmission of effects. Few physicists nowadays cling to either as a matter of principle; the only question is: which best explains observed phenomena? Both views have in common a belief in physical determinism, i.e. a belief that what happens in the world dealt with by physics happens according to laws such that, if we knew the whole state of the physical world during a finite time, however short, we could theoretically infer its state at any earlier or later time. This is the kernel of materialism from the standpoint of ethics, religion, sociology, etc., though not from the standpoint of metaphysics. If physical determinism is true—if, that is to say, everything that we commonly regard as the motion of matter is subject to laws of the above kind—then, although there may be a concurrent world of mind, all its manifestations in human and animal behaviour will be such as an ideally skilful physicist could calculate from purely physical data. Physics may still be unable to tell us anything about a man's thoughts, but it will be able to predict all that he will say and do. Under these circumstances, a man will be, for all practical purposes, an automaton, since his mental life can only be communicated to others or displayed in action by physical means. Even his thoughts can be inferred from physics, unless he is content never to give utterance to them.

This point of view resulted from Cartesianism, though most Cartesians attempted to escape from its consequences. Lamettrie, author of *L'homme machine*, justly claimed that he had derived his philosophy from Descartes. Descartes, who knew about the conservation of *vis viva*, but not about the conservation of momentum, endeavoured to safeguard human freedom by maintaining that the will could alter the direction of motion of the animal spirits, though not the amount of their motion. He did not, however, extend this freedom to animals, which he regarded as automata. Nowadays no one would dream of drawing such a distinction between men and animals. And even his immediate followers had to abandon his position on this point, owing to the discovery of the conservation of momentum, which showed that the quantity of motion in each direction must be constant. From that day to our own, many philosophers have advocated the theory of two parallel series, one mental and one physical, each subject to its own laws, and neither influencing the other. This theory has less plausibility in our time than it had formerly; but apart from the question of its truth, it is worth while to realize that it does not afford an escape from the more disagreeable consequences of materialism.

If there is parallelism between the physical and mental series, as this theory supposes, every physical law must have its psychological counterpart, and therefore psychology must be as rigidly deterministic as physics. There will be, so to speak, a dictionary, by which physical events can be translated into the concurrent mental events. Given this dictionary, the Laplacean calculator can, by physics alone, deduce the state of the material world at any given time, and discover from the dictionary what must be the corresponding state of the mental world. Clearly, the emancipation from physics which anti-materialists desire is not to be achieved along these lines.

There is, however, no good reason to accept the theory of psychophysical parallelism. The dualism of mind and matter is probably not ultimate, and the supposed impossibility of interaction rests upon nothing better than scholastic dogmas. To common sense it appears that our minds are affected by what we see and hear, and that, conversely, our bodies are affected by our volitions whenever we will to make any movement. There is no reason whatever to suppose that common sense is mistaken in this view, although, of course, there is great need of analysis as to what really takes place when we perceive or will.

Lange advances, quite justly, as an argument against materialism, the fact that we only know about matter through its appearances to us, which, according to materialism itself, are profoundly affected by our own physical organization. What we see depends not only upon what is there to be seen, but also upon the eye, the optic nerve, and the brain. But the eye, the optic nerve, and the brain are only known through being seen by the physiologist. In this way materialism is driven back to sensationalism. If it is to escape sensationalism, it must abandon the empirical scientific method, substituting for it the dogmatism of an *a priori* meta-physic, which professes to know what is behind appearances. Historically, we may regard materialism as a system of dogma set up to combat orthodox dogma. As a rule, the materialistic dogma has not been set up by men who loved dogma, but by men who felt that nothing less definite would enable them to fight the dogmas they disliked. They were in the position of men who raise armies to enforce peace. Accordingly we find that, as ancient orthodoxies disintegrate, materialism more and more gives way to scepti-cism. At the present day, the chief protagonists of materialism are certain men of science in America and certain politicians in Russia, because it is in those two countries that traditional theology is still powerful.

The two dogmas that constitute the essence of materialism are: First, the sole reality of matter; secondly, the reign of law. The belief that matter alone is real will not survive the sceptical arguments derived from the physiological mechanism of sensation. But it has received recently another blow, from the quarter whence it was least to be expected, namely, from physics. The theory of relativity, by merging time into space-time, has damaged the traditional notion of substance more than all the arguments of philosophers. Matter, for common sense, is something which persists in time and moves in space. But for modern relativity-physics this view is no longer tenable. A piece of matter has become, not a persistent thing with varying states, but a system of inter-related events. The old solidity is gone, and with it the characteristics that, to the materialist, made matter seem more real than fleeting thoughts. Nothing is permanent, nothing endures; the prejudice that the real is the persistent must be abandoned.

The notion of substance has not been regarded by philosophers as metaphysically valid since the time of Hume and Kant, but it persisted in the practice of physics. Its defeat, within physics, by the abandonment of a single cosmic time affords a purely scientific argument against the older type of materialism, which utilized the belief that substance is what persists through time.

The reign of law raises more difficult and also more important questions. The outlook with which the phrase 'reign of law' seems to belong most naturally is that of Newton, especially as developed by his disciples. Belief in the reign of law is often combined with strict theological ortho-doxy, but in that case human volitions are excepted, at any rate in certain cases. The reign of law only becomes part of the materialistic outlook when it is believed to have no exceptions, not even human volitions. It is in this form that we have to consider it. It will be necessary first to define the phrase, and then to inquire what ground there is for believing it applicable to the world.

The definition of the reign of law is by no means so easy as seems often to be supposed. The idea is derived from such instances as the law of gravitation in the solar system, where a simple formula enables us to predict the motions of the planets and their satellites. But this instance is deceptive in several respects. In the first place, there is no reason to suppose that the laws in other cases are equally simple. In the second place, it turns out that the Newtonian form of the law of gravitation is only approximate, and that the exact law is enormously more complicated. In the third place, the geography (if one may use such a term) of the solar system is amazingly schematic. To a first approximation, it may be regarded as consisting of a small number of mass-points, whose individual motions are easily observable. This point of view is not adequate for dealing with such matters as tides, but it suffices for the deduction of Kepler's laws from the law of gravitation, which was Newton's most spectacular achievement. It is obviously a very different matter to obtain laws applicable to individual electrons and protons, because of the greater geographical complexity involved. For these reasons, among others, it is rash to regard the Newtonian astronomy as typical of what is to be expected in physics.

The least that can be meant by the reign of law is this: given any phenomenon, there exists some formula of finite complexity such that, from a sufficient (finite) number of data at other times the phenomenon in question can be calculated. In practice, the 'other times' will usually be earlier times, but this is not always the case—for example, in speculations as to the geological history of the earth or the origin of the solar system. Theoretically, it should be irrelevant whether the 'other times' are earlier or later than that of the phenomenon concerned.

In elucidation of the above definition, there are one or two observations to be made. The reason for saying that the formula must be of finite complexity is that otherwise nothing is asserted beyond a logical truism. By admitting formulae of infinite complexity, any series of events whatever could be brought within the compass of a single law, and therefore we should assert nothing in asserting the reign of law. The reason for insisting that the number of data required must be finite is similar, but is reinforced by another, namely, that we cannot manipulate an infinite number of data, and could therefore never discover evidence either for or against a law which required them.

There is a further point which should be borne in mind. None of our observations is completely accurate; there is always a margin of error. Consequently we can never prove that events obey *exactly* any law which is found to work within the margin of error, nor, conversely, need we trouble ourselves about inaccuracies which must remain below this margin. For example: it is always assumed in physics that continuous functions can be differentiated, although, as a matter of pure mathematics, this is known to be only sometimes the case. There is no harm in this from the physicist's standpoint, because, given any continuous function which cannot be differentiated, there will always be another which can be differentiated, and which differs from the first by less than the probable error in our observations. Approximations are all that we can achieve, and therefore all that we need attempt.

The question now arises: Is there any reason to believe in the reign of law in the above sense? In the world of pure physics there are a number of fundamental occurrences which cannot at present be reduced to law. No one knows why some atoms of a radio-active element disintegrate while others do not; we know statistical averages, but what goes on in the individual atom is completely obscure. Again, the spectrum of an element is caused by electrons jumping from one possible orbit to another. We know a great deal about the possible orbits, and about what happens when a jump takes place, and about the proportion that choose one possible jump as compared to those that choose another. But we do not know what (if anything) decides the particular moment at which an electron jumps, or the particular jump that it sees fit to make when several are possible. Here, again, it is statistical averages that we know. It is therefore open to anybody to say that, while averages are subject to law, the actions of individual electrons have a certain range of caprice, within which there is no evidence for the reign of law. A man who maintained such a view dogmatically would be very rash, since tomorrow he might be refuted by some new discovery. But a man who merely maintains that, in the present state of physics, it is a possibility to be borne in mind, is displaying a proper scientific caution. Thus even within the pure physics of inorganic matter the reign of law cannot be asserted to be indubitably universal.

This doubt cannot but be increased when we pass on to biology and psychology. I do not mean that there is any positive evidence against the reign of law in this region; I mean only that the evidence in its favour is less strong, because fewer laws are known, and prediction is as yet only possible within very narrow limits. The discovery of quanta in physics shows how rash it is to dogmatize as to the further surprises which even an advanced science may have in store for us; and psychology is by no means an advanced science.

In the present condition of human knowledge, therefore, either to assert or to deny the universal reign of law is a mark of prejudice; the rational man will regard the question as open. All perennial controversies, such as that between determinists and believers in free will, spring from a conflict between opposing passions, both widespread, but one stronger in one man and the other in another. In this case, the conflict is between the passion for power and the passion for safety, because if the external world behaves according to law we can adapt ourselves to it. We desire the reign of law for the sake of safety, and freedom for the sake of power. Common sense assumes that law governs inanimate nature and one's neighbours, while freedom is reserved for oneself. In this way both passions are gratified to the full. But philosophy demands some more subtle reconciliation, and is therefore never weary of inventing new ways of combining freedom with determination. The sceptic can merely observe this struggle with detachment, and he is fortunate if his detachment does not degenerate into cynicism.

It has always been customary, and since the time of Kant it has been thought even respectable, to invoke moral considerations in support of freedom. While, however, the sceptic has a good case as against the dogmatic believer in the universal reign of law, he is not likely to admit the opposite claim that a dogmatic disbelief in this principle is helpful to morals. If he is a sceptic worthy of the name, he will begin by saying that no one knows what beliefs are helpful to morals, or even whether beliefs have any noticeable influence on conduct. But if he is a student of history, he will observe that, as a practical postulate, belief in natural law has borne good fruit by producing such knowledge as we possess, whereas its rejection has been associated with intolerance and obscurantism. He will say that, though possibly there may be phenomena not reducible to law, this is a mere speculative possibility, of which it is unnecessary to take account in the actual practice of science, since science can only advance by the discovery of laws, and where (if anywhere) there are no laws, there is also no possible science.

In our own time, the old battle of materialism persists chiefly in biology and physiology. Some men of science maintain that the phenomena of living organisms cannot be explained solely in terms of chemistry and physics; others maintain that such explanation is always theoretically possible. Professor J. S. Haldane may be regarded, in this country, as the leading exponent of the former view; in Germany it is associated with Driesch. One of the most effective champions of the mechanistic view was Jacques Loeb, who showed (*inter alia*) that a sea-urchin could have a pin for its father, and afterwards extended this result to animals much higher in the scale. The controversy may be expected to last for a long time, since, even if the mechanists are in the right, they are not likely soon to find explanations of all vital phenomena of the sort that their theory postulates. It will be a severe blow to the vitalists when protoplasm is manufactured in the laboratory, but they will probably take refuge in saying that their theories only apply to multi-cellular organisms. Later, they will confine vitalism to vertebrates, then to mammals, then to men, and last of all to white men—or perhaps it will be yellow men by that time. Ordinary scientific probability suggests, however, that the sphere of mechanistic explanation in regard to vital phenomena is likely to be indefinitely extended by the progress of biological knowledge.

Psychology, which might have been expected to be more opposed to materialism than any other science, has, on the contrary, shown decided leanings in that direction. The behaviourist school maintains that psychology should only concern itself with what can be seen by external observation, and denies totally that introspection is an independent source of scientific knowledge. This view would make all the phenomena with which psychology is concerned physical phenomena, thereby conceding to materialism the utmost of its claims. Apart, however, from other difficulties, there is the difficulty already noted, that the data of physics are sensations, which are infected with the subjectivity of the observer. Physics seeks to discover material occurrences not dependent upon the physiological and psychical peculiarities of the observer. But its facts are only discovered by means of observers, and therefore only afford data for physics in so far as means exist of eliminating the observer's contribution to the phenomenon. This elimination is not an easy matter. It might be argued, on philosophical grounds, that it is impossible, and this is no doubt true if *complete* elimination is meant. But to a certain extent the problem can be treated scientifically, without raising metaphysical issues. It is then found that subjectivity is of three kinds, physical, physiological, and psychical. The first of these is satisfactorily dealt with by the theory of relativity: the method of tensors is its complete theoretical solution. The second and third are perhaps not really distinct; they can be dealt with in so far as one man's perceptions differ from another's, but it is difficult to see any method of eliminating subjective elements in which all men are alike.

There is one other respect in which psychology has been tending towards the point of view advocated by materialists. We used to hear much of such supposed faculties as 'consciousness', 'thought', and 'reason'. Many modern psychologists, following William James, are inclined to dismiss 'consciousness' as a term destitute of any clear meaning. 'Thought' and 'reason', meanwhile, are found to be analogous to processes of learning among animals, which are ultimately reducible to the law of habit. All this, of course, is still controversial; but if it should prove correct, the psychological difficulties of materialism will be greatly diminished.

The conclusion of the above discussion would seem to be that, as a practical maxim of scientific method, materialism may be accepted if it means that the goal of every science is to be merged in physics. But it must be added that physics itself is not materialistic in the old sense, since it no longer assumes matter as permanent substance. And it must also be remembered that there is no good reason to suppose materialism metaphysically true: it is a point of view which has hitherto proved useful in research, and is likely to continue useful wherever new scientific laws are being discovered, but which may well not cover the whole field, and cannot be regarded as definitely true without a wholly unwarranted dogmatism.

(Introduction to *A History of Materialism*, by F. A. Lange. London: Lund Humphries, 1925; New York: The Humanities Press, 1950.)

30

LANGUAGE AND METAPHYSICS

IN the present chapter I propose to consider whether anything, and, if so, what, can be inferred from the structure of language as to the structure of the world. There has been a tendency, especially among logical positivists, to treat language as an independent realm, which can be studied without regard to non-linguistic occurrences. To some extent, and in a limited field, this separation of language from other facts is possible; the detached study of logical syntax has undoubtedly yielded valuable results. But I think it is easy to exaggerate what can be achieved by syntax alone. There is, I think, a discoverable relation between the structure of sentences and the structure of the occurrences to which the sentences refer. I do not think the structure of non-verbal facts is wholly unknowable, and I believe that, with sufficient caution, the properties of language may help us to understand the structure of the world.

With regard to the relation of words to non-verbal facts, most philosophers can be divided into three broad types:

A. Those who infer properties of the world from properties of language. These are a very distinguished party; they include Parmenides, Plato, Spinoza, Leibniz, Hegel, and Bradley.

B. Those who maintain that knowledge is only of words. Among these are the Nominalists and some of the Logical Positivists.

C. Those who maintain that there is knowledge not expressible in words, and use words to tell us what this knowledge is. These include the mystics, Bergson and Wittgenstein; also certain aspects of Hegel and Bradley.

Of these three parties, the third can be dismissed as self-contradictory. The second comes to grief on the empirical fact that we can know what words occur in a sentence, and that this is not a verbal fact, although it is indispensable to the verbalists. If, therefore, we are confined to the above three alternatives, we must make the best of the first.

We may divide our problem into two parts: first, what is implied by the correspondence theory of truth, in the measure in which we have accepted this theory? Second, is there anything in the world corresponding to the distinction between different parts of speech, as this appears in a logical language?

As regards 'correspondence', we have been led to the belief that, when a proposition is true, it is true in virtue of one or more occurrences which are called its 'verifiers'. If it is a proposition containing no variable, it cannot have more than one verifier. We may confine ourselves to this case, since it involves the whole of the problem with which we are concerned. We have thus to inquire whether, given a sentence (supposed true) which contains no variable, we can infer anything as to the structure of the verifier from that of the sentence. In this inquiry we shall presuppose a logical language.

Consider first a group of sentences which all contain a certain name (or a synonym for it). These sentences all have something in common. Can we say that their verifiers also have something in common?

Here we must distinguish according to the kind of name concerned. If W is a complete group of qualities, such as we considered in the last chapter, and we form a number of judgements of perception, such as 'W is red', 'W is round', 'W is bright', etc., these all have one single verifier, namely W. But if I make a number of true statements concerning a given shade of colour C, they all have different verifiers. These all have a common part C, just as the statements have a common part 'C'. It will be seen that here, as in the last chapter, we are led to a view which, syntactically, is scarcely distinguishable from the subject-predicate view, from which it differs only in that it regards the 'subject' as a bundle of compresent qualities. We may state what has just been said as follows: given a number of subject-predicate sentences expressing judgements of perception, such as 'this is red', if they all have the same subject they all have the same verifier, which is what the subject designates; if they all have the same predicate, the verifiers all have a common part, which is what the predicate designates.

This theory is not applicable to such a sentence as 'A is to the left of B', where 'A' and 'B' are names for two parts of my visual field. So far as 'A' and 'B' are concerned, we considered this sentence sufficiently in the last chapter. What I now wish to examine is the question: what, if anything, is common to the verifiers of a number of different sentences of the form 'A is to the left of B'?

The question involved is the old question of 'universals'. We might have investigated this question in connection with predicates—say 'red is a colour', or 'high C is a sound'. But since we have explained the more apparently obvious subject-predicate sentences—e.g. 'this is red'—as really not subject-predicate sentences, we shall find it more convenient to discuss 'universals' in connection with relations.

Sentences—except object-words used in an exclamatory manner— require words other than names. Such words, generically, we call 'relation-

words', including predicates as words for monadic relations. The definition, as explained in Chapter VI, is syntactical: a 'name' is a word which
can occur significantly in an atomic sentence of any form; a 'relation-
word' is one which can occur in some atomic sentences, but only in such
as contain the appropriate number of names.

It is generally agreed that language requires relation-words; the question
at issue is: 'What does this imply as regards the verifiers of sentences?'
A 'universal' may be defined as 'the meaning (if any) of a relation-word'.
Such words as 'if' and 'or' have no meaning in isolation, and it may be
that the same is true of relation-words.

It may be suggested (erroneously, as I think and shall try to prove)
that we need not assume universals, but only a set of stimuli to the making
of one of a set of similar noises. The matter is, however, not quite straightforward. A defender of universals, if attacked, might begin in this way:
'You say that two cats, because they are similar, stimulate the utterance
of two similar noises which are both instances of the word "cat". But the
cats must be *really* similar to each other, and so must the noises. And if
they are *really* similar, it is impossible that "similarity" should be just a
word. It is a word which you utter on certain occasions, namely, when
there *is* similarity. Your tricks and devices', he will say, 'may seem to
dispose of other universals, but only by putting all the work on to this
one remaining universal, similarity; of that you cannot get rid, and therefore you might as well admit all the rest.'

The question of universals is difficult, not only to decide, but to formulate. Let us consider 'A is to the left of B'. Places in the momentary visual
field, as we have seen, are absolute, and are defined by relation to the
centre of the field of vision. They may be defined by the two relations
right-and-left, up-and-down; these relations, at any rate, suffice for
topological purposes. In order to study momentary visual space, it is
necessary to keep the eyes motionless and attend to things near the peri-
phery as well as in the centre of the field of vision. If we are not deliberately
keeping our eyes motionless, we shall look directly at whatever we notice;
the natural way to examine a series of places is to look at each in turn.
But if we want to study what we can see at one moment, this method
will not do, since a given physical object, as a visual datum, is different
when it is seen directly and when it is far from the centre of the field. In
fact, however, this makes very little difference. We cannot escape from
the fact that visual positions form a two-dimensional series, and that such
series demand dyadic asymmetrical relations. The view we take as to
colours makes no difference in this respect.

It seems that there is no escape from admitting relations as parts of
the non-linguistic constitution of the world; similarity, and perhaps also
asymmetrical relations, cannot be explained away, like 'or' and 'not', as
belonging only to speech. Such words as 'before' and 'above', just as

truly as proper names, 'mean' something which occurs in objects of perception. It follows that there is a valid form of analysis which is not that of whole and part. We can perceive A-before-B as a whole, but if we perceived it *only* as a whole we should not know whether we had seen it or B-before-A. The whole-and-part analysis of the datum A-before-B yields only A and B, and leaves out 'before'. In a logical language, therefore, there will be *some* distinctions of parts of speech which correspond to objective distinctions.

Let us examine once more the question whether asymmetrical relations are needed as well as similarity; and let us take, for the purpose, 'A is above B', where 'A' and 'B' are proper names of events. We shall suppose that we perceive that A is above B. Now it is clear, to begin with a trivial point, that we do not need the word 'below' as well as the word 'above'; either alone suffices. I shall therefore assume that our language contains no word 'below'. The whole percept, A-above-B, resembles other percepts C-above-D, E-above F, etc., in a manner which makes us call them all facts of vertical order. So far, we do not need a concept 'above'; we may have merely a group of similar occurrences, all called 'vertical orders', i.e. all causing a noise similar to 'above'. So far, we can do with only similarity.

But now we must consider asymmetry. When you say 'A is above B', how does your hearer know that you have not said 'B is above A'? In exactly the same way as *you* know that A is above B; he perceives that the noise 'A' precedes the noise 'B'.

Thus the vital matter is the distinction between A-first-and-then-B, B-first-and-then-A; or, in writing, between AB and BA. Consider, then, the two following shapes: AB and BA. I want to make it clear that I am speaking of just these, not of others like them. Let S_1 be the proper name of the first shape, S_2 that of the second; let A_1, A_2 be the proper names of the two A's, and B_1, B_2 of the two B's. Then S_1, S_2 each consist of two parts, and one part of S_1 is closely similar to one part of S_2, while the other part is closely similar to the other part. Moreover, the ordering relation is the same in both cases. Nevertheless, the two wholes are not very similar. Perhaps asymmetry could be explained in this way: given a number of A's and a number of B's, arranged in pairs, the resulting wholes fall into two classes, members of the same class being closely similar to each other, while members of different classes are very dissimilar. If we give the proper names S_3, S_4 to the following two shapes: AB and BA, then it is obvious that S_1 and S_3 are very similar, and so are S_2 and S_4, but S_1 and S_3 are not very similar to S_2 and S_4. (Observe that, in describing S_1 and S_2, we shall have to say: S_1 consists of A_1 before B_1, S_2 consists of B_2 before A_2.) Perhaps in this way it is possible to explain asymmetry in terms of similarity, though the explanation is not very satisfactory.

Assuming that we can, in the above manner or in some other, get rid of all universals except similarity, it remains to be considered whether similarity itself could be explained away.

We will consider this in the simplest possible case. Two patches of red (not necessarily of exactly the same shade) are similar, and so are two instances of the word 'red'. Let us suppose that we are being shown a number of coloured discs and asked to name their colours—say in a test for colour-blindness. We are shown two red discs in succession, and each time we say 'red'. We have been saying that, in the primary language, similar stimuli produce similar reactions; our theory of meaning has been based on this. In our case, the two discs are similar, and the two utterances of the word 'red' are similar. Are we saying the *same* thing about the discs and about the utterances when we say the discs are similar and when we say the utterances are similar, or are we only saying similar things? In the former case, similarity is a true universal; in the latter case, not. The difficulty, in the latter case, is the endless regress; but are we sure that this difficulty is inseparable? We shall say, if we adopt this alternative: if A and B are perceived to be similar, and C and D are also perceived to be similar, that means that AB is a whole of a certain kind and CD is a whole of the same kind; i.e. since we do not want to define the kind by a universal, AB and CD are *similar* wholes. I do not see how we are to avoid an endless regress of the vicious kind if we attempt to explain similarity in this way.

I conclude, therefore, though with hesitation, that there are universals, and not merely general words. Similarity, at least, will have to be admitted; and in that case it seems hardly worth while to adopt elaborate devices for the exclusion of other universals.

It should be observed that the above argument only proves the necessity of the word 'similar', not of the word 'similarity'.

Some propositions containing the word 'similarity' can be replaced by equivalent propositions containing the word 'similar', while others cannot. These latter need not be admitted. Suppose, for example, I say 'similarity exists'. If 'exists' means what it does when I say 'the President of the United States exists', my statement is nonsense. What I can mean may, to begin with, be expressed in the statement: 'There are occurrences which require for their verbal description sentences of the form "*a* is similar to *b*".' But this linguistic fact seems to imply a fact about the occurrences described, namely the sort of fact that is asserted when I say '*a* is similar to *b*'. When I say 'similarity exists', it is this fact about the world, not a fact about language, that I mean to assert. The word 'yellow' is necessary because there are yellow things; the word 'similar' is necessary because there are pairs of similar things. And the similarity of two things is as truly a non-linguistic fact as the yellowness of one thing.

We have arrived, in this chapter, at a result which has been, in a sense, the goal of all our discussions. The result I have in mind is this: that complete metaphysical agnosticism is not compatible with the maintenance of linguistic propositions. Some modern philosophers hold that we know much about language, but nothing about anything else. This view forgets that language is an empirical phenomenon like another, and that a man who is metaphysically agnostic must deny that he knows when he uses a word. For my part, I believe that, partly by means of the study of syntax, we can arrive at considerable knowledge concerning the structure of the world.

> (*An Inquiry into Meaning and Truth*, London: Allen & Unwin; New York: W. W. Norton, 1940.)

31

THE RETREAT FROM PYTHAGORAS

M Y philosophical development, since the early years of the present century, may be broadly described as a gradual retreat from Pythagoras. The Pythagoreans had a peculiar form of mysticism which was bound up with mathematics. This form of mysticism greatly affected Plato and had, I think, more influence upon him than is generally acknowledged. I had, for a time, a very similar outlook and found in the nature of mathematical logic, as I then supposed its nature to be, something profoundly satisfying in some important emotional respects.

As a boy, my interest in mathematics was more simple and ordinary: it had more affinity with Thales than with Pythagoras. I was delighted when I found things in the real world obeying mathematical laws. I liked the lever and the pulley and the fact that falling bodies describe parabolas. Although I could not play billiards, I liked the mathematical theory of how billiard balls behave. On one occasion, when I had a new tutor, I spun a penny and he said, 'Why does the penny spin?' I replied, 'Because I make a couple with my fingers'. He was surprised and remarked, 'What do you know about couples?' I replied airily, 'Oh, I know all about couples'. When, on one occasion, I had to mark the tennis court myself, I used the theorem of Pythagoras to make sure that the lines were at right angles with each other. An uncle of mine took me to call on Tyndall, the eminent physicist. While they were talking to each other, I had to find my own amusement. I got hold of two walking-sticks, each with a crook. I balanced them on one finger, inclining them in opposite directions so that they crossed each other at a certain point. Tyndall looked round and asked what I was doing. I replied that I was thinking of a practical way of determining the centre of gravity, because the centre of gravity of each stick must be vertically below my finger and therefore at the point where the sticks crossed each other. Presumably in consequence of this remark, Tyndall gave me one of his books, *The Forms of Water*. I hoped, at that time, that all science could become mathematical, including psychology. The parallelogram of forces shows that a body acted on by two forces simultaneously will pursue a middle course, inclining more towards the stronger force. I hoped that there might be a similar 'parallelogram of motives'—a foolish idea, since a man who comes to a fork in the road and is equally attracted to both roads, does not go across the fields between them. Science had not then arrived at the 'all-or-nothing principle' of which the importance was only discovered during the present century. I thought, when I was young, that two divergent attractions would lead to a Whig compromise, whereas it has appeared since that very often one of them prevails completely. This has justified Dr Johnson in the opinion that the Devil, not the Almighty, was the first Whig.

My interest in the applications of mathematics was gradually replaced by an interest in the principles upon which mathematics is based. This change came about through a wish to refute mathematical scepticism. A great deal of the argumentation that I had been told to accept was obviously fallacious, and I read whatever books I could find that seemed to offer a firmer foundation for mathematical beliefs. This kind of research led me gradually further and further from applied mathematics into more and more abstract regions, and finally into mathematical logic. I came to think of mathematics, not primarily as a tool for understanding and manipulating the sensible world, but as an abstract edifice subsisting in a Platonic heaven and only reaching the world of sense in an impure and degraded form. My general outlook, in the early years of this century, was profoundly ascetic. I disliked the real world and sought refuge in a timeless world, without change or decay or the will-o'-the-wisp of progress. Although this outlook was very serious and sincere, I sometimes expressed it in a frivolous manner. My brother-in-law, Logan Pearsall Smith, had a set of questions that he used to ask people. One of them was, 'What do you particularly like?' I replied, 'Mathematics and the sea, and theology and heraldry, the two former because they are inhuman, the two latter because they are absurd'. This answer, however, took the form that it did from a desire to win the approval of the questioner.

My attitude to mathematics at this time was expressed in an article called 'The Study of Mathematics', which was printed in *The New Quarterly* in 1907, and reprinted in *Philosophical Essays* (1910). Some quotations from this essay illustrate what I then felt:

'Mathematics, rightly viewed, possesses not only truth, but supreme beauty—a beauty cold and austere, like that of sculpture, without appeal to any part of our weaker nature, without the gorgeous trappings of painting or music, yet sublimely pure, and capable of a stern perfection such as only the greatest art can show. The true spirit of delight, the exaltation, the sense of being more than man, which is the touchstone of the highest excellence, is to be found in mathematics as surely as in poetry. What is best in mathematics deserves not merely to be learnt as a task, but to be assimilated as a part of daily thought, and brought again and again before the mind with ever-renewed encouragement. Real life is, to most men, a long second-best, a perpetual compromise between the ideal and the possible; but the world of pure reason knows no compromise, no practical limitations, no barrier to the creative activity embodying in splendid edifices the passionate aspiration after the perfect from which all great work springs. Remote from human passions, remote even from the pitiful facts of nature, the generations have gradually created an ordered cosmos, where pure thought can dwell as in its natural home, and where one, at least, of our nobler impulses can escape from the dreary exile of the actual world.'

'The contemplation of what is non-human, the discovery that our minds are capable of dealing with material not created by them, above all, the realization that beauty belongs to the outer world as to the inner, are the chief means of overcoming the terrible sense of impotence, of weakness, of exile amid hostile powers, which is too apt to result from acknowledging the all-but omnipotence of alien forces. To reconcile us, by the exhibition of its awful beauty, to the reign of Fate—which is merely the literary personification of these forces—is the task of tragedy. But mathematics takes us still further from what is human, into the region of absolute necessity, to which not only the actual world, but every possible world must conform; and even here it builds a habitation, or rather finds a habitation eternally standing, where our ideals are fully satisfied and our best hopes are not thwarted.'

'Too often it is said that there is no absolute truth but only opinion and private judgment; that each of us is conditioned, in his view of the world, by his own peculiarities, his own taste and bias; that there is no external kingdom of truth to which, by patience, by discipline, we may at last obtain admittance, but only truth for me, for you, for every separate person. By this habit of mind one of the chief ends of human effort is denied, and the supreme virtue of candour, of fearless acknowledgment of what is, disappears from our moral vision.'

'In a world so full of evil and suffering, retirement into the cloister of contemplation, to the enjoyment of delights which, however noble, must always be for the few only, cannot but appear as a somewhat selfish refusal to share the burden imposed upon others by accidents in which justice plays no part. Have any of us the right, we ask, to withdraw from present evils, to leave our fellow-men unaided, while we live a life which, though arduous and austere, is yet plainly good in its own nature?'

All this, though I still remember the pleasure of believing it, has come to seem to me largely nonsense, partly for technical reasons and partly from a change in my general outlook upon the world. Mathematics has ceased to seem to me non-human in its subject-matter. I have come to believe, though very reluctantly, that it consists of tautologies. I fear that, to a mind of sufficient intellectual power, the whole of mathematics would appear trivial, as trivial as the statement that a four-footed animal is an animal. I think that the timelessness of mathematics has none of the sublimity that it once seemed to me to have, but consists merely in the fact that the pure mathematician is not talking about time. I cannot any longer find any mystical satisfaction in the contemplation of mathematical truth.

The aesthetic pleasure to be derived from an elegant piece of mathematical reasoning remains. But here, too, there were disappointments. The solution of the contradictions mentioned in an earlier chapter seemed to be only possible by adopting theories which might be true but were not beautiful. I felt about the contradictions much as an earnest Catholic must feel about wicked Popes. And the splendid certainty which I had always hoped to find in mathematics was lost in a bewildering maze. All this would have made me sad but for the fact that the ascetic mood had begun to fade. It had had so strong a hold upon me that Dante's *Vita Nuova* appeared to me psychologically quite natural, and its strange symbolism appealed to me as emotionally satisfying. But this mood began to pass, and was finally dispelled by the First World War.

One effect of that War was to make it impossible for me to go on living in a world of abstraction. I used to watch young men embarking in troop trains to be slaughtered on the Somme because generals were stupid. I felt an aching compassion for these young men, and found myself united to the actual world in a strange marriage of pain. All the high-flown thoughts that I had had about the abstract world of ideas seemed to me thin and rather trivial in view of the vast suffering that surrounded me. The non-human world remained as an occasional refuge, but not as a country in which to build one's permanent habitation.

In this change of mood, something was lost, though something also was gained. What was lost was the hope of finding perfection and finality and certainty. What was gained was a new submission to some truths which were to me repugnant. My abandonment of former beliefs was, however, never complete. Some things remained with me, and still remain: I still think that truth depends upon a relation to fact, and that facts in general are non-human; I still think that man is cosmically unimportant, and that a Being, if there were one, who could view the universe impartially, without the bias of *here* and *now*, would hardly mention man, except perhaps in a footnote near the end of the volume; but I no longer have the wish to thrust out human elements from regions where they belong; I have no longer the feeling that intellect is superior to sense, and that only Plato's world of ideas gives access to the 'real' world. I used to think of sense, and of thought which is built on sense, as a prison from which we can be freed by thought which is emancipated from sense. I now have no such feelings. I think of sense, and of thoughts built on sense, as windows, not as prison bars. I think that we can, however imperfectly, mirror the world, like Leibniz's monads; and I think it is the duty of the philosopher to make himself as undistorting a mirror as he can. But it is also his duty to recognize such distortions as are inevitable from our very nature. Of these, the most fundamental is that we view the world from the point of view of the *here* and *now*, not with that large impartiality which theists attribute to the Deity. To achieve such impartiality is impossible for us, but we can travel a certain distance towards it. To show the road to this end is the supreme duty of the philosopher.

(*My Philosophical Development*, London: Allen & Unwin; New York: Simon & Schuster, 1959.)

PART VII

Historian of Philosophy

'Many histories of philosophy exist and I should not wish to add one to their number', wrote Russell in the preface to his own *A History of Western Philosophy*, but he wrote that monumental survey and followed it by the more recent, more current, *Wisdom of the West*. In both of these volumes and in other essays in the field, he not only ably expounds what each philosopher thought but also exhibits what a leading philosopher thinks of each philosopher reviewed.

Historians of philosophy in the past have been prone to make philosophy even more dull in its historical setting than it already appeared in its technical attire. Russell's works succeed in showing that philosophy can be both interesting and instructive to the general reader.

32

PHILOSOPHY IN THE TWENTIETH CENTURY

EVER since the end of the Middle Ages philosophy has steadily declined in social and political importance. William of Ockham, one of the greatest of medieval philosophers, was hired by the Kaiser to write pamphlets against the Pope; in those days many burning questions were bound up with disputes in the schools. The advances of philosophy in the seventeenth century were more or less connected with political opposition to the Catholic Church; Malebranche, it is true, was a priest, but priests are not now allowed to accept his philosophy. The disciples of Locke in eighteenth-century France, and the Benthamites in nineteenth-century England, were for the most part extreme Radicals in politics, and created the modern bourgeois liberal outlook. But the correlation between philosophical and political opinions grows less definite as we advance. Hume was a Tory in politics, though an extreme Radical in philosophy. Only in Russia, which remained medieval till the revolution, has any clear connection of philosophy and politics survived. Bolsheviks are materialists, while Whites are idealists. In Tibet the connection is even closer; the second official in the State is called the 'metaphysician in chief'. Elsewhere philosophy is no longer held in such high esteem.

Academic philosophy, throughout the twentieth century, has been mainly divided into three groups. The first consists of the adherents of the classical German philosophy, usually Kant, but sometimes Hegel. The second consists of the pragmatists and Bergson. The third consists of those who attach themselves to the sciences, believing that philosophy has no special brand of truth and no peculiar method of arriving at it; these men, for convenience, may be called realists, though in fact there are many among them to whom this name is not strictly applicable. The distinction between the different schools is not sharp, and individuals belong partly to one, partly to another. William James may be regarded as almost the founder of both realism and pragmatism. Dr Whitehead's recent books employ the methods of realists in defence of a more or less Bergsonian metaphysic. Many philosophers, not without a considerable show of reason, regard Einstein's doctrines as affording a scientific basis for Kant's belief in the subjectivity of time and space. The distinctions in fact are thus less clear than the distinctions in logic. Nevertheless the distinctions in logic are useful as affording a framework for the classification of opinions.

German idealism, throughout the twentieth century, has been on the defensive. The new books that have been recognized as important by others than professors have represented newer schools, and a person who judged by book reviews might imagine that these schools had now the upper hand. But in fact most teachers of philosophy, in Germany, France, and Great Britain, though perhaps not America, still adhere to the classical tradition. It is certainly much easier for a young man to get a post if he belongs to this party than if he does not. Its opponents made an attempt to show that it shared the wickedness of everything German, and was in some way responsible for the invasion of Belgium.[1] But its adherents were too eminent and respectable for this line of attack to be successful. Two of them, Émile Boutroux and Bernard Bosanquet, were until their deaths the official spokesmen of French and British philosophy respectively at international congresses. Religion and conservatism look mainly to this school for defence against heresy and revolution. They have the strength and weakness of those who stand for the *status quo*: the strength that comes of tradition, and the weakness that comes of lack of fresh thought.

In the English-speaking world, this position was only acquired just before the beginning of the twentieth century. I began the serious study of philosophy in the year 1893, the year which saw the publication of Mr Bradley's *Appearance and Reality*. Mr Bradley was one of those who had had to fight to win proper recognition of German philosophy in England, and his attitude was very far from that of one who defends a traditional orthodoxy. To me, as to most of my contemporaries, his *Logic* and his *Appearance and Reality* made a profound appeal. I still regard these books with the greatest respect, though I have long ceased to agree with their doctrines.

The outlook of Hegelianism is characterized by the belief that logic alone can tell us a great deal about the real world. Mr Bradley shares this belief; he contends that the world as it seems to be is self-contradictory, and therefore illusory, while the real world, since it must be logically self-consistent, is bound to have certain characteristics of a surprising kind. It cannot be in time and space, it cannot contain a variety of inter-related things, it cannot contain separate selves, or even that degree of division between subject and object which is involved in knowing. It consists therefore of a single Absolute, timelessly engaged in something more analogous to feeling than to thinking or willing. Our sublunary world is all illusion, and what seems to happen in it does not really matter. This doctrine ought to destroy morality, but morality is temperamental and

---

[1] See e.g. Santayana's *Egotism in German Philosophy*.

defies logic. Hegelians in fact urge as their basic moral principle that we ought to behave as if the Hegelian philosophy were true; but they do not notice that if it were true it would not matter how we behave.

The attack upon this philosophy came from two sides. On the one side were the logicians, who pointed to fallacies in Hegel, and contended that relations and plurality, space and time, are in fact not self-contradictory. On the other side were those who disliked the regimentation and order-liness involved in a world created by logic; of these the chief were William James and Bergson. The two lines of attack were not logically inconsistent, except in some of their accidental manifestations, but they were temperamentally different, and were inspired by different kinds of knowledge. Moreover their appeal was quite different; the appeal of the one was academic, that of the other was human. The academic appeal argued that Hegelianism was false: the human appeal argued that it was disagreeable: Naturally the latter had more popular success.

In the English-speaking world, the greatest influence in the overthrow of German idealism was William James—not as he appears in his *Psychology*, but as he came to be known through the series of small books which were published in the last years of his life and after his death. In an article published in *Mind* so long ago as 1884, reprinted in the posthumous volume *Essays in Radical Empiricism*,[1] he sets out his temperamental bias with extraordinary charm:

Since we are in the main not sceptics, we might go on and frankly confess to each other the motives for our several faiths. I frankly confess mine—I cannot but think that at bottom they are of an aesthetic and not of a logical sort. The 'through-and-through' universe seems to suffocate me with its infallible impeccable all-pervasiveness. Its necessity, with no possibilities; its relations, with no subjects, make me feel as if I had entered into a contract with no reserved rights, or rather as if I had to live in a large seaside boarding-house with no private bedroom in which I might take refuge from the society of the place. I am distinctly aware, moreover, that the old quarrel of sinner and pharisee has something to do with the matter. Certainly, to my personal knowledge, all Hegelians are not prigs, but I somehow feel as if all prigs ought to end, if developed, by becoming Hegelians. There is a story of two clergymen asked by mistake to conduct the same funeral. One came first and had got no further than 'I am the Resurrection and the Life' when the other entered. '*I* am the Resurrection and the Life', cried the latter. The 'through-and through' philosophy, as it actually exists, reminds many of us of that clergyman. It seems too buttoned-up and white-chokered and clean-shaven a thing to speak for the vast slow-breathing unconscious Kosmos with its dread abysses and its unknown tides.

[1] Pp. 276–8.

I think it may be wagered that no one except William James has ever lived who would have thought of comparing Hegelianism to a seaside boarding-house. In 1884 this article had no effect, because Hegelianism was still on the up-grade, and philosophers had not learnt to admit that their temperaments had anything to do with their opinions. In 1912 (the date of the reprint) the atmosphere had changed through many causes—among others the influence of William James upon his pupils. I cannot claim to have known him more than superficially except from his writings, but it seems to me that one may distinguish three strands in his nature, all of which contributed to form his outlook. Last in time but first in its philosophical manifestations was the influence of his training in physiology and medicine, which gave him a scientific and slightly materialistic bias as compared to purely literary philosophers who derived their inspiration from Plato, Aristotle and Hegel. This strand dominates his *Psychology* except in a few crucial passages, such as his discussion of free will. The second element in his philosophical make-up was a mystical and religious bias inherited from his father and shared with his brother. This inspired the *Will to Believe* and his interest in psychical research. Thirdly, there was an attempt, made with all the earnestness of a New England conscience, to exterminate the natural fastidiousness which he also shared with his brother, and replace it by democratic sentiment à la Walt Whitman. The fastidiousness is visible in the above quotation, where he expresses horror of a boarding-house with no private bedroom (which Whitman would have loved). The wish to be democratic is visible in the claim that he is a sinner, not a pharisee. Certainly he was not a pharisee, but he probably committed as few sins as any man who ever lived. On this point he fell short of his usual modesty.

The best people usually owe their excellence to a combination of qualities which might have been supposed incompatible, and so it was in the case of James, whose importance was greater than was thought by most of his contemporaries. He advocated pragmatism as a method of presenting religious hopes as scientific hypotheses, and he adopted the revolutionary view that there is no such thing as 'consciousness', as a way of overcoming the opposition between mind and matter without giving predominance to either. In these two parts of his philosophy he had different allies: Schiller and Bergson as regards the former, the new realists as regards the latter. Only Dewey, among eminent men, was with him on both issues. The two parts have different histories and affiliations, and must be considered separately.

James's *Will to Believe* dates from 1897; his *Pragmatism* from 1907. Schiller's *Humanism* and Dewey's *Studies in Logical Theory* both date from 1903. Throughout the early years of the twentieth century the philosophical world was excited about pragmatism; then Bergson outbid it in appealing to the same tastes. The three founders of pragmatism differ greatly *inter se*; we may distinguish James, Schiller, and Dewey as respectively its religious, literary, and scientific protagonists—for, though James was many-sided, it was chiefly his religious side which found an outlet in pragmatism. But let us ignore these differences and try to present the doctrine as a unity.

The basis of the doctrine is a certain kind of scepticism. Traditional philosophy professed to be able to prove the fundamental doctrines of religion; its opponents professed to be able to disprove them, or at least, like Spencer, to prove that they could not be proved. It seemed, however, that if they could not be proved, they also could not be disproved. And this appeared to be the case with many doctrines which such men as Spencer regarded as unshakable: causality, the reign of law, the general trustworthiness of memory, the validity of induction, and so on. All these, from a purely rational point of view, should be embraced in the agnostic's suspense of judgment, since, so far as we can see, they are radically incapable of proof or disproof. James argued that, as practical men, we cannot remain in doubt on these issues if we are to survive. We must assume, for instance, that the sort of food which has nourished us in the past will not poison us in the future. Sometimes we are mistaken and die. The test of a belief is not conformity with 'fact', since we can never reach the facts concerned; the test is its success in promoting life and the achievement of our desires. From this point of view, as James tried to show in *The Varieties of Religious Experience*, religious beliefs often pass the test, and are therefore to be called 'true'. It is in no other sense—so he contends—that the most accredited theories of science can be called 'true': they work in practice, and that is all we know about it.

As applied to the general hypotheses of science and religion, there is a great deal to be said for this view. Given a careful definition of what is meant by 'working', and a proviso that the cases concerned are those where we do not really know the truth, there is no need to quarrel with the doctrine in this region. But let us take humbler examples, where real truth is not so hard to obtain. Suppose you see a flash of lightning, you may expect to hear thunder, or you may judge that the flash was too distant for the thunder to be audible, or you may not think about the matter at all. This last is usually the most sensible course, but let us suppose that you adopt one of the other two. When you hear the thunder, your belief is verified or refuted, not by any advantage or disadvantage it has brought you, but by a 'fact', the sensation of hearing thunder. Pragmatists attend mainly to beliefs which are incapable of being verified by any facts that come within our experience. Most of our everyday beliefs about mundane affairs—e.g. that so-and-so's address is such-and-such—are capable of verification within our experience, and in these cases the pragmatist's criterion is unnecessary. In many cases like the above instance of the thunder, it is quite inapplicable, since the true belief has no practical advantage over the false one, and neither is as advantageous as thinking about something else. It is a common defect of philosophers to like 'grand' examples rather than such as come from ordinary daily life.

Although pragmatism may not contain ultimate philosophical truth, it has certain important merits. First, it realizes that the truth that *we* can attain to is merely human truth, fallible and changeable like everything human. What lies outside the cycle of human occurrences is not truth, but fact (of certain kinds). Truth is a property of beliefs, and beliefs are psychical events. Moreover their relation to facts does not have the schematic simplicity which logic assumes; to have pointed this out is a second merit in pragmatism. Beliefs are vague and complex, pointing not to one precise fact, but to several vague regions of fact. Beliefs, therefore, unlike the schematic propositions of logic, are not sharply opposed as true or false, but are a blur of truth and falsehood; they are of varying shades of grey, never white or black. People who speak with reverence of the 'Truth' would do better to speak about Fact, and to realize that the reverend qualities to which they pay homage are not to be found in human beliefs. There are practical as well as theoretical advantages in this, since people persecute each other because they believe that they know the 'Truth'. Speaking psycho-analytically, it may be laid down that any 'great ideal' which people mention with awe is really an excuse for inflicting pain on their enemies. Good wine needs no bush, and good morals need no bated breath.

In practice, however, pragmatism has a more sinister side. The truth, it says, is what pays in the way of beliefs. Now a belief may be made to pay through the operation of the criminal law. In the seventeenth century, Catholicism paid in Catholic countries and Protestantism in Protestant countries. Energetic people can manufacture 'truth' by getting hold of the Government and persecuting opinions other than their own. These consequences flow from an exaggeration into which pragmatism has fallen. Granted that, as pragmatists point out, truth is a matter of degree, and is a property of purely human occurrences, namely beliefs, it still does not follow that the degree of truth possessed by a belief depends upon purely human conditions. In increasing the degree of truth in our beliefs, we are approximating to an ideal, and the ideal is determined by Fact, which is only within our control to a certain very limited extent, as regards some of the minor circumstances on or near the surface of a certain planet. The theory of the pragmatist is derived from the practice of the advertiser, who, by saying repeatedly that his pills are worth a guinea a box, makes people willing to give sixpence a box for them, and thus makes his assertion more nearly true than if it had been made with less confidence. Such instances of man-made truth are interesting, but their scope is very limited. By exaggerating their scope, people become involved in an orgy of propaganda, which is ultimately brought to an abrupt end by hard facts in the shape of war, pestilence, and famine. The recent history of Europe is an object-lesson of the falsehood of pragmatism in this form.

It is a curious thing that Bergson should have been hailed as an ally by the pragmatists, since, on the face of it, his philosophy is the exact antithesis to theirs. While pragmatists teach that utility is the test of truth, Bergson teaches, on the contrary, that our intellect, having been fashioned by practical needs, ignores all the aspects of the world which it does not pay to notice, and is in fact an obstacle to the apprehension of truth. We have, he thinks, a faculty called 'intuition' which we can use if we take the trouble, and which will enable us to know, in theory at least, everything past and present, though apparently not the future. But since it would be inconvenient to be troubled with so much knowledge, we have developed a brain, the function of which is to forget. But for the brain we should remember everything; owing to its sieve-like operations, we usually remember only what is useful, and that all wrong. Utility, for Bergson, is the source of error, while truth is arrived at by a mystic contemplation from which all thought of practical advantage is absent. Nevertheless Bergson, like the pragmatists, prefers action to reason, Othello to Hamlet; he thinks it better to kill Desdemona by intuition than to let the King live because of intellect. It is this that makes pragmatists regard him as an ally.

Bergson's *Données Immédiates de la Conscience* was published in 1889, and his *Matière et Mémoire* in 1896. But his great reputation began with *L'Evolution Créatrice*, published in 1907—not that this book was better than the others, but that it contained less argument and more rhetoric, so that it had more persuasive effect. This book contains, from beginning to end, no argument, and therefore no bad argument; it contains merely a poetical picture appealing to the fancy. There is nothing in it to help us to a conclusion as to whether the philosophy which it advocates is true or false; this question, which might be thought not unimportant, Bergson has left to others. But according to his own theories he is right in this, since truth is to be attained by intuition, not by intellect, and is therefore not a matter of argument.

A great part of Bergson's philosophy is merely traditional mysticism expressed in slightly novel language. The doctrine of interpenetration, according to which different things are not really separate, but are merely so conceived by the analytic intellect, is to be found in every mystic, eastern or western, from Parmenides to Mr Bradley. Bergson has given an air of novelty to this doctrine by means of two devices. First he connects 'intuition' with the instincts of animals; he suggests that intuition is what enables the solitary wasp Ammophila to sting the larva in which it lays its eggs exactly so as to paralyse it without killing it. (The instance is unfortunate, since Dr and Mrs Peckham have shown that this poor wasp is no more unerring than a mere man of science with his blundering intellect.) This gives a flavour of modern science to his doctrines, and enables him to adduce zoological instances which make the unwary think that his views are based upon the latest results of biological research. Secondly, he gives the name 'space' to the separateness of things as they appear to the analytic intellect, and the name 'time' or 'duration' to their interpenetration as revealed to intuition. This enables him to say many new things about 'space' and 'time', which sound very profound and original when they are supposed to be about what is ordinarily meant by those words. 'Matter', being that which is in 'space', is of course a fiction created by the intellect, and is seen to be such as soon as we place ourselves at the point of view of intuition.

In this part of his philosophy, apart from phraseology, Bergson has added nothing to Plotinus. The invention of the phraseology certainly shows great ability, but it is that of the company-promoter rather than the philosopher. It is not this part of his philosophy, however, which has won him his wide popularity. He owes that to his doctrine of the *élan vital* and real becoming. His great and remarkable innovation is to have combined mysticism with a belief in the reality of time and progress. It is worth while to see how he achieved this feat.

Traditional mysticism has been contemplative, convinced of the unreality of time, and essentially a lazy man's philosophy. The psychological prelude to the mystic illumination is the dark 'night of the soul', which arises when a man is hopelessly balked in his practical activities, or for some reason suddenly loses interest in them. Activity being thus ruled out, he takes to contemplation. It is a law of our being that, whenever it is in any way possible, we adopt such beliefs as will preserve our self-respect. Psycho-analytic literature is full of grotesque examples of this law. Accordingly the man who has been driven to contemplation presently discovers that contemplation is the true end of life, and that the real world is hidden from those who are immersed in mundane activities. From this basis the remaining doctrines of traditional mysticism can be deduced. Lao-Tze, perhaps the first of the great mystics, wrote his book (so tradition avers) at a custom-house while he was waiting to have his baggage examined;[1] and, as might be expected, it is full of the doctrine that action is futile.

But Bergson sought to adapt mysticism to those who believe in activity and 'life', who believe in the reality of progress and are in no way disillusioned about our existence here below. The mystic is usually a temperamentally active man forced into inaction; the vitalist is a temperamentally inactive man with a romantic admiration for action. Before 1914 the world was full of such people, 'Heartbreak House' people. Their temperamental basis is boredom and scepticism, leading to love of excitement and longing for an irrational faith—a faith they found ultimately in the belief that it

---

[1] The chief argument against this tradition is that the book is not very long.

was their duty to make other people kill each other. But in 1907 they had not this outlet, and Bergson provided a good substitute.

Bergson's view is sometimes expressed in language which might mislead, because things which he regards as illusory are occasionally mentioned in a way which suggests that they are real. But when we avoid these possibilities of misunderstanding, I think his doctrine of time is as follows. Time is not a series of separate moments or events, but a continuous growth, in which the future cannot be foreseen because it is genuinely new and therefore unimaginable. Everything that really happens persists, like the successive rings in the growth of a tree. (This is not his illustration.) Thus the world is perpetually growing fuller and richer. Everything that has happened persists in the pure memory of intuition, as opposed to the pseudo-memory of the brain. This persistence is 'duration', while the impulse to new creation is the '*élan vital*'. To recover the pure memory of intuition is a matter of self-discipline. We are not told how to do it, but one suspects something not unlike the practices of Yogis.

If one might venture to apply to Bergson's philosophy so vulgar a thing as logic, certain difficulties would appear in this philosophy of change. Bergson is never tired of pouring scorn upon the mathematician for regarding time as a series, whose parts are mutually external. But if there is indeed genuine novelty in the world, as he insists (and without this feature his philosophy loses its attractive qualities), and if whatever really comes into the world persists (which is the simple essence of his doctrine of duration), then the sum-total of existence at any earlier time is part of the sum-total at any later time. Total states of the world at various times form a series in virtue of this relation of whole and part, and this series has all the properties that the mathematician wants and that Bergson professes to have banished. If the new elements which are added in later states of the world are not external to the old elements, there is no genuine novelty, creative evolution has created nothing, and we are back in the system of Plotinus. Of course Bergson's answer to this dilemma is that what happens is 'growth', in which everything changes and yet remains the same. This conception, however, is a mystery, which the profane cannot hope to fathom. At bottom, Bergson's appeal is to mystical faith, not to reason; but into the regions where faith is above logic we cannot follow him.

Meanwhile, from many directions, a philosophy grew up which is often described as 'realism', but is really characterized by analysis as a method and pluralism as a metaphysic. It is not necessarily realistic, since it is, in some forms, compatible with Berkeleian idealism. It is not compatible with Kantian or Hegelian idealism, because it rejects the logic upon which those systems are based. It tends more and more to the adoption and development of James's view, that the fundamental stuff of the world is neither mental nor material, but something simpler and more fundamental, out of which both mind and matter are constructed.

In the 'nineties, James was almost the only eminent figure, except among the very old, that stood out against German idealism. Schiller and Dewey had not yet begun to make themselves felt, and even James was regarded as a psychologist who need not be taken very seriously in philosophy. But with the year 1900 a revolt against German idealism began, not from a pragmatist point of view, but from a severely technical standpoint. In Germany, apart from the admirable works of Frege (which begin in 1879, but were not read until recent years), Husserl's *Logische Untersuchungen*, a monumental work published in 1900, soon began to exert a great effect. Meinong's *Ueber Annahmen* (1902) and *Gegenstandstheorie und Psychologie* (1904) were influential in the same direction. In England, G. E. Moore and I began to advocate similar views. His article on *The Nature of Judgment* was published in 1899; his *Principia Ethica* in 1903. My *Philosophy of Leibniz* appeared in 1900, and *Principles of Mathematics* in 1903. In France, the same kind of philosophy was vigorously championed by Couturat. In America, William James's radical empiricism (without his pragmatism) was blended with the new logic to produce a radically new philosophy, that of the *New Realists*, somewhat later in date, but more revolutionary, than the European works mentioned above, although Mach's *Analyse der Empfindungen* had anticipated part of its teaching.

The new philosophy which was thus inaugurated has not yet reached a final form, and is still in some respects immature. Moreover, there is a very considerable measure of disagreement among its various advocates. It is in parts somewhat abstruse. For these reasons, it is impossible to do more than set forth some of its salient features.

The first characteristic of the new philosophy is that it abandons the claim to a special philosophical method or a peculiar brand of knowledge to be obtained by its means. It regards philosophy as essentially one with science, differing from the special sciences merely by the generality of its problems, and by the fact that it is concerned with the formation of hypotheses where empirical evidence is still lacking, It conceives that all knowledge is scientific knowledge, to be ascertained and proved by the methods of science. It does not aim, as previous philosophy has usually done, at statements about the universe as a whole, nor at the construction of a comprehensive system. It believes, on the basis of its logic, that there is no reason to deny the apparently piecemeal and higgledy-piggledy nature of the world.   It does not regard the world as 'organic', in the sense that, from any part adequately understood, the whole could be inferred as the skeleton of an extinct monster can be inferred from a single bone.   In particular, it does not attempt, as German idealism did, to deduce the nature of the world as a whole from the nature of knowledge. It regards knowledge as a natural fact like another, with no mystic significance and no cosmic importance.

The new philosophy had originally three main sources: theory of knowledge, logic and the principles of mathematics. Ever since Kant, knowledge had been conceived as an interaction, in which the thing known was modified by our knowledge of it, and therefore always had certain characteristics due to our knowledge. It was also held (though not by Kant) to be logically impossible for a thing to exist without being known. Therefore the properties acquired through being known were properties which everything must have. In this way, it was contended, we can discover a great deal about the real world by merely studying the conditions of knowledge. The new philosophy maintained, on the contrary, that knowledge, as a rule, makes no difference to what is known, and that there is not the slightest reason why there should not be things which are not known to any mind. Consequently theory of knowledge ceases to be a magic key to open the door to the mysteries of the universe, and we are thrown back upon the plodding investigations of science.

In logic, similarly, atomism replaced the 'organic' view. It had been maintained that everything is affected in its intrinsic nature by its relations to everything else, so that a thorough knowledge of one thing would involve a thorough knowledge of the whole universe. The new logic maintained that the intrinsic character of a thing does not logically enable us to deduce its relations to other things. An example will make the point clear. Leibniz maintains somewhere (and in this he agrees with modern idealists) that if a man is in Europe and his wife dies in India, there is an intrinsic change in the man at the moment of his wife's death. Common sense would say that there is no intrinsic change in the man until he hears of his bereavement. This view is adopted by the new philosophy; its consequences are more far-reaching than they might appear to be at first sight.

The principles of mathematics have always had an important relation to philosophy. Mathematics apparently contains *a priori* knowledge of a high degree of certainty, and most philosophy aspires to *a priori* knowledge. Ever since Zeno the Eleatic, philosophers of an idealistic caste have sought to throw discredit on mathematics by manufacturing contradictions which were designed to show that mathematicians had not arrived at real metaphysical truth, and that the philosophers were able to supply a better brand. There is a great deal of this in Kant, and still more in Hegel. During the nineteenth century, the mathematicians destroyed this part of Kant's philosophy. Lobatchevski, by inventing non-Euclidean geometry, undermined the mathematical argument of Kant's transcendental aesthetic. Weierstrass proved that continuity does not involve infinitesimals; Georg Cantor invented a theory of continuity and a theory of infinity which did away with all the old paradoxes upon which philosophers had battened. Frege showed that arithmetic follows from logic, which Kant had denied. All these results were obtained by ordinary mathematical methods, and were as indubitable as the multiplication table. Philosophers met the situation by not reading the authors concerned. Only the new philosophy assimilated the new results, and thereby won an easy argumentative victory over the partisans of continued ignorance.

The new philosophy is not merely critical. It is constructive, but as science is constructive, bit by bit and tentatively. It has a special technical method of construction, namely, mathematical logic, a new branch of mathematics, much more akin to philosophy than any of the traditional branches. Mathematical logic makes it possible, as it never was before, to see what is the outcome, for philosophy, of a given body of scientific doctrine, what entities must be assumed, and what relations between them. The philosophy of mathematics and physics has made immense advances by the help of this method; part of the outcome for physics has been set forth by Dr Whitehead in three recent works.[1] There is reason to hope that the method will prove equally fruitful in other fields, but it is too technical to be set forth here.

A good deal of modern pluralist philosophy has been inspired by the logical analysis of propositions. At first this method was applied with too much respect for grammar; Meinong, for example, maintained that, since we can say truly 'the round square does not exist', there must be such an object as the round square, although it must be a non-existent object. The present writer was at first not exempt from this kind of reasoning, but discovered in 1905 how to escape from it by means of the theory of 'descriptions', from which it appears that the round square is not mentioned when we say 'the round square does not exist'. It may seem absurd to spend time on such a ridiculous topic as the round square, but such topics often afford the best tests of logical theories. Most logical theories are condemned by the fact that they lead to absurdities; therefore the logician must be aware of absurdities and on the lookout for them. Many laboratory experiments would seem trivial to anyone who did not know their relevance, and absurdities are the experiments of the logician.

From preoccupation with the logical analysis of propositions, the new philosophy had at first a strong tincture of Platonic and medieval realism; it regarded abstracts as having the same kind of existence that concretes have. From this view, as its logic perfected itself, it became gradually more free. What remains is not such as to shock common sense.

Although pure mathematics was more concerned than any other science in the first beginnings of the new philosophy, the most important influence in the present day is physics. This has come about chiefly through the work of Einstein, which has fundamentally altered our notions of space, time and matter. This is not the place for an explanation of the theory of relativity, but a few words on some of its philosophical consequences are unavoidable.

[1] *The Principles of Natural Knowledge*, 1919; *The Concept of Nature*, 1920; *The Principle of Relativity*, 1922. All published by the Cambridge University Press.

Two specially important items in the theory of relativity, from the philosophical point of view, are: (1) that there is not a single all-embracing time in which all the events in the universe have their place; (2) that the conventional or subjective part in our observation of physical phenomena, though much greater than was formerly supposed, can be eliminated by means of a certain mathematical method known as the tensor calculus. I shall say nothing on this latter topic, as it is intolerably technical.

As regards time, it must be understood, to begin with, that we are not dealing with a philosophical speculation, but with a theory necessitated by experimental results and embodied in mathematical formulae. There is the same sort of difference between the two as there is between the theories of Montesquieu and the American Constitution. What emerges is this: that while the events that happen to a given piece of matter have a definite time-order from the point of view of an observer who shares its motion, events which happen to pieces of matter in different places have not always a definite time-order. To be precise: if a light-signal is sent from the earth to the sun, and reflected back to the earth, it will return to the earth about sixteen minutes after it was sent out. The events which happen on the earth during those sixteen minutes are neither earlier nor later than the arrival of the light-signal at the sun. If we imagine observers moving in all possible ways with respect to the earth and the sun, observing the events on the earth during those sixteen minutes, and also the arrival of the light-signal at the sun; if we assume that all these observers allow for the velocity of light and employ perfectly accurate chronometers; then some of these observers will judge any given event on earth during those sixteen minutes to be earlier than the arrival of the light-signal at the sun, some will judge it to be simultaneous, and some will judge it to be later. All are equally right or equally wrong. From the impersonal standpoint of physics, the events on earth during those sixteen minutes are neither earlier nor later than the arrival of the light-signal at the sun, nor yet simultaneous with it. We cannot say that an event A in one piece of matter is definitely earlier than an event B in another unless light can travel from A to B, starting when the earlier event happens (according to A's time), and arriving before the later event happens (according to B's time). Otherwise the apparent time-order of the two events will vary according to the observer, and will therefore not represent any physical fact.

If velocities comparable with that of light were common in our experience, it is probable that the physical world would have seemed too complicated to be tackled by scientific methods, so that we should have been content with medicine men down to the present day. But if physics *had* been discovered, it would have had to be the physics of Einstein, because Newtonian physics would have been obviously inapplicable. Radio-active substances send out particles which move very nearly with the velocity of light, and the behaviour of these particles would be unintelligible without the new physics of relativity. There is no doubt that the old physics is faulty, and from a philosophical point of view it is no excuse to say that the fault is 'only a little one'. We have to make up our minds to the fact that, within certain limits, there is no definite time-order between events which happen in different places. This is the fact which has led to the introduction of the single manifold called 'space-time' instead of the two separate manifolds called 'space' and 'time'. The time that we have been regarding as cosmic is really 'local time', a time bound up with the notion of the earth, with as little claim to universality as that of a ship which does not alter its clocks in crossing the Atlantic.

When we consider the part that time plays in all our common notions, it becomes evident that our outlook would be profoundly changed if we really imaginatively realized what the physicists have done. Take the notion of 'progress': if the time-order is arbitrary, there will be progress or retrogression according to the convention adopted in measuring time. The notion of distance in space is of course also affected: two observers who employ every possible device for ensuring accuracy will arrive at different estimates of the distance between two places, if the observers are in rapid relative motion. It is obvious that the very idea of distance has become vague, because distance must be between material things, not points of empty space (which are fictions); and it must be the distance at a given time, because the distance between any two bodies is continually changing; and a given time is a subjective notion, dependent upon the way the observer is travelling. We can no longer speak of a body at a given time, but must speak simply of an event. Between two events there is, quite independently of any observer, a certain relation called the 'interval' between them. This interval will be differently analysed by different observers into a spatial and a temporal component, but this analysis has no objective validity. The interval is an objective physical fact, but its separation into spatial and temporal elements is not.

It is obvious that our old comfortable notion of 'solid matter' cannot survive. A piece of matter is nothing but a series of events obeying certain laws. The conception of matter arose at a time when philosophers had no doubts as to the validity of the conception of 'substance'. Matter was substance which was in space and time, mind was substance which was in time only. The notion of substance grew more shadowy in metaphysics as time went on, but it survived in physics because it did no harm—until relativity was invented. Substance, traditionally, was a notion compounded of two elements. First, a substance had the logical property that it could only occur as subject in a proposition, not as predicate, Secondly, it was something that persisted through time, or, in the case of God, was outside time altogether. These two properties had no necessary connection, but this was not perceived because physics taught that bits of matter are immortal and theology taught that the soul is immortal. Both, therefore, were thought to have both the characteristics of substance. Now, however, physics compels us to regard evanescent events as substances in the logical sense, i.e. as subjects which cannot be predicates. A piece of matter, which we took to be a single persistent entity, is really a string of entities, like the apparently persistent objects in a cinema. And there is no reason why we should not say the same of a mind: the persistent ego seems as fictitious as the permanent atom. Both are only strings of events having certain interesting relations to each other.

Modern physics enables us to give body to the suggestion of Mach and James, that the 'stuff' of the mental and physical worlds is the same. 'Solid matter' was obviously very different from thoughts and also from the persistent ego. But if matter and the ego are both only convenient aggregations of events, it is much less difficult to imagine them composed out of the same materials. Moreover, what has hitherto seemed one of the most marked peculiarities of mind, namely subjectivity, or the possession of a point of view, has now invaded physics, and is found not to involve mind: photographic cameras in different places may photograph the 'same' event, but they will photograph it differently. Even chronometers and measuring-rods become subjective in modern physics; what they directly record is not a physical fact, but their relation to a physical fact. Thus physics and psychology have approached each other, and the old dualism of mind and matter has broken down.

It is perhaps worth while to point out that modern physics knows nothing of 'force' in the old or popular sense of that word. We used to think that the sun exerted a 'force' on the earth. Now we think that space-time, in the neighbourhood of the sun, is so shaped that the earth finds it less trouble to move as it does than in any other way. The great principle of modern physics is the 'principle of least action', that in going from one place to another a body always chooses the route which involves least action. (Action is a technical term, but its meaning need not concern us at present.) Newspapers and certain writers who wish to be thought forceful are fond of the word 'dynamic'. There is nothing 'dynamic' in dynamics, which, on the contrary, finds everything deducible from a law of universal laziness. And there is no such thing as one body 'controlling' the movements of another. The universe of modern science is much more like that of Lao-Tze than that of those who prate of 'great laws' and 'natural forces'.

The modern philosophy of pluralism and realism has, in some ways, less to offer than earlier philosophies. In the Middle Ages, philosophy was the handmaid of theology; to this day, they come under one heading in booksellers' catalogues. It has been generally regarded as the business of philosophy to prove the great truths of religion. The new realism does not profess to be able to prove them, or even to disprove them. It aims only at clarifying the fundamental ideas of the sciences, and synthesizing the different sciences in a single comprehensive view of that fragment of the world that science has succeeded in exploring. It does not know what lies beyond; it possesses no talisman for transforming ignorance into know-ledge. It offers intellectual delights to those who value them, but it does not attempt to flatter human conceit as most philosophies do. If it is dry and technical, it lays the blame on the universe, which has chosen to work in a mathematical way rather than as poets or mystics might have desired. Perhaps this is regrettable, but a mathematician can hardly be expected to regret it.

(*Sceptical Essays*, London: Allen & Unwin; New York: W. W. Norton, 1928.)

33

ARISTOTLE'S LOGIC

ARISTOTLE'S influence, which was very great in many different fields, was greatest of all in logic. In late antiquity, when Plato was still supreme in metaphysics, Aristotle was the recognized authority in logic, and he retained this position throughout the Middle Ages. It was not till the thirteenth century that Christian philosophers accorded him supremacy in the field of metaphysics. This supremacy was largely lost after the Renaissance, but his supremacy in logic survived. Even at the present day, all Catholic teachers of philosophy and many others still obstinately reject the discoveries of modern logic, and adhere with a strange tenacity to a system which is as definitely antiquated as Ptolemaic astronomy. This makes it difficult to do historical justice to Aristotle. His present-day influence is so inimical to clear thinking that it is hard to remember how great an advance he made upon all his predecessors (including Plato), or how admirable his logical work would still seem if it had been a stage in a continual progress, instead of being (as in fact it was) a dead end, followed by over two thousand years of stagnation. In dealing with the predecessors of Aristotle, it is not necessary to remind the reader that they are not verbally inspired; one can therefore praise them for their ability without being supposed to subscribe to all their doctrines. Aristotle, on the contrary, is still, especially in logic, a battle-ground, and cannot be treated in a purely historical spirit.

Aristotle's most important work in logic is the doctrine of the syllogism. A syllogism is an argument consisting of three parts, a major premiss, a minor premiss, and a conclusion. Syllogisms are of a number of different kinds, each of which has a name given by the scholastics. The most familiar is the kind called 'Barbara':

All men are mortal (Major premiss).
Socrates is a man (Minor premiss).
Therefore: Socrates is mortal (Conclusion).

Or: all men are mortal.
All Greeks are men.
Therefore: All Greeks are mortal.

(Aristotle does not distinguish between these two forms; this, as we shall see later, is a mistake.)

Other forms are: No fishes are rational, all sharks are fishes, therefore no sharks are rational. (This is called 'Celarent'.)

All men are rational, some animals are men, therefore some animals are rational. (This is called 'Darii'.)

No Greeks are black, some men are Greeks, therefore some men are not black. (This is called 'Ferro'.)

These four make up the 'first figure'; Aristotle adds a second and third figure, and the schoolmen added a fourth. It is shown that the three later figures can be reduced to the first by various devices.

There are some inferences that can be made from a single premiss. From 'some men are mortal' we can infer that 'some mortals are men'. According to Aristotle, this can be also inferred from 'all men are mortal'. From 'no gods are mortal' we can infer 'no mortals are gods,' but from 'some men are not Greeks' it does not follow that 'some Greeks are not men'.

Apart from such inferences as the above, Aristotle and his followers thought that all deductive inference, when strictly stated, is syllogistic. By setting forth all the valid kinds of syllogism, and setting out any suggested argument in syllogistic form, it should therefore be possible to avoid all fallacies.

This system was the beginning of formal logic, and, as such, was both important and admirable. But considered as the end, not the beginning, of formal logic, it is open to three kinds of criticism:

(1) Formal defects within the system itself.

(2) Over-estimation of the syllogism, as compared to other forms of deductive argument.

(3) Over-estimation of deduction as a form of argument.

On each of these three, something must be said.

(1) *Formal defects.* Let us begin with the two statements 'Socrates is a man' and 'all Greeks are men'. It is necessary to make a sharp distinction between these two, which is not done in Aristotelian logic. The statement 'all Greeks are men' is commonly interpreted as implying that there are Greeks; without this implication, some of Aristotle's syllogisms are not valid. Take for instance:

'All Greeks are men, all Greeks are white, therefore some men are white.' This is valid if there are Greeks, but not otherwise. If I were to say:

'All golden mountains are mountains, all golden mountains are golden, therefore some mountains are golden,' my conclusion would be false, though in some sense my premisses would be true. If we are to be explicit, we must therefore divide the one statement 'all Greeks are men' into two, one saying 'there are Greeks', and the other saying 'if anything is a Greek it is a man'. The latter statement is purely hypothetical, and does not imply that there are Greeks.

The statement 'all Greeks are men' is thus much more complex in form than the statement 'Socrates is a man'. 'Socrates is a man' has Socrates for its subject, but 'all Greeks are men' does not have 'all Greeks' for its subject, for there is nothing about 'all Greeks' either in the statement 'there are Greeks', or in the statement 'if anything is a Greek it is a man'.

This purely formal error was a source of errors in metaphysics and theory of knowledge. Consider the state of our knowledge in regard to the two propositions 'Socrates is mortal' and 'all men are mortal'. In order to know the truth of 'Socrates is mortal', most of us are content to rely upon testimony; but if testimony is to be reliable, it must lead us back to someone who knew Socrates and saw him dead. The one perceived fact —the dead body of Socrates—together with the knowledge that this was called 'Socrates', was enough to assure us of the mortality of Socrates. But when it comes to 'all men are mortal', the matter is different. The question of our knowledge of such general propositions is a very difficult one. Sometimes they are merely verbal: 'All Greeks are men' is known because nothing is called 'a Greek' unless it is a man. Such general statements can be ascertained from the dictionary; they tell us nothing about the world except how words are used. But 'all men are mortal' is not of this sort; there is nothing logically self-contradictory about an immortal man. We believe the proposition on the basis of induction, because there is no well-authenticated case of a man living more than (say) one hundred and fifty years; but this only makes the proposition probable, not certain. It cannot be certain so long as living men exist.

Metaphysical errors arose through supposing that 'all men' is the subject of 'all men are mortal' in the same sense as that in which 'Socrates' is the subject of 'Socrates is mortal'. It made it possible to hold that, in some sense, 'all men' denotes an entity of the same sort as that denoted by 'Socrates'. This led Aristotle to say that in a sense a species is a substance. He is careful to qualify this statement, but his followers, especially Porphyry, showed less caution.

Another error into which Aristotle falls through this mistake is to think that a predicate of a predicate can be a predicate of the original subject. If I say 'Socrates is Greek, all Greeks are human', Aristotle thinks that 'human' is a predicate of 'Greek', while 'Greek' is a predicate of 'Socrates', and obviously 'human' is a predicate of 'Socrates'. But in fact 'human' is not a predicate of 'Greek'. The distinction between names and predicates, or in metaphysical language, between particulars and universals, is thus blurred, with disastrous consequences to philosophy. One of the resulting confusions was to suppose that a class with only one member is identical with that one member. This made it impossible to have a correct theory of the number *one*, and led to endless bad metaphysics about unity.

(2) *Over-estimation of the syllogism.* The syllogism is only one kind of deductive argument. In mathematics, which is wholly deductive, syllogisms hardly ever occur. Of course, it would be possible to re-write mathematical arguments in syllogistic form, but this would be very artificial and would not make them any more cogent. Take arithmetic, for example. If I buy goods worth 16s 3d, and tender a £1 note in payment, how much change is due to me? To put this simple sum in the form of a syllogism would be absurd, and would tend to conceal the real nature of the argument. Again, within logic there are non-syllogistic inferences such as: 'A horse is an animal, therefore a horse's head is an animal's head.' Valid syllogisms, in fact, are only some among valid deductions, and have no logical priority over others. The attempt to give pre-eminence to the syllogism in deduction misled philosophers as to the nature of mathematical reasoning. Kant, who perceived that mathematics is not syllogistic, inferred that it uses extra-logical principles, which, however, he supposed to be as certain as those of logic. He, like his predecessors, though in a different way, was misled by respect for Aristotle.

(3) *Over-estimation of deduction.* The Greeks in general attached more importance to deduction as a source of knowledge than modern philosophers do. In this respect, Aristotle was less at fault than Plato; he repeatedly admitted the importance of induction, and he devoted considerable attention to the question: How do we know the first premisses from which deduction must start? Nevertheless he, like other Greeks, gave undue prominence to deduction in his theory of knowledge. We shall agree that Mr Smith (say) is mortal, and we may, loosely, say that we know this because we know that all men are mortal. But what we really know is not 'all men are mortal'; we know rather something like 'all men born more than one hundred and fifty years ago are mortal, and so are almost all men born more than one hundred years ago'. This is our reason for thinking that Mr Smith will die. But this argument is an induction, not a deduction. It has less cogency than a deduction, and yields only a probability, not a certainty; but on the other hand it gives *new* knowledge, which deduction does not. All the importance inferences outside logic and pure mathematics are inductive, not deductive; the only exceptions are law and theology, each of which derives its first principles from an unquestionable text, viz. the statute books or the scriptures.

Apart from *The Prior Analytics*, which deals with the syllogism, there are other logical writings of Aristotle which have considerable importance in the history of philosophy. One of these is the short work on *The Categories*. Porphyry the Neoplatonist wrote a commentary on this book, which had a very notable influence on medieval philosophy; but for the present let us ignore Porphyry and confine ourselves to Aristotle.

What, exactly, is meant by the word 'category', whether in Aristotle or in Kant and Hegel, I must confess that I have never been able to understand. I do not myself believe that the term 'category' is in any way useful in philosophy, as representing any clear idea. There are, in Aristotle, ten categories: substance, quantity, quality, relation, place, time, position, state, action and affection. The only definition offered of the term 'category' is: 'Expressions which are in no way composite signify'—and then follows the above list. This seems to mean that every word of which the meaning is not compounded of the meanings of other words signifies a substance or a quantity or etc. There is no suggestion of any principle on which the list of ten categories has been compiled.

'Substance' is primarily what is not predicable of a subject nor present in a subject. A thing is said to be 'present in a subject' when, though not a part of the subject, it cannot exist without the subject. The instances given are a piece of grammatical knowledge which is present in a mind, and a certain whiteness which may be present in a body. A substance in the above primary sense is an individual thing or person or animal. But in a secondary sense a species or a genus—e.g. 'man' or 'animal'—may be called a substance. This secondary sense seems indefensible, and opened the door, in later writers, to much bad metaphysics.

The Posterior Analytics is a work largely concerned with a question which must trouble any deductive theory, namely: How are first premisses obtained? Since deduction must start from somewhere, we must begin with something unproved, which must be known otherwise than by demonstration. I shall not give Aristotle's theory in detail, since it depends upon the notion of *essence*. A definition, he says, is a statement of a thing's essential nature. The notion of essence is an intimate part of every philosophy subsequent to Aristotle, until we come to modern times. It is, in my opinion, a hopelessly muddle-headed notion, but its historical importance requires us to say something about it.

The 'essence' of a thing appears to have meant 'those of its properties which it cannot change without losing its identity'. Socrates may be sometimes happy, sometimes sad; sometimes well, sometimes ill. Since he can change these properties without ceasing to be Socrates, they are no part of his essence. But it is supposed to be of the essence of Socrates that he is a man, though a Pythagorean, who believes in transmigration, will not admit this. In fact, the question of 'essence' is one as to the use of words. We apply the same name, on different occasions, to somewhat different occurrences, which we regard as manifestations of a single 'thing' or 'person'. In fact, however, this is only a verbal convenience. The 'essence' of Socrates thus consists of those properties in the absence of which we should not use the name 'Socrates'. The question is purely linguistic: a *word* may have an essence, but a *thing* cannot.

The conception of 'substance', like that of 'essence', is a transference to metaphysics of what is only a linguistic convenience. We find it convenient, in describing the world, to describe a certain number of occurrences as events in the life of 'Socrates', and a certain number of others as events in the life of 'Mr Smith'. This leads us to think of 'Socrates' or 'Mr Smith' as denoting something that persists through a certain number of years, and as in some way more 'solid' and 'real' than the events that happen to him. If Socrates is ill, we think that Socrates, at other times, is well, and therefore the being of Socrates is independent of his illness; illness, on the other hand, requires somebody to be ill. But although Socrates need not be ill, *something* must be occurring to him if he is to be considered to exist. He is not, therefore, really any more 'solid' than the things that happen to him.

'Substance', when taken seriously, is a concept impossible to free from difficulties. A substance is supposed to be the subject of properties, and to be something distinct from all its properties. But when we take away the properties, and try to imagine the substance by itself, we find that there is nothing left. To put the matter in another way: What distinguishes one substance from another? Not difference of properties, for, according to the logic of substance, difference of properties presupposes numerical diversity between the substances concerned. Two substances, therefore, must be *just* two, without being, in themselves, in any way distinguishable. How, then, are we ever to find out that they *are* two?

'Substance', in fact, is merely a convenient way of collecting events into bundles. What can we know about Mr Smith? When we look at him, we see a pattern of colours; when we listen to him talking, we hear a series of sounds. We believe that, like us, he has thoughts and feelings. But what is Mr Smith apart from all these occurrences? A mere imaginary hook, from which the occurrences are supposed to hang. They have in fact no need of a hook, any more than the earth needs an elephant to rest upon. Anyone can see, in the analogous case of a geographical region, that such a word as 'France' (say) is only a linguistic convenience, and that there is not a *thing* called 'France' over and above its various parts. The same holds of 'Mr Smith'; it is a collective name for a number of occurrences. If we take it as anything more, it denotes something completely unknowable, and therefore not needed for the expression of what we know.

'Substance', in a word, is a metaphysical mistake, due to transference to the world-structure of the structure of sentences composed of a subject and a predicate.

I conclude that the Aristotelian doctrines with which we have been concerned in this chapter are wholly false, with the exception of the formal theory of the syllogism, which is unimportant. Any person in the present day who wishes to learn logic will be wasting his time if he reads Aristotle or any of his disciples. None the less, Aristotle's logical writings show great ability, and would have been useful to mankind if they had appeared at a time when intellectual originality was still active. Unfortunately, they appeared at the very end of the creative period of Greek thought, and therefore came to be accepted as authoritative. By the time that logical originality revived, a reign of two thousand years had made Aristotle very difficult to dethrone. Throughout modern times, practically every advance in science, in logic, or in philosophy has had to be made in the teeth of opposition from Aristotle's disciples.

(*A History of Western Philosophy*, London: Allen & Unwin: New York: Simon & Schuster, 1946).

34

ST THOMAS AQUINAS

THOMAS AQUINAS (b. 1225 or 1226, d. 1274) is regarded as the greatest of scholastic philosophers. In all Catholic educational institutions that teach philosophy his system has to be taught as the only right one; this has been the rule since a rescript of 1879 by Leo XIII. St Thomas, therefore, is not only of historical interest, but is a living influence, like Plato, Aristotle, Kant and Hegel—more, in fact, than the latter two. In most respects, he follows Aristotle so closely that the Stagyrite has, among Catholics, almost the authority of one of the Fathers; to criticize him in matters of pure philosophy has come to be thought almost impious.[1] This was not always the case. In the time of Aquinas, the battle for Aristotle, as against Plato, still had to be fought. The influence of Aquinas secured the victory until the Renaissance; then Plato, who became better known than in the Middle Ages, again acquired supremacy in the opinion of most philosophers. In the seventeenth century, it was possible to be orthodox and a Cartesian; Malebranche, though a priest, was never censured. But in our day such freedoms are a thing of the past; Catholic ecclesiastics must accept St Thomas if they concern themselves with philosophy.

St Thomas was the son of the Count of Aquino, whose castle, in the kingdom of Naples, was close to Monte Cassino, where the education of the 'angelic doctor' began. He was for six years at Frederick II's university of Naples; then he became a Dominican and went to Cologne, to study under Albertus Magnus, who was the leading Aristotelian among the philosophers of the time. After a period in Cologne and Paris, he returned to Italy in 1259, where he spent the rest of his life except for the three years 1269–72. During these three years he was in Paris, where the Dominicans, on account of their Aristotelianism, were in trouble with the university authorities, and were suspected of heretical sympathy with the Averroists, who had a powerful party in the university. The Averroists held, on the basis of their interpretation of Aristotle, that the soul, in so far as it is individual, is not immortal; immortality belongs only to the intellect, which is impersonal, and identical in different

[1] When I did so in a broadcast, very many protests from Catholics resulted.

intellectual beings. When it was forcibly brought to their notice that this doctrine is contrary to the Catholic faith, they took refuge in the subterfuge of 'double truth': one sort, based on reason, in philosophy, and another, based on revelation, in theology. All this brought Aristotle into bad odour, and St Thomas, in Paris, was concerned to undo the harm done by too close adherence to Arabian doctrines. In this he was singularly successful.

Aquinas, unlike his predecessors, had a really competent knowledge of Aristotle. His friend William of Moerbeke provided him with translations from the Greek, and he himself wrote commentaries. Until his time, men's notions of Aristotle had been obscured by Neoplatonic accretions. He, however, followed the genuine Aristotle, and disliked Platonism, even as it appears in St Augustine. He succeeded in persuading the Church that Aristotle's system was to be preferred to Plato's as the basis of Christian philosophy, and that Mohammedans and Christian Averroists had misinterpreted Aristotle. For my part, I should say that the *De Anima* leads much more naturally to the view of Averroes than to that of Aquinas; however, the Church, since St Thomas, has thought otherwise. I should say, further, that Aristotle's views on most questions of logic and philosophy were not final, and have since been proved to be largely erroneous; this opinion, also, is not allowed to be professed by any Catholic philosopher or teacher of philosophy.

St Thomas's most important work, the *Summa contra Gentiles*, was written during the years 1259–64. It is concerned to establish the truth of the Christian religion by arguments addressed to a reader supposed to be not already a Christian; one gathers that the imaginary reader is usually thought of as a man versed in the philosophy of the Arabs. He wrote another book, *Summa Theologiae*, of almost equal importance, but of somewhat less interest to us because less designed to use arguments not assuming in advance the truth of Christianity.

What follows is an abstract of the *Summa contra Gentiles*.

Let us first consider what is meant by 'wisdom'. A man may be wise in some particular pursuit, such as making houses; this implies that he knows the means to some particular end. But all particular ends are subordinate to the end of the universe, and wisdom *per se* is concerned with the end of the universe. Now the end of the universe is the good of the intellect, i.e. *truth*. The pursuit of wisdom in this sense is the most perfect, sublime, profitable, and delightful of pursuits. All this is proved by appeal to the authority of 'The Philosopher', i.e. Aristotle.

My purpose (he says) is to declare the truth which the Catholic Faith professes. But here I must have recourse to natural reason, since the gentiles do not accept the authority of Scripture. Natural reason, however, is deficient in the things of God; it can prove some parts of the faith, but not others. It can prove the existence of God and the immortality of the soul, but not the Trinity, the Incarnation, or the Last Judgment. Whatever is demonstrable is, so far as it goes, in accordance with the Christian faith, and nothing in revelation is *contrary* to reason. But it is important to separate the parts of the faith which can be proved by reason from those which cannot. Accordingly, of the four books into which the *Summa* is divided, the first three make no appeal to revelation, except to show that it is in accordance with conclusions reached by reason; only in the fourth book are matters treated which cannot be known apart from revelation.

The first step is to prove the existence of God. Some think this unnecessary, since the existence of God (they say) is self-evident. If we knew God's essence, this would be true, since (as is proved later) in God, essence and existence are one. But we do not know His essence, except very imperfectly. Wise men know more of His essence than do the ignorant, and angels know more than either; but no creature knows enough of it to be able to deduce God's existence from His essence. On this ground, the ontological argument is rejected.

It is important to remember that religious truths which can be proved can also be known by faith. The proofs are difficult, and can only be understood by the learned; but faith is necessary also to the ignorant, to the young, and to those who, from practical preoccupations, have not the leisure to learn philosophy. For them, revelation suffices.

Some say that God is *only* knowable by faith. They argue that, if the principles of demonstration became known to us through experience derived from the senses, as is said in the *Posterior Analytics*, whatever transcends sense cannot be proved. This, however, is false; and even if it were true, God could be known from His sensible effects.

The existence of God is proved, as in Aristotle, by the argument of the unmoved mover.[1] There are things which are only moved, and other things which both move and are moved. Whatever is moved is moved by something, and, since an endless regress is impossible, we must arrive somewhere at something which moves other things without being moved. This unmoved mover is God. It might be objected that this argument involves the eternity of movement, which Catholics reject. This would be an error: it is valid on the hypothesis of the eternity of movement, but is only strengthened by the opposite hypothesis, which involves a beginning, and therefore a First Cause.

In the *Summa Theologiae*, five proofs of God's existence are given. First, the argument of the unmoved mover, as above. Second, the argument of the First Cause, which again depends upon the impossibility of an infinite regress. Third, that there must be an ultimate source of all necessity; this is much the same as the second argument. Fourth, that we find various perfections in the world, and that these must have their source in something completely perfect. Fifth, that we find even lifeless

---

[1] But in Aristotle the argument leads to 47 or 55 gods.

things serving a purpose, which must be that of some being outside them, since only living things can have an internal purpose.

To return to the *Summa contra Gentiles*, having proved the existence of God, we can now say many things about Him, but these are all, in a sense, negative; God's nature is only known to us through what it is not. God is eternal, since He is unmoved; He is unchanging, since He contains no passive potentiality. David of Dinant (a materialistic pantheist of the early thirteenth century) 'raved' that God is the same as primary matter; this is absurd, since primary matter is pure passivity, and God is pure activity. In God, there is no composition, therefore He is not a body, because bodies have parts.

God is His own essence, since otherwise He would not be simple, but would be compounded of essence and existence. (This point is important.) In God, essence and existence are identical. There are no accidents in God. He cannot be specified by any substantial difference; He is not in any genus; He cannot be defined. But He lacks not the excellence of any genus. Things are in some ways like God, in others not. It is more fitting to say that things are like God than that God is like things.

God is good, and is His own goodness; He is the good of every good. He is intelligent, and His act of intelligence is His essence. He understands by His essence, and understands Himself perfectly. (John the Scot, it will be remembered, thought otherwise.)

Although there is no composition in the divine intellect, God understands many things. This might seem a difficulty, but the things that He understands have no distinct being in Him. Nor do they exist *per se*, as Plato thought, because forms of natural things cannot exist or be understood apart from matter. Nevertheless, God must understand forms before creating. The solution of this difficulty is as follows: 'The concept of the divine intellect, according as He understands Himself, which concept is His Word, is the likeness not only of God Himself understood, but also of all the things of which the divine essence is the likeness. Accordingly many things can be understood by God, by one intelligible species which is the divine essence, and by one understood intention which is the divine Word.'[1] Every form, so far as it is something positive, is a perfection. God's intellect includes in His essence what is proper to each thing, by understanding where it is like Him and where unlike; for instance life, not knowledge, is the essence of a plant, and knowledge, not intellect, is the essence of an animal. Thus a plant is like God in being alive, but unlike in not having knowledge; an animal is like God in having knowledge, but unlike in not having intellect. It is always by a negation that a creature differs from God.

God understands all things at the same instant. His knowledge is not a

[1] *Summa contra Gentiles*, Book I, chapter liii.

habit, and is not discursive or argumentative. God is truth. (This is to be understood literally.)

We come now to a question which had already troubled both Plato and Aristotle. Can God know particular things, or does He only know universals and general truths? A Christian, since he believes in Providence, must hold that God knows particular things; nevertheless, there are weighty arguments against this view. St Thomas enumerates seven such arguments, and then proceeds to refute them. The seven arguments are as follows:

1. Singularity being signate matter, nothing immaterial can know it.

2. Singulars do not always exist, and cannot be known when they do not exist; therefore they cannot be known by an unchanging being.

3. Singulars are contingent, not necessary; therefore there can be no certain knowledge of them except when they exist.

4. Some singulars are due to volitions, which can only be known to the person willing.

5. Singulars are infinite in number, and the infinite as such is unknown.

6. Singulars are too petty for God's attention.

7. In some singulars there is evil, but God cannot know evil.

Aquinas replies that God knows singulars as their cause; that He knows things that do not yet exist, just as an artificer does when he is making something; that He knows future contingents, because He sees each thing in time as if present, He Himself being not in time; that He knows our minds and secret wills, and that He knows an infinity of things, although we cannot do so. He knows trivial things, because nothing is *wholly* trivial, and everything has *some* nobility; otherwise God would know only Himself. Moreover the order of the universe is very noble, and this cannot be known without knowing even the trivial parts. Finally, God knows evil things, because knowing anything good involves knowing the opposite evil.

In God there is Will; His Will is His essence, and its principal object is the divine essence. In willing Himself, God wills other things also, for God is the end of all things, He wills even things that are not yet. He wills His own being and goodness, but other things, though He wills them, He does not will *necessarily*. There is free will in God; a *reason* can be assigned for His volition, but not a *cause*. He cannot will things impossible in themselves; for example, He cannot make a contradiction true. The Saint's example of something beyond even divine power is not an altogether happy one; he says that God could not make a man be an ass.

In God are delight and joy and love; God hates nothing, and possesses the contemplative and active virtues. He is happy, and is His own happiness.

We come now (in Book II) to the consideration of creatures. This is useful for refuting errors against God. God created the world out of nothing, contrary to the opinions of the ancients. The subject of the things that God cannot do is resumed. He cannot be a body, or change Himself; He cannot fail; He cannot be weary, or forget, or repent, or be angry or sad; He cannot make a man have no soul, or make the sum of the angles of a triangle be not two right angles. He cannot undo the past, commit sins, make another God, or make Himself not exist.

Book II is mainly occupied with the soul in man. All intellectual substances are immaterial and incorruptible; angels have no bodies, but in men the soul is united to a body. It is the form of the body, as in Aristotle. There are not three souls in man, but only one. The whole soul is present entire in every part of the body. The souls of animals, unlike those of men, are not immortal. The intellect is part of each man's soul; there is not, as Averroes maintained, only one intellect, in which various men participate. The soul is not transmitted with the semen, but is created afresh with each man. There is, it is true, a difficulty: when a man is born out of wedlock, this seems to make God an accomplice in adultery. This objection, however, is only specious. (There is a grave objection, which troubled St Augustine, and that is as to the transmission of original sin. It is the soul that sins, and if the soul is not transmitted, but created afresh, how can it inherit the sin of Adam? This is not discussed.)

In connection with the intellect, the problem of universals is discussed. St Thomas's position is that of Aristotle. Universals do not subsist outside the soul, but the intellect, in understanding universals, understands things that are outside the soul.

The Third Book is largely concerned with ethical questions. Evil is unintentional, not an essence, and has an accidental cause which is good. All things tend to be like God who is the end of all things. Human happiness does not consist in carnal pleasures, honour, glory, wealth, worldly power, or goods of the body, and is not seated in the senses. Man's ultimate happiness does not consist in acts of moral virtue, because these are means; it consists in the contemplation of God. But the knowledge of God possessed by the majority does not suffice; nor the knowledge of Him obtained by demonstration; nor even the knowledge obtained by faith. In this life, we cannot see God in His essence, or have ultimate happiness; but hereafter we shall see Him face to face. (Not literally, we are warned, because God has no face.) This will happen, not by our natural power, but by the divine light; and even then, we shall not see all of Him. By this vision we become partakers of eternal life, i.e. of life outside time.

Divine Providence does not exclude evil, contingency, free will, chance or luck. Evil comes through second causes, as in the case of a good artist with bad tools.

Angels are not all equals; there is an order among them. Each angel is the sole specimen of his species, for, since angels have no bodies, they can only be distinct through specific differences, not through position in space.

Astrology is to be rejected, for the usual reason. In answer to the question 'Is there such a thing as fate?' Aquinas replies that we *might* give the name 'fate' to the order impressed by Providence, but it is wiser not to do so, as 'fate' is a pagan word. This leads to an argument that prayer is useful although Providence is unchangeable. (I have failed to follow this argument.) God sometimes works miracles, but no one else can. Magic, however, is possible with the help of demons; this is not properly miraculous, and is not by the help of the stars.

Divine law directs us to love God; also, in a lesser degree, our neighbour. It forbids fornication, because the father should stay with the mother while the children are being reared. It forbids birth control, as being against nature; it does not, however, on this account forbid life-long celibacy. Matrimony should be indissoluble, because the father is needed in the education of the children, both as more rational than the mother, and as having more physical strength when punishment is required. Not all carnal intercourse is sinful, since it is natural; but to think the married state as good as continence is to fall into the heresy of Jovinian. There must be strict monogamy; polygyny is unfair to women, and polyandry makes paternity uncertain. Incest is to be forbidden because it would complicate family life. Against brother-sister incest there is a very curious argument: that if the love of husband and wife were combined with that of brother and sister, mutual attraction would be so strong as to cause unduly frequent intercourse.

All these arguments on sexual ethics, it is to be observed, appeal to purely rational considerations, not to divine commands and prohibitions. Here, as throughout the first three books, Aquinas is glad, at the end of a piece of reasoning, to quote texts showing that reason has led him to a conclusion in harmony with the Scriptures, but he does not appeal to authority until his result has been reached.

There is a most lively and interesting discussion of voluntary poverty, which, as one might expect, arrives ultimately at a conclusion in harmony with the principles of the mendicant Orders, but states the objections with a force and realism which shows them to be such as he had actually heard urged by the secular clergy.

He then passes on to sin, predestination, and election, on which his view is broadly that of Augustine. By mortal sin a man forfeits his last end to all eternity, and therefore eternal punishment is his due. No man can be freed from sin except by grace, and yet the sinner is to be blamed if he is not converted. Man needs grace to persevere in good, but no one can *merit* divine assistance. God is not the cause of sinning, but some He leaves in sin, while others He delivers from it. As regards predestination, St Thomas seems to hold, with St Augustine, that no reason can be given why some are elected and go to heaven, while others are left reprobate and go to hell. He holds also that no man can enter heaven unless he has been baptized. This is not one of the truths that can be proved by the unaided reason; it is revealed in John iii. 5.[1]

The fourth book is concerned with the Trinity, the Incarnation, the supremacy of the Pope, the sacraments, and the resurrection of the body. In the main, it is addressed to theologians rather than philosophers, and I shall therefore deal with it briefly.

There are three ways of knowing God: by reason, by revelation, and by intuition of things previously known only by revelation. Of the third way, however, he says almost nothing. A writer inclined to mysticism would have said more of it than of either of the others, but Aquinas's temperament is ratiocinative rather than mystical.

The Greek Church is blamed for denying the double procession of the Holy Ghost and the supremacy of the Pope. We are warned that, although Christ was conceived of the Holy Ghost, we must not suppose that He was the son of the Holy Ghost according to the flesh.

The sacraments are valid even when dispensed by wicked ministers. This was an important point in Church doctrine. Very many priests lived in mortal sin, and pious people feared that such priests could not administer the sacraments. This was awkward; no one could know if he was really married, or if he had received valid absolution. It led to heresy and schism, since the puritanically minded sought to establish a separate priesthood of more impeccable virtue. The Church, in consequence, was obliged to assert with great emphasis that sin in a priest did not incapacitate him for the performance of his functions.

One of the last questions discussed is the resurrection of the body. Here, as elsewhere, Aquinas states very fairly the arguments that have been brought against the orthodox position. One of these, at first sight, offers great difficulties. What is to happen, asks the Saint, to a man who never, throughout his life, ate anything but human flesh, and whose parents did likewise? It would seem unfair to his victims that they should be deprived of their bodies at the last day as a consequence of his greed; yet, if not, what will be left to make up his body? I am happy to say that this difficulty, which might at first sight seem insuperable, is triumphantly met. The identity of the body, St Thomas points out, is not dependent on the persistence of the same material particles; during life, by the processes of eating and digesting, the matter composing the body undergoes perpetual change. The cannibal may, therefore, receive the same body at the resurrection, even if it is not composed of the same matter as was in his body when he died. With this comforting thought we may end our abstract of the *Summa contra Gentiles*.

[1] 'Jesus answered, verily, verily, I say unto thee, except a man be born of water and of the Spirit, he cannot enter into the kingdom of God.'

In its general outlines, the philosophy of Aquinas agrees with that of Aristotle, and will be accepted or rejected by a reader in the measure in which he accepts or rejects the philosophy of the Stagyrite. The originality of Aquinas is shown in his adaptation of Aristotle to Christian dogma, with a minimum of alteration. In his day he was considered a bold innovator; even after his death many of his doctrines were condemned by the universities of Paris and Oxford. He was even more remarkable for systematizing than for originality. Even if every one of his doctrines were mistaken, the *Summa* would remain an imposing intellectual edifice. When he wishes to refute some doctrine, he states it first, often with great force, and almost always with an attempt at fairness. The sharpness and clarity with which he distinguishes arguments derived from reason and arguments derived from revelation are admirable. He knows Aristotle well, and understands him thoroughly, which cannot be said of any earlier Catholic philosopher.

These merits, however, seem scarcely sufficient to justify his immense reputation. The appeal to reason is, in a sense, insincere, since the conclusion to be reached is fixed in advance. Take, for example, the indissolubility of marriage. This is advocated on the ground that the father is useful in the education of the children, (*a*) because he is more rational than the mother, (*b*) because, being stronger, he is better able to inflict physical punishment. A modern educator might retort (*a*) that there is no reason to suppose men in general more rational than women, (*b*) that the sort of punishment that requires great physical strength is not desirable in education. He might go on to point out that fathers, in the modern world, have scarcely any part in education. But no follower of St Thomas would, on that account, cease to believe in lifelong monogamy, because the real grounds of belief are not those which are alleged.

Or take again the arguments professing to prove the existence of God. All of these, except the one from teleology in lifeless things, depend upon the supposed impossibility of a series having no first term. Every mathematician knows that there is no such impossibility; the series of negative integers ending with minus one is an instance to the contrary. But here again no Catholic is likely to abandon belief in God even if he becomes convinced that St Thomas's arguments are bad; he will invent other arguments, or take refuge in revelation.

The contentions that God's essence and existence are one and the same, that God *is* His own goodness, His own power, and so on, suggest a confusion, found in Plato, but supposed to have been avoided by Aristotle, between the manner of being of particulars and the manner of being of universals. God's essence is, one must suppose, of the nature of universals, while His existence is not. It is difficult to state this difficulty satisfactorily, since it occurs within a logic that can no longer be accepted. But it points clearly to some kind of syntactical confusion, without which much of the argumentation about God would lose its plausibility.

There is little of the true philosophic spirit in Aquinas. He does not, like the Platonic Socrates, set out to follow wherever the argument may lead. He is not engaged in an inquiry, the result of which it is impossible to know in advance. Before he begins to philosophize, he already knows the truth; it is declared in the Catholic faith. If he can find apparently rational arguments for some parts of the faith, so much the better; if he cannot, he need only fall back on revelation. The finding of arguments for a conclusion given in advance is not philosophy, but special pleading. I cannot, therefore, feel that he deserves to be put on a level with the best philosophers either of Greece or of modern times.

(*A History of Western Philosophy*, London: Allen & Unwin; New York: Simon & Schuster, 1946.)

35

CURRENTS OF THOUGHT
IN THE NINETEENTH CENTURY

THE intellectual life of the nineteenth century was more complex than that of any previous age. This was due to several causes. First: the area concerned was larger than ever before; America and Russia made important contributions, and Europe became more aware than formerly of Indian philosophies, both ancient and modern. Second: science, which had been a chief source of novelty since the seventeenth century, made new conquests, especially in geology, biology and organic chemistry. Third: machine production profoundly altered the social structure and gave men a new conception of their powers in relation to the physical environment. Fourth: a profound revolt, both philosophical and political, against traditional systems in thought, in politics and in economics, gave rise to attacks upon many beliefs and institutions that had hitherto been regarded as unassailable. This revolt had two very different forms, one romantic, the other rationalistic. (I am using these words in a liberal sense.) The romantic revolt passes from Byron, Schopenhauer and Nietzsche to Mussolini and Hitler; the rationalistic revolt begins with the French philosophers of the Revolution, passes on, somewhat softened, to the philosophical radicals in England, then acquires a deeper form in Marx and issues in Soviet Russia.

The intellectual predominance of Germany is a new factor, beginning with Kant. Leibniz, though a German, wrote almost always in Latin or French, and was very little influenced by Germany in his philosophy. German idealism after Kant, as well as later German philosophy was, on the contrary, profoundly influenced by German history; much of what seems strange in German philosophical speculation reflects the state of mind of a vigorous nation deprived, by historical accidents, of its natural share of power. Germany had owed its international position to the Holy Roman Empire, but the Emperor had gradually lost control of his nominal subjects. The last powerful Emperor was Charles V, and he owed his power to his possessions in Spain and the Low Countries. The Reformation and the Thirty Years' War destroyed what had been left of German unity, leaving a number of petty principalities which were at the mercy of France. In the eighteenth century only one German state, Prussia, had successfully resisted the French; that is why Frederick was called the Great. But Prussia itself had failed to stand against Napoleon, being utterly defeated in the battle of Jena. The resurrection of Prussia under Bismarck appeared as a revival of the heroic past of Alaric, Charlemagne and Barbarossa. (To Germans, Charlemagne is a German, not a Frenchman.) Bismarck showed his sense of history when he said, 'We will not go to Canossa'.

Prussia, however, though politically predominant, was culturally less advanced than much of Western Germany; this explains why many eminent Germans, including Goethe, did not regret Napoleon's success at Jena. Germany, at the beginning of the nineteenth century, presented an extraordinary cultural and economic diversity. In East Prussia serfdom still survived; the rural aristocracy were largely immersed in bucolic ignorance, and the labourers were completely without even the rudiments of education. Western Germany, on the other hand, had been in part subject to Rome in antiquity; it had been under French influence since the seventeenth century; it had been occupied by French revolutionary armies, and had acquired institutions as liberal as those of France. Some of the princes were intelligent, patrons of the arts and sciences, imitating Renaissance princes in their courts; the most notable example was Weimar, where the Grand Duke was Goethe's patron. The princes were, naturally, for the most part opposed to German unity, since it would destroy their independence. They were therefore anti-patriotic, and so were many of the eminent men who depended on them, to whom Napoleon appeared the missionary of a higher culture than that of Germany.

Gradually, during the nineteenth century, the culture of Protestant Germany became increasingly Prussian. Frederick the Great, as a freethinker and an admirer of French philosophy, had struggled to make Berlin a cultural centre; the Berlin Academy had as its perpetual President an eminent Frenchman, Maupertuis, who, however, unfortunately became the victim of Voltaire's deadly ridicule. Frederick's endeavours, like those of the other enlightened despots of the time, did not include economic or political reform; all that was really achieved was a claque of hired intellectuals. After his death, it was again in Western Germany that most of the men of culture were to be found.

German philosophy was more connected with Prussia than were German literature and art. Kant was a subject of Frederick the Great; Fichte and Hegel were professors at Berlin. Kant was little influenced by Prussia; indeed he got into trouble with the Prussian Government for his liberal theology. But both Fichte and Hegel were philosophic mouthpieces of Prussia, and did much to prepare the way for the later identification of German patriotism with admiration for Prussia. Their work in this respect was carried on by the great German historians, particularly by Mommsen and Treitschke. Bismarck finally persuaded the German nation to accept unification under Prussia, and thus gave the victory to the less internationally-minded elements in German culture.

Throughout the whole period after the death of Hegel, most academic philosophy remained traditional, and therefore not very important. British empiricist philosophy was dominant in England until near the end of the century, and in France until a somewhat earlier time; then, gradually, Kant and Hegel conquered the universities of France and England, so far as their teachers of technical philosophy were concerned. The general educated public, however, was very little affected by this movement, which had few adherents among men of science. The writers who carried on the academic tradition—John Stuart Mill on the empiricist side, Lotze, Sigwart, Bradley and Bosanquet on the side of German idealism—were none of them quite in the front rank among philosophers, that is to say, they were not the equals of the men whose systems they, on the whole, adopted. Academic philosophy has often before been out of touch with the most vigorous thought of the age, for instance, in the sixteenth and seventeenth centuries, when it was still mainly scholastic. Whenever this happens, the historian of philosophy is less concerned with the professors than with the unprofessional heretics.

Most of the philosophers of the French Revolution combined science with beliefs associated with Rousseau. Helvetius and Condorcet may be regarded as typical in their combination of rationalism and enthusiasm.

Helvetius (1715–71) had the honour of having his book *De l'Esprit* (1758) condemned by the Sorbonne and burnt by the hangman. Bentham read him in 1769 and immediately determined to devote his life to the principles of legislation, saying: 'What Bacon was to the physical world, Helvetius was to the moral. The moral world has therefore had its Bacon, but its Newton is still to come'. James Mill took Helvetius as his guide in the education of his son John Stuart.

Following Locke's doctrine that the mind is a *tabula rasa*, Helvetius considered the differences between individuals entirely due to differences of education: in every individual, his talents and his virtues are the effect of his instruction. Genius, he maintains, is often due to chance: if Shakespeare had not been caught poaching, he would have been a wool merchant. His interest in legislation comes from the doctrine that the principal instructors of adolescence are the forms of government and the consequent manners and customs. Men are born ignorant, not stupid; they are made stupid by education.

In ethics, Helvetius was a utilitarian; he considered pleasure to be the good. In religion, he was a deist, and vehemently anti-clerical. In theory of knowledge, he adopted a simplified version of Locke: 'Enlightened by Locke, we know that it is to the sense-organs we owe our ideas, and consequently our mind'. Physical sensibility, he says, is the sole cause of our actions, our thoughts, our passions and our sociability. He strongly disagrees with Rousseau as to the value of knowledge, which he rates very highly.

His doctrine is optimistic, since only a perfect education is needed to make men perfect. There is a suggestion that it would be easy to find a perfect education if the priests were got out of the way.

Condorcet (1743–94) has opinions similar to those of Helvetius, but more influenced by Rousseau. The rights of man, he says, are all deduced from this one truth, that he is a sensitive being, capable of making reasonings and acquiring moral ideas, from which it follows that men can no longer be divided into rulers and subjects, liars and dupes. 'These principles, for which the generous Sidney gave his life and to which Locke attached the authority of his name, were afterwards developed more precisely by Rousseau.' Locke, he says, first showed the limits of human knowledge. His 'method soon became that of all philosophers, and it is by applying it to morals, politics and economics, that they have succeeded in pursuing in these sciences a road almost as sure as that of the natural sciences'.

Condorcet much admires the American Revolution. 'Simple common sense taught the inhabitants of the British Colonies that Englishmen born on the other side of the Atlantic Ocean had precisely the same rights as those born on the meridian of Greenwich.' The United States Constitution, he says, is based on natural rights, and the American Revolution made the rights of man known to all Europe from the Neva to the Guadalquivir. The principles of the French Revolution, however, are 'purer, more precise, deeper than those that guided the Americans'. These words were written while he was in hiding from Robespierre; shortly afterwards, he was caught and imprisoned. He died in prison, but the manner of his death is uncertain.

He was a believer in the equality of women. He was also the inventor of Malthus's theory of population, which, however, had not for him the gloomy consequences that it had for Malthus, because he coupled it with the necessity of birth control. Malthus's father was a disciple of Condorcet, and it was in this way that Malthus came to know of the theory.

Condorcet is even more enthusiastic and optimistic than Helvetius. He believes that, through the spread of the principles of the French Revolution, all the major social ills will soon disappear. Perhaps he was fortunate in not living beyond 1794.

The doctrines of the French revolutionary philosophers, made less enthusiastic and much more precise, were brought to England by the philosophical radicals, of whom Bentham was the recognized chief. Bentham was, at first, almost exclusively interested in law; gradually, as he grew older, his interests widened and his opinions became more subversive. After 1808, he was a republican, a believer in the equality of women, an enemy of imperialism, and an uncompromising democrat. Some of these opinions he owed to James Mill. Both believed in the omnipotence of education. Bentham's adoption of the principle of 'the greatest happiness of the greatest number' was no doubt due to democratic feeling, but it involved opposition to the doctrine of the rights of man, which he bluntly characterized as 'nonsense'.

The philosophical radicals differed from men like Helvetius and Condorcet in many ways. Temperamentally, they were patient and fond of working out their theories in practical detail. They attached great importance to economics, which they believed themselves to have developed as a science. Tendencies to enthusiasm, which existed in Bentham and John Stuart Mill, but not in Malthus or James Mill, were severely held in check by this 'science', and particularly by Malthus's gloomy version of the theory of population, according to which most wage-earners must always, except just after a pestilence, earn the smallest amount that will keep them and their families alive. Another great difference between the Benthamites and their French predecessors was that in industrial England there was violent conflict between employers and wage-earners, which gave rise to trade unionism and socialism. In this conflict the Benthamites, broadly speaking, sided with the employers against the working class. Their last representative, John Stuart Mill, however, gradually ceased to give adherence to his father's stern tenets, and became, as he grew older, less and less hostile to socialism, and less and less convinced of the eternal truth of classical economics. According to his autobiography, this softening process was begun by the reading of the romantic poets.

The Benthamites, though at first revolutionary in a rather mild way, gradually ceased to be so, partly through success in converting the British Government to some of their views, partly through opposition to the growing strength of socialism and trade unionism. Men who were in revolt against tradition, as already mentioned, were of two kinds, rationalistic and romantic, though in men like Condorcet both elements were combined. The Benthamites were almost wholly rationalistic, and so were the Socialists who rebelled against them as well as against the existing economic order. This movement does not acquire a complete philosophy until we come to Marx, who will be considered in a later chapter.

The romantic form of revolt is very different from the rationalist form, though both are derived from the French Revolution and the philosophers who immediately preceded it. The romantic form is to be seen in Byron in an unphilosophical dress, but in Schopenhauer and Nietzsche it has learnt the language of philosophy. It tends to emphasize the will at the expense of the intellect, to be impatient of chains of reasoning, and to glorify violence of certain kinds. In practical politics it is important as an ally of nationalism. In tendency, if not always in fact, it is definitely hostile to what is commonly called reason, and tends to be anti-scientific. Some of its most extreme forms are to be found among Russian anarchists, but in Russia it was the rationalist form of revolt that finally prevailed. It was Germany, always more susceptible to romanticism than any other country, that provided a governmental outlet for the anti-rational philosophy of naked will.

So far, the philosophies that we have been considering have had an inspiration which was traditional, literary, or political. But there were two other sources of philosophical opinion, namely science and machine production. The second of these began its theoretical influence with Marx, and has grown gradually more important ever since. The first has been important since the seventeenth century, but took new forms during the nineteenth century.

What Galileo and Newton were to the seventeenth century, Darwin was to the nineteenth. Darwin's theory had two parts. On the one hand there was the doctrine of evolution, which maintained that the different forms of life had developed gradually from a common ancestry. This doctrine, which is now generally accepted, was not new. It had been maintained by Lamarck and by Darwin's grandfather Erasmus, not to mention Anaximander. Darwin supplied an immense mass of evidence for the doctrine, and in the second part of his theory believed himself to have discovered the cause of evolution. He thus gave to the doctrine a popularity and a scientific force which it had not previously possessed, but he by no means originated it.

The second part of Darwin's theory was the struggle for existence and the survival of the fittest. All animals and plants multiply faster than nature can provide for them; therefore in each generation many perish before the age for reproducing themselves. What determines which will survive? To some extent, no doubt, sheer luck, but there is another cause of more importance. Animals and plants are, as a rule, not exactly like their parents, but differ slightly by excess or defect in every measurable characteristic. In a given environment, members of the same species compete for survival, and those best adapted to the environment have the best chance. Therefore among chance variations those that are favourable will preponderate among adults in each generation. Thus from age to age deer run more swiftly, cats stalk their prey more silently, and giraffes' necks become longer. Given enough time, this mechanism, so Darwin contended, could account for the whole long development from the protozoa to *homo sapiens*.

This part of Darwin's theory has been much disputed, and is regarded by most biologists as subject to many important qualifications. That, however, is not what most concerns the historian of nineteenth-century ideas. From the historical point of view, what is interesting is Darwin's extension to the whole of life of the economics that characterized the philosophical radicals. The motive force of evolution, according to him, is a kind of biological economics in a world of free competition. It was Malthus's doctrine of population, extended to the world of animals and plants, that suggested to Darwin the struggle for existence and the survival of the fittest as the source of evolution.

Darwin himself was a liberal, but his theories had consequences in some degree inimical to traditional liberalism. The doctrine that all men are born equal, and that the differences between adults are due wholly to education, was incompatible with his emphasis on congenital differences between members of the same species. If, as Lamarck held, and as Darwin himself was willing to concede up to a point, acquired characteristics were inherited, this opposition to such views as those of Helvetius could have been somewhat softened; but it has appeared that only congenital characteristics are inherited, apart from certain not very important exceptions. Thus the congenital differences between men acquire fundamental importance.

There is a further consequence of the theory of evolution, which is independent of the particular mechanism suggested by Darwin. If men and animals have a common ancestry, and if men developed by such slow stages that there were creatures which we should not know whether to classify as human or not, the question arises: at what stage in evolution did men, or their semi-human ancestors, begin to be all equal? Would *Pithecanthropus erectus*, if he had been properly educated, have done work as good as Newton's? Would the Piltdown Man have written Shakespeare's poetry if there had been anybody to convict him of poaching? A resolute egalitarian who answers these questions in the affirmative will find himself forced to regard apes as the equals of human beings. And why stop with apes? I do not see how he is to resist an argument in favour of Votes for Oysters. An adherent of evolution should maintain that not only the doctrine of the equality of all men, but also that of the rights of man, must be condemned as unbiological, since it makes too emphatic a distinction between men and other animals.

There is, however, another aspect of liberalism which was greatly strengthened by the doctrine of evolution, namely the belief in progress. So long as the state of the world allowed optimism, evolution was welcomed by liberals, both on this ground and because it gave new arguments against orthodox theology. Marx himself, though his doctrines are in some respects pre-Darwinian, wished to dedicate his book to Darwin.

The prestige of biology caused men whose thinking was influenced by science to apply biological rather than mechanistic categories to the world. Everything was supposed to be evolving, and it was easy to imagine an immanent goal. In spite of Darwin, many men considered that evolution justified a belief in cosmic purpose. The conception of organism came to be thought the key to both scientific and philosophical explanations of natural laws, and the atomic thinking of the eighteenth century came to be regarded as out of date. This point of view has at last influenced even theoretical physics. In politics it leads naturally to emphasis upon the community as opposed to the individual. This is in harmony with the growing power of the State; also with nationalism, which can appeal to the Darwinian doctrine of survival of the fittest applied, not to individuals, but to nations. But here we are passing into the region of extra-scientific views suggested to a large public by scientific doctrines imperfectly understood.

While biology has militated against a mechanistic view of the world, modern economic technique has had an opposite effect. Until about the end of the eighteenth century, scientific technique, as opposed to scientific doctrines, had no important effect upon opinion. It was only with the rise of industrialism that technique began to affect men's thought. And even then, for a long time, the effect was more or less indirect. Men who produce philosophical theories are, as a rule, brought into very little contact with machinery. The romantics noticed and hated the ugliness that industrialism was producing in places hitherto beautiful, and the vulgarity (as they considered it) of those who had made money in 'trade'. This led them into an opposition to the middle class which sometimes brought them into something like an alliance with the champions of the proletariat. Engels praised Carlyle, not perceiving that what Carlyle desired was not the emancipation of wage-earners, but their subjection to the kind of masters they had had in the Middle Ages. The Socialists welcomed industrialism, but wished to free industrial workers from subjection to the power of employers. They were influenced by industrialism in the problems that they considered, but not much in the ideas that they employed in the solution of their problems.

The most important effect of machine production on the imaginative picture of the world is an immense increase in the sense of human power. This is only an acceleration of a process which began before the dawn of history, when men diminished their fear of wild animals by the invention of weapons and their fear of starvation by the invention of agriculture. But the acceleration has been so great as to produce a radically new outlook in those who wield the powers that modern technique has created. In old days, mountains and waterfalls were natural phenomena; now, an inconvenient mountain can be abolished and a convenient waterfall can be created. In old days, there were deserts and fertile regions; now, the desert can, if people think it worth while, be made to blossom like the rose, while fertile regions are turned into deserts by insufficiently scientific optimists. In old days, peasants lived as their parents and grandparents had lived, and believed as their parents and grandparents had believed; not all the power of the Church could eradicate pagan ceremonies, which had to be given a Christian dress by being connected with local saints.

Now the authorities can decree what the children of peasants shall learn in school, and can transform the mentality of agriculturists in a generation; one gathers that this has been achieved in Russia.

There thus arises, among those who direct affairs or are in touch with those who do so, a new belief in power: first, the power of man in his conflicts with nature, and then the power of rulers as against the human beings whose beliefs and aspirations they seek to control by scientific propaganda, especially education. The result is a diminution of fixity; no change seems impossible. Nature is raw material; so is that part of the human race which does not effectively participate in government. There are certain old conceptions which represent men's belief in the limits of human power; of these the two chief are God and truth. (I do not mean that these two are *logically* connected.) Such conceptions tend to melt away; even if not explicitly negated, they lose importance, and are retained only superficially. This whole outlook is new, and it is impossible to say how mankind will adapt itself to it. It has already produced immense cataclysms, and will no doubt produce others in the future. To frame a philosophy capable of coping with men intoxicated with the prospect of almost unlimited power and also with the apathy of the powerless is the most pressing task of our time.

Though many still sincerely believe in human equality and theoretical democracy, the imagination of modern people is deeply affected by the pattern of social organization suggested by the organization of industry in the nineteenth century, which is essentially undemocratic. On the one hand there are the captains of industry, and on the other the mass of workers. This disruption of democracy from within is not yet acknowledged by ordinary citizens in democratic countries, but it has been a preoccupation of most philosophers from Hegel onwards, and the sharp opposition which they discovered between the interests of the many and those of the few has found practical expression in Fascism. Of the philosophers, Nietzsche was unashamedly on the side of the few, Marx wholeheartedly on the side of the many. Perhaps Bentham was the only one of importance who attempted a reconciliation of conflicting interests; he therefore incurred the hostility of both parties.

To formulate any satisfactory modern ethic of human relationships, it will be essential to recognize the necessary limitations of men's power over the non-human environment, and the desirable limitations of their power over each other.

(*A History of Western Philosophy*, London: Allen & Unwin; New York: Simon & Schuster, 1946.)

36

THE PHILOSOPHY OF LOGICAL ANALYSIS

IN philosophy ever since the time of Pythagoras there has been an opposition between the men whose thought was mainly inspired by mathematics and those who were more influenced by the empirical sciences. Plato, Thomas Aquinas, Spinoza and Kant belong to what may be called the mathematical party; Democritus, Aristotle and the modern empiricists from Locke onwards, belong to the opposite party. In our day a school of philosophy has arisen which sets to work to eliminate Pythagoreanism from the principles of mathematics, and to combine empiricism with an interest in the deductive parts of human knowledge. The aims of this school are less spectacular than those of most philosophers in the past, but some of its achievements are as solid as those of the men of science.

The origin of this philosophy is in the achievements of mathematicians who set to work to purge their subject of fallacies and slipshod reasoning. The great mathematicians of the seventeenth century were optimistic and anxious for quick results; consequently they left the foundations of analytical geometry and the infinitesimal calculus insecure. Leibniz believed in actual infinitesimals, but although this belief suited his metaphysics it had no sound basis in mathematics. Weierstrass, soon after the middle of the nineteenth century, showed how to establish the calculus without infinitesimals, and thus at last made it logically secure. Next came Georg Cantor, who developed the theory of continuity and infinite number. 'Continuity' had been, until he defined it, a vague word, convenient for philosophers like Hegel, who wished to introduce metaphysical muddles into mathematics. Cantor gave a precise significance to the word, and showed that continuity, as he defined it, was the concept needed by mathematicians and physicists. By this means a great deal of mysticism, such as that of Bergson, was rendered antiquated.

Cantor also overcame the long-standing logical puzzles about infinite number. Take the series of whole numbers from 1 onwards; how many of them are there? Clearly the number is not finite. Up to a thousand, there are a thousand numbers; up to a million, a million. Whatever finite number you mention, there are evidently more numbers than that, because from 1 up to the number in question there are just that number of numbers, and then there are others that are greater. The number of finite whole numbers must, therefore, be an infinite number. But now comes a curious fact: the number of even numbers must be the same as the number of all whole numbers. Consider the two rows:

$$1, 2, 3, 4, \quad 5, \quad 6, \ldots.$$
$$2, 4, 6, 8, \quad 10, \quad 12, \ldots.$$

There is one entry in the lower row for every one in the top row; therefore the number of terms in the two rows must be the same, although the lower row consists of only half the terms in the top row. Leibniz, who noticed this, thought it a contradiction, and concluded that, though there are infinite collections, there are no infinite numbers. Georg Cantor, on the contrary, boldly denied that it is a contradiction. He was right; it is only an oddity.

Georg Cantor defined an 'infinite' collection as one which has parts containing as many terms as the whole collection contains. On this basis he was able to build up a most interesting mathematical theory of infinite numbers, thereby taking into the realm of exact logic a whole region formerly given over to mysticism and confusion.

The next man of importance was Frege, who published his first work in 1879, and his definition of 'number' in 1884; but, in spite of the epoch-making nature of his discoveries, he remained wholly without recognition until I drew attention to him in 1903. It is remarkable that, before Frege, every definition of number that had been suggested contained elementary logical blunders. It was customary to identify 'number' with 'plurality'. But an instance of 'number' is a particular number, say 3, and an instance of 3 is a particular triad. The triad is a plurality, but the class of all triads— which Frege identified with the number 3—is a plurality of pluralities, and number in general, of which 3 is an instance, is a plurality of pluralities. The elementary grammatical mistake of confounding this with the simple plurality of a given triad made the whole philosophy of number, before Frege, a tissue of nonsense in the strictest sense of the term 'nonsense'.

From Frege's work it followed that arithmetic, and pure mathematics generally, is nothing but a prolongation of deductive logic. This disproved Kant's theory that arithmetical propositions are 'synthetic' and involve a reference to time. The development of pure mathematics from logic was set forth in detail in *Principia Mathematica*, by Whitehead and myself.

It gradually became clear that a great part of philosophy can be reduced to something that may be called 'syntax', though the word has to be used in a somewhat wider sense than has hitherto been customary. Some men, notably Carnap, have advanced the theory that all philosophical problems are really syntactical, and that, when errors in syntax are avoided, a philosophical problem is thereby either solved or shown to be insoluble. I think, and Carnap now agrees, that this is an overstatement, but there can be no doubt that the utility of philosophical syntax in relation to traditional problems is very great.

I will illustrate its utility by a brief explanation of what is called the theory of descriptions. By a 'description' I mean a phrase such as 'The present President of the United States', in which a person or thing is designated, not by name, but by some property which is supposed or known to be peculiar to him or it. Such phrases had given a lot of trouble. Suppose I say 'The golden mountain does not exist', and suppose you ask 'What is it that does not exist?' It would seem that, if I say 'It is the golden mountain', I am attributing some sort of existence to it. Obviously I am not making the same statement as if I said, 'The round square does not exist'. This seemed to imply that the golden mountain is one thing and the round square is another, although neither exists. The theory of descriptions was designed to meet this and other difficulties.

According to this theory, when a statement containing a phrase of the form 'the so-and-so' is rightly analysed, the phrase 'the so-and-so' disappears. For example, take the statement 'Scott was the author of *Waverley*'. The theory interprets this statement as saying:

'One and only one man wrote *Waverley*, and that man was Scott.' Or, more fully:

'There is an entity c such that the statement "x wrote *Waverley*" is true if x is c and false otherwise; moreover c is Scott.'

The first part of this, before the word 'moreover', is defined as meaning: 'The author of *Waverley* exists (or existed or will exist)'. Thus 'The golden mountain does not exist' means:

'There is no entity c such that "x is golden and mountainous" is true when x is c, but not otherwise.'

With this definition the puzzle as to what is meant when we say 'The golden mountain does not exist' disappears.

'Existence', according to this theory, can only be asserted of descriptions. We can say 'The author of *Waverley* exists', but to say 'Scott exists' is bad grammar, or rather bad syntax. This clears up two millennia of muddle-headedness about 'existence', beginning with Plato's *Theatetus*.

One result of the work we have been considering is to dethrone mathematics from the lofty place that it has occupied since Pythagoras and Plato, and to destroy the presumption against empiricism which has been derived from it. Mathematical knowledge, it is true, is not obtained by induction from experience; our reason for believing that 2 and 2 are 4 is not that we have so often found, by observation, that one couple and another couple together make a quartet. In this sense, mathematical knowledge is still not empirical. But it is also not *a priori* knowledge about the world. It is, in fact, merely verbal knowledge. '3' means '2 + 1', and

'4' means '3 + 1'. Hence it follows (though the proof is long) that '4' means the same as '2 + 2'. Thus mathematical knowledge ceases to be mysterious. It is all of the same nature as the 'great truth' that there are three feet in a yard.

Physics, as well as pure mathematics, has supplied material for the philosophy of logical analysis. This has occurred especially through the theory of relativity and quantum mechanics.

What is important to the philosopher in the theory of relativity is the substitution of space-time for space and time. Common sense thinks of the physical world as composed of 'things' which persist through a certain period of time and move in space. Philosophy and physics developed the notion of 'thing' into that of 'material substance', and thought of material substance as consisting of particles, each very small, and each persisting throughout all time. Einstein substituted events for particles; each event had to each other a relation called 'interval', which could be analysed in various ways into a time-element and a space-element. The choice between these various ways was arbitrary, and no one of them was theoretically preferable to any other. Given two events A and B, in different regions, it might happen that according to one convention they were simultaneous, according to another A was earlier than B, and according to yet another B was earlier than A. No physical facts correspond to these different conventions.

From all this it seems to follow that events, not particles, must be the 'stuff' of physics. What has been thought of as a particle will have to be thought of as a series of events. The series of events that replaces a particle has certain important physical properties, and therefore demands our attention; but it has no more substantiality than any other series of events that we might arbitrarily single out. Thus 'matter' is not part of the ultimate material of the world, but merely a convenient way of collecting events into bundles.

Quantum theory reinforces this conclusion, but its chief philosophical importance is that it regards physical phenomena as possibly discontinuous. It suggests that, in an atom (interpreted as above), a certain state of affairs persists for a certain time, and then suddenly is replaced by a finitely different state of affairs. Continuity of motion, which had always been assumed, appears to have been a mere prejudice. The philosophy appropriate to quantum theory, however, has not yet been adequately developed. I suspect that it will demand even more radical departures from the traditional doctrine of space and time than those demanded by the theory of relativity.

While physics has been making matter less material, psychology has been making mind less mental. We had occasion in a former chapter to compare the association of ideas with the conditioned reflex. The latter, which has replaced the former, is obviously much more physiological.

(This is only one illustration; I do not wish to exaggerate the scope of the conditioned reflex.) Thus from both ends physics and psychology have been approaching each other, and making more possible the doctrine of 'neutral monism' suggested by William James's criticism of 'consciousness'. The distinction of mind and matter came into philosophy from religion, although, for a long time, it seemed to have valid grounds. I think that both mind and matter are merely convenient ways of grouping events. Some single events, I should admit, belong only to material groups, but others belong to both kinds of groups, and are therefore at once mental and material. This doctrine effects a great simplification in our picture of the structure of the world.

Modern physics and physiology throw a new light upon the ancient problem of perception. If there is to be anything that can be called 'perception', it must be in some degree an effect of the object perceived, and it must more or less resemble the object if it is to be a source of knowledge of the object. The first requisite can only be fulfilled if there are causal chains which are, to a greater or less extent, independent of the rest of the world. According to physics, this is the case. Light-waves travel from the sun to the earth, and in doing so obey their own laws. This is only roughly true. Einstein has shown that light-rays are affected by gravitation. When they reach our atmosphere, they suffer refraction, and some are more scattered than others. When they reach a human eye, all sorts of things happen which would not happen elsewhere, ending up with what we call 'seeing the sun'. But although the sun of our visual experience is very different from the sun of the astronomer, it is still a source of knowledge as to the latter, because 'seeing the sun' differs from 'seeing the moon' in ways that are causally connected with the difference between the astronomer's sun and the astronomer's moon. What we can know of physical objects in this way, however, is only certain abstract properties of structure. We can know that the sun is round in a sense, though not quite the sense in which what we see is round; but we have no reason to suppose that it is bright or warm, because physics can account for its seeming so without supposing that it is so. Our knowledge of the physical world, therefore, is only abstract and mathematical.

Modern analytical empiricism, of which I have been giving an outline, differs from that of Locke, Berkeley and Hume by its incorporation of mathematics and its development of a powerful logical technique. It is thus able, in regard to certain problems, to achieve definite answers, which have the quality of science rather than of philosophy. It has the advantage, as compared with the philosophies of the system-builders, of being able to tackle its problems one at a time, instead of having to invent at one stroke a block theory of the whole universe. Its methods, in this respect, resemble those of science. I have no doubt that, in so far as philosophical knowledge is possible, it is by such methods that it must be sought; I have also no doubt that, by these methods, many ancient problems are completely soluble.

There remains, however, a vast field, traditionally included in philosophy, where scientific methods are inadequate. This field includes ultimate questions of value; science alone, for example, cannot prove that it is bad to enjoy the infliction of cruelty. Whatever can be known, can be known by means of science; but things which are legitimately matters of feeling lie outside its province.

Philosophy, throughout its history, has consisted of two parts inharmoniously blended: on the one hand a theory as to the nature of the world, on the other an ethical or political doctrine as to the best way of living. The failure to separate these two with sufficient clarity has been a source of much confused thinking. Philosophers, from Plato to William James, have allowed their opinions as to the constitution of the universe to be influenced by the desire for edification: knowing, as they supposed, what beliefs would make men virtuous, they have invented arguments, often very sophistical, to prove that these beliefs are true. For my part I reprobate this kind of bias, both on moral and on intellectual grounds. Morally, a philosopher who uses his professional competence for anything except a disinterested search for truth is guilty of a kind of treachery. And when he assumes, in advance of inquiry, that certain beliefs, whether true or false, are such as to promote good behaviour, he is so limiting the scope of philosophical speculation as to make philosophy trivial; the true philosopher is prepared to examine *all* preconceptions. When any limits are placed, consciously or unconsciously, upon the pursuit of truth, philosophy becomes paralysed by fear, and the ground is prepared for a government censorship punishing those who utter 'dangerous thoughts'— in fact, the philosopher has already placed such a censorship over his own investigations.

Intellectually, the effect of mistaken moral considerations upon philosophy has been to impede progress to an extraordinary extent. I do not myself believe that philosophy can either prove or disprove the truth of religious dogmas, but ever since Plato most philosophers have considered it part of their business to produce 'proofs' of immortality and the existence of God. They have found fault with the proofs of their predecessors— St Thomas rejected St Anselm's proofs, and Kant rejected Descartes's— but they have supplied new ones of their own. In order to make their proofs seem valid, they have had to falsify logic, to make mathematics mystical, and to pretend that deep-seated prejudices were heaven-sent intuitions.

All this is rejected by the philosophers who make logical analysis the main business of philosophy. They confess frankly that the human intellect is unable to find conclusive answers to many questions of profound importance to mankind, but they refuse to believe that there is some 'higher' way of knowing, by which we can discover truths hidden from science and the intellect. For this renunciation they have been rewarded by the discovery that many questions, formerly obscured by the fog of metaphysics, can be answered with precision, and by objective methods which introduce nothing of the philosopher's temperament except the desire to understand. Take such questions as: What is number? What are space and time? What is mind, and what is matter? I do not say that we can here and now give definitive answers to all these ancient questions, but I do say that a method has been discovered by which, as in science, we can make successive approximations to the truth, in which each new stage results from an improvement, not a rejection, of what has gone before.

In the welter of conflicting fanaticisms, one of the few unifying forces is scientific truthfulness, by which I mean the habit of basing our beliefs upon observations and inferences as impersonal, and as much divested of local and temperamental bias, as is possible for human beings. To have insisted upon the introduction of this virtue into philosophy, and to have invented a powerful method by which it can be rendered fruitful, are the chief merits of the philosophical school of which I am a member. The habit of careful veracity acquired in the practice of this philosophical method can be extended to the whole sphere of human activity, producing, wherever it exists, a lessening of fanaticism with an increasing capacity of sympathy and mutual understanding. In abandoning a part of its dogmatic pretensions, philosophy does not cease to suggest and inspire a way of life.

(*A History of Western Philosophy*, London: Allen & Unwin; New York: Simon & Schuster, 1946.)

PART VIII

The Psychologist

Certainly no psychologist today takes seriously the Platonic doctrine that there is a sharp and irreducible dichotomy between mind and matter. The ancient view that there is an absolute division between these two entities finds no support in modern physics and psychology. Both mind and matter are outmoded terms which should be abandoned. Russell's own view is that both are composed of groups or series of events. A mind and a piece of matter, therefore, are structurally the same. The only significant difference is that there is a variance in arrangement, like considering people according to geographical order or chronological order. Some samples of his application of psychological theory follow.

37

PSYCHOLOGICAL AND PHYSICAL CAUSAL LAWS

T HE traditional conception of cause and effect is one which modern science shows to be fundamentally erroneous, and requiring to be replaced by a quite different notion, that of *laws of change*. In the traditional conception, a particular event A caused a particular event B, and by this it was implied that, given any event B, some earlier event A could be discovered which had a relation to it, such that—

(1) Whenever A occurred, it was followed by B;
(2) In this sequence, there was something 'necessary', not a mere *de facto* occurrence of A first and then B.

The second point is illustrated by the old discussion as to whether it can be said that day causes night, on the ground that day is always followed by night. The orthodox answer was that day could not be called the cause of night, because it would not be followed by night if the earth's rotation were to cease, or rather to grow so slow that one complete rotation would take a year. A cause, it was held, must be such that under no conceivable circumstances could it fail to be followed by its effect.

As a matter of fact, such sequences as were sought by believers in the traditional form of causation have not so far been found in nature. Everything in nature is apparently in a state of continuous change,[1] so that what we call one 'event' turns out to be really a process. If this event is to cause another event, the two will have to be contiguous in time; for if there is any interval between them, something may happen during that interval to prevent the expected effect. Cause and effect, therefore, will have to be temporally contiguous processes. It is difficult to believe, at any rate where physical laws are concerned, that the earlier part of the process which is the cause can make any difference to the effect, so long as the later part of the process which is the cause remains unchanged. Suppose,

---

[1] The theory of quanta suggests that the continuity is only apparent. If so, we shall be able theoretically to reach events which are not processes. But in what is directly observable there is still apparent continuity, which justifies the above remarks for the present.

for example, that a man dies of arsenic poisoning, we say that his taking arsenic was the cause of death. But clearly the process by which he acquired the arsenic is irrelevant: everything that happened before he swallowed it may be ignored, since it cannot alter the effect except in so far as it alters his condition at the moment of taking the dose. But we may go further: swallowing arsenic is not really the proximate cause of death, since a man might be shot through the head immediately after taking the dose, and then it would not be of arsenic that he would die. The arsenic produces certain physiological changes, which take a finite time before they end in death. The earlier parts of these changes can be ruled out in the same way as we can rule out the process by which the arsenic was acquired. Proceeding in this way, we can shorten the process which we are calling the cause more and more. Similarly we shall have to shorten the effect. It may happen that immediately after the man's death his body is blown to pieces by a bomb. We cannot say what will happen after the man's death, through merely knowing that he has died as the result of arsenic poisoning. Thus, if we are to take the cause as one event and the effect as another, both must be shortened indefinitely. The result is that we merely have, as the embodiment of our causal law, a certain direction of change at each moment. Hence we are brought to differential equations as embodying causal laws. A physical law does not say 'A will be followed by B', but tells us what acceleration a particle will have under given circumstances, i.e. it tells us how the particle's motion is changing at each moment, not where the particle will be at some future moment.

Laws embodied in differential equations may possibly be exact, but cannot be known to be so. All that we can know empirically is approximate and liable to exceptions; the exact laws that are assumed in physics are known to be somewhere near the truth, but are not known to be true just as they stand. The laws that we actually know empirically have the form of the traditional causal laws, except that they are not to be regarded as universal or necessary. 'Taking arsenic is followed by death' is a good empirical generalization; it may have exceptions, but they will be rare. As against the professedly exact laws of physics, such empirical generalizations have the advantage that they deal with observable phenomena. We cannot observe infinitesimals, whether in time or space; we do not even know whether time and space are infinitely divisible. Therefore rough empirical generalizations have a definite place in science, in spite of not being exact or universal. They are the data for more exact laws, and the grounds for believing that they are *usually* true are stronger than the grounds for believing that the more exact laws are *always* true.

Science starts, therefore, from generalizations of the form, 'A is usually followed by B'. This is the nearest approach that can be made to a causal law of the traditional sort. It may happen in any particular instance that A is *always* followed by B, but we cannot know this, since we cannot foresee all the perfectly possible circumstances that might make the sequence fail, or know that none of them will actually occur. If, however, we know of a very large number of cases in which A is followed by B, and few or none in which the sequence fails, we shall in *practice* be justified in saying 'A causes B', provided we do not attach to the notion of cause any of the metaphysical superstitions that have gathered about the word.

There is another point, besides lack of universality and necessity, which it is important to realize as regards causes in the above sense, and that is the lack of uniqueness. It is generally assumed that, given any event, there is some one phenomenon which is *the* cause of the event in question. This seems to be a mere mistake. Cause, in the only sense in which it can be practically applied, means 'nearly invariable antecedent'. We cannot in practice obtain an antecedent which is *quite* invariable, for this would require us to take account of the whole universe, since something not taken account of may prevent the expected effect. We cannot distinguish, among nearly invariable antecedents, one as *the* cause, and the others as merely its concomitants: the attempt to do this depends upon a notion of cause which is derived from will, and will (as we shall see later) is not at all the sort of thing that it is generally supposed to be, nor is there any reason to think that in the physical world there is anything even remotely analogous to what will is supposed to be. If we could find one antecedent, and only one, that was *quite* invariable, we could call that one *the* cause without introducing any notion derived from mistaken ideas about will. But in fact we cannot find any antecedent that we know to be quite invariable, and we can find many that are nearly so. For example, men leave a factory for dinner when the hooter sounds at twelve o'clock. You may say the hooter is *the* cause of their leaving. But innumerable other hooters in other factories, which also always sound at twelve o'clock, have just as good a right to be called the cause. Thus every event has many nearly invariable antecedents, and therefore many antecedents which may be called its cause.

The laws of traditional physics, in the form in which they deal with movements of matter or electricity, have an apparent simplicity which somewhat conceals the empirical character of what they assert. A piece of matter, as it is known empirically, is not a single existing thing, but a system of existing things. When several people simultaneously see the same table, they all see something different; therefore 'the' table, which they are supposed all to see, must be either a hypothesis or a construction. 'The' table is to be neutral as between different observers: it does not favour the aspect seen by one man at the expense of that seen by another. It was natural, though to my mind mistaken, to regard the 'real' table as the common cause of all the appearances which the table presents (as we say) to different observers. But why should we suppose that there is some one common cause of all these appearances? As we have just seen, the notion of 'cause' is not so reliable as to allow us to infer the existence of something that, by its very nature, can never be observed.

Instead of looking for an impartial source, we can secure neutrality by the equal representation of all parties. Instead of supposing that there is some unknown cause, the 'real' table, behind the different sensations of those who are said to be looking at the table, we may take the whole set of these sensations (together possibly with certain other particulars) as actually *being* the table. That is to say, the table which is neutral as between different observers (actual and possible) is the set of all those particulars which would naturally be called 'aspects' of the table from different points of view. (This is a first approximation, modified later.)

It may be said: If there is no single existent which is the source of all these 'aspects', how are they collected together? The answer is simple: Just as they would be if there were such a single existent. The supposed 'real' table underlying its appearances is, in any case, not itself perceived, but inferred, and the question whether such and such a particular is an 'aspect' of this table is only to be settled by the connection of the particular in question with the one or more particulars by which the table is defined. That is to say, even if we assume a 'real' table, the particulars which are its aspects have to be collected together by their relations to each other, not to it, since it is merely inferred from them. We have only, therefore, to notice how they are collected together, and we can then keep the collection without assuming any 'real' table as distinct from the collection. When different people see what they call the same table, they see things which are not exactly the same, owing to difference of point of view, but which are sufficiently alike to be described in the same words, so long as no great accuracy or minuteness is sought. These closely similar particulars are collected together by their similarity primarily and, more correctly, by the fact that they are related to each other approximately according to the laws of perspective and of reflection and diffraction of light. I suggest, as a first approximation, that these particulars, together with such correlated others as are unperceived, jointly *are* the table; and that a similar definition applies to all physical objects.[1]

In order to eliminate the reference to our perceptions, which introduces an irrelevant psychological suggestion, I will take a different illustration, namely, stellar photography. A photographic plate exposed on a clear night reproduces the appearance of the portion of the sky concerned, with more or fewer stars according to the power of the telescope that is being used. Each separate star which is photographed produces its separate effect on the plate, just as it would upon ourselves if we were looking at the sky. If we assume, as science normally does, the continuity of physical processes, we are forced to conclude that, at the place where the plate is, and at all places between it and a star which it photographs, *something* is

---

[1] See *Our Knowledge of the External World* (Allen & Unwin), chapters iii and iv.

happening which is specially connected with that star. In the days when the aether was less in doubt, we should have said that what was happening was a certain kind of transverse vibration in the aether. But it is not necessary or desirable to be so explicit: all that we need say is that *something* happens which is specially connected with the star in question. It must be something specially connected with that star, since that star produces its own special effect upon the plate. Whatever it is must be the end of a process which starts from the star and radiates outwards, partly on general grounds of continuity, partly to account for the fact that light is transmitted with a certain definite velocity. We thus arrive at the conclusion that, if a certain star is visible at a certain place, or could be photographed by a sufficiently sensitive plate at that place, something is happening there which is specially connected with that star. Therefore in every place at all times a vast multitude of things must be happening, namely, at least one for every physical object which can be seen or photographed from that place. We can classify such happenings on either of two principles:

(1) We can collect together all the happenings in one place, as is done by photography so far as light is concerned;

(2) We can collect together all the happenings, in different places, which are connected in the way that common sense regards as being due to their emanating from one object.

Thus, to return to the stars, we can collect together either—

(1) All the appearances of different stars in a given place, or,
(2) All the appearances of a given star in different places.

But when I speak of 'appearances', I do so only for brevity: I do not mean anything that must 'appear' to somebody, but only that happening, whatever it may be, which is connected, at the place in question, with a given physical object—according to the old orthodox theory, it would be a transverse vibration in the aether. Like the different appearances of the table to a number of simultaneous observers, the different particulars that belong to one physical object are to be collected together by continuity and inherent laws of correlation, not by their supposed causal connection with an unknown assumed existent called a piece of matter, which would be a mere unnecessary metaphysical thing in itself. A piece of matter, according to the definition that I propose, is, as a first approximation,[1] the collection of all those correlated particulars which would normally be regarded as its appearances or effects in different places. Some further elaborations are desirable, but we can ignore them for the present. I shall return to them at the end of this lecture.

According to the view that I am suggesting, a physical object or piece

[1] The exact definition of a piece of matter as a construction will be given later.

of matter is the collection of all those correlated particulars which would be regarded by common sense as its effects or appearances in different places. On the other hand, all the happenings in a given place represent what common sense would regard as the appearances of a number of different objects as viewed from that place. All the happenings in one place may be regarded as the view of the world from that place. I shall call the view of the world from a given place a 'perspective'. A photograph represents a perspective. On the other hand, if photographs of the stars were taken in all points throughout space, and in all such photographs a certain star, say Sirius, were picked out whenever it appeared, all the different appearances of Sirius, taken together, would represent Sirius. For the understanding of the difference between psychology and physics it is vital to understand these two ways of classifying particulars, namely:

(1) According to the place where they occur;
(2) According to the system of correlated particulars in different places to which they belong, such system being defined as a physical object.

Given a system of particulars which is a physical object, I shall define that one of the system which is in a given place (if any) as the 'appearance of that object in that place'.

When the appearance of an object in a given place changes, it is found that one or other of two things occurs. The two possibilities may be illustrated by an example. You are in a room with a man, whom you see: you may cease to see him either by shutting your eyes or by his going out of the room. In the first case, his appearance to other people remains unchanged; in the second, his appearance changes from all places. In the first case, you say that it is not he who has changed, but your eyes; in the second, you say that he has changed. Generalizing, we distinguish—

(1) Cases in which only certain appearances of the object change, while others, and especially appearances from places very near to the object, do not change;
(2) Cases where all, or almost all, the appearances of the object undergo a connected change.

In the first case, the change is attributed to the medium between the object and the place; in the second, it is attributed to the object itself.[1]

It is the frequency of the latter kind of change, and the comparatively simple nature of the laws governing the simultaneous alterations of appearances in such cases, that have made it possible to treat a physical object as one thing, and to overlook the fact that it is a system of particulars.

[1] The application of this distinction to motion raises complications due to relativity, but we may ignore these for our present purposes.

When a number of people at a theatre watch an actor, the changes in their several perspectives are so similar and so closely correlated that all are popularly regarded as identical with each other and with the changes of the actor himself. So long as all the changes in the appearances of a body are thus correlated there is no pressing *prima facie* need to break up the system of appearances, or to realize that the body in question is not really one thing but a set of correlated particulars. It is especially and primarily such changes that physics deals with, i.e. it deals primarily with processes in which the unity of a physical object need not be broken up because all its appearances change simultaneously according to the same law—or, if not all, at any rate all from places sufficiently near to the object, with increasing accuracy as we approach the object.

The changes in appearances of an object which are due to changes in the intervening medium will not affect, or will affect only very slightly, the appearances from places close to the object. If the appearances from sufficiently neighbouring places are either wholly unchanged, or changed to a diminishing extent which has zero for its limit, it is usually found that the changes can be accounted for by changes in objects which are between the object in question and the places from which its appearance has changed appreciably. Thus physics is able to reduce the laws of most changes with which it deals to changes in physical objects, and to state most of its fundamental laws in terms of matter. It is only in those cases in which the unity of the system of appearances constituting a piece of matter has to be broken up, that the statement of what is happening cannot be made exclusively in terms of matter. The whole of psychology, we shall find, is included among such cases; hence their importance for our purposes.

We can now begin to understand one of the fundamental differences between physics and psychology. Physics treats as a unit the whole system of appearances of a piece of matter, whereas psychology is interested in certain of these appearances themselves. Confining ourselves for the moment to the psychology of perceptions, we observe that perceptions are certain of the appearances of physical objects. From the point of view that we have been hitherto adopting, we might define them as the appearances of objects at places from which sense-organs and the suitable parts of the nervous system form part of the intervening medium. Just as a photographic plate receives a different impression of a cluster of stars when a telescope is part of the intervening medium, so a brain receives a different impression when an eye and an optic nerve are part of the intervening medium. An impression due to this sort of intervening medium is called a perception, and is interesting to psychology on its own account, not merely as one of the set of correlated particulars which is the physical object of which (as we say) we are having a perception.

We spoke earlier of two ways of classifying particulars. One way collects together the appearances commonly regarded as a given object from different places; this is, broadly speaking, the way of physics, leading to the construction of physical objects as sets of such appearances. The other way collects together the appearances of different objects from a given place, the result being what we call a perspective. In the particular case where the place concerned is a human brain, the perspective belonging to the place consists of all the perceptions of a certain man at a given time. Thus classification by perspectives is irrelevant to psychology, and is essential in defining what we mean by one mind.

I do not wish to suggest that the way in which I have been defining perceptions is the only possible way, or even the best way. It is the way that arose naturally out of our present topic. But when we approach psychology from a more introspective standpoint, we have to distinguish sensations and perceptions, if possible, from other mental occurrences, if any. We have also to consider the psychological effects of sensations, as opposed to their physical causes and correlates. These problems are quite distinct from those with which we have been concerned in the present lecture, and I shall not deal with them until a later stage.

It is clear that psychology is concerned essentially with actual particulars, not merely with systems of particulars. In this it differs from physics, which, broadly speaking, is concerned with the cases in which all the particulars which make up one physical object can be treated as a single causal unit, or rather the particulars which are sufficiently near to the object of which they are appearances can be so treated. The laws which physics seeks can, broadly speaking, be stated by treating such systems of particulars as causal units. The laws which psychology seeks cannot be so stated, since the particulars themselves are what interests the psychologist. This is one of the fundamental differences between physics and psychology; and to make it clear has been the main purpose of this lecture.

I will conclude with an attempt to give a more precise definition of a piece of matter. The appearances of a piece of matter from different places change partly according to intrinsic laws (the laws of perspective, in the case of visual shape), partly according to the nature of the intervening medium—fog, blue spectacles, telescopes, microscopes, sense-organs, etc. As we approach nearer to the object, the effect of the intervening medium grows less. In a generalized sense, all the intrinsic laws of change of appearance may be called 'laws of perspective'. Given any appearance of an object, we can construct hypothetically a certain system of appearances to which the appearance in question would belong if the laws of perspective alone were concerned. If we construct this hypothetical system for each appearance of the object in turn, the system corresponding to a given appearance x will be independent of any distortion due to the medium beyond x, and will only embody such distortion as is due to the medium between x and the object. Thus, as the appearance by which our hypothetical system is defined is moved nearer and nearer to the object, the hypothetical system of appearances defined by its means embodies less and less of the effect of the medium. The different sets of appearances resulting from moving x nearer and nearer to the object will approach to a limiting set, and this limiting set will be that system of appearances which the object would present if the laws of perspective alone were operative and the medium exercised no distorting effect. This limiting set of appearances may be defined, for purposes of physics, as the piece of matter concerned.

(*The Analysis of Mind*, London: Allen & Unwin; New York: The Macmillan Co., 1921.)

38

TRUTH AND FALSEHOOD

T HE definition of truth and falsehood, which is our topic today, lies strictly outside our general subject, namely, the analysis of mind. From the psychological standpoint, there may be different kinds of belief, and different degrees of certainty, but there cannot be any purely psychological means of distinguishing between true and false beliefs. A belief is rendered true or false by relation to a fact, which may lie outside the experience of the person entertaining the belief. Truth and falsehood, except in the case of beliefs about our own minds, depend upon the relations of mental occurrences to outside things, and thus take us beyond the analysis of mental occurrences as they are in themselves. Nevertheless, we can hardly avoid the consideration of truth and falsehood. We wish to believe that our beliefs, sometimes at least, yield *knowledge*, and a belief does not yield knowledge unless it is true. The question whether our minds are instruments of knowledge, and, if so, in what sense, is so vital that any suggested analysis of mind must be examined in relation to this question. To ignore this question would be like describing a chronometer without regard to its accuracy as a timekeeper, or a thermometer without mentioning the fact that it measures temperature.

Many difficult questions arise in connection with knowledge. It is difficult to define knowledge, difficult to decide whether we have any knowledge, and difficult, even if it is conceded that we sometimes have knowledge, to discover whether we can ever know that we have knowledge in this or that particular case. I shall divide the discussion into four parts:

I. We may regard knowledge, from a behaviourist standpoint, as exhibited in a certain kind of response to the environment. This response must have some characteristics which it shares with those of scientific instruments, but must also have others that are peculiar to knowledge. We shall find that this point of view is important, but not exhaustive of the nature of knowledge.

II. We may hold that the beliefs that constitute knowledge are distinguished from such as are erroneous or uncertain by properties which are intrinsic either to single beliefs or to systems of beliefs, being in either case discoverable without reference to outside fact. Views of this kind have been widely held among philosophers, but we shall find no reason to accept them.

III. We believe that some beliefs are true, and some false. This raises the problem of *verifiability*: are there any circumstances which can justifiably give us an unusual degree of certainty that such and such a belief is true? It is obvious that there are circumstances which in fact cause a certainty of this sort, and we wish to learn what we can from examining these circumstances.

IV. Finally, there is the formal problem of defining truth and falsehood, and deriving the objective reference of a proposition from the meanings of its component words.

We will consider these four problems in succession.

I. We may regard a human being as an instrument, which makes various responses to various stimuli. If we observe these responses from outside, we shall regard them as showing knowledge when they display two characteristics, *accuracy* and *appropriateness*. These two are quite distinct, and even sometimes incompatible. If I am being pursued by a tiger, accuracy is furthered by turning round to look at him, but appropriateness by running away without making any search for further knowledge of the beast. I shall return to the question of appropriateness later; for the present it is accuracy that I wish to consider.

When we are viewing a man from the outside, it is not his beliefs, but his bodily movements, that we can observe. His knowledge must be inferred from his bodily movements, and especially from what he says and writes. For the present we may ignore beliefs, and regard a man's knowledge as actually consisting in what he says and does. That is to say, we will construct, as far as possible, a purely behaviouristic account of truth and falsehood.

If you ask a boy 'What is twice two?' and the boy says 'four', you take that as *prima facie* evidence that the boy knows what twice two is. But if you go on to ask what is twice three, twice four, twice five, and so on, and the boy always answers 'four', you come to the conclusion that he knows nothing about it. Exactly similar remarks apply to scientific instruments. I know a certain weathercock which has the pessimistic habit of always pointing to the north-east. If you were to see it first on a cold March day, you would think it an excellent weathercock; but with the first warm day of spring your confidence would be shaken. The boy and the weathercock have the same defect: they do not vary their response when the stimulus is varied. A good instrument, or a person with much knowledge, will give different responses to stimuli which differ in relevant ways. This is the first point in defining accuracy of response.

We will now assume another boy, who also, when you first question him, asserts that twice two is four. But with this boy, instead of asking him different questions, you make a practice of asking him the same question every day at breakfast. You find that he says five, or six, or seven, or any other number at random, and you conclude that he also does not know what twice two is, though by good luck he answered right the first time. This boy is like a weathercock which, instead of being stuck fast, is always going round and round, changing without any change of wind. This boy and weathercock have the opposite defect to that of the previous pair: they give different responses to stimuli which do not differ in any relevant way.

In connection with vagueness in memory, we already had occasion to consider the definition of accuracy. Omitting some of the niceties of our previous discussion, we may say that an instrument is *accurate* when it avoids the defects of the two boys and weathercocks, that is to say, when—

(*a*) It gives different responses to stimuli which differ in relevant ways;
(*b*) It gives the same response to stimuli which do not differ in relevant ways.

What are relevant ways depends upon the nature and purpose of the instrument. In the case of a weathercock, the direction of the wind is relevant, but not its strength; in the case of the boy, the meaning of the words of your question is relevant, but not the loudness of your voice, or whether you are his father or his schoolmaster. If, however, you were a boy of his own age, that would be relevant, and the appropriate response would be different.

It is clear that knowledge is displayed by accuracy of response to certain kinds of stimuli, e.g. examinations. Can we say, conversely, that it consists wholly of such accuracy of response? I do not think we can; but we can go a certain distance in this direction. For this purpose we must define more carefully the kind of accuracy and the kind of response that may be expected where there is knowledge.

From our present point of view, it is difficult to exclude perception from knowledge; at any rate, knowledge is displayed by actions based upon perception. A bird flying among trees avoids bumping into their branches; its avoidance is a response to visual sensations. This response has the characteristic of accuracy, in the main, and leads us to say that the bird 'knows', by sight, what objects are in its neighbourhood. For a behaviourist, this must certainly count as knowledge, however it may be viewed by analytic psychology. In this case, what is known, roughly, is the stimulus; but in more advanced knowledge the stimulus and what is known become different. For example, you look in your calendar and find that Easter will be early next year. Here the stimulus is the calendar, whereas the response concerns the future. Even this can be paralleled among instruments: the behaviour of the barometer has a present stimulus, but foretells the future, so that the barometer might be said, in a sense, to know the future. However that may be, the point I am emphasizing as regards knowledge is that what is known may be quite different from the stimulus, and no part of the cause of the knowledge-response. It is only in sense-knowledge that the stimulus and what is known are, with qualifications, identifiable. In knowledge of the future, it is obvious that they are totally distinct, since otherwise the response would precede the stimulus. In abstract knowledge also they are distinct, since abstract facts have no date. In knowledge of the past there are complications, which we must briefly examine.

Every form of memory will be, from our present point of view, in one sense a delayed response. But this phrase does not quite clearly express what is meant. If you light a fuse and connect it with a heap of dynamite, the explosion of the dynamite may be spoken of, in a sense, as a delayed response to your lighting of the fuse. But that only means that it is a somewhat late portion of a continuous process of which the earlier parts have less emotional interest. This is not the case with habit. A display of habit has two sorts of causes: (a) the past occurrences which generated the habit, (b) the present occurrence which brings it into play. When you drop a weight on your toe, and say what you do say, the habit has been caused by imitation of your undesirable associates, whereas it is brought into play by the dropping of the weight. The great bulk of our knowledge is a habit in this sense: whenever I am asked when I was born, I reply correctly by mere habit. It would hardly be correct to say that getting born was the stimulus, and that my reply is a delayed response. But in cases of memory this way of speaking would have an element of truth. In an habitual memory, the event remembered was clearly an essential part of the stimulus to the formation of the habit. The present stimulus which brings the habit into play produces a different response from that which it would produce if the habit did not exist. Therefore the habit enters into the causation of the response, and so do, at one remove, the causes of the habit. It follows that an event remembered is an essential part of the causes of our remembering.

In spite, however, of the fact that what is known is *sometimes* an indispensable part of the cause of the knowledge, this circumstance is, I think, irrelevant to the general question with which we are concerned, namely: What sort of response to what sort of stimulus can be regarded as displaying knowledge? There is one characteristic which the response must have, namely, it must consist of voluntary movements. The need of this characteristic is connected with the characteristic of *appropriateness*, which I do not wish to consider as yet. For the present I wish only to obtain a clearer idea of the sort of *accuracy* that a knowledge-response must have. It is clear from many instances that accuracy, in other cases, may be purely mechanical. The most complete form of accuracy consists in giving correct answers to questions, an achievement in which calculating machines far surpass human beings. In asking a question of a calculating machine, you must use its language: you must not address it in English, any more than you would address an Englishman in Chinese. But if you address it in the language it understands, it will tell you what is 34,521 times 19,987, without a moment's hesitation or a hint of inaccuracy. We do not say the machine *knows* the answer, because it has no purpose of its own in giving the answer: it does not wish to impress you with its cleverness, or feel proud of being such a good machine. But as far as mere accuracy goes, the machine leaves nothing to be desired.

Accuracy of response is a perfectly clear notion in the case of answers to questions, but in other cases it is much more obscure. We may say generally that an object whether animate or inanimate, is 'sensitive' to a certain feature of the environment if it behaves differently according to the presence or absence of that feature. Thus iron is sensitive to anything magnetic. But sensitiveness does not constitute knowledge, and knowledge of a fact which is not sensible is not sensitiveness to *that* fact, as we have seen in distinguishing the fact known from the stimulus. As soon as we pass beyond the simple case of question and answer, the definition of knowledge by means of behaviour demands the consideration of purpose. A carrier pigeon flies home, and so we say it 'knows' the way. But if it merely flew to some place at random, we should not say that it 'knew' the way to that place, any more than a stone rolling down hill knows the way to the valley.

On the features which distinguish knowledge from accuracy of response in general, not much can be said from a behaviourist point of view without referring to purpose. But the necessity of *something* besides accuracy of response may be brought out by the following consideration: Suppose two persons, of whom one believed whatever the other disbelieved, and disbelieved whatever the other believed. So far as accuracy and sensitiveness of response alone are concerned, there would be nothing to choose between these two persons. A thermometer which went down for warm weather and up for cold might be just as accurate as the usual kind; and a person who always believes falsely is just as sensitive an instrument as a person who always believes truly. The observable and practical difference between them would be that the one who always believed falsely would quickly come to a bad end. This illustrates once more that accuracy of response to stimulus does not alone show knowledge, but must be reinforced by appropriateness, i.e. suitability for realizing one's purpose. This applies even in the apparently simple case of answering questions: if the purpose of the answers is to deceive, their falsehood, not their truth, will be evidence of knowledge. The proportion of the combination of appropriateness with accuracy in the definition of knowledge is difficult; it seems that both enter in, but that appropriateness is only required as regards the general type of response, not as regards each individual instance.

II. I have so far assumed as unquestionable the view that the truth or falsehood of a belief consists in a relation to a certain fact, namely the objective of the belief. This view has, however, been often questioned. Philosophers have sought some intrinsic criterion by which true and false beliefs could be distinguished.[1] I am afraid their chief reason for this search has been the wish to feel more certainty than seems otherwise possible as to what is true and what is false. If we could discover the truth of a belief by examining its intrinsic characteristics, or those of some collection of beliefs of which it forms part, the pursuit of truth, it is thought, would be a less arduous business than it otherwise appears to be. But the attempts which have been made in this direction are not encouraging. I will take two criteria which have been suggested, namely, (1) self-evidence, (2) mutual coherence. If we can show that these are inadequate, we may feel fairly certain that no intrinsic criterion hitherto suggested will suffice to distinguish true from false beliefs.

(1) *Self-evidence.*—Some of our beliefs seem to be peculiarly indubitable. One might instance the belief that two and two are four, that two things cannot be in the same place at the same time, nor one thing in two places, or that a particular buttercup that we are seeing is yellow. The suggestion we are to examine is that such beliefs have some recognizable quality which secures their truth, and the truth of whatever is deduced from them according to self-evident principles of inference. This theory is set forth, for example, by Meinong in his book, *Ueber die Erfahrungs-grundlagen unseres Wissens.*

If this theory is to be logically tenable, self-evidence must not consist merely in the fact that we believe a proposition. We believe that our beliefs are sometimes erroneous, and we wish to be able to select a certain class of beliefs which are never erroneous. If we are to do this, it must be by some mark which belongs only to certain beliefs, not to all; and

[1] The view that such a criterion exists is generally held by those whose views are in any degree derived from Hegel. It may be illustrated by the following passage from Lossky, *The Intuitive Basis of Knowledge* (Macmillan, 1919), p. 268: 'Strictly speaking, a false judgment is not a judgment at all. The predicate does not follow from the subject S alone, but from the subject plus a certain addition C, *which in no sense belongs to the content of the judgment*. What takes place may be a process of association of ideas, of imagining, or the like, but is not a process of judging. An experienced psychologist will be able by careful observation to detect that in this process there is wanting just the specific element of the objective dependence of the predicate upon the subject which is characteristic of a judgment. It must be admitted, however, that an exceptional power of observation is needed in order to distinguish, by means of introspection, mere combinations of ideas from judgments.'

among those to which it belongs there must be none that are mutually inconsistent. If, for example, two propositions p and q were self-evident, and it were also self-evident that p and q could not both be true, that would condemn self-evidence as a guarantee of truth. Again, self-evidence must not be the same thing as the absence of doubt or the presence of complete certainty. If we are completely certain of a proposition, we do not seek a ground to support our belief. If self-evidence is alleged as a ground of belief, that implies that doubt has crept in, and that our self-evident proposition has not wholly resisted the assaults of scepticism. To say that any given person believes some things so firmly that he cannot be made to doubt them is no doubt true. Such beliefs he will be willing to use as premises in reasoning, and to him personally they will seem to have as much evidence as any belief can need. But among the propositions which one man finds indubitable there will be some that another man finds it quite possible to doubt. It used to seem self-evident that there could not be men at the Antipodes, because they would fall off, or at best grow giddy from standing on their heads. But New Zealanders find the falsehood of this proposition self-evident. Therefore, if self-evidence is a guarantee of truth, our ancestors must have been mistaken in thinking their beliefs about the Antipodes self-evident. Meinong meets this difficulty by saying that some beliefs are falsely thought to be self-evident, but in the case of others it is self-evident that they are self-evident, and these are wholly reliable. Even this, however, does not remove the practical risk of error, since we may mistakenly believe it self-evident that a certain belief is self-evident. To remove all risk of error, we shall need an endless series of more and more complicated self-evident beliefs, which cannot possibly be realized in practice. It would seem, therefore, that self-evidence is useless as a practical criterion for insuring truth.

The same result follows from examining instances. If we take the four instances mentioned at the beginning of this discussion, we shall find that three of them are logical, while the fourth is a judgment of perception. The proposition that two and two are four follows by purely logical deduction from definitions: that means that its truth results, not from the properties of objects, but from the meanings of symbols. Now symbols, in mathematics, mean what we choose; thus the feeling of self-evidence, in this case, seems explicable by the fact that the whole matter is within our control. I do not wish to assert that this is the whole truth about mathematical propositions, for the question is complicated, and I do not know what the whole truth is. But I do wish to suggest that the feeling of self-evidence in mathematical propositions has to do with the fact that they are concerned with the meanings of symbols, not with properties of the world such as external observation might reveal.

Similar considerations apply to the impossibility of a thing being in two places at once, or of two things being in one place at the same time. These impossibilities result logically, if I am not mistaken, from the definitions of one thing and one place. That is to say, they are not laws of physics, but only part of the intellectual apparatus which we have manufactured for manipulating physics. Their self-evidence, if this is so, lies merely in the fact that they represent our decision as to the use of words, not a property of physical objects.

Judgments of perception, such as 'this buttercup is yellow', are in a quite different position from judgments of logic, and their self-evidence must have a different explanation. In order to arrive at the nucleus of such a judgment, we will eliminate, as far as possible, the use of words which take us beyond the present fact, such as 'buttercup' and 'yellow'. The simplest kind of judgment underlying the perception that a buttercup is yellow would seem to be the perception of similarity in two colours seen simultaneously. Suppose we are seeing two buttercups, and we perceive that their colours are similar. This similarity is a physical fact, not a matter of symbols or words; and it certainly seems to be indubitable in a way that many judgments are not.

The first thing to observe, in regard to such judgments, is that as they stand they are vague. The word 'similar' is a vague word, since there are degrees of similarity, and no one can say where similarity ends and dissimilarity begins. It is unlikely that our two buttercups have *exactly* the same colour, and if we judged that they had we should have passed altogether outside the region of self-evidence. To make our proposition more precise, let us suppose that we are also seeing a red rose at the same time. Then we may judge that the colours of the buttercups are more similar to each other than to the colour of the rose. This judgment seems more complicated, but has certainly gained in precision. Even now, however, it falls short of complete precision, since similarity is not *prima facie* measurable, and it would require much discussion to decide what we mean by greater or less similarity. To this process of the pursuit of precision there is strictly no limit.

The next thing to observe (although I do not personally doubt that most of our judgments of perception are true) is that it is very difficult to define any class of such judgments which can be known, by its intrinsic quality, to be always exempt from error. Most of our judgments of perception involve correlations, as when we judge that a certain noise is that of a passing cart. Such judgments are all obviously liable to error, since there is no correlation of which we have a right to be certain that it is invariable. Other judgments of perception are derived from recognition, as when we say 'this is a buttercup', or even merely 'this is yellow'. All such judgments entail some risk of error, though sometimes perhaps a very small one; some flowers that look like buttercups are marigolds, and colours that some would call yellow others might call orange. Our subjective certainty is usually a result of habit, and may lead us astray in circumstances which are unusual in ways of which we are unaware.

For such reasons, no form of self-evidence seems to afford an absolute criterion of truth. Nevertheless, it is perhaps true that judgments having a high degree of subjective certainty are more apt to be true than other judgments. But if this be the case, it is a result to be demonstrated, not a premiss from which to start in defining truth and falsehood. As an initial guarantee, therefore, neither self-evidence nor subjective certainty can be accepted as adequate.

(2) *Coherence.*—Coherence as the definition of truth is advocated by idealists, particularly by those who in the main follow Hegel. It is set forth ably in Mr Joachim's book, *The Nature of Truth* (Oxford, 1906). According to this view, any set of propositions other than the whole of truth can be condemned on purely logical grounds, as internally inconsistent; a single proposition, if it is what we should ordinarily call false, contradicts itself irremediably, while if it is what we should ordinarily call true, it has implications which compel us to admit other propositions, which in turn lead to others, and so on, until we find ourselves committed to the whole of truth. One might illustrate by a very simple example: if I say 'so-and-so is a married man', that is not a self-subsistent proposition. We cannot logically conceive of a universe in which this proposition constituted the whole of truth. There must be also someone who is a married woman, and who is married to the particular man in question. The view we are considering regards everything that can be said about any one object as relative in the same sort of way as 'so-and-so is a married man'. But everything, according to this view, is relative, not to one or two other things, but to all other things, so that from one bit of truth the whole can be inferred.

The fundamental objection to this view is logical, and consists in a criticism of its doctrine as to relations. I shall omit this line of argument, which I have developed elsewhere.[1] For the moment I will content myself with saying that the powers of logic seem to me very much less than this theory supposes. If it were taken seriously, its advocates ought to profess that any one truth is logically inferable from any other, and that, for example, the fact that Caesar conquered Gaul, if adequately considered, would enable us to discover what the weather will be tomorrow. No such claim is put forward in practice, and the necessity of empirical observation is not denied; but according to the theory it ought to be.

Another objection is that no endeavour is made to show that we cannot form a consistent whole composed partly or wholly of false propositions, as in a novel. Leibniz's conception of many possible worlds seems to

---

[1] In the article on 'The Monistic Theory of Truth' in *Philosophical Essays* (Longmans, 1910), reprinted from the *Proceedings of the Aristotelian Society*, 1906-7.

accord much better with modern logic and with the practical empiricism which is now universal. The attempt to deduce the world by pure thought is attractive, and in former times was largely supposed capable of success. But nowadays most men admit that beliefs must be tested by observation, and not merely by the fact that they harmonize with other beliefs. A consistent fairy-tale is a different thing from truth, however elaborate it may be. But to pursue this topic would lead us into difficult technicalities; I shall therefore assume, without further argument, that coherence is not sufficient as a definition of truth.

III. Many difficult problems arise as regards the verifiability of beliefs. We believe various things, and while we believe them we think we know them. But it sometimes turns out that we were mistaken, or at any rate we come to think we were. We must be mistaken either in our previous opinion or in our subsequent recantation; therefore our beliefs are not all correct, and there are cases of belief which are not cases of knowledge. The question of verifiability is in essence this: can we discover any set of beliefs which are never mistaken or any test which, when applicable, will always enable us to discriminate between true and false beliefs? Put thus broadly and abstractly, the answer must be negative. There is no way hitherto discovered of wholly eliminating the risk of error, and no infallible criterion. If we believe we have found a criterion, this belief itself may be mistaken; we should be begging the question if we tried to test the criterion by applying the criterion to itself.

But although the notion of an absolute criterion is chimerical, there may be relative criteria, which increase the probability of truth. Common sense and science hold that there are. Let us see what they have to say.

One of the plainest cases of verification, perhaps ultimately the only case, consists in the happening of something expected. You go to the station believing that there will be a train at a certain time; you find the train, you get into it, and it starts at the expected time. This constitutes verification, and is a perfectly definite experience. It is, in a sense, the converse of memory: instead of having first sensations and then images accompanied by belief, we have first images accompanied by belief and then sensations. Apart from differences as to the time-order and the accompanying feelings, the relation between image and sensation is closely similar in the two cases of memory and expectation; it is a relation of similarity, with difference as to causal efficacy—broadly, the image has the psychological but not the physical effects that the sensation would have. When an image accompanied by an expectation-belief is thus succeeded by a sensation which is the 'meaning' of the image, we say that the expectation-belief has been verified. The experience of verification in this sense is exceedingly familiar; it happens every time that

*

accustomed activities have results that are not surprising, in eating and walking and talking and all our daily pursuits.

But although the experience in question is common, it is not wholly easy to give a theoretical account of it. How do we know that the sensation resembles the previous image? Does the image persist in presence of the sensation, so that we can compare the two? And even if *some* image does persist, how do we know that it is the previous image unchanged? It does not seem as if this line of inquiry offered much hope of a successful issue. It is better, I think, to take a more external and causal view of the relation of expectation to expected occurrence. If the occurrence, when it comes, gives us the feeling of expectedness, and if the expectation, beforehand, enabled us to act in a way which proves appropriate to the occurrence, that must be held to constitute the maximum of verification. We have first an expectation, then a sensation with the feeling of expectedness related to memory of the expectation. This whole experience, when it occurs, may be defined as verification, and as constituting the truth of the expectation. Appropriate action, during the period of expectation, may be regarded as additional verification, but is not essential. The whole process may be illustrated by looking up a familiar quotation, finding it in the expected words, and in the expected part of the book. In this case we can strengthen the verification by writing down beforehand the words which we expect to find.

I think all verification is ultimately of the above sort. We verify a scientific hypothesis indirectly, by deducing consequences as to the future, which subsequent experience confirms. If somebody were to doubt whether Caesar had crossed the Rubicon, verification could only be obtained from the future. We could proceed to display manuscripts to our historical sceptic, in which it was said that Caesar had behaved in this way. We could advance arguments, verifiable by future experience, to prove the antiquity of the manuscript from its texture, colour, etc. We could find inscriptions agreeing with the historian on other points, and tending to show his general accuracy. The causal laws which our arguments would assume could be verified by the future occurrence of events inferred by means of them. The existence and persistence of causal laws, it is true, must be regarded as a fortunate accident, and how long it will continue we cannot tell. Meanwhile verification remains often practically possible. And since it is sometimes possible, we can gradually discover what kinds of beliefs tend to be verified by experience, and what kinds tend to be falsified; to the former kinds we give an increased degree of assent, to the latter kinds a diminished degree. The process is not absolute or infallible, but it has been found capable of sifting beliefs and building up science. It affords no theoretical refutation of the sceptic, whose position must remain logically unassailable; but if complete scepticism is rejected, it gives the practical method by which the system of our beliefs grows gradually towards the unattainable ideal of impeccable knowledge.

IV. I come now to the purely formal definition of the truth or falsehood of a belief. For this definition it is necessary first of all to consider the derivation of the objective reference of a proposition from the meanings of its component words or images.

Just as a word has meaning, so a proposition has an objective reference. The objective reference of a proposition is a function (in the mathematical sense) of the meanings of its component words. But the objective reference differs from the meaning of a word through the duality of truth and falsehood. You may believe the proposition 'today is Tuesday' both when, in fact, today is Tuesday, and when today is not Tuesday. If today is not Tuesday, this fact is the objective of your belief that today is Tuesday. But obviously the relation of your belief to the fact is different in this case from what it is in the case when today is Tuesday. We may say, metaphorically, that when today is Tuesday, your belief that it is Tuesday points *towards* the fact, whereas when today is not Tuesday your belief points *away from* the fact. Thus the objective reference of a belief is not determined by the fact alone, but by the direction of the belief towards or away from the fact.[1] If, on a Tuesday, one man believes that it is Tuesday while another believes that it is not Tuesday, their beliefs have the same objective, namely the fact that it is Tuesday, but the true belief points towards the fact while the false one points away from it. Thus, in order to define the reference of a proposition we have to take account not only of the objective, but also of the direction of pointing, towards the objective in the case of a true proposition and away from it in the case of a false one.

This mode of stating the nature of the objective reference of a proposition is necessitated by the circumstance that there are true and false propositions, but not true and false facts. If today is Tuesday, there is not a false objective 'today is not Tuesday', which could be the objective of the false belief 'today is not Tuesday'. This is the reason why two beliefs which are each other's contradictories have the same objective. There is, however, a practical inconvenience, namely that we cannot determine the objective reference of a proposition, according to this definition, unless we know whether the proposition is true or false. To avoid this inconvenience, it is better to adopt a slightly different phraseology, and say: The 'meaning' of the proposition 'today is Tuesday' consists in pointing to the fact 'today is Tuesday' if that is a fact, or away from the fact 'today is not Tuesday' if that is a fact. The 'meaning' of the proposition 'today is not Tuesday' will be exactly the opposite. By this hypothetical form we are able to speak of the meaning of a pro-

[1] I owe this way of looking at the matter to my friend Ludwig Wittgenstein.

position without knowing whether it is true or false. According to this definition, we know the meaning of a proposition when we know what would make it true and what would make it false, even if we do not know whether it is in fact true or false.

The meaning of a proposition is derivative from the meanings of its constituent words. Propositions occur in pairs, distinguished (in simple cases) by the absence or presence of the word 'not'. Two such propositions have the same objective, but opposite meanings: when one is true, the other is false, and when one is false, the other is true.

The purely formal definition of truth and falsehood offers little difficulty. What is required is a formal expression of the fact that a proposition is true when it points towards its objective, and false when it points away from it. In very simple cases we can give a very simple account of this: we can say that true propositions actually resemble their objectives in a way in which false propositions do not. But for this purpose it is necessary to revert to image-propositions instead of word-propositions. Let us take again the illustration of a memory-image of a familiar room, and let us suppose that in the image the window is to the left of the door. If in fact the window is to the left of the door, there is a correspondence between the image and the objective; there is the same relation between the window and the door as between the images of them. The image-memory consists of the image of the window to the left of the image of the door. When this is true, the very same relation relates the terms of the objective (namely the window and the door) as relates the images which mean them. In this case the correspondence which constitutes truth is very simple.

In the case we have just been considering the objective consists of two parts with a certain relation (that of left-to-right), and the proposition consists of images of these parts with the very same relation. The same proposition, if it were false, would have a less simple formal relation to its objective. If the image-proposition consists of an image of the window to the left of an image of the door, while in fact the window is not to the left of the door, the proposition does not result from the objective by the mere substitution of images for their prototypes. Thus in this unusually simple case we can say that a true proposition 'corresponds' to its objective in a formal sense in which a false proposition does not. Perhaps it may be possible to modify this notion of formal correspondence in such a way as to be more widely applicable, but if so, the modifications required will be by no means slight. The reasons for this must now be considered.

To begin with, the simple type of correspondence we have been exhibiting can hardly occur when words are substituted for images, because, in word-propositions, relations are usually expressed by words, which are not themselves relations. Take such a proposition as 'Socrates precedes

Plato'. Here the word 'precedes' is just as solid as the words 'Socrates' and 'Plato'; it *means* a relation, but is not a relation. Thus the objective which makes our proposition true consists of *two* terms with a relation between them, whereas our proposition consists of *three* terms with a relation of order between them. Of course, it would be perfectly possible, theoretically, to indicate a few chosen relations, not by words, but by relations between the other words. 'Socrates–Plato' might be used to mean 'Socrates precedes Plato'; 'Pla-Socrates-to' might be used to mean 'Plato was born before Socrates and died after him'; and so on. But the possibilities of such a method would be very limited. For aught I know, there may be languages that use it, but they are not among the languages with which I am acquainted. And in any case, in view of the multiplicity of relations that we wish to express, no language could advance far without words for relations. But as soon as we have words for relations, word-propositions have necessarily more terms than the facts to which they refer, and cannot therefore correspond so simply with their objectives as some image-propositions can.

The consideration of negative propositions and negative facts introduces further complications. An image-proposition is necessarily positive: we can image the window to the left of the door, or to the right of the door, but we can form no image of the bare negative 'the window not to the left of the door'. We can *disbelieve* the image-proposition expressed by 'the window to the left of the door', and our disbelief will be true if the window is not to the left of the door. But we can form no image of the fact that the window is not to the left of the door. Attempts have often been made to deny such negative facts, but, for reasons which I have given elsewhere,[1] I believe these attempts to be mistaken, and I shall assume that there are negative facts.

Word-propositions, like image-propositions, are always positive facts. The fact that Socrates precedes Plato is symbolized in English by the fact that the word 'precedes' occurs between the words 'Socrates' and 'Plato'. But we cannot symbolize the fact that Plato does not precede Socrates by not putting the word 'precedes' between 'Plato' and 'Socrates'. A negative fact is not sensible, and language, being intended for communication, has to be sensible. Therefore we symbolize the fact that Plato does not precede Socrates by putting the words 'does not precede' between 'Plato' and 'Socrates'. We thus obtain a series of words which is just as positive a fact as the series 'Socrates precedes Plato'. The propositions asserting negative facts are themselves positive facts; they are merely different positive facts from those asserting positive facts.

We have thus, as regards the opposition of positive and negative, three different sorts of duality, according as we are dealing with facts, image-propositions, or word-propositions. We have, namely:

[1] *Monist*, January 1919, pp. 42 ff.

(1) Positive and negative facts;

(2) Image-propositions, which may be believed or disbelieved, but do not allow any duality of content corresponding to positive and negative facts;

(3) Word-propositions, which are always positive facts, but are of two kinds: one verified by a positive objective, the other by a negative objective.

Owing to these complications, the simplest type of correspondence is impossible when either negative facts or negative propositions are involved.

Even when we confine ourselves to relations between two terms which are both imaged, it may be impossible to form an image-proposition in which the relation of the terms is represented by the same relation of the images. Suppose we say 'Caesar was 2,000 years before Foch', we express a certain temporal relation between Caesar and Foch; but we cannot allow 2,000 years to elapse between our image of Caesar and our image of Foch. This is perhaps not a fair example, since '2,000 years before' is not a direct relation. But take a case where the relation is direct, say, 'the sun is brighter than the moon'. We can form visual images of sunshine and moonshine, and it may happen that our image of the sunshine is the brighter of the two, but this is by no means either necessary or sufficient. The act of comparison, implied in our judgment, is something more than the mere co-existence of two images, one of which is in fact brighter than the other. It would take us too far from our main topic if we were to go into the question what actually occurs when we make this judgment. Enough has been said to show that the correspondence between the belief and its objective is more complicated in this case than in that of the window to the left of the door, and this was all that had to be proved.

In spite of these complications, the general nature of the formal correspondence which makes truth is clear from our instances. In the case of the simpler kind of propositions, namely those that I call 'atomic' propositions, where there is only one word expressing a relation, the objective which would verify our proposition, assuming that the word 'not' is absent, is obtained by replacing each word by what it means, the word meaning a relation being replaced by this relation among the meanings of the other words. For example, if the proposition is 'Socrates precedes Plato', the objective which verifies it results from replacing the word 'Socrates' by Socrates, the word 'Plato' by Plato, and the word 'precedes' by the relation of preceding between Socrates and Plato. If the result of this process is a fact, the proposition is true; if not, it is false. When our proposition is 'Socrates does not precede Plato', the conditions of truth and falsehood are exactly reversed. More complicated propositions can be dealt with on the same lines. In fact, the purely formal question, which has occupied us in this last section, offers no very formidable difficulties.

I do not believe that the above formal theory is untrue, but I do believe that it is inadequate. It does not, for example, throw any light upon our preference for true beliefs rather than false ones. This preference is only explicable by taking account of the causal efficacy of beliefs, and of the greater appropriateness of the responses resulting from true beliefs. But appropriateness depends upon purpose, and purpose thus becomes a vital part of theory of knowledge.

(*The Analysis of Mind*, London: Allen & Unwin;
New York: The Macmillan Co., 1921.)

39

KNOWLEDGE BEHAVIOURISTICALLY CONSIDERED

THE word 'knowledge', like the word 'memory', is avoided by the behaviourist. Nevertheless there is a phenomenon commonly called 'knowledge', which is tested behaviouristically in examinations. I want to consider this phenomenon with a view to deciding whether there is anything in it that the behaviourist cannot deal with adequately.

It will be remembered that, in Chapter II, we were led to the view that knowledge is a characteristic of the complete process from stimulus to reaction, or even, in the cases of sight and hearing, from an external object to a reaction, the external object being connected with the stimulus by a chain of physical causation in the outer world. Let us, for the moment, leave on one side such cases as sight and hearing, and confine ourselves, for the sake of definiteness, to knowledge derived from touch.

We can observe touch producing reactions in quite humble animals, such as worms and sea anemones. Are we to say that they have 'knowledge' of what they touch? In some sense, yes. Knowledge is a matter of degree. When it is regarded in a purely behaviouristic manner, we shall have to concede that it exists, in some degree, wherever there is a characteristic reaction to a stimulus of a certain kind, and this reaction does not occur in the absence of the right kind of stimulus. In this sense, 'knowledge' is indistinguishable from 'sensitivity', which we considered in connection with perception. We might say that a thermometer 'knows' the temperature, and that a compass 'knows' the direction of the magnetic north. This is the only sense in which, on grounds of observation, we can attribute knowledge to animals that are low in the scale. Many animals, for example, hide themselves when exposed to light, but as a rule not otherwise. In this, however, they do not differ from a radiometer. No doubt the mechanism is different, but the observed molar motion has similar characteristics. Whenever there is a reflex, an animal may be said, in a sense, to 'know' the stimulus. This is, no doubt, not the usual sense of 'knowledge', but it is the germ out of which knowledge in the usual sense has grown, and without which no knowledge would be possible.

Knowledge in any more advanced sense is only possible as a result of learning, in the sense considered in Chapter III. The rat that has learned the maze 'knows' the way out of it; the boy who has learned certain verbal reactions 'knows' the multiplication table. Between these two cases there is no important difference. In both cases, we say that the subject 'knows' something because he reacts in a manner advantageous to himself, in which he could not react before he had had certain experiences. I do not think, however, that we ought to use such a notion as 'advantageous' in connection with knowledge. What we can observe, for instance, with the rat in the maze, is violent activity until the food is reached, followed by eating when it is reached; also a gradual elimination of acts which do not lead to the food. Where this sort of behaviour is observed, we may say that it is directed towards the food, and that the animal 'knows' the way to the food when he gets to it by the shortest possible route.

But if this view is right, we cannot define any knowledge acquired by learning except with reference to circumstances towards which an animal's activity is directed. We should say, popularly, that the animal 'desires' such circumstances. 'Desire', like 'knowledge', is capable of a behaviouristic definition, and it would seem that the two are correlative. Let us, then, spend a little time on the behaviouristic treatment of 'desire'.

The best example of desire, from this point of view, is hunger. The stimulus to hunger is a certain well-ascertained bodily condition. When in this condition, an animal moves restlessly; if he sees or smells food, he moves in a manner which, in conditions to which he is accustomed, would bring him to the food; if he reaches it, he eats it, and if the quantity is sufficient he then becomes quiescent. This kind of behaviour may be summarized by saying that a hungry animal 'desires' food. It is behaviour which is in various ways different from that of inanimate matter, because restless movements persist until a certain condition is realized. These movements may or may not be the best adapted to realizing the condition in question. Everyone knows about the pike that was put on one side of a glass partition, with minnows on the other side. He continually bumped his nose on the glass, and after six weeks gave up the attempt to catch them. When, after this, the partition was removed, he still refrained from pursuing them. I do not know whether the experiment was tried of leaving a possibility of getting to the minnows by a roundabout route. To have learned to take a roundabout route would perhaps have required a degree of intelligence beyond the capacity of fishes; this is a matter, however, which offers little difficulty to dogs or monkeys.

What applies to hunger applies equally to other forms of 'desire'. Every animal has a certain congenital apparatus of 'desires'; that is to say, in certain bodily conditions he is stimulated to restless activities which tend towards the performance of some reflex, and if a given situation is often repeated the animal arrives more and more quickly at the performance of the reflex. This last, however, is only true of the higher animals; in the lower, the whole process from beginning to end is reflex, and can therefore only succeed in normal circumstances. The higher animals, and more especially men, have a larger proportion of learning and a smaller proportion of reflexes in their behaviour, and are therefore better able to adapt themselves to new circumstances. The helplessness of infants is a necessary condition for the adaptability of adults; infants have fewer useful reflexes than the young of animals, but have far more power of forming useful habits, which can be adapted to circumstances and are not fatally fixed from birth. This fact is intimately connected with the superiority of the human intelligence above that of the brutes.

Desire is extremely subject to 'conditioning'. If A is a primitive desire and B has on many occasions been a means to A, B comes to be desired in the same sense in which A was previously desired. It may even happen, as in misers, that the desire for B completely displaces the desire for A, so that B, when attained, is no longer used as a means to A. This, however, is more or less exceptional. In general, the desire for A persists, although the desire for B has a more or less independent life.

The 'conditioning' of primitive desires in human beings is the source of much that distinguishes our life from that of animals. Most animals only seek food when they are hungry; they may, then, die of starvation before they find it. Men, on the contrary, must have early acquired pleasure in hunting as an art, and must have set out on hunting expeditions before they were actually hungry. A further stage in the conditioning of hunger came with domestic animals; a still further stage with agriculture. Nowadays, when a man sets to work to earn his living, his activity is still connected, though not very directly, with hunger and the other primitive desires that can be gratified by means of money. These primitive desires are still, so to speak, the power station, though their energy is widely distributed to all sorts of undertakings that seem, at first sight, to have no connection with them. Consider 'freedom' and the political activities it inspires; this is derivable, by 'conditioning', from the emotion of rage which Dr Watson observed in infants whose limbs are not 'free'. Again we speak of the 'fall' of empires and of 'fallen' women; this is connected with the fear which infants display when left without support.

After this excursion into the realm of desire, we can now return to 'knowledge', which, as we saw, is a term correlative to 'desire', and applicable to another feature of the same kind of activity. We may say, broadly, that a response to a stimulus of the kind involving desire in the above sense shows 'knowledge' if it leads by the quickest or easiest route to the state of affairs which, in the above sense, is behaviouristically the object of desire. Knowledge is thus a matter of degree: the rat, during its progressive improvements in the maze, is gradually acquiring more and more knowledge. Its 'intelligence quotient', so far as that particular task is concerned, will be the ratio of the time it took on the first trial to the time it takes now to get out of the maze. Another point, if our definition of knowledge is accepted, is, that there is no such thing as purely contemplative knowledge: knowledge exists only in relation to the satisfaction of desire, or, as we say, in the capacity to choose the right means to achieve our ends.

But can such a definition as the above really stand? Does it represent at all the sort of thing that would commonly be called knowledge? I think it does in the main, but there is need of some discussion to make this clear.

In some cases, the definition is obviously applicable. These are the cases that are analogous to the rat in the maze, the consideration of which led us to our definition. Do you 'know' the way from Trafalgar Square to St Pancras? Yes, if you can walk it without taking any wrong turnings. In practice, you can give verbal proof of such knowledge, without actually having to walk the distance; but that depends upon the correlation of names with streets, and is part of the process of substituting words for things. There may, it is true, come doubtful cases. I was once on a bus in Whitehall, and my neighbour asked 'What street is this?' I answered him, not without surprise at his ignorance. He then said, 'What building is that?' and I replied 'The Foreign Office'. To this he retorted, 'But I thought the Foreign Office was in Downing Street'. This time, it was his knowledge that surprised me. Should we say that he knew where the Foreign Office is? The answer is yes or no according to his purpose. From the point of view of sending a letter to it, he knew; from the point of view of walking to it, he did not know. He had, in fact, been a British Consul in South America, and was in London for the first time.

But now let us come to cases less obviously within the scope of our definition. The reader 'knows' that Columbus crossed the ocean in 1492. What do we mean by saying that he 'knows' this? We mean, no doubt, primarily that writing down this statement is the way to pass examinations, which is just as useful to us as getting out of the maze is to the rat. But we do not mean only this. There is historical evidence of the fact, at least I suppose there is. The historical evidence consists of printed books and manuscripts. Certain rules have been developed by historians as to the conditions in which statements in books or manuscripts may be accepted as true, and the evidence in our case is (I presume) in accordance with these rules. Historical facts often have importance in the present; for example, wills, or laws not yet repealed. The rules for weighing historical evidence are such as will, in general, bring out self-consistent results. Two results are self-consistent when, in relation to a desire to which both are relevant, they enjoin the same action, or actions which can form part of one movement towards the goal. At Coton, near Cambridge, there is (or was in my time) a signpost with two arms pointing in diametrically opposite directions, and each arm said 'To Cambridge'. This was a perfect example of self-contradiction, since the two arms made statements representing exactly opposite actions. And this case illustrates why self-contradiction is to be avoided. But the avoidance of self-contradiction makes great demands upon us; Hegel and Bradley imagined that we could know the nature of the universe by means of this principle alone. In this they were pretty certainly mistaken, but nevertheless a great deal of our 'knowledge' depends upon this principle to a greater or less extent.

Most of our knowledge is like that in a cookery book, maxims to be followed when occasion arises, but not useful at every moment of every day. Since knowledge may be useful at any time, we get gradually, through conditioning, a general desire for knowledge. The learned man who is helpless in practical affairs is analogous to the miser, in that he has become absorbed in a means. It should be observed, also, that knowledge is neutral as among different purposes. If you know that arsenic is a poison, that enables you equally to avoid it if you wish to remain in health, and to take it if you wish to commit suicide. You cannot judge from a man's conduct in relation to arsenic whether he knows that it is a poison or not, unless you know his desires. He may be tired of life, but avoid arsenic because he has been told that it is a good medicine; in this case, his avoidance of it is evidence of *lack* of knowledge.

But to return to Columbus: surely, the reader will say, Columbus really did cross the Atlantic in 1492, and that is why we call this statement 'knowledge'. This is the definition of 'truth' as 'correspondence with fact'. I think there is an important element of correctness in this definition, but it is an element to be elicited at a later stage, after we have discussed the physical world. And it has the defect—as pragmatists have urged—that there seems no way of getting at 'facts' and comparing them with our beliefs: all that we ever reach consists of other beliefs. I do not offer our present behaviouristic and pragmatic definition of 'knowledge' as the only possible one, but I offer it as the one to which we are led if we wish to regard knowledge as something causally important, to be exemplified in our reactions to stimuli. This is the appropriate point of view when we are studying man from without, as we have been doing hitherto.

There is, however, within the behaviourist philosophy, one important addition to be made to our definition. We began this chapter with sensitivity, but we went on to the consideration of learned reactions, where the learning depended upon association. But there is another sort of learning —at least it is *prima facie* another sort—which consists of increase of sensitivity. All sensitivity in animals and human beings must count as a sort of knowledge; that is to say, if an animal behaves, in the presence of a stimulus of a certain kind, as it would not behave in the absence of that stimulus, then, in an important sense, it has 'knowledge' as regards the stimulus. Now it appears that practice—e.g. in music—very greatly increases sensitivity. We learn to react differently to stimuli which only differ slightly; what is more, we learn to react to differences. A violin-player can react with great precision to an interval of a fifth; if the interval is very slightly greater or less, his behaviour in tuning is influenced by the difference from a fifth. And as we have already had occasion to notice, we become, through practice, increasingly sensitive to form. All this increased sensitivity must count as increase of knowledge.

But in saying this we are not saying anything inconsistent with our earlier definition of knowledge. Sensitivity is essential to choosing the right reaction in many cases. To take the cookery book again: when it says 'take a pinch of salt', a good cook knows how much to take, which is an instance of sensitivity. Accurate scientific observation, which is of great practical importance, depends upon sensitivity. And so do many of our practical dealings with other people: if we cannot 'feel' their moods, we shall be always getting at cross purposes.

The extent to which sensitivity is improved by practice is astonishing. Town-bred people do not know whether the weather is warm or cold until they read the weather reports in the paper. An entomologist perceives vastly more beetles in the course of a country walk than other people do. The subtlety with which connoisseurs can distinguish among wines and cigars is the despair of youths who wish to become men of the world. Whether this increase of sensitivity can be accounted for by the law of association, I do not know. In many cases, probably, it can, but I think sensitiveness to form, which is the essential element in the more difficult forms of abstract thought as well as in many other matters, cannot be regarded as derivative from the law of association, but is more analogous to the development of a new sense. I should therefore include improvement in sensitivity as an independent element in the advancement of knowledge. But I do so with some hesitation.

The above discussion does not pretend to cover the whole of the ground that has to be covered in discussing the definition of 'knowledge'. There are other points of view, which are also necessary to a complete consideration of the question. But these must wait until, after considering the physical world, we come to the discussion of man as viewed from within.

(*An Outline of Philosophy*, London: Allen & Unwin;
Philosophy, New York: W. W. Norton, 1927.)

PART IX

The Moral Philosopher

Perhaps no philosopher in modern times has been subject to more scathing criticism of his views on ethics than Russell. Few major thinkers have, however, dared to utter opinions that were so out of tune with current stereotyped beliefs. Whether history will later confirm or deny the wisdom of Russell's views on ethics, his desire to champion unpopular ideas and to question any idea which seemed irrational deserves admiration. Those who see morality as a settled body of knowledge will obviously derive no pleasure from reading Russell's terse criticism of traditional beliefs, many of which have deep roots in ancient superstitions.

It is, of course, on the topic of sex that Russell has encountered most unfavourable criticism (and loss of position as in the case of City College) for here he strikes deeply at superstitions. But sex is not the whole subject-matter of ethics as the selections which follow amply demonstrate. Russell, as a scientific humanist, has had deep concern for the problems of human conduct and the theories of their solution for the individual and society, the more so since he finds these solutions outside of organized religion. In this field of moral theory, we find once more a gradual change and development of viewpoint as his ideas of language, logic and philosophy in general have altered over the years.

40

STYLES IN ETHICS

IN all ages and nations positive morality has consisted almost wholly of prohibitions of various classes of actions, with the addition of a small number of commands to perform certain other actions. The Jews, for example, prohibited murder and theft, adultery and incest, the eating of pork and seething the kid in its mother's milk. To us the last two precepts may seem less important than the others, but religious Jews have observed them far more scrupulously than what seem to us fundamental principles of morality. South Sea Islanders could imagine nothing more utterly wicked than eating out of a vessel reserved for the use of the chief. My friend Dr Brogan made a statistical investigation into the ethical valuations of undergraduates in certain American colleges. Most considered Sabbath-breaking more wicked than lying, and extra-conjugal sexual relations more wicked than murder. The Japanese consider disobedience to parents the most atrocious of crimes. I was once at a charming spot on the outskirts of Kioto with several Japanese socialists, men who were among the most advanced thinkers in the country. They told me that a certain well beside which we were standing was a favourite spot for suicides, which were very frequent. When I asked why so many occurred they replied that most were those of young people in love whose parents had forbidden them to marry. To my suggestion that perhaps it would be better if parents had less power they all returned an emphatic negative. To Dr Brogan's undergraduates this power of Japanese parents to forbid love would seem monstrous, but the similar power of husbands or wives would seem a matter of course. Neither they nor the Japanese would examine the question rationally; both would decide unthinkingly on the basis of moral precepts learned in youth.

When we study in the works of anthropologists the moral precepts which men have considered binding in different times and places we find the most bewildering variety. It is quite obvious to any modern reader that most of these customs are absurd. The Aztecs held that it was a duty to sacrifice and eat enemies captured in war, since otherwise the light of the sun would go out. The Book of Leviticus enjoins that when a married man dies without children his brother shall marry the widow, and the first son born shall count as the dead man's son. The Romans, the Chinese, and many other nations secured a similar result by adoption. This custom originated in ancestor-worship; it was thought that the ghost would make himself a nuisance unless he had descendants (real or putative) to worship him. In India the remarriage of widows is traditionally considered something too horrible to contemplate. Many primitive races feel horror at the thought of marrying anyone belonging to one's own totem, though there may be only the most distant blood-relationship. After studying these various customs it begins at last to occur to the reader that possibly the customs of his own age and nation are not eternal, divine ordinances, but are susceptible of change, and even, in some respects, of improvement. Books such as Westermarck's *History of Human Marriage* or Müller-Lyer's *Phasen der Liebe*, which relate in a scientific spirit the marriage customs that have existed and the reasons which have led to their growth and decay, produce evidence which must convince any rational mind that our own customs are sure to change and that there is no reason to expect a change to be harmful. It thus becomes impossible to cling to the position of many who are earnest advocates of *political* reform and yet hold that reform in our moral precepts is not needed. Moral precepts, like everything else, can be improved, and the true reformer will be as open-minded in regard to them as in regard to other matters.

Müller-Lyer, from the point of view of family institutions, divides the history of civilization into three periods—the clan period, the family period, and the personal period. Of these the last is only now beginning; the other two are each divided into three stages—early, middle and late. He shows that sexual and family ethics have at all times been dominated by economic considerations; hunting, pastoral, agricultural and industrial tribes or nations have each their own special kinds of institutions. Economic causes determine whether a tribe will practise polygamy, polyandry, group marriage, or monogamy, and whether monogamy will be lifelong or dissoluble. Whatever the prevailing practice in a tribe it is thought to be the only one compatible with virtue, and all departures from it are regarded with moral horror. Owing to the force of custom it may take a long time for institutions to adapt themselves to economic circumstances; the process of adaptation may take centuries. Christian sexual ethics, according to this author, belong to the middle-family period; the personal period, now beginning, has not yet been embodied in the laws of most Christian countries, and even the late-family period, since it admits divorce under certain circumstances, involves an ethic to which the Church is usually opposed.

Müller-Lyer suggests a general law to the effect that where the state is strong the family is weak and the position of women is good, whereas where the state is weak the family is strong and the position of women is bad. It is of course obvious that where the family is strong the position of women must be bad, and vice versa, but the connection of these with the strength or weakness of the state is less obvious, though probably in the main no less true. Traditional China and Japan afforded good instances. In both the state was much weaker than in modern Europe, the family much stronger, and the position of women much worse. It is true that in modern Japan the state is very strong, yet the family also is strong and the position of women is bad; but this is a transitional condition. The whole tendency in Japan is for the family to grow weaker and the position of women to grow better. This tendency encounters grave difficulties. I met in Japan only one woman who appeared to be what we should consider emancipated in the West—she was charming, beautiful, high-minded, and prepared to make any sacrifice for her principles. After the earthquake in Tokio the officer in charge of the forces concerned in keeping order in the district where she lived, seized her and the man with whom she lived in a free union and her twelve-year-old nephew, whom he believed to be her son; he took them to the police station and there murdered them by slow strangulation, taking about ten minutes over each except the boy. In his account of the matter he stated that he had not had much difficulty with the boy, because he had succeeded in making friends with him on the way to the police station. The boy was an American citizen. At the funeral, the remains of all three were seized by armed reactionaries and destroyed, with the passive acquiescence of the police. The question whether the murderer deserved well of his country is now set in schools, half the children answering affirmatively. We have here a dramatic confrontation of middle-family ethics with personal ethics. The officer's views were those of feudalism, which is a middle-family system; his victims' views were those of the nascent personal period. The Japanese state, which belongs to the late-family period, disapproved of both.

The middle-family system involves cruelty and persecution. The indissolubility of marriage results in appalling misery for the wives of drunkards, sadists and brutes of all kinds, as well as great unhappiness for many men and the unedifying spectacle of daily quarrels for the unfortunate children of ill-assorted couples. It involves also an immense amount of prostitution, with its inevitable consequence of widespread venereal disease. It makes marriage, in most cases, a matter of financial bargain between parents, and virtually proscribes love. It considers sexual intercourse always justifiable within marriage, even if no mutual affection exists. It is impossible to be too thankful that this system is nearly extinct in the Western nations (except France). But it is foolish to pretend that this ideal held by the Catholic church and in some degree by most Protestant churches is a lofty one. It is intolerant, gross, cruel and hostile to all the best potentialities of human nature. Nothing is gained by continuing to pay lip-service to this musty Moloch.

The American attitude on marriage is curious. America, in the main, does not object to easy divorce laws, and is tolerant of those who avail themselves of them. But it holds that those who live in countries where divorce is difficult or impossible ought to submit to hardships from which Americans are exempt, and deserve to be held up to obloquy if they do not do so. An interesting example of this attitude was afforded by the treatment of Gorki when he visited the United States.

There are two different lines of argument by which it is possible to attack the general belief that there are universal absolute rules of moral conduct, and that anyone who infringes them is wicked. One line of argument emerges from the anthropological facts which we have already considered. Broadly speaking, the views of the average man on sexual ethics are those appropriate to the economic system existing in the time of his great-grandfather. Morality has varied as economic systems have varied, lagging always about three generations behind. As soon as people realize this they find it impossible to suppose that the particular brand of marriage customs prevailing in their own age and nation represents eternal verities, whereas all earlier and later marriage customs, and all those prevailing in other latitudes and longitudes, are vicious and degraded. This shows that we ought to be prepared for changes in marriage customs, but does not tell us what changes we ought to desire.

The second line of argument is more positive and more important. Popular morality—including that of the churches, though not that of the great mystics—lays down rules of conduct rather than ends of life. The morality that ought to exist would lay down ends of life rather than rules of conduct. Christ says: 'Thou shalt love thy neighbour as thyself'; this lays down one of the ends of life. The Decalogue says: 'Remember that thou keep holy the Sabbath Day'; this lays down a rule of action. Christ's conduct to the woman taken in adultery showed the conflict between love and moral rules. All His priests, down to our own day, have gone directly contrary to His teachings on this point, and have shown themselves invariably willing to cast the first stone. The belief in the importance of rules of conduct is superstitious; what is important is to care for good ends. A good man is a man who cares for the happiness of his relations and friends, and, if possible, for that of mankind in general, or, again, a man who cares for art and science. Whether such a man obeys the moral rules laid down by the Jews thousands of years ago is quite unimportant. Moreover a man may obey all these rules and yet be extremely bad.

Let us take some illustrations. I have a friend, a high-minded man, who has taken part in arduous and dangerous enterprises of great public importance and is almost unbelievably kind in all his private relations.

This man has a wife who is a dipsomaniac, who has become imbecile, and has to be kept in an institution. She cannot divorce him because she is imbecile; he cannot divorce her because she affords him no ground for divorce. He does not consider himself morally bound to her and is therefore, from a conventional point of view, a wicked man. On the other hand a man who is perpetually drunk, who kicks his wife when she is pregnant, and begets ten imbecile children, is not generally regarded as particularly wicked. A business man who is generous to all his employees but falls in love with his stenographer is wicked; another who bullies his employees but is faithful to his wife is virtuous. This attitude is rank superstition, and it is high time that it was got rid of.

Sexual morality, freed from superstition, is a simple matter. Fraud and deceit, assault, seduction of persons under age, are proper matters for the criminal law. Relations between adults who are free agents are a private matter, and should not be interfered with either by the law or by public opinion, because no outsider can know whether they are good or bad. When children are involved the state becomes interested to the extent of seeing that they are properly educated and cared for, and it ought to ensure that the father does his duty by them in the way of maintenance. But neither the state nor public opinion ought to insist on the parents living together if they are incompatible; the spectacle of parents' quarrels is far worse for children than the separation of the parents could possibly be.

The ideal to be aimed at is not lifelong monogamy enforced by legal or social penalties. The ideal to be aimed at is that all sexual intercourse should spring from the free impulse of both parties, based upon mutual inclination and nothing else. At present a woman who sells herself successively to different men is branded as a prostitute, whereas a woman who sells herself for life to one rich man whom she does not love becomes a respected society leader. The one is exactly as bad as the other. The individual should not be condemned in either case; but the institutions producing the individual's action should be condemned equally in both cases. The cramping of love by institutions is one of the major evils of the world. Every person who allows himself to think that an adulterer must be wicked adds his stone to the prison in which the source of poetry and beauty and life is incarcerated by 'priests in black gowns'.

Perhaps there is not, strictly speaking, any such thing as 'scientific' ethics. It is not the province of science to decide on the ends of life. Science can show that an ethic is unscientific, in the sense that it does not minister to any desired end. Science also can show how to bring the interest of the individual into harmony with that of society. We make laws against theft, in order that theft may become contrary to self-interest. We might, on the same ground, make laws to diminish the number of imbecile children born into the world. There is no evidence that existing marriage laws, particularly where they are very strict, serve any social purpose; in this sense we may say that they are unscientific. But to proclaim the ends of life, and make men conscious of their value, is not the business of science; it is the business of the mystic, the artist and the poet.

(Our Changing Morality, ed. Freda Kirchwey,
New York: Albert & Charles Boni, 1924.)

41

THE PLACE OF SEX AMONG HUMAN VALUES

THE writer who deals with a sexual theme is always in danger of being accused, by those who think that such themes should not be mentioned, of an undue obsession with his subject. It is thought that he would not risk the censure of prudish and prurient persons unless his interest in the subject were out of all proportion to its importance. This view, however, is only taken in the case of those who advocate changes in the conventional ethic. Those who stimulate the appeals to harry prostitutes and those who secure legislation nominally against the White Slave Traffic, but really against voluntary and decent extra-marital relations; those who denounce women for short skirts and lipsticks; and those who spy upon sea beaches in the hopes of discovering inadequate bathing costumes, are none of them supposed to be the victims of a sexual obsession. Yet in fact they probably suffer much more in this way than do writers who advocate greater sexual freedom. Fierce morality is generally a reaction against lustful emotions, and the man who gives expression to it is generally filled with indecent thoughts—thoughts which are rendered indecent, not by the mere fact that they have a sexual content, but by the fact that morality has incapacitated the thinker from thinking cleanly and wholesomely on this topic. I am quite in agreement with the Church in thinking that obsession with sexual topics is an evil, but I am not in agreement with the Church as to the best methods of avoiding this evil. It is notorious that St Anthony was more obsessed by sex than the most extreme voluptuary who ever lived; I will not adduce more recent examples for fear of giving offence. Sex is a natural need, like food and drink. We blame the gormandizer and the dipsomaniac, because in the case of each an interest which has a certain legitimate place in life has usurped too large a share of his thoughts and emotions. But we do not blame a man for a normal and healthy enjoyment of a reasonable quantity of food. Ascetics, it is true, have done so, and have considered that a man should cut down his nutriment to the lowest point compatible with survival, but this view is not now common, and may be ignored. The Puritans, in their determination to avoid the pleasures of sex, became somewhat more conscious than people had been before of the pleasures of the table. As a seventeenth-century critic of Puritanism says:

> Would you enjoy gay nights and pleasant dinners?
> Then must you board with saints and bed with sinners.

It would seem, therefore, that the Puritans did not succeed in subduing the purely corporeal part of our human nature, since what they took away from sex they added to gluttony. Gluttony is regarded by the Catholic Church as one of the seven deadly sins, and those who practise it are placed by Dante in one of the deeper circles of hell; but it is a somewhat vague sin, since it is hard to say where legitimate interest in food ceases and guilt begins to be incurred. Is it wicked to eat anything that is not nourishing? If so, with every salted almond we risk damnation. Such views, however, are out of date. We all know a glutton when we see one, and although he may be somewhat despised, he is not severely reprobated. In spite of this fact, undue obsession with food is rare among those who have never suffered want. Most people eat their meals and then think about other things until the next meal. Those, on the other hand, who, having adopted an ascetic philosophy, have deprived themselves of all but the minimum of food, become obsessed by visions of banquets and dreams of demons bearing luscious fruits. And marooned Antarctic explorers, reduced to a diet of whale's blubber, spend their days planning the dinner they will have at the Carlton when they get home.

Such facts suggest that, if sex is not to be an obsession, it should be regarded by the moralists as food has come to be regarded, and not as food was regarded by the hermits of the Thebaid. Sex is a natural human need like food and drink. It is true that men can survive without it, whereas they cannot survive without food and drink, but from a psychological standpoint the desire for sex is precisely analogous to the desire for food and drink. It is enormously enhanced by abstinence, and temporarily allayed by satisfaction. While it is urgent, it shuts out the rest of the world from the mental purview. All other interests fade for the moment, and actions may be performed which will subsequently appear insane to the man who has been guilty of them. Moreover, as in the case of food and drink, the desire is enormously stimulated by prohibition. I have known children refuse apples at breakfast and go straight out into the orchard and steal them, although the breakfast apples were ripe and the stolen apples unripe. I do not think it can be denied that the desire for alcohol among well-to-do Americans is much stronger than it was twenty years ago. In like manner, Christian teaching and Christian authority have immensely stimulated interest in sex. The generation which first ceases to believe in the conventional teaching is bound, therefore, to indulge in sexual freedom to a degree far beyond what is to be expected of those whose views on sex are unaffected by superstitious teaching, whether positively or negatively. Nothing but freedom will prevent undue obsession with sex, but even freedom will not have this effect unless it has become habitual and has been associated with a wise education as regards sexual matters. I wish to repeat, however, as emphatically as I can, that I regard an undue preoccupation with this topic as an evil, and that I think this evil widespread at the present day, especially in America, where I find it particularly pronounced among the sterner moralists, who display it markedly by their readiness to believe falsehoods concerning those whom they regard as their opponents. The glutton, the voluptuary, and the ascetic are all self-absorbed persons whose horizon is limited by their own desires, either by way of satisfaction or by way of renunciation. A man who is healthy in mind and body will not have his interests thus concentrated upon himself. He will look out upon the world and find in it objects that seem to him worthy of his attention. Absorption in self is not, as some have supposed, the natural condition of unregenerate man. It is a disease brought on, almost always, by some thwarting of natural impulses. The voluptuary who gloats over thoughts of sexual gratification is in general the result of some kind of deprivation, just as the man who hoards food is usually a man who has lived through a famine or a period of destitution. Healthy, outward-looking men and women are not to be produced by the thwarting of natural impulse, but by the equal and balanced development of all the impulses essential to a happy life.

I am not suggesting that there should be no morality and no self-restraint in regard to sex, any more than in regard to food. In regard to food we have restraints of three kinds, those of law, those of manners, and those of health. We regard it as wrong to steal food, to take more than our share at a common meal, and to eat in ways that are likely to make us ill. Restraints of a similar kind are essential where sex is concerned, but in this case they are much more complex and involve much more self-control. Moreover, since one human being ought not to have property in another, the analogue of stealing is not adultery, but rape, which obviously must be forbidden by law. The questions that arise in regard to health are concerned almost entirely with venereal disease, a subject which we have already touched upon in connection with prostitution. Clearly, the diminution of professional prostitution is the best way, apart from medicine, of dealing with this evil, and diminution of professional prostitution can be best effected by that greater freedom among young people which has been growing up in recent years.

A comprehensive sexual ethic cannot regard sex merely as a natural hunger and a possible source of danger. Both these points of view are important, but it is even more important to remember that sex is connected with some of the greatest goods in human life. The three that seem paramount are lyric love, happiness in marriage, and art. Of lyric love and marriage we have already spoken. Art is thought by some to be independent of sex, but this view has fewer adherents now than it had in former times. It is fairly clear that the impulse to every kind of aesthetic creation is psychologically connected with courtship, not necessarily in any direct or obvious way, but none the less profoundly. In order that the sexual impulse may lead to artistic expression, a number of conditions are necessary. There must be artistic capacity; but artistic capacity, even within a given race, appears as though it were common at one time and uncommon at another, from which it is safe to conclude that environment, as opposed to native talent, has an important part to play in the development of the artistic impulse. There must be a certain kind of freedom, not the sort that consists in rewarding the artist, but the sort that consists in not compelling him or inducing him to form habits which turn him into a Philistine. When Julius II imprisoned Michelangelo, he did not in any way interfere with that kind of freedom which the artist needs. He imprisoned him because he considered him an important man, and he would not tolerate the slightest offence to him from anybody whose rank was less than papal. When, however, an artist is compelled to kotow to rich patrons or town councillors, and to adapt his work to their aesthetic canons, his artistic freedom is lost. And when he is compelled by fear of social and economic persecution to go on living in a marriage which has become intolerable, he is deprived of the energy which artistic creation requires. Societies that have been conventionally virtuous have not produced great art. Those which have, have been composed of men such as Idaho would sterilize. America at present imports most of its artistic talent from Europe, where, as yet, freedom lingers; but already the Americanization of Europe is making it necessary to turn to the negroes. The last home of art, it seems, is to be somewhere on the Upper Congo, if not in the uplands of Tibet. But its final extinction cannot be long delayed, since the rewards which America is prepared to lavish upon foreign artists are such as must inevitably bring about their artistic death. Art in the past has had a popular basis, and this has depended upon joy of life. Joy of life, in its turn, depends upon a certain spontaneity in regard to sex. Where sex is repressed, only work remains, and a gospel of work for work's sake never produced any work worth doing. Let me not be told that someone has collected statistics of the number of sexual acts *per diem* (or shall we say *per noctem?*) performed in the United States, and that it is at least as great per head as in any other country. I do not know whether this is the case or not, and I am not in any way concerned to deny it. One of the most dangerous fallacies of the conventional moralists is the reduction of sex to the sexual act, in order to be the better able to belabour it. No civilized man, and no savage that I have ever heard of, is satisfied in his instinct by the bare sexual act. If the impulse which leads to the act is to be satisfied, there must be courtship, there must be love, there must be companionship. Without these, while the physical hunger may be appeased for the moment, the mental hunger remains unabated, and no profound satisfaction can be obtained. The sexual freedom that the artist needs is freedom to love, not the gross freedom to relieve the bodily need with some unknown woman; and freedom to love is what, above all, the conventional moralists will not concede. If art is to revive after the world has been Americanized, it will be necessary that America should change, that its moralists should become less moral and its immoralists less immoral, that both, in a word, should recognize the higher values involved in sex, and the possibility that joy may be of more value than a bank account. Nothing in America is so painful to the traveller as the lack of joy. Pleasure is frantic and bacchanalian, a matter of momentary oblivion, not of delighted self-expression. Men whose grandfathers danced to the music of the pipe in Balkan or Polish villages sit throughout the day glued to their desks, amid typewriters and telephones, serious, important and worthless. Escaping in the evening to drink and a new kind of noise, they imagine that they are finding happiness, whereas they are finding only a frenzied and incomplete oblivion of the hopeless routine of money that breeds money, using for the purpose the bodies of human beings whose souls have been sold into slavery.

It is not my intention to suggest, what I by no means believe, that all that is best in human life is connected with sex. I do not myself regard science, either practical or theoretical, as connected with it, nor yet certain kinds of important social and political activities. The impulses that lead to the complex desires of adult life can be arranged under a few simple heads. Power, sex and parenthood appear to me to be the source of most of the things that human beings do, apart from what is necessary for self-preservation. Of these three, power begins first and ends last. The child, since he has very little power, is dominated by the desire to have more. Indeed, a large proportion of his activities spring from this desire. His other dominant desire is vanity—the wish to be praised and the fear of being blamed or left out. It is vanity that makes him a social being and gives him the virtues necessary for life in a community. Vanity is a motive closely intertwined with sex, though in theory separable from it. But power has, so far as I can see, very little connection with sex, and it is love of power, at least as much as vanity, that makes a child work at his lessons and develop his muscles. Curiosity and the pursuit of knowledge should, I think, be regarded as a branch of the love of power. If knowledge is power, then the love of knowledge is the love of power. Science, therefore, except for certain branches of biology and physiology, must be regarded as lying outside the province of the sexual emotions. As the Emperor Frederick II is no longer alive, this opinion must remain more or less hypothetical. If he were still alive, he would no doubt decide it by castrating an eminent mathematician and an eminent composer and observing the effects upon their repective labours. I should expect the former to be nil and the latter to be considerable. Seeing that the pursuit of knowledge is one of the most valuable elements in human nature, a very important sphere of activity is, if we are right, exempted from the domination of sex.

Power is also the motive to most political activity, understanding this word in its widest sense. I do not mean to suggest that a great statesman is indifferent to the public welfare; on the contrary, I believe him to be a man in whom parental feeling has become widely diffused. But unless he has also a considerable love of power he will fail to sustain the labours necessary for success in a political enterprise. I have known many high-minded men in public affairs, but unless they had an appreciable dose of personal ambition they seldom had the energy to accomplish the good at which they aimed. On a certain crucial occasion, Abraham Lincoln made a speech to two recalcitrant senators, beginning and ending with the words: 'I am the President of the United States, clothed with great power'. It can hardly be questioned that he found some pleasure in asserting this fact. Throughout all politics, both for good and for evil, the two chief forces are the economic motive and the love of power; an attempt to interpret politics on Freudian lines is, to my mind, a mistake.

If we are right in what we have been saying, most of the greatest men, other than artists, have been actuated in their important activities by motives unconnected with sex. If such activities are to persist, and are, in their humbler forms, to become common, it is necessary that sex should not over-shadow the remainder of a man's emotional and passionate nature. The desire to understand the world and the desire to reform it are the two great engines of progress, without which human society would stand still or retrogress. It may be that too complete a happiness would cause the impulses to knowledge and reform to fade. When Cobden wished to enlist John Bright in the free trade campaign, he based a personal appeal upon the sorrow that Bright was experiencing owing to his wife's recent death. It may be that without this sorrow Bright would have had less sympathy with the sorrows of others. And many a man has been driven to abstract pursuits by despair of the actual world. To a man of sufficient energy, pain may be a valuable stimulus, and I do not deny that if we were all perfectly happy we should not exert ourselves to become happier. But I cannot admit that it is any part of the duty of human beings to provide others with pain on the off-chance that it may prove fruitful. In ninety-nine cases out of a hundred pain proves merely crushing. In the hundredth case it is better to trust to the natural shocks that flesh is heir to. So long as there is death there will be sorrow, and so long as there is sorrow it can be no part of the duty of human beings to increase its amount, in spite of the fact that a few rare spirits know how to transmute it.

(*Marriage and Morals*, London: Allen & Unwin;
New York: Liveright Publishing Corporation, 1929.)

42

INDIVIDUAL AND SOCIAL ETHICS

I N this last lecture I wish to do two things. First, to repeat briefly the conclusions reached in earlier lectures; second, to relate social and political doctrines to the individual ethics by which a man should guide his personal life, and after the evils we have recognized and the dangers that we have acknowledged, to hold out nevertheless, as resulting from our survey, certain high hopes for the not too distant future of mankind, which I, for my part, believe to be justified on a sober estimate of possibilities.

To begin with recapitulation. Broadly speaking, we have distinguished two main purposes of social activities: on the one hand, security and justice require centralized governmental control, which must extend to the creation of a world government if it is to be effective. Progress, on the contrary, requires the utmost scope for personal initiative that is compatible with social order.

The method of securing as much as possible of both these aims is *devolution*. The world government must leave national governments free in everything not involved in the prevention of war; national governments, in their turn, must leave as much scope as possible to local authorities. In industry, it must not be thought that all problems are solved when there is nationalization. A large industry—e.g. railways—should have a large measure of self-government; the relation of employees to the State in a nationalized industry should not be a mere reproduction of their former relation to private employers. Everything concerned with opinion, such as newspapers, books and political propaganda, must be left to genuine competition, and carefully safeguarded from governmental control, as well as from every other form of monopoly. But the competition must be cultural and intellectual, not economic, and still less military or by means of the criminal law.

In cultural matters, diversity is a condition of progress. Bodies that have a certain independence of the State, such as universities and learned societies, have great value in this respect. It is deplorable to see, as in present-day Russia, men of science compelled to subscribe to obscurantist nonsense at the behest of scientifically ignorant politicians who are able and willing to enforce their ridiculous decisions by the use of economic and police power. Such pitiful spectacles can only be prevented by limiting the activities of politicians to the sphere in which they may be supposed competent. They should not presume to decide what is good music, or good biology, or good philosophy. I should not wish such matters to be decided in this country by the personal taste of any Prime Minister, past, present, or future, even if, by good luck, his taste were impeccable.

I come now to the question of personal ethics, as opposed to the question of social and political institutions. No man is wholly free, and no man is wholly a slave. To the extent to which a man has freedom, he needs a personal morality to guide his conduct. There are some who would say that a man need only obey the accepted moral code of his community. But I do not think any student of anthropology could be content with this answer. Such practices as cannibalism, human sacrifice, and head hunting have died out as a result of moral protests against conventional moral opinion. If a man seriously desires to live the best life that is open to him, he must learn to be critical of the tribal customs and tribal beliefs that are generally accepted among his neighbours.

But in regard to departures, on conscientious grounds, from what is thought right by the society to which a man belongs, we must distinguish between the authority of custom and the authority of law. Very much stronger grounds are needed to justify an action which is illegal than to justify one which only contravenes conventional morality. The reason is that respect for law is an indispensable condition for the existence of any tolerable social order. When a man considers a certain law to be bad, he has a right, and may have a duty, to try to get it changed, but it is only in rare cases that he does right to break it. I do not deny that there are situations in which law-breaking becomes a duty: it is a duty when a man profoundly believes that it would be a sin to obey. This covers the case of the conscientious objector. Even if you are quite convinced that he is mistaken, you cannot say that he ought not to act as his conscience dictates. When legislators are wise, they avoid, as far as possible, framing laws in such a way as to compel conscientious men to choose between sin and what is legally a crime.

I think it must also be admitted that there are cases in which revolution is justifiable. There are cases where the legal government is so bad that it is worth while to overthrow it by force in spite of the risk of anarchy that is involved. This risk is very real. It is noteworthy that the most successful revolutions—that of England in 1688 and that of America in 1776—were carried out by men who were deeply imbued with a respect for law. Where this is absent, revolution is apt to lead to either anarchy or dictatorship. Obedience to the law, therefore, though not an *absolute* principle, is one to which great weight must be attached, and to which exceptions should only be admitted in rare cases after mature consideration.

We are led by such problems to a deep duality in ethics, which, however perplexing, demands recognition.

Throughout recorded history, ethical beliefs have had two very different sources, one political, the other concerned with personal religious and moral convictions. In the Old Testament the two appear quite separately, one as the Law, the other as the Prophets. In the Middle Ages there was the same kind of distinction between the official morality inculcated by the hierarchy and the personal holiness that was taught and practised by the great mystics. This duality of personal and civic morality, which still persists, is one of which any adequate ethical theory must take account. Without civic morality communities perish; without personal morality their survival has no value. Therefore civic and personal morality are equally necessary to a good world.

Ethics is not concerned *solely* with duty to my neighbour, however rightly such duty may be conceived. The performance of public duty is not the whole of what makes a good life; there is also the pursuit of private excellence. For man, though partly social, is not wholly so. He has thoughts and feelings and impulses which may be wise or foolish, noble or base, filled with love or inspired by hate. And for the better among these thoughts and feelings and impulses, if his life is to be tolerable, there must be scope. For although few men can be happy in solitude, still fewer can be happy in a community which allows no freedom of individual action.

Individual excellence, although a great part of it consists in right behaviour towards other people, has also another aspect. If you neglect your duties for the sake of trivial amusement, you will have pangs of conscience; but if you are tempted away for a time by great music or a fine sunset, you will return with no sense of shame and no feeling that you have been wasting your time. It is dangerous to allow politics and social duty to dominate too completely our conception of what constitutes individual excellence. What I am trying to convey, although it is not dependent upon any theological belief, is in close harmony with Christian ethics. Socrates and the Apostles laid it down that we ought to obey God rather than man, and the Gospels enjoin love of God as emphatically as love of our neighbours. All great religious leaders, and also all great artists and intellectual discoverers, have shown a sense of moral compulsion to fulfil their creative impulses, and a sense of moral exaltation when they have done so. This emotion is the basis of what the Gospels call duty to God, and is (I repeat) separable from theological belief. Duty to my neighbour, at any rate as my neighbour conceives it, may not be the whole of my duty. If I have a profound conscientious conviction that I ought to act in a way that is condemned by governmental authority, I ought to follow my conviction. And conversely, society ought to allow me freedom to follow my convictions except when there are very powerful reasons for restraining me.

But it is not only acts inspired by a sense of duty that should be free from excessive social pressure. An artist or a scientific discoverer may be doing what is of most social utility, but he cannot do his proper work from a sense of duty alone. He must have a spontaneous impulse to paint or to discover, for, if not, his painting will be worthless and his discoveries unimportant.

The sphere of individual action is not to be regarded as ethically inferior to that of social duty. On the contrary, some of the best of human activities are, at least in feeling, rather personal than social. As I said in Lecture III, prophets, mystics, poets, scientific discoverers, are men whose lives are dominated by a vision; they are essentially solitary men. When their dominant impulse is strong, they feel that they cannot obey authority if it runs counter to what they profoundly believe to be good. Although, on this account, they are often persecuted in their own day, they are apt to be, of all men, those to whom posterity pays the highest honour. It is such men who put into the world the things that we most value, not only in religion, in art, and in science, but also in our way of feeling towards our neighbour, for improvements in the sense of social obligation, as in everything else, have been largely due to solitary men whose thoughts and emotions were not subject to the dominion of the herd.

If human life is not to become dusty and uninteresting, it is important to realize that there are things that have a value which is quite independent of utility. What is useful is useful because it is a means to something else, and the something else, if it is not in turn merely a means, must be valued for its own sake, for otherwise the usefulness is illusory.

To strike the right balance between ends and means is both difficult and important. If you are concerned to emphasize means, you may point out that the difference between a civilized man and a savage, between an adult and a child, between a man and an animal, consists largely in a difference as to the weight attached to ends and means in conduct. A civilized man insures his life, a savage does not; an adult brushes his teeth to prevent decay, a child does not except under compulsion; men labour in the fields to provide food for the winter, animals do not. Forethought, which involves doing unpleasant things now for the sake of pleasant things in the future, is one of the most essential marks of mental development. Since forethought is difficult and requires control of impulse, moralists stress its necessity, and lay more stress on the virtue of present sacrifice than on the pleasantness of the subsequent reward. You must do right because it is right, and not because it is the way to get to heaven. You must save because all sensible people do, and not because you may ultimately secure an income that will enable you to enjoy life. And so on.

But the man who wishes to emphasize ends rather than means may advance contrary arguments with equal truth. It is pathetic to see an elderly rich business man, who from work and worry in youth has become dyspeptic, so that he can eat only dry toast and drink only water while his careless guests feast; the joys of wealth, which he had anticipated throughout long laborious years, elude him, and his only pleasure is the use of financial power to compel his sons to submit in their turn to a similar futile drudgery. Misers, whose absorption in means is pathological, are generally recognized to be unwise, but minor forms of the same malady are apt to receive undue commendation. Without some consciousness of ends, life becomes dismal and colourless; ultimately the need for excitement too often finds a worse outlet than it would otherwise have done, in war or cruelty or intrigue or some other destructive activity.

Men who boast of being what is called 'practical' are for the most part exclusively preoccupied with means. But theirs is only one-half of wisdom. When we take account of the other half, which is concerned with ends, the economic process and the whole of human life take on an entirely new aspect. We ask no longer: what have the producers produced, and what has consumption enabled the consumers in their turn to produce? We ask instead: what has there been in the lives of consumers and producers to make them glad to be alive? What have they felt or known or done that could justify their creation? Have they experienced the glory of new knowledge? Have they known love and friendship? Have they rejoiced in sunshine and the spring and the smell of flowers? Have they felt the joy of life that simple communities express in dance and song? Once in Los Angeles I was taken to see the Mexican colony—idle vagabonds, I was told, but to me they seemed to be enjoying more of what makes life a boon and not a curse than fell to the lot of my anxious hardworking hosts. When I tried to explain this feeling, however, I was met with a blank and total lack of comprehension.

People do not always remember that politics, economics, and social organization generally, belong in the realm of means, not ends. Our political and social thinking is prone to what may be called the 'administrator's fallacy', by which I mean the habit of looking upon a society as a systematic whole, of a sort that is thought good if it is pleasant to contemplate as a model of order, a planned organism with parts neatly dovetailed into each other. But a society does not, or at least should not, exist to satisfy an external survey, but to bring a good life to the individuals who compose it. It is in the individuals, not in the whole, that ultimate value is to be sought. A good society is a means to a good life for those who compose it, not something having a separate kind of excellence on its own account.

When it is said that a nation is an organism, an analogy is being used which may be dangerous if its limitations are not recognized. Men and the higher animals are organisms in a strict sense: whatever good or evil befalls a man befalls *him* as a single person, not this or that part of him. If I have tooth-ache, or a pain in my toe, it is *I* that have the pain, and it would not exist if no nerves connected the part concerned with my brain. But when a farmer in Herefordshire is caught in a blizzard, it is not the government in London that feels cold. That is why the individual man is the bearer of good and evil, and not, on the one hand, any separate part of a man, or on the other hand, any collection of men. To believe that there can be good or evil in a collection of human beings, over and above the good or evil in the various individuals, is an error; moreover, it is an error which leads straight to totalitarianism, and is therefore dangerous.

There are some among philosophers and statesmen who think that the State can have an excellence of its own, and not merely as a means to the welfare of the citizens. I cannot see any reason to agree with this view. 'The State' is an abstraction; it does not feel pleasure or pain, it has no hopes or fears, and what we think of as its purposes are really the purposes of individuals who direct it. When we think concretely, not abstractly, we find, in place of 'the State', certain people who have more power than falls to the share of most men. And so glorification of 'the State' turns out to be, in fact, glorification of a governing minority. No democrat can tolerate such a fundamentally unjust theory.

There is another ethical theory, which to my mind is also inadequate; it is that which might be called the 'biological' theory, though I should not wish to assert that it is held by biologists. This view is derived from a contemplation of evolution. The struggle for existence is supposed to have gradually led to more and more complex organisms, culminating (so far) in man. In this view, survival is the supreme end, or rather, survival of one's own species. Whatever increases the human population of the globe, if this theory is right, is to count as 'good', and whatever diminishes the population is to count as 'bad'.

I cannot see any justification for such a mechanical and arithmetical outlook. It would be easy to find a single acre containing more ants than there are human beings in the whole world, but we do not on that account acknowledge the superior excellence of ants. And what humane person would prefer a large population living in poverty and squalor to a smaller population living happily with a sufficiency of comfort?

It is true, of course, that survival is the necessary condition for everything else, but it is only a *condition* of what has value, and may have no value on its own account. Survival, in the world that modern science and technique have produced, demands a great deal of government. But what is to give value to survival must come mainly from sources that lie outside government. The reconciling of these two opposite requisites has been our problem in these discussions.

And now, gathering up the threads of our discussions, and remembering all the dangers of our time, I wish to reiterate certain conclusions, and, more particularly, to set forth the hopes which I believe we have rational grounds for entertaining.

Between those who care most for social cohesion and those who primarily value individual initiative there has been an age-long battle ever since the time of the ancient Greeks. In every such perennial controversy there is sure to be truth on both sides; there is not likely to be a clear-cut solution, but at best one involving various adjustments and compromises.

Throughout history, as I suggested in my second lecture, there has been a fluctuation between periods of excessive anarchy and periods of too strict governmental control. In our day, except (as yet) in the matter of world government, there has been too much tendency towards authority, and too little care for the preservation of initiative. Men in control of vast organizations have tended to be too abstract in their outlook, to forget what actual human beings are like, and to try to fit men to systems rather than systems to men.

The lack of spontaneity from which our highly organized societies tend to suffer is connected with excessive control over large areas by remote authorities.

One of the advantages to be gained from decentralization is that it provides new opportunities for hopefulness and for individual activities that embody hopes. If our political thoughts are all concerned with vast problems and dangers of world catastrophe, it is easy to become despairing. Fear of war, fear of revolution, fear of reaction, may obsess you according to your temperament and your party bias. Unless you are one of a very small number of powerful individuals, you are likely to feel that you cannot do much about these great issues. But in relation to smaller problems—those of your town, or your trade union, or the local branch of your political party, for example—you can hope to have a successful influence. This will engender a hopeful spirit, and a hopeful spirit is what is most needed if a way is to be found of dealing successfully with the larger problems. War and shortages and financial stringency have caused almost universal fatigue, and have made hopefulness seem shallow and insincere. Success, even if, at first, it is on a small scale, is the best cure for this mood of pessimistic weariness. And success, for most people, means breaking up our problems, and being free to concentrate on those that are not too desperately large.

The world has become the victim of dogmatic political creeds, of which, in our day, the most powerful are Capitalism and Communism. I do not believe that either, in a dogmatic and unmitigated form, offers a cure for preventable evils. Capitalism gives opportunity of initiative to a few; Communism could (though it does not in fact) provide a servile kind of security for all. But if people can rid themselves of the influence of unduly simple theories and the strife that they engender, it will be possible, by a wise use of scientific technique, to provide both opportunity for all and security for all. Unfortunately our political theories are less intelligent than our science, and we have not yet learnt how to make use of our knowledge and our skill in the ways that will do most to make life happy and even glorious. It is not only the experience and the fear of war that oppresses mankind, though this is perhaps the greatest of all the evils of our time. We are oppressed also by the great impersonal forces that govern our daily life, making us still slaves of circumstance though no longer slaves in law. This need not be the case. It has come about through the worship of false gods. Energetic men have worshipped power rather than simple happiness and friendliness; men of less energy have acquiesced, or have been deceived by a wrong diagnosis of the sources of sorrow.

Ever since mankind invented slavery, the powerful have believed that their happiness could be achieved by means that involved inflicting misery on others. Gradually, with the growth of democracy, and with the quite modern application of Christian ethics to politics and economics, a better ideal than that of the slave-holders has begun to prevail, and the claims of justice are now acknowledged as they never were at any former time. But in seeking justice by means of elaborate systems we have been in danger of forgetting that justice alone is not enough. Daily joys, times of liberation from care, adventure and opportunity for creative activities, are at least as important as justice in bringing about a life that men can feel to be worth living. Monotony may be more deadening than an alternation of delight and agony. The men who think out administrative reforms and schemes of social amelioration are for the most part earnest men who are no longer young. Too often they have forgotten that to most people not only spontaneity but some kind of personal pride is necessary for happiness. The pride of a great conqueror is not one that a well-regulated world can allow, but the pride of the artist, of the discoverer, of the man who has turned a wilderness into a garden or has brought happiness where, but for him, there would have been misery—such pride is good, and our social system should make it possible, not only for the few, but for very many.

The instincts that long ago prompted the hunting and fighting activities of our savage ancestors demand an outlet; if they can find no other, they will turn to hatred and thwarted malice. But there are outlets for these very instincts that are not evil. For fighting it is possible to substitute emulation and active sport; for hunting, the joy of adventure and discovery and creation. We must not ignore these instincts, and we need not regret them; they are the source, not only of what is bad, but of what is best in human achievement. When security has been achieved, the most important task for those who seek human welfare will be to find for these ancient and powerful instincts neither merely restraints nor the outlets that make for destruction, but as many as possible of the outlets that give joy and pride and splendour to human life.

Throughout the ages of human development men have been subject to miseries of two kinds: those imposed by external nature, and those that human beings misguidedly inflicted upon each other. At first, by far the worst evils were those that were due to the environment. Man was a rare species, whose survival was precarious. Without the agility of the monkey, without any coating of fur, he had difficulty in escaping from wild beasts, and in most parts of the world could not endure the winter's cold. He had only two biological advantages: the upright posture freed his hands, and intelligence enabled him to transmit experience. Gradually these two advantages gave him supremacy. The numbers of the human species increased beyond those of any other large mammals. But nature could still assert her power by means of flood and famine and pestilence, and by exacting from the great majority of mankind incessant toil in the securing of daily bread.

In our own day our bondage to external nature is fast diminishing, as a result of the growth of scientific intelligence. Famines and pestilences still occur, but we know better, year by year, what should be done to prevent them. Hard work is still necessary, but only because we are unwise: given peace and co-operation, we could subsist on a very moderate amount of toil. With existing techniques, we can, whenever we choose to exercise wisdom, be free of many ancient forms of bondage to external nature.

But the evils that men inflict upon each other have not diminished in the same degree. There are still wars, oppressions and hideous cruelties, and greedy men still snatch wealth from those who are less skilful or less ruthless than themselves. Love of power still leads to vast tyrannies, or to mere obstruction when its grosser forms are impossible. And fear— deep, scarcely conscious fear—is still the dominant motive in very many lives.

All this is unnecessary; there is nothing in human nature that makes these evils inevitable. I wish to repeat, with all possible emphasis, that I disagree completely with those who infer from our combative impulses that human nature demands war and other destructive forms of conflict. I firmly believe the very opposite of this. I maintain that combative impulses have an essential part to play, and in their harmful forms can be enormously lessened.

Greed of possession will grow less when there is no fear of destitution. Love of power can be satisfied in many ways that involve no injury to others: by the power over nature that results from discovery and invention, by the production of admired books or works of art, and by successful persuasion. Energy and the wish to be effective are beneficent if they can find the right outlet, and harmful if not—like steam, which can either drive the train or burst the boiler.

Our emancipation from bondage to external nature has made possible a greater degree of human well-being than has ever hitherto existed. But if this possibility is to be realized, there must be freedom of initiative in all ways not positively harmful, and encouragement of those forms of initiative that enrich the life of Man. We shall not create a good world by trying to make men tame and timid, but by encouraging them to be bold and adventurous and fearless except in inflicting injuries upon their fellow-men. In the world in which we find ourselves, the possibilities of good are almost limitless, and the possibilities of evil no less so. Our present predicament is due more than anything else to the fact that we have learnt to understand and control to a terrifying extent the forces of nature outside us, but not those that are embodied in ourselves. Self-control has always been a watchword of the moralists, but in the past it has been a control without understanding. In these lectures I have sought for a wider understanding of human needs than is assumed by most politicians and economists, for it is only through such an understanding that we can find our way to the realization of those hopes which, though as yet they are largely frustrated by our folly, our skill has placed within our reach.

(*Authority and the Individual*, London: Allen & Unwin; New York: Simon & Schuster, 1949.)

43

WHAT I BELIEVE'

What I Believe was published as a little book in 1925. In it, Russell wrote in the preface, 'I have tried to say what I think of man's place in the universe, and of his possibilities in the way of achieving the good life. . . . In human affairs, we can see that there are forces making for happiness, and forces making for misery. We do not know which will prevail, but to act wisely we must be aware of both'. In the New York court proceedings in 1940 *What I Believe* was one of the books presented as evidence that Russell was unfit to teach at City College. Extracts from it were also widely quoted in the press, usually in such a way as to give quite a false impression of Russell's views.

I. NATURE AND MAN

MAN is a part of Nature, not something contrasted with Nature. His thoughts and his bodily movements follow the same laws that describe the motions of stars and atoms. The physical world is large compared with Man—larger than it was thought to be in Dante's time, but not so large as it seemed a hundred years ago. Both upward and downward, both in the large and in the small, science seems to be reaching limits. It is thought that the universe is of finite extent in space, and that light could travel round it in a few hundred millions of years. It is thought matter consists of electrons and protons, which are of finite size and of which there are only a finite number in the world. Probably their changes are not continuous, as used to be thought, but proceed by jerks, which are never smaller than a certain minimum jerk. The laws of these changes can apparently be summed up in a small number of very general principles, which determine the past and the future of the world when any small section of its history is known.

Physical science is thus approaching the stage when it will be complete, and therefore uninteresting. Given the laws governing the motions of electrons and protons, the rest is merely geography—a collection of particular facts telling their distribution throughout some portion of the world's history. The total number of facts of geography required to determine the world's history is probably finite; theoretically they could all be written down in a big book to be kept at Somerset House with a calculating machine attached which, by turning a handle, would enable the inquirer to find out the facts at other times than those recorded. It is difficult to imagine anything less interesting or more different from the passionate delights of incomplete discovery. It is like climbing a high mountain and finding nothing at the top except a restaurant where they sell ginger beer, surrounded by fog but equipped with wireless. Perhaps in the times of Ahmes the multiplication table was exciting.

Of this physical world, uninteresting in itself, Man is a part. His body, like other matter, is composed of electrons and protons, which, so far as we know, obey the same laws as those not forming part of animals or plants. There are some who maintain that physiology can never be reduced to physics, but their arguments are not very convincing and it seems prudent to suppose that they are mistaken. What we call our 'thoughts' seem to depend upon the organization of tracks in the brain in the same sort of way in which journeys depend upon roads and railways. The energy used in thinking seems to have a chemical origin; for instance, a deficiency of iodine will turn a clever man into an idiot. Mental phenomena seem to be bound up with material structure. If this be so, we cannot suppose that a solitary electron or proton can 'think'; we might as well expect a solitary individual to play a football match. We also cannot suppose that an individual's thinking survives bodily death, since that destroys the organization of the brain, and dissipates the energy which utilized the brain tracks.

God and immortality, the central dogmas of the Christian religion, find no support in science. It cannot be said that either doctrine is essential to religion, since neither is found in Buddhism. (With regard to immortality, this statement in an unqualified form might be misleading, but it is correct in the last analysis.) But we in the West have come to think of them as the irreducible minimum of theology. No doubt people will continue to entertain these beliefs, because they are pleasant, just as it is pleasant to think ourselves virtuous and our enemies wicked. But for my part I cannot see any ground for either. I do not pretend to be able to prove that there is no God. I equally cannot prove that Satan is a fiction. The Christian God may exist; so may the Gods of Olympus, or of ancient Egypt, or of Babylon. But no one of these hypotheses is more probable than any other: they lie outside the region of even probable knowledge, and therefore there is no reason to consider any of them. I shall not enlarge upon this question, as I have dealt with it elsewhere.[1]

The question of personal immortality stands on a somewhat different footing. Here evidence either way is possible. Persons are part of the everyday world with which science is concerned, and the conditions which determine their existence are discoverable. A drop of water is not immortal; it can be resolved into oxygen and hydrogen. If, therefore, a drop of water were to maintain that it had a quality of aqueousness which would survive its dissolution we should be inclined to be sceptical. In like manner

[1] See my *Philosophy of Leibniz*, Chapter XV.

we know that the brain is not immortal, and that the organized energy of a living body becomes, as it were, demobilized at death, and therefore not available for collective action. All the evidence goes to show that what we regard as our mental life is bound up with brain structure and organized bodily energy. Therefore it is rational to suppose that mental life ceases when bodily life ceases. The argument is only one of probability, but it is as strong as those upon which most scientific conclusions are based.

There are various grounds upon which this conclusion might be attacked. Psychial research professes to have actual scientific evidence of survival, and undoubtedly its procedure is, in principle, scientifically correct. Evidence of this sort might be so overwhelming that no one with a scientific temper could reject it. The weight to be attached to the evidence, however, must depend upon the antecedent probability of the hypothesis of survival. There are always different ways of accounting for any set of phenomena and of these we should prefer the one which is antecedentally least improbable. Those who already think it likely that we survive death will be ready to view this theory as the best explanation of psychical phenomena. Those who, on other grounds, regard this theory as implausible will seek for other explanations. For my part, I consider the evidence so far adduced by psychical research in favour of survival much weaker than the physiological evidence on the other side. But I fully admit that it might at any moment become stronger, and in that case it would be unscientific to disbelieve in survival.

Survival of bodily death is, however, a different matter from immortality: it may only mean a postponement of psychical death. It is immortality that men desire to believe in. Believers in immortality will object to physiological arguments, such as I have been using, on the ground that soul and body are totally disparate, and that the soul is something quite other than its empirical manifestations through our bodily organs. I believe this to be a metaphysical superstition. Mind and matter alike are for certain purposes convenient terms, but are not ultimate realities. Electrons and protons, like the soul, are logical fictions; each is really a history, a series of events, not a single persistent entity. In the case of the soul, this is obvious from the facts of growth. Whoever considers conception, gestation, and infancy cannot seriously believe that the soul is an indivisible something, perfect and complete throughout this process. It is evident that it grows like the body, and that it derives both from the spermatozoon and from the ovum, so that it cannot be indivisible. This is not materialism: it is merely the recognition that everything interesting is a matter of organization, not of primal substance.

Metaphysicians have advanced innumerable arguments to prove that the soul must be immortal. There is one simple test by which all these arguments can be demolished. They all prove equally that the soul must pervade all space. But as we are not so anxious to be fat as to live long, none of the metaphysicians in question have ever noticed this application of their reasonings. This is an instance of the amazing power of desire in blinding even very able men to fallacies which would otherwise be obvious at once. If we were not afraid of death, I do not believe that the idea of immortality would ever have arisen.

Fear is the basis of religious dogma, as of so much else in human life. Fear of human beings, individually or collectively, dominates much of our social life, but it is fear of nature that gives rise to religion. The antithesis of mind and matter is, as we have seen, more or less illusory; but there is another antithesis which is more important—that, namely, between things that can be affected by our desires and things that cannot be so affected. The line between the two is neither sharp nor immutable— as science advances, more and more things are brought under human control. Nevertheless there remain things definitely on the other side. Among these are all the *large* facts of our world, the sort of facts that are dealt with by astronomy. It is only facts on or near the surface of the earth that we can, to some extent, mould to suit our desires. And even on the surface of the earth our powers are very limited. Above all, we cannot prevent death, although we can often delay it.

Religion is an attempt to overcome this antithesis. If the world is controlled by God, and God can be moved by prayer, we acquire a share in omnipotence. In former days, miracles happened in answer to prayer; they still do in the Catholic Church, but Protestants have lost this power. However, it is possible to dispense with miracles, since Providence has decreed that the operation of natural laws shall produce the best possible results. Thus belief in God still serves to humanize the world of nature, and to make men feel that physical forces are really their allies. In like manner immortality removes the terror from death. People who believe that when they die they will inherit eternal bliss may be expected to view death without horror, though, fortunately for medical men, this does not invariably happen. It does, however, soothe men's fears somewhat even when it cannot allay them wholly.

Religion, since it has its source in terror, has dignified certain kinds of fear, and made people think them not disgraceful. In this it has done mankind a great disservice: *all* fear is bad. I believe that when I die I shall rot, and nothing of my ego will survive. I am not young, and I love life. But I should scorn to shiver with terror at the thought of annihilation. Happiness is none the less true happiness because it must come to an end, nor do thought and love lose their value because they are not everlasting. Many a man has borne himself proudly on the scaffold; surely the same pride should teach us to think truly about man's place in the world. Even if the open windows of science at first make us shiver after the cosy indoor warmth of traditional humanizing myths, in the end the fresh air brings vigour, and the great spaces have a splendour of their own.

The philosophy of nature is one thing, the philosophy of value is quite another. Nothing but harm can come of confusing them. What we think good, what we should like, has no bearing whatever upon what is, which is the question for the philosophy of nature. On the other hand, we cannot be forbidden to value this or that on the ground that the non-human world does not value it, nor can we be compelled to admire anything because it is a 'law of nature'. Undoubtedly we are part of nature, which has produced our desires, our hopes and fears, in accordance with laws which the physicist is beginning to discover. In this sense we are part of nature, we are subordinated to nature, the outcome of natural laws, and their victims in the long run.

The philosophy of nature must not be unduly terrestrial; for it, the earth is merely one of the smaller planets of one of the smaller stars of the Milky Way. It would be ridiculous to warp the philosophy of nature in order to bring out results that are pleasing to the tiny parasites of this insignificant planet. Vitalism as a philosophy, and evolutionism, show, in this respect, a lack of sense of proportion and logical relevance. They regard the facts of life, which are personally interesting to us, as having a cosmic significance, not a significance confined to the earth's surface. Optimism and pessimism, as cosmic philosophies, show the same naïve humanism; the great world, so far as we know it from the philosophy of nature, is neither good nor bad, and is not concerned to make us happy or unhappy. All such philosophies spring from self-importance, and are best corrected by a little astronomy.

But in the philosophy of value the situation is reversed. Nature is only a part of what we can imagine; everything, real or imagined, can be appraised by us, and there is no outside standard to show that our valuation is wrong. We are ourselves the ultimate and irrefutable arbiters of value, and in the world of value Nature is only a part. Thus in this world we are greater than Nature. In the world of values, Nature in itself is neutral, neither good nor bad, deserving of neither admiration nor censure. It is we who create value and our desires which confer value. In this realm we are kings, and we debase our kingship if we bow down to Nature. It is for us to determine the good life, not for Nature—not even for Nature personified as God.

II. THE GOOD LIFE

There have been at different times and among different people many varying conceptions of the good life. To some extent the differences were amenable to argument; this was when men differed as to the means to achieve a given end. Some think that prison is a good way of preventing crime; others hold that education would be better. A difference of this sort can be decided by sufficient evidence. But some differences cannot be tested in this way. Tolstoy condemned all war; others had held the life of a soldier doing battle for the right to be very noble. Here there was probably involved a real difference as to ends. Those who praise the soldier usually consider the punishment of sinners a good thing in itself; Tolstoy did not think so. On such a matter no argument is possible. I cannot, therefore, prove that my view of the good life is right; I can only state my view, and hope that as many as possible will agree. My view is this:

The good life is one inspired by love and guided by knowledge.

Knowledge and love are both indefinitely extensible; therefore, however good a life may be, a better life can be imagined. Neither love without knowledge, nor knowledge without love can produce a good life. In the Middle Ages, when pestilence appeared in a country, holy men advised the population to assemble in churches and pray for deliverance; the result was that the infection spread with extraordinary rapidity among the crowded masses of supplicants. This was an example of love without knowledge. The late war afforded an example of knowledge without love. In each case, the result was death on a large scale.

Although both love and knowledge are necessary, love is in a sense more fundamental, since it will lead intelligent people to seek knowledge, in order to find out how to benefit those whom they love. But if people are not intelligent, they will be content to believe what they have been told, and may do harm in spite of the most genuine benevolence. Medicine affords, perhaps, the best example of what I mean. An able physician is more useful to a patient than the most devoted friend, and progress in medical knowledge does more for the health of the community than ill-informed philanthropy. Nevertheless, an element of benevolence is essential even here if any but the rich are to profit by scientific discoveries.

Love is a word which covers a variety of feelings; I have used it purposely, as I wish to include them all. Love as an emotion—which is what I am speaking about, for love 'on principle' does not seem to me genuine—moves between two poles: on one side, pure delight in contemplation; on the other, pure benevolence. Where inanimate objects are concerned, delight alone enters in; we cannot feel benevolence towards a landscape or a sonata. This type of enjoyment is presumably the source of art. It is stronger, as a rule, in very young children than in adults, who are apt to view objects in a utilitarian spirit. It plays a large part in our feelings towards human beings, some of whom have charm and some the reverse, when considered simply as objects of aesthetic contemplation.

The opposite pole of love is pure benevolence. Men have sacrificed their lives to helping lepers; in such a case the love they felt cannot have had any element of aesthetic delight. Parental affection, as a rule, is accompanied by pleasure in the child's appearance, but remains strong when this element is wholly absent. It would seem odd to call a mother's interest in a sick child 'benevolence', because we are in the habit of using this word to describe a pale emotion nine parts humbug. But it is difficult to find any other word to describe the desire for another person's welfare. It is a fact that a desire of this sort may reach any degree of strength in the case of parental feeling. In other cases it is far less intense: indeed it would seem likely that all altruistic emotion is a sort of overflow of parental feeling, or sometimes a sublimation of it. For want of a better word, I shall call this emotion 'benevolence'. But I want to make it clear that I am speaking of an emotion, not a principle, and that I do not include in it any feeling of superiority such as is sometimes associated with the word. The word 'sympathy' expresses part of what I mean, but leaves out the element of activity that I wish to include.

Love at its fullest is an indissoluble combination of the two elements, delight and well-wishing. The pleasure of a parent in a beautiful and successful child combines both elements; so does sex-love at its best. But in sex-love benevolence will only exist where there is secure possession, since otherwise jealousy will destroy it, while perhaps actually increasing the delight in contemplation. Delight without well-wishing may be cruel; well-wishing without delight easily tends to become cold and a little superior. A person who wishes to be loved wishes to be the object of a love containing both elements, except in cases of extreme weakness, such as infancy and severe illness. In these cases benevolence may be all that is desired. Conversely, in cases of extreme strength, admiration is more desired than benevolence: this is the state of mind of potentates and famous beauties. We only desire other people's good wishes in proportion as we feel ourselves in need of help or in danger of harm from them. At least, that would seem to be the biological logic of the situation, but it is not quite true to life. We desire affection in order to escape from the feeling of loneliness, in order to be, as we say, 'understood'. This is a matter of sympathy, not merely of benevolence; the person whose affection is satisfactory to us must not merely wish us well, but must know in what our happiness consists. But this belongs to the other element of the good life, namely knowledge.

In a perfect world, every sentient being would be to every other the object of the fullest love, compounded of delight, benevolence and understanding inextricably blended. It does not follow that, in this actual world, we ought to attempt to have such feelings toward all the sentient beings whom we encounter. There are many in whom we cannot feel delight, because they are disgusting; if we were to do violence to our nature by trying to see beauties in them, we should merely blunt our susceptibilities to what we naturally find beautiful. Not to mention human beings there are fleas and bugs and lice. We should have to be as hard pressed as the Ancient Mariner before we could feel delight in contemplating these creatures. Some saints, it is true, have called them 'pearls of

God', but what these men delighted in was the opportunity of displaying their own sanctity.

Benevolence is easier to extend widely, but even benevolence has its limits. If a man wished to marry a lady, we should not think the better of him for withdrawing if he found that someone else also wished to marry her: we should regard this as a fair field for competition. Yet his feelings towards a rival cannot be *wholly* benevolent. I think that in all descriptions of the good life here on earth we must assume a certain basis of animal vitality and animal instinct; without this, life becomes tame and uninteresting. Civilization should be something added to this, not substituted for it; the ascetic saint and the detached sage fail in this respect to be complete human beings. A small number of them may enrich a community; but a world composed of them would die of boredom.

These considerations lead to a certain emphasis on the element of delight as an ingredient in the best love. Delight, in this actual world, is unavoidably selective, and prevents us from having the same feelings toward all mankind. When conflicts arise between delight and benevolence, they must, as a rule, be decided by a compromise, not by a complete surrender of either. Instinct has its rights, and if we do violence to it beyond a point it takes vengeance in subtle ways. Therefore in aiming at a good life the limits of human possibility must be borne in mind. Here again, however, we are brought back to the necessity of knowledge.

When I speak of knowledge as an ingredient of the good life, I am not thinking of ethical knowledge, but of scientific knowledge and knowledge of particular facts. I do not think there is, strictly speaking, such a thing as ethical knowledge. If we desire to achieve some end, knowledge may show us the means, and this knowledge may loosely pass as ethical. But I do not believe that we can decide what sort of conduct is right or wrong except by reference to its probable consequences. Given an end to be achieved, it is a question for science to discover how to achieve it. All moral rules must be tested by examining whether they tend to realize ends that we desire. I say ends that we desire, not ends that we *ought* to desire. What we 'ought' to desire is merely what someone else wishes us to desire. Usually it is what the authorities wish us to desire—parents, schoolmasters, policemen and judges. If you say to me 'you ought to do so-and-so', the motive power of your remark lies in my desire for your approval—together, possibily, with rewards or punishments attached to your approval or disapproval. Since all behaviour springs from desire, it is clear that ethical notions can have no importance except as they influence desire. They do this through the desire for approval and the fear of disapproval. These are powerful social forces, and we shall naturally endeavour to win them to our side if we wish to realize any social purpose. When I say that the morality of conduct is to be judged by its probable consequences, I mean that I desire to see approval given to behaviour likely to realize social purposes which we desire, and disapproval to opposite behaviour. At present this is not done; there are certain traditional rules according to which approval and disapproval are meted out quite regardless of consequences. But this is a topic with which we shall deal in the next section.

The superfluity of theoretical ethics is obvious in simple cases. Suppose, for instance, your child is ill. Love makes you wish to cure it, and science tells you how to do so. There is not an intermediate stage of ethical theory, where it is demonstrated that your child had better be cured. Your act springs directly from desire for an end, together with knowledge of means. This is equally true of all acts, whether good or bad. The ends differ, and the knowledge is more adequate in some cases than in others. But there is no conceivable way of making people do things they do not wish to do. What is possible is to alter their desires by a system of rewards and penalties, among which social approval and disapproval are not the least potent. The question for the legislative moralist is, therefore: How shall this system of rewards and punishments be arranged so as to secure the maximum of what is desired by the legislative authority? If I say that the legislative authority has bad desires, I mean merely that its desires conflict with those of some section of the community to which I belong. Outside human desires there is no moral standard.

Thus, what distinguishes ethics from science is not any special kind of knowledge but merely desire. The knowledge required in ethics is exactly like the knowledge elsewhere; what is peculiar is that certain ends are desired, and that right conduct is what conduces to them. Of course, if the definition of right conduct is to make a wide appeal, the ends must be such as large sections of mankind desire. If I defined right conduct as that which increases my own income, readers would disagree. The whole effectiveness of any ethical argument lies in its scientific part, i.e. in the proof that one kind of conduct, rather than some other, is a means to an end which is widely desired. I distinguish, however, between ethical argument and ethical education. The latter consists in strengthening certain desires and weakening others. This is quite a different process, which will be separately discussed at a later stage.

We can now explain more exactly the purport of the definition of the good life with which this chapter began. When I said that the good life consists of love guided by knowledge, the desire which prompted me was the desire to live such a life as far as possible, and to see others living it; and the logical content of the statement is that, in a community where men live in this way, more desires will be satisfied than in one where there is less love or less knowledge. I do not mean that such a life is 'virtuous' or that its opposite is 'sinful', for these are conceptions which seem to me to have no scientific justification.

III. MORAL RULES

The practical need of morals arises from the conflict of desires, whether of different people or of the same person at different times or even at one time. A man desires to drink, and also to be fit for his work next morning. We think him immoral if he adopts the course which gives him the smaller total satisfaction of desire. We think ill of people who are extravagant or reckless, even if they injure no one but themselves. Bentham supposed that the whole of morality could be derived from 'enlightened self-interest', and that a person who always acted with a view to his own maximum satisfaction in the long run would always act rightly. I cannot accept this view. Tyrants have existed who derived exquisite pleasure from watching the infliction of torture; I cannot praise such men when prudence led them to spare their victims' lives with a view to further sufferings another day. Nevertheless, other things being equal, prudence is a part of the good life. Even Robinson Crusoe had occasion to practise industry, self-control and foresight which must be reckoned as moral qualities, since they increased his total satisfaction without counterbalancing injury to others. This part of morals plays a great part in the training of young children, who have little inclination to think of the future. If it were more practised in later life, the world would quickly become a paradise, since it would be quite sufficient to prevent wars, which are acts of passion, not reason. Nevertheless, in spite of the importance of prudence, it is not the most interesting part of morals. Nor is it the part that raises intellectual problems, since it does not require an appeal to anything beyond self-interest.

The part of morality that is not included in prudence is, in essence, analogous to law, or the rules of a club. It is a method of enabling men to live together in a community in spite of the possibility that their desires may conflict. But here two very different methods are possible. There is the method of criminal law, which aims at a merely external harmony by attaching disagreeable consequences to acts which thwart other men's desires in certain ways. This is also the method of social censure: to be thought ill of by one's own society is a form of punishment, to avoid which most people avoid being known to transgress the code of their set. But there is another method, more fundamental, and far more satisfactory when it succeeds. This is to alter men's characters and desires in such a way as to minimize occasions of conflict by making the success of one man's desires as far as possible consistent with that of another's. That is why love is better than hate, because it brings harmony instead of conflict into the desires of the persons concerned. Two people between whom there is love succeed or fail together, but when two people hate each other the success of either is the failure of the other.

If we were right in saying that the good life is inspired by love and guided by knowledge, it is clear that the moral code of any community is not ultimate and self-sufficient, but must be examined with a view to seeing whether it is such as wisdom and benevolence would have decreed. Moral codes have not always been faultless. The Aztecs considered it their painful duty to eat human flesh for fear the light of the sun should grow dim. They erred in their science; and perhaps they would have perceived the scientific error if they had had any love for the sacrifical victims. Some tribes immure girls in the dark from the age of ten to the age of seventeen, for fear the sun's rays should render them pregnant. But surely our modern codes of morals contain nothing analogous to these savage practices? Surely we only forbid things which are really harmful, or at any rate so abominable that no decent person could defend them? I am not so sure.

Current morality is a curious blend of utilitarianism and superstition, but the superstitious part has the stronger hold, as is natural, since superstition is the origin of moral rules. Originally, certain acts were thought displeasing to the gods, and were forbidden by law because the divine wrath was apt to descend upon the community, not merely upon the guilty individuals. Hence arose the conception of sin, as that which is displeasing to God. No reason can be assigned as to why certain acts should be thus displeasing; it would be very difficult to say, for instance, why it was displeasing that the kid should be seethed in its mother's milk. But it was known by Revelation that this was the case. Sometimes the Divine commands have been curiously interpreted. For example, we are told not to work on Saturdays, and Protestants take this to mean that we are not to play on Sundays. But the same sublime authority is attributed to the new prohibition as to the old.

It is evident that a man with a scientific outlook on life cannot let himself be intimidated by texts of Scripture or by the teaching of the Church. He will not be content to say 'such-and-such an act is sinful, and that ends the matter'. He will inquire whether it does any harm or whether, on the contrary, the belief that it is sinful does harm. And he will find that, especially in what concerns sex, our current morality contains a very great deal of which the origin is purely superstitious. He will find also that this superstition, like that of the Aztecs, involves needless cruelty, and would be swept away if people were actuated by kindly feelings towards their neighbours. But the defenders of traditional morality are seldom people with warm hearts, as may be seen from the love of militarism displayed by Church dignitaries. One is tempted to think that they value morals as affording a legitimate outlet for their desire to inflict pain; the sinner is fair game, and therefore away with tolerance!

Let us follow an ordinary human life from conception to the grave, and note the points where superstitious morals inflict preventable suffering. I begin with conception, because here the influence of superstition is particularly noteworthy. If the parents are not married, the child has a stigma, as clearly undeserved as anything could be. If either of the parents has venereal disease, the child is likely to inherit it. If they already have too many children for the family income, there will be poverty, under-feeding, overcrowding, very likely incest. Yet the great majority of moralists agree that the parents had better not know how to prevent this misery by preventing conception.[1] To please these moralists, a life of torture is inflicted upon millions of human beings who ought never to have existed, merely because it is supposed that sexual intercourse is wicked unless accompanied by desire for offspring, but not wicked when this desire is present, even though the offspring is humanly certain to be wretched. To be killed suddenly and then eaten, which was the fate of the Aztecs' victims, is a far less degree of suffering than is inflicted upon a child born in miserable surroundings and tainted with venereal disease. Yet it is the greater suffering which is deliberately inflicted by bishops and politicians in the name of morality. If they had even the smallest spark of love or pity for children they could not adhere to a moral code involving this fiendish cruelty.

At birth, and in early infancy, the average child suffers more from economic causes than from superstition. When well-to-do women have children, they have the best doctors, the best nurses, the best diet, the best rest and the best exercise. Working-class women do not enjoy these advantages, and frequently their children die for lack of them. A little is done by the public authorities in the way of care of mothers, but very grudgingly. At a moment when the supply of milk to nursing mothers is being cut down to save expense, public authorities will spend vast sums on paving rich residential districts where there is little traffic. They must know that in taking this decision they are condemning a certain number of working-class children to death for the crime of poverty. Yet the ruling party are supported by the immense majority of ministers of religion, who, with the Pope at their head, have pledged the vast forces of super-stition throughout the world to the support of social injustice.

In all stages of education the influence of superstition is disastrous. A certain percentage of children have the habit of thinking; one of the aims of education is to cure them of this habit. Inconvenient questions are met with 'hush, hush', or with punishment. Collective emotion is used to instil certain kinds of belief, more particularly nationalistic kinds. Capitalists, militarists, and ecclesiastics co-operate in education, because all depend for their power upon the prevalence of emotionalism and the rarity of critical judgment. With the aid of human nature, education

[1] This is fortunately no longer true. The vast majority of Protestant and Jewish leaders do not now object to birth control. Russell's statement is a perfectly accurate description of conditions in 1925. It is also significant that, with one or two exceptions, all the great pioneers of contraception—Francis Place, Richard Carlile, Charles Knowlton, Charles Bradlaugh, and Margaret Sanger were prominent free-thinkers. (Editor's note.)

succeeds in increasing and intensifying these propensities of the average man.

Another way in which superstition damages education is through its influence on the choice of teachers. For economic reasons, a women teacher must not be married; for moral reasons, she must not have extra-marital sexual relations. And yet everybody who has taken the trouble to study morbid psychology knows that prolonged virginity is, as a rule, extraordinarily harmful to women, so harmful that, in a sane society, it would be severely discouraged in teachers. The restrictions imposed lead more and more to a refusal, on the part of energetic and enterprising women, to enter the teaching profession. This is all due to the lingering influence of superstitious asceticism.

At middle and upper class schools the matter is even worse. There are chapel services, and the care of morals is in the hands of clergymen. Clergymen, almost necessarily, fail in two ways as teachers of morals. They condemn acts which do no harm and they condone acts which do great harm. They all condemn sexual relations between unmarried people who are fond of each other but not yet sure that they wish to live together all their lives. Most of them condemn birth control. None of them condemns the brutality of a husband who causes his wife to die of too frequent pregnancies. I knew a fashionable clergyman whose wife had nine children in nine years. The doctors told him that if she had another she would die. Next year she had another and died. No one condemned him; he retained his benefice and married again. So long as clergymen continue to condone cruelty and condemn innocent pleasure, they can only do harm as guardians of the morals of the young.

Another bad effect of superstition on education is the absence of instruction about the facts of sex. The main physiological facts ought to be taught quite simply and naturally before puberty at a time when they are not exciting. At puberty, the elements of an unsuperstitious sexual morality ought to be taught. Boys and girls should be taught that nothing can justify sexual intercourse unless there is mutual inclination. This is contrary to the teaching of the Church, which holds that, provided the parties are married and the man desires another child, sexual inter-course is justified however great may be the reluctance of the wife. Boys and girls should be taught respect for each other's liberty; they should be made to feel that nothing gives one human being rights over another, and that jealousy and possessiveness kill love. They should be taught that to bring another human being into the world is a very serious matter, only to be undertaken when the child will have a reasonable prospect of health, good surroundings and parental care. But they should also be taught methods of birth control, so as to ensure that children shall only come when they are wanted. Finally, they should be taught the dangers of venereal disease, and the methods of prevention and cure. The increase of human happiness to be expected from sex education on these lines is immeasurable.

It should be recognized that, in the absence of children, sexual relations are a purely private matter, which does not concern either the State or the neighbours. Certain forms of sex which do not lead to children are at present punished by the criminal law: this is purely superstitious, since the matter is one which affects no one except the parties directly concerned. Where there are children, it is a mistake to suppose that it is necessarily to their interest to make divorce very difficult. Habitual drunkenness, cruelty, insanity are grounds upon which divorce is necessary for the children's sake quite as much as for the sake of the wife or husband. The peculiar importance attached, at present, to adultery is quite irrational. It is obvious that many forms of misconduct are more fatal to married happiness than an occasional infidelity. Masculine insistence on a child a year, which is not conventionally misconduct or cruelty, is the most fatal of all.

Moral rules ought not to be such as to make instinctive happiness impossible. Yet that is an effect of strict monogamy in a community where the numbers of the two sexes are very unequal. Of course, under such circumstances, the moral rules are infringed. But when the rules are such that they can only be obeyed by greatly diminishing the happiness of the community, and when it is better they should be infringed than observed, surely it is time that the rules were changed. If this is not done, many people who are acting in a way not contrary to the public interest are faced with the undeserved alternative of hypocrisy or obloquy. The Church does not mind hypocrisy, which is a flattering tribute to its power; but elsewhere it has come to be recognized as an evil which we ought not lightly to inflict.

Even more harmful than theological superstition is the superstition of nationalism, of duty to one's own State and to no other. But I do not propose on this occasion to discuss the matter beyond pointing out that limitation to one's compatriots is contrary to the principle of love which we recognized as constituting the good life. It is also, of course, contrary to enlightened self-interest, since an exclusive nationalism does not pay even the victorious nations.

One other respect in which our society suffers from the theological conception of 'sin' is the treatment of criminals. The view that criminals are 'wicked' and 'deserve' punishment is not one which a rational morality can support. Undoubtedly certain people do things which society wishes to prevent, and does right in preventing as far as possible. We may take murder as the plainest case. Obviously, if a community is to hold together and we are to enjoy its pleasures and advantages, we cannot allow people to kill each other whenever they feel an impulse to do so. But this problem should be treated in a purely scientific spirit. We should ask simply:

What is the best method of preventing murder? Of two methods which are equally effective in preventing murder, the one involving least harm to the murderer is to be preferred. The harm to the murderer is wholly regrettable, like the pain of a surgical operation. It may be equally necessary, but it is not a subject for rejoicing. The vindictive feeling called 'moral indignation' is merely a form of cruelty. Suffering to the criminal can never be justified by the notion of vindictive punishment. If education combined with kindness is equally effective, it is to be preferred; still more is it to be preferred if it is more effective. Of course, the prevention of crime and the punishment of crime are two different questions; the object of causing pain to the criminal is presumably deterrent. If prisons were so humanized that a prisoner got a good education for nothing, people might commit crimes in order to qualify for entrance. No doubt prison must be less pleasant than freedom; but the best way to secure this result is to make freedom more pleasant than it sometimes is at present. I do not wish, however, to embark upon the subject of Penal Reform. I merely wish to suggest that we should treat the criminal as we treat a man suffering from plague. Each is a public danger, each must have his liberty curtailed until he has ceased to be a danger. But the man suffering from plague is an object of sympathy and commiseration, whereas the criminal is an object of execration. This is quite irrational. And it is because of this difference of attitude that our prisons are so much less successful in curing criminal tendencies than our hospitals are in curing disease.

IV. SALVATION: INDIVIDUAL AND SOCIAL

One of the defects of traditional religion is its individualism, and this defect belongs also to the morality associated with it. Traditionally, the religious life was, as it were, a duologue between the soul and God. To obey the will of God was virtue; and this was possible for the individual quite regardless of the state of the community. Protestant sects developed the idea of 'finding salvation', but it was always present in Christian teaching. This individualism of the separate soul had its value at certain stages of history, but in the modern world we need rather a social than an individual conception of welfare. I want to consider, in this section, how this affects our conception of the good life.

Christianity arose in the Roman Empire among populations, wholly destitute of political power, whose national States had been destroyed and merged into a vast impersonal aggregate. During the first three centuries of the Christian era the individuals who adopted Christianity could not alter the social or political institutions under which they lived, although they were profoundly convinced of their badness. In these circumstances, it was natural that they should adopt the belief that an individual may be perfect in an imperfect world, and that the good life has nothing to do with this world. What I mean may become plain by comparison with Plato's Republic. When Plato wanted to describe the good life, he described a whole community, not an individual; he did so in order to define justice, which is an essentially social conception. He was accustomed to citizenship of a republic, and political responsibility was something which he took for granted. With the loss of Greek freedom comes the rise of Stoicism, which is like Christianity, and unlike Plato, in having an individualistic conception of the good life.

We, who belong to great democracies, should find a more appropriate morality in free Athens than in despotic Imperial Rome. In India, where the political circumstances are very similar to those of Judea in the time of Christ, we find Gandhi preaching a very similar morality to Christ's and being punished for it by the christianized successors of Pontius Pilate. But the more extreme Indian nationalists are not content with individual salvation: they want national salvation. In this they have taken on the outlook of the free democracies of the West. I want to suggest some respects in which this outlook, owing to Christian influences, is not yet sufficiently bold and self-conscious, but is still hampered by the belief in individual salvation.

The good life, as we conceive it, demands a multitude of social conditions, and cannot be realized without them. The good life, we said, is a life inspired by love and guided by knowledge. The knowledge required can only exist where governments or millionaires devote themselves to its discovery and diffusion. For example, the spread of cancer is alarming—what are we to do about it? At the moment, no one can answer the question for lack of knowledge; and the knowledge is not likely to emerge except through endowed research. Again, knowledge of science, history, literature and art ought to be attainable by all who desire it; this requires elaborate arrangements on the part of public authorities, and is not to be achieved by means of religious conversion. Then there is foreign trade, without which half the inhabitants of Great Britain would starve; and if we were starving very few of us would live the good life. It is needless to multiply examples. The important point is that, in all that differentiates between a good life and a bad one, the world is a unity, and the man who pretends to live independently is a conscious or unconscious parasite.

The idea of individual salvation, with which the early Christians consoled themselves for their political subjection, becomes impossible as soon as we escape from a very narrow conception of the good life. In the orthodox Christian conception, the good life is the virtuous life, and virtue consists in obedience to the will of God, and the will of God is revealed to each individual through the voice of conscience. This whole conception is that of men subject to an alien despotism. The good life involves much beside virtue—intelligence, for instance. And conscience is a most fallacious guide, since it consists of vague reminiscences of precepts heard in early youth, so that it is never wiser than its possessor's nurse or mother. To live a good life in the fullest sense a man must have a good education, friends, love, children (if he desires them), a sufficient income to keep him from want and grave anxiety, good health, and work which is not uninteresting. All these things, in varying degrees, depend upon the community, and are helped or hindered by political events. The good life must be lived in a good society, and is not fully possible otherwise.

This is the fundamental defect of the aristocratic ideal. Certain good things, such as art and science and friendship, can flourish very well in an aristocratic society. They existed in Greece on a basis of slavery; they exist among ourselves on a basis of exploitation. But love, in the form of sympathy, or benevolence, cannot exist freely in an aristocratic society. The aristocrat has to persuade himself that the slave or proletarian or coloured man is of inferior clay, and that his sufferings do not matter. At the present moment, polished English gentlemen flog Africans so severely that they die after hours of unspeakable anguish. Even if these gentlemen are well-educated, artistic and admirable conversationalists, I cannot admit that they are living the good life. Human nature imposes some limitation of sympathy, but not such a degree as that. In a democratically-minded society, only a maniac would behave in this way. The limitation of sympathy involved in the aristocratic ideal is its condemnation. Salvation is an aristocratic ideal, because it is individualistic. For this reason, also, the idea of personal salvation, however interpreted and expanded, cannot serve for the definition of the good life.

Another characteristic of salvation is that it results from a catastrophic change, like the conversion of Saint Paul. Shelley's poems afford an illustration of this conception applied to societies; the moment comes when everybody is converted, the 'anarchs' fly and 'the world's great age begins anew'. It may be said that a poet is an unimportant person, whose ideas are of no consequence. But I am persuaded that a large proportion of revolutionary leaders have had ideas extremely like Shelley's. They have thought that misery and cruelty and degradation were due to tyrants or priests or capitalists or Germans, and that if these sources of evil were overthrown there would be a general change of heart and we should all live happy ever after. Holding these beliefs, they have been willing to wage a 'war to end wars'. Comparatively fortunate were those who had suffered defeat or death; those who had the misfortune to emerge victorious were reduced to cynicism and despair by the failure of all their glowing hopes. The ultimate source of these hopes was the Christian doctrine of catastrophic conversion as the road to salvation.

I do not wish to suggest that revolutions are never necessary, but I do wish to suggest that they are not short cuts to the millennium. There is no short cut to the good life, whether individual or social. To build up the good life, we must build up intelligence, self-control and sympathy. This is a quantitative matter, a matter of gradual improvement, of early training, of educational experiment. Only impatience prompts the belief in the possibility of sudden improvement. The gradual improvement that is possible, and the methods by which it may be achieved, are a matter for future science. But something can be said now. Some part of what can be said I shall try to indicate in a final section.

V. SCIENCE AND HAPPINESS

The purpose of the moralist is to improve men's behaviour. This is a laudable ambition, since their behaviour is for the most part deplorable. But I cannot praise the moralist either for the particular improvements he desires or for the methods he adopts for achieving them. His ostensible method is moral exhortation; his real method (if he is orthodox) is a system of economic rewards and punishments. The former effects nothing permanent or important; the influence of revivalists, from Savonarola downwards, has always been very transitory. The latter—the rewards and punishments—have a very considerable effect. They cause a man, for example, to prefer casual prostitutes to a quasi-permanent mistress, because it is necessary to adopt the method which is most easily concealed. They thus keep up the numbers of a very dangerous profession, and secure the prevalence of venereal disease. These are not the objects desired by the moralist, and he is too unscientific to notice that they are the objects which he actually achieves.

Is there anything better to be substituted for this unscientific mixture of preaching and bribery? I think there is.

Men's actions are harmful either from ignorance or from bad desires. 'Bad' desires, when we are speaking from a social point of view, may be defined as those which tend to thwart the desires of others, or more exactly, those which thwart more desires than they assist. It is not necessary to dwell upon the harmfulness that springs from ignorance; here, more knowledge is all that is wanted, so that the road to improvement lies in more research and more education. But the harmfulness that springs from bad desires is a more difficult matter.

In the ordinary man and women there is a certain amount of active malevolence, both special ill-will directed to particular enemies and general impersonal pleasure in the misfortunes of others. It is customary to cover this over with fine phrases; about half of conventional morality is a cloak for it. But it must be faced if the moralists' aim of improving our actions is to be achieved. It is shown in a thousand ways, great and small: in the glee with which people repeat and believe scandal, in the unkind treatment of criminals in spite of clear proof that better treatment would have more effect in reforming them, in the unbelievable barbarity with which all white races treat negroes, and in the gusto with which old ladies and clergymen pointed out the duty of military service to young men during the war. Even children may be the objects of wanton cruelty: David Copperfield and Oliver Twist are by no means imaginary. This active malevolence is the worst feature of human nature and the one which it is most necessary to change if the world is to grow happier. Probably this one cause has more to do with war than all the economic and political causes put together.

Given this problem of preventing malevolence, how shall we deal with it? First let us try to understand its causes. These are, I think, partly social, partly physiological. The world, now as much as at any former time, is based upon life-and-death competition; the question at issue in the War was whether German or Allied children should die of want and starvation. (Apart from malevolence on both sides there was not the slightest reason why both should not survive.) Most people have in the background of their minds a haunting fear of ruin; this is especially true of people who have children. The rich fear that Bolsheviks will confiscate their investments; the poor fear that they will lose their job or their health. Everyone is engaged in the frantic pursuit of 'security' and imagines that this is to be achieved by keeping potential enemies in subjection. It is in moments of panic that cruelty becomes most widespread and most atrocious. Reactionaries everywhere appeal to fear: in England, to fear of Bolshevism; in France, to fear of Germany; in Germany, to fear of France. And the sole effect of their appeals is to increase the danger against which they wish to be protected.

It must, therefore, be one of the chief concerns of the scientific moralist to combat fear. This can be done in two ways: by increasing security, and by cultivating courage. I am speaking of fear as an irrational passion, not of the rational prevision of possible misfortune. When a theatre catches fire, the rational man foresees disaster just as clearly as the man stricken with panic, but he adopts methods likely to diminish the disaster, whereas the man stricken with panic increases it. Europe since 1914 has been like a panic-stricken audience in a theatre on fire; what is needed is calm authoritative directions as to how to escape without trampling each other to pieces in the process. The Victorian Age, for all its humbug, was a period of rapid progress, because men were dominated by hope rather than fear. If we are again to have progress, we must again be dominated by hope.

Everything that increases the general security is likely to diminish cruelty. This applies to prevention of war, whether through the instrumentality of the League of Nations or otherwise; to prevention of destitution; to better health by improvement in medicine, hygiene and sanitation; and to all other methods of lessening the terrors that lurk in the abysses of men's minds and emerge as nightmares when they sleep. But nothing is accomplished by an attempt to make a portion of mankind secure at the expense of another portion—Frenchmen at the expense of Germans, capitalists at the expense of wage-earners, white men at the expense of yellow men, and so on. Such methods only increase terror in the dominant group, lest just resentment should lead the oppressed to rebel. Only justice can give security; and by 'justice' I mean the recognition of the equal claims of all human beings.

In addition to social changes designed to bring security there is, however, another and more direct means of diminishing fear, namely by a regimen designed to increase courage. Owing to the importance of courage in battle, men early discovered means of increasing it by education and diet—eating human flesh, for example, was supposed to be useful. But military courage was to be the prerogative of the ruling caste: Spartans were to have more than helots, British officers than Indian privates, men than women, and so on. For centuries it was supposed to be the privilege of of the aristocracy. Every increase of courage in the ruling caste was used to increase the burdens on the oppressed, and therefore to increase the grounds for fear in the oppressors, and therefore to leave the causes of cruelty undiminished. Courage must be democratized before it can make men humane.

To a great extent, courage has already been democratized by recent events. The suffragettes showed that they possessed as much courage as the bravest men; this demonstration was essential in winning them the vote. The common soldier in the War needed as much courage as a captain or lieutenant, and much more than a general; this had much to do with his lack of servility after demobilization. The Bolsheviks, who proclaim themselves the champions of the proletariat, are not lacking in courage, whatever else may be said of them; this is proved by their prerevolutionary record. In Japan, where formerly the Samurai had a monopoly of martial ardour, conscription brought the need of courage throughout the male population. Thus among all the Great Powers much has been done during the past half-century to make courage no longer an aristocratic monopoly: if this were not the case, the danger to democracy would be far greater than it is.

But courage in fighting is by no means the only form, nor perhaps even the most important. There is courage in facing poverty, courage in facing derision, courage in facing the hostility of one's own herd. In these, the bravest soldiers are often lamentably deficient. And above all there is the courage to think calmly and rationally in the face of danger, and to control the impulse of panic fear or panic rage. There are certainly things which education can help to give. And the teaching of every form of courage is rendered easier by good health, good physique, adequate nourishment and free play for fundamental vital impulses. Perhaps the physiological sources of courage could be discovered by comparing the blood of a cat with that of a rabbit. In all likelihood there is no limit to what science could do in the way of increasing courage, by example, experience of danger, an athletic life, and a suitable diet. All these things our upper class boys to a great extent enjoy, but as yet they are in the main the prerogative of wealth. The courage so far encouraged in the poorer sections of the community is courage under orders, not the kind that involves initiative and leadership. When the qualities that now confer leadership have become universal, there will no longer be leaders and followers, and democracy will have been realized at last.

But fear is not the only source of malevolence; envy and disappointment also have their share. The envy of cripples and hunchbacks is proverbial as a source of malignity, but other misfortunes than theirs produce similar results. A man or women who has been thwarted sexually is apt to be full of envy; this generally takes the form of moral condemnation of the more fortunate. Much of the driving force of revolutionary movements is due to envy of the rich. Jealousy is, of course, a special form of envy—envy of love. The old often envy the young; when they do, they are apt to treat them cruelly.

There is, so far as I know, no way of dealing with envy except to make the lives of the envious happier and fuller, and to encourage in youth the idea of collective enterprises rather than competition. The worst forms of envy are in those who have not had a full life in the way of marriage, or children, or career. Such misfortunes could in most cases be avoided by better social institutions. Still, it must be admitted that a residuum of envy is likely to remain. There are many instances in history of generals so jealous of each other that they preferred defeat to enhancement of the other's reputation. Two politicians of the same party, or two artists of the same school, are almost sure to be jealous of one another. In such cases, there seems nothing to be done except to arrange, as far as possible, that each competitor shall be unable to injure the other, and shall only be able to win by superior merit. An artist's jealousy of a rival does little harm usually, because the only effective way of indulging it is to paint better pictures than his rival's, since it is not open to him to destroy his rival's pictures. Where envy is unavoidable it must be used as a stimulus to one's own efforts, not to the thwarting of the efforts of rivals.

The possibilities of science in the way of increasing human happiness are not confined to diminishing those aspects of human nature which make for mutual defeat, and which we therefore call 'bad'. There is probably no limit to what science can do in the way of increasing positive excellence. Health has already been greatly improved; in spite of the lamentations of those who idealize the past, we live longer and have fewer illnesses than any class or nation in the eighteenth century. With a little more application of the knowledge we already possess, we might be much healthier than we are. And future discoveries are likely to accelerate this process enormously.

So far, it has been physical science that has had most effect upon our lives, but in the future physiology and psychology are likely to be far more potent. When we have discovered how character depends upon physiological conditions, we shall be able, if we choose, to produce far more of the type of human being that we admire. Intelligence, artistic capacity, benevolence—all these things no doubt could be increased by science. There seems scarcely any limit to what *could* be done in the way of producing a good world, if only men would use science wisely. I have expressed elsewhere my fears that men may not make a wise use of the power they derive from science.[1] At present I am concerned with the good that men could do if they chose, not with the question whether they will choose rather to do harm.

There is a certain attitude about the application of science to human life with which I have some sympathy, though I do not, in the last analysis, agree with it. It is the attitude of those who dread what is 'unnatural'. Rousseau is, of course, the great protagonist of this view in Europe. In Asia, Lao-Tze has set it forth even more persuasively, and 2,400 years sooner. I think there is a mixture of truth and falsehood in the admiration of 'nature', which it is important to disentangle. To begin with, what is 'natural'? Roughly speaking, anything to which the speaker was accustomed in childhood. Lao-Tze objects to roads and carriages and boats, all of which were probably unknown in the village where he was born. Rousseau has got used to these things, and does not regard them as against nature. But he would no doubt have thundered against railways if he had lived to see them. Clothes and cooking are too ancient to be denounced by most of the apostles of nature, though they all object to new fashions in either. Birth control is thought wicked by people who tolerate celibacy, because the former is a new violation of nature and the latter an ancient one. In all these ways those who preach 'nature' are inconsistent, and one is tempted to regard them as mere conservatives.

Nevertheless, there is something to be said in their favour. Take for instance vitamins, the discovery of which has produced a revulsion in favour of 'natural' foods. It seems, however, that vitamins can be supplied by cod-liver oil and electric light, which are certainly not part of the 'natural' diet of a human being. This case illustrates that, in the absence of knowledge, unexpected harm may be done by a new departure from nature; but when the harm has come to be understood it can usually be remedied by some new artificiality. As regards our physical environment and our physical means of gratifying our desires, I do not think the doctrine of 'nature' justifies anything beyond a certain experimental caution in the adoption of new expedients. Clothes, for instance, are contrary to

[1] See *Icarus*.

nature, and need to be supplemented by another unnatural practice, namely washing, if they are not to bring disease. But the two practices together make a man healthier than the savage who eschews both.

There is more to be said for 'nature' in the realm of human desires. To force upon man, woman or child a life which thwarts their strongest impulses is both cruel and dangerous; in this sense, a life according to 'nature' is to be commended with certain provisos. Nothing could be more artificial than an underground electric railway, but no violence is done to a child's nature when it is taken to travel in one; on the contrary, almost all children find the experience delightful. Artificialities which gratify the desires of ordinary human beings are good, other things being equal. But there is nothing to be said for ways of life which are artificial in the sense of being imposed by authority or economic necessity. Such ways of life are, no doubt, to some extent necessary at present; ocean travel would become very difficult if there were no stokers on steamers. But necessities of this kind are regrettable, and we ought to look for ways of avoiding them. A certain amount of work is not a thing to complain of; indeed, in nine cases out of ten, it makes a man happier than complete idleness. But the amount and kind of work that most people have to do at present is a grave evil: especially bad is the life-long bondage to routine. Life should not be too closely regulated or too methodical; our impulses, when not positively destructive or injurious to others, ought if possible to have free play; there should be room for adventure. Human nature we should respect, because our impulses and desires are the stuff out of which our happiness is to be made. It is no use to give men something abstractedly considered 'good'; we must give them something desired or needed if we are to add to their happiness. Science may learn in time to mould our desires so that they shall not conflict with those of other people to the same extent as they do now; then we shall be able to satisfy a larger proportion of our desires than at present. In that sense, but in that sense only, our desires will then have become 'better'. A single desire is no better and no worse, considered in isolation, than any other; but a group of desires is better than another group if all of the first group can be satisfied simultaneously, while in the second group some are inconsistent with others. That is why love is better than hatred.

To respect physical nature is foolish; physical nature should be studied with a view to making it serve human ends as far as possible, but it remains ethically neither good nor bad. And where physical nature and human nature interact, as in the population question, there is no need to fold our hands in passive adoration and accept war, pestilence and famine as the only possible means of dealing with excessive fertility. The divines say: it is wicked, in this matter, to apply science to the physical side of the problem; we must (they say) apply morals to the human side and practise abstinence. Apart from the fact that everyone, including the divines, knows that their advice will not be taken, why should it be wicked to solve the population question by adopting physical means for preventing conception? No answer is forthcoming except one based upon antiquated dogmas. And clearly the violence to nature advocated by the divines is at least as great as that involved in birth control. The divines prefer a violence to human nature, which, when successfully practised, involves unhappiness, envy, a tendency to persecution, often madness. I prefer a 'violence' to physical nature which is of the same sort as that involved in the steam engine or even in the use of an umbrella. This instance shows how ambiguous and uncertain is the application of the principle that we should follow 'nature'.

Nature, even human nature, will cease more and more to be an absolute datum; more and more it will become what scientific manipulation has made it. Science can, if it chooses, enable our grandchildren to live the good life, by giving them knowledge, self-control and characters productive of harmony rather than strife. At present it is teaching our children to kill each other, because many men of science are willing to sacrifice the future of mankind to their own momentary prosperity. But this phase will pass when men have acquired the same domination over their own passions that they already have over the physical forces of the external world. Then at last we shall have won our freedom.

(Reprinted in *Why I am not a Christian*, London: Allen & Unwin; New York: Simon & Schuster, 1957.)

44

THE EXPANDING MENTAL UNIVERSE

THE effects of modern knowledge upon our mental life have been many and various, and seem likely, in future, to become even greater than they have been hitherto. The life of the mind is traditionally divided into three aspects: thinking, willing, and feeling. There is no great scientific validity in this division, but it is convenient for purposes of discussion, and I shall, therefore, follow it.

It is obvious that the primary effect of modern knowledge is on our thinking, but it has already had important effects in the sphere of will, and should have equally important effects in the sphere of feeling, though as yet these are very imperfectly developed. I will begin with the purely intellectual effects.

The physical universe, according to a theory widely held by astronomers, is continually expanding. Everything not quite near to us is moving away from us, and the more remote it is, the faster it is receding. Those who hold this theory think that very distant parts of the universe are perpetually slipping into invisibility because they are moving away from us with a velocity greater than that of light. I do not know whether this theory of the expanding physical universe will continue to hold the field or not, but there can be no doubt about the expanding mental universe. Those who are aware of the cosmos as science has shown it to be have to stretch their imaginations both in space and in time to an extent which was unknown in former ages, and which to many in our time is bewilderingly painful.

The expansion of the world in space was begun by the Greek astronomers. Anaxagoras, whom Pericles imported into Athens to teach the Athenians philosophy, maintained that the sun is as large as the Peloponnesus, but his contemporaries thought that this must be a wild exaggeration. Before long, however, the astronomers discovered ways of calculating the distance of the sun and moon from the earth, and, although their calculations were not correct, they sufficed to show that the sun must be many times larger than the earth. Poseidonius, who was Cicero's tutor, made the best estimate of the sun's distance that was made in antiquity. His estimate was about half of the right value. Ancient astronomers after his time were farther from the mark than he was, but all of them remained aware that, in comparison with the solar system, the size of the earth is insignificant.

In the Middle Ages there was an intellectual recession, and much knowledge that had been possessed by the Greeks was forgotten. The best imaginative picture of the universe, as conceived in the Middle Ages, is in Dante's Paradiso. In this picture there are a number of concentric spheres containing the moon, the sun, the various planets, the fixed stars, and the Empyrean. Dante, guided by Beatrice, traverses all of them in twenty-four hours. His cosmos, to a modern mind, is unbelievably small and tidy. Its relation to the universe with which we have to live is like that of a painted Dutch interior to a raging ocean in storm. His physical world contains no mysteries, no abysses, no unimaginable accumulation of uncatalogued worlds. It is comfortable and cosy and human and warm; but, to those who have lived with modern astronomy, it seems claustrophobic and with an orderliness which is more like that of a prison than that of the free air of heaven.

Ever since the early seventeenth century our conception of the universe has grown in space and time, and, until quite recent years, there has not seemed to be any limit to this growth. The distance of the sun was found to be much greater than any Greek had supposed and some of the planets were found to be very much more distant than the sun. The fixed stars, even the nearest, turned out to be vastly farther off than the sun. The light of the sun takes about eight minutes to reach us, but the light of the nearest fixed star takes about four years. The stars that we can see separately with the naked eye are our immediate neighbours in a vast assemblage called 'The Galaxy', or, in more popular parlance, 'The Milky Way'. This is one assemblage of stars which contains almost all that we can see with the naked eye, but it is only one of many millions of such assemblages. We do not know how many there may be.

A few figures may help the imagination. The distance of the nearest fixed star is about twenty-five million million miles. The Milky Way, which is, so to speak, our parish, contains about three hundred thousand million stars. There are many million assemblages similar to The Milky Way, and the distance from one such assemblage to the next takes about two million years for light to traverse. There is a considerable amount of matter in the universe. The sun weighs about two billion billion billion tons. The Milky Way weighs about a hundred and sixty thousand million times as much as the sun, and there are many million assemblages comparable to The Milky Way. But, although there is so much matter, the immensely large part of the universe is empty, or very nearly empty.

In regard to time, a similar stretching of our thoughts is necessary. This necessity was first shown by geology and paleontology. Fossils, sedimentary rocks and igneous rocks gave a backward history of the earth which was, of necessity, very long. Then came theories of the origin of the solar system and of the nebulae. Now, with the most powerful existing telescopes, we can see objects so distant that the light from them has taken about five hundred million years to reach us, so that what we see is not what is happening now, but what was happening in that immensely distant past.

What I have been saying concerns the expansion of our mental universe in the sphere of thought. I come now to the effects this expansion has, and should have, in the realms of will and feeling.

To those who have lived entirely amid terrestrial events and who have given little thought to what is distant in space and time, there is at first something bewildering and oppressive, and perhaps even paralysing, in the realization of the minuteness of man and all his concerns in comparison with astronomical abysses. But this effect is not rational and should not be lasting. There is no reason to worship mere size. We do not necessarily respect a fat man more than a thin man. Sir Isaac Newton was very much smaller than a hippopotamus, but we do not on that account value him less than the larger beast. The size of a man's mind—if such a phrase is permissible—is not to be measured by the size of a man's body. It is to be measured, in so far as it can be measured, by the size and complexity of the universe that he grasps in thought and imagination. The mind of the astronomer can grow, and should grow, step by step with the universe of which he is aware. And when I say that his mind should grow, I mean his total mind, not only its intellectual aspect. Will and feeling should keep pace with thought if man is to grow as his knowledge grows. If this cannot be achieved—if, while knowledge becomes cosmic, will and feeling remain parochial—there will be a lack of harmony producing a kind of madness of which the effects must be disasterous.

We have considered knowledge, but I wish now to consider wisdom, which is a harmony of knowledge, will and feeling, and by no means necessarily grows with the growth of knowledge.

Let us begin with will. There are things that a man can achieve and other things that he cannot achieve. The story of Canute's forbidding the tide to rise was intended to show the absurdity of willing something that is beyond human power. In the past, the things that men could do were very limited. Bad men, even with the worst intentions, could do only a very finite amount of harm. Good men, with the best intentions, could do only a very limited amount of good. But with every increase in knowledge, there has been an increase in what men could achieve. In our scientific world, and presumably still more in the more scientific world of the not distant future, bad men can do more harm, and good men can do more good, than had seemed possible to our ancestors even in their wildest dreams.

Until the end of the Middle Ages, it was thought that there were only

four kinds of matter, the so-called elements of earth, water, air and fire.
As the inadequacy of this theory became increasingly evident the number
of elements admitted by men of science increased until it was estimated
at ninety-two. The modern study of the atom has made it possible to
manufacture new elements which do not occur in nature. It is a regrettable
fact that all these new elements are deleterious and that quite moderate
quantities of them can kill large numbers of people. In this respect recent
science has not been beneficent. *Per contra*, science has achieved what
might almost seem like miracles in the way of combating diseases and
prolonging human life.

These increases of human power remain terrestrial: we have become
able, as never before, to mould life on earth, or to put an end to it if the
whim should seize us. But, unless by some such whim we put an end to
man, we are on the threshold of a vast extension of human power. We
could now, if the expenditure were thought worth while, send a projectile
to the moon, and there are those who hold that we could in time make
the moon capable of supporting human life. There is no reason to suppose
that Mars and Venus will long remain unconquered. Meanwhile, as
Senator Johnson told the Senate, scientific power could have astonishing
effects upon our own planet. It could, to quote his own words, 'have the
power to control the earth's weather, to cause drought and flood, to change
the tides and raise the levels of the sea, to divert the Gulf Stream and
change temperate climates to frigid'.

When we have acquired these immense powers, to what end shall we use
them? Man has survived, hitherto, by virtue of ignorance and inefficiency.
He is a ferocious animal, and there have always been powerful men who
did all the harm they could. But their activities were limited by the
limitations of their technique. Now, these limitations are fading away.
If, with our increased cleverness, we continue to pursue aims no more
lofty than those pursued by tyrants in the past, we shall doom ourselves
to destruction and shall vanish as the dinosaurs vanished. They, too,
were once the lords of creation. They developed innumerable horns to
give them victory in the contests of their day. But, though no other
dinosaur could conquer them, they became extinct and left the world
to smaller creatures such as rats and mice.

We shall court a similar fate if we develop cleverness without wisdom.
I foresee rival projectiles landing simultaneously on the moon, each
equipped with H-bombs and each successfully engaged in exterminating
the other. But until we have set our own house in order, I think that we
had better leave the moon in peace. As yet, our follies have been only
terrestrial; it would seem a doubtful victory to make them cosmic.

If the increased power which science has conferred upon human
volitions is to be a boon and not a curse, the ends to which those volitions
are directed must grow commensurately with the growth of power to

carry them out. Hitherto, although we have been told on Sundays to love our neighbour, we have been told on weekdays to hate him, and there are six times as many weekdays as Sundays. Hitherto, the harm that we could do to our neighbour by hating him was limited by our incompetence, but in the new world upon which we are entering there will be no such limit, and the indulgence of hatred can lead only to disaster.

These considerations bring us to the sphere of feeling. It is feeling that determines the ends we shall pursue. It is feeling that decides what use we shall make of the enormous increases in human power. Feeling, like the rest of our mental capacities, has been gradually developed in the struggle for existence. From a very early time, human beings have been divided into groups which have gradually grown larger, passing, in the course of ages, from families to tribes, from tribes to nations, and from nations to federations. Throughout this process, biological needs have generated two opposite systems of morality: one for dealings with our own social group; the other for dealings with outsiders. The Decalogue tells us not to murder or steal, but outside our own group this prohibition is subject to many limitations. Many of the men who are most famous in history derive their fame from skill in helping their own group to kill people of other groups and steal from them. To this day, aristocratic families in England are proud if they can prove that their ancestors were Norman and were cleverer at killing Saxons than Saxons were at killing them.

Our emotional life is conditioned to a degree which has now become biologically disadvantageous by this opposition between one's own tribe and the alien tribes against which it collectively competes. In the new world created by modern technique, economic prosperity is to be secured by means quite different from those that were formerly advocated. A savage tribe, if it can exterminate a rival tribe, not only eats its enemies but appropriates their lands and lives more comfortably than it did before. To a continually diminishing degree these advantages of conquest survived until recent times.

But now the opposite is the case. Two nations which co-operate are more likely to achieve economic prosperity than either can achieve if they compete. Competition continues because our feelings are not yet adapted to our technique. It continues because we cannot make our emotions grow at the same rate as our skills.

Increase of skill without a corresponding enlargement in feeling produces a technical integration which fails of success for lack of an integration of purpose. In a technically developed world, what is done in one region may have enormous effects in a quite different region. So long as, in our feeling, we take account only of our own region, the machine as a whole fails to work smoothly. The process is one which, in varying forms, has persisted throughout evolution. A sponge, while it is living in the sea, is like a block of flats, a common abode of a number of separate little animals each almost entirely independent of the others and in no way obliged to concern itself with their interests. In the body of a more developed animal, each cell remains in some degree a separate creature, but it cannot prosper except through the prosperity of the whole. In cancer, a group of cells engages in a career of imperialism, but, in bringing the rest of the body to death, it decrees also its own extinction. A human body is a unit from the point of view of self-interest. One cannot set the interest of the great toe in opposition to that of the little finger. If any part of the body is to prosper, there must be co-operation to the common ends of the body as a whole.

The same sort of unification is taking place, though as yet very imperfectly, in human society, which is gradually approximating to the kind of unity that belongs to a single human body. When you eat, if you are in health, the nourishment profits every part of your body, but you do not think how kind and unselfish your mouth is to take all this trouble for something else. It is this kind of unification and expansion of self-interest that will have to take place if a scientific society is to prove capable of survival. This enlargement in the sphere of feeling is being rendered necessary by the new interdependence of different parts of the world.

Let us take an illustration from a quite probable future. Suppose some country in the southern hemisphere sets to work to make the Antarctic continent habitable. The first step will be to melt the ice—a feat which future science is likely to find possible. The melting of the ice will raise the level of the sea everywhere and will submerge most of Holland and Louisiana as well as many other low-lying lands. Clearly the inhabitants of such countries will object to projects that would drown them. I have chosen a somewhat fantastic illustration as I am anxious to avoid those that might excite existing political passions. The point is that close interdependence necessitates common purposes if disaster is to be avoided, and that common purposes will not prevail unless there is some community of feeling. The proverbial Kilkenny cats fought each other until nothing was left but the tips of their tails: if they had felt kindly toward each other, both might have lived happily.

Religion has long taught that it is our duty to love our neighbour and to desire the happiness of others rather than their misery. Unfortunately, active men have paid little attention to this teaching. But in the new world, the kindly feeling towards others which religion has advocated will be not only a moral duty but an indispensable condition of survival. A human body could not long continue to live if the hands were in conflict with the feet, and the stomach were at war with the liver. Human society as a whole is becoming, in this respect, more and more like a single human body; and if we are to continue to exist, we shall have to acquire feelings directed toward the welfare of the whole in the same sort of way in which our feelings of individual welfare concern the whole body and not only this or that portion of it. At any time such a way of feeling would have been admirable, but now, for the first time in human history, it is becoming necessary if any human being is to be able to achieve anything of what he would wish to enjoy.

Seers and poets have long had visions of the kind of expansion of the ego which I am trying to adumbrate. They have taught that men are capable of something which is called wisdom, something which does not consist of knowledge alone, or of will alone, or of feeling alone, but is a synthesis and intimate union of all three.

Some of the Greeks, and notably Socrates, thought that knowledge alone would suffice to produce the perfect man. According to Socrates, no one sins willingly, and, if we all had enough knowledge, we should all behave perfectly. I do not think that this is true. One could imagine a satanic being with immense knowledge and equally immense malevolence —and, alas, approximations to such a being have actually occurred in human history. It is not enough to seek knowledge rather than error. It is necessary, also, to feel benevolence rather than its opposite. But, although knowledge alone is not enough, it is a very essential ingredient of wisdom.

The world of a newborn infant is confined to his immediate environment. It is a tiny world bounded by what is immediately apparent to the senses. It is shut up within the walls of the here-and-now. Gradually, as knowledge grows, these walls recede. Memory and experience make what is past and what is distant gradually more vivid in the life of the growing child. If a child develops into a man of science, his world comes to embrace those very distant portions of space and time of which I spoke earlier. If he is to achieve wisdom, his feelings must grow as his knowledge grows. Theologians tell us that God views the universe as one vast whole, without any here-and-now, without that partiality of sense and feeling to which we are, in a greater or less degree, inevitably condemned. We cannot achieve this complete impartiality, and we could not survive if we did, but we can, and should, move as far toward it as our human limitations permit.

We are beset in our daily lives by fret and worry and frustrations. We find ourselves too readily pinned down to thoughts of what seems obstructive in our immediate environment. But it is possible, and authentic wise men have proved that it is possible, to live in so large a world that the vexations of daily life come to feel trivial and that the purposes which stir our deeper emotions take on something of the immensity of our cosmic contemplations. Some can achieve this in a greater degree, some only in a lesser, but all who care to do so can achieve this in some degree and, in so far as they succeed in this, they will win a kind of peace which will leave activity unimpeded but not turbulent.

The state of mind which I have been trying to describe is what I mean by wisdom, and it is undoubtedly more precious than rubies. The world needs this kind of wisdom as it has never needed it before. If mankind can acquire it, our new powers over nature offer a prospect of happiness and well-being such as men have never experienced and could scarcely even imagine. If mankind cannot, every increase in cleverness will bring us only nearer to irretrievable disaster. Men have done many good things and many bad ones. Some of the good things have been very good. All those who care for these good things must hope, with what confidence they can command, that in this moment of decision the wise choice will be made.

(No. 31 in series 'Adventures of the Mind', *The Saturday Evening Post*, July 18, 1959. Vol. 322, No. 3. Reprinted in *Adventures of the Mind*, ed. Richard Thruelson and John Kobler, New York: Alfred A. Knopf, 1959.)

PART X

The Philosopher of Education

Theories and practices in education have been both varied and numerous. Any philosophy of education will, however, ultimately be tested by the degree to which it coincides with objective evidence of the worth of its proffered ideal.

Although Russell's views on education were somewhat novel and created considerable newspaper publicity, his contributions to logic, mathematical philosophy, and philosophy in general, far outshadow his impact on educational theory. This is not altogether surprising in view of the fact that newspapers are out to stir up excitement and most readers are more interested in reading about unconventional ideas or popular themes than they are in hearing about mathematical advances. The publicity Russell received during the time he and Dora Russell headed the unorthodox Beacon Hill School (1927–1935) exaggerated the trivial and ignored the important.

Whether Russell is right or wrong in his philosophy of education is not the only issue. What is equally important is that scandalous tales often emerge about any famous writer who advocates unpopular ideas. A typical example of this sort of thing was the reputed occurrence of a small girl, without any clothes on, answering the door bell at Beacon Hill School. The local rector stared and said, 'Good God!' The girl replied as she closed the door: 'There *is* no God!'

The selections that follow are indicative of the import of Russell's philosophy of education and the great value Russell places upon the *function* of a teacher and the vital significance of a sound education in a troubled world.

45

EDUCATION

No political theory is adequate unless it is applicable to children as well as to men and women. Theorists are mostly childless, or, if they have children, they are carefully screened from the disturbances which would be caused by youthful turmoil. Some of them have written books on education, but without, as a rule, having any actual children present to their minds while they wrote. Those educational theorists who have had a knowledge of children, such as the inventors of Kindergarten and the Montessori system,[1] have not always had enough realization of the ultimate goal of education to be able to deal successfully with advanced instruction. I have not the knowledge either of children or of education which would enable me to supply whatever defects there may be in the writings of others. But some questions, concerning education as a political institution, are involved in any hope of social reconstruction, and are not usually considered by writers on educational theory. It is these questions that I wish to discuss.

The power of education in forming character and opinion is very great and very generally recognized. The genuine beliefs, though not usually the professed precepts, of parents and teachers are almost unconsciously acquired by most children; and even if they depart from these beliefs in later life, something of them remains deeply implanted, ready to emerge in a time of stress or crisis. Education is, as a rule, the strongest force on the side of what exists and against fundamental change: threatened institutions, while they are still powerful, possess themselves of the educational machine, and instil a respect for their own excellence into the malleable minds of the young. Reformers retort by trying to oust their opponents from their position of vantage. The children themselves are not considered by either party; they are merely so much material, to be recruited into one army or the other. If the children themselves were considered, education would not aim at making them belong to this party or that, but at enabling them to choose intelligently between the parties; it would aim at making them able to think, not at making them think

---

[1] As regards the education of young children, Madame Montessori's methods seem to me full of wisdom.

what their teachers think. Education as a political weapon could not exist if we respected the rights of children. If we respected the rights of children, we should educate them so as to give them the knowledge and the mental habits required for forming independent opinions; but education as a political institution endeavours to form habits and to circumscribe knowledge in such a way as to make one set of opinions inevitable.

The two principles of *justice* and *liberty*, which cover a very great deal of the social reconstruction required, are not by themselves sufficient where education is concerned. Justice, in the literal sense of equal rights, is obviously not wholly possible as regards children. And as for liberty, it is, to begin with, essentially negative: it condemns all avoidable interference with freedom, without giving a positive principle of construction. But education is essentially constructive, and requires some positive conception of what constitutes a good life. And although liberty is to be respected in education as much as is compatible with instruction, and although a very great deal more liberty than is customary can be allowed without loss to instruction, yet it is clear that some departure from complete liberty is unavoidable if children are to be taught anything, except in the case of unusually intelligent children who are kept isolated from more normal companions. This is one reason for the great responsibility which rests upon teachers: the children must, necessarily, be more or less at the mercy of their elders, and cannot make themselves the guardians of their own interests. Authority in education is to some extent unavoidable, and those who educate have to find a way of exercising authority in accordance with the *spirit* of liberty.

Where authority is unavoidable, what is needed is *reverence*. A man who is to educate really well, and is to make the young grow and develop into their full stature, must be filled through and through with the spirit of reverence. It is reverence towards others that is lacking in those who advocate machine-made cast-iron systems: militarism, capitalism, Fabian scientific organization and all the other prisons into which reformers and reactionaries try to force the human spirit. In education, with its codes of rules emanating from a Government office, its large classes and fixed curriculum and overworked teachers, its determination to produce a dead level of glib mediocrity, the lack of reverence for the child is all but universal. Reverence requires imagination and vital warmth; it requires most imagination in respect of those who have least actual achievement or power. The child is weak and superficially foolish, the teacher is strong, and in an everyday sense wiser than the child. The teacher without reverence, or the bureaucrat without reverence, easily despises the child for these outward inferiorities. He thinks it is his duty to 'mould' the child: in imagination he is the potter with the clay. And so he gives to the child some unnatural shape, which hardens with age, producing strains and spiritual dissatisfactions, out of which grow cruelty and envy, and the belief that others must be compelled to undergo the same distortions.

The man who has reverence will not think it his duty to 'mould' the young. He feels in all that lives, but especially in human beings, and most of all in children, something sacred, indefinable, unlimited, something individual and strangely precious, the growing principle of life, an embodied fragment of the dumb striving of the world. In the presence of a child he feels an unaccountable humility—a humility not easily defensible on any rational ground, and yet somehow nearer to wisdom than the easy self-confidence of many parents and teachers. The outward helplessness of the child and the appeal of dependence make him conscious of the responsibility of a trust. His imagination shows him what the child may become, for good or evil, how its impulses may be developed or thwarted, how its hopes must be dimmed and the life in it grow less living, how its trust will be bruised and its quick desires replaced by brooding will. All this gives him a longing to help the child in its own battle; he would equip and strengthen it, not for some outside end proposed by the State or by any other impersonal authority, but for the ends which the child's own spirit is obscurely seeking. The man who feels this can wield the authority of an educator without infringing the principle of liberty.

It is not in a spirit of reverence that education is conducted by States and Churches and the great institutions that are subservient to them. What is considered in education is hardly ever the boy or girl, the young man or young woman, but almost always, in some form, the maintenance of the existing order. When the individual is considered, it is almost exclusively with a view to worldly success—making money or achieving a good position. To be ordinary, and to acquire the art of getting on, is the ideal which is set before the youthful mind, except by a few rare teachers who have enough energy of belief to break through the system within which they are expected to work. Almost all education has a political motive: it aims at strengthening some group, national or religious or even social, in the competition with other groups. It is this motive, in the main, which determines the subjects taught, the knowledge offered and the knowledge withheld, and also decides what mental habits the pupils are expected to acquire. Hardly anything is done to foster the inward growth of mind and spirit; in fact, those who have had most education are very often atrophied in their mental and spiritual life, devoid of impulse, and possessing only certain mechanical aptitudes which take the place of living thought.

Some of the things which education achieves at present must continue to be achieved by education in any civilized country. All children must continue to be taught how to read and write, and some must continue to acquire the knowledge needed for such professions as medicine or law or engineering. The higher education required for the sciences and the arts is necessary for those to whom it is suited. Except in history and religion and kindred matters, the actual instruction is only inadequate, not positively harmful. The instruction might be given in a more liberal spirit, with more attempt to show its ultimate uses; and of course much of it is traditional and dead. But in the main it is necessary, and would have to form a part of any educational system.

It is in history and religion and other controversial subjects that the actual instruction is positively harmful. These subjects touch the interests by which schools are maintained; and the interests maintain the schools in order that certain views on these subjects may be instilled. History, in every country, is so taught as to magnify that country: children learn to believe that their own country has always been in the right and almost always victorious, that it has produced almost all the great men, and that it is in all respects superior to all other countries. Since these beliefs are flattering, they are easily absorbed, and hardly ever dislodged from instinct by later knowledge.

To take a simple and almost trivial example: the facts about the battle of Waterloo are known in great detail and with minute accuracy; but the facts as taught in elementary schools will be widely different in England, France, and Germany. The ordinary English boy imagines that the Prussians played hardly any part; the ordinary German boy imagines that Wellington was practically defeated when the day was retrieved by Blücher's gallantry. If the facts were taught accurately in both countries, national pride would not be fostered to the same extent, neither nation would feel so certain of victory in the event of war, and the willingness to fight would be diminished. It is this result which has to be prevented. Every State wishes to promote national pride, and is conscious that this cannot be done by unbiased history. The defenceless children are taught by distortions and suppressions and suggestions. The false ideas as to the history of the world which are taught in the various countries are of a kind which encourages strife and serves to keep alive a bigoted nationalism. If good relations between States were desired, one of the first steps ought to be to submit all teaching of history to an international commission, which should produce neutral textbooks free from the patriotic bias which is now demanded everywhere.[1]

[1] THE TEACHING OF PATRIOTISM. HIS MAJESTY'S APPROVAL

THE King has been graciously pleased to accept a copy of the little book containing suggestions to local education authorities and teachers in Wales as to the teaching of patriotism which has just been issued by the Welsh Department of the Board of Education in connection with the observance of the National Anniversary of St David's Day. His Private Secretary (Lord Stamfordham), in writing to Mr Alfred T. Davies, the Permanent Secretary of the Welsh Department, says that His Majesty is much pleased with the contents of the book, and trusts that the principles inculcated in it will bear good fruit in the lives and characters of the coming generation.—*Morning Post*, January 29, 1916.

Exactly the same thing applies to religion. Elementary schools are practically always in the hands either of some religious body or of a State which has a certain attitude towards religion. A religious body exists through the fact that its members all have certain definite beliefs on subjects as to which the truth is not ascertainable. Schools conducted by religious bodies have to prevent the young, who are often inquiring by nature, from discovering that these definite beliefs are opposed by others which are no more unreasonable, and that many of the men best qualified to judge think that there is no good evidence in favour of any definite belief. When the State is militantly secular, as in France, State schools become as dogmatic as those that are in the hands of the Churches (I understand that the word 'God' must not be mentioned in a French elementary school). The result in all these cases is the same: free inquiry is checked, and on the most important matter in the world the child is met with dogma or with stony silence.

It is not only in elementary education that these evils exist. In more advanced education they take subtler forms, and there is more attempt to conceal them, but they are still present. Eton and Oxford set a certain stamp upon a man's mind, just as a Jesuit College does. It can hardly be said that Eton and Oxford have a *conscious* purpose, but they have a purpose which is none the less strong and effective for not being formulated. In almost all who have been through them they produce a worship of 'good form', which is as destructive to life and thought as the medieval Church. 'Good form' is quite compatible with a superficial open-mindedness, a readiness to hear all sides, and a certain urbanity towards opponents. But it is not compatible with fundamental open-mindedness, or with any inward readiness to give weight to the other side. Its essence is the assumption that what is most important is a certain kind of behaviour, a behaviour which minimizes friction between equals and delicately impresses inferiors with a conviction of their own crudity. As a political weapon for preserving the privileges of the rich in a snobbish democracy it is unsurpassable. As a means of producing an agreeable social *milieu* for those who have money with no strong beliefs or unusual desires it has some merit. In every other respect it is abominable.

The evils of 'good form' arise from two sources: its perfect assurance of its own rightness, and its belief that correct manners are more to be desired than intellect, or artistic creation, or vital energy, or any of the other sources of progress in the world. Perfect assurance, by itself, is enough to destroy all mental progress in those who have it. And when it is combined with contempt for the angularities and awkwardnesses that are almost invariably associated with great mental power, it becomes a source of destruction to all who come in contact with it. 'Good form' is itself dead and incapable of growth; and by its attitude to those who are without it it spreads its own death to many who might otherwise have life.

The harm which it has done to well-to-do Englishmen, and to men whose abilities have led the well-to-do to notice them, is incalculable.

The prevention of free inquiry is unavoidable so long as the purpose of education is to produce belief rather than thought, to compel the young to hold positive opinions on doubtful matters rather than to let them see the doubtfulness and be encouraged to independence of mind. Education ought to foster the wish for truth, not the conviction that some particular creed is the truth. But it is creeds that hold men together in fighting organizations: Churches, States, political parties. It is intensity of belief in a creed that produces efficiency in fighting: victory comes to those who feel the strongest certainty about matters on which doubt is the only rational attitude. To produce this intensity of belief and this efficiency in fighting, the child's nature is warped, and its free outlook is cramped, by cultivating inhibitions as a check to the growth of new ideas. In those whose minds are not very active the result is the omnipotence of prejudice; while the few whose thought cannot be wholly killed become cynical, intellectually hopeless, destructively critical, able to make all that is living seem foolish, unable themselves to supply the creative impulses which they destroy in others.

The success in fighting which is achieved by suppressing freedom of thought is brief and very worthless. In the long run mental vigour is as essential to success as it is to a good life. The conception of education as a form of drill, a means of producing unanimity through slavishness, is very common, and is defended chiefly on the ground that it leads to victory. Those who enjoy parallels from ancient history will point to the victory of Sparta over Athens to enforce their moral. But it is Athens that has had power over men's thoughts and imagination, not Sparta: any one of us, if we could be born again into some past epoch, would rather be born an Athenian than a Spartan. And in the modern world so much intellect is required in practical affairs that even the external victory is more likely to be won by intelligence than by docility. Education in credulity leads by quick stages to mental decay; it is only by keeping alive the spirit of free inquiry that the indispensable minimum of progress can be achieved.

Certain mental habits are commonly instilled by those who are engaged in educating: obedience and discipline, ruthlessness in the struggle for worldly success, contempt towards opposing groups, and an unquestioning credulity, a passive acceptance of the teacher's wisdom. All these habits are against life. Instead of obedience and discipline, we ought to aim at preserving independence and impulse. Instead of ruthlessness, education should try to develop justice in thought. Instead of contempt, it ought to instil reverence, and the attempt at understanding; towards the opinions of others it ought to produce, not necessarily acquiescence, but only such opposition as is combined with imaginative apprehension and a clear realization of the grounds for opposition. Instead of credulity, the object should be to stimulate constructive doubt, the love of mental adventure, the sense of worlds to conquer by enterprise and boldness in thought. Contentment with the *status quo*, and subordination of the individual pupil to political aims, owing to indifference to the things of the mind, are the immediate causes of these evils; but beneath these causes there is one more fundamental, the fact that education is treated as a means of acquiring power over the pupil, not as a means of nourishing his own growth. It is in this that lack of reverence shows itself; and it is only by more reverence that a fundamental reform can be effected.

Obedience and discipline are supposed to be indispensable if order is to be kept in a class, and if any instruction is to be given. To some extent this is true; but the extent is much less than it is thought to be by those who regard obedience and discipline as in themselves desirable. Obedience, the yielding of one's will to outside direction, is the counterpart of authority. Both may be necessary in certain cases. Refractory children, lunatics and criminals may require authority, and may need to be forced to obey. But in so far as this is necessary it is a misfortune: what is to be desired is the free choice of ends with which it is not necessary to interfere. And educational reformers have shown that this is far more possible than our fathers would ever have believed.[1]

What makes obedience seem necessary in schools is the large classes and overworked teachers demanded by a false economy. Those who have no experience of teaching are incapable of imagining the expense of spirit entailed by any really living instruction. They think that teachers can reasonably be expected to work as many hours as bank clerks. Intense fatigue and irritable nerves are the result, and an absolute necessity of performing the day's task mechanically. But the task cannot be performed mechanically except by exacting obedience.

If we took education seriously, and thought it as important to keep alive the minds of children as to secure victory in war, we should conduct education quite differently: we should make sure of achieving the end, even if the expense were a hundredfold greater than it is. To many men and women a small amount of teaching is a delight, and can be done with a fresh zest and life which keeps most pupils interested without any need of discipline. The few who do not become interested might be separated from the rest, and given a different kind of instruction. A teacher ought to have only as much teaching as can be done, on most days, with actual pleasure in the work, and with an awareness of the pupil's mental needs. The result would be a relation of friendliness instead of hostility between teacher and pupil, a realization on the part of most pupils that education serves to develop their own lives and is not merely an outside imposition, interfering with play and demanding many hours of sitting still. All that

---

[1] What Madame Montessori has achieved in the way of minimizing obedience and discipline with advantage to education is almost miraculous.

is necessary to this end is a greater expenditure of money, to secure teachers with more leisure and with a natural love of teaching.

Discipline, as it exists in schools, is very largely an evil. There is a kind of discipline which is necessary to almost all achievement, and which perhaps is not sufficiently valued by those who react against the purely external discipline of traditional methods. The desirable kind of discipline is the kind that comes from within, which consists in the power of pursuing a distant object steadily, forgoing and suffering many things on the way. This involves the subordination of minor impulses to will, the power of a directing action by large creative desires even at moments when they are not vividly alive. Without this, no serious ambition, good or bad, can be realized, no consistent purpose can dominate. This kind of discipline is very necessary, but can only result from strong desires for ends not immediately attainable, and can only be produced by education if education fosters such desires, which it seldom does at present. Such discipline springs from one's own will, not from outside authority. It is not this kind which is sought in most schools, and it is not this kind which seems to me an evil.

Although elementary education encourages the undesirable discipline that consists in passive obedience, and although hardly any existing education encourages the moral discipline of consistent self-direction, there is a certain kind of purely mental discipline which is produced by the traditional higher education. The kind I mean is that which enables a man to concentrate his thoughts at will upon any matter that he has occasion to consider, regardless of preoccupations or boredom or intellectual difficulty. This quality, though it has no important intrinsic excellence, greatly enhances the efficiency of the mind as an instrument. It is this that enables a lawyer to master the scientific details of a patent case which he forgets as soon as judgment has been given, or a civil servant to deal quickly with many different administrative questions in succession. It is this that enables men to forget private cares during business hours. In a complicated world it is a very necessary faculty for those whose work requires mental concentration.

Success in producing mental discipline is the chief merit of traditional higher education. I doubt whether it can be achieved except by compelling or persuading active attention to a prescribed task. It is for this reason chiefly that I do not believe methods such as Madame Montessori's applicable when the age of childhood has been passed. The essence of her method consists in giving a choice of occupations, any one of which is interesting to most children, and all of which are instructive. The child's attention is wholly spontaneous, as in play; it enjoys acquiring knowledge in this way, and does not acquire any knowledge which it does not desire. I am convinced that this is the best method of education with young children: the actual results make it almost impossible to think otherwise.

But it is difficult to see how this method can lead to control of attention by the will. Many things which must be thought about are uninteresting, and even those that are interesting at first often become very wearisome before they have been considered as long as is necessary. The power of giving prolonged attention is very important, and it is hardly to be widely acquired except as a habit induced originally by outside pressure. Some few boys, it is true, have sufficiently strong intellectual desires to be willing to undergo all that is necessary by their own initiative and free will; but for all others an external inducement is required in order to make them learn any subject thoroughly. There is among educational reformers a certain fear of demanding great efforts, and in the world at large a growing unwillingness to be bored. Both these tendencies have their good side, but both also have their dangers. The mental discipline which is jeopardized can be preserved by mere advice without external compulsion whenever a boy's intellectual interest and ambition can be sufficiently stimulated. A good teacher ought to be able to do this for any boy who is capable of much mental achievement; and for many of the others the present purely bookish education is probably not the best. In this way, so long as the importance of mental discipline is realized, it can probably be attained, whenever it is attainable, by appealing to the pupil's consciousness of his own needs. So long as teachers are not expected to succeed by this method, it is easy for them to slip into a slothful dullness, and blame their pupils when the fault is really their own.

Ruthlessness in the economic struggle will almost unavoidably be taught in schools so long as the economic structure of society remains unchanged. This must be particularly the case in middle-class schools, which depend for their numbers upon the good opinion of parents, and secure the good opinion of parents by advertising the successes of pupils. This is one of many ways in which the competitive organization of the State is harmful. Spontaneous and disinterested desire for knowledge is not at all uncommon in the young, and might be easily aroused in many in whom it remains latent. But it is remorselessly checked by teachers who think only of examinations, diplomas and degrees. For the abler boys there is no time for thought, no time for the indulgence of intellectual taste, from the moment of first going to school until the moment of leaving the university. From first to last there is nothing but one long drudgery of examination tips and textbook facts. The most intelligent, at the end, are disgusted with learning, longing only to forget it and to escape into a life of action. Yet there, as before, the economic machine holds them prisoners, and all their spontaneous desires are bruised and thwarted.

The examination system, and the fact that instruction is treated mainly as training for a livelihood, leads the young to regard knowledge from a purely utilitarian point of view, as the road to money, not as the gateway to wisdom. This would not matter so much if it affected only those who have no genuine intellectual interests. But unfortunately it affects most those whose intellectual interests are strongest, since it is upon them that the pressure of examinations falls with most severity. To them most, but to all in some degree, education appears as a means of acquiring superiority over others; it is infected through and through with ruthlessness and glorification of social inequality. Any free, disinterested consideration shows that, whatever inequalities might remain in a Utopia, the actual inequalities are almost all contrary to justice. But our educational system tends to conceal this from all except the failures, since those who succeed are on the way to profit by the inequalities, with every encouragement from the men who have directed their education.

Passive acceptance of the teacher's wisdom is easy to most boys and girls. It involves no effort of independent thought, and seems rational because the teacher knows more than his pupils; it is moreover the way to win the favour of the teacher unless he is a very exceptional man. Yet the habit of passive acceptance is a disastrous one in later life. It causes men to seek a leader, and to accept as a leader whoever is established in that position. It makes the power of Churches, Governments, party caucuses, and all the other organizations by which plain men are misled into supporting old systems which are harmful to the nation and to themselves. It is possible that there would not be much independence of thought even if education did everything to promote it; but there would certainly be more than there is at present. If the object were to make pupils think, rather than to make them accept certain conclusions, education would be conducted quite differently: there would be less rapidity of instruction and more discussion, more occasions when pupils are encouraged to express themselves, more attempt to make education concern itself with matters in which the pupils feel some interest.

Above all, there would be an endeavour to rouse and stimulate the love of mental adventure. The world in which we live is various and astonishing: some of the things that seem plainest grow more and more difficult the more they are considered; other things, which might have been thought quite impossible to discover, have nevertheless been laid bare by genius and industry. The powers of thought, the vast regions which it can master, the much more vast regions which it can only dimly suggest to imagination, give to those whose minds have travelled beyond the daily round an amazing richness of material, an escape from the triviality and wearisomeness of familiar routine, by which the whole of life is filled with interest, and the prison walls of the commonplace are broken down. The same love of adventure which takes men to the South Pole, the same passion for a conclusive trial of strength which leads some men to welcome war, can find in creative thought an outlet which is neither wasteful nor cruel, but increases the dignity of man by incarnating in life some of that shining splendour which the human spirit is bringing down out of the unknown.

To give this joy, in a greater or less measure, to all who are capable of it, is the supreme end for which the education of the mind is to be valued.

It will be said that the joy of mental adventure must be rare, that there are few who can appreciate it, and that ordinary education can take no account of so aristocratic a good. I do not believe this. The joy of mental adventure is far commoner in the young than in grown men and women. Among children it is very common, and grows naturally out of the period of make-believe and fancy. It is rare in later life because everything is done to kill it during education. Men fear thought as they fear nothing else on earth—more than ruin, more even than death. Thought is subversive and revolutionary, destructive and terrible; thought is merciless to privilege, established institutions, and comfortable habits; thought is anarchic and lawless, indifferent to authority, careless of the well-tried wisdom of the ages. Thought looks into the pit of hell and is not afraid. It sees man, a feeble speck, surrounded by unfathomable depths of silence; yet it bears itself proudly, as unmoved as if it were lord of the universe. Thought is great and swift and free, the light of the world, and the chief glory of man.

But if thought is to become the possession of many, not the privilege of the few, we must have done with fear. It is fear that holds men back—fear lest their cherished beliefs should prove delusions, fear lest the institutions by which they live should prove harmful, fear lest they themselves should prove less worthy of respect than they have supposed themselves to be. 'Should the working man think freely about property? Then what will become of us, the rich? Should young men and young women think freely about sex? Then what will become of morality? Should soldiers think freely about war? Then what will become of military discipline? Away with thought! Back into the shades of prejudice, lest property, morals, and war should be endangered! Better men should be stupid, slothful, and oppressive than that their thoughts should be free. For if their thoughts were free they might not think as we do. And at all costs this disaster must be averted.' So the opponents of thought argue in the unconscious depths of their souls. And so they act in their churches, their schools, and their universities.

No institution inspired by fear can further life. Hope, not fear, is the creative principle in human affairs. All that has made man great has sprung from the attempt to secure what is good, not from the struggle to avert what was thought evil. It is because modern education is so seldom inspired by a great hope that it so seldom achieves a great result. The wish to preserve the past rather than the hope of creating the future dominates the minds of those who control the teaching of the young. Education should not aim at a passive awareness of dead facts, but at an activity directed towards the world that our efforts are to create. It should be inspired, not by a regretful hankering after the extinct beauties of

Greece and the Renaissance, but by a shining vision of the society that is to be, of the triumphs that thought will achieve in the time to come, and of the ever-widening horizon of man's survey over the universe. Those who are taught in this spirit will be filled with life and hope and joy, able to bear their part in bringing to mankind a future less sombre than the past, with faith in the glory that human effort can create.

(*Principles of Social Reconstruction*, London: Allen & Unwin; *Why Men Fight*, New York: The Century Companies (Appleton–Century–Crofts), 1916.)

46

THE AIMS OF EDUCATION

BEFORE considering how to educate, it is well to be clear as to the sort of result which we wish to achieve. Dr Arnold wanted 'humbleness of mind', a quality not possessed by Aristotle's 'magnanimous man'. Nietzsche's ideal is not that of Christianity. No more is Kant's: for while Christ enjoins love, Kant teaches that no action of which love is the motive can be truly virtuous. And even people who agree as to the ingredients of a good character may differ as to their relative importance. One man will emphasize courage, another learning, another kindliness, and another rectitude. One man, like the elder Brutus, will put duty to the State above family affection; another, like Confucius, will put family affection first. All these divergences will produce differences as to education. We must have some conception of the kind of person we wish to produce, before we can have any definite opinion as to the education which we consider best.

Of course, an educator may be foolish, in the sense that he produces results other than those at which he was aiming. Uriah Heep was the outcome of lessons in humility at a Charity School, which had had an effect quite different from what was intended. But in the main the ablest educators have been fairly successful. Take as examples the Chinese literati, the modern Japanese, the Jesuits, Dr Arnold, and the men who direct the policy of the American public schools. All these, in their various ways, have been highly successful. The results aimed at in the different cases were utterly different, but in the main the results were achieved. It may be worth while to spend a few moments on these different systems, before attempting to decide what we should ourselves regard as the aims which education should have in view.

Traditional Chinese education was, in some respects, very similar to that of Athens in its best days. Athenian boys were made to learn Homer by heart from beginning to end; Chinese boys were made to learn the Confucian classics with similar thoroughness. Athenians were taught a kind of reverence for the gods which consisted in outward observances, and placed no barrier in the way of free intellectual speculation. Similarly, the Chinese were taught certain rites connected with ancestor-worship, but were by no means obliged to have the beliefs which the rites would seem to imply. An easy and elegant scepticism was the attitude expected of an educated adult: anything might be discussed, but it was a trifle vulgar to reach very positive conclusions. Opinions should be such as could be discussed pleasantly at dinner, not such as men would fight for. Carlyle calls Plato 'a lordly Athenian gentleman, very much at his ease in Zion'. This characteristic of being 'at his ease in Zion' is also found in Chinese sages, and is, as a rule, absent from the sages produced by Christian civilizations, except when, like Goethe, they have deeply imbibed the spirit of Hellenism. The Athenians and the Chinese alike wished to enjoy life, and had a conception of enjoyment which was refined by an exquisite sense of beauty.

There were, however, great differences between the two civilizations, owing to the fact that, broadly speaking, the Greeks were energetic and the Chinese were lazy. The Greeks devoted their energies to art and science and mutual extermination, in all of which they achieved unprecedented success. Politics and patriotism afforded practical outlets for Greek energy: when a politician was ousted, he led a band of exiles to attack his native city. When a Chinese official was disgraced, he retired to the hills and wrote poems on the pleasures of country life. Accordingly, the Greek civilization destroyed itself, but the Chinese civilization could only be destroyed from without. These differences, however, seem not wholly attributable to education, since Confucianism in Japan never produced the indolent cultured scepticism which characterized the Chinese literati, except in the Kyoto nobility, who formed a kind of Faubourg Saint Germain.

Chinese education produced stability and art; it failed to produce progress or science. Perhaps this may be taken as what is to be expected of scepticism. Passionate beliefs produce either progress or disaster, not stability. Science, even when it attacks traditional beliefs, has beliefs of its own, and can scarcely flourish in an atmosphere of literary scepticism. In a pugnacious world which has been unified by modern inventions, energy is needed for national self-preservation. And without science, democracy is impossible: the Chinese civilization was confined to the small percentage of educated men, and the Greek civilization was based on slavery. For these reasons, the traditional education of China is not suited to the modern world, and has been abandoned by the Chinese themselves. Cultivated eighteenth-century gentlemen, who in some respects resembled Chinese literati, have become impossible for the same reasons.

Modern Japan affords the clearest illustration of a tendency which is prominent among all the Great Powers—the tendency to make national greatness the supreme purpose of education. The aim of Japanese education is to produce citizens who shall be devoted to the State through the training of their passions, and useful to it through the knowledge they have acquired. I cannot sufficiently praise the skill with which this double purpose has been pursued. Ever since the advent of Commodore Perry's squadron, the Japanese have been in a situation in which self-perservation was very difficult; their success affords a justification of their methods, unless we are to hold that self-preservation itself may be culpable. But only a desperate situation could have justified their educational methods, which would have been culpable in any nation not in imminent peril. The Shinto religion, which must not be called in question even by university professors, involves history which is just as dubious as Genesis; the Dayton trial pales into insignificance beside the theological tyranny in Japan. There is an equal ethical tyranny; nationalism, filial piety, Mikado-worship, etc., must not be called in question, and therefore many kinds of progress are scarcely possible. The great danger of a cast-iron system of this sort is that it may provoke revolution as the sole method of progress. This danger is real, though not immediate, and is largely caused by the educational system.

We have thus in modern Japan a defect opposite to that of ancient China. Whereas the Chinese literati were too sceptical and lazy, the products of Japanese education are likely to be too dogmatic and energetic. Neither acquiescence in scepticism nor acquiescence in dogma is what education should produce. What it should produce is a belief that knowledge is attainable in a measure, though with difficulty; that much of what passes for knowledge at any given time is likely to be more or less mistaken, but that the mistakes can be rectified by care and industry. In acting upon our beliefs, we should be very cautious where a small error would mean disaster; nevertheless it is upon our beliefs that we must act. This state of mind is rather difficult: it requires a high degree of intellectual culture without emotional atrophy. But though difficult, it is not impossible; it is in fact the scientific temper. Knowledge, like other good things, is difficult, but not impossible; the dogmatist forgets the difficulty, the sceptic denies the possibility. Both are mistaken, and their errors, when widespread, produce social disaster.

The Jesuits, like the modern Japanese, made the mistake of subordinating education to the welfare of an institution—in their case, the Catholic Church. They were not concerned primarily with the good of the particular pupil, but with making him a means to the good of the Church. If we accept their theology, we cannot blame them: to save souls from hell is more important than any merely terrestrial concern, and is only to be achieved by the Catholic Church. But those who do not accept this dogma will judge Jesuit education by its results. These results, it is true, were sometimes quite as undesired as Uriah Heep: Voltaire was a product of Jesuit methods. But on the whole, and for a long time, the intended results were achieved: the counter-reformation, and the collapse of Protestantism in France, must be largely attributed to Jesuit efforts. To achieve these ends, they made art sentimental, thought superficial, and morals loose; in the end, the French Revolution was needed to sweep away the harm that they had done. In education, their crime was that they were not actuated by love of their pupils, but by ulterior ends.

Dr Arnold's system, which has remained in force in English public schools to the present day, had another defect, namely that it was aristocratic. The aim was to train men for positions of authority and power, whether at home or in distant parts of the empire. An aristocracy, if it is to survive, needs certain virtues: these were to be imparted at school. The product was to be energetic, stoical, physically fit, possessed of certain unalterable beliefs, with high standards of rectitude, and convinced that it had an important mission in the world. To a surprising extent, these results were achieved. Intellect was sacrificed to them, because intellect might produce doubt. Sympathy was sacrificed, because it might interfere with governing 'inferior' races or classes. Kindliness was sacrificed for the sake of toughness; imagination, for the sake of firmness. In an unchanging world, the result might have been a permanent aristocracy, possessing the merits and defects of the Spartans. But aristocracy is out of date, and subject populations will no longer obey even the most wise and virtuous rulers. The rulers are driven into brutality, and brutality further encourages revolt. The complexity of the modern world increasingly requires intelligence, and Dr Arnold sacrificed intelligence to 'virtue'. The battle of Waterloo may have been won on the playing fields of Eton, but the British Empire is being lost there. The modern world needs a different type, with more imaginative sympathy, more intellectual suppleness, less belief in bull-dog courage and more belief in technical knowledge. The administrator of the future must be the servant of free citizens, not the benevolent ruler of admiring subjects. The aristocratic tradition embedded in British higher education is its bane. Perhaps this tradition can be eliminated gradually; perhaps the older educational institutions will be found incapable of adapting themselves. As to that, I do not venture an opinion.

The American public schools achieve successfully a task never before attempted on a large scale: the task of transforming a heterogeneous selection of mankind into a homogeneous nation. This is done so ably, and is on the whole such a beneficent work, that on the balance great praise is due to those who accomplish it. But America, like Japan, is placed in a peculiar situation, and what the special circumstances justify is not necessarily an ideal to be followed everywhere and always. America has had certain advantages and certain difficulties. Among the advantages were: a higher standard of wealth; freedom from the danger of defeat in war; comparative absence of cramping traditions inherited from the Middle Ages. Immigrants found in America a generally diffused sentiment of democracy and an advanced stage of industrial technique. These,

I think, are the two chief reasons why almost all of them came to admire America more than their native countries. But actual immigrants, as a rule, retain a dual patriotism; in European struggles they continue to take passionately the side of the nation to which they originally belonged. Their children, on the contrary, lose all loyalty to the country from which their parents have come, and become merely and simply Americans. The attitude of the parents is attributable to the general merits of America; that of the children is very largely determined by their school education. It is only the contribution of the school that concerns us.

In so far as the school can rely upon the genuine merits of America, there is no need to associate the teaching of American patriotism with the inculcation of false standards. But where the old world is superior to the new, it becomes necessary to instil a contempt for genuine excellences. The intellectual level in Western Europe and the artistic level in Eastern Europe are, on the whole, higher than in America. Throughout Western Europe, except in Spain and Portugal, there is less theological superstition than in America. In almost all European countries the individual is less subject to herd domination than in America: his inner freedom is greater even where his political freedom is less. In these respects, the American public schools do harm. The harm is essential to the teaching of an exclusive American patriotism. The harm, as with the Japanese and the Jesuits, comes from regarding the pupils as means to an end, not as ends in themselves. The teacher should love his children better than his State or his Church; otherwise he is not an ideal teacher.

When I say that pupils should be regarded as ends, not as means, I may be met by the retort that, after all, everybody is more important as a means than as an end. What a man is as an end perishes when he dies; what he produces as a means continues to the end of time. We cannot deny this, but we can deny the consequences deduced from it. A man's importance as a means may be for good or for evil; the remote effects of human actions are so uncertain that a wise man will tend to dismiss them from his calculations. Broadly speaking, good men have good effects, and bad men bad effects. This, of course, is not an invariable law of nature. A bad man may murder a tyrant, because he has committed crimes which the tyrant intends to punish; the effects of his act may be good, though he and his act are bad. Nevertheless, as a broad general rule, a community of men and women who are intrinsically excellent will have better effects than one composed of people who are ignorant and malevolent. Apart from such considerations, children and young people feel instinctively the difference between those who genuinely wish them well and those who regard them merely as raw material for some scheme. Neither character nor intelligence will develop as well or as freely where the teacher is deficient in love; and love of this kind consists essentially in *feeling* the child as an end. We all have this feeling about ourselves: we desire good things for ourselves without first demanding a proof that some great purpose will be furthered by our obtaining them. Every ordinarily affectionate parent feels the same sort of thing about his or her children. Parents want their children to grow, to be strong and healthy, to do well at school, and so on, in just the same way in which they want things for themselves; no effort of self-denial and no abstract principle of justice is involved in taking trouble about such matters. This parental instinct is not always strictly confined to one's own children. In its diffused form, it must exist in anyone who is to be a good teacher of little boys and girls. As the pupils grow older, it grows less important. But only those who possess it can be trusted to draw up schemes of education. Those who regard it as one of the purposes of male education to produce men willing to kill and be killed for frivolous reasons are clearly deficient in diffused parental feeling; yet they control education in all civilized countries except Denmark and China.

But it is not enough that the educator should love the young; it is necessary also that he should have a right conception of human excellence. Cats teach their kittens to catch mice and play with them; militarists do likewise with the human young. The cat loves the kitten, but not the mouse; the militarist may love his own son, but not the sons of his country's enemies. Even those who love all mankind may err through a wrong conception of the good life. I shall try, therefore, before going any further, to give an idea of what I consider excellent in men and women, quite without regard to practicality, or to the educational methods by which it might be brought into being. Such a picture will help us afterwards, when we come to consider the details of education; we shall know the direction in which we wish to move.

We must first make a distinction: some qualities are desirable in a certain proportion of mankind, others are desirable universally. We want artists, but we also want men of science. We want great administrators, but we also want ploughmen and millers and bakers. The qualities which produce a man of great eminence in some one direction are often such as might be undesirable if they were universal. Shelley describes the day's work of a poet as follows:

> He will watch from dawn to gloom
> The lake-reflected sun illume
> The yellow-bees in the ivy bloom,
> Nor heed nor see what things they be.

These habits are praiseworthy in a poet, but not—shall we say—in a postman. We cannot therefore frame our education with a view to giving everyone the temperament of a poet. But some characteristics are universally desirable, and it is these alone that I shall consider at this stage.

I make no distinction whatever between male and female excellence. A certain amount of occupational training is desirable for a woman who is to have the care of babies, but that only involves the same sort of difference as there is between a farmer and a miller. It is in no degree fundamental, and does not demand consideration at our present level.

I will take four characteristics which seem to me jointly to form the basis of an ideal character: vitality, courage, sensitiveness, and intelligence. I do not suggest that this list is complete, but I think it carries us a good way. Moreover, I firmly believe that, by proper physical, emotional, and intellectual care of the young, these qualities could all be made very common. I shall consider each in turn.

Vitality is rather a physiological than a mental characteristic; it is presumably always present where there is perfect health, but it tends to ebb with advancing years, and gradually dwindles to nothing in old age. In vigorous children it quickly rises to a maximum before they reach school age, and then tends to be diminished by education. Where it exists, there is pleasure in feeling alive, quite apart from any specific pleasant circumstance. It heightens pleasures and diminishes pains. It makes it easy to take an interest in whatever occurs, and thus promotes objectivity, which is an essential of sanity. Human beings are prone to become absorbed in themselves, unable to be interested in what they see and hear or in anything outside their own skins. This is a great misfortune to themselves, since it entails at best boredom and at worst melancholia; it is also a fatal barrier to usefulness, except in very exceptional cases. Vitality promotes interest in the outside world; it also promotes the power of hard work. Moreover, it is a safeguard against envy, because it makes one's own existence pleasant. As envy is one of the great sources of human misery, this is a very important merit in vitality. Many bad qualities are of course compatible with vitality—for example, those of a healthy tiger. And many of the best qualities are compatible with its absence: Newton and Locke, for example, had very little. Both these men, however, had irritabilities and envies from which better health would have set them free. Probably the whole of Newton's controversy with Leibniz, which ruined English mathematics for over a hundred years, would have been avoided if Newton had been robust and able to enjoy ordinary pleasures. In spite of its limitations, therefore, I reckon vitality among the qualities which it is important that all men should possess.

Courage—the second quality on our list—has several forms, and all of them are complex. Absence of fear is one thing, and the power of controlling fear is another. And absence of fear, in turn, is one thing when the fear is rational, another when it is irrational. Absence of irrational fear is clearly good; so is the power of controlling fear. But absence of rational fear is a matter as to which debate is possible. However, I shall postpone this question until I have said something about the other forms of courage.

Irrational fear plays an extraordinarily large part in the instinctive emotional life of most people. In its pathological forms, as persecution mania, anxiety complex, or what not, it is treated by alienists. But in milder forms it is common among those who are considered sane. It may be a general feeling that there are dangers about, more correctly termed 'anxiety', or a specific dread of things that are not dangerous, such as mice or spiders.[1] It used to be supposed that many fears were instinctive, but this is now questioned by most investigators. There are apparently a few instinctive fears—for instance, of loud noises—but the great majority arise either from experience or from suggestion. Fear of the dark, for example, seems to be entirely due to suggestion. Vertebrates, there is reason to think, do not usually feel instinctive fear of their natural enemies, but catch this emotion from their elders. When human beings bring them up by hand, many fears usual among the species are found to be absent. But fear is exceedingly infectious: children catch it from their elders even when their elders are not aware of having shown it. Timidity in mothers or nurses is very quickly imitated by children through suggestion. Hitherto, men have thought it attractive in women to be full of irrational terrors, because it gave men a chance to seem protective without incurring any real danger. But the sons of these men have acquired the terrors from their mothers, and have had to be afterwards trained to regain a courage which they need never have lost if their fathers had not desired to despise their mothers. The harm that has been done by the subjection of women is incalculable; this matter of fear affords only one incidental illustration.

I am not at the moment discussing the methods by which fear and anxiety may be minimized; that is a matter which I shall consider later. There is, however, one question which arises at this stage, namely: can we be content to deal with fear by means of repression, or must we find some more radical cure? Traditionally, aristocracies have been trained not to show fear, while subject nations, classes and sexes have been encouraged to remain cowardly. The test of courage has been crudely behaviouristic: a man must not run away in battle; he must be proficient in 'manly' sports; he must retain self-command in fires, shipwrecks, earthquakes, etc. He must not merely do the right thing, but he must avoid turning pale, or trembling, or gasping for breath, or giving any other easily observed sign of fear. All this I regard as of great importance: I should wish to see courage cultivated in all nations, in all classes, and in both sexes. But when the method adopted is repressive, it entails the evils usually associated with that practice. Shame and disgrace have

[1] On fear and anxiety in childhood, see e.g. William Stern, *Psychology of Early Childhood*, chapter xxxv. (George Allen & Unwin, Ltd., 1924.)

always been potent weapons in producing the appearance of courage; but in fact they merely cause a conflict of terrors, in which it is hoped that the dread of public condemnation will be the stronger. 'Always speak the truth except when something frightens you' was a maxim taught to me in childhood. I cannot admit the exception. Fear should be overcome not only in action, but in feeling; and not only in conscious feeling, but in the unconscious as well. The purely external victory over fear, which satisfies the aristocratic code, leaves the impulse operative underground, and produces evil twisted reactions which are not recognized as the off-spring of terror. I am not thinking of 'shell shock', in which the connection with fear is obvious. I am thinking rather of the whole system of oppression and cruelty by which dominant castes seek to retain their ascendancy. When recently in Shanghai a British officer ordered a number of unarmed Chinese students to be shot in the back without warning, he was obviously actuated by terror just as much as a soldier who runs away in battle. But military aristocracies are not sufficiently intelligent to trace such actions to their psychological source; they regard them rather as showing firmness and a proper spirit.

From the point of view of psychology and physiology, fear and rage are closely analogous emotions; the man who feels rage is not possessed of the highest kind of courage. The cruelty invariably displayed in sup-pressing negro insurrections, communist rebellions, and other threats to aristocracy, is an offshoot of cowardice, and deserves the same contempt as is bestowed upon the more obvious forms of that vice. I believe that it is possible so to educate ordinary men and women that they shall be able to live without fear. Hitherto, only a few heroes and saints have achieved such a life; but what they have done others could do if they were shown the way.

For the kind of courage which does not consist in repression, a number of factors must be combined. To begin with the humblest: health and vitality are very helpful, though not indispensable. Practice and skill in dangerous situations are very desirable. But when we come to consider, not courage in this or that respect, but universal courage, something more fundamental is wanted. What is wanted is a combination of self-respect with an impersonal outlook on life. To begin with self-respect: some men live from within, while others are mere mirrors of what is felt and said by their neighbours. The latter can never have true courage: they must have admiration, and are haunted by the fear of losing it. The teaching of 'humility', which used to be thought desirable, was the means of producing a perverted form of this same vice. 'Humility' suppressed self-respect, but not the desire for the respect of others; it merely made nominal self-abasement the means of acquiring credit. Thus it produced hypocrisy and falsification of instinct. Children were taught unreasoning submission, and proceeded to exact it when they grew up; it was said that only those who have learned to obey know how to command. What I suggest is that no one should learn how to obey, and no one should attempt to command. I do not mean, of course, that there should not be leaders in co-operative enterprises; but their authority should be like that of a captain of a football team, which is suffered voluntarily in order to achieve a common purpose. Our purposes should be our own, not the result of external authority; and our purposes should never be forcibly imposed upon others. This is what I mean when I say no one should command and no one should obey.

There is one thing more required for the highest courage, and that is what I called just now an impersonal outlook on life. The man whose hopes and fears are all centred upon himself can hardly view death with equanimity, since it extinguishes his whole emotional universe. Here, again, we are met by a tradition urging the cheap and easy way of repression: the saint must learn to renounce Self, must mortify the flesh, and forgo instinctive joys. This can be done, but its consequences are bad. Having renounced pleasure for himself, the ascetic saint renounces it for others also, which is easier. Envy persists underground, and leads him to the view that suffering is ennobling, and may therefore be legitimately inflicted. Hence arises a complete inversion of values: what is good is thought bad, and what is bad is thought good. The source of all the harm is that the good life has been sought in obedience to a negative imperative, not in broadening and developing natural desires and instincts. There are certain things in human nature which take us beyond Self without effort. The commonest of these is love, more particularly parental love, which in some is so generalized as to embrace the whole human race. Another is knowledge. There is no reason to suppose that Galileo was particularly benevolent, yet he lived for an end which was not defeated by his death. Another is art. But in fact every interest in something outside a man's own body makes his life to that degree impersonal. For this reason, paradoxical as it may seem, a man of wide and vivid interests finds less difficulty in leaving life than is experienced by some miserable hypochondriac whose interests are bounded by his own ailments. Thus the perfection of courage is found in the man of many interests, who *feels* his ego to be but a small part of the world, not through despising himself, but through valuing much that is not himself. This can hardly happen except where instinct is free and intelligence is active. From the union of the two grows a comprehensiveness of outlook unknown both to the voluptuary and to the ascetic; and to such an outlook personal death appears a trivial matter. Such courage is positive and instinctive, not negative and repressive. It is courage in this positive sense that I regard as one of the major ingredients in a perfect character.

Sensitiveness, the third quality in our list, is in a sense a corrective of mere courage. Courageous behaviour is easier for a man who fails to apprehend dangers, but such courage may often be foolish. We cannot regard as satisfactory any way of acting which is dependent upon ignorance or forgetfulness: the fullest possible knowledge and realization are an essential part of what is desirable. The cognitive aspect, however, comes under the head of intelligence; sensitiveness, in the sense in which I am using the term, belongs to the emotions. A purely theoretical definition would be that a person is emotionally sensitive when many stimuli produce emotions in him; but taken thus broadly the quality is not necessarily a good one. If sensitiveness is to be good, the emotional reaction must be in some sense *appropriate*: mere intensity is not what is needed. The quality I have in mind is that of being affected pleasurably or the reverse by many things, and by the right things. What are the right things, I shall try to explain. The first step, which most children take at the age of about five months, is to pass beyond mere pleasures of sensation, such as food and warmth, to the pleasure of social approbation. This pleasure, as soon as it has arisen, develops very rapidly: every child loves praise and hates blame. Usually the wish to be thought well of remains one of the dominant motives throughout life. It is certainly very valuable as a stimulus to pleasant behaviour, and as a restraint upon impulses of greed. If we were wiser in our admirations, it might be much more valuable. But so long as the most admired heroes are those who have killed the greatest number of people, love of admiration cannot alone be adequate to the good life.

The next stage in the development of a desirable form of sensitiveness is sympathy. There is a purely physical sympathy: a very young child will cry because a brother or sister is crying. This, I suppose, affords the basis for the further developments. The two enlargements that are needed are: first, to feel sympathy even when the sufferer is not an object of special affection; secondly, to feel it when the suffering is merely known to be occurring, not sensibly present. The second of these enlargements depends largely upon intelligence. It may only go so far as sympathy with suffering which is portrayed vividly and touchingly, as in a good novel; it may, on the other hand, go so far as to enable a man to be moved emotionally by statistics. This capacity for abstract sympathy is as rare as it is important. Almost everybody is deeply affected when someone he loves suffers from cancer. Most people are moved when they see the sufferings of unknown patients in hospitals. Yet when they read that the death-rate from cancer is such-and-such, they are as a rule only moved to momentary personal fear lest they or someone dear to them should acquire the disease. The same is true of war: people think it dreadful when their son or brother is mutilated, but they do not think it a million times as dreadful that a million people should be mutilated. A man who is full of kindliness in all personal dealings may derive his income from incitement to war or from the torture of children in 'backward' countries. All these familiar phenomena are due to the fact that sympathy is not stirred, in most people, by a merely abstract stimulus. A large proportion of the evils in the modern world would cease if this could be remedied. Science has greatly increased our power of affecting the lives of distant people, without increasing our sympathy for them. Suppose you are a shareholder in a company which manufactures cotton in Shanghai. You may be a busy man, who has merely followed financial advice in making the investment; neither Shanghai nor cotton interest you, but only your dividends. Yet you become part of the force leading to massacres of innocent people, and your dividends would disappear if little children were not forced into unnatural and dangerous toil. You do not mind, because you have never seen the children, and an abstract stimulus cannot move you. That is the fundamental reason why large-scale industrialism is so cruel, and why oppression of subject races is tolerated. An education producing sensitiveness to abstract stimuli would make such things impossible.

Cognitive sensitiveness, which should also be included, is practically the same thing as a habit of observation, and this is more naturally considered in connection with intelligence. Aesthetic sensitiveness raises a number of problems which I do not wish to discuss at this stage. I will therefore pass on to the last of the four qualities we enumerated, namely, intelligence.

One of the great defects of traditional morality has been the low estimate it placed upon intelligence. The Greeks did not err in this respect, but the Church led men to think that nothing matters except virtue, and virtue consists in abstinence from a certain list of actions arbitrarily labelled 'sin'. So long as this attitude persists, it is impossible to make men realize that intelligence does more good than an artificial conventional 'virtue'. When I speak of intelligence, I include both actual knowledge and receptivity to knowledge. The two are, in fact, closely connected. Ignorant adults are unteachable; on such matters as hygiene or diet, for example, they are totally incapable of believing what science has to say. The more a man has learnt, the easier it is for him to learn still more—always assuming that he has not been taught in a spirit of dogmatism. Ignorant people have never been compelled to change their mental habits, and have stiffened into an unchangeable attitude. It is not only that they are credulous where they should be sceptical; it is just as much that they are incredulous where they should be receptive. No doubt the word 'intelligence' properly signifies rather an aptitude for acquiring knowledge than knowledge already acquired; but I do not think this aptitude is acquired except by exercise, any more than the aptitude of a pianist or an acrobat. It is, of course, possible to impart information in ways that do not train intelligence; it is not only possible, but easy, and frequently done. But I do not believe that it is possible to train intelligence without imparting information, or at any rate causing knowledge to be acquired. And without intelligence our complex modern world cannot subsist; still less can it make progress. I regard the cultivation of intelligence, therefore, as one of the major purposes of education. This might seem a commonplace, but in fact it is not. The desire to instil what are regarded as correct beliefs has made educationists too often indifferent to the training of intelligence. To make this clear, it is necessary to define intelligence a little more closely, so as to discover the mental habits which it requires. For this purpose I shall consider only the aptitude for acquiring knowledge, not the store of actual knowledge which might legitimately be included in the definition of intelligence.

The instinctive foundation of the intellectual life is curiosity, which is found among animals in its elementary forms. Intelligence demands an alert curiosity, but it must be of a certain kind. The sort that leads village neighbours to try to peer through curtains after dark has no very high value. The widespread interest in gossip is inspired, not by a love of knowledge, but by malice: no one gossips about other people's secret virtues, but only about their secret vices. Accordingly most gossip is untrue, but care is taken not to verify it. Our neighbour's sins, like the consolations of religion, are so agreeable that we do not stop to scrutinize the evidence closely. Curiosity properly so-called, on the other hand, is inspired by a genuine love of knowledge. You may see this impulse, in a moderately pure form, at work in a cat which has been brought to a strange room, and proceeds to smell every corner and every piece of furniture. You will see it also in children, who are passionately interested when a drawer or cupboard, usually closed, is open for their inspection. Animals, machines, thunderstorms, and all forms of manual work, arouse the curiosity of children, whose thirst for knowledge puts the most intelligent adult to shame. This impulse grows weaker with advancing years until at last what is unfamiliar inspires only disgust, with no desire for a closer acquaintance. This is the stage at which people announce that the country is going to the dogs, and that 'things are not what they were in my young days'. The thing which is not the same as it was in that far-off time is the speaker's curiosity. And with the death of curiosity we may reckon that active intelligence, also, has died.

But although curiosity lessens in intensity and in extent after childhood, it may for a long time improve in quality. Curiosity about general propositions shows a higher level of intelligence than curiosity about particular facts; broadly speaking, the higher the order of generality, the greater is the intelligence involved. (This rule, however, must not be taken too strictly.) Curiosity dissociated from personal advantage shows a higher development than curiosity (say) with a chance of food. The cat that sniffs in a new room is not a wholly disinterested scientific inquirer, but probably also wants to find out whether there are mice about.

Perhaps it is not quite correct to say that curiosity is best when it is dis-interested, but rather that it is best when the connection with other interests is not direct and obvious, but discoverable only by means of a certain degree of intelligence. This point, however, it is not necessary for us to decide.

If curiosity is to be fruitful, it must be associated with a certain technique for the acquisition of knowledge. There must be habits of observation, belief in the possibility of knowledge, patience and industry. These things will develop of themselves, given the original fund of curiosity and the proper intellectual education. But since our intellectual life is only a part of our activity, and since curiosity is perpetually coming into conflict with other passions, there is need of certain intellectual virtues, such as open-mindedness. We become impervious to new truth both from habit and from desire; we find it hard to disbelieve what we have emphatically believed for a number of years, and also what ministers to self-esteem or any other fundamental passion. Open-mindedness should therefore be one of the qualities that education aims at producing. At present, this is only done to a very limited extent, as is illustrated by the following paragraph from the *Daily Herald*, July 31, 1925:

A special committee, appointed to inquire into the allegations of the subversion of children's minds in Bootle schools by their school teachers, has placed its findings before the Bootle Borough Council. The Committee was of opinion that the allegations were substantiated, but the Council deleted the word 'substantiated' and stated that 'the allegations gave cause for reasonable inquiry'. A recommendation made by the Com-mittee, and adopted by the Council, was that in future appointments of teachers they shall undertake to train the scholars in habits of reverence towards God and religion, and of respect for the civil and religious insti-tutions of the country.

Thus whatever may happen elsewhere, there is to be no open-minded-ness in Bootle. It is hoped that the Borough Council will shortly send a deputation to Dayton, Tennessee, to obtain further light upon the best methods of carrying out their programme. But perhaps that is unnecessary. From the wording of the resolution, it would seem as if Bootle needed no instruction in obscurantism.

Courage is essential to intellectual probity, as well as to physical hero-ism. The real world is more unknown than we like to think; from the first day of life we practise precarious inductions, and confound our mental habits with laws of external nature. All sorts of intellectual systems —Christianity, Socialism, Patriotism, etc.—are ready, like orphan asylums, to give safety in return for servitude. A free mental life cannot be as warm and comfortable and sociable as a life enveloped in a creed: only a creed can give the feeling of a cosy fireside while the winter storms are raging without.

This brings us to a somewhat difficult question: to what extent should the good life be emancipated from the herd? I hesitate to use the phrase 'herd instinct', because there are controversies as to its correctness. But, however interpreted, the phenomena which it describes are familiar. We like to stand well with those whom we feel to be the group with which we wish to co-operate—our family, our neighbours, our colleagues, our political party, or our nation. This is natural, because we cannot obtain any of the pleasures of life without co-operation. Moreover, emotions are infectious, especially when they are felt by many people at once. Very few people can be present at an excited meeting without getting excited: if they are opponents, their opposition becomes excited. And to most people such opposition is only possible if they can derive support from the thought of a different crowd in which they will win approbation. That is why the Communion of Saints has afforded such comfort to the persecuted. Are we to acquiesce in this desire for co-operation with a crowd, or shall our education try to weaken it? There are arguments on both sides, and the right answer must consist in finding a just proportion, not in a whole-hearted decision for either party.

I think myself that the desire to please and to co-operate should be strong and normal, but should be capable of being overcome by other desires on certain important occasions. The desirability of a wish to please has already been considered in connection with sensitiveness. Without it, we should all be boors, and all social groups, from the family upwards, would be impossible. Education of young children would be very difficult if they did not desire the good opinion of their parents. The contagious character of emotions also has its uses, when the contagion is from a wiser person to a more foolish one. But in the case of panic fear and panic rage it is of course the very reverse of useful. Thus the question of emotional receptivity is by no means simple. Even in purely intellectual matters, the issue is not clear. The great discoverers have had to withstand the herd, and incur hostility by their independence. But the average man's opinions are much less foolish than they would be if he thought for himself: in science, at least, his respect for authority is on the whole beneficial.

I think that in the life of a man whose circumstances are not very exceptional there should be a large sphere where what is vaguely termed herd instinct dominates, and a small sphere into which it does not penetrate. The small sphere should contain the region of his special competence. We think ill of a man who cannot admire a woman unless everybody else also admires her: we think that in the choice of a wife a man should be guided by his own independent feelings, not by a reflection of the feelings of his society. It is no matter if his judgments of people in general agree with those of his neighbours, but when he falls in love he ought to be guided by his own independent feelings. Much the same thing applies in other directions. A farmer should follow his own judgment as to the capacities of the fields which he cultivates himself, though his judgment should be formed after acquiring a knowledge of scientific agriculture. An economist should form an independent judgment on currency questions but an ordinary mortal had better follow authority. Wherever there is special competence, there should be independence. But a man should not make himself into a kind of hedgehog, all bristles to keep the world at a distance. The bulk of our ordinary activities must be co-operative, and co-operation must have an instinctive basis. Nevertheless, we should all learn to be able to think for ourselves about matters that are particularly well known to us, and we ought all to have acquired the courage to proclaim unpopular opinions when we believe them to be important. The application of these broad principles in special cases may, of course, be difficult. But it will be less difficult than it is at present in a world where men commonly have the virtues we have been considering in this chapter. The persecuted saint, for instance, would not exist in such a world. The good man would have no occasion to bristle and become self-conscious; his goodness would result from following his impulses, and would be combined with instinctive happiness. His neighbours would not hate him, because they would not fear him; the hatred of pioneers is due to the terror they inspire, and this terror would not exist among men who had acquired courage. Only a man dominated by fear would join the Ku Klux Klan or the Fascisti. In a world of brave men, such persecuting organizations could not exist, and the good life would involve far less resistance to instinct than it does at present. The good world can only be created and sustained by fearless men, but the more they succeed in their task the fewer occasions there will be for the exercise of their courage.

A community of men and women possessing vitality, courage, sensitiveness and intelligence, in the highest degree that education can produce, would be very different from anything that has hitherto existed. Very few people would be unhappy. The main causes of unhappiness at present are: ill-health, poverty and an unsatisfactory sex life. All of these would become very rare. Good health could be almost universal, and even old age could be postponed. Poverty, since the industrial revolution, is only due to collective stupidity. Sensitiveness would make people wish to abolish it, intelligence would show them the way, and courage would lead them to adopt it. (A timid person would rather remain miserable than do anything unusual.) Most people's sex life, at present, is more or less unsatisfactory. This is partly due to bad education, partly to persecution by the authorities and Mrs Grundy. A generation of women brought up without irrational sex fears would soon make an end of this. Fear has been thought the only way to make women 'virtuous', and they have been deliberately taught to be cowards, both physically and mentally. Women in whom love is cramped encourage brutality and hypocrisy in their husbands, and distort the instincts of their children. One generation of fearless women could transform the world, by bringing into it a generation of fearless children, not contorted into unnatural shapes, but stiaight and candid, generous, affectionate, and free. Their ardour would sweep away the cruelty and pain which we endure because we are lazy, cowardly, hard-hearted, and stupid. It is education that gives us these bad qualities, and education that must give us the opposite virtues. Education is the key to the new world.

(*On Education*, London: Allen & Unwin; *Education and the Good Life*, New York: Boni & Liveright, 1926.)

47

EMOTION AND DISCIPLINE

EDUCATION has at all times had a twofold aim, namely instruction and training in good conduct. The conception of good conduct varies with the political institutions and social traditions of the community. In the middle ages, when there was a hierarchical organization proceeding from the serf by gradual stages up to God, the chief virtue was obedience. Children were taught to obey their parents and to reverence their social superiors, to feel awe in the presence of the priest and submission in the presence of the Lord of the Manor. Only the Emperor and the Pope were free, and, since the morality of the time afforded no guidance to free men, they spent their time in fighting each other. The moderns differ from the men of the thirteenth century both in aim and in method. Democracy has substituted co-operation for submission and herd instinct for reverence; the group in regard to which herd instinct is to be most operative has become the nation, which was formerly rendered unimportant by the universality of the Church. Meanwhile propaganda has become persuasive rather than forceful, and has learnt to proceed by the instilling of suitable sentiments in early youth. Church music, school songs, and the flag determine, by their influence on the boy, the subsequent actions of the man in moments of strong emotion. Against these influences the assaults of reason have but little power.

The influence of political conceptions on early education is not always obvious, and is often unconcious on the part of the educator. For the present, therefore, I wish to consider education in behaviour with as little regard as possible to the social order, to which I shall return at a later stage.

When it is sought to produce a certain kind of behaviour in a child or animal, there are two different techniques which may be followed. We may, on the one hand, by means of rewards and punishments cause the child or animal to perform or abstain from certain precise acts; or we may, on the other hand, seek to produce in the child or animal such emotions as will lead, on the whole, to acts of the kind desired.

By a suitable distribution of rewards and punishments, it is possible to control a very large part of overt behaviour.

Usually the only form of reward or punishment required will be praise or blame. By this method boys who are naturally timid can acquire physical courage, and children who are sensitive to pain can be taught a stoical endurance. Good manners, if not imposed earlier, can be learnt in adolescence by means of no worse punishment than the contemptuous lifting of an eyebrow. What is called 'good form' is acquired by almost all who are exposed to it, merely from fear of the bad opinion incurred by infringing it. Those who have been taught from an early age to fear the displeasure of their group as the worst of misfortunes will die on the battlefield, in a war of which they understand nothing, rather than suffer the contempt of fools. The English public schools have carried this system to perfection, and have largely sterilized intelligence by making it cringe before the herd. This is what is called making a boy manly.

As a social force, the behaviourist method of 'conditioning' is therefore very powerful and very successful. It can and does cause men to act in ways quite different from those in which they would otherwise have acted, and it is capable of producing an impressive uniformity of overt behaviour. Nevertheless, it has its limitations.

It was through Freud that these limitations first became known in a scientific manner, though men of psychological insight had long ago perceived them in an intuitive way. For our purposes, the essential discovery of psycho-analysis is this: that an impulse which is prevented, by behaviourist methods, from finding overt expression in action, does not necessarily die, but is driven underground, and finds some new outlet which has not been inhibited by training. Often the new outlet will be more harmful than the one that has been prevented, and in any case the deflection involves emotional disturbance and unprofitable expenditure of energy. It is therefore necessary to pay more attention to emotion, as opposed to overt behaviour, than is done by those who advocate conditioning as alone sufficient in the training of character.

There are, moreover, some undesirable habits in regard to which the method of rewards and punishments fails completely, even from its own point of view. One of these is bed-wetting. When this persists beyond the age at which it usually stops, punishment only makes it more obstinate. Although this fact has long been known to psychologists, it is still unknown to most schoolmasters, who for years on end punish boys having this habit, without ever noticing that the punishment does not produce reform. The cause of the habit, in older boys, is usually some deep-seated unconscious psychological disturbance, which must be brought to the surface before a cure can be effected.

The same kind of psychological mechanism applies in many less obvious instances. In the case of definite nervous disorders this is now widely recognized. Kleptomania, for example, is not uncommon in children, and, unlike ordinary thieving, it cannot be cured by punishment, but only by ascertaining and removing its psychological cause. What is less recognized is that we all suffer, to a greater or less degree, from nervous disorders having an emotional origin. A man is called sane when he is as sane as the average of his contemporaries; but in the average man many of the mechanisms which determine his opinions and actions are quite fantastic, so much so that in a world of real sanity they would be called insane. It is dangerous to produce good social behaviour by means which leave the anti-social emotions untouched. So long as these emotions, while persisting, are denied all outlet, they will grow stronger and stronger, leading to impulses of cruelty which will at last become irresistible. In the man of weak will, these impulses may break out in crime, or in some form of behaviour to which social penalties are attached. In the man of strong will, they take even more undesirable forms. He may be a tyrant in the home, ruthless in business, bellicose in politics, persecuting in his social morality; for all these qualities other men with similar defects of character will admire him; he will die universally respected, after having spread hatred and misery over a city, a nation, or an epoch according to his ability and his opportunities. Correct behaviour combined with bad emotions is not enough, therefore, to make a man a contributor to the happiness of mankind. If this is our criterion of desirable conduct, something more must be sought in the education of character.

Such considerations, as well as the sympathetic observation of children, suggest that the behaviourist method of training character is inadequate, and needs to be supplemented by a quite different method.

Experience of children shows that it is possible to operate upon feeling, and not only upon outward behaviour, by giving children an environment in which desirable emotions shall become common and undesirable emotions rare. Some children (and some adults) are of a cheerful disposition, others are morose; some are easily contented with any pleasure that offers, while others are inconsolable unless they can have the particular pleasure on which their hearts are set; some, in the absence of evidence, regard the bulk of human beings with friendly confidence, while others regard most people with terrified suspicion. The prevalent emotional attitude of the child generally remains that of the adult, though in later life men learn to conceal their timidities and grudges by disguises of greater or lesser effectiveness. It is therefore very important that children should have predominantly those emotional attitudes which, both in childhood and subsequently, will make them happy, successful, and useful, rather than those that lead to unhappiness, failure, and malevolence. There is no doubt that it is within the power of psychology to determine the kind of environment that promotes desirable emotions, and that often intelligent affection without science can arrive at the right result. When this method is rightly used, its effect on character is more radical and far more satisfactory than the effect to be obtained by rewards and punishments.

The right emotional environment for a child is a delicate matter, and of course varies with the child's age. Throughout childhood, though to a continually diminishing extent, there is need of the feeling of safety. For this purpose, kindness and a pleasant routine are the essentials. The relation with adults should be one of play and physical ease, but not of emotional caresses. There should be close intimacy with other children. Above all, there should be opportunity for initiative in construction, in exploration, and in intellectual and artistic directions. The child has two opposite needs, safety and freedom, of which the latter gradually grows at the expense of the former. The affection given by adults should be such as to cause a feeling of safety, but not such as to limit freedom or to arouse a deep emotional response in the child. Play, which is a vital need of childhood, should be contributed not only by other children, but also by parents, and is essential to the best relation between parents and children.

Freedom is the most difficult element to secure under existing conditions. I am not an advocate of absolute freedom, for reasons which we considered in an earlier chapter; but I am an advocate of certain forms of freedom which most adults find unendurable. There should be no enforced respect for grown-ups, who should allow themselves to be called fools whenever children wish to call them so. We cannot prevent our children from thinking us fools by merely forbidding them to utter their thoughts; in fact, they are more likely to think ill of us if they dare not say so. Children should not be forbidden to swear—not because it is desirable that they should swear, but because it is desirable that they should think that it does not matter whether they do or not, since this is a true proposition. They should be free entirely from the sex taboo, and not checked when their conversation seems to inhibited adults to be indecent. If they express opinions on religion or politics or morals, they may be met with argument, provided it is genuine argument, but not if it is really dogma: the adult may, and should, suggest considerations to them, but should not impose conclusions.

Given such conditions, children may grow up fearless and fundamentally happy, without the resentment that comes of thwarting or the excessive demands that are produced by an atmosphere of hothouse affection. Their intelligence will be untrammelled, and their views on human affairs will have the kindliness that comes of contentment. A world of human beings with this emotional equipment would make short work of our social system, with its wars, its oppressions, its economic injustice, its horror of free speech and free inquiry, and its superstitious moral code. The toleration of these evils depends upon timidity in thought and malevolent feeling due to lack of freedom. Dr Watson, who minimizes the congenital aspects of character, nevertheless allows, as one of the unlearnt reactions of infants, rage at any constriction of the limbs. This instinctive emotion is the basis of the love of freedom. The man whose tongue is constricted by laws or taboos against free speech, whose pen is constricted by the censorship, whose loves are constricted by an ethic which considers jealousy a better thing than affection, whose childhood has been imprisoned in a code of manners and whose youth has been drilled in a cruel orthodoxy, will feel against the world that hampers him the same rage that is felt by the infant whose arms and legs are held motionless. In his rage he will turn to destruction, becoming a revolutionary, a militarist, or a persecuting moralist according to temperament and opportunity. To make human beings who will create a better world is a problem in emotional psychology: it is the problem of making human beings who have a free intelligence combined with a happy disposition. This problem is not beyond the powers of science; it is the will, not the power, that is lacking.

(*Education and the Social Order*, London: Allen & Unwin; *Education and the Modern World*, New York: W. W. Norton, 1932.)

48

THE FUNCTIONS OF A TEACHER

TEACHING, more even than most other professions, has been transformed during the last hundred years from a small, highly skilled profession concerned with a minority of the population, to a large and important branch of the public service. The profession has a great and honourable tradition, extending from the dawn of history until recent times, but any teacher in the modern world who allows himself to be inspired by the ideals of his predecessors is likely to be made sharply aware that it is not his function to teach what he thinks, but to instil such beliefs and prejudices as are thought useful by his employers. In former days a teacher was expected to be a man of exceptional knowledge or wisdom, to whose words men would do well to attend. In antiquity, teachers were not an organized profession, and no control was exercised over what they taught. It is true that they were often punished afterwards for their subversive doctrines. Socrates was put to death and Plato is said to have been thrown into prison, but such incidents did not interfere with the spread of their doctrines. Any man who has the genuine impulse of the teacher will be more anxious to survive in his books than in the flesh. A feeling of intellectual independence is essential to the proper fulfilment of the teacher's functions, since it is his business to instil what he can of knowledge and reasonableness into the process of forming public opinion. In antiquity he performed this function unhampered except by occasional spasmodic and ineffective interventions of tyrants or mobs. In the middle ages teaching became the exclusive prerogative of the Church, with the result that there was little progress either intellectual or social. With the Renaissance, the general respect for learning brought back a very considerable measure of freedom to the teacher. It is true that the Inquisition compelled Galileo to recant, and burnt Giordano Bruno at the stake, but each of these men had done his work before being punished. Institutions such as universities largely remained in the grip of the dogmatists, with the result that most of the best intellectual work was done by independent men of learning. In England, especially, until near the end of the nineteenth century, hardly any men of first-rate eminence except Newton were connected with universities. But the social system was such that this interfered little with their activities or their usefulness.

In our more highly organized world we face a new problem. Something called education is given to everybody, usually by the State, but sometimes by the Churches. The teacher has thus become, in the vast majority of cases, a civil servant obliged to carry out the behests of men who have not his learning, who have no experience of dealing with the young, and whose only attitude towards education is that of the propagandist. It is not very easy to see how, in these circumstances, teachers can perform the functions for which they are specially fitted.

State education is obviously necessary, but as obviously involves certain dangers against which there ought to be safeguards. The evils to be feared were seen in their full magnitude in Nazi Germany and are still seen in Russia. Where these evils prevail no man can teach unless he subscribes to a dogmatic creed which few people of free intelligence are likely to accept sincerely. Not only must he subscribe to a creed, but he must condone abominations and carefully abstain from speaking his mind on current events. So long as he is teaching only the alphabet and the multiplication table, as to which no controversies arise, official dogmas do not necessarily warp his instruction; but even while he is teaching these elements he is expected, in totalitarian countries, not to employ the methods which he thinks most likely to achieve the scholastic result, but to instil fear, subservience, and blind obedience by demanding unquestioned submission to his authority. And as soon as he passes beyond the bare elements, he is obliged to take the official view on all controversial questions. The result is that the young in Nazi Germany became, and Russia become, fanatical bigots, ignorant of the world outside their own country, totally unaccustomed to free discussion, and not aware that their opinions can be questioned without wickedness. This state of affairs, bad as it is, would be less disastrous than it is if the dogmas instilled were, as in medieval Catholicism, universal and international; but the whole conception of an international culture is denied by the modern dogmatists, who preached one creed in Germany, another in Italy, another in Russia and yet another in Japan. In each of these countries fanatical nationalism was what was most emphasized in the teaching of the young, with the result that the men of one country have no common ground with the men of another, and that no conception of a common civilization stands in the way of warlike ferocity.

The decay of cultural internationalism has proceeded at a continually increasing pace ever since the First World War. When I was in Leningrad in 1920, I met the Professor of Pure Mathematics, who was familiar with London, Paris, and other capitals, having been a member of various international congresses. Nowadays the learned men of Russia are very seldom permitted such excursions, for fear of their drawing comparisons unfavourable to their own country. In other countries nationalism in learning is less extreme, but everywhere it is far more powerful than it was. There is a tendency in England (and, I believe, in the United States) to dispense with Frenchmen and Germans in the teaching of French and German. The practice of considering a man's nationality rather than his competence in appointing him to a post is damaging to education and an offence against the ideal of international culture, which was a heritage from the Roman Empire and the Catholic Church, but is now being submerged under a new barbarian invasion, proceeding from below rather than from without.

In democratic countries these evils have not yet reached anything like the same proportions, but it must be admitted that there is grave danger of similar developments in education, and that this danger can only be averted if those who believe in liberty of thought are on the alert to protect teachers from intellectual bondage. Perhaps the first requisite is a clear conception of the services which teachers can be expected to perform for the community. I agree with the governments of the world that the imparting of definite uncontroversial information is one of the least of the teacher's functions. It is, of course, the basis upon which the others are built, and in a technical civilization such as ours it has undoubtedly a considerable utility. There must exist in a modern community a sufficient number of men who possess the technical skill required to preserve the mechanical apparatus upon which our physical comforts depend. It is, moreover, inconvenient if any large percentage of the population is unable to read and write. For these reasons we are all in favour of universal compulsory education. But governments have perceived that it is easy, in the course of giving instruction, to instil beliefs on controversial matters and to produce habits of mind which may be convenient or inconvenient to those in authority. The defence of the state in all civilized countries is quite as much in the hands of teachers as in those of the armed forces. Except in totalitarian countries, the defence of the state is desirable, and the mere fact that education is used for this purpose is not in itself a ground of criticism. Criticism will only arise if the state is defended by obscurantism and appeals to irrational passion. Such methods are quite unnecessary in the case of any state worth defending. Nevertheless, there is a natural tendency towards their adoption by those who have no first-hand knowledge of education. There is a widespread belief that nations are made strong by uniformity of opinion and by the suppression of liberty. One hears it said over and over again that democracy weakens a country in war, in spite of the fact that in every important war since the year 1700 the victory has gone to the more democratic side. Nations have been brought to ruin much more often by insistence upon a narrow-minded doctrinal uniformity than by free discussion and the toleration of divergent opinions. Dogmatists the world over believe that although the truth is known to them, others will be led into false beliefs provided they are allowed to hear the arguments on both sides. This is a view which leads to one or another of two misfortunes: either one set of dogmatists conquers the world and prohibits all new ideas, or, what is worse, rival dogmatists conquer different regions and preach the gospel of hate against each other, the former of these evils existing in the middle ages, the latter during the wars of religion, and again in the present day. The first makes civilization static, the second tends to destroy it completely. Against both, the teacher should be the main safeguard.

It is obvious that organized party spirit is one of the greatest dangers of our time. In the form of nationalism it leads to wars between nations, and in other forms it leads to civil war. It should be the business of teachers to stand outside the strife of parties and endeavour to instil into the young the habit of impartial inquiry, leading them to judge issues on their merits and to be on their guard against accepting *ex parte* statements at their face value. The teacher should not be expected to flatter the prejudices either of the mob or of officials. His professional virtue should consist in a readiness to do justice to all sides, and in an endeavour to rise above controversy into a region of dispassionate scientific investigation. If there are people to whom the results of his investigation are inconvenient, he should be protected against their resentment, unless it can be shown that he has lent himself to dishonest propaganda by the dissemination of demonstrable untruths.

The function of the teacher, however, is not merely to mitigate the heat of current controversies. He has more positive tasks to perform, and he cannot be a great teacher unless he is inspired by a wish to perform these tasks. Teachers are more than any other class the guardians of civilization. They should be intimately aware of what civilization is, and desirous of imparting a civilized attitude to their pupils. We are thus brought to the question: what constitutes a civilized community?

This question would very commonly be answered by pointing to merely material tests. A country is civilized if it has much machinery, many motor cars, many bathrooms, and a great deal of rapid locomotion. To these things, in my opinion, most modern men attach much too much importance. Civilization in the more important sense, is a thing of the mind, not of material adjuncts to the physical side of living. It is a matter partly of knowledge, partly of emotion. So far as knowledge is concerned, a man should be aware of the minuteness of himself and his immediate environment in relation to the world in time and space. He should see his own country not *only* as home, but as one among the countries of the world, all with an equal right to live and think and feel. He should see his own age in relation to the past and the future, and be aware that its own controversies will seem as strange to future ages as those of the past seem to us now. Taking an even wider view, he should be conscious of the vastness of geological epochs and astronomical abysses; but he should be aware of all this, not as a weight to crush the individual human spirit, but as a vast panorama which enlarges the mind that contemplates it. On the side of the emotions, a very similar enlargement from the purely personal is needed if a man is to be truly civilized. Men pass from birth to death, sometimes happy, sometimes unhappy; sometimes generous, sometimes grasping and petty; sometimes heroic, sometimes cowardly and servile. To the man who views the procession as a whole, certain things stand out as worthy of admiration. Some men have been inspired by love of mankind; some by supreme intellect have helped us to understand the world in which we live; and some by exceptional sensitiveness have created beauty. These men have produced something of positive good to outweigh the long record of cruelty, oppression, and superstition. These men have done what lay in their power to make human life a better thing than the brief turbulence of savages. The civilized man, where he cannot admire, will aim rather at understanding than at reprobating. He will seek rather to discover and remove the impersonal causes of evil than to hate the men who are in its grip. All this should be in the mind and heart of the teacher, and if it is in his mind and heart he will convey it in his teaching to the young who are in his care.

No man can be a good teacher unless he has feelings of warm affection towards his pupils and a genuine desire to impart to them what he himself believes to be of value. This is not the attitude of the propagandist. To the propagandist his pupils are potential soldiers in an army. They are to serve purposes that lie outside their own lives, not in the sense in which every generous purpose transcends self, but in the sense of ministering to unjust privilege or to despotic power. The propagandist does not desire that his pupils should survey the world and freely choose a purpose which to them appears of value. He desires, like a topiarian artist, that their growth shall be trained and twisted to suit the gardener's purpose. And in thwarting their natural growth he is apt to destroy in them all generous vigour, replacing it by envy, destructiveness, and cruelty. There is no need for men to be cruel; on the contrary, I am persuaded that most cruelty results from thwarting in early years, above all from thwarting what is good.

Repressive and persecuting passions are very common, as the present state of the world only too amply proves. But they are not an inevitable part of human nature. On the contrary, they are, I believe, always the outcome of some kind of unhappiness. It should be one of the functions of the teacher to open vistas before his pupils showing them the possibility of activities that will be as delightful as they are useful, thereby letting loose their kind impulses and preventing the growth of a desire to rob others of joys that they will have missed. Many people decry happiness as an end, both for themselves and for others, but one may suspect them of sour grapes. It is one thing to forgo personal happiness for a public end, but it is quite another to treat the general happiness as a thing of no account. Yet this is often done in the name of some supposed heroism. In those who take this attitude there is generally some vein of cruelty based probably upon an unconscious envy, and the source of the envy will usually be found in childhood or youth. It should be the aim of the educator to train adults free from these psychological misfortunes, and not anxious to rob others of happiness because they themselves have not been robbed of it.

As matters stand today, many teachers are unable to do the best of which they are capable. For this there are a number of reasons, some more or less accidental, others very deep-seated. To begin with the former, most teachers are overworked and are compelled to prepare their pupils for examinations rather than to give them a liberalizing mental training. The people who are not accustomed to teaching—and this includes practically all educational authorities—have no idea of the expense of spirit that it involves. Clergymen are not expected to preach sermons for several hours every day, but the analogous effort is demanded of teachers. The result is that many of them become harassed and nervous, out of touch with recent work in the subjects that they teach, and unable to inspire their students with a sense of the intellectual delights to be obtained from new understanding and new knowledge.

This, however, is by no means the gravest matter. In most countries certain opinions are recognized as correct, and others as dangerous. Teachers whose opinions are not correct are expected to keep silent about them. If they mention their opinions it is propaganda, while the mentioning of correct opinions is considered to be merely sound instruction. The result is that the inquiring young too often have to go outside the class-room to discover what is being thought by the most vigorous minds of their own time. There is in America a subject called civics, in which, perhaps more than in any other, the teaching is expected to be misleading. The young are taught a sort of copybook account of how public affairs are supposed to be conducted, and are carefully shielded from all knowledge as to how in fact they are conducted. When they grow up and discover the truth, the result is too often a complete cynicism in which all public ideals are lost; whereas if they had been taught the truth carefully and with proper comment at an earlier age they might have become men able to combat evils in which, as it is, they acquiesce with a shrug.

The idea that falsehood is edifying is one of the besetting sins of those who draw up educational schemes. I should not myself consider that a man could be a good teacher unless he had made a firm resolve never in the course of his teaching to conceal truth because it is what is called 'unedifying'. The kind of virtue that can be produced by guarded ignorance is frail and fails at the first touch of reality. There are, in this world, many men who deserve admiration, and it is good that the young should be taught to see the ways in which these men are admirable. But it is not good to teach them to admire rogues by concealing their roguery. It is thought that the knowledge of things as they are will lead to cynicism, and so it may do if the knowledge comes suddenly with a shock of surprise and horror. But if it comes gradually, duly intermixed with a knowledge of what is good, and in the course of a scientific study inspired by the wish to get at the truth, it will have no such effect. In any case, to tell lies to the young, who have no means of checking what they are told, is morally indefensible.

The thing, above all, that a teacher should endeavour to produce in his pupils if democracy is to survive, is the kind of tolerance that springs from an endeavour to understand those who are different from ourselves. It is perhaps a natural human impulse to view with horror and disgust all manners and customs different from those to which we are used. Ants and savages put strangers to death. And those who have never travelled either physically or mentally find it difficult to tolerate the queer ways and outlandish beliefs of other nations and other times, other sects and other political parties. This kind of ignorant intolerance is the antithesis of a civilized outlook, and is one of the gravest dangers to which our overcrowded world is exposed. The educational system ought to be designed to correct it, but much too little is done in this direction at present. In every country nationalistic feeling is encouraged, and school children are taught, what they are only too ready to believe, that the inhabitants of other countries are morally and intellectually inferior to those of the country in which the school children happen to reside. Collective hysteria, the most mad and cruel of all human emotions, is encouraged instead of being discouraged, and the young are encouraged to believe what they hear frequently said rather than what there is some rational ground for believing. In all this the teachers are not to blame. They are not free to teach as they would wish. It is they who know most intimately the needs of the young. It is they who through daily contact have come to care for them. But it is not they who decide what shall be taught or what the methods of instruction are to be. There ought to be a great deal more freedom than there is for the scholastic profession. It ought to have more opportunities of self-determination, more independence from the interference of bureaucrats and bigots. No one would consent in our day to subject the medical men to the control of non-medical authorities as to how they should treat their patients, except of course where they depart criminally from the purpose of medicine, which is to cure the patient. The teacher is a kind of medical man whose purpose is to cure the patient of childishness, but he is not allowed to decide for himself on the basis of experience what methods are most suitable to this end. A few great historic universities, by the weight of their prestige, have secured virtual self-determination, but the immense majority of educational institutions are hampered and controlled by men who do not understand the work with which they are interfering. The only way to prevent totalitarianism in our highly organized world is to secure a certain degree of independence for bodies performing useful public work, and among such bodies teachers deserve a foremost place.

The teacher, like the artist, the philosopher, and the man of letters, can only perform his work adequately if he feels himself to be an individual directed by an inner creative impulse, not dominated and fettered by an outside authority. It is very difficult in this modern world to find a place for the individual. He can subsist at the top as a dictator in a totalitarian state or a plutocratic magnate in a country of large industrial enterprises, but in the realm of the mind it is becoming more and more difficult to preserve independence of the great organized forces that control the livelihoods of men and women. If the world is not to lose the benefit to be derived from its best minds, it will have to find some method of allowing them scope and liberty in spite of organization. This involves a deliberate restraint on the part of those who have power, and a conscious realization that there are men to whom free scope must be afforded. Renaissance Popes could feel in this way towards Renaissance artists, but the powerful men of our day seem to have more difficulty in feeling respect for exceptional genius. The turbulence of our times is inimical to the fine flower of culture. The man in the street is full of fear, and therefore unwilling to tolerate freedoms for which he sees no need. Perhaps we must wait for quieter times before the claims of civilization can again override the claims of party spirit. Meanwhile, it is important that some at least should continue to realize the limitations of what can be done by organization. Every system should allow loopholes and exceptions, for if it does not it will in the end crush all that is best in man.

(*Harper's Magazine*, June 1940, subsequently reprinted in *Unpopular Essays*, London: Allen & Unwin; New York: Simon & Schuster, 1950.)

PART XI

The Philosopher of Politics

Few technical philosophers have shown such keen insight and astute observance of political theories and trends as Russell. The title of his Nobel Prize Acceptance Speech was 'Politically Important Desires', and as the *New York Times* observed, it was 'as witty as it was penetrating'.

Russell, even in his earliest writings, displayed an uncanny foresight in being able to predict with remarkable accuracy events that would follow. In his first book, *German Social Democracy*, published in 1896, he acutely observed the seeds which later developed into Germany's future of dictatorship and war. This book showed what was to become Russell's most characteristic asset, his ability to discuss any problem in a scientific, objective and dispassionate way. When Russell changed his views, as he frequently did, he always held steadfastly to the belief that any approximation of truth can only be obtained by examining the available evidence at the moment.

The analysis of power has been Russell's key concept in the theory of politics. To his thinking in this area he has brought to bear his critical acumen which serves to point to the fallacious theories that abound in Fascism and Communism. He has long been outspoken not only as a political theorist but as an analyst of the practical import of these theories in the daily political scene.

49

THE RECONCILIATION OF INDIVIDUALITY
AND CITIZENSHIP

IN our first chapter we proposed a question: Can the fullest individual development be combined with the necessary minimum of social coherence? This has led us to consider the various ways in which education is affected by politics and economics, most of which, we have found, are harmful to the boys and girls concerned. Is it necessary that the effects of politics and economics on the individual should always be harmful? Or is this a temporary misfortune of our own time? And, in the latter case, what hope is there of a greater harmony between individuality and citizenship in the not too distant future?

The harm that is done to education by politics arises chiefly from two sources: first, that the interests of some partial group are placed before the interests of mankind; second, that there is too great a love of uniformity both in the herd and in the bureaucrat. Of these two evils, the first is at present the greater; but if the first were overcome, the second might become very grave.

It has been the custom for education to favour one's own State, one's own religion, the male sex, and the rich. In countries where various religions exist side by side, the State is not able to favour any one of them in its schools, but this has led to the creation of schools belonging to various sects, or, as in New York City and Boston, to distortion, in the Catholic interest, of the history taught in the public schools.[1] The male sex can no longer be favoured as it used to be. But education, outside Russia, is still so conducted as to further the interests of the rich; and of course everywhere it teaches an exclusive loyalty to one's own State.

The result of this state of affairs is that education has become part of the struggle for power between religions, classes, and nations. The pupil is not considered for his own sake, but as a recruit: the educational machine is not concerned with his welfare, but with ulterior political purposes. There is no reason to suppose that the State will ever place the interests of the child before its own interests; we have, therefore, to inquire whether

[1] In New York City, for example, teachers have to speak of the Reformation as 'the Protestant Revolt'.

there is any possibility of a State whose interests, where education is concerned, will be approximately identical with those of the child.

It is obvious that the first requisite for this purpose is the elimination of large-scale wars. If this were achieved by the establishment of an international authority, the teaching of militant nationalism would no longer serve any purpose, and would soon diminish to a point where it would be innocuous. There would no longer be any need for Officers' Training Corps, or for compulsory military service, or for the teaching of false history. Moral training would no longer have homicide as the apex of a virtuous life, to which everything else leads up. The establishment of an international authority sufficiently strong to impose its settlement of disputes upon recalcitrant States is, I am convinced, the most important reform from an educational as well as from every other point of view.

There are, however, formidable obstacles to the establishment of such an authority—obstacles much more formidable than most pacifists realize. Consider such an issue as that between communism and capitalism. It is extremely improbable that this issue will be settled peaceably: on both sides men consider it sufficiently vital to be worth fighting about, and it is difficult to imagine any international machinery strong enough to prevent it from leading to war. Imagine (say) a civil war in Germany between communists and nationalists. Would France and Russia look on passively? If France and Russia joined in, would Great Britain remain neutral? Would the United States risk the spread of Communism over the whole Continent of Europe? Would China and India fail to profit by the opportunity? Until the issue between Communism and capitalism is decided in one way or another, world peace cannot be secure, whatever machinery may be created. And it is difficult to see how this issue can be decided except by the victory of Communism, at any rate throughout Europe. Capitalism will no longer bring contentment. Before very long, the general standard of comfort may be higher in Russia than elsewhere; the propagandist effect of such a state of affairs will be irresistible. It seems, therefore, not improbable that the shortest road to world peace lies through Russian propaganda. If so, it is short-sighted to object to the somewhat crude methods employed by the Soviet Government in teaching Communism to its boys and girls. I do not positively assert all this; I merely suggest it as an hypothesis which is by no means improbable.

It is, of course, clear that there cannot be secure peace until Germany ceases to be punished for having been defeated in the war. And this will not happen until France ceases to dominate Europe. And France will perhaps not cease to dominate except as the result of a war.

It is doubtful, also, whether the liberation of India from the domination of England and of China from that of Japan can be achieved except through a first-class war.

All these large questions will have to be solved before there is any serious hope of the preservation of peace by the creation of an international authority. They may all be solved by the victory of Communism within the next twenty years, but I am scarcely enough of an optimist to expect this.

Next to the elimination of war, the most important requisite in the reconciliation of the individual and the citizen is the elimination of superstition. For this purpose, I define a belief as superstitious if its sole basis is traditional or emotional. When people consider the preservation of such beliefs important, they create systems of education involving respect for the wisdom of our ancestors and a habit of deciding questions on other than rational grounds. Holders of power, almost inevitably, desire their subjects to be emotional rather than rational, since this renders it easier to make those who are victims of an unjust social system contented with their lot. Superstition thus becomes the natural ally of injustice, and only where the economic and political institutions are just is governmental education likely to promote a rational outlook.

It is, of course, by no means certain that, if a just economic system were established as the result of a long conflict, it would, at first, be unaccompanied by superstition. In war-time, false beliefs are used to generate enthusiasm, and a strict intellectual discipline is found useful in preventing doubts as to the importance of the cause. Russian Communism already has its body of theological dogma, its hagiology, and its sacred history. If, after a century of struggle, the Russian doctrine converts the world, it will, in the interval, have created many myths and acquired great doctrinal rigidity. The man who, when that time comes, shall venture to say that Marx and Lenin were not the greatest men that ever lived, is likely to be considerably persecuted. It is possible—though I do not think it is probable—that the Communist party may come to occupy a position somewhat similar to that of the Church in the Dark Ages. It is possible that the wars preceding the victory of Communism will destroy all the industrial plant in the world and cause the death of all men of science and competent technicians. In that case, when it is found recorded in the Scriptures that Lenin expected salvation from 'Electrification', people may wonder what this word meant, and may conclude that it denoted mystic union with Karl Marx. It is, therefore, not inconceivable that there may come to be a world State with a just economic system and nevertheless dominated by superstition. But this can hardly happen except on the hypothesis of appallingly destructive wars. On any other hypothesis, it is to be expected that the elements of superstition which are at present associated with the Soviet Government will fade when victory has removed the need of a war mentality. In the long run, even a belief in Communism will cease to seem important, since no other system will come within the purview of practical politics.

I come now to a second danger, which is that of a too great love of uniformity. This may exist, as we said before, both in the bureaucrat and in the herd. Children are instinctively hostile to anything 'odd' in other children, especially in the ages from ten to fifteen. If the authorities realize that this conventionality is undesirable, they can guard against it in various ways, and they can, as was suggested in an earlier chapter, place the cleverer children in separate schools. The intolerance of eccentricity that I am speaking of is strongest in the stupidest children, who tend to regard the peculiar tastes of clever children as affording just grounds for persecution. When the authorities also are stupid (which may occur), they will tend to side with the stupid children, and acquiesce, at least tacitly, in rough treatment for those who show intelligence. In that case, a society will be produced in which all the important positions will be won by those whose stupidity enables them to please the herd. Such a society will have corrupt politicians, ignorant schoolmasters, policemen who cannot catch criminals, and judges who condemn innocent men. Such a society, even if it inhabits a country full of natural wealth, will in the end grow poor from inability to choose able men for important posts. Such a society, though it may prate of Liberty and even erect statues in her honour, will be a persecuting society, which will punish the very men whose ideas might save it from disaster. All this will spring from the too intense pressure of the herd, first at school and then in the world at large. Where such excessive pressure exists, those who direct education are not, as a rule, aware that it is an evil; indeed, they are quite apt to welcome it as a force making for good behaviour. It is important, therefore, to consider what circumstances cause schoolmasters and education officials to fall into this error, and whether any system is likely to prevent them from doing so.

There are, in the teaching profession, two very different types. There are those who have an enthusiasm for some subject, and who love to teach it and implant their own enthusiasm in their pupils. On the other hand, there are those who enjoy the position of power and easy superiority, who like governing but have not enough skill to govern grown men. Some systems favour the former type, some the latter; modern efficiency tends more and more to favour the man who governs rather than teaches. I do not deny that the governing type has its uses: I once knew a lady who had taught in a public school in Texas, and had found it necessary always to come armed with a revolver. But except in remote and sparsely populated regions, boys or girls who are abnormally refractory can be isolated, with the result that those who remain, having lost their ringleader, will become amenable to less drastic methods. The teacher who is inspired by love of his subject, combined with affection for children, can in most circumstances achieve far more in the way of imparting knowledge and civilization than can ever be achieved by the man who loves order and method and efficiency but lacks knowledge and hates children. Unfortunately, in any large school there is a considerable amount of administrative routine, which is generally done best by the worst teachers; and as the higher authorities see the administrative work but are apt not to see the teaching, there is a tendency for credit to be quite wrongly apportioned. Moreover, in any great administrative machine the officials at the head of it naturally consider administration the most honourable and difficult kind of work, with the result that a better status and a higher salary are given to those who do the administrative work of schools than to those who actually teach. All this tends to produce the wrong type of teacher. It is the executive type that encourages uniformity, while the other type will rejoice in ability (which is in itself an eccentricity), and for the sake of ability will readily tolerate other forms of oddity. It is therefore very important, in combating the danger of uniformity, to encourage teachers who love teaching rather than those who love governing.

We come here upon one aspect of a problem which is likely to grow increasingly serious as the world becomes more organized. A man who has a position of power in a great organization requires a definite type of ability, namely, that which is called executive or administrative; it makes very little difference what the matter is that the organization handles, the kind of skill required at the top will be always the same. A man who can organize successfully (let us say) the Lancashire cotton trade will also be successful if he tackles the air defences of London, the exploration of Central Asia, or the transport of timber from British Columbia to England. For these various undertakings he will require no knowledge of cotton, no knowledge of aerial warfare, no knowledge of the buried cities of Turkestan, and no acquaintance with forestry or navigation. His helpers in subordinate positions will, in the several cases, require these several kinds of skill; but his skill is, in a sense, abstract, and does not depend upon specialized knowledge. It thus happens, as organizations increase in size, that the important positions of power tend, more and more, to be in the hands of men who have no intimate familiarity with the purposes of the work that they organize. While this is unavoidable, it has its dangers; and, to return to our theme, it has its dangers in the sphere of education.

In the sphere of education, the danger of the administrator arises through his love of classification and statistics. It is impossible that he should not have this passion, since he must deal quickly with vast masses of material, which only classification will enable him to do. Now in some kinds of material, classification is fairly satisfactory; this occurs where there are well-marked natural kinds. The greengrocer sells peas and beans and spinach and cabbage, and is never obliged to stop and ask himself: 'Is this object a pea or a cauliflower?' With children the matter is otherwise. The question whether a given child is mentally deficient is often a border-line question, to which, speaking scientifically, no precise answer can be given. But speaking administratively, a precise answer *must* be given: the child must either be sent to a special school or kept in the ordinary school. The administrator, therefore, looks about for some means of reaching a precision which does not exist in nature; this is one of the reasons for which he tends to love intelligence tests. And what applies in the case of the mentally deficient applies also in the case of any other mental classification. The man who deals affectionately with a small group of children knows them as individuals, and feels things about them which it would be difficult to put into words; often it is what is peculiar to a child that such a man likes best. But the man who views children from a distance, through a mist of official reports, is impatient of this sort of thing. He wishes all children were exactly alike, since that would make his work easy, but he is compelled to admit classification by age, sex, nationality and religion. The most enlightened also admit classification by intelligence tests. But even the most enlightened like everything cut and dried, and forget the quality of individual life which makes each human being different from every other. For this reason there is a danger lest education officials should encourage a uniformity towards which, in any case, the world is tending.

This is an administrative problem, and it has an administrative solution, namely, devolution. If there were a world government, it would no doubt exercise a certain degree of supervision over all education: it would forbid excessive teaching of local patriotism, and it might prohibit doctrines which it considered subversive. But in all other respects it would, no doubt, leave education to be organized locally. If it were inspired by a scientific spirit, it would also permit various experiments in new methods. The experimental spirit is, at present, foreign to most administrators, but if education were more scientific it would become much commoner. It is to the growth of the experimental spirit that we must look for the toleration of loopholes and exceptions in the scientific State. Without loopholes and exceptions, there will be little progress and insufficient diversity; but this, I think, may come to be believed by officials when they have all had a sound scientific education, not only in physics and chemistry, but also in biology.

Individualism, although it is important not to forget its just claims, needs, in a densely populated industrial world, to be more controlled, even in individual psychology, than in former times. Those of us who have lived in large cities have all acquired ways of behaviour in crowds which are such as to prevent confusion: we keep to the right, move at the proper speed, and cross streets where we should. These are small and external matters, but something of the same sort is required in more serious concerns. St John the Baptist used to go about insufficiently clad, exclaiming 'Repent ye: for the Kingdom of Heaven is at hand'. If a man were to do this in London or New York, he would collect such a crowd that the traffic would be blocked, and the police would have to tell him that he must hire a hall before again uttering his sentiments. Very few men in an industrial society are independent units in their work; the vast majority belong to organizations, and have to carry out their portion of a collective undertaking. A sense of citizenship, of social co-operation, is therefore more necessary than it used to be; but it remains important that this should be secured without too great a diminution of individual judgment and individual initiative.

If a man's life is to be satisfactory, whether from his own point of view or from that of the world at large, it requires two kinds of harmony: an internal harmony of intelligence, emotion and will, and an external harmony with the wills of others. In both these respects, existing education is defective. Internal harmony is prevented by the religious and moral teaching given in infancy and youth, which usually continues to govern the emotions but not the intelligence in later life, while the will is left vacillating, inclining to one side or the other according as emotion or intelligence has momentarily the upper hand. Such conflicts could be prevented if the young were taught doctrines which adult intelligence can accept. This can be done in private schools on a small scale, but without the co-operation of the State it cannot be done on a sufficiently large scale to produce results having other than experimental importance.

The matter of external harmony with the wills of others is more difficult, and not capable of a complete solution. Competition and co-operation are both natural human activities, and it is difficult to suppress competition completely without destroying individuality. But it is not individual and unorganized competition that does the harm in the modern world. Two men may compete for the same woman without harm to anyone, provided their rivalry stops short of murder. The dangerous form of disharmony in the modern world is the organized form, between nations and between classes. So long as this form of disharmony persists, the world cannot enjoy the advantages which science and technical skill have made possible. The disharmony between nations is encouraged by education in the present day, and could be brought to an end by the introduction of internationalist propaganda in schools. This, however, is hardly possible without a previous victory of political internationalism. Education can consolidate political achievements, but is not likely to cause them so long as it is controlled by national States.

There have been times when competition in the form of war was advantageous to the victors. Those times are past. It is obvious now, to every thinking person, that every nation would be happier if all armed forces everywhere were disbanded and all disputes between nations were settled by an international tribunal and all tariffs were abolished and all men could move freely from one country to another. Science has so altered our technique as to make the world one economic unit. But our political institutions and beliefs lag behind our technique, and each nation makes itself artificially poor by economic isolation. We invent labour-saving devices and are troubled by unemployment. When we cannot sell our products, we cut down wages, under the impression, apparently, that the less men earn the more they will spend. All these evils arise from one source, that, while our technique demands co-operation of the whole human race as a single producing and consuming unit, our passions and our political beliefs persist in demanding competition.

Our world is a mad world. Ever since 1914 it has ceased to be constructive, because men will not follow their intelligence in creating international co-operation, but persist in retaining the division of mankind into hostile groups. This collective failure to use the intelligence that men possess for purposes of self-preservation is due, in the main, to the insane and destructive impulses which lurk in the unconscious of those who have been unwisely handled in infancy, childhood, and adolescence. In spite of continually improving technique in production, we all grow poorer. In spite of being well aware of the horrors of the next war, we continue to cultivate in the young those sentiments which will make it inevitable. In spite of science, we react against the habit of considering problems rationally. In spite of increasing command over nature, most men feel more hopeless and impotent than they have felt since the Middle Ages. The source of all this does not lie in the external world, nor does it lie in the purely cognitive part of our nature, since we know more than men ever knew before. It lies in our passions; it lies in our emotional habits; it lies in the sentiments instilled in youth, and in the phobias created in infancy. The cure for our problem is to make men sane, and to make men sane they must be educated sanely. At present the various factors we have been considering all tend towards social disaster. Religion encourages stupidity, and an insufficient sense of reality; sex education frequently produces nervous disorders, and where it fails to do so overtly, too often plants discords in the unconscious which make happiness in adult life impossible; nationalism as taught in schools implies that the most important duty of young men is homicide; class feeling promotes acquiescence in economic injustice; and competition promotes ruthlessness in the social struggle. Can it be wondered at that a world in which the forces of the State are devoted to producing in the young insanity, stupidity, readiness for homicide, economic injustice and ruthlessness—can it be wondered at, I say, that such a world is not a happy one? Is a man to be condemned as immoral and subversive because he wishes to substitute for these elements in the moral education of the present day intelligence, sanity, kindliness, and a sense of justice? The world has become so intolerably tense, so charged with hatred, so filled with misfortune and pain that men have lost the power of balanced judgment which is needed for emergence from the slough in which mankind is staggering. Our age is so painful that many of the best men have been seized with despair. But there is no rational ground for despair: the means of happiness for the human race exist, and it is only necessary that the human race should choose to use them.

(*Education and the Social Order*, London: Allen & Unwin; *Education and the Modern World*, New York; W. W. Norton, 1932.)

50

PHILOSOPHY AND POLITICS

THE British are distinguished among the nations of modern Europe, on the one hand by the excellence of their philosophers, and on the other hand by their contempt for philosophy. In both respects they show their wisdom. But contempt for philosophy, if developed to the point at which it becomes systematic, is itself a philosophy; it is the philosophy which, in America, is called 'instrumentalism'. I shall suggest that philosophy, if it is bad philosophy, may be dangerous, and therefore deserves that degree of negative respect which we accord to lightning and tigers. What positive respect may be due to 'good' philosophy I will leave for the moment an open question.

The connection of philosophy with politics, which is the subject of my lecture, has been less evident in Britain than in Continental countries. Empiricism, broadly speaking, is connected with liberalism, but Hume was a Tory; what philosophers call 'idealism' has, in general, a similar connection with conservatism, but T. H. Green was a Liberal. On the Continent distinctions have been more clear-cut, and there has been a greater readiness to accept or reject a block of doctrines as a whole, without critical scrutiny of each separate part.

In most civilized countries at most times, philosophy has been a matter in which the authorities had an official opinion, and except where liberal democracy prevails this is still the case. The Catholic Church is connected to the philosophy of Aquinas, the Soviet Government to that of Marx. The Nazis upheld German idealism, though the degree of allegiance to be given to Kant, Fichte or Hegel respectively was not clearly laid down. Catholics, Communists, and Nazis all consider that their views on practical politics are bound up with their views on theoretical philosophy. Democratic liberalism, in its early successes, was connected with the empirical philosophy developed by Locke. I want to consider this relation of philosophies to political systems as it has in fact existed, and to inquire how far it is a valid logical relation, and how far, even if not logical, it has a kind of psychological inevitability. In so far as either kind of relation exists, a man's philosophy has practical importance, and a prevalent philosophy may have an intimate connection with the happiness or misery of large sections of mankind.

The word 'philosophy' is one of which the meaning is by no means fixed. Like the word 'religion', it has one sense when used to describe certain features of historical cultures, and another when used to denote a study or an attitude of mind which is considered desirable in the present day. Philosophy, as pursued in the universities of the Western democratic world, is, at least in intention, part of the pursuit of knowledge, aiming at the same kind of detachment as is sought in science, and not required by the authorities to arrive at conclusions convenient to the government. Many teachers of philosophy would repudiate, not only the intention to influence their pupils' politics, but also the view that philosophy should inculcate virtue. This, they would say, has as little to do with the philosopher as with the physicist or the chemist. Knowledge, they would say, should be the sole purpose of university teaching; virtue should be left to parents, schoolmasters, and Churches.

But this view of philosophy, with which I have much sympathy, is very modern, and even in the modern world exceptional. There is a quite different view, which has prevailed since antiquity, and to which philosophy has owed its social and political importance.

Philosophy, in this historically usual sense, has resulted from the attempt to produce a synthesis of science and religion, or, perhaps more exactly, to combine a doctrine as to the nature of the universe and man's place in it with a practical ethic inculcating what was considered the best way of life. Philosophy was distinguished from religion by the fact that, nominally at least, it did not appeal to authority or tradition; it was distinguished from science by the fact that an essential part of its purpose was to tell men how to live. Its cosmological and ethical theories were closely interconnected: sometimes ethical motives influenced the philosopher's views as to the nature of the universe, sometimes his views as to the universe led him to ethical conclusions. And with most philosophers ethical opinions involved political consequences: some valued democracy, others oligarchy; some praised liberty, others discipline. Almost all types of philosophy were invented by the Greeks, and the controversies of our own day were already vigorous among the pre-Socratics.

The fundamental problem of ethics and politics is that of finding some way of reconciling the needs of social life with the urgency of individual desires. This has been achieved, in so far as it has been achieved, by means of various devices. Where a government exists, the criminal law can be used to prevent anti-social action on the part of those who do not belong to the government, and law can be reinforced by religion wherever religion teaches that disobedience is impiety. Where there is a priesthood sufficiently influential to enforce its moral code on lay rulers, even the rulers become to some extent subject to law; of this there are abundant instances in the

Old Testament and in medieval history. Kings who genuinely believe in the Divine government of the world, and in a system of rewards and punishments in the next life, feel themselves not omnipotent, and not able to sin with impunity. This feeling is expressed by the King in *Hamlet*, when he contrasts the inflexibility of Divine justice with the subservience of earthly judges to the royal power.

Philosophers, when they have tackled the problem of preserving social coherence, have sought solutions less obviously dependent upon dogma than those offered by official religions. Most philosophy has been a reaction against scepticism; it has arisen in ages when authority no longer sufficed to produce the socially necessary minimum of belief, so that nominally rational arguments had to be invented to secure the same result. This motive has led to a deep insincerity infecting most philosophy, both ancient and modern. There has been a fear, often unconscious, that clear thinking would lead to anarchy, and this fear has led philosophers to hide in mists of fallacy and obscurity.

There have, of course, been exceptions; the most notable are Protagoras in antiquity, and Hume in modern times. Both, as a result of scepticism, were politically conservative. Protagoras did not know whether the gods exist, but he held that in any case they ought to be worshipped. Philosophy, according to him, had nothing edifying to teach, and for the survival of morals we must rely upon the thoughtlessness of the majority and their willingness to believe what they had been taught. Nothing, therefore, must be done to weaken the popular force of tradition.

The same sort of thing, up to a point, may be said about Hume. After setting forth his sceptical conclusions, which, he admits, are not such as men can live by, he passes on to a piece of practical advice which, if followed, would prevent anybody from reading him. 'Carelessness and inattention', he says, 'alone can afford us any remedy. For this reason I rely entirely upon them.' He does not, in this connection, set forth his reasons for being a Tory, but it is obvious that 'carelessness and inattention', while they may lead to acquiescence in the *status quo*, cannot, unaided, lead a man to advocate this or that scheme of reform.

Hobbes, though less sceptical than Hume, was equally persuaded that government is not of divine origin, and was equally led, by the road of disbelief, to advocacy of extreme conservatism.

Protagoras was 'answered' by Plato, and Hume by Kant and Hegel. In each case the philosophical world heaved a sigh of relief, and refrained from examining too nicely the intellectual validity of the 'answer', which in each case had political as well as theoretical consequences—though in the case of the 'answer' to Hume it was not the Liberal Kant but the reactionary Hegel who developed the *political* consequences.

But thorough-going sceptics, such as Protagoras and Hume, have never been influential, and have served chiefly as bugbears to be used by reactionaries in frightening people into irrational dogmatism. The really powerful adversaries against whom Plato and Hegel had to contend were not sceptics, but empiricists, Democritus in the one case and Locke in the other. In each case empiricism was associated with democracy and with a more or less utilitarian ethic. In each case the new philosophy succeeded in presenting itself as nobler and more profound than the philosophy of pedestrian common sense which it superseded. In each case, in the name of all that was most sublime, the new philosophy made itself the champion of injustice, cruelty, and opposition to progress. In the case of Hegel this has come to be more or less recognized; in the case of Plato it is still something of a paradox, though it has been brilliantly advocated in a recent book by Dr K. R. Popper.[1]

Plato, according to Diogenes Laertius, expressed the view that all the books of Democritus ought to be burnt. His wish was so far fulfilled that none of the writings of Democritus survive. Plato, in his Dialogues, never mentioned him; Aristotle gave some account of his doctrines; Epicurus vulgarized him; and finally Lucretius put the doctrines of Epicurus into verse. Lucretius just survived, by a happy accident. To reconstruct Democritus from the controversy of Aristotle and the poetry of Lucretius is not easy; it is almost as if we had to reconstruct Plato from Locke's refutation of innate ideas and Vaughan's 'I saw eternity the other night'. Nevertheless enough can be done to explain and condemn Plato's hatred.

Democritus is chiefly famous as (along with Leucippus) the founder of atomism, which he advocated in spite of the objections of metaphysicians —objections which were repeated by their successors down to and including Descartes and Leibniz. His atomism, however, was only part of his general philosophy. He was a materialist, a determinist, a free-thinker, a utilitarian who disliked all strong passions, a believer in evolution, both astronomical and biological.

Like the men of similar opinions in the eighteenth century, Democritus was an ardent democrat. 'Poverty in a democracy', he says, 'is as much to be preferred to what is called prosperity under despots as freedom is to slavery.' He was a contemporary of Socrates and Protagoras, and a fellow-townsman of the latter; he flourished during the early years of the Peloponnesian war, but may have died before it ended. That war concentrated the struggle that was taking place throughout the Hellenic world between democracy and oligarchy. Sparta stood for oligarchy; so did Plato's family and friends, who were thus led to become Quislings. Their treachery is held to have contributed to the defeat of Athens. After that defeat, Plato set to work to sing the praises of the victors by constructing a Utopia of which the main features were suggested by the constitution of Sparta.

---

[1] *The Open Society and its Enemies.* The same thesis is maintained in my *History of Western Philosophy.*

Such, however, was his artistic skill that Liberals never noticed his reactionary tendencies until his disciples Lenin and Hitler had supplied them with a practical exegesis.[1]

That Plato's Republic should have been admired, on its political side, by decent people, is perhaps the most astonishing example of literary snobbery in all history. Let us consider a few points in this totalitarian tract. The main purpose of education, to which everything else is subordinated, is to produce courage in battle. To this end, there is to be a rigid censorship of the stories told by mothers and nurses to young children; there is to be no reading of Homer, because that degraded versifier makes heroes lament and gods laugh; the drama is to be forbidden, because it contains villains and women; music is to be only of certain kinds, which, in modern terms would be 'Rule Britannia' and 'The British Grenadiers'. The government is to be in the hands of a small oligarchy, who are to practise trickery and lying—trickery in manipulating the drawing of lots for eugenic purposes, and elaborate lying to persuade the population that there are biological differences between the upper and lower classes. Finally, there is to be a large-scale infanticide when children are born otherwise than as a result of governmental swindling in the drawing of lots.

Whether people are happy in this community does not matter, we are told, for excellence resides in the whole, not in the parts. Plato's city is a copy of the eternal city laid up in heaven; perhaps in heaven we shall enjoy the kind of existence it offers us, but if we do not enjoy it here on earth, so much the worse for us.

This system derives its persuasive force from the marriage of aristocratic prejudice and 'divine philosophy'; without the latter, its repulsiveness would be obvious. The fine talk about the good and the unchanging makes it possible to lull the reader into acquiescence in the doctrine that the wise should rule, and that their purpose should be to preserve the status quo, as the ideal state in heaven does. To every man of strong political convictions—and the Greeks had amazingly vehement political passions—it is obvious that 'the good' are those of his own party, and that, if they could establish the constitution they desire, no further change would be necessary. So Plato thought, but by concealing his thought in a metaphysical mist he gave it an impersonal and disinterested appearance which deceived the world for ages.

The ideal of static perfection, which Plato derived from Parmenides and embodied in his theory of ideas, is one which is now generally recognized as inapplicable to human affairs. Man is a restless animal, not content, like the boa-constrictor, to have a good meal once a month and sleep the rest of the time. Man needs, for his happiness, not only the enjoyment of this or that, but hope and enterprise and change. As Hobbes

[1] In 1920 I compared the Soviet State to Plato's Republic, to the equal indignation of Communists and Platonists.

says, 'felicity consisteth in prospering, not in having prospered'. Among modern philosophers, the ideal of unending and unchanging bliss has been replaced by that of evolution, in which there is supposed to be an orderly progress towards a goal which is never quite attained or at any rate has not been attained at the time of writing. This change of outlook is part of the substitution of dynamics for statics which began with Galileo, and which has increasingly affected all modern thinking, whether scientific or political.

Change is one thing, progress is another. 'Change' is scientific, 'progress' is ethical; change is indubitable, whereas progress is a matter of controversy. Let us first consider change, as it appears in science.

Until the time of Galileo, astronomers, following Aristotle, believed that everything in the heavens, from the moon upwards, is unchanging and incorruptible. Since Laplace, no reputable astronomer has held this view. Nebulae, stars and planets, we now believe, have all developed gradually. Some stars, for instance, the companion of Sirius, are 'dead'; they have at some time undergone a cataclysm which has enormously diminished the amount of light and heat radiating from them. Our own planet, in which philosophers are apt to take a parochial and excessive interest, was once too hot to support life, and will in time be too cold. After ages during which the earth produced harmless trilobites and butterflies, evolution progressed to the point at which it generated Neros, Genghis Khans and Hitlers. This, however, is a passing nightmare; in time the earth will become again incapable of supporting life, and peace will return.

But this purposeless see-saw, which is all that science has to offer, has not satisfied the philosophers. They have professed to discover a formula of progress, showing that the world was becoming gradually more and more to their liking. The recipe for a philosophy of this type is simple. The philosopher first decides which are the features of the existing world that give him pleasure, and which are the features that give him pain. He then, by a careful selection among facts, persuades himself that the universe is subject to a general law leading to an increase of what he finds pleasant and a decrease of what he finds unpleasant. Next, having formulated his law of progress, he turns on the public and says: 'It is fated that the world must develop as I say; therefore those who wish to be on the winning side, and do not care to wage a fruitless war against the inevitable, will join my party'. Those who oppose him are condemned as unphilosophic, unscientific and out of date, while those who agree with him feel assured of victory, since the universe is on their side. At the same time the winning side, for reasons which remain somewhat obscure, is represented as the side of virtue.

The man who first fully developed this point of view was Hegel. Hegel's philosophy is so odd that one would not have expected him to be able to get sane men to accept it, but he did. He set it out with so much obscurity that people thought it must be profound. It can quite easily be expounded lucidly in words of one syllable, but then its absurdity becomes obvious. What follows is not a caricature, though of course Hegelians will maintain that it is.

Hegel's philosophy, in outline, is as follows. Real reality is timeless, as in Parmenides and Plato, but there is also an apparent reality, consisting of the every-day world in space and time. The character of real reality can be determined by logic alone, since there is only one sort of possible reality that is not self-contradictory. This is called the 'Absolute Idea'. Of this he gives the following definition: '*The Absolute Idea*. The idea, as unity of the subjective and objective Idea, is the notion of the Idea—a notion whose object is the Idea as such, and for which the objective is Idea—an Object which embraces all characteristics in its unity.' I hate to spoil the luminous clarity of this sentence by any commentary, but in fact the same thing would be expressed by saying 'The Absolute Idea is pure thought thinking about pure thought'. Hegel has already proved to his satisfaction that all Reality is thought, from which it follows that thought cannot think about anything but thought, since there is nothing else to think about. Some people might find this a little dull; they might say: 'I like thinking about Cape Horn and the South Pole and Mount Everest and the great nebula in Andromeda; I enjoy contemplating the ages when the earth was cooling while the sea boiled and volcanoes rose and fell between night and morning. I find your precept, that I should fill my mind with the lucubrations of word-spinning professors, intolerably stuffy, and really, if that is your "happy ending", I don't think it was worth while to wade through all the verbiage that led up to it.' And with these words they would say goodbye to philosophy and live happy ever after.

But if we agreed with these people we should be doing Hegel an injustice, which God forbid. For Hegel would point out that, while the Absolute, like Aristotle's God, never thinks about anything but itself, because it knows that all else is illusion, yet we, who are forced to live in the world of phenomena, as slaves of the temporal process, seeing only the parts, and only dimly apprehending the whole in moments of mystic insight, we, illusory products of illusion, are compelled to think as though Cape Horn were self-subsistent and not merely an idea in the Divine Mind. When we think we think about Cape Horn, what happens in Reality is that the Absolute is aware of a Cape-Horny thought. It really does have such a thought, or rather such an aspect of the one thought that it time-lessly thinks and is, and this is the only reality that belongs to Cape Horn. But since we cannot reach such heights, we are doing our best in thinking of it in the ordinary geographical way.

But what, someone may say, has all this to do with politics? At first sight, perhaps, not very much. To Hegel, however, the connection is obvious. It follows from his metaphysic that true liberty consists in obedience to an arbitrary authority, that free speech is an evil, that absolute monarchy is good, that the Prussian State was the best existing at the time when he wrote, that war is good, and that an international organization for the peaceful settlement of disputes would be a misfortune.

It is just possible that some among my readers may not see at once how these consequences follow, so I hope I may be pardoned for saying a few words about the intermediate steps.

Although time is unreal, the series of appearances which constitutes history has a curious relation to Reality. Hegel discovered the nature of Reality by a purely logical process called the 'dialectic', which consists of discovering contradictions in abstract ideas and correcting them by making them less abstract. Each of these abstract ideas is conceived as a stage in the development of 'The Idea', the last stage being the 'Absolute Idea'.

Oddly enough, for some reason which Hegel never divulged, the temporal process of history repeats the logical development of the dialectic. It might be thought, since the metaphysic professes to apply to all Reality, that the temporal process which parallels it would be cosmic, but not a bit of it: it is purely terrestrial, confined to recorded history, and (incredible as this may seem) to the history that Hegel happened to know. Different nations, at different times, have embodied the stages of the Idea that the dialectic had reached at those times. Of China, Hegel knew only that it *was*, therefore China illustrated the category of mere Being. Of India he knew only that Buddhists believed in Nirvana, therefore India illustrated the category of Nothing. The Greeks and Romans got rather further along the list of categories, but all the late stages have been left to the Germans, who, since the time of the fall of Rome, have been the sole standard-bearers of the Idea, and had already in 1830 very nearly realized the Absolute Idea.

To anyone who still cherishes the hope that man is a more or less rational animal, the success of this farrago of nonsense must be astonishing. In his own day, his system was accepted by almost all academically educated young Germans, which is perhaps explicable by the fact that it flattered German self-esteem. What is more surprising is its success outside Germany. When I was young, most teachers of philosophy in British and American universities were Hegelians, so that, until I read Hegel, I supposed there must be some truth in his system; I was cured, however, by discovering that everything he said on the philosophy of mathematics was plain nonsense.

Most curious of all was his effect on Marx, who took over some of his most fanciful tenets, more particularly the belief that history develops according to a logical plan, and is concerned, like the purely abstract dialectic, to find ways of avoiding self-contradiction. Over a large part of the earth's surface you will be liquidated if you question this dogma, and eminent Western men of science, who sympathize politically with Russia, show their sympathy by using the word 'contradiction' in ways that no self-respecting logician can approve.

In tracing a connection between the politics and the metaphysics of a man like Hegel, we must content ourselves with certain very general features of his practical programme. That Hegel glorified Prussia was something of an accident; in his earlier years he ardently admired Napoleon and only became a German patriot when he became an employee of the Prussian State. Even in the latest form of his Philosophy of History, he still mentions Alexander, Caesar, and Napoleon as men great enough to have a right to consider themselves exempt from the obligations of the moral law. What his philosophy constrained him to admire was not Germany as against France, but order, system, regulation and intensity of governmental control. His deification of the State would have been just as shocking if the State concerned had been Napoleon's despotism. In his own opinion, he knew what the world needed, though most men did not; a strong government might compel men to act for the best, which democracy could never do. Heraclitus, to whom Hegel was deeply indebted says: 'Every beast is driven to the pasture with blows'. Let us, in any case, make sure of the blows; whether they lead to a pasture is a matter of minor importance—except, of course, to the 'beasts'.

It is obvious that an autocratic system, such as that advocated by Hegel or by Marx's present-day disciples, is only theoretically justifiable on a basis of unquestioned dogma. If you know for certain what is the purpose of the universe in relation to human life, what is going to happen, and what is good for people even if they do not think so; if you can say, as Hegel does, that his theory of history is 'a result which happens to be known to *me*, because I have traversed the entire field'—then you will feel that no degree of coercion is too great, provided it leads to the goal.

The only philosophy that affords a theoretical justification of democracy, and that accords with democracy in its temper of mind, is empiricism. Locke, who may be regarded, so far as the modern world is concerned, as the founder of empiricism, makes it clear how closely this is connected with his views on liberty and toleration, and with his opposition to absolute monarchy. He is never tired of emphasizing the uncertainty of most of our knowledge, not with a sceptical intention such as Hume's, but with the intention of making men aware that they *may* be mistaken, and that they should take account of this possibility in all their dealings with men of opinions different from their own. He had seen the evils wrought, both by the 'enthusiasm' of the sectaries and by the dogma of the divine right of kings; to both he opposed a piecemeal and patchwork political doctrine, to be tested at each point by its success in practice.

What may be called, in a broad sense, the Liberal theory of politics is a recurrent product of commerce. The first known example of it was in the Ionian cities of Asia Minor, which lived by trading with Egypt and Lydia. When Athens, in the time of Pericles, became commercial, the Athenians became Liberal. After a long eclipse, Liberal ideas revived in the Lombard cities of the Middle Ages, and prevailed in Italy until they were extinguished by the Spaniards in the sixteenth century. But the Spaniards failed to reconquer Holland or to subdue England, and it was these countries that were the champions of Liberalism and the leaders in commerce in the seventeenth century. In our day the leadership has passed to the United States.

The reasons for the connection of commerce with Liberalism are obvious. Trade brings men into contact with tribal customs different from their own, and in so doing destroys the dogmatism of the untravelled. The relation of buyer and seller is one of negotiation between two parties who are both free; it is most profitable when the buyer or seller is able to understand the point of view of the other party. There is, of course, imperialistic commerce, where men are forced to buy at the point of the sword; but this is not the kind that generates Liberal philosophies, which have flourished best in trading cities that have wealth without much military strength. In the present day, the nearest analogue to the commercial cities of antiquity and the Middle Ages is to be found in small countries such as Switzerland, Holland, and Scandinavia.

The Liberal creed, in practice, is one of live-and-let-live, of toleration and freedom so far as public order permits, of moderation and absence of fanaticism in political programmes. Even democracy, when it becomes fanatical, as it did among Rousseau's disciples in the French Revolution, ceases to be Liberal; indeed, a fanatical belief in democracy makes democratic institutions impossible, as appeared in England under Cromwell and in France under Robespierre. The genuine Liberal does not say 'this is true', he says 'I am inclined to think that under present circumstances this opinion is probably the best'. And it is only in this limited and undogmatic sense that he will advocate democracy.

What has theoretical philosophy to say that is relevant to the validity or otherwise of the Liberal outlook?

The essence of the Liberal outlook lies not in *what* opinions are held, but in *how* they are held: instead of being held dogmatically, they are held tentatively, and with a consciousness that new evidence may at any moment lead to their abandonment. This is the way in which opinions are held in science, as opposed to the way in which they are held in theology. The decisions of the Council of Nicaea are still authoritative, but in science fourth-century opinions no longer carry any weight. In the USSR the dicta of Marx on dialectical materialism are so unquestioned that they help to determine the views of geneticists on how to obtain the best breed of wheat,[1] though elsewhere it is thought that experiment is the right way to study such problems. Science is empirical, tentative, and undogmatic; all immutable dogma is unscientific. The scientific outlook, accordingly, is the intellectual counterpart of what is, in the practical sphere, the outlook of Liberalism.

Locke, who first developed in detail the empiricist theory of knowledge, preached also religious toleration, representative institutions, and the limitation of governmental power by the system of checks and balances. Few of his doctrines were new, but he developed them in a weighty manner at just the moment when the English government was prepared to accept them. Like the other men of 1688, he was only reluctantly a rebel, and he disliked anarchy as much as he disliked despotism. Both in intellectual and in practical matters he stood for order without authority; this might be taken as the motto both of science and of Liberalism. It depends, clearly, upon consent or assent. In the intellectual world it involves standards of evidence which, after adequate discussion, will lead to a measure of agreement among experts. In the practical world it involves submission to the majority after all parties have had an opportunity to state their case.

In both respects his moment was a fortunate one. The great controversy between the Ptolemaic and Copernican systems had been decided, and scientific questions could no longer be settled by an appeal to Aristotle. Newton's triumphs seemed to justify boundless scientific optimism.

In the practical world, a century and a half of wars of religion had produced hardly any change in the balance of power as between Protestants and Catholics. Enlightened men had begun to view theological controversies as an absurdity, caricatured in Swift's war between the Big-endians and the Little-endians. The extreme Protestant sects, by relying upon the inner light, had made what professed to be Revelation into an anarchic force. Delightful enterprises, scientific and commercial, invited energetic men to turn aside from barren disputation. Fortunately they accepted the invitation, and two centuries of unexampled progress resulted.

We are now again in an epoch of wars of religion, but a religion is now called an 'ideology'. At the moment, the Liberal philosophy is felt by many to be too tame and middle-aged: the idealistic young look for something with more bite in it, something which has a definite answer to all their questions, which calls for missionary activity and gives hope of a millennium brought about by conquest. In short, we have been plunging into a renewed age of faith. Unfortunately the atomic bomb is a swifter exterminator than the stake, and cannot safely be allowed so long a run. We must hope that a more rational outlook can be made to prevail, for

[1] See *The New Genetics in the Soviet Union*, by Hudson and Richens. School of Agriculture, Cambridge, 1946.

only through a revival of Liberal tentativeness and tolerance can our world survive.

The empiricist's theory of knowledge—to which, with some reservations, I adhere—is half way between dogma and scepticism. Almost all knowledge, it holds, is in some degree doubtful, though the doubt, if any, is negligible as regards pure mathematics and facts of present sense-perception. The doubtfulness of what passes for knowledge is a matter of degree; having recently read a book on the Anglo-Saxon invasion of Britain, I am now convinced of the existence of Hengist, but very doubtful about Horsa. Einstein's general theory of relativity is probably broadly speaking true, but when it comes to calculating the circumference of the universe we may be pardoned for expecting later investigations to give a somewhat different result. The modern theory of the atom has pragmatic truth, since it enables us to construct atomic bombs: its consequences are what instrumentalists facetiously call 'satisfactory'. But it is not improbable that some quite different theory may in time be found to give a better explanation of the observed facts. Scientific theories are accepted as useful hypotheses to suggest further research, and as having some element of truth in virtue of which they are able to colligate existing observations; but no sensible person regards them as immutably perfect.

In the sphere of practical politics, this intellectual attitude has important consequences. In the first place, it is not worth while to inflict a comparatively certain present evil for the sake of a comparatively doubtful future good. If the theology of former times was entirely correct, it was worth while burning a number of people at the stake in order that the survivors might go to heaven, but if it was doubtful whether heretics would go to hell, the argument for persecution was not valid. If it is certain that Marx's eschatology is true, and that as soon as private capitalism has been abolished we shall all be happy ever after, then it is right to pursue this end by means of dictatorships, concentration camps, and world wars; but if the end is doubtful or the means not sure to achieve it, present misery becomes an irresistible argument against such drastic methods. If it were certain that without Jews the world would be a paradise, there could be no valid objection to Auschwitz; but if it is much more probable that the world resulting from such methods would be a hell, we can allow free play to our natural humanitarian revulsion against cruelty.

Since, broadly speaking, the distant consequences of actions are more uncertain than the immediate consequences, it is seldom justifiable to embark on any policy on the ground that, though harmful in the present, it will be beneficial in the long run. This principle, like all others held by empiricists, must not be held absolutely; there are cases where the future consequences of one policy are fairly certain and very unpleasant, while the present consequences of the other, though not agreeable, are easily endurable. This applies, for instance, to saving food for the winter, investing capital in machinery, and so on. But even in such cases uncertainty should not be lost sight of. During a boom there is much investment that turns out to have been unprofitable, and modern economists recognize that the habit of investing rather than consuming may easily be carried too far.

It is commonly urged that, in a war between Liberals and fanatics, the fanatics are sure to win, owing to their more unshakable belief in the righteousness of their cause. This belief dies hard, although all history, including that of the last few years, is against it. Fanatics have failed, over and over again, because they have attempted the impossible, or because, even when what they aimed at was possible, they were too unscientific to adopt the right means; they have failed also because they roused the hostility of those whom they wished to coerce. In every important war since 1700 the more democratic side has been victorious. This is partly because democracy and empiricism (which are intimately interconnected) do not demand a distortion of facts in the interests of theory. Russia and Canada, which have somewhat similar climatic conditions, are both interested in obtaining better breeds of wheat; in Canada this aim is pursued experimentally, in Russia by interpreting the Marxist Scriptures.

Systems of dogma without empirical foundation, such as those of scholastic theology, Marxism, and Fascism, have the advantage of producing a great degree of social coherence among their disciples. But they have the disadvantage of involving persecution of valuable sections of the population. Spain was ruined by the expulsion of the Jews and Moors; France suffered by the emigration of Huguenots after the Revocation of the Edict of Nantes; Germany would probably have been first in the field with the atomic bomb but for Hitler's hatred of Jews. And, to repeat, dogmatic systems have the two further disadvantages of involving false beliefs on practically important matters of fact, and of rousing violent hostility in those who do not share the fanaticism in question. For these various reasons, it is not to be expected that, in the long run, nations addicted to a dogmatic philosophy will have the advantage over those of a more empirical temper. Nor is it true that dogma is necessary for social coherence when social coherence is called for; no nation could have shown more of it than the British showed in 1940.

Empiricism, finally, is to be commended not only on the ground of its greater truth, but also on ethical grounds. Dogma demands authority, rather than intelligent thought, as the source of opinion; it requires persecution of heretics and hostility to unbelievers; it asks of its disciples that they should inhibit natural kindliness in favour of systematic hatred. Since argument is not recognized as a means of arriving at truth, adherents of rival dogmas have no method except war by means of which to reach a decision. And war, in our scientific age, means, sooner or later, universal death.

I conclude that, in our day as in the time of Locke, empiricist Liberalism (which is not incompatible with *democratic* socialism) is the only philosophy that can be adopted by a man who, on the one hand, demands some scientific evidence for his beliefs, and, on the other hand, desires human happiness more than the prevalence of this or that party or creed. Our confused and difficult world needs various things if it is to escape disaster, and among these one of the most necessary is that, in the nations which still uphold Liberal beliefs, these beliefs should be whole-hearted and profound, not apologetic towards dogmatisms of the right and of the left, but deeply persuaded of the value of liberty, scientific freedom and mutual forbearance. For without these beliefs life on our politically divided but technically unified planet will hardly continue to be possible.

(Cambridge, National Book League, 1947. Subsequently reprinted in *Unpopular Essays*; London: Allen & Unwin; New York: Simon & Schuster, 1950.)

51

POLITICALLY IMPORTANT DESIRES

I WILL begin the discussion of political theory with this subject because I think that most current discussions of politics and political theory take insufficient account of psychology. Economic facts, population statistics, constitutional organization, and so on, are set forth minutely. There is no difficulty in finding out how many South Koreans and how many North Koreans there were when the Korean War began. If you will look into the right books you will be able to ascertain what was their average income per head, and what were the sizes of their respective armies. But if you want to know what sort of person a Korean is, and whether there is any appreciable difference between a North Korean and a South Korean; if you wish to know what they respectively want out of life, what are their discontents, what their hopes and what their fears; in a word what it is that, as they say, 'makes them tick', you will look through the reference books in vain. And so you cannot tell whether the South Koreans are enthusiastic about UNO, or would prefer union with their cousins in the North. Nor can you guess whether they are willing to forgo land reform for the privilege of voting for some politician they have never heard of. It is neglect of such questions by the eminent men who sit in remote capitals, that so frequently causes disappointment. If politics is to become scientific, and if the event is not to be constantly surprising, it is imperative that our political thinking should penetrate more deeply into the springs of human action. What is the influence of hunger upon slogans? How does their effectiveness fluctuate with the number of calories in your diet? If one man offers you democracy and another offers you a bag of grain, at what stage of starvation will you prefer the grain to the vote? Such questions are far too little considered. However, let us, for the present, forget the Koreans and consider the human race.

All human activity is prompted by desire or impulse. There is a wholly fallacious theory advanced by some earnest moralists to the effect that it is possible to resist desire in the interests of duty and moral principle. I say this is fallacious, not because no man ever acts from a sense of duty, but because duty has no hold on him unless he desires to be dutiful. If you wish to know what men will do, you must know not only, or principally, their material circumstances, but rather the whole system of their desires with their relative strengths.

There are some desires which, though very powerful, have not, as a rule, any great *political* importance. Most men at some period of their lives desire to marry, but as a rule they can satisfy this desire without having to take any political action. There are, of course, exceptions; the rape of the Sabine women is a case in point. And the development of Northern Australia is seriously impeded by the fact that the vigorous young men who ought to do the work dislike being wholly deprived of female society. But such cases are unusual, and in general the interest that men and women take in each other has little influence upon politics.

The desires that are politically important may be divided into a primary and a secondary group. In the primary group come the necessities of life: food and shelter and clothing. When these things become very scarce, there is no limit to the efforts that men will make, or to the violence that they will display, in the hope of securing them. It is said by students of the earliest history that, on four separate occasions, drought in Arabia caused the population of that country to overflow into surrounding regions, with immense effects political, cultural and religious. The last of these four occasions was the rise of Islam. The gradual spread of Germanic tribes from Southern Russia to England, and thence to San Francisco, had similar motives. Undoubtedly the desire for food has been, and still is, one of the main causes of great political events.

But man differs from other animals in one very important respect, and that is that he has some desires which are, so to speak, infinite, which can never be fully gratified, and which would keep him restless even in Paradise. The boa constrictor, when he has had an adequate meal, goes to sleep, and does not wake until he needs another meal. Human beings, for the most part, are not like this. When the Arabs, who had been used to living sparingly on a few dates, acquired the riches of the Eastern Roman Empire, and dwelt in palaces of almost unbelievable luxury, they did not, on that account, become inactive. Hunger could no longer be a motive, for Greek slaves supplied them with exquisite viands at the slightest nod. But other desires kept them active: four in particular, which we can label acquisitiveness, rivalry, vanity, and love of power.

Acquisitiveness—the wish to possess as much as possible of goods, or the title to goods—is a motive which, I suppose, has its origin in a combination of fear with the desire for necessaries. I once befriended two little girls from Esthonia, who had narrowly escaped death from starvation in a famine. They lived in my family, and of course had plenty to eat. But they spent all their leisure visiting neighbouring farms and stealing potatoes, which they hoarded. Rockefeller, who in his infancy had experienced great poverty, spent his adult life in a similar manner. Similarly the Arab chieftains on their silken Byzantine divans could not forget the desert, and hoarded riches far beyond any possible physical need. But whatever may be the psycho-analysis of acquisitiveness, no one can deny that it is one of the great motives—especially among the more powerful, for, as I said before, it is one of the infinite motives. However much you may acquire, you will always wish to acquire more; satiety is a dream which will always elude you.

But acquisitiveness, although it is the mainspring of the capitalist system, is by no means the most powerful of the motives that survive the conquest of hunger. Rivalry is a much stronger motive. Over and over again in Mohammedan history, dynasties have come to grief because the sons of a sultan by different mothers could not agree, and in the resulting civil war universal ruin resulted. The same sort of thing happens in modern Europe. When the British Government very unwisely allowed the Kaiser to be present at a naval review at Spithead, the thought which arose in his mind was not the one which we had intended. What he thought was: 'I must have a Navy as good as Grandmamma's'. And from this thought have sprung all our subsequent troubles. The world would be a happier place than it is if acquisitiveness were always stronger than rivalry. But in fact, a great many men will cheerfully face impoverishment if they can thereby secure complete ruin for their rivals. Hence the present level of taxation.

Vanity is a motive of immense potency. Anyone who has much to do with children knows how they are constantly performing some antic, and saying 'Look at me'. 'Look at me' is one of the most fundamental desires of the human heart. It can take innumerable forms, from buffoonery to the pursuit of posthumous fame. There was a Renaissance Italian princeling who was asked by the priest on his deathbed if he had anything to repent of. 'Yes', he said. 'There is one thing. On one occasion I had a visit from the Emperor and the Pope simultaneously. I took them to the top of my tower to see the view, and I neglected the opportunity to throw them both down, which would have given me immortal fame.' History does not relate whether the priest gave him absolution. One of the troubles about vanity is that it grows with what it feeds on. The more you are talked about, the more you will wish to be talked about. The condemned murderer who is allowed to see the account of his trial in the Press is indignant if he finds a newspaper which has reported it inadequately. And the more he finds about himself in other newspapers, the more indignant he will be with the one whose reports are meagre. Politicians and literary men are in the same case. And the more famous they become, the more difficult the press cutting agency finds it to satisfy them. It is scarcely possible to exaggerate the influence of vanity throughout the range of human life, from the child of three to the potentate at whose frown the world trembles.

Mankind have even committed the impiety of attributing similar desires to the Deity, whom they imagine avid for continual praise.

But great as is the influence of the motives we have been considering, there is one which outweighs them all. I mean the love of power. Love of power is closely akin to vanity, but it is not by any means the same thing. What vanity needs for its satisfaction is glory, and it is easy to have glory without power. The people who enjoy the greatest glory in the United States are film stars, but they can be put in their place by the Committee for Un-American Activities, which enjoys no glory whatever. In England, the King has more glory than the Prime Minister, but the Prime Minister has more power than the King. Many people prefer glory to power, but on the whole these people have less effect upon the course of events than those who prefer power to glory. When Blücher, in 1814, saw Napoleon's palaces, he said: 'Wasn't he a fool to have all this and to go running after Moscow.' Napoleon, who certainly was not destitute of vanity, preferred power when he had to choose. To Blücher, this choice seemed foolish. Power, like vanity, is insatiable. Nothing short of omnipotence could satisfy it completely. And as it is especially the vice of energetic men, the causal efficacy of love of power is out of all proportion to its frequency. It is, indeed, by far the strongest motive in the lives of important men.

Love of power is greatly increased by the experience of power, and this applies to petty power as well as to that of potentates. In the happy days before 1914, when well-to-do ladies could acquire a host of servants, their pleasure in exercising power over the domestics steadily increased with age. Similarly, in any autocratic régime, the holders of power become increasingly tyrannical with experience of the delights that power can afford. Since power over human beings is shown in making them do what they would rather not do, the man who is actuated by love of power is more apt to inflict pain than to permit pleasure. If you ask your boss for leave of absence from the office on some legitimate occasion, his love of power will derive more satisfaction from a refusal than from a consent. If you require a building permit, the petty official concerned will obviously get more pleasure from saying 'No' than from saying 'Yes'. It is this sort of thing which makes the love of power such a dangerous motive.

But it has other sides which are more desirable. The pursuit of know-ledge is, I think, mainly actuated by love of power. And so are all advances in scientific technique. In politics, also, a reformer may have just as strong a love of power as a despot. It would be a complete mistake to decry love of power altogether as a motive. Whether you will be led by this motive to actions which are useful, or to actions which are pernicious, depends upon the social system, and upon your capacities. If your capacities are theoretical or technical, you will contribute to knowledge or technique, and, as a rule, your activity will be useful. If you are a politician you *may* be actuated by love of power, but as a rule this motive will join itself on to the desire to see some state of affairs realized which, for some reason, you prefer to the *status quo*. A great general may, like Alcibiades, be quite indifferent as to which side he fights on, but most generals have preferred to fight for their own country, and have, therefore, had other motives besides love of power. The politician may change sides so frequently as to find himself always in the majority, but most politicians have a preference for one party to the other, and subordinate their love of power to this preference. Love of power as nearly pure as possible is to be seen in various different types of men. One type is the soldier of fortune, of whom Napoleon is the supreme example. Napoleon had, I think, no ideological preference for France over Corsica, but if he had become Emperor of Corsica he would not have been so great a man as he became by pretending to be a Frenchman. Such men, however, are not quite pure examples, since they also derive immense satisfaction from vanity. The purest type is that of the *Eminence Grise*—the power behind the throne that never appears in public, and merely hugs itself with the secret thought: 'How little these puppets know who is pulling the strings'. Baron Holstein, who controlled the foreign policy of the German Empire from 1890 to 1906, illustrates this type to perfection. He lived in a slum; he never appeared in society; he avoided meeting the Emperor, except on one single occasion when the Emperor's importunity could not be resisted; he refused all invitations to Court functions, on the ground that he possessed no court dress. He had acquired secrets which enabled him to blackmail the Chancellor and many of the Kaiser's intimates. He used the power of blackmail, not to acquire wealth, or fame, or any other obvious advantage, but merely to compel the adoption of the foreign policy he preferred. In the East, similar characters were not very uncommon among eunuchs.

I come now to other motives which, though in a sense less fundamental than those we have been considering, are still of considerable importance. The first of these is love of excitement. Human beings show their superiority to the brutes by their capacity for boredom, though I have sometimes thought, in examining the apes at the Zoo, that they, perhaps, have the rudiments of this tiresome emotion. However that may be, experience shows that escape from boredom is one of the really powerful desires of almost all human beings. When white men first effect contact with some unspoilt race of savages, they offer them all kinds of benefits, from the light of the Gospel to pumpkin pie. These, however, much as we may regret it, most savages receive with indifference. What they really value among the gifts that we bring to them is intoxicating liquor, which enables them, for the first time in their lives, to have the illusion, for a few brief moments, that it is better to be alive than dead. Red Indians, while they were still unaffected by white men, would smoke their pipes, not calmly as we do, but orgiastically, inhaling so deeply that they sank into a faint. And when excitement by means of nicotine failed, a patriotic orator would stir them up to attack a neighbouring tribe, which would give them all the enjoyment that we (according to our temperament) derive from a horse race or a General Election. The pleasure of gambling consists almost entirely in excitement. Monsieur Huc describes Chinese traders at the Great Wall in winter, gambling until they have lost all their cash, then proceeding to lose all their merchandise, and at last gambling away their clothes and going out naked to die of cold. With civilized men, as with primitive Red Indian tribes, it is, I think, chiefly love of excitement which makes the populace applaud when war breaks out; the emotion is exactly the same as at a football match, although the results are sometimes somewhat more serious.

It is not altogether easy to decide what is the root cause of the love of excitement. I incline to think that our mental make-up is adapted to the stage when men lived by hunting. When a man spent a long day with very primitive weapons in stalking a deer with the hope of dinner, and when, at the end of the day, he dragged the carcase triumphantly to his cave, he sank down in contented weariness, while his wife dressed and cooked the meat. He was sleepy, and his bones ached, and the smell of cooking filled every nook and cranny of his consciousness. At last, after eating, he sank into deep sleep. In such a life there was neither time nor energy for boredom. But when he took to agriculture, and made his wife do all the heavy work in the fields, he had time to reflect upon the vanity of human life, to invent mythologies and systems of philosophy, and to dream of the life hereafter in which he would perpetually hunt the wild boar of Valhalla. Our mental make-up is suited to a life of very severe physical labour. I used, when I was younger, to take my holidays walking. I would cover twenty-five miles a day, and when the evening came I had no need of anything to keep me from boredom, since the delight of sitting amply sufficed. But modern life cannot be conducted on these physically strenuous principles. A great deal of work is sedentary, and most manual work exercises only a few specialized muscles. When crowds assemble in Trafalgar Square to cheer to the echo an announcement that the government has decided to have them killed, they would not do so if they had all walked twenty-five miles that day. This cure for bellicosity is, however, impracticable, and if the human race is to survive—a thing which is, perhaps, undesirable—other means must be found for securing an innocent outlet for the unused physical energy that produces love of excitement. This is a matter which has been too little considered, both by moralists and by social reformers. The social reformers are of the opinion that they have more serious things to consider. The moralists, on the other hand, are immensely impressed with the seriousness of all the permitted outlets of the love of excitement; the seriousness, however, in their minds, is that of Sin. Dance halls, cinemas, this age of jazz, are all, if we may believe our ears, gateways to Hell, and we should be better employed sitting at home contemplating our sins. I find myself unable to be in entire agreement with the grave men who utter these warnings. The devil has many forms, some designed to deceive the young, some designed to deceive the old and serious. If it is the devil that tempts the young to enjoy themselves, is it not, perhaps, the same personage that persuades the old to condemn their enjoyment? And is not condemnation perhaps merely a form of excitement appropriate to old age? And is it not, perhaps, a drug which—like opium—has to be taken in continually stronger doses to produce the desired effect? Is it not to be feared that, beginning with the wickedness of the cinema, we should be led step by step to condemn the opposite political party, dagoes, wops, Asiatics, and, in short, everybody except the fellow members of our club? And it is from just such condemnations, when widespread, that wars proceed. I have never heard of a war that proceeded from dance halls.

What is serious about excitement is that so many of its forms are destructive. It is destructive in those who cannot resist excess in alcohol or gambling. It is destructive when it takes the form of mob violence. And above all it is destructive when it leads to war. It is so deep a need that it will find harmful outlets of this kind unless innocent outlets are at hand. There are such innocent outlets at present in sport, and in politics so long as it is kept within constitutional bounds. But these are not sufficient, especially as the kind of politics that is most exciting is also the kind that does most harm. Civilized life has grown altogether too tame, and, if it is to be stable, it must provide harmless outlets for the impulses which our remote ancestors satisfied in hunting. In Australia, where people are few and rabbits are many, I watched a whole populace satisfying the primitive impulse in the primitive manner by the skilful slaughter of many thousands of rabbits. But in London or New York, where people are many and rabbits are few, some other means must be found to gratify primitive impulse. I think every big town should contain artificial water falls that people could descend in very fragile canoes, and they should contain bathing-pools full of mechanical sharks. Any person found advocating a preventive war should be condemned to two hours a day with these ingenious monsters. More seriously, pains should be taken to provide constructive outlets for the love of excitement. Nothing in the world is more exciting than a moment of sudden discovery or invention, and many more people are capable of experiencing such moments than is sometimes thought.

Interwoven with many other political motives are two closely related passions to which human beings are regrettably prone: I mean fear and hate. It is normal to hate what we fear, and it happens frequently, though not always, that we fear what we hate. I think it may be taken as the rule among primitive men, that they both fear and hate whatever is unfamiliar. They have their own herd, originally a very small one. And within one herd, all are friends, unless there is some special ground of enmity. Other herds are potential or actual enemies; a single member of one of them who strays by accident will be killed. An alien herd as a whole will be avoided or fought according to circumstances. It is this primitive mechanism which still controls our instinctive reaction to foreign nations. The completely untravelled person will view all foreigners as the savage regards a member of another herd. But the man who has travelled, or who has studied international politics, will have discovered that, if his herd is to prosper, it must, to some degree, become amalgamated with other herds. If you are English and someone says to you: 'The French are your brothers', your first instinctive feeling will be: 'Nonsense, they shrug their shoulders, and talk French. And I am even told that they eat frogs'. If he explains to you that we may have to fight the Russians, that, if so, it will be desirable to defend the line of the Rhine, and that, if the line of the Rhine is to be defended, the help of the French is essential, you will begin to see what he means when he says that the French are your brothers. But if some fellow-traveller were to go on to say that the Russians also are your brothers, he would be unable to persuade you, unless he could show that we are in danger from the Martians. We love those who hate our enemies, and if we had no enemies there would be very few people whom we should love.

All this, however, is only true so long as we are concerned solely with attitudes towards other human beings. You might regard the soil as your enemy because it yields reluctantly a niggardly subsistence. You might regard Mother Nature in general as your enemy, and envisage human life as a struggle to get the better of Mother Nature. If men viewed life in this way, co-operation of the whole human race would become easy. And men could easily be brought to view life in this way if schools, newspapers, and politicians devoted themselves to this end. But schools are out to teach patriotism; newspapers are out to stir up excitement; and politicians are out to get re-elected. None of the three, therefore, can do anything towards saving the human race from reciprocal suicide.

There are two ways of coping with fear: one is to diminish the external danger, and the other is to cultivate stoic endurance. The latter can be reinforced, except where immediate action is necessary, by turning our thoughts away from the cause of fear. The conquest of fear is of very great importance. Fear is in itself degrading; it easily becomes an obsession; it produces hate of that which is feared, and it leads headlong to excesses of cruelty. Nothing has so beneficent an effect on human beings as security. If an international system could be established which would remove the fear of war, the improvement in the everyday mentality of everyday people would be enormous and very rapid. Fear, at present, overshadows the world. The atom bomb and the bacterial bomb, wielded by the wicked communist or the wicked capitalist as the case may be, makes Washington and the Kremlin tremble, and drives men further and further along the road towards the abyss. If matters are to improve, the first and essential step is to find a way of diminishing fear. The world at present is obsessed by the conflict of rival ideologies, and one of the apparent causes of conflict is the desire for the victory of our own ideology and the defeat of the other. I do not think that the fundamental motive here has much to do with ideologies. I think the ideologies are merely a way of grouping people, and that the passions involved are merely those which always arise between rival groups. There are, of course, various reasons for hating Communists. First and foremost, we believe that they wish to take away our property. But so do burglars, and although we disapprove of burglars, our attitude towards them is very different indeed from our attitude towards Communists—chiefly because they do not inspire the same degree of fear. Secondly, we hate the Communists because they are irreligious. But the Chinese have been irreligious since the eleventh century, and we only began to hate them when they turned out Chiang Kai-shek. Thirdly, we hate the Communists because they do not believe in democracy, but we consider this no reason for hating Franco. Fourthly, we hate them because they do not allow liberty; this we feel so strongly that we have decided to imitate them. It is obvious that none of these are the real grounds for our hatred. We hate them because we fear them and they threaten us. If the Russians still adhered to the Greek Orthodox religion, if they had instituted parliamentary government, and if they had a completely free press which daily vituperated us, then—provided they still had armed forces as powerful as they have now—we should still hate them if they gave us ground for thinking them hostile. There is, of course, the *odium theologicum*, and it can be a cause of enmity. But I think that this is an offshoot of herd feeling: the man who has a different theology feels strange, and whatever is strange must be dangerous. Ideologies, in fact, are one of the methods by which herds are created, and the psychology is much the same however the herd may have been generated.

You may have been feeling that I have allowed only for bad motives, or, at best, such as are ethically neutral. I am afraid they are, as a rule, more powerful than more altruistic motives, but I do not deny that altruistic motives exist, and may, on occasion, be effective. The agitation against slavery in England in the early nineteenth century was indubitably altruistic, and was thoroughly effective. Its altruism was proved by the fact that in 1833 British taxpayers paid many millions in compensation to Jamaican landowners for the liberation of their slaves, and also by the fact that at the Congress of Vienna the British Government was prepared to make important concessions with a view to inducing other nations to abandon the slave trade. This is an instance from the past, but present day America has afforded instances equally remarkable. I will not, however, go into these, as I do not wish to become embarked in current controversies.

I do not think it can be questioned that sympathy is a genuine motive, and that some people at some times are made somewhat uncomfortable by the sufferings of some other people. It is sympathy that has produced the many humanitarian advances of the last hundred years. We are shocked when we hear stories of the ill-treatment of lunatics, and there are now quite a number of asylums in which they are not ill-treated. Prisoners in Western countries are not supposed to be tortured, and when they are, there is an outcry if the facts are discovered. We do not approve of treating orphans as they are treated in *Oliver Twist*. Protestant countries disapprove of cruelty to animals. In all these ways sympathy has been politically effective. If the fear of war were removed, its effectiveness would become much greater. Perhaps the best hope for the future of mankind is that ways will be found of increasing the scope and intensity of sympathy.

To sum up our discussion: Politics is concerned with herds rather than with individuals, and the passions which are important in politics are, therefore, those in which the various members of a given herd can feel alike. The broad instinctive mechanism upon which political edifices have to be built is one of co-operation within the herd and hostility towards other herds. The co-operation within the herd is never perfect. There are members who do not conform, who are, in the etymological sense, 'egregious', that is to say, outside the flock. These members are those who have fallen below, or risen above, the ordinary level. They are: idiots, criminals, prophets, and discoverers. A wise herd will learn to tolerate the eccentricity of those who rise above the average, and to treat with a minimum of ferocity those who fall below it.

As regards relations to other herds, modern technique has produced a conflict between self-interest and instinct. In old days, when two tribes went to war, one of them exterminated the other, and annexed its territory. From the point of view of the victor, the whole operation was thoroughly satisfactory. The killing was not at all expensive, and the excitement was agreeable. It is not to be wondered at that, in such circumstances, war persisted. Unfortunately we still have the emotions appropriate to such primitive warfare, while the actual operations of war have changed completely. Killing an enemy in a modern war is a very expensive operation. If you consider how many Germans were killed in the late war, and how much the victors are paying in income tax, you can, by a sum in long division, discover the cost of a dead German, and you will find it considerable. In the East, it is true, the enemies of the Germans have secured the ancient advantages of turning out the defeated population and occupying their lands. The Western victors, however, have secured no such advantages. It is obvious that modern war is not good business from a financial point of view. Although we won both the world wars, we should now be much richer if they had not occurred. If men were actuated by self-interest, which they are not—except in the case of a few saints—the whole human race would co-operate. There would be no more wars, no more armies, no more navies, no more atom bombs. There would not be armies of propagandists employed in poisoning the minds of Nation A against Nation B, and reciprocally of Nation B against Nation A. There would not be armies of officials at frontiers to prevent the entry of foreign books and foreign ideas, however excellent in themselves. There would not be customs barriers to ensure the existence of many small enterprises where one big enterprise would be more economic. All this would happen very quickly if men desired their own happiness as ardently as they desire the misery of their neighbours. But, you will tell me, what is the use of these Utopian dreams? Moralists will see to it that we do not become wholly selfish, and until we do the millennium will be impossible.

I do not wish to seem to end upon a note of cynicism. I do not deny that there are better things than selfishness, and that some people achieve these things. I maintain, however, on the one hand, that there are few occasions upon which large bodies of men, such as politics is concerned with, can rise above selfishness, while, on the other hand, there are a very great many circumstances in which populations will fall below selfishness, if selfishness is interpreted as enlightened self-interest.

And among those occasions on which people fall below self-interest are most of the occasions on which they are convinced that they are acting from idealistic motives. Much that passes as idealism is disguised hatred or disguised love of power. When you see large masses of men swayed by what appear to be noble motives, it is as well to look below the surface and ask yourself what it is that makes these motives effective. It is partly because it is so easy to be taken in by a façade of nobility that a psychological inquiry, such as I have been attempting, is worth making. I would say, in conclusion, that if what I have said is right, the main thing needed to make the world happy is intelligence. And this, after all, is an optimistic conclusion, because intelligence is a thing that can be fostered by known methods of education.

(The Nobel Prize Acceptance Speech. Subsequently reprinted in *Human Society in Ethics and Politics*, London: Allen & Unwin, 1954; New York: Simon & Schuster, 1955.)

52

WHY I AM NOT A COMMUNIST[1]

IN relation to any political doctrine there are two questions to be asked: (1) Are its theoretical tenets true? (2) Is its practical policy likely to increase human happiness? For my part, I think the theoretical tenets of Communism are false, and I think its practical maxims are such as to produce an immeasurable increase of human misery.

The theoretical doctrines of Communism are for the most part derived from Marx. My objections to Marx are of two sorts: one, that he was muddle-headed; and the other, that his thinking was almost entirely inspired by hatred. The doctrine of surplus value, which is supposed to demonstrate the exploitation of wage-earners under capitalism, is arrived at: (*a*) by surreptitiously accepting Malthus's doctrine of population, which Marx and all his disciples explicitly repudiate; (*b*) by applying Ricardo's theory of value to wages, but not to the prices of manufactured articles. He is entirely satisfied with the result, not because it is in accordance with the facts or because it is logically coherent, but because it is calculated to rouse fury in wage-earners. Marx's doctrine that all historical events have been motivated by class conflicts is a rash and untrue extension to world history of certain features prominent in England and France a hundred years ago. His belief that there is a cosmic force called Dialectical Materialism which governs human history independently of human volitions, is mere mythology. His theoretical errors, however, would not have mattered so much but for the fact that, like Tertullian and Carlyle, his chief desire was to see his enemies punished, and he cared little what happened to his friends in the process.

Marx's doctrine was bad enough, but the developments which it underwent under Lenin and Stalin made it much worse. Marx had taught that there would be a revolutionary transitional period following the victory of the proletariat in a civil war and that during this period the proletariat, in accordance with the usual practice after a civil war, would deprive its vanquished enemies of political power. This period was to be that of the dictatorship of the proletariat. It should not be forgotten that

[1] Originally appeared in the Background Book, *Why I Opposed Communism*, published by Phoenix House, Ltd.

in Marx's prophetic vision the victory of the proletariat was to come after it had grown to be the vast majority of the population. The dictatorship of the proletariat therefore as conceived by Marx was not essentially anti-democratic. In the Russia of 1917, however, the proletariat was a small percentage of the population, the great majority being peasants. It was decreed that the Bolshevik party was the class-conscious part of the proletariat, and that a small committee of its leaders was the class-conscious part of the Bolshevik party. The dictatorship of the proletariat thus came to be the dictatorship of a small committee, and ultimately of one man—Stalin. As the sole class-conscious proletarian, Stalin condemned millions of peasants to death by starvation and millions of others to forced labour in concentration camps. He even went so far as to decree that the laws of heredity are henceforth to be different from what they used to be, and that the germ-plasm is to obey Soviet decrees but not that reactionary priest Mendel. I am completely at a loss to understand how it came about that some people who are both humane and intelligent could find something to admire in the vast slave camp produced by Stalin.

I have always disagreed with Marx. My first hostile criticism of him was published in 1896. But my objections to modern Communism go deeper than my objections to Marx. It is the abandonment of democracy that I find particularly disastrous. A minority resting its powers upon the activities of a secret police is bound to be cruel, oppressive and obscurantist. The dangers of irresponsible power came to be generally recognized during the eighteenth and nineteenth centuries, but those who have been dazzled by the outward success of the Soviet Union have forgotten all that was painfully learnt during the days of absolute monarchy, and have gone back to what was worst in the Middle Ages under the curious delusion that they were in the vanguard of progress.

There are signs that in course of time the Russian régime will become more liberal. But, although this is possible, it is very far from certain. In the meantime, all those who value not only art and science but a sufficiency of daily bread and freedom from the fear that a careless word by their children to a schoolteacher may condemn them to forced labour in a Siberian wilderness, must do what lies in their power to preserve in their own countries a less servile and more prosperous manner of life.

There are those who, oppressed by the evils of Communism, are led to the conclusion that the only effective way to combat these evils is by means of a world war. I think this a mistake. At one time such a policy might have been possible, but now war has become so terrible and Communism has become so powerful that no one can tell what would be left after a world war, and whatever might be left would probably be at least as bad as present-day Communism. This forecast does not depend upon which side, if either, is nominally victorious. It depends only upon the inevitable effects of mass destruction by means of hydrogen and cobalt bombs and perhaps of ingeniously propagated plagues. The way to combat Communism is not war. What is needed in addition to such armaments as will deter Communists from attacking the West, is a diminution of the grounds for discontent in the less prosperous parts of the non-Communist world. In most of the countries of Asia, there is abject poverty which the West ought to alleviate as far as it lies in its power to do so. There is also a great bitterness which was caused by the centuries of European insolent domination in Asia. This ought to be dealt with by a combination of patient tact with dramatic announcements renoucing such relics of white domination as survive in Asia. Communism is a doctrine bred of poverty, hatred and strife. Its spread can only be arrested by diminishing the area of poverty and hatred.

(*Portraits from Memory*, London: Allen & Unwin;
New York: Simon & Schuster, 1956.)

PART XII

The Philosopher in the Field of Economics

Despite the fact that Russell has made no major contribution to economic theory his views on economics have not gone unnoticed. As far back as 1896, when his first hostile criticism of Marx was published, Russell had shown a keen interest in economic problems. He has repeatedly stressed the fact that an exclusively economic point of view is an oversimplification.

Although some of his views have undergone 'repeated changes', as he admits in his preface to this volume, he has at times held steadfast to some of his earlier views. For example, he has always disagreed with Marx's theory of surplus value and his rigid doctrine that all historical events have been motivated by class conflicts. The selections that follow indicate his recognition of the psychological and other factors which bear upon man's activities in the economic as well as other spheres.

53

PROPERTY

AMONG the many gloomy novelists of the realistic school, perhaps the most full of gloom is Gissing. In common with all his characters, he lives under the weight of a great oppression: the power of the fearful and yet adored idol of Money. One of his typical stories is 'Eve's Ransom', where the heroine, with various discreditable subterfuges, throws over the poor man whom she loves in order to marry the rich man whose income she loves still better. The poor man, finding that the rich man's income has given her a fuller life and a better character than the poor man's love could have given her, decides that she has done quite right, and that he deserves to be punished for his lack of money. In this story, as in his other books, Gissing has set forth, quite accurately, the actual dominion of money, and the impersonal worship which it exacts from the great majority of civilized mankind.

Gissing's facts are undeniable, and yet his attitude produces a revolt in any reader who has vital passions and masterful desires. His worship of money is bound up with his consciousness of inward defeat. And in the modern world generally, it is the decay of life which has promoted the religion of material goods; and the religion of material goods, in its turn, has hastened the decay of life on which it thrives. The man who worships money has ceased to hope for happiness through his own efforts or in his own activities: he looks upon happiness as a passive enjoyment of pleasures derived from the outside world. The artist or the lover does not worship money in his moments of ardour, because his desires are specific, and directed towards objects which only he can create. And conversely, the worshipper of money can never achieve greatness as an artist or a lover.

Love of money has been denounced by moralists since the world began. I do not wish to add another to the moral denunciations, of which the efficacy in the past has not been encouraging. I wish to show how the worship of money is both an effect and a cause of diminishing vitality, and how our institutions might be changed so as to make the worship of money grow less and the general vitality grow more. It is not the desire for money as a means to definite ends that is in question. A struggling artist may desire money in order to have leisure for his art, but this desire is finite, and can be satisfied fully by a very modest sum. It is the *worship* of money that I wish to consider: the belief that all values may be measured in terms of money, and that money is the ultimate test of success in life. This belief is held in fact, if not in words, by multitudes of men and women, and yet it is not in harmony with human nature, since it ignores vital needs and the instinctive tendency towards some specific kind of growth. It makes men treat as unimportant those of their desires which run counter to the acquisition of money, and yet such desires are, as a rule, more important to well-being than any increase of income. It leads men to mutilate their own natures from a mistaken theory of what constitutes success, and to give admiration to enterprises which add nothing to human welfare. It promotes a dead uniformity of character and purpose, a diminution in the joy of life, and a stress and strain which leaves whole communities weary, discouraged, and disillusioned.

America, the pioneer of Western progress, is thought by many to display the worship of money in its most perfect form. A well-to-do American, who already has more than enough money to satisfy all reasonable requirements, very often continues to work at his office with an assiduity which would only be pardonable if starvation were the alternative.

But England, except among a small minority, is almost as much given over to the worship of money as America. Love of money in England takes, as a rule, the form of snobbishly desiring to maintain a certain social status, rather than of striving after an indefinite increase of income. Men postpone marriage until they have an income enabling them to have as many rooms and servants in their house as they feel that their dignity requires. This makes it necessary for them while they are young to keep a watch upon their affections, lest they should be led into an imprudence: they acquire a cautious habit of mind, and a fear of 'giving themselves away', which makes a free and vigorous life impossible. In acting as they do they imagine that they are being virtuous, since they would feel it a hardship for a woman to be asked to descend to a lower social status than that of her parents, and a degradation to themselves to marry a woman whose social status was not equal to their own. The things of nature are not valued in comparison with money. It is not thought a hardship for a women to have to accept, as her only experience of love, the prudent and limited attentions of a man whose capacity for emotion has been lost during years of wise restraint or sordid relations with women whom he did not respect. The woman herself does not know that it is a hardship; for she, too, has been taught prudence for fear of a descent in the social scale, and from early youth she has had it instilled into her that strong feeling does not become a young woman. So the two unite to slip through life in ignorance of all that is worth knowing. Their ancestors were not restrained from passion by the fear of hell-fire, but they are restrained effectually by a worse fear, the fear of coming down in the world.

The same motives which lead men to marry late also lead them to limit their families. Professional men wish to send their sons to a public school, though the education they will obtain is no better than at a grammar school, and the companions with whom they will associate are more vicious. But snobdom has decided that public schools are best, and from its verdict there is no appeal. What makes them the best is that they are the most expensive. And the same social struggle, in varying forms, runs through all classes except the very highest and the very lowest. For this purpose men and women make great moral efforts, and show amazing powers of self-control; but all their efforts and all their self-control, being not used for any creative end, serve merely to dry up the well-spring of life within them, to make them feeble, listless, and trivial. It is not in such a soil that the passion which produces genius can be nourished. Men's souls have exchanged the wilderness for the drawing-room: they have become cramped and pretty and deformed, like Chinese women's feet. Even the horrors of war have hardly awakened them from the smug somnambulism of respectability. And it is chiefly the worship of money that has brought about this death-like slumber of all that makes men great.

In France the worship of money takes the form of thrift. It is not easy to make a fortune in France, but an inherited competence is very common, and where it exists the main purpose of life is to hand it on undiminished, if not increased. The French *rentier* is one of the great forces in international politics: it is he through whom France has been strengthened in diplomacy and weakened in war, by increasing the supply of French capital and diminishing the supply of French men. The necessity of providing a *dot* for daughters, and the subdivision of property by the law of inheritance, have made the family more powerful, as an institution, than in any other civilized country. In order that the family may prosper, it is kept small, and the individual members are often sacrificed to it. The desire for family continuity makes men timid and unadventurous: it is only in the organized proletariat that the daring spirit survives which made the Revolution and led the world in political thought and practice. Through the influence of money, the strength of the family has become a weakness to the nation by making the population remain stationary and even tend to decline. The same love of safety is beginning to produce the same effects elsewhere; but in this, as in many better things, France has led the way.

In Germany the worship of money is more recent than in France, England, and America; indeed, it hardly existed until after the Franco-Prussian War. But it has been adopted now with the same intensity and whole-heartedness which have always marked German beliefs. It is characteristic that, as in France the worship of money is associated with

the family, so in Germany it is associated with the State. Liszt, in deliberate
revolt against the English economists, taught his compatriots to think of
economics in national terms, and the German who develops a business is
felt, by others as well as by himself, to be performing a service to the
State. Germans believe that England's greatness is due to industrialism
and Empire, and that our success in these is due to an intense nationalism.
The apparent internationalism of our Free Trade policy they regard as
mere hyprocrisy. They have set themselves to imitate what they believe
we really are, with only the hyprocrisy omitted. It must be admitted that
their success has been amazing. But in the process they have destroyed
almost all that made Germany of value to the world, and they have not
adopted whatever of good there may have been among us, since that was
all swept aside in the wholesale condemnation of 'hypocrisy'. And in adopting our worst faults, they have made them far worse by a system, a
thoroughness and a unanimity of which we are happily incapable.
Germany's religion is of great importance to the world, since Germans
have a power of real belief, and have the energy to acquire the virtues and
vices which their creed demands. For the sake of the world, as well as for
the sake of Germany, we must hope that they will soon abandon the
worship of wealth which they have unfortunately learnt from us.

Worship of money is no new thing, but it is a more harmful thing
than it used to be, for several reasons. Industrialism has made work more
wearisome and intense, less capable of affording pleasure and interest by
the way to the man who has undertaken it for the sake of money. The
power of limiting families has opened a new field for the operation of
thrift. The general increase in education and self-discipline has made
men more capable of pursuing a purpose consistently in spite of tempta-
tions, and when the purpose is against life it becomes more destructive
with every increase of tenacity in those who adopt it. The greater productivity resulting from industrialism has enabled us to devote more
labour and capital to armies and navies for the protection of our wealth
from envious neighbours, and for the exploitation of inferior races, which
are ruthlessly wasted by the capitalist régime. Through the fear of losing
money, forethought and anxiety eat away men's power of happiness, and
the dread of misfortune becomes a greater misfortune than the one which
is dreaded. The happiest men and women, as we can all testify from our
own experience, are those who are indifferent to money because they have
some positive purpose which shuts it out. And yet all our political thought,
whether Imperialist, Radical, or Socialist, continues to occupy itself
almost exclusively with men's economic desires, as though they alone had
real importance.

In judging of an industrial system, whether the one under which we
live or one proposed by reformers, there are four main tests which may
be applied. We may consider whether the system secures (1) the maximum

of production, or (2) justice in distribution, or (3) a tolerable existence for producers, or (4) the greatest possible freedom and stimulus to vitality and progress. We may say, broadly, that the present system aims only at the first of these objects, while Socialism aims at the second and third. Some defenders of the present system contend that technical progress is better promoted by private enterprise than it would be if industry were in the hands of the State; to this extent they recognize the fourth of the objects we have enumerated. But they recognize it only on the side of the goods and the capitalist, not on the side of the wage-earner. I believe that the fourth is much the most important of the objects to be aimed at, that the present system is fatal to it, and that orthodox Socialism might well prove equally fatal.

One of the least-questioned assumptions of the capitalist system is, that production ought to be increased in amount by every possible means: by new kinds of machinery, by employment of women and boys, by making hours of labour as long as is compatible with efficiency. Central African natives, accustomed to living on the raw fruits of the earth and defeating Manchester by dispensing with clothes, are compelled to work by a hut tax which they can only pay by taking employment under European capitalists. It is admitted that they are perfectly happy while they remain free from European influences, and that industrialism brings upon them, not only the unwonted misery of confinement, but also death from diseases to which white men have become partially immune. It is admitted that the best negro workers are the 'raw natives', fresh from the bush, uncontaminated by previous experience of wage-earning. Nevertheless, no one effectively contends that they ought to be preserved from the deterioration which we bring, since no one effectively doubts that it is good to increase the world's production at no matter what cost.

The belief in the importance of production has a fanatical irrationality and ruthlessness. So long as something is produced, what it is that is produced seems to be thought a matter of no account. Our whole economic system encourages this view, since fear of unemployment makes any kind of work a boon to wage-earners. The mania for increasing production has turned men's thoughts away from much more important problems, and has prevented the world from getting the benefits it might have got out of the increased productivity of labour.

When we are fed and clothed and housed, further material goods are needed only for ostentation.[1] With modern methods, a certain proportion of the population, without working long hours, could do all the work that is really necessary in the way of producing commodities. The time which is now spent in producing luxuries could be spent partly in enjoyment and country holidays, partly in better education, partly in work that is not manual or subserving manual work. We could, if we wished, have

---

[1] Except by that small minority who are capable of artistic enjoyment.

far more science and art, more diffused knowledge and mental cultivation, more leisure for wage-earners, and more capacity for intelligent pleasures. At present not only wages, but almost all earned incomes, can only be obtained by working much longer hours than men ought to work. A man who earns £800 a year by hard work could not, as a rule, earn £400 a year by half as much work. Often he could not earn anything if he were not willing to work practically all day and every day. Because of the excessive belief in the value of production, it is thought right and proper for men to work long hours, and the good that might result from shorter hours is not realized. And all the cruelties of the industrial system, not only in Europe but even more in the tropics, arouse only an occasional feeble protest from a few philanthropists. This is because, owing to the distortion produced by our present economic methods, men's conscious desires, in such matters, cover only a very small part, and that not the most important part, of the real needs affected by industrial work. If this is to be remedied, it can only be by a different economic system, in which the relation of activity to needs will be less concealed and more direct.

The purpose of maximizing production will not be achieved in the long run if our present industrial system continues. Our present system is wasteful of human material, partly through damage to the health and efficiency of industrial workers, especially when women and children are employed, partly through the fact that the best workers tend to have small families and that the more civilized races are in danger of gradual extinction. Every great city is a centre of race-deterioration. For the case of London this has been argued with a wealth of statistical detail by Sir H. Llewelyn Smith;[1] and it cannot easily be doubted that it is equally true in other cases. The same is true of material resources: the minerals, the virgin forests, and the newly developed wheatfields of the world are being exhausted with a reckless prodigality which entails almost a certainty of hardship for future generations.

Socialists see the remedy in State ownership of land and capital, combined with a more just system of distribution. It cannot be denied that our present system of distribution is indefensible from every point of view, including the point of view of justice. Our system of distribution is regulated by law, and is capable of being changed in many respects which familiarity makes us regard as natural and inevitable. We may distinguish four chief sources of recognized legal rights to private property: (1) a man's right to what he has made himself; (2) the right to interest on capital which has been lent; (3) the ownership of land; (4) inheritance. These form a crescendo of respectability: capital is more respectable than labour, land is more respectable than capital, and any form of wealth is more respectable when it is inherited than when it has been acquired by our own exertions.

[1] Booth's *Life and Labour of the People,* Vol. iii.

A man's right to the produce of his own labour has never, in fact, had more than a very limited recognition from the law. The early Socialists, especially the English forerunners of Marx, used to insist upon this right as the basis of a just system of distribution, but in the complication of modern industrial processes it is impossible to say what a man has produced. What proportion of the goods carried by a railway should belong to the goods porters concerned in their journey? When a surgeon saves a man's life by an operation, what proportion of the commodities which the man subsequently produces can the surgeon justly claim? Such problems are insoluble. And there is no special justice, even if they were soluble, in allowing to each man what he himself produces. Some men are stronger, healthier, cleverer, than others, but there is no reason for increasing these natural injustices by the artificial injustices of the law. The principle recommends itself partly as a way of abolishing the very rich, partly as a way of stimulating people to work hard. But the first of these objects can be better obtained in other ways, and the second ceases to be obviously desirable as soon as we cease to worship money.

Interest arises naturally in any community in which private property is unrestricted and theft is punished, because some of the most economical processes of production are slow, and those who have the skill to perform them may not have the means of living while they are being completed. But the power of lending money gives such great wealth and influence to private capitalists that unless strictly controlled it is not compatible with any real freedom for the rest of the population. Its effects at present, both in the industrial world and in international politics, are so bad that it seems imperatively necessary to devise some means of curbing its power.

Private property in land has no justification except historically through power of the sword. In the beginning of feudal times, certain men had enough military strength to be able to force those whom they disliked not to live in a certain area. Those whom they chose to leave on the land became their serfs, and were forced to work for them in return for the gracious permission to stay. In order to establish law in place of private force, it was necessary, in the main, to leave undisturbed the rights which had been acquired by the sword. The land became the property of those who had conquered it, and the serfs were allowed to give rent instead of service. There is no justification for private property in land, except the historical necessity to conciliate turbulent robbers who would not otherwise have obeyed the law. This necessity arose in Europe many centuries ago, but in Africa the whole process is often quite recent. It is by this process, slightly disguised, that the Kimberley diamond-mines and the Rand gold-mines were acquired in spite of prior native rights. It is a singular example of human inertia that men should have continued until now to endure the tyranny and extortion which a small minority are able to inflict by their possession of the land. No good to the community, of any sort or kind, results from the private ownership of land. If men were reasonable, they would decree that it should cease tomorrow, with no compensation beyond a moderate life income to the present holders.

The mere abolition of rent would not remove injustice, since it would confer a capricious advantage upon the occupiers of the best sites and the most fertile land. It is necessary that there should be rent, but it should be paid to the State or to some body which performs public services; or, if the total rental were more than is required for such purposes, it might be paid into a common fund and divided equally among the population. Such a method would be just, and would not only help to relieve poverty, but would prevent wasteful employment of land and the tyranny of local magnates. Much that appears as the power of capital is really the power of the landowner—for example, the power of railway companies and mine-owners. The evil and injustice of the present system are glaring, but men's patience of preventable evils to which they are accustomed is so great that it is impossible to guess when they will put an end to this strange absurdity.

Inheritance, which is the source of the greater part of the unearned income in the world, is regarded by most men as a natural right. Sometimes, as in England, the right is inherent in the owner of property, who may dispose of it in any way that seems good to him. Sometimes, as in France, his right is limited by the right of his family to inherit at least a portion of what he has to leave. But neither the right to dispose of property by will nor the right of children to inherit from parents has any basis outside the instincts of possession and family pride. There may be reasons for allowing a man whose work is exceptionally fruitful—for instance, an inventor—to enjoy a larger income than is enjoyed by the average citizen, but there can be no good reason for allowing this privilege to descend to his children and grandchildren and so on for ever. The effect is to produce an idle and exceptionally fortunate class, who are influential through their money, and opposed to reform for fear it should be directed against themselves. Their whole habit of thought becomes timid, since they dread being forced to acknowledge that their position is indefensible; yet snobbery and the wish to secure their favour lead almost the whole middle class to ape their manners and adopt their opinions. In this way they become a poison infecting the outlook of almost all educated people.

It is sometimes said that without the incentive of inheritance men would not work so well. The great captains of industry, we are assured, are actuated by the desire to found a family, and would not devote their lives to unremitting toil without the hope of gratifying this desire. I do not believe that any large proportion of really useful work is done from this motive. Ordinary work is done for the sake of a living, and the very best work is done for the interest of the work itself. Even the captains of industry, who are thought (perhaps by themselves as well as by others) to be aiming at founding a family, are probably more actuated by love of power and by the adventurous pleasure of great enterprises. And if there were some slight diminution in the amount of work done, it would be well worth while in order to get rid of the idle rich, with the oppression, feebleness, and corruption which they inevitably introduce.

The present system of distribution is not based upon any principle. Starting from a system imposed by conquest, the arrangements made by the conquerors for their own benefit were stereotyped by the law, and have never been fundamentally reconstructed. On what principles ought the reconstruction to be based?

Socialism, which is the most widely advocated scheme of reconstruction, aims chiefly at *justice*: the present inequalities of wealth are unjust, and Socialism would abolish them. It is not essential to Socialism that all men should have the same income, but it is essential that inequalities should be justified, in each case, by inequality of need or of service performed. There can be no disputing that the present system is grossly unjust, and that almost all that is unjust in it is harmful. But I do not think justice alone is a sufficient principle upon which to base an economic reconstruction. Justice would be secured if all were equally unhappy, as well as if all were equally happy. Justice, by itself, when once realized, contains no source of new life. The old type of Marxian revolutionary socialist never dwelt, in imagination, upon the life of communities after the establishment of the millennium. He imagined that, like the Prince and Princess in a fairy story, they would live happily ever after. But that is not a condition possible to human nature. Desire, activity, purpose, are essential to a tolerable life, and a millennium, though it may be a joy in prospect, would be intolerable if it were actually achieved.

The more modern Socialists, it is true, have lost most of the religious fervour which characterized the pioneers, and view Socialism as a tendency rather than a definite goal. But they still retain the view that what is of most political importance to a man is his income, and that the principal aim of a democratic politician ought to be to increase the wages of labour. I believe this involves too passive a conception of what constitutes happiness. It is true that, in the industrial world, large sections of the population are too poor to have any possibility of a good life; but it is not true that a good life will come of itself with a diminution of poverty. Very few of the well-to-do classes have a good life at present, and perhaps Socialism would only substitute the evils which now afflict the more prosperous in place of the evils resulting from destitution.

In the existing labour movement, although it is one of the most vital sources of change, there are certain tendencies against which reformers ought to be on their guard. The labour movement is in essence a movement in favour of justice, based upon the belief that the sacrifice of the many to the few is not necessary now, whatever may have been the case in the past. When labour was less productive and education was less widespread, an aristocratic civilization may have been the only one possible: it may have been necessary that the many should contribute to the life of the few, if the few were to transmit and increase the world's possessions in art and thought and civilized existence. But this necessity is past or rapidly passing, and there is no longer any valid objection to the claims of justice. The labour movement is morally irresistible, and is not now seriously opposed except by prejudice and simple self-assertion. All living thought is on its side; what is against it is traditional and dead. But although it itself is living, it is not by any means certain that it will make for life.

Labour is led by current political thought in certain directions which would become repressive and dangerous if they were to remain strong after labour had triumphed. The aspirations of the labour movement are, on the whole, opposed by the great majority of the educated classes, who feel a menace, not only or chiefly to their personal comfort, but to the civilized life in which they have their part, which they profoundly believe to be important to the world. Owing to the opposition of the educated classes, labour, when it is revolutionary and vigorous, tends to despise all that the educated classes represent. When it is more respectful, as its leaders tend to be in England, the subtle and almost unconscious influence of educated men is apt to sap revolutionary ardour, producing doubt and uncertainty instead of the swift, simple assurance by which victory might have been won. The very sympathy which the best men in the well-to-do classes extend to labour, their very readiness to admit the justice of its claims, may have the effect of softening the opposition of labour leaders to the *status quo*, and of opening their minds to the suggestion that no fundamental change is possible. Since these influences affect leaders much more than the rank and file, they tend to produce in the rank and file a distrust of leaders, and a desire to seek out new leaders who will be less ready to concede the claims of the more fortunate classes. The result may be in the end a labour movement as hostile to the life of the mind as some terrified property-owners believe it to be at present.

The claims of justice, narrowly interpreted, may reinforce this tendency. It may be thought unjust that some men should have larger incomes or shorter hours of work than other men. But efficiency in mental work, including the work of education, certainly requires more comfort and longer periods of rest than are required for efficiency in physical work, if only because mental work is not physiologically wholesome. If this is not recognized, the life of the mind may suffer through short-sightedness even more than through deliberate hostility.

Education suffers at present, and may long continue to suffer, through the desire of parents that their children should earn money as soon as possible. Everyone knows that the half-time system, for example, is bad, but the power of organized labour keeps it in existence. It is clear that the cure for this evil, as for those that are concerned with the population question, is to relieve parents of the expense of their children's education, and at the same time to take away their right to appropriate their children's earnings.

The way to prevent any dangerous opposition of labour to the life of the mind is not to oppose the labour movement, which is too strong to be opposed with justice. The right way is to show by actual practice that thought is useful to labour, that without thought its positive aims cannot be achieved, and that there are men in the world of thought who are willing to devote their energies to helping labour in its struggle. Such men, if they are wise and sincere, can prevent labour from becoming destructive of what is living in the intellectual world.

Another danger in the aims of organized labour is the danger of conservatism as to methods of production. Improvements of machinery or organization bring great advantages to employers, but involve temporary and sometimes permanent loss to the wage-earners. For this reason, and also from mere instinctive dislike of any change of habits, strong labour organizations are often obstacles to technical progress. The ultimate basis of all social progress must be increased technical efficiency, a greater result from a given amount of labour. If labour were to offer an effective opposition to this kind of progress, it would in the long run paralyse all other progress. The way to overcome the opposition of labour is not by hostility or moral homilies, but by giving to labour the direct interest in economical processes which now belongs to the employers. Here, as elsewhere, the unprogressive part of a movement which is essentially progressive is to be eliminated, not by decrying the whole movement, but by giving it a wider sweep, making it more progressive, and leading it to demand an even greater change in the structure of society than any that it had contemplated in its inception.

The most important purpose that political institutions can achieve is to keep alive in individuals creativeness, vigour, vitality, and the joy of life. These things existed, for example, in Elizabethan England in a way in which they do not exist now. They stimulated adventure, poetry, music, fine architecture and set going the whole movement out of which England's greatness has sprung in every direction in which England has been great. These things co-existed with injustice, but outweighed it, and made a national life more admirable than any that is likely to exist under Socialism.

What is wanted in order to keep men full of vitality is opportunity, not only security. Security is merely a refuge from fear; opportunity is the source of hope. The chief test of an economic system is not whether it makes men prosperous, or whether it secures distributive justice (though these are both very desirable), but whether it leaves men's instinctive growth unimpeded. To achieve this purpose, there are two main conditions which it should fulfil: it should not cramp men's private affections, and it should give the greatest possible outlet to the impulse of creation. There is in most men, until it becomes atrophied by disuse, an instinct of constructiveness, a wish to make something. The men who achieve most are, as a rule, those in whom this instinct is strongest: such men become artists, men of science, statesmen, empire-builders, or captains of industry, according to the accidents of temperament and opportunity. The most beneficient and the most harmful careers are inspired by this impulse. Without it, the world would sink to the level of Tibet: it would subsist, as it is always prone to do, on the wisdom of its ancestors, and each generation would sink more deeply into a lifeless traditionalism.

But it is not only the remarkable men who have the instinct of constructiveness, though it is they who have it most strongly. It is almost universal in boys, and in men it usually survives in a greater or less degree, according to the greater or less outlet which it is able to find. Work inspired by this instinct is satisfying, even when it is irksome and difficult, because every effort is as natural as the effort of a dog pursuing a hare. The chief defect of the present capitalistic system is that work done for wages very seldom affords any outlet for the creative impulse. The man who works for wages has no choice as to what he shall make: the whole creativeness of the process is concentrated in the employer who orders the work to be done. For this reason the work becomes a merely external means to a certain result, the earning of wages. Employers grow indignant about the trade union rules for limitation of output, but they have no right to be indignant, since they do not permit the men whom they employ to have any share in the purpose for which the work is undertaken. And so the process of production, which should form one instinctive cycle, becomes divided into separate purposes, which can no longer provide any satisfaction of instinct for those who do the work.

This result is due to our industrial system, but it would not be avoided by State Socialism. In a Socialist community, the State would be the employer, and the individual workman would have almost as little control over his work as he has at present. Such control as he could exercise would be indirect, through political channels, and would be too slight and roundabout to afford any appreciable satisfaction. It is to be feared that instead of an increase of self-direction, there would only be an increase of mutual interference.

The total abolition of private capitalistic enterprise, which is demanded by Marxian Socialism, seems scarcely necessary. Most men who construct sweeping systems of reform, like most of those who defend the *status quo*, do not allow enough for the importance of exceptions and the undesirability of rigid system. Provided the sphere of capitalism is restricted, and a large proportion of the population are rescued from its dominion, there is no reason to wish it wholly abolished. As a competitor and a rival, it might serve a useful purpose in preventing more democratic enterprises from sinking into sloth and technical conservatism. But it is of the very highest importance that capitalism should become the exception rather than the rule, and that the bulk of the world's industry should be conducted on a more democratic system.

Much of what is to be said against militarism in the State is also to be said against capitalism in the economic sphere. Economic organizations, in the pursuit of efficiency, grow larger and larger, and there is no possibility of reversing this process. The causes of their growth are technical, and large organizations must be accepted as an essential part of civilized society. But there is no reason why their government should be centralized and monarchical. The present economic system, by robbing most men of initiative, is one of the causes of the universal weariness which devitalizes urban and industrial populations, making them perpetually seek excitement, and leading them to welcome even the outbreak of war as a relief from the dreary monotony of their daily lives.

If the vigour of the nation is to be preserved, if we are to retain any capacity for new ideas, if we are not to sink into a Chinese condition of stereotyped immobility, the monarchical organization of industry must be swept away. All large businesses must become democratic and federal in their government. The whole wage-earning system is an abomination, not only because of the social injustice which it causes and perpetuates, but also because it separates the man who does the work from the purpose for which the work is done. The whole of the controlling purpose is concentrated in the capitalist; the purpose of the wage-earner is not the produce, but the wages. The purpose of the capitalist is to secure the maximum of work for the minimum of wages; the purpose of the wage-earner is to secure the maximum of wages for the minimum of work. A system involving this essential conflict of interests cannot be expected to work smoothly or successfully, or to produce a community with any pride in efficiency.

Two movements exist, one already well advanced, the other in its infancy, which seem capable, between them, of suggesting most of what is needed. The two movements I mean are the co-operative movement and syndicalism. The co-operative movement is capable of replacing the wages system over a very wide field, but it is not easy to see how it could be applied to such things as railways. It is just in these cases that the principles of syndicalism are most easily applicable.

If organization is not to crush individuality, membership of an organization ought to be voluntary, not compulsory, and ought always to carry with it a voice in the management. This is not the case with economic organizations, which give no opportunity for the pride and pleasure that men find in an activity of their own choice, provided it is not utterly monotonous.

It must be admitted, however, that much of the mechanical work which is necessary in industry is probably not capable of being made interesting in itself. But it will seem less tedious than it does at present if those who do it have a voice in the management of their industry. And men who desire leisure for other occupations might be given the opportunity of doing uninteresting work during a few hours of the day for a low wage; this would give an opening to all who wished for some activity not immediately profitable to themselves. When everything that is possible has been done to make work interesting, the residue will have to be made endurable, as almost all work is at present, by the inducement of rewards outside the hours of labour. But if these rewards are to be satisfactory, it is essential that the uninteresting work should not necessarily absorb a man's whole energies, and that opportunities should exist for more or less continuous activities during the remaining hours. Such a system might be an immeasurable boon to artists, men of letters, and others who produce for their own satisfaction works which the public does not value soon enough to secure a living for the producers; and apart from such rather rare cases, it might provide an opportunity for young men and women with intellectual ambitions to continue their education after they have left school, or to prepare themselves for careers which require an exceptionally long training.

The evils of the present system result from the separation between the several interests of consumer, producer, and capitalist. No one of these three has the same interests as the community or as either of the other two. The co-operative system amalgamates the interests of consumer and capitalist; syndicalism would amalgamate the interests of producer and capitalist. Neither amalgamates all three, or makes the interests of those who direct industry quite identical with those of the community. Neither, therefore, would wholly prevent industrial strife, or obviate the need of the State as arbitrator. But either would be better than the present system, and probably a mixture of both would cure most of the evils of industrialism as it exists now. It is surprising that, while men and women have struggled to achieve political democracy, so little has been done to introduce democracy in industry. I believe incalculable benefits might result from industrial democracy, either on the co-operative model or with recognition of a trade or industry as a unit for purposes of government, with some kind of Home Rule such as syndicalism aims at securing. There is no reason why all governmental units should be geographical: this system was necessary in the past because of the slowness of means of communication, but it is not necessary now. By some such system many men might come to feel again a pride in their work, and to find again that outlet for the creative impulse which is now denied to all but a fortunate few. Such a system requires the abolition of the landowner and the restriction of the capitalist, but does not entail equality of earnings. And unlike Socialism, it is not a static or final system: it is hardly more than a framework for energy and initiative. It is only by some such method, I believe, that the free growth of the individual can be reconciled with the huge technical organizations which have been rendered necessary by industrialism.

(*Principles of Social Reconstruction*, London: Allen & Unwin; *Why Men Fight*, New York: The Century Companies (Appleton–Century–Crofts), 1916.)

54

DIALECTICAL MATERIALISM

THE contributions of Marx and Engels to theory were twofold: there was Marx's theory of surplus value, and there was their joint theory of historical development, called 'dialectical materialism'. We will consider first the latter, which seems to me both more true and more important than the former.

Let us, in the first place, endeavour to be clear as to what the theory of dialectical materialism is. It is a theory which has various elements. Metaphysically it is materialistic: in method it adopts a form of dialectic suggested by Hegel, but differing from his in many important respects. It takes over from Hegel an outlook which is evolutionary, and in which the stages in evolution can be characterized in clear logical terms. These changes are of the nature of development, not so much in an ethical as in a logical sense—that is to say, they proceed according to a plan which a man of sufficient intellect could, thoeretically, foretell, and which Marx himself professes to have foretold, in its main outlines, up to the moment of the universal establishment of Communism. The materialism of its meta-physics is translated, where human affairs are concerned, into the doctrine that the prime cause of all social phenomena is the method of production and exchange prevailing at any given period. The clearest statements of the theory are to be found in Engels, in his *Anti-Dühring*, of which the relevant parts have appeared in England under the title: *Socialism, Utopian and Scientific*. A few extracts will help to provide us with our text:

'It was seen that *all* past history, with the exception of its primitive stages, was the history of class struggles: that these warring classes of society are always the products of the modes of production and of exchange —in a word, of the economic conditions of their time; that the *economic* structure of society always furnishes the real basis, starting from which we can alone work out the ultimate explanation of the whole superstructure of juridical and political institutions as well as of the religious, philo-sophical, and other ideas of a given historical period.'

The discovery of this principle, according to Marx and Engels, showed that the coming of Socialism was inevitable.

'From that time forward Socialism was no longer an accidental discovery of this or that ingenious brain, but the necessary outcome of the struggle between two historically developed classes—the proletariat and the bourgeoisie. Its task was no longer to manufacture a system of society as perfect as possible, but to examine the historico-economic succession of events from which these classes and their antagonism had of necessity sprung, and to discover in the economic conditions thus created the means of ending the conflict. But the Socialism of earlier days was as incompatible with this materialistic conception as the conception of Nature of the French materialists was with dialectics and modern natural science. The Socialism of earlier days certainly criticized the existing capitalistic mode of production and its consequences. But it could not explain them, and, therefore, could not get the mastery of them. It could only simply reject them as bad. The more strongly this earlier Socialism denounced the exploitation of the working class, inevitable under Capitalism, the less able was it clearly to show in what this exploitation consisted and how it arose.'

The same theory which is called Dialectical Materialism is also called the Materialist Conception of History. Engels says: 'The materialist conception of history starts from the proposition that the production of the means to support human life and, next to production, the exchange of things produced, is the basis of all social structure; that in every society that has appeared in history, the manner in which wealth is distributed and society divided into classes or orders, is dependent upon what is produced, how it is produced, and how the products are exchanged. From this point of view the final causes of all social changes and political revolutions are to be sought, not in men's brains, not in man's better insight into eternal truth and justice, but in changes in the modes of production and exchange. They are to be sought, not in the *philosophy*, but in the *economics* of each particular epoch. The growing perception that existing social institutions are unreasonable and unjust, that reason has become unreason, and right wrong, is only proof that in the modes of production and exchange changes have silently taken place, with which the social order, adapted to earlier economic conditions, is no longer in keeping. From this it also follows that the means of getting rid of the incongruities that have been brought to light, must also be present, in a more or less developed condition, within the changed modes of production themselves. These means are not to be invented by deduction from fundamental principles, but are to be discovered in the stubborn facts of the existing system of production.'

The conflicts which lead to political upheavals are not primarily mental conflicts in the opinions and passions of human beings.

'This conflict between productive forces and modes of production is not a conflict engendered in the mind of man, like that between original sin and divine justice. It exists, in fact, objectively outside us, independently of the will and actions even of the men that have brought it on. Modern Socialism is nothing but the reflex, in thought, of this conflict in fact; its ideal reflection in the minds, first, of the class directly suffering under it, the working class.'

There is a good statement of the materialist theory of history in an early joint work of Marx and Engels (1845-6), called *German Ideology*. It is there said that the materialist theory starts with the actual process of production of an epoch, and regards as the basis of history the form of economic life connected with this form of production and generated by it. This, they say, shows civil society in its various stages and in its action as the State. Moreover, from the economic basis the materialist theory explains such matters as religion, philosophy, and morals, and the reasons for the course of their development.

These quotations perhaps suffice to show what the theory is. A number of questions arise as soon as it is examined critically. Before going on to economics one is inclined to ask, first, whether materialism is true in philosophy, and second, whether the elements of Hegelian dialectic which are embedded in the Marxist theory of development can be justified apart from a full-fledged Hegelianism. Then comes the further question whether these metaphysical doctrines have any relevance to the historical thesis as regards economic development, and last of all comes the examination of this historical thesis itself. To state in advance what I shall be trying to prove, I hold (1) that materialism, in some sense, may be true, though it cannot be known to be so; (2) that the elements of dialectic which Marx took over from Hegel made him regard history as a more rational process than it has in fact been, convincing him that all changes must be in some sense progressive, and giving him a feeling of certainty in regard to the future, for which there is no scientific warrant; (3) that the whole of his theory of economic development may perfectly well be true if his metaphysic is false, and false if his metaphysic is true, and that but for the influence of Hegel it would never have occurred to him that a matter so purely empirical could depend upon abstract metaphysics; (4) with regard to the economic interpretation of history, it seems to me very largely true, and a most important contribution to sociology; I cannot, however, regard it as *wholly* true, or feel any confidence that all great historical changes can be viewed as developments. Let us take these points one by one.

(1) *Materialism.* Marx's materialism was of a peculiar kind, by no means identical with that of the eighteenth century. When he speaks of the 'materialist conception of history', he never emphasizes philosophical materialism, but only the economic causation of social phenomena. His philosophical position is best set forth (though very briefly) in his *Eleven Theses on Feuerbach* (1845). In these he says:

'The chief defect of all previous materialism—including that of

Feuerbach—is that the object (Gegenstand), the reality, sensibility, is only apprehended under the form of the object (Objekt) or of contemplation (Anschauung), but not as human sensible activity or practice, not subjectively. Hence it came about that the active side was developed by idealism in opposition to materialism. . . .

'The question whether objective truth belongs to human thinking is not a question of theory, but a practical question. The truth, i.e. the reality and power, of thought must be demonstrated in practice. The contest as to the reality or non-reality of a thought which is isolated from practice, is a purely scholastic question. . . .

'The highest point that can be reached by contemplative materialism, i.e. by materialism which does not regard sensibility as a practical activity, is the contemplation of isolated individuals in "bourgeois society".

'The standpoint of the old materialism is "bourgeois" society; the standpoint of the new is *human* society or socialized (vergesellschaftete) humanity.

'Philosophers have only *interpreted* the world in various ways, but the real task is to *alter* it.'

The philosophy advocated in the earlier part of these theses is that which has since become familiar to the philosophical world through the writings of Dr Dewey, under the name of pragmatism or instrumentalism. Whether Dr Dewey is aware of having been anticipated by Marx, I do not know, but undoubtedly their opinions as to the metaphysical status of matter are virtually identical. In view of the importance attached by Marx to his theory of matter, it may be worth while to set forth his view rather more fully.

The conception of 'matter', in old-fashioned materialism, was bound up with the conception of 'sensation'. Matter was regarded as the cause of sensation, and originally also as its object, at least in the case of sight and touch. Sensation was regarded as something in which a man is passive, and merely receives impressions from the outer world. This conception of sensation as passive is, however—so the instrumentalists contend—an unreal abstraction, to which nothing actual corresponds. Watch an animal receiving impressions connected with another animal: its nostrils dilate, its ears twitch, its eyes are directed to the right point, its muscles become taut in preparation for appropriate movements. All this is action, mainly of a sort to improve the informative quality of impressions, partly such as to lead to fresh action in relation to the object. A cat seeing a mouse is by no means a passive recipient of purely contemplative impressions. And as a cat with a mouse, so is a textile manufacturer with a bale of cotton. The bale of cotton is an opportunity for action, it is something to be transformed. The machinery by which it is to be transformed is explicitly and obviously a product of human activity. Roughly speaking, all matter, according to Marx, is to be thought of as we naturally think of machinery: it has a raw material giving opportunity for action, but in its completed form it is a human product.

Philosophy has taken over from the Greeks a conception of passive contemplation, and has supposed that knowledge is obtained by means of contemplation. Marx maintains that we are always active, even when we come nearest to pure 'sensation': we are never merely apprehending our environment, but always at the same time altering it. This necessarily makes the older conception of knowledge inapplicable to our actual relations with the outer world. In place of knowing an object in the sense of passively receiving an impression of it, we can only know it in the sense of being able to act upon it successfully. That is why the test of all truth is practical. And since we change the object when we act upon it, truth ceases to be static, and becomes something which is continually changing and developing. That is why Marx calls his materialism 'dialectical', because it contains within itself, like Hegel's dialectic, an essential principle of progressive change.

I think it may be doubted whether Engels quite understood Marx's views on the nature of matter and on the pragmatic character of truth; no doubt he thought he agreed with Marx, but in fact he came nearer to orthodox materialism.[1] Engels explains 'historical materialism', as he understands it, in an Introduction, written in 1892, to his *Socialism, Utopian and Scientific*. Here, the part assigned to action seems to be reduced to the conventional task of scientific verification. He says: 'The proof of the pudding is in the eating. From the moment we turn to our own use these objects, according to the qualities we perceive in them, we put to an infallible test the correctness or otherwise of our sense-perceptions. . . . Not in one single instance, so far, have we been led to the conclusion that our sense-perceptions, scientifically controlled, induce in our minds ideas respecting the outer world that are, by their very nature, at variance with reality, or that there is an inherent incompatibility between the outer world and our sense-perceptions of it.'

There is no trace, here, of Marx's pragmatism, or of the doctrine that sensible objects are largely the products of our own activity. But there is also no sign of any consciousness of disagreement with Marx. It may be that Marx modified his views in later life, but it seems more probable that, on this subject as on some others, he held two different views simultaneously, and applied the one or the other as suited the purpose of his argument. He certainly held that some propositions were 'true' in a more than pragmatic sense. When, in *Capital*, he sets forth the cruelties of the industrial system as reported by Royal Commissions, he certainly holds that these cruelties really took place, and not only that successful action will result from supposing that they took place. Similarly, when he prophesies the Communist revolution, he believes that there will be such an

[1] Cf. Sidney Hook, *Towards the Understanding of Karl Marx*, p. 32.

event, not merely that it is convenient to think so. His pragmatism must, therefore, have been only occasional—in fact when, on pragmatic grounds, it was justified by being convenient.

It is worth noting that Lenin, who does not admit any divergence between Marx and Engels, adopts in his *Materialism and Empirio-Criticism* a view which is more nearly that of Engels than that of Marx.

For my part, while I do not think that materialism can be *proved*, I think Lenin is right in saying that it is not *dis*proved by modern physics. Since his time, and largely as a reaction against his success, respectable physicists have moved further and further from materialism, and it is naturally supposed, by themselves and by the general public, that it is physics which has caused this movement. I agree with Lenin that no substantially new argument has emerged since the time of Berkeley, with one exception. This one exception, oddly enough, is the argument set forth by Marx in his theses on Feuerbach, and completely ignored by Lenin. If there is no such thing as sensation, if matter as something which we passively apprehend is a delusion, and if 'truth' is a practical rather than a theoretical conception, then old-fashioned materialism, such as Lenin's, becomes untenable. And Berkeley's view becomes equally untenable, since it removes the object in relation to which we are active. Marx's instrumentalist theory, though he calls it materialistic, is really not so. As against materialism, its arguments have indubitably much force. Whether it is ultimately valid is a difficult question, as to which I have deliberately refrained from expressing an opinion, since I could not do so without writing a complete philosophical treatise.

(2) *Dialectic in history.* The Hegelian dialectic was a full-blooded affair. If you started with any partial concept and meditated on it, it would presently turn into its opposite; it and its opposite would combine into a synthesis, which would, in turn, become the starting point of a similar movement, and so on until you reached the Absolute Idea, on which you could reflect as long as you liked without discovering any new contradictions. The historical development of the world in time was merely an objectification of this process of thought. This view appeared possible to Hegel, because for him mind was the ultimate reality; for Marx, on the contrary, matter is the ultimate reality. Nevertheless he continues to think that the world develops according to a logical formula. To Hegel, the development of history is as logical as a game of chess. Marx and Engels keep the rules of chess, while supposing that the chessmen move themselves in accordance with the laws of physics, without the intervention of a player. In one of the quotations from Engels which I gave earlier, he says: 'The means of getting rid of the incongruities that have been brought to light, *must* also be present, in a more or less developed condition, within the changed modes of production themselves.' This 'must' betrays

a relic of the Hegelian belief that logic rules the world. Why should the outcome of a conflict in politics always be the establishment of some more developed system? This has not, in fact, been the case in innumerable instances. The barbarian invasion of Rome did not give rise to more developed economic forms, nor did the expulsion of the Moors from Spain, or the destruction of the Albigenses in the South of France. Before the time of Homer the Mycenaean civilization had been destroyed, and it was many centuries before a developed civilization again emerged in Greece. The examples of decay and retrogression are at least as numerous and as important in history as the examples of development. The opposite view, which appears in the works of Marx and Engels, is nothing but nineteenth-century optimism.

This is a matter of practical as well as theoretical importance. Communists always assume that conflicts between Communism and capitalism, while they may for a time result in partial victories for capitalism, must in the end lead to the establishment of Communism. They do not envisage another possible result, quite as probable, namely, a return to barbarism. We all know that modern war is a somewhat serious matter, and that in the next world war it is likely that large populations will be virtually exterminated by poison gases and bacteria. Can it be seriously supposed that after a war in which the great centres of population and most important industrial plant had been wiped out, the remaining population would be in a mood to establish scientific Communism? Is it not practically certain that the survivors would be in a mood of gibbering and superstitious brutality, fighting all against all for the last turnip or the last mangel-wurzel? Marx used to do his work in the British Museum, but after the Great War the British Government placed a tank just outside the museum, presumably to teach the intellectuals their place. Communism is a highly intellectual, highly civilized doctrine, which can, it is true, be established, as it was in Russia, after a slight preliminary skirmish, such as that of 1914–18, but hardly after a really serious war. I am afraid the dogmatic optimism of the Communist doctrine must be regarded as a relic of Victorianism.

There is another curious point about the Communist interpretation of the dialectic. Hegel, as everyone knows, concluded his dialectical account of history with the Prussian State, which, according to him, was the perfect embodiment of the Absolute Idea. Marx, who had no affection for the Prussian State, regarded this as a lame and impotent conclusion. He said that the dialectic should be essentially revolutionary, and seemed to suggest that it could not reach any final static resting-place. Nevertheless we hear nothing about the further revolutions that are to happen after the establishment of Communism. In the last paragraph of *La Misère de la Philosophie* he says:

'It is only in an order of things in which there will no longer be classes or class-antagonism that *social evolutions* will cease to be *political revolutions.*'

What these social evolutions are to be, or how they are to be brought about without the motive power of class conflict, Marx does not say. Indeed, it is hard to see how, on his theory, any further evolution would be possible. Except from the point of view of present-day politics, Marx's dialectic is no more revolutionary than that of Hegel. Moreover, since all human development has, according to Marx, been governed by conflicts of classes, and since under Communism there is to be only one class, it follows that there can be no further development, and that mankind must go on for ever and ever in a state of Byzantine immobility. This does not seem plausible, and it suggests that there must be other possible causes of political events besides those of which Marx has taken account.

(3) *Irrelevance of Metaphysics.* The belief that metaphysics has any bearing upon practical affairs is, to my mind, a proof of logical incapacity. One finds physicists with all kinds of opinions: some follow Hume, some Berkeley, some are conventional Christians, some are materialists, some are sensationalists, some even are solipsists. This makes no difference whatever to their physics. They do not take different views as to when eclipses will occur, or what are the conditions of the stability of a bridge. That is because, in physics, there is some genuine knowledge, and whatever metaphysical beliefs a physicist may hold must adapt themselves to this knowledge. In so far as there is any genuine knowledge in the social sciences, the same thing is true. Whenever metaphysics is really useful in reaching a conclusion, that is because the conclusion cannot be reached by scientific means, i.e. because there is no good reason to suppose it true. What can be known can be known without metaphysics, and whatever needs metaphysics for its proof cannot be proved. In actual fact Marx advances in his books much detailed historical argument, in the main perfectly sound, but none of this in any way depends upon materialism. Take, for example, the fact that free competition tends to end in monopoly. This is an empirical fact, the evidence for which is equally patent whatever one's metaphysic may happen to be. Marx's metaphysic comes in in two ways: on the one hand, by making things more cut and dried and precise than they are in real life; on the other hand, in giving him a certainty about the future which goes beyond what a scientific attitude would warrant. But in so far as his doctrines of historical development can be shown to be true, his metaphysic is irrelevant. The question whether Communism is going to become universal is quite independent of metaphysics. It may be that a metaphysic is helpful in the fight: early Mohammedan conquests were much facilitated by the belief that the faithful who died in battle went straight to Paradise, and similarly the efforts of Communists may be stimulated by the belief that there is a God called Dialectical Materialism who is fighting on their side,

and will, in His own good time, give them the victory. On the other hand, there are many people to whom it is repugnant to have to profess belief in propositions for which they see no evidence, and the loss of such people must be reckoned as a disadvantage resulting from the Communist metaphysic.

(4) *Economic Causation in History*. In the main I agree with Marx that economic causes are at the bottom of most of the great movements in history, not only political movements, but also those in such departments as religion, art, and morals. There are, however, important qualifications to be made. In the first place, Marx does not allow nearly enough for the time-lag. Christianity, for example, arose in the Roman Empire, and in many respects bears the stamp of the social system of that time, but Christianity has survived through many changes. Marx treats it as moribund. 'When the ancient world was in its last throes, the ancient religions were overcome by Christianity. When Christian ideas succumbed in the eighteenth century to rationalist ideas, feudal society fought its death-battle with the then revolutionary bourgeoisie.' (*Manifesto of the Communist Party* by Karl Marx and F. Engels.) Nevertheless, in his own country it remained the most powerful obstacle to the realization of his own ideas,[1] and throughout the Western world its political influence is still enormous. I think it may be conceded that *new* doctrines that have any success must bear some relation to the economic circumstances of their age, but old doctrines can persist for many centuries without any such relation of any vital kind.

Another point where I think Marx's theory of history is too definite is that he does not allow for the fact that a small force may tip the balance when two great forces are in approximate equilibrium. Admitting that the great forces are generated by economic causes, it often depends upon quite trivial and fortuitous events which of the great forces gets the victory. In reading Trotsky's account of the Russian Revolution, it is difficult to believe that Lenin made no difference, but it was touch and go whether the German Government allowed him to get to Russia. If the minister concerned had happened to be suffering from dyspepsia on a certain morning, he might have said 'No' when in fact he said 'Yes', and I do not think it can be rationally maintained that without Lenin the Russian Revolution would have achieved what it did. To take another instance: if the Prussians had happened to have a good general at the battle of Valmy, they might have wiped out the French Revolution. To take an even more fantastic example, it may be maintained quite plausibly that if Henry VIII had not fallen in love with Anne Boleyn, the United States would not now exist. For it was owing to this event that England broke with the Papacy, and therefore did not acknowledge the Pope's

---

[1] 'For Germany', wrote Marx in 1844, 'the critique of religion is essentially completed.'

gift of the Americas to Spain and Portugal. If England had remained Catholic, it is probable that what is now the United States would have been part of Spanish America.

This brings me to another point in which Marx's philosophy of history was faulty. He regards economic conflicts as always conflicts between classes, whereas the majority of them have been between races or nations. English industrialism of the early nineteenth century was internationalist, because it expected to retain its monopoly of industry. It seemed to Marx, as it did to Cobden, that the world was going to be increasingly cosmopolitan. Bismarck, however, gave a different turn to events, and industrialism ever since has grown more and more nationalistic. Even the conflict between capitalism and Communism takes increasingly the form of a conflict between nations. It is true, of course, that the conflicts between nations are very largely economic, but the grouping of the world by nations is itself determined by causes which are in the main not economic.

Another set of causes which have had considerable importance in history are those which may be called medical. The Black Death, for example, was an event of whose importance Marx was well aware, but the causes of the Black Death were only in part economic. Undoubtedly it would not have occurred among populations at a higher economic level, but Europe had been quite as poor for many centuries as it was in 1348, so that the proximate cause of the epidemic cannot have been poverty. Take again such a matter as the prevalence of malaria and yellow fever in the tropics, and the fact that these diseases have now become preventable. This is a matter which has very important economic effects, though not itself of an economic nature.

Much the most necessary correction in Marx's theory is as to the causes of changes in methods of production. Methods of production appear in Marx as prime causes, and the reasons for which they change from time to time are left completely unexplained. As a matter of fact, methods of production change, in the main, owing to intellectual causes, owing, that is to say, to scientific discoveries and inventions. Marx thinks that discoveries and inventions are made when the economic situation calls for them. This, however, is a quite unhistorical view. Why was there practically no experimental science from the time of Archimedes to the time of Leonardo? For six centuries after Archimedes the economic conditions were such as should have made scientific work easy. It was the growth of science after the Renaissance that led to modern industry. This intellectual causation of economic processes is not adequately recognized by Marx.

History can be viewed in many ways, and many general formulae can be invented which cover enough of the ground to seem adequate if the facts are carefully selected. I suggest, without undue solemnity, the following alternative theory of the causation of the industrial revolution:

industrialism is due to modern science, modern science is due to Galileo, Galileo is due to Copernicus, Copernicus is due to the Renaissance, the Renaissance is due to the fall of Constantinople, the fall of Constantinople is due to the migration of the Turks, the migration of the Turks is due to the desiccation of Central Asia. Therefore the fundamental study in searching for historical causes is hydrography.

(*Freedom and Organization*, London: Allen & Unwin; *Freedom Versus Organization*, New York: W. W. Norton, 1934.)

55

THE THEORY OF SURPLUS VALUE

MARX'S theory of surplus value is simple in its main outline, though complicated in its details. He argues that a wage-earner produces goods equal in value to his wages in a portion of the working day, often assumed to be about half, and in the remainder of his working day produces goods which become the property of the capitalist although he has not had to make any payment for them. Thus the wage earner produces more than he is paid for; the value of this additional product is what Marx calls 'surplus value'. Out of surplus value come profits, rent, tithes, taxes—in a word, everything except wages.

This view is based upon an economic argument which is not altogether easy to follow, the more so as it is partly valid, partly fallacious. It is, however, very necessary to analyse Marx's argument, since it has had a profound effect upon the development of Socialism and Communism.

Marx starts from the orthodox economic doctrine that the exchange value of a commodity is proportional to the amount of labour required for its production. We have already considered this doctrine in connection with Ricardo, and have seen that it is true only partially and in certain circumstances. It is true in so far as the cost of production is represented by wages, and there is competition among capitalists which keeps the price as low as possible. If the capitalists have formed themselves into a Trust or Cartel, or if the cost of raw material is a large part of the total cost of production, the theory is no longer true. Marx, however, accepted the theory from the economists of his day, although he despised them, apparently without any examination of the grounds in its favour.

The next step in the argument is derived (without adequate acknowledgement) from Malthus. It followed from Malthus's theory of population that there would always be competition among wage-earners, which would ensure that the value of labour, like that of other commodities, should be measured by its cost of production (and reproduction). That is to say, wages would suffice for the bare necessaries of the labourer and his family, and under a competitive system they could not rise above this level.

Malthus's theory of population, like Ricardo's theory of value, is subject to limitations which we have already considered. Marx always rejects it contemptuously, and is bound to do so, since, as Malthus was careful to point out, it would, if valid, make all communistic Utopias impossible. But Marx does not advance any reasoned argument against Malthus, and, what is still more remarkable, he accepts without question the law that wages must always (under a competitive system) be at subsistence level, which depends upon the acceptance of the very theory that he at other times rejects.

From these premisses, the labour theory of value and the iron law of wages, the theory of surplus value seems to follow. The wage-earner, let us say, works twelve hours a day, and in six hours produces the value of his labour. What he produces in the remaining six hours represents the capitalist's exploitation, his surplus value. Although the capitalist does not have to pay for the last six hours, yet, for some unexplained reason, he is able to make the price of his product proportional to labour-time required for production. Marx forgets that this whole theory depended upon the assumption that all labour had to be paid for, and the further assumption that the capitalists competed with each other.[1] In the absence of these assumptions, there is no reason why value should be proportional to the labour-time of production.

If we assume that there are many competing capitalists in the business in question, then, supposing the state of affairs to have been initially as Marx supposes, it will be possible to lower the price and still make a profit, which will therefore be done as a result of competition. The capitalist, it is true, will have to pay rent, and probably interest on borrowed money; but so far as he is concerned, he will be forced down to the lowest profit at which he thinks it worth while to carry on the business. If, on the other hand, there is no competition, the price will be fixed, as with all monopolies, by the principle of 'what the traffic will bear', which has nothing to do with the amount of labour involved.

While, therefore, it is undeniable that men make fortunes by exploiting labour, Marx's analysis of the economic process by which this is done appears to be faulty. And the main reason why it is not correct is the acceptance of Ricardo's theory of value.

I have written above as though (apart from currency fluctuations) value could be measured by price. This, indeed, follows from the definition of value, which is the amount of other commodities for which a given commodity will exchange. Price is merely a means of expressing the exchange values of different commodities in commensurable terms: if we wish to compare the values of a number of different commodities, we do so most easily by means of their price, i.e. (under a gold currency) by their exchange value in relation to gold. In so far as value means 'exchange

[1] Though this is stated by Engels in his introduction to *La Misère de la Philosophie*.

value', the fact that (at any given moment) value is measured by price is a mere logical consequence of the definition.

But Marx has another conception of value which obscurely conflicts with the definition of value as exchange value. This other conception, which never emerges clearly, is ethical or metaphysical; it seems to mean 'what a commodity *ought* to exchange for'. A few quotations will illustrate the difficulty of arriving at Marx's meaning on this point.

'Price', he says, 'is the money-name of the labour realized in a commodity. Hence the expression of the equivalence of a commodity with the sum of money constituting its price, is a tautology, just as in general the expression of the relative value of a commodity is a statement of the equivalence of two commodities. But although price, being the exponent of the magnitude of a commodity's value, is the exponent of its exchange-ratio with money, it does not follow that the exponent of this exchange-ratio is necessarily the exponent of the magnitude of the commodity's value. . . . Magnitude of value expresses a relation of social production, it expresses the connection that necessarily exists between a certain article and the portion of the total labour-time of society required to produce it. As soon as the magnitude of value is converted into price, the above necessary relation takes the shape of a more or less accidental exchange-ratio between a single commodity and another, the money-commodity. But this exchange-ratio may express either the real magnitude of that commodity's value, or the quantity of gold deviating from that value, for which, according to circumstances, it may be parted with. The possibility, therefore, of quantitative incongruity between price and magnitude of value, or the deviation of the former from the latter, is inherent in the price-form itself.'

So far it might be supposed that Marx is thinking only of accidental fluctuations, such as might be due to the relative shrewdness or impecuniosity of buyer and seller. He goes on, however, to a more serious distinction between price and value, which, if he had followed it up, would have raised difficulties for him of which he apparently remained unaware. He says:

'The price-form, however, is not only compatible with the possibility of a quantitative incongruity between magnitude of value and price, i.e. between the former and its expression in money, but it may also conceal a qualitative inconsistency, so much so, that, although money is nothing but the value-form of commodities, price ceases altogether to express value. Objects that in themselves are no commodities, such as conscience, honour, &c., are capable of being offered for sale by their holders, and of thus acquiring, through their price, the form of commodities. Hence an object may have a price without having value. The price in that case is imaginary, like certain quantities in mathematics. On the other hand, the imaginary price-form may sometimes conceal either a direct or indirect real value-relation; for instance, the price of uncultivated land, which is without value, because no human labour has been incorporated in it.'

It is of course necessary for Marx, with his labour theory of value, to maintain that virgin land has no value. Since it often has a price, the distinction between price and value is essential to him at this point. Exchange-value, it now appears, is not the actual amount of other goods for which a given commodity can, in fact, be exchanged; it is the amount of goods for which the commodity could be exchanged *if* people valued commodities in proportion to the amount of labour required for their production. Marx concedes that people do not so value commodities when they are buying and selling, for, if they did, it would be impossible to exchange virgin land, upon which no labour has been expended, for gold, which has had to be mined. Accordingly when Marx says that the value of a commodity is measured by the amount of labour required for its production, he does not mean to say anything about what the commodity is likely to fetch in the market. What, then, does he mean?

He may mean either of two things. He may be giving a mere verbal definition of the word 'value': when I speak of the 'value' of a commodity (he may be saying), I mean the amount of labour required to produce it, or rather, such quantity of other commodities as an equivalent amount of labour would produce. Or, again, he may be using 'value' in an ethical sense: he may mean that goods *ought* to exchange in proportion to the labour involved, and would do so in a world ruled by economic justice. If he adopts the first of these alternatives, most of the propositions in his theory of value become trivial, while those which assert a connection between value and price become arbitrary and remain partly false. If he adopts the second alternative, he is no longer analysing economic facts, but setting up an economic ideal. Moreover, this ideal would be an impossible one, for the reasons emphasized in Ricardo's theory of rent: a bushel of wheat grown on bad land embodies more labour than one grown on good land, but could not in any imaginable economic system be sold at a higher price. Either the verbal or the ethical alternative as to the meaning of 'value', therefore, reduces Marx's economic theory to a state of confusion.

The ethical interpretation of 'value', nevertheless, seems to have had some influence, not only on Marx, but on all those who upheld the labour theory of value. In the case of Marx, this is borne out by the fact that, in connection with the price of virgin land, he mentions such things as the price of a man's honour, where we feel that there is something ethically reprehensible in the existence of a price. In the case of other economists, it is interesting to observe that Hodgskin, from whom Marx learned much, and who first among theorists applied the labour theory of value in the interests of the proletariat, finds the source of this theory in Locke's doctrine that the justification of private property is a man's right to the produce of his own labour.[1] If he exchanges the produce of his own labour for the produce of an equal amount of someone else's labour, justice is preserved; the labour theory is therefore in conformity with ethics. This point of view, perhaps unconsciously, seems to have influenced Marx: where price and value diverged, he felt that price represented the wickedness of capitalism.

Much of the efficacy of Marx's writing depends upon tacit assumptions in his arithmetical illustrations. Let us take one of these as typical of many.

'One more example. Jacob gives the following calculation for the year 1815. Owing to the previous adjustment of several items it is very imperfect; nevertheless for our purpose it is sufficient. In it he assumes the price of wheat to be 8s a quarter, and the average yield per acre to be twenty-two bushels.

Value Produced Per Acre

	£	s	d		£	s	d
Seed	1	9	0	Tithes, Rates, and Taxes	1	1	0
Manure	2	10	0	Rent	1	8	0
Wages	3	10	0	Farmer's Profit and Interest . . .	1	2	0
Total . . .	7	9	0	Total . . .	3	11	0

'Assuming that the price of the product is the same as its value, we here find the surplus value distributed under the various heads of profit, interest, rent, &c. We have nothing to do with these in detail; we simply add them together, and the sum is a surplus value of £3 11s 0d. The sum of £3 19s 0d, paid for seed and manure, is constant capital, and we put it equal to zero. There is left the sum of £3 10s 0d, which is the variable capital advanced: and we see that a new value of £3 10s 0d + £3 11s 0d has been produced in its place. Therefore $\frac{s}{v} = \frac{\text{£3 11s 0d}}{\text{£3 10s 0d}}$, giving a rate of surplus value of more than 100 per cent. The labourer employs more than one-half of his working day in producing the surplus value, which different persons, under different pretexts, share amongst themselves.'

In this illustration, s means surplus value, and v means variable capital, i.e. wages. It will be seen that Marx includes in surplus value the whole of what the farmer makes, and the whole of the rates and taxes. It is therefore implied in the calculation (a) that the farmer does no work, (b) that the rates and taxes are wholly handed over to the idle rich. Marx would not, of course, make either of these assumptions in explicit terms,

[1] Halévy, *Thomas Hodgskin*, pp. 208-9, Société Nouvelle de Librairie et d'édition, Paris, 1903.

but they are implicit in his figures, both in this case and in every analogous illustration. In 1815, the year to which the above example applies, the rates were mainly expended in wages, under the old Poor Law. The taxes, it is true, went chiefly to the fund-holders, but of the remainder some part was certainly spent in useful ways—for example, in keeping up the British Museum, without which Marx could not have written his *magnum opus*.

More important than the question of rates and taxes is the question of the capitalist's work. In the case of a small capitalist, such as a farmer, it is ridiculous to treat him as one of the idle rich. If a farm were run by the State, it would need an overseer, and a competent overseer could probably obtain a salary about equal to the farmer's profit, taking one year with another. The cotton manufacturers of the years before 1846, who formed Engels's conception of the capitalist, and thence Marx's, were largely men in a rather small way, who worked almost entirely on borrowed capital. Their income depended upon their skill in using the money that had been lent to them. It is true that they were brutal, but it is not true that they were idle. Somebody has to organize a factory, somebody has to buy the machinery and sell the product, somebody has to do the day-to-day supervision. In the early days of capitalism, all this was done by the employer; yet Marx regards the whole of his earnings as entirely due to appropriation of the surplus value created by the employees. I know there are passages where the opposite is admitted, but they are isolated, whereas the assumption that the employer does no work is pervasive.

In the modern large-scale developments of capitalistic enterprise, it is true, the capitalist is often idle. The shareholders of railways do nothing, and the directors do not do much, in the way of managing the business. The work of management, in all large concerns, tends to fall more and more into the hands of salaried experts, leaving the capitalists as mere recipients of interest. In so far as Socialism represents a more scientific organization of industry, less chaotic and less lacking in forethought, salaried experts might be expected to sympathize with it. They seldom do so, however, because, as a result of the bias given by Marx, Socialism has tended to stand, not only for the workers as against the idle rich, but for the manual workers as against both the rich and the brain workers. Marx, by ignoring the functions of the small-scale capitalist in managing his business, produced a theory which could not do justice to the salaried experts who do the work of management in large-scale capitalism. The glorification of manual work as against brain work was a theoretical error, and its political effects have been disastrous.

It may be said that it is of no importance whether Marx was right in the niceties of his economic analysis. He was right in maintaining that the proletariat were brutally exploited, and that their exploitation was due to the power of the rich. To distinguish one class of rich men from another was, from this point of view, unprofitable; the important thing was to end exploitation, and this could only be done by conquering power in a fight against the rich collectively.

To this there are two objections. The first is, that the abolition of exploitation, if unwisely carried out, might leave the proletariat even more destitute than before; the second, that Marx has not rightly analysed where the power of money resides, and has therefore given himself an unnecessary number of enemies.

The first of these objections applies to the destruction of any system in which power is unequally distributed. The holders of power will always use their position to obtain special advantages for themselves; at the same time, they will in general wish to prevent chaos, and to insure a certain efficiency in the system by which they profit. They will tend to have a monopoly of experience in government and management. It may well happen that, if they are suddenly dispossessed, lack of knowledge and experience on the part of those previously oppressed will cause them to fall into even greater sufferings than those from which they have escaped. If this is not to happen, there must be, on the side of the newly emancipated, a sufficient amount of governmental and technical intelligence to carry on the political and economic life of the community. Successful revolutions, such as the French Revolution, have had more knowledge and intelligence on the side of the rebels than among the defenders of the old system. Where this condition is not fulfilled, the transition is bound to be arduous, and may never succeed in producing any improvement. It is doubtful whether the population of Haiti has been happier since it threw off the power of the French.

As regards the analysis of the power of money, I think that Henry George was more nearly right than Marx. Henry George, following Spence and the French physiocrats, found the source of economic power in land, and held that the only necessary reform was the payment of rent to the State rather than to private landowners. This was also the view of Herbert Spencer until he became old and respected. In its older forms, it is scarcely applicable to the modern world, but it contains an important element of truth, which Marx unfortunately missed. Let us try to restate the matter in modern terms.

All power to exploit others depends upon the possession of some complete or partial, permanent or temporary monopoly, but this monopoly may be of the most diverse kinds. Land is the most obvious. If I own land in London or New York, I can, owing to the law of trespass, invoke the whole of the forces of the State to prevent others from making use of my land without my consent. Those who wish to live or work on my land must therefore pay me rent, and if my land is very advantageous they must pay me much rent. I do not have to do anything at all in return for the rent. The capitalist has to organize a business, the professional man has to exercise his skill, but the landowner can levy toll on their industry without doing anything at all. Similarly if I own coal or iron or any other mineral, I can make my own terms with those who wish to mine it, so long as I leave them an average rate of profit. Every improvement in industry, every increase in the population of cities, automatically augments what the landowner can exact in the form of rent. While others work, he remains idle; but their work enables him to grow richer and richer.

Land, however, is by no means the only form of monopoly. The owners of capital, collectively, are monopolists as against borrowers; that is why they are able to charge interest. The control of credit is a form of monopoly quite as important as land. Those who control credit can encourage or ruin a business as their judgement may direct; they can even, within limits, decide whether industry in general is to be prosperous or depressed. This power they owe to monopoly.

The men who have most economic power in the modern world derive it from land, minerals, and credit, in combination. Great bankers control iron ore, coalfields, and railways; smaller capitalists are at their mercy, almost as completely as proletarians. The conquest of economic power demands as its first step the ousting of the monopolists. It will then remain to be seen whether, in a world in which there is no private monopoly, much harm is done by men who have achieved success by skill without the aid of ultimate economic power. It is questionable whether, on the balance, the world would now be the better if Mr Henry Ford had been prevented from making cheap cars; and the harm that is done by great industrialists is usually dependent upon their access to some source of monopoly power. In labour disputes, the employer is the immediate enemy, but is often no more than a private in the opposing army. The real enemy is the monopolist.

(*Freedom and Organization*, London: Allen & Unwin; *Freedom Versus Organization*, New York: W. W. Norton, 1934.)

PART XIII

The Philosopher of History

Despite Russell's own admission that he is not a professional historian and that he approaches the subject with 'considerable trepidation', he does show keen insight into some of the crucial problems of history. Russell was intensely interested in history as a youth and ever kept alive this fascination in later life. With such an intense interest in the panorama of history, it is not surprising to find the philosopher early turning to the philosophy of history.

In addition to this interest in history for philosophers of history, Russell thinks that history should be of concern not only to academicians but that it should be 'an essential part of the furniture' of any educated mind. The man whose interests are governed by the short span between his birth and death has a myopic vision and limitation of outlook. On the other hand, one with a sense of history can foresee the tragedy of repeated blunders and face with stoic endurance the follies of the present. The selections that follow also show Russell's critical appraisal of theories of history and the practice of the writing of history.

56

ON HISTORY

OF all the studies by which men acquire citizenship of the intellectual commonwealth, no single one is so indispensable as the study of the past. To know how the world developed to the point at which our individual memory begins; how the religions, the institutions, the nations among which we live, became what they are; to be acquainted with the great of other times, with customs and beliefs differing widely from our own—these things are indispensable to any consciousness of our position, and to any emancipation from the accidental circumstances of our education. It is not only to the historian that history is valuable, not only to the professed student of archives and documents, but to all who are capable of a contemplative survey of human life. But the value of history is so multiform that those to whom some one of its sides appeals with especial force are in constant danger of forgetting all the others.

I

History is valuable, to begin with, because it is true; and this, though not the whole of its value, is the foundation and condition of all the rest. That all knowledge, as such, is in some degree good, would appear to be at least probable; and the knowledge of every historical fact possesses this element of goodness, even if it possesses no other. Modern historians, for the most part, seem to regard truth as constituting the whole of the value of history. On this ground they urge the self-effacement of the historian before the document; every intrusion of his own personality, they fear, will involve some degree of falsification. Objectivity before all things is to be sought, they tell us; let the facts be merely narrated, and allowed to speak for themselves—if they can find tongues. It follows, as a part of the position, that all facts are equally important; and, although this doctrine can never be quite conformed to in practice, it seems nevertheless to float before many minds as an ideal towards which research may gradually approximate.

That the writing of history should be based on the study of documents is an opinion which it would be absurd to controvert. For they alone contain evidence as to what really occurred; and it is plain that untrue history can have no great value. Moreover, there is more life in one document than in fifty histories (omitting a very few of the best); by the mere fact that it contains what belongs to that actual past time, it has a strangely vivid life-in-death, such as belongs to our own past when some sound or scent awakens it. And a history written after the event can hardly make us realize that the actors were ignorant of the future; it is difficult to believe that the late Romans did not know their empire was about to fall, or that Charles I was unaware of so notorious a fact as his own execution.

But if documents are, in so many ways, superior to any deliberate history, what function remains to the historian? There is, to begin with, the business of selection. This would be admitted by all; for the materials are so vast that it is impossible to present the whole of them. But it is not always realized that selection involves a standard of value among facts, and therefore implies that truth is not the sole aim in recording the past. For all facts are equally true; and selection among them is only possible by means of some other criterion than their truth. And the existence of some such criterion is obvious; no one would maintain, for example, that the little Restoration scandals recorded by Grammont are as important as the letters on the Piedmontese massacres, by which Milton, in the name of Cromwell, summoned the tardy potentates of Europe.

It may be said, however, that the only true principle of selection is the purely scientific one; those facts are to be regarded as important which lead to the establishment of general laws. Whether there ever will be a science of history it is quite impossible to guess; at any rate it is certain that no such science exists at present, except to some slight degree in the province of economics. In order that the scientific criterion of importance among facts should be applicable, it is necessary that two or more hypotheses should have been invented, each accounting for a large number of the facts, and that then a crucial fact should be discovered which discriminates between the rivals. Facts are important, in the inductive sciences, solely in relation to theories; and new theories give importance to new facts. So, for example, the doctrine of Natural Selection brought into prominence all transitional and intermediate species, the existence of rudiments, and the embryological record of descent. But it will hardly be maintained that history has reached, or is soon likely to reach, a point where such standards are applicable to its facts. History, considered as a body of truth, seems destined long to remain almost purely descriptive. Such generalizations as have been suggested—omitting the sphere of economics—are, for the most part, so plainly unwarranted as to be not even worthy of refutation. Burke argued that all revolutions end in military tyrannies, and predicted Napoleon. In so far as his argument was based on the analogy of Cromwell, it was a very lucky hit; but certainly not a scientific law. It is true that numerous instances are not always necessary to establish a law, provided the essential and relevant circumstances can be easily disentangled. But, in history, so many circumstances of a small and accidental nature are relevant that no broad and simple uniformities are possible.

And there is a further point against this view of history as solely or chiefly a causal science. Where our main endeavour is to discover general laws, we regard these as intrinsically more valuable than any of the facts which they interconnect. In astronomy, the law of gravitation is plainly better worth knowing than the position of a particular planet on a particular night, or even on every night throughout a year. There are in the law a splendour and simplicity and sense of mastery which illuminate a mass of otherwise uninteresting details. And so again in biology: until the theory of evolution put meaning into the bewildering variety of organic structures, the particular facts were interesting only to the professed naturalist. But in history the matter is far otherwise. In economics, it is true, the data are often subordinate to the attempts at science which are based upon them; but in all other departments, the data are more interesting, and the scientific superstructure less satisfactory. Historical facts, many of them, have an intrinsic value, a profound interest on their own account, which makes them worthy of study, quite apart from any possibility of linking them together by means of causal laws.

The study of history is often recommended on the ground of its utility in regard to the problems of present-day politics. That history has great utility in this respect it is impossible to deny; but it is necessary very carefully to limit and define the kind of guidance to be expected from it. The 'teachings of history', in the crude sense, presuppose the discovery of causal laws, usually of a very sweeping kind; and 'teachings' of this sort, though in certain cases they may do no harm, are always theoretically unsound. In the eighteenth century perpetually, and in our own day occasionally, arguments as to the value of liberty or democracy are drawn from Greece and Rome; their greatness or their decay, according to the bias of the author, is attributed to these causes. What can be more grotesque than to hear the rhetoric of the Romans applied to the circumstances of the French Revolution! The whole organization of a City State, based on slavery, without representative institutions, and without printing, is so utterly remote from any modern democracy as to make all analogy, except of the vaguest kind, totally frivolous and unreal. So with regard to imperialism, arguments are drawn from the successes and failures of the ancients. Shall we believe, for example, that Rome was ruined by the perpetual extension of her frontiers? Or shall we believe, with Mommsen, that the failure to conquer the Germans between the Rhine and the Danube was one of her most fatal errors? All such arguments will always be conducted according to the prejudices of the author; and all alike, even if they have some measure of truth in regard to the past, must be quite inapplicable to the present.

This evil is greatest when history is regarded as teaching some general philosophical doctrine, such as: Right, in the long run, is Might; Truth always prevails in the end; or, Progress is a universal law of society. All such doctrines require, for their support, a careful choice of place and time, and, what is worse, a falsification of values. A very flagrant instance of this danger is Carlyle. In the case of Puritanism, it led him to justify all Cromwell's acts of impatience and illegality, and arbitrarily to arrest his survey in 1658; how he accounted for the Restoration it is impossible to say. In other cases, it led him still further astray. For it is often hard to discover on which side the Right lies, but the Might is visible to all men; thus the doctrine that Right is Might slides insensibly into the belief that Might is Right. Hence the praise of Frederick and Napoleon and Bismarck, the pitiless contempt for the negroes, the Irish, and the 'thirty-thousand distressed needlewomen'. In some such way, every general theory that all is for the best must be forced by the facts into defence of the indefensible.

Nevertheless, history has a function in regard to current affairs, but a function less direct, less exact, and less decisive. It may, in the first place, suggest minor maxims, whose truth, when they are once propounded, can be seen without the help of the events that suggested them. This is largely the case in economics, where most of the motives concerned are simple. It is the case also, for a similar reason, in regard to strategy. Wherever, out of the facts, a simple deductive argument from indubitable premises can be elicited, history may yield useful precepts. But these will only apply where the end is given, and are therefore of a technical nature. They can never tell the statesman what end to pursue, but only, within certain limits, how some of the more definite ends, such as wealth, or victory in war, are to be attained.

II

Another and a greater utility, however, belongs also to history. It enlarges the imagination, and suggests possibilities of action and feeling which would not have occurred to an uninstructed mind. It selects from past lives the elements which were significant and important; it fills our thoughts with splendid examples, and with the desire for greater ends than unaided reflection would have discovered. It relates the present to the past, and thereby the future to the present. It makes visible and living the growth and greatness of nations, enabling us to extend our hopes beyond the span of our own lives. In all these ways, a knowledge of history is capable of giving to statesmanship, and to our daily thoughts, a breadth and scope unattainable by those whose view is limited to the present.

What the past does for us may be judged, perhaps, by the consideration of those younger nations whose energy and enterprise are winning the envy of Europe. In them we see developing a type of man, endowed with all the hopefulness of the Renaissance or of the Age of Pericles, persuaded that his more vigorous efforts can quickly achieve whatever has proved too difficult for the generations that preceded him. Ignorant and contemptuous of the aims that inspired those generations, unaware of the complex problems that they attempted to solve, his rapid success in comparatively simple achievements encourages his confident belief that the future belongs to him. But to those who have grown up surrounded by monuments of men and deeds whose memory they cherish, there is a curious thinness about the thoughts and emotions that inspire this confidence; optimism seems to be sustained by a too exclusive pursuit of what can be easily achieved; and hopes are not transmuted into ideals by the habit of appraising current events by their relation to the history of the past. Whatever is different from the present is despised. That among those who contributed nothing to the dominion of Mammon great men lived, that wisdom may reside in those whose thoughts are not dominated by the machine, is incredible to this temper of mind. Action, Success, Change, are its watchwords; whether the action is noble, the success in a good cause, or the change an improvement in anything except wealth, are questions which there is no time to ask. Against this spirit, whereby all leisure, all care for the ends of life, are sacrificed to the struggle to be first in a worthless race, history and the habit of living with the past are the surest antidotes; and in our age, more than ever before, such antidotes are needed.

The record of great deeds is a defeat of Time; for it prolongs their power through many ages after they and their authors have been swallowed by the abyss of the non-existent. And, in regard to the past, where contemplation is not obscured by desire and the need for action, we see, more clearly than in the lives about us, the value for good and evil, of the aims men have pursued and the means they have adopted. It is good, from time to time, to view the present as already past, and to examine what elements it contains that will add to the world's store of permanent possessions, that will live and give life when we and all our generation have perished. In the light of this contemplation all human experience is transformed, and whatever is sordid or personal is purged away. And, as we grow in wisdom, the treasure-house of the ages opens to our view; more and more we learn to know and love the men through whose devotion all this wealth has become ours. Gradually, by the contemplation of great lives, a mystic communion becomes possible, filling the soul like music from an invisible choir. Still, out of the past, the voices of heroes call us. As, from a lofty promontory, the bell of an ancient cathedral, unchanged since the day when Dante returned from the kingdom of the dead, still sends its solemn warning across the waters, so their voice still sounds across the intervening sea of time; still, as then, its calm deep tones speak to the solitary tortures of cloistered aspiration, putting the serenity of things eternal in place of the doubtful struggle against ignoble joys and transient pleasures. Not by those about them were they heard; but they spoke to the winds of heaven, and the winds of heaven tell the tale to the great of later days. The great are not solitary; out of the night come the voices of those who have gone before, clear and courageous; and so through the ages they march, a mighty procession, proud, undaunted, unconquerable. To join in this glorious company, to swell the immortal paeon of those whom fate could not subdue—this may not be happiness; but what is happiness to those whose souls are filled with that celestial music? To them is given what is better than happiness: to know the fellowship of the great, to live in the inspiration of lofty thoughts, and to be illumined in every perplexity by the fire of nobility and truth.

But history is more than the record of individual men, however great: it is the province of history to tell the biography, not only of men, but of Man; to present the long procession of generations as but the passing thoughts of one continuous life; to transcend their blindness and brevity in the slow unfolding of the tremendous drama in which all play their part. In the migrations of races, in the birth and death of religions, in the rise and fall of empires, the unconscious units, without any purpose beyond the moment, have contributed unwittingly to the pageant of the ages; and, from the greatness of the whole, some breath of greatness breathes over all who participated in the march. In this lies the haunting power of the dim history beyond written records. There, nothing is known but the cloudy outlines of huge events; and, of all the separate lives that came and went, no memory remains. Through unnumbered generations, forgotten sons worshipped at the tombs of forgotten fathers, forgotten mothers bore warriors whose bones whitened the silent steppes of Asia. The clash of arms, the hatreds and oppressions, the blind conflicts of dumb nations, are all still, like a distant waterfall; but slowly, out of the strife, the nations that we know emerged, with a heritage of poetry and piety transmitted from the buried past.

And this quality, which is all that remains of pre-historic times, belongs also to the later periods where the knowledge of details is apt to obscure the movement of the whole. We, too, in all our deeds, bear our part in a process of which we cannot guess the development: even the obscurest are actors in a drama of which we know only that it is great. Whether any purpose that we value will be achieved, we cannot tell; but the drama itself, in any case, is full of Titanic grandeur. This quality it is the business of the historian to extract from the bewildering multitude of irrelevant details. From old books, wherein the loves, the hopes, the faiths of bygone generations lie embalmed, he calls pictures before our minds, pictures of high endeavours and brave hopes, living still through his care, in spite of failure and death. Before all is wrapped in oblivion, the historian must compose afresh, in each succeeding age, the epitaph upon the life of Man.

The past alone is truly real: the present is but a painful, struggling birth into the immutable being of what is no longer. Only the dead exist fully. The lives of the living are fragmentary, doubtful, and subject to change; but the lives of the dead are complete, free from the sway of Time, the all-but omnipotent lord of the world. Their failures and successes, their hopes and fears, their joys and pains, have become eternal—our efforts cannot now abate one jot of them. Sorrows long buried in the grave, tragedies of which only a fading memory remains, loves immortalized by Death's hallowing touch—these have a power, a magic, an untroubled calm, to which no present can attain.

Year by year, comrades die, hopes prove vain, ideals fade; the enchanted land of youth grows more remote, the road of life more wearisome; the burden of the world increases until the labour and the pain become almost too heavy to be borne; joy fades from the weary nations of the earth and the tyranny of the future saps men's vital force; all that we love is waning, waning from the dying world. But the past, ever devouring the transient offspring of the present, lives by the universal death; steadily, irresistibly, it adds new trophies to its silent temple, which all the ages build; every great deed, every splendid life, every achievement and every heroic failure, is there enshrined. On the banks of the river of Time, the sad procession of human generations is marching slowly to the grave; in the quiet country of the Past, the march is ended, the tired wanderers rest, and all their weeping is hushed.

(*The Independent Review*, July 1904.)

57

THE MATERIALISTIC THEORY OF HISTORY

THE materialistic conception of history, as it is called, is due to Marx, and underlies the whole Communist philosophy. I do not mean, of course, that a man could not be a Communist without accepting it, but that in fact it is accepted by the Communist Party, and that it profoundly influences their views as to politics and tactics. The name does not convey at all accurately what is meant by the theory. It means that all the mass-phenomena of history are determined by economic motives. This view has no essential connection with materialism in the philosophic sense. Materialism in the philosophic sense may be defined as the theory that all apparently mental occurrences either are really physical, or at any rate have purely physical causes. Materialism in this sense also was preached by Marx, and is accepted by all orthodox Marxians. The arguments for and against it are long and complicated, and need not concern us, since, in fact, its truth or falsehood has little or no bearing on politics.

In particular, philosophic materialism does not prove that economic causes are fundamental in politics. The view of Buckle, for example, according to which climate is one of the decisive factors, is equally compatible with materialism. So is the Freudian view, which traces everything to sex. There are innumerable ways of viewing history which are materialistic in the philosophic sense without being economic or falling within the Marxian formula. Thus the 'materialistic conception of history' may be false even if materialism in the philosophic sense should be true.

On the other hand, economic causes might be at the bottom of all political events even if philosophic materialism were false. Economic causes operate through men's desire for possessions, and would be supreme if this desire were supreme, even if desire could not, from a philosophic point of view, be explained in materialistic terms.

There is, therefore, no logical connection either way between philosophic materialism and what is called the 'materialistic conception of history'.

It is of some moment to realize such facts as this, because otherwise political theories are both supported and opposed for quite irrelevant reasons, and arguments of theoretical philosophy are employed to determine questions which depend upon concrete facts of human nature. This mixture damages both philosophy and politics, and is therefore important to avoid.

For another reason, also, the attempt to base a political theory upon philosophical doctrine is undesirable. The philosophical doctrine of materialism, if true at all, is true everywhere and always; we cannot expect exceptions to it, say, in Buddhism or in the Hussite movement. And so it comes about that people whose politics are supposed to be a consequence of their metaphysics grow absolute and sweeping, unable to admit that a general theory of history is likely, at best, to be only true on the whole and in the main. The dogmatic character of Marxian Communism finds support in the supposed philosophic basis of the doctrine; it has the fixed certainty of Catholic theology, not the changing fluidity and sceptical practicality of modern science.

Treated as a practical approximation, not as an exact metaphysical law, the materialistic conception of history has a very large measure of truth. Take, as an instance of its truth, the influence of industrialism upon ideas. It is industrialism, rather than the arguments of Darwinians and Biblical critics, that has led to the decay of religious belief in the urban working class. At the same time, industrialism has revived religious belief among the rich. In the eighteenth century French aristocrats mostly became free-thinkers; now their descendants are mostly Catholics, because it has become necessary for all the forces of reaction to unite against the revolutionary proletariat. Take, again, the emancipation of women. Plato, Mary Wolstonecraft, and John Stuart Mill produced admirable arguments, but influenced only a few impotent idealists. The war came, leading to the employment of women in industry on a large scale, and instantly the arguments in favour of votes for women were seen to be irresistible. More than that, traditional sexual morality collapsed, because its whole basis was the economic dependence of women upon their fathers and husbands. Changes in such a matter as sexual morality bring with them profound alterations in the thoughts and feelings of ordinary men and women; they modify law, literature, art, and all kinds of institutions that seem remote from economics.

Such facts as these justify Marxians in speaking, as they do, of 'bourgeois ideology', meaning that kind of morality which has been imposed upon the world by the possessors of capital. Contentment with one's lot may be taken as typical of the virtues preached by the rich to the poor. They honestly believe it is a virtue—at any rate they did formerly. The more religious among the poor also believed it, partly from the influence of authority, partly from an impulse to submission, what MacDougall calls 'negative self-feeling', which is commoner than some people think. Similarly men preached the virtue of female chastity, and women usually accepted their teaching; both really believed the doctrine, but its persistence was only possible through the economic power of men. This led erring women to punishment here on earth, which made further punishment hereafter seem probable. When the economic penalty ceased, the conviction of sinfulness gradually decayed. In such changes we see the collapse of 'bourgeois ideology'.

But in spite of the fundamental importance of economic facts in determining the politics and beliefs of an age or nation, I do not think that non-economic factors can be neglected without risks of errors which may be fatal in practice.

The most obvious non-economic factor, and the one the neglect of which has led Socialists most astray, is nationalism. Of course a nation, once formed, has economic interests which largely determine its politics; but it is not, as a rule, economic motives that decide what group of human beings shall form a nation. Trieste, before the war, considered itself Italian, although its whole prosperity as a port depended upon its belonging to Austria. No economic motive can account for the opposition between Ulster and the rest of Ireland. In Eastern Europe, the Balkanization produced by self-determination has been obviously disastrous from an economic point of view, and was demanded for reasons which were in essence sentimental. Throughout the war wage-earners, with only a few exceptions, allowed themselves to be governed by nationalist feeling, and ignored the traditional Communist exhortation: 'Workers of the world, unite.' According to Marxian orthodoxy, they were misled by cunning capitalists, who made their profit out of the slaughter. But to anyone capable of observing psychological facts, it is obvious that this is largely a myth. Immense numbers of capitalists were ruined by the war; those who were young were just as liable to be killed as the proletarians were. No doubt commercial rivalry between England and Germany had a great deal to do with causing the war; but rivalry is a different thing from profit-seeking. Probably by combination English and German capitalists could have made more than they did out of rivalry, but the rivalry was instinctive, and its economic form was accidental. The capitalists were in the grip of nationalist instinct as much as their proletarian 'dupes'. In both classes some have gained by the war; but the universal will to war was not produced by the hope of gain. It was produced by a different set of instincts, and one which Marxian psychology fails to recognize adequately.

The Marxian assumes that a man's 'herd', from the point of view of herd-instinct, is his class, and that he will combine with those whose economic class-interest is the same as his. This is only very partially true in fact. Religion has been the most decisive factor in determining a man's herd throughout long periods of the world's history. Even now a Catholic working man will vote for a Catholic capitalist rather than for an unbelieving Socialist. In America the divisions in local elections are mainly on religious lines. This is no doubt convenient for the capitalists, and tends to make them religious men; but the capitalists alone could not produce the result. The result is produced by the fact that many working men prefer the advancement of their creed to the improvement of their livelihood. However deplorable such a state of mind may be, it is not necessarily due to capitalist lies.

All politics are governed by human desires. The materialist theory of history, in the last analysis, requires the assumption that every politically conscious person is governed by one single desire—the desire to increase his own share of commodities; and, further, that his method of achieving this desire will usually be to seek to increase the share of his class, not only his own individual share. But this assumption is very far from the truth. Men desire power, they desire satisfactions for their pride and their self-respect. They desire victory over rivals so profoundly that they will invent a rivalry for the unconscious purpose of making a victory possible. All these motives cut across the pure economic motive in ways that are practically important.

There is need of a treatment of political motives by the methods of psycho-analysis. In politics, as in private life, men invent myths to rationalize their conduct. If a man thinks that the only reasonable motive in politics is economic self-advancement, he will persuade himself that the things he wishes to do will make him rich. When he wants to fight the Germans, he tells himself that their competition is ruining his trade. If, on the other hand, he is an 'idealist', who holds that his politics should aim at the advancement of the human race, he will tell himself that the crimes of the Germans demand their humiliation. The Marxian sees through this latter camouflage, but not through the former. To desire one's own economic advancement is comparatively reasonable; to Marx, who inherited eighteenth-century rationalist psychology from the British orthodox economists, self-enrichment seemed the natural aim of a man's political actions. But modern psychology has dived much deeper into the ocean of insanity upon which the little barque of human reason insecurely floats. The intellectual optimism of a bygone age is no longer possible to the modern student of human nature. Yet it lingers in Marxism, making Marxians rigid and Procrustean in their treatment of the life of instinct. Of this rigidity the materialistic conception of history is a prominent instance.

In the next chapter I shall attempt to outline a political psychology which seems to me more nearly true than that of Marx.

(*The Practice and Theory of Bolshevism*,
London: Allen & Unwin, 1920.)

58

HISTORY AS AN ART

I AM approaching the subject of this lecture with considerable trepidation. I know that among my hearers there are professional historians whom I greatly respect, and I should not at all wish to seem desirous of instructing them as to how their work should be done. I shall speak as a consumer, not a producer. In shops they have a maxim: 'The customer is always right.' But academic persons (among whom I should wish to include myself) are more lordly than shopkeepers: if the consumer does not like what he is offered, that is because he is a Philistine and because he does not know what is good for him. Up to a point I sympathize with this attitude. It would never do for a mathematician to try to please the general reader. The physical sciences in their serious aspects must be addressed primarily to specialists, though their more adventurous practitioners write occasional books designed to make your flesh creep. But such books are not regarded by their fellow-scientists as part of their serious work, and detract from, rather than add to, their professional reputation. I think that in this respect history is in a position different from that of mathematics and physical science. There have to be physicists, worse luck, and there have to be mathematicians until calculating machines become cheaper, but when that happy consummation has been reached, there will be no point in teaching anybody to do sums, and the multiplication table can be placed alongside the birch as an out-of-date instrument of education. But history seems to me to be in a different category. The multiplication table, though useful, can hardly be called beautiful. It is seldom that essential wisdom in regard to human destiny is to be found by remembering even its more difficult items. History, on the other hand, is—so I shall contend—a desirable part of everybody's mental furniture in the same kind of way as is generally recognized in the case of poetry. If history is to fulfil this function, it can only do so by appealing to those who are not professional historians. I have myself always found very great interest in the reading of history, and I have been grateful to those historians who gave me what I, as a consumer, though not a producer, was looking for in their books. It is from this point of view that I wish to speak. I wish to set forth what those who are not historians ought to get from history. And this is a theme upon which you will, I think, admit that non-historians have a right to express an opinion.

There has been much argumentation, to my mind somewhat futile, as to whether history is a science or an art. It should, I think, have been entirely obvious that it is both. Trevelyan's *Social History of England* indubitably deserves praise from the artistic point of view, but I remember finding in it a statement to the effect that England's maritime greatness was due to a change in the habits of herrings. I know nothing about herrings, so I accept this statement on authority. My point is that it is a piece of science, and that its scientific character in no way detracts from the artistic value of Trevelyan's work. Nevertheless, the work of historians can be divided into two branches, according as the scientific or the artistic motive predominates.

When people speak of history as a science, there are two very different things that may be meant. There is a comparatively pedestrian sense in which science is involved in ascertaining historical facts. This is especially important in early history, where evidence is both scarce and obscure, but it arises also in more recent times whenever, as is apt to be the case, there is a conflict of testimony. How much are we to believe of Procopius? Is there anything of historical value to be made out of Napoleon's lucubrations in St Helena? Such questions are in a sense scientific, since they concern the weight to be attached to different sources of evidence. They are matters as to which the historian may justifiably address himself to other historians, since the considerations involved are likely to be obscure and specialized. Work of this sort is presupposed in any attempt to write large-scale history. History, however much it may be pursued as an art, has to be controlled by the attempt to be true to fact. Truth to fact is a rule of the art, but does not in itself confer artistic excellence. It is like the rules of the sonnet, which can be scrupulously observed without conferring merit on the result. But history cannot be praiseworthy, even from the most purely artistic point of view, unless the historian does his utmost to preserve fidelity to the facts. Science in this sense is absolutely essential to the study of history.

There is another sense in which history attempts to be scientific, and this sense raises more difficult questions. In this sense history seeks to discover causal laws connecting different facts, in the same sort of way in which physical sciences have succeeded in discovering interconnections among facts. The attempt to discover such causal laws in history is entirely praiseworthy, but I do not think that it is what gives the most value to historical studies. I found an admirable discussion of this matter in an essay which I had read forty years ago and largely forgotten: I mean George Trevelyan's *Clio, a Muse*. He points out that in history we are interested in the particular facts and not only in their causal relations. It may be, as some have suggested, that Napoleon lost the battle of Leipzig because he ate a peach after the battle of Dresden. If this is the case, it is no doubt not without interest. But the events which it connects are on their own account much more interesting. In physical science, exactly the opposite is true. Eclipses, for example, are not very interesting in themselves except when they give fixed points in very early history, as is the case with the eclipse in Asia Minor which helps to date Thales and the eclipse in China in 776 B.C. (some authorities say that it was in 775 B.C. I leave this question to historians and astronomers). But although most eclipses are not interesting in themselves, the laws which determine their recurrence are of the very highest interest, and the discovery of these laws was of immense importance in dispelling superstition. Similarly, the experimental facts upon which modern physics is based would be totally uninteresting if it were not for the causal laws that they help to establish. But history is not like this. Most of the value of history is lost if we are not interested in the things that happen for their own sakes. In this respect history is like poetry. There is a satisfaction to curiosity in discovering why Coleridge wrote 'Kubla Khan' as he did, but this satisfaction is a trivial affair compared to that which we derive from the poem itself.

I do not mean to deny that it is a good thing to discover causal sequences in history when it is possible, but I think the possibility exists only in rather limited fields. Gresham's law that bad money drives out good is an example of one of the best established of such causal sequences. The whole science of economics, in so far as it is valid, consists of causal laws illustrated by historical facts. But as everybody now recognizes, supposed laws of economics have a much more temporary and local validity than was thought a hundred years ago. One of the difficulties in searching for such laws is that there is not so much recurrence in history as in astronomy. It may be true, as Meyers maintains in his little book on *The Dawn of History*, that on four separate occasions drought in Arabia has caused a wave of Semitic conquest, but it is hardly to be supposed that the same cause would produce the same effect at the present day. Even when historical causal sequences are established as regards the past, there is not much reason to expect that they will hold in the future, because the relevant facts are so complex that unforeseeable changes may falsify our predictions. No historian, however scientific, could have predicted in the fourteenth century the changes brought about by Columbus and Vasco da Gama. For these reasons I think that scientific laws in history are neither so important nor so discoverable as is sometimes maintained.

This applies with especial force to those large schemes of historical development which have fascinated many eminent men from St Augustine to Professor Toynbee. In modern times, the most important inventors of general theories as to human development have been Hegel and his disciple Marx. Both believed that the history of the past obeyed a logical *schema,* and that this same *schema* gave a means of foretelling the future. Neither foresaw the hydrogen bomb, and no doctrine of human development hitherto concocted enables us to foresee the effects of this ingenious device. If this reflection seems gloomy, I will add another of a more cheerful sort: I cannot accept the view of Spengler that every society must inevitably grow old and decay like an individual human body. I think this view results from unduly pressing the analogy between a social and an individual organism. Most societies have perished by assassination, and not by old age. Some might maintain that Chinese society has been decrepit ever since the fall of the Han dynasty; but it survived because the countries immediately to the West of China were sparsely inhabited. What has put an end to the traditional civilization of China is not any new inherent weakness, but the improvement in means of communication with the West. Some among the Stoics thought that the world would be periodically destroyed by fire and then recreated. There is evidently something in this view which suits men's preconceptions, and in milder forms it underlies almost all general theories of human development that historians have invented. All alike, I should say, are no more than myths, agreeable or disagreeable according to the temperaments of their inventors.

There is a department of history which has always interested me, perhaps beyond its intrinsic importance. It is that of by-paths in history: communities which have become isolated from the main current of their parent countries, but have trickled by unforeseen courses into the main stream of quite other rivers. From this point of view I have long been fascinated by the Bactrian Greeks. I thought that they had been completely lost, like a river absorbed by the desert, and then I learnt, to my no small delight, that they had become the source of Buddhist art and had inspired the statuary of the East through many ages and in many lands. Another example of the same kind of by-path is that of the Bogomils in Bulgaria, who were obscure disciples of Marcian and Mani, and whose doctrines, by means of certain misguided crusaders, were adopted by the Cathari in northern Italy and the Albigenses in Southern France. A still more remarkable example of the same kind of thing appears in the history of New England. From early boyhood I had known of Pride's Purge, when the haughty soldier caused the Long Parliament to tremble in the name of theological truth and the wages due to the army. But it had never occurred to me to wonder what became of Pride after 1660. In 1896 I was taken to a place in New England called Pride's Crossing, and was informed that it was called after the eponymous hero of the Purge. I learnt that he had had to leave his native country and settle upon a wild and rocky shore where the winter was long, the soil infertile, and the Indians dangerous. It might have seemed to Charles II and his courtiers that Pride had met his deserts, but after two and a half centuries his descendants rule the world and the descendants of Charles II tremble at their frown.

I come now to my main theme, which is what history can do and should do for the general reader. I am not thinking of what history does for historians; I am thinking of history as an essential part of the furniture of an educated mind. We do not think that poetry should only be read by poets, or that music should only be heard by composers. And, in like manner, history should not be known only to historians. But clearly the kind of history which is to contribute to the mental life of those who are not historians must have certain qualities that more professional work need not have, and, conversely, does not require certain things which one would look for in a learned monograph. I will try to say—though I find it very difficult—what I feel that I personally have derived from the reading of history. I should put first and foremost something like a new dimension in the individual life, a sense of being a drop in a great river rather than a tightly bounded separate entity. The man whose interests are bounded by the short span between his birth and death has a myopic vision and a limitation of outlook which can hardly fail to narrow the scope of his hopes and desires. And what applies to an individual man, applies also to a community. Those communities that have as yet little history make upon a European a curious impression of thinness and isolation. They do not feel themselves the inheritors of the ages, and for that reason what they aim at transmitting to their successors seems jejune and emotionally poor to one in whom the past is vivid and the future is illuminated by knowledge of the slow and painful achievements of former times. History makes one aware that there is no finality in human affairs; there is not a static perfection and an unimprovable wisdom to be achieved. Whatever wisdom we may have achieved is a small matter in comparison with what is possible. Whatever beliefs we may cherish, even those that we deem most important, are not likely to last for ever; and, if we imagine that they embody eternal verities, the future is likely to make a mock of us. Cock-sure certainty is the source of much that is worst in our present world, and it is something of which the contemplation of history ought to cure us, not only or chiefly because there were wise men in the past, but because so much that was thought wisdom turned out to be folly— which suggests that much of our own supposed wisdom is no better.

I do not mean to maintain that we should lapse into a lazy scepticism. We should hold our beliefs, and hold them strongly. Nothing great is achieved without passion, but underneath the passion there should always be that large impersonal survey which sets limits to actions that our passions inspire. If you think ill of Communism or capitalism, should you exterminate the human race in order that there may be no more Communists or capitalists as the case may be? Few people would deliber- ately assert that this would be wise, and yet it is a consummation towards which some politicians who are not historically minded seem to be leading mankind. This is an extreme example, but it is by no means difficult to think of innumerable others.

Leaving these general and rather discursive considerations, let us come to the question how history should be written if it is to produce the best possible result in the non-historical reader. Here there is first of all an extremely simple requirement: it must be interesting. I mean that it must be interesting not only to men who for some special reason wish to know some set of historical facts, but to those who are reading in the same spirit in which one reads poetry or a good novel. This requires first and foremost that the historian should have feelings about the events that he is relating and the characters that he is portraying. It is of course imperative that the historian should not distort facts, but it is not imperative that he should not take sides in the clashes and conflicts that fill his pages. An historian who is impartial, in the sense of not liking one party better than another and not allowing himself to have heroes and villains among his characters, will be a dull writer. If the reader is to be interested, he must be allowed to take sides in the drama. If this causes an historian to be one-sided, the only remedy is to find another historian with an opposite bias. The history of the Reformation, for example, can be interesting when it is written by a Protestant historian, and can be equally interesting when it is written by a Catholic historian. If you wish to know what it felt like to live at the time of the Wars of Religion you will perhaps succeed if you read both Protestant and Catholic histories, but you will not succeed if you read only men who view the whole series of events with complete detachment. Carlyle said about his history of the French Revolution that his book was itself a kind of French Revolution. This is true, and it gives the book a certain abiding merit in spite of its inadequacy as an historical record. As you read it you understand why people did what they did, and this is one of the most important things that a history ought to do for the reader. At one time I read what Diodorus Siculus has to say about Agathocles, who appeared as an unmitigated ruffian. I looked up Agathocles afterwards in a modern reference book and found him represented as bland and statesmanlike and probably innocent of all the crimes imputed to him. I have no means of knowing which of these two accounts is the more true, but I know that the white-washing account was completely uninteresting. I do not like a tendency, to which some modern historians are prone, to tone down everything dramatic and make out that heroes were not so very heroic and villains not so very villainous. No doubt a love of drama can lead an historian astray; but there is drama in plenty that requires no falsification, though only literary skill can convey it to the reader.

'Literary skill' is a large and general phrase, and it may be worth while to give it a more specific meaning. There is, first of all, style in the narrow sense of the word, especially diction and rhythm. Some words, especially those invented for scientific purposes, have merely a dictionary meaning. If you found the word 'tetrahedron' on a page, you would at once begin to feel bored. But the word 'pyramid' is a fine, rich word, which brings Pharaohs and Aztecs floating into the mind. Rhythm is a matter dependent upon emotion: what is strongly felt will express itself naturally in a rhythmical and varied form. For this reason, among others, a writer needs a certain freshness of feeling which is apt to be destroyed by fatigue and by the necessity of consulting authorities. I think—though this is perhaps counsel of perfection—that before an historian actually composes a chapter, he should have the material so familiarly in his mind that his pen never has to pause for verification of what he is saying. I do not mean that verification is unnecessary, because everybody's memory plays tricks, but that it should come after, and not during, composition. Style, when it is good, is a very personal expression of the writer's way of feeling and for that reason, among others, it is fatal to imitate even the most admirable style. Somewhere in Milman's *History of Christianity* (I speak from memory), he says: 'Rhetoric was still studied as a fine, though considered as a mere, art.' The shade of Gibbon, if it was looking over Milman's shoulder, must have been pained by this sentence.

If expository prose is to be interesting, there has to be a period of incubation, after the necessary knowledge has been acquired, when the bare facts will become clothed with such associations as are appropriate, of analogy or pathos or irony or what not, and when they will compose themselves into the unity of a pattern as in a play. This sort of thing is hardly likely to happen adequately unless the author has a fair amount of leisure and not an unfair amount of fatigue. Conscientious people are apt to work too hard and to spoil their work by doing so. Bagehot speaks somewhere of men he knew in the City who went bankrupt because they worked eight hours a day, but would have been rich if they had confined themselves to four hours. I think many learned men could profit by this analogy.

Within the compass of history as an art there are various kinds of history, each of which has its own peculiar kind of merit. One of these kinds of merit is especially exemplified by Gibbon, who offers us a stately procession of characters marching through the ages, all in court dress and yet all individual. Not long ago I was reading about Zenobia in the *Cambridge Ancient History*, but I regret to say that she appeared completely uninteresting. I remembered somewhat dimly a much more lively account in Gibbon. I looked it up, and at once the masterful lady came alive. Gibbon had had his feelings about her, and had imagined what it would be like to be at her Court. He had written with lively fancy, and not merely with cold desire to chronicle known facts. It is odd that one does not more resent the fact that his characters all have to be fitted into an eighteenth-

century mould. I remember that somewhere in dealing with the Vandals
after the time of Genseric he speaks of 'the polished tyrants of Africa'. I
am quite unable to believe that these men were polished, though I have
no difficulty in believing that they were tyrants. But somehow, in spite of
such limitations, Gibbon conveys an extraordinarily vivid sense of the
march of events throughout the centuries with which he deals. His book
illustrates what I am firmly persuaded is true, that great history must be
the work of a single man and cannot possibly be achieved by a compen-
dium in which each contributor deals with his own speciality. Learning
has grown so multifarious and complex that it has been thought impossible
for any one mind to embrace a large field. I am sure that this is a most
unfortunate mistake. If a book is to have value except as a work of reference
it must be the work of one mind. It must be the result of holding together
a great multiplicity within the unity of a single temperament. I will admit
at once that this is growing more and more difficult, but I think means
can be devised by which it will still be possible, and I think they must
be devised if great histories are not to be a thing of the past.

What is needed is division of labour. Gibbon profited by Tillemont,
and probably could not otherwise have achieved his work in a lifetime. The
archaeologist or the man who delves in unpublished manuscript material
is likely to have neither the time nor the energy for large-scale history.
The man who proposes to write large-scale history should not be expected
himself to do the spade work. In the sciences, this sort of thing is recognized. Kepler's laws were based upon the observations of Tycho Brahe.
Clerk Maxwell's theories rested upon the experiments of Faraday.
Einstein did not himself make the observations upon which his doctrines
are based. Broadly speaking the amassing of facts is one thing, and the
digesting of them is another. Where the facts are numerous and complex,
it is scarcely possible for one man to do both. Suppose, for example, you
wish to know the effect of the Minoan civilization on the classical civilization of Greece. You will hardly expect the most balanced or the best
informed opinion from a man who has been engaged in the very difficult
work of ascertaining Minoan facts. The same sort of thing applies to less
recondite problems, say, for example, the influence of Plutarch on the
French Revolution.

The name of Plutarch brings to mind another department of history.
History is not concerned only with large-scale pageants, nor with the
delineation of different kinds of societies. It is concerned also, and equally,
with individuals who are noteworthy on their own account. Plutarch's
Lives of the Noble Grecians and Romans has inspired in many ambitious
young men valiant careers upon which they might not otherwise have
ventured. I think there is a tendency in our time to pay too little attention
to the individual and too much to the mass. We are so persuaded that we
live in the Age of the Common Man that men become common even when

they might be otherwise. There has been a movement, especially in teaching history to the young, towards emphasis on types of culture as opposed to the doings of individual heroes. Up to a point, this is entirely praiseworthy. We get a better sense of the march of events if we are told something about the manner of life of Cromagnon man or Neanderthal man, and it is wholesome to know about the tenement houses in Rome where the Romans lived whom Plutarch does not mention. A book like the Hammonds' *Village Labourer* presents a whole period from a point of view of which there is nothing in the older conventional histories. All this is true and important. But what, though important, is not true, but most perniciously false, is the suggestion, which easily grows up when history is studied *only* in this way, that individuals do not count and that those who have been regarded as heroes are only embodiments of social forces, whose work would have been done by someone else if it had not been done by them, and that, broadly speaking, no individual can do better than let himself be borne along by the current of his time. What is worst about this view is that, if it is held, it tends to become true. Heroic lives are inspired by heroic ambitions, and the young man who thinks that there is nothing important to be done is pretty sure to do nothing important. For such reasons I think the kind of history that is exemplified by Plutarch's *Lives* is quite as necessary as the more generalized kind. Very few people can make a community: Lenin and Stalin are the only ones who have achieved it in modern times. But a very much larger number of men can achieve an individual life which is significant. This applies not only to men whom we may regard as models to be imitated, but to all those who afford new material for imagination. The Emperor Frederick II, for example, most certainly does not deserve to be imitated, but he makes a splendid piece in one's mental furniture. The Wonder of the World, tramping hither and thither with his menagerie, completed at last by his Prime Minister in a cage, debating with Moslem sages, winning crusades in spite of being excommunicate, is a figure that I should be sorry not to know about. We all think it worth while to know about the great heroes of tragedy—Agamemnon, Oedipus, Hamlet and the rest—but there have been real men whose lives had the same quality as that of the great tragic heroes, and had the additional merit of having actually existed. All forms of greatness, whether divine or diabolic, share a certain quality, and I do not wish to see this quality ironed out by the worship of mediocrity. When I first visited America nearly sixty years ago, I made the acquaintance of a lady who had lately had a son. Somebody remarked lightly, 'perhaps he will be a genius'. The lady, in tones of heart-felt horror, replied, 'Oh, I hope not!' Her wish, alas, was granted.

I do not mean to subscribe to Carlyle's cult of heroes, still less to Nietzsche's exaggeration of it. I do not wish for one moment to suggest that the common man is unimportant, or that the study of masses of men is less worth pursuing than the study of notable individuals. I wish only to preserve a balance between the two. I believe that remarkable individuals have done a great deal to mould history. I think that, if the hundred ablest men of science of the seventeenth century had all died in infancy, the life of the common man in every industrial community would now be quite different from what it is. I do not think that if Shakespeare and Milton had not existed someone else would have composed their works. And yet this is the sort of thing that some 'scientific' historians seem to wish one to believe.

I will go a step farther in agreement with those who emphasize the individual. I think that what is most worthy to be known and admired in human affairs has to do with individuals rather than with communities. I do not believe in the independent value of a collection of human beings over and above the value contained in their several lives, and I think it is dangerous if history neglects individual value in order to glorify a State, a Nation, a Church, or any other such collective entity. But I will not pursue this theme farther for fear of being led into politics.

The interest of the general reader in history has, I think, declined during the present century, and for my part I greatly regret this decline. There are a number of reasons for it. In the first place, reading altogether has declined. People go to the movies, or listen to the radio, or watch television. They indulge a curious passion for changing their position on the earth's surface as quickly as possible, which they combine with an attempt to make all parts of the earth's surface look alike. But even those who persist in the habit of serious reading spend less of their time on history than serious readers formerly did. My friend Whitehead at one time employed Paolo Sarpi's *History of the Council of Trent* as a bed book. I doubt whether there is now any person living who does likewise. History has ceased to be as interesting as it used to be, partly because the present is so full of important events, and so packed with quick-moving changes, that many people find neither time nor inclination to turn their attention to former centuries. A life of Hitler or Lenin or Stalin or Trotsky can be quite as interesting in itself as a life of Napoleon, and has, in addition, more relevance to present problems. But I am afraid we must admit that there is another cause for the decline of historical reading, and that is the decline of historical writing in the grand manner. I do not know how eagerly their contemporaries lapped up Herodotus or Thucydides or Polybius or Plutarch or Tacitus, but we all know the eagerness with which historians were welcomed in the eighteenth and nineteenth centuries. In Britain there was a long procession from Clarendon's *History of the Rebellion* to Macaulay. In France, from the time of Voltaire onwards, history was a battleground of rival philosophies. In Germany, under the inspiration of Hegel, historians combined brilliance and wickedness in equal proportions. I do not think it would be unfair to Mommsen to say that his history had two themes: one, the greatness of Caesar because he destroyed liberty; the other, that Carthage was like England and Rome was like Germany and that the future Punic Wars to which he looked forward would have an outcome analogous to that of their predecessors. The influence of Treitschke in spreading a pernicious myth is generally recognized. When we speak of the importance of history, we must admit its importance for evil as well as for good. This applies especially to the popular myths which have gradually become a part of folk-lore. I went once to Ireland with my two young children. My daughter, aged five, made friends with a peasant woman who treated her with great kindness. But, as we went away, the woman said: 'She's a bonny girl, in spite of Cromwell.' It seemed a pity that the woman did not know either more history or less.

The decay in the writing of great histories is only part of the decay in the writing of great books. Men of science nowadays do not write books comparable to Newton's *Principia* or Darwin's *Origin of Species*. Poets no longer write epics. In the learned world, everything moves so fast that a massive book would be out of date before it could be published. Contributions to learning appear in periodicals, not in separate books, and few men in any branch of learning feel that there is time for that leisurely survey from which great books formerly sprang. There are of course exceptions. One of the most noteworthy is Professor Toynbee, whose work is as massive as any of those of former times. But the exceptions are not sufficiently numerous to disprove the general trend. I suppose the trend will remain until the world settles down to some form of progress less helter-skelter than the present race towards the abyss.

I think that in bringing sanity to our intoxicated age, history has an important part to play. I do not mean that this is to be brought about by any supposed 'lessons of history', or indeed by anything easily put into a verbal formula. What history can and should do, not only for historians but for all whose education has given them any breadth of outlook, is to produce a certain temper of mind, a certain way of thinking and feeling about contemporary events and their relation to the past and the future. I do not know whether one should accept Cornford's thesis that Thucydides modelled his history on Attic tragedy; but, if he did, the events that he recorded fully justified his doing so, and the Athenians, if they had seen themselves in the light of actors in a possible tragedy, might have had the wisdom to avert the tragic outcome. It is an ancient doctrine that tragedy comes of hubris, but it is none the less true for being ancient, and hubris recurs in every age among those who have forgotten the disasters to which it has always led. In our age, mankind collectively has given itself over to a degree of hubris surpassing everything known in former ages. In the past, Prometheus was regarded as a would-be liberator, restrained in his beneficent work by the tyranny of Zeus, but now we begin to wish that there were some Zeus to restrain the modern followers of Prometheus. Prometheus aimed to serve mankind: his modern followers serve the passions of mankind, but only in so far as they are mad and destructive. In the modern world there are clever men in laboratories and fools in power. The clever men are slaves, like djinns in the Arabian Nights. Mankind collectively, under the guidance of the fools and by the ingenuity of the clever slaves, is engaged in the great task of preparing its own extermination. I wish there were a Thucydides to treat this theme as it deserves. I cannot but think that if the men in power were impregnated with a sense of history they would find a way of avoiding the catastrophe which all see approaching and which none desire, for history is not only an account of this nation or that, nor even of this continent or that; its theme is Man, that strange product of evolution which has risen by means of skill to a mastery over all other forms of life, and even, at great peril to himself, to mastery over the forces of inanimate nature. But Man, in spite of his cleverness, has not learnt to think of the human family as one. Although he has abolished the jungle, he still allows himself to be governed by the law of the jungle. He has little sense of the common tasks of humanity, of its achievements in the past and its possible greater achievements in the future. He sees his fellow-man not as a collaborator in a common purpose, but as an enemy who will kill if he is not killed. Whatever his sect or party may be, he believes that it embodies ultimate and eternal wisdom, and that the opposite party embodies ultimate and absolute folly. To any person with any historical culture such a view is absurd. No portion of mankind in the past was as good as it thought itself, or as bad as it was thought by its enemies; but, in the past, humanity could achieve its common purposes in spite of strife, though haltingly and with temporarily disastrous setbacks. But in our age the new cleverness is only compatible with survival if accompanied by a new wisdom. The wisdom that is needed is new only in one sense: that it must appeal to masses of men, and above all, to those who control great power. It is not new in the sense that it has never been proclaimed before. It has been proclaimed by wise men for many ages, but their wisdom has not been heeded. Now, the time is past when wisdom could be treated as nothing but the idle dream of visionaries. Sometimes in the moments when I am most oppressed by the fear of coming disaster, I am tempted to think that what the world needs is a prophet who will proclaim, with a voice combining thunder with the deepest compassion, that the road upon which mankind is going is the wrong road—a road leading to the death of our children and to the extinction of all hope—but that there is another road which men can pursue if they will, and that this other road leads to a better world than any that has existed in the past. But, although this vision of a prophet can afford a momentary consolation, what the world needs is something more difficult, more rare. If a prophet were to arise in the East, he would be liquidated; if a prophet were to arise in the West, he would not be heard in the East and in the West would be condemned to obloquy. It it is not by the action of any one individual, however great and however eloquent, that the world can be saved. It can be saved only when rulers and their followers in the most powerful countries of the world become aware that they have been pursuing a will-o'-the-wisp which is tempting them only toward ignominious death in a mire of futile hatred. The collective folly is not yet universal. Some nations stand wholly outside it, some are only partially victims to it. It is not too late to hope that mankind may have a future as well as a past. I believe that if men are to feel this hope with sufficient vividness to give it dynamic power, the awareness of history is one of the greatest forces of which the beneficent appeal must be felt.

(*Portraits from Memory*, London: Allen & Unwin; New York: Simon & Schuster, 1956.)

PART XIV

The Philosopher of Culture: East and West

Philosophers for the most part are not world travellers. Few have observed, first hand, the atmosphere of even their own continent; Kant, for instance, never travelled more than forty miles beyond the limits of his native Königsberg. Among the major philosophers of the twentieth century, few have travelled as extensively and understood so well the diverse economic and political problems of culture East and West.

Russell has taught and lectured on four continents. Following his travels in Russia, Japan and China in the early twenties and his frequent trips and extended stays in the United States, he wrote informatively of what he saw and critically of what each civilization boded.

59

CHINESE AND WESTERN CIVILIZATION
CONTRASTED

THERE is at present in China, as we have seen in previous chapters, a close contact between our civilization and that which is native to the Celestial Empire. It is still a doubtful question whether this contact will breed a new civilization better than either of its parents, or whether it will merely destroy the native culture and replace it by that of America. Contacts between different civilizations have often in the past proved to be landmarks in human progress. Greece learnt from Egypt, Rome from Greece, the Arabs from the Roman Empire, medieval Europe from the Arabs, and Renaissance Europe from the Byzantines. In many of these cases, the pupils proved better than their masters. In the case of China, if we regard the Chinese as the pupils, this may be the case again. In fact, we have quite as much to learn from them as they from us, but there is far less chance of our learning it. If I treat the Chinese as our pupils, rather than vice versa, it is only because I fear we are unteachable.

I propose in this chapter to deal with the purely cultural aspects of the questions raised by the contact of China with the West. In the three following chapters, I shall deal with questions concerning the internal condition of China, returning finally, in a concluding chapter, to the hopes for the future which are permissible in the present difficult situation.

With the exception of Spain and America in the sixteenth century, I cannot think of any instance of two civilizations coming into contact after such a long period of separate development as has marked those of China and Europe. Considering this extraordinary separateness, it is surprising that mutual understanding between Europeans and Chinese is not more difficult. In order to make this point clear, it will be worth while to dwell for a moment on the historical origins of the two civilizations.

Western Europe and America have a practically homogeneous mental life, which I should trace to three sources: (1) Greek culture; (2) Jewish religion and ethics; (3) modern industrialism, which itself is an outcome of modern science. We may take Plato, the Old Testament and Galileo as representing these three elements, which have remained singularly separable down to the present day. From the Greeks we derive literature and the arts, philosophy and pure mathematics; also the more urbane portions of our social outlook. From the Jews we derive fanatical belief, which its friends call 'faith'; moral fervour, with the conception of sin; religious intolerance, and some part of our nationalism. From science, as applied in industrialism, we derive power and the sense of power, the belief that we are as gods, and may justly be the arbiters of life and death for unscientific races. We derive also the empirical method, by which almost all real knowledge has been acquired. These three elements, I think, account for most of our mentality.

No one of these three elements has had any appreciable part in the development of China, except that Greece indirectly influenced Chinese painting, sculpture, and music. China belongs, in the dawn of its history, to the great river empires, of which Egypt and Babylonia contributed to our origins, by the influence which they had upon the Greeks and Jews. Just as these civilizations were rendered possible by the rich alluvial soil of the Nile, the Euphrates and the Tigris, so the original civilization of China was rendered possible by the Yellow River. Even in the time of Confucius, the Chinese Empire did not stretch far either to south or north of the Yellow River. But in spite of this similarity in physical and economic circumstances, there was very little in common between the mental outlook of the Chinese and that of the Egyptians and Babylonians. Lao-Tze and Confucius, who both belong to the sixth century B.C., have already the characteristics which we should regard as distinctive of the modern Chinese. People who attribute everything to economic causes would be hard put to it to account for the differences between the ancient Chinese and the ancient Egyptians and Babylonians. For my part, I have no alternative theory to offer. I do not think science can, at present, account wholly for national character. Climate and economic circumstances account for part, but not the whole. Probably a great deal depends upon the character of dominant individuals who happen to emerge at a formative period, such as Moses, Mahomet, and Confucius.

The oldest known Chinese sage is Lao-Tze, the founder of Taoism. 'Lao-Tze' is not really a proper name, but means merely 'the old philosopher'. He was (according to tradition) an older contemporary of Confucius, and his philosophy is to my mind far more interesting. He held that every person, every animal and every thing has a certain way or manner of behaving which is natural to him, or her, or it, and that we ought to conform to this way ourselves and encourage others to conform to it. 'Tao' means 'way', but used in a more or less mystical sense, as in the text: 'I am the Way and the Truth and the Life.' I think he fancied that death was due to departing from the 'way', and that if we all lived strictly according to nature we should be immortal, like the heavenly bodies. In later times Taoism degenerated into mere magic, and was largely concerned with the search for the elixir of life. But I think the hope of escaping from death was an element in Taoist philosophy from the first.

Lao-Tze's book, or rather the book attributed to him, is very short, but his ideas were developed by his disciple Chuang-Tze, who is more interesting than his master. The philosophy which both advocated was one of freedom. They thought ill of government, and of all interferences with Nature. They complained of the hurry of modern life, which they contrasted with the calm existence of those whom they called 'the pure men of old'. There is a flavour of mysticism in the doctrine of the Tao, because in spite of the multiplicity of living things the Tao is in some sense one, so that if all live according to it there will be no strife in the world. But both sages have already the Chinese characteristics of humour, restraint, and understatement. Their humour is illustrated by Chuang-Tze's account of Po-Lo who 'understood the management of horses', and trained them till five out of every ten died. Their restraint and understatement are evident when they are compared with Western mystics. Both characteristics belong to all Chinese literature and art, and to the conversation of cultivated Chinese in the present day. All classes in China are fond of laughter, and never miss a chance of a joke. In the educated classes, the humour is sly and delicate, so that Europeans often fail to see it, which adds to the enjoyment of the Chinese. Their habit of understatement is remarkable. I met one day in Peking a middle-aged man who told me he was academically interested in the theory of politics; being new to the country, I took his statement at its face value, but I afterwards discovered that he had been governor of a province, and had been for many years a very prominent politician. In Chinese poetry there is an apparent absence of passion which is due to the same practice of understatement. They consider that a wise man should always remain calm, and though they have their passionate moments (being in fact a very excitable race), they do not wish to perpetuate them in art, because they think ill of them. Our romantic movement, which led people to like vehemence, has, so far as I know, no analogue in their literature. Their old music, some of which is very beautiful, makes so little noise that one can only just hear it. In art they aim at being exquisite, and in life at being reasonable. There is no admiration for the ruthless strong man, or for the unrestrained expression of passion. After the more blatant life of the West, one misses at first all the effects at which they are aiming; but gradually the beauty and dignity of their existence become visible, so that the foreigners who have lived longest in China are those who love the Chinese best.

The Taoists, though they survive as magicians, were entirely ousted from the favour of the educated classes by Confucianism. I must confess that I am unable to appreciate the merits of Confucius. His writings are

largely occupied with trivial points of etiquette, and his main concern is
to teach people how to behave correctly on various occasions. When one
compares him, however, with the traditional religious teachers of some
other ages and races, one must admit that he has great merits, even if
they are mainly negative. His system, as developed by his followers, is
one of pure ethics, without religious dogma; it has not given rise to a
powerful priesthood, and it has not led to persecution. It certainly has
succeeded in producing a whole nation possessed of exquisite manners
and perfect courtesy. Nor is Chinese courtesy merely conventional; it
is quite as reliable in situations for which no precedent has been provided.
And it is not confined to one class; it exists even in the humblest coolie.
It is humiliating to watch the brutal insolence of white men received by
the Chinese with a quiet dignity which cannot demean itself to answer
rudeness with rudeness. Europeans often regard this as weakness, but it
is really strength, the strength by which the Chinese have hitherto conquered all their conquerors.

There is one, and only one, important foreign element in the traditional
civilization of China, and that is Buddhism. Buddhism came to China
from India in the early centuries of the Christian era, and acquired a
definite place in the religion of the country. We, with the intolerant outlook which we have taken over from the Jews, imagine that if a man
adopts one religion he cannot adopt another. The dogmas of Christianity
and Mohammedanism, in their orthodox forms, are so framed that no
man can accept both. But in China this incompatibility does not exist; a
man may be both a Buddhist and a Confucian, because nothing in either
is incompatible with the other. In Japan, similarly, most people are both
Buddhists and Shintoists. Nevertheless there is a temperamental difference
between Buddhism and Confucianism, which will cause any individual
to lay stress on one or other even if he accepts both. Buddhism is a religion
in the sense in which we understand the word. It has mystic doctrines
and a way of salvation and a future life. It has a message to the world
intended to cure the despair which it regards as natural to those who have
no religious faith. It assumes an instinctive pessimism only to be cured
by some gospel. Confucianism has nothing of all this. It assumes people
fundamentally at peace with the world, wanting only instruction as to
how to live, not encouragement to live at all. And its ethical instruction
is not based upon any metaphysical or religious dogma; it is purely mundane. The result of the co-existence of these two religions in China has
been that the more religious and contemplative natures turned to Buddhism, while the active administrative type was content with Confucianism,
which was always the official teaching, in which candidates for the civil
service were examined. The result is that for many ages the Government
of China has been in the hands of literary sceptics, whose administration
has been lacking in those qualities of energy and destructiveness which

Western nations demand of their rulers. In fact, they have conformed very closely to the maxims of Chuang-Tze. The result has been that the population has been happy except where civil war brought misery; that subject nations have been allowed autonomy; and that foreign nations have had no need to fear China, in spite of its immense population and resources.

Comparing the civilization of China with that of Europe, one finds in China most of what was to be found in Greece, but nothing of the other two elements of our civilization, namely Judaism and science. China is practically destitute of religion, not only in the upper classes, but throughout the population. There is a very definite ethical code, but it is not fierce or persecuting, and does not contain the notion 'sin'. Except quite recently, through European influence, there has been no science and no industrialism.

What will be the outcome of the contact of this ancient civilization with the West? I am not thinking of the political or economic outcome, but of the effect on the Chinese mental outlook. It is difficult to dissociate the two questions altogether, because of course the cultural contact with the West must be affected by the nature of the political and economic contact. Nevertheless, I wish to consider the cultural question as far as I can in isolation.

There is, in China, a great eagerness to acquire Western learning, not simply in order to acquire national strength and be able to resist Western aggression, but because a very large number of people consider learning a good thing in itself. It is traditional in China to place a high value on knowledge, but in old days the knowledge sought was only of the classical literature. Nowadays it is generally realized that Western knowledge is more useful. Many students go every year to universities in Europe, and still more to America, to learn science or economics or law or political theory. These men, when they return to China, mostly become teachers or civil servants or journalists or politicians. They are rapidly modernizing the Chinese outlook, especially in the educated classes.

The traditional civilization of China had become unprogressive, and had ceased to produce much of value in the way of art and literature. This was not due, I think, to any decadence in the race, but merely to lack of new material. The influx of Western knowledge provides just the stimulus that was needed. Chinese students are able and extraordinarily keen. Higher education suffers from lack of funds and absence of libraries, but does not suffer from any lack of the finest human material. Although Chinese civilization has hitherto been deficient in science, it never contained anything hostile to science, and therefore the spread of scientific knowledge encounters no such obstacles as the Church put in its way in Europe. I have no doubt that if the Chinese could get a stable government and sufficient funds, they would, within the next thirty years, begin to produce remarkable work in science. It is quite likely that they might outstrip us, because they come with fresh zest and with all the ardour of a renaissance. In fact, the enthusiasm for learning in Young China reminds one constantly of the renaissance spirit in fifteenth-century Italy.

It is very remarkable, as distinguishing the Chinese from the Japanese, that the things they wish to learn from us are not those that bring wealth or military strength, but rather those that have either an ethical and social value, or a purely intellectual interest. They are not by any means uncritical of our civilization. Some of them told me that they were less critical before 1914, but that the war made them think there must be imperfections in the Western manner of life. The habit of looking to the West for wisdom was, however, very strong, and some of the younger ones thought that Bolshevism could give what they were looking for. That hope also must be suffering disappointment, and before long they will realize that they must work out their own salvation by means of a new synthesis. The Japanese adopted our faults and kept their own, but it is possible to hope that the Chinese will make the opposite selection, keeping their own merits and adopting ours.

The distinctive merit of our civilization, I should say, is the scientific method; the distinctive merit of the Chinese is a just conception of the ends of life. It is these two that one must hope to see gradually uniting.

Lao-Tze describes the operation of Tao as 'production without possession, action without self-assertion, development without domination'. I think one could derive from these words a conception of the ends of life as reflective Chinese see them, and it must be admitted that they are very different from the ends which most white men set before themselves. Possession, self-assertion, domination, are eagerly sought, both nationally and individually. They have been erected into a philosophy by Nietzsche, and Nietzsche's disciples are not confined to Germany.

But, it will be said, you have been comparing Western practice with Chinese theory; if you had compared Western theory with Chinese practice, the balance would have come out quite differently. There is, of course, a great deal of truth in this. Possession, which is one of the three things that Lao-Tze wishes us to forgo, is certainly dear to the heart of the average Chinaman. As a race, they are tenacious of money— not perhaps more so than the French, but certainly more than the English or the Americans. Their politics are corrupt, and their powerful men make money in disgraceful ways. All this it is impossible to deny.

Nevertheless, as regards the other two evils, self-assertion and domination, I notice a definite superiority to ourselves in Chinese practice. There is much less desire than among the white races to tyrannize over other people. The weakness of China internationally is quite as much due to this virtue as to the vices of corruption and so on which are usually assigned as the sole reason. If any nation in the world could ever be 'too proud to fight', that nation would be China. The natural Chinese attitude is one of tolerance and friendliness, showing courtesy and expecting it in return. If the Chinese chose, they could be the most powerful nation in the world. But they only desire freedom, not domination. It is not improbable that other nations may compel them to fight for their freedom, and if so, they may lose their virtues and acquire a taste for empire. But at present, though they have been an imperial race for two thousand years, their love of empire is extraordinarily slight.

Although there have been many wars in China, the natural outlook of the Chinese is very pacifistic. I do not know of any other country where a poet would have chosen, as Po-Chui did in one of the poems translated by Mr Waley, called by him *The Old Man with the Broken Arm*, to make a hero of a recruit who maimed himself to escape military service. Their pacifism is rooted in their contemplative outlook, and in the fact that they do not desire to change whatever they see. They take a pleasure— as their pictures show—in observing characteristic manifestations of different kinds of life, and they have no wish to reduce everything to a preconceived pattern. They have not the ideal of progress which dominates the Western nations, and affords a rationalization of our active impulses. Progress is, of course, a very modern ideal even with us; it is part of what we owe to science and industrialism. The cultivated conservative Chinese of the present day talk exactly as their earliest sages write. If one points out to them that this shows how little progress there has been, they will say: 'Why seek progress when you already enjoy what is excellent?' At first, this point of view seems to a European unduly indolent; but gradually doubts as to one's own wisdom grow up, and one begins to think that much of what we call progress is only restless change, bringing us no nearer to any desirable goal.

It is interesting to contrast what the Chinese have sought in the West with what the West has sought in China. The Chinese in the West seek knowledge, in the hope—which I fear is usually vain—that knowledge may prove a gateway to wisdom. White men have gone to China with three motives: to fight, to make money, and to convert the Chinese to our religion. The last of these motives has the merit of being idealistic, and has inspired many heroic lives. But the soldier, the merchant, and the missionary are alike concerned to stamp our civilization upon the world; they are all three, in a certain sense, pugnacious. The Chinese have no wish to convert us to Confucianism; they say 'religions are many, but reason is one', and with that they are content to let us go our way. They are good merchants, but their methods are quite different from those of European merchants in China, who are perpetually seeking concessions, monopolies, railways, and mines, and endeavouring to get their claims supported by gunboats. The Chinese are not, as a rule, good soldiers, because the causes for which they are asked to fight are not worth fighting for, and they know it. But that is only a proof of their reasonableness.

I think the tolerance of the Chinese is in excess of anything that Europeans can imagine from their experience at home. We imagine ourselves tolerant, because we are more so than our ancestors. But we still practise political and social persecution, and what is more, we are firmly persuaded that our civilization and our way of life are immeasurably better than any other, so that when we come across a nation like the Chinese, we are convinced that the kindest thing we can do to them is to make them like ourselves. I believe this to be a profound mistake. It seemed to me that the average Chinaman, even if he is miserably poor, is happier than the average Englishman, and is happier because the nation is built upon a more humane and civilized outlook than our own. Restlessness and pugnacity not only cause obvious evils, but fill our lives with discontent, incapacitate us for the enjoyment of beauty, and make us almost incapable of the contemplative virtues. In this respect we have grown rapidly worse during the last hundred years. I do not deny that the Chinese go too far in the other direction; but for that very reason I think contact between East and West is likely to be fruitful to both parties. They may learn from us the indispensable minimum of practical efficiency, and we may learn from them something of that contemplative wisdom which has enabled them to persist while all the other nations of antiquity have perished.

When I went to China, I went to teach; but every day that I stayed I thought less of what I had to teach them and more of what I had to learn from them. Among Europeans who had lived a long time in China, I found this attitude not uncommon; but among those whose stay is short, or who go only to make money, it is sadly rare. It is rare because the Chinese do not excel in the things we really value—military prowess and industrial enterprise. But those who value wisdom or beauty, or even the simple enjoyment of life, will find more of these things in China than in the distracted and turbulent West, and will be happy to live where such things are valued. I wish I could hope that China, in return for our scientific knowledge, may give us something of her large tolerance and contemplative peace of mind.

> (*The Problem of China*, London: Allen & Unwin;
> New York: The Century Companies, (Appleton-
> Century-Crofts) 1922.)

60

EASTERN AND WESTERN IDEALS OF HAPPINESS

EVERYBODY knows Wells's Time Machine, which enabled its possessor to travel backwards or forwards in time, and see for himself what the past was like and what the future will be. But people do not always realize that a great deal of the advantages of Wells's device can be secured by travelling about the world at the present day. A European who goes to New York and Chicago sees the future, the future to which Europe is likely to come if it escapes economic disaster. On the other hand, when he goes to Asia he sees the past. In India, I am told, he can see the Middle Ages; in China he can see the eighteenth century. If George Washington were to return to earth, the country which he created would puzzle him dreadfully. He would feel a little less strange in England, still less strange in France; but he would not feel really at home until he reached China. There, for the first time in his ghostly wanderings, he would find men who still believe in 'life, liberty, and the pursuit of happiness', and who conceive these things more or less as Americans of the War of Independence conceived them. And I think it would not be long before he became President of the Chinese Republic.

Western civilization embraces North and South America, Europe excluding Russia, and the British self-governing dominions. In this civilization the United States leads the van; all the characteristics that distinguish the West from the East are most marked and furthest developed in America. We are accustomed to take progress for granted: to assume without hesitation that the changes which have happened during the last hundred years were unquestionably for the better, and that further changes for the better are sure to follow indefinitely. On the Continent of Europe, the war and its consequences have administered a blow to this confident belief, and men have begun to look back to the time before 1914 as a golden age, not likely to recur for centuries. In England there has been much less of this shock to optimism, and in America still less. For those of us who have been accustomed to take progress for granted, it is especially interesting to visit a country like China, which has remained where we were one hundred and fifty years ago, and to ask ourselves whether, on the balance, the changes which have happened to us have brought any real improvement.

The civilization of China, as everyone knows, is based upon the teaching of Confucius, who flourished five hundred years before Christ. Like the Greeks and Romans, he did not think of human society as naturally progressive; on the contrary, he believed that in remote antiquity rulers had been wise, and the people had been happy to a degree which the degenerate present could admire but hardly achieve. This, of course, was a delusion. But the practical result was that Confucius, like other teachers of antiquity, aimed at creating a stable society, maintaining a certain level of excellence, but not always striving after new successes. In this he was more successful than any other man who ever lived. His personality has been stamped on Chinese civilization from his day to our own. During his lifetime the Chinese occupied only a small part of present-day China, and were divided into a number of warring states. During the next three hundred years they established themselves throughout what is now China proper, and founded an empire exceeding in territory and population any other that existed until the last fifty years. In spite of barbarian invasions, Mongol and Manchu dynasties, and occasional longer or shorter periods of chaos and civil war, the Confucian system survived, bringing with it art and literature and a civilized way of life. It is only in our own day, through contact with the West and with the westernized Japanese, that this system has begun to break down.

A system which has had this extraordinary power of survival must have great merits, and certainly deserves our respect and consideration. It is not a religion, as we understand the word, because it is not associated with the supernatural or with mystical beliefs. It is a purely ethical system, but its ethics, unlike those of Christianity, are not too exalted for ordinary men to practise. In essence, what Confucius teaches is something very like the old-fashioned ideal of a 'gentleman' as it existed in the eighteenth century. One of his sayings will illustrate this (I quote from Lionel Giles's *Sayings of Confucius*):

The true gentleman is never contentious. If a spirit of rivalry is anywhere unavoidable, it is at a shooting-match. Yet even here he courteously salutes his opponents before taking up his position, and again when, having lost, he retires to drink the forfeit-cup. So that even when competing he remains a true gentleman.

He speaks much, as a moral teacher is bound to do, about duty and virtue and such matters, but he never exacts anything contrary to nature and the natural affections. This is shown in the following conversation:

The Duke of She addressed Confucius, saying: We have an upright man in our country. His father stole a sheep, and the son bore witness against him.—In our country, Confucius replied, uprightness is something different from this. A father hides the guilt of his son, and a son hides the guilt of his father. It is in such conduct that true uprightess is to be found.

Confucius was in all things moderate, even in virtue. He did not believe that we ought to return good for evil. He was asked on one occasion: 'How do you regard the principle of returning good for evil?' And he replied: 'What, then, is to be the return for good? Rather should you return justice for injustice, and good for good.' The principle of returning good for evil was being taught in his day in China by the Taoists, whose teaching is much more akin to that of Christianity than is the teaching of Confucius. The founder of Taoism, Lao-Tze (supposed to have been an older contemporary of Confucius), says: 'To the good I would be good; to the not-good I would also be good, in order to make them good. With the faithful I would keep faith; with the unfaithful I would also keep faith, in order that they may become faithful. Even if a man is bad, how can it be right to cast him off? Requite injury with kindness.' Some of Lao-Tze's words are amazingly like parts of the Sermon on the Mount. For instance, he says:

He that humbles himself shall be preserved entire. He that bends shall be made straight. He that is empty shall be filled. He that is worn out shall be renewed. He who has little shall succeed. He who has much shall go astray.

It is characteristic of China that it was not Lao-Tze but Confucius who became the recognized national sage. Taoism has survived, but chiefly as magic and among the uneducated. Its doctrines have appeared visionary to the practical men who administered the empire, while the doctrines of Confucius were eminently calculated to avoid friction. Lao-Tze preached a doctrine of inaction: 'The empire', he says, 'has ever been won by letting things take their course. He who must always be doing is unfit to obtain the empire.' But Chinese governors naturally preferred the Confucian maxims of self-control, benevolence, and courtesy, combined, as they were, with a great emphasis upon the good that could be done by wise government. It never occurred to the Chinese, as it has to all modern white nations, to have one system of ethics in theory and another in practice. I do not mean that they always live up to their own theories, but that they attempt to do so and are expected to do so, whereas there are large parts of the Christian ethic which are universally admitted to be too good for this wicked world.

We have, in fact, two kinds of morality side by side: one which we preach but do not practise, and another which we practise but seldom preach. Christianity, like all religions except Mormonism, is Asiatic in origin; it had in the early centuries that emphasis on individualism and other-worldliness which is characteristic of Asiatic mysticism. From this point of view, the doctrine of non-resistance was intelligible. But when Christianity became the nominal religion of energetic European princes, it was found necessary to maintain that some texts were not to be taken literally, while others, such as 'render unto Caesar the things that are Caesar's', acquired great popularity. In our own day, under the influence of competitive industrialism, the slightest approach to non-resistance is despised, and men are expected to be able to keep their end up. In practice, our effective morality is that of material success achieved by means of a struggle; and this applies to nations as well as to individuals. Anything else seems to us soft and foolish.

The Chinese do not adopt either our theoretical or our practical ethic. They admit in theory that there are occasions when it is proper to fight, and in practice that these occasions are rare; whereas we hold in theory that there are no occasions when it is proper to fight and in practice that such occasions are very frequent. The Chinese sometimes fight, but are not a combative race, and do not greatly admire success in war or in business. Traditionally, they admire learning more than anything else; next to that, and usually in combination with it, they admire urbanity and courtesy. For ages past, administrative posts have been awarded in China on the results of competitive examinations. As there has been no hereditary aristocracy for two thousand years—with the sole exception of the family of Confucius, the head of which is a Duke—learning has drawn to itself the kind of respect which, in feudal Europe, was given to powerful nobles, as well as the respect which it inspired on its own account. The old learning, however, was very narrow, consisting merely in an uncritical study of the Chinese classics and their recognized commentators. Under the influence of the West, it has come to be known that geography, economics, geology, chemistry, and so on, are of more practical use than the moralizings of former ages. Young China—that is to say, the students who have been educated on European lines—recognize modern needs, and have perhaps hardly enough respect for the old tradition. Nevertheless, even the most modern, with few exceptions, retain the traditional virtues of moderation, politeness, and a pacific temper. Whether these virtues will survive a few more decades of Western and Japanese tuition is perhaps doubtful. If I were to try to sum up in a phrase the main difference between the Chinese and ourselves, I should say that they, in the main, aim at enjoyment, while we, in the main, aim at power. We like power over our fellow-men, and we like power over Nature. For the sake of the former we have built up strong states, and for the sake of the latter we have built up Science. The Chinese are too lazy and too good-natured for such pursuits. To say that they are lazy is, however, only true in a certain sense. They are not lazy in the way that Russians are, that is to say, they will work hard for their living. Employers of labour find them extraordinarily industrious. But they will not work, as Americans and Western Europeans do, simply because they would be bored if they did not work, nor do they love hustle for its own sake. When they have enough to live on, they live on it, instead of trying to augment it by hard work. They have an infinite capacity for leisurely amusements—going to the theatre, talking while they drink tea, admiring the Chinese art of earlier times, or walking in beautiful scenery. To our way of thinking, there is something unduly mild about such a way of spending one's life; we respect more a man who goes to his office every day, even if all that he does in his office is harmful.

Living in the East has, perhaps, a corrupting influence upon a white man, but I must confess that, since I came to know China, I have regarded laziness as one of the best qualities of which men in the mass are capable. We achieve certain things by being energetic, but it may be questioned whether, on the balance, the things that we achieve are of any value. We develop wonderful skill in manufacture, part of which we devote to making ships, automobiles, telephones, and other means of living luxuriously at high pressure, while another part is devoted to making guns, poison gases, and aeroplanes for the purpose of killing each other wholesale. We have a first-class system of administration and taxation, part of which is devoted to education, sanitation, and such useful objects, while the rest is devoted to war. In England at the present day most of the national revenue is spent on past and future wars and only the residue on useful objects. On the Continent, in most countries, the proportion is even worse. We have a police system of unexampled efficiency, part of which is devoted to the detection and prevention of crime and part to imprisoning anybody who has any new constructive political ideas. In China, until recently, they had none of these things. Industry was too inefficient to produce either automobiles or bombs; the State too inefficient to educate its own citizens or to kill those of other countries; the police too inefficient to catch either bandits or Bolsheviks. The result was that in China, as compared to any white man's country, there was freedom for all, and a degree of diffused happiness which was amazing in view of the poverty of all but a tiny minority.

Comparing the actual outlook of the average Chinese with that of the average Westerner, two differences strike one: first, that the Chinese do not admire activity unless it serves some useful purpose; secondly, that they do not regard morality as consisting in checking our own impulses and interfering with those of others. The first of these differences has been already discussed, but the second is perhaps equally important. Professor Giles, the eminent Chinese scholar, at the end of his Gifford Lectures on 'Confucianism and its Rivals', maintains that the chief obstacle to the success of Christian missions in China has been the doctrine of original sin. The traditional doctrine of orthodox Christianity—still preached by most Christian missionaries in the Far East—is that we are all born wicked, so wicked as to deserve eternal punishment. The Chinese might have no difficulty in accepting this doctrine if it applied only to white men, but when they are told that their own parents and grandparents are in hell-fire they grow indignant. Confucius taught that men are born good, and that if they become wicked, that is through the force of evil example or corrupting manners. This difference from traditional Western orthodoxy has a profound influence on the outlook of the Chinese.

Among ourselves, the people who are regarded as moral luminaries are those who forgo ordinary pleasures themselves and find compensation in interfering with the pleasures of others. There is an element of the busybody in our conception of virtue: unless a man makes himself a nuisance to a great many people, we do not think he can be an exceptionally good man. This attitude comes from our notion of sin. It leads not only to interference with freedom, but also to hypocrisy, since the conventional standard is too difficult for most people to live up to. In China this is not the case. Moral precepts are positive rather than negative. A man is expected to be respectful to his parents, kind to his children, generous to his poor relations, and courteous to all. These are not very difficult duties, but most men actually fulfil them, and the result is perhaps better than that of our higher standard, from which most people fall short.

Another result of the absence of the notion of sin is that men are much more willing to submit their differences to argument and reason than they are in the West. Among ourselves, differences of opinion quickly become questions of 'principle': each side thinks that the other side is wicked, and that any yielding to it involves sharing in its guilt. This makes our disputes bitter, and involves in practice a great readiness to appeal to force. In China, although there were military men who were ready to appeal to force, no one took them seriously, not even their own soldiers. They fought battles which were nearly bloodless, and they did much less harm than we should expect from our experience of the fiercer conflicts of the West. The great bulk of the population, including the civil administration, went about its business as though these generals and their armies did not exist. In ordinary life, disputes are usually adjusted by the friendly mediation of some third party. Compromise is the accepted principle, because it is necessary to save the face of both parties. Saving face, though in some forms it makes foreigners smile, is a most valuable national institution, making social and political life far less ruthless than it is with us.

There is one serious defect, and only one, in the Chinese system, and that is, that it does not enable China to resist more pugnacious nations. If the whole world were like China, the whole world could be happy;

but so long as others are warlike and energetic, the Chinese, now that they are no longer isolated, will be compelled to copy our vices to some degree if they are to preserve their national independence. But let us not flatter ourselves that this imitation will be an improvement.

(*Sceptical Essays*, London: Allen & Unwin; New York; W. W. Norton, 1928.)

PART XV

The Philosopher of Religion

The finest minds will always be attracted to ultimate questions that remain unsolved. Lesser minds are content with 'answers' to questions for which there is no evidence.

Since his youth, Russell has found no reason to change his agnostic position in religion. It was while reading John Stuart Mill's *Autobiography* at the age of eighteen that he became convinced of the fallacy in the argument of the First Cause. His concern with religious problems and the philosophy of religion has been active over the years.

Any critic of religion is, of course, prone to attack from all sides. What is particularly significant perhaps is that religious apologists are especially fervent in their attacks upon eminent intellectuals. Philosophers in the twentieth century have, for the most part, tended to avoid expressing any view which touched the *core* of religious sensitivity. Whether thinkers like Russell are right or wrong, perhaps only history can decide. Anyone who can keep an open mind, or who is permitted to keep an open mind, in this controversial area can gain much from the frank and fearless articles Russell has contributed to the subject.

61

THE ESSENCE OF RELIGION

THE decay of traditional religious beliefs, bitterly bewailed by upholders of the Churches, welcomed with joy by those who regard the old creeds as mere superstition, is an undeniable fact. Yet when the dogmas have been rejected, the question of the place of religion in life is by no means decided. The dogmas have been valued, not so much on their own account, as because they were believed to facilitate a certain attitude towards the world, an habitual direction of our thoughts, a life in the whole, free from the finiteness of self and providing an escape from the tyranny of desire and daily cares. Such a life in the whole is possible without dogma, and ought not to perish through the indifference of those to whom the beliefs of former ages are no longer credible. Acts inspired by religion have some quality of infinity in them: they seem done in obedience to a command, and though they may achieve great ends, yet it is no clear knowledge of these ends that makes them seem imperative. The beliefs which underlie such acts are often so deep and so instinctive as to remain unknown to those whose lives are built upon them. Indeed, it may be not belief but feeling that makes religion: a feeling which, when brought into the sphere of belief, may involve the conviction that this or that is good, but may, if it remains untouched by intellect, be only a feeling and yet be dominant in action. It is the quality of infinity that makes religion, the selfless, untrammelled life in the whole which frees men from the prison house of eager wishes and little thoughts. This liberation from the prison is given by religion, but only by a religion without fettering dogmas; and dogmas become fettering as soon as assent to them becomes unnatural.

The soul of man is a strange mixture of God and brute, a battleground of two natures, the one particular, finite, self-centred, the other universal, infinite, and impartial. The finite life, which man shares with the brutes, is tied to the body, and views the world from the standpoint of the *here* and *now*. All those loves and hatreds which are based upon some service to the self belong to the finite life. The love of man and woman, and the love of parents and children, when they do not go beyond the promptings of instinct, are still part of the animal nature: they do not pass into the infinite life until they overcome instinct and cease to be subservient only to the purposes of the finite self. The hatred of enemies and the love of allies in battle are part of what man shares with other gregarious animals: they view the universe as grouped about one point, the single struggling self. Thus the finite part of our life contains all that makes the individual man essentially separate from other men and from the rest of the universe, all those thoughts and desires that cannot, in their nature, be shared by the inhabitant of a different body, all the distortions that make error, and all the insistent claims that lead to strife.

The infinite part of our life does not see the world from one point of view: it shines impartially, like the diffused light on a cloudy sea. Distant ages and remote regions of space are as real to it as what is present and near. In thought, it rises above the life of the senses, seeking always what is general and open to all men. In desire and will, it aims simply at the good, without regarding the good as mine or yours. In feeling, it gives love to all, not only to those who further the purposes of self. Unlike the finite life, it is impartial: its impartiality leads to truth in thought, justice in action, and universal love in feeling. Unlike the nature which man shares with the brutes, it has a life without barriers, embracing in its survey the whole universe of existence and essence; nothing in it is essentially private, but its thoughts and desires are such as all may share, since none depend upon the exclusiveness of *here* and *now* and *me*. Thus the infinite nature is the principle of union in the world, as the finite nature is the principle of division. Between the infinite nature in one man and the infinite nature in another, there can be no essential conflict: if its embodiments are incomplete, they supplement each other; its division among different men is accidental to its character, and the infinite in all constitutes one universal nature. There is thus a union of all the infinite natures of different men in a sense in which there is no union of all the finite natures. In proportion as the infinite grows strong in us, we live more completely the life of that one universal nature which embraces what is infinite in each of us.

The finite self, impelled by the desire for self-preservation, builds prison walls round the infinite part of our nature, and endeavours to restrain it from that free life in the whole which constitutes its being. The finite self aims at dominion: it sees the world in concentric circles round the *here* and *now*, and itself as the God of that wished-for heaven. The universal soul mocks at this vision, but the finite self hopes always to make it true, and thus to quiet its troublesome critic. In many men, the finite self remains always the gaoler of the universal soul; in others, there is a rare and momentary escape; in a few, the prison walls are demolished wholly, and the universal soul remains free through life. It is the escape from prison that gives to some moments and some thoughts a quality of infinity, like light breaking through from some greater world beyond. Sudden beauty in the midst of strife, uncalculating love, or the night wind in the trees, seem to suggest the possibility of a life free from the conflicts and pettinesses of our everyday world, a life where there is peace which no misfortune can disturb. The things which have this quality of infinity seem to give an insight deeper than the piecemeal knowledge of our daily life. A life dominated by this insight, we feel, would be a life free from struggle, a life in harmony with the whole, outside the prison walls built by the instinctive desires of the finite self.

It is this experience of sudden wisdom which is the source of what is essential in religion. Mysticism interprets this experience as a contact with a deeper, truer, more unified world than that of our common beliefs. Behind a thin veil, it sees the glory of God, dimly as a rule, sometimes with dazzling brightness. All the evils of our daily world it regards as merely shadows on the veil, illusions, nothings, which vanish from the sight of those who see the splendour beyond. But in this interpretation mysticism diminishes the value of the experience upon which it is based. The quality of infinity, which we feel, is not to be accounted for by the perception of new objects, other than those that at most times seem finite; it is to be accounted for, rather, by a different way of regarding the same objects, a contemplation more impersonal, more vast, more filled with love, than the fragmentary, disquiet consideration we give to things when we view them as means to help or hinder our own purposes. It is not in some other world that that beauty and that peace are to be found; it is in this actual everyday world, in the midst of action and the business of life. But it is in the everyday world as viewed by the universal soul, and in the midst of action and business inspired by its vision. The evils and the smallnesses are not illusions, but the universal soul finds within itself a love to which imperfections are no barrier, and thus unifies the world by the unity of its own contemplation.

The transition from the life of the finite self to the infinite life in the whole requires a moment of absolute self-surrender, when all personal will seems to cease, and the soul feels itself in passive submission to the universe. After passionate struggle for some particular good, there comes some inward or outward necessity to abandon the pursuit of the object which has absorbed all our desire, and no other desire is ready to replace the one that has been relinquished. Hence arises a state of suspension of the will, when the soul no longer seeks to impose itself upon the world, but is open to every impression that comes to it from the world. It is at such a time that the contemplative vision first comes into being, bringing with it universal love and universal worship. From universal worship comes joy, from universal love comes a new desire, and thence the birth of that seeking after universal good which constitutes the will of our infinite nature. Thus from the moment of self-surrender, which to the finite self appears like death, a new life begins, with a larger vision, a new happiness, and wider hopes.

The self-surrender in which the infinite life is born may be made easier to some men by belief in an all-wise God to whom submission is a duty. But it is not in its essence dependent upon this belief or upon any other. The religions of the past, it is true, have all depended to a greater or less degree upon dogma, upon some theory as to the nature and the purpose of the universe. But the decay of traditional beliefs has made every religion that rests on dogma precarious, and even impossible, to many whose nature is strongly religious. Hence those who cannot accept the creeds of the past, and yet believe that a religious outlook requires dogma, lose what is infinite in life, and become limited in their thoughts to everyday matters; they lose consciousness of the life of the whole, they lose that inexplicable sense of union which gives rise to compassion and the unhesitating service of humanity. They do not see in beauty the adumbration of a glory which a richer vision would see in every common thing, or in love a gateway to that transfigured world in which our union with the universe is fulfilled. Thus their outlook is impoverished, and their life is rendered smaller even in its finite parts. For right action they are thrown back upon bare morality; and bare morality is very inadequate as a motive for those who hunger and thirst after the infinite. Thus it has become a matter of the first importance to preserve religion without any dependence upon dogmas to which an intellectually honest assent grows daily more difficult.

There are in Christianity three elements which it is desirable to preserve if possible: worship, acquiescence, and love. Worship is given by Christianity to God; acquiescence is given to the inevitable because it is the will of God; love is enjoined towards my neighbours, my enemies, and, in fact, towards all men. The love which Christianity enjoins, and indeed any love which is to be universal and yet strong, seems in some way dependent upon worship and acquiescence. Yet these, in the form in which they appear in Christianity, depend upon belief in God, and are therefore no longer possible to those who cannot entertain this belief. Something, in worship, must be lost when we lose belief in the existence of supreme goodness and power combined. But much can be preserved, and what can be preserved seems sufficient to constitute a very strong religious life. Acquiescence, also, is rendered more difficult by loss of belief in God, since it takes away the assurance that apparent evil in the constitution of the world is really good. But it is not rendered impossible; and in consequence of its greater difficulty it becomes, when achieved, nobler, deeper, more filled by self-surrender than any acquiescence which Christianity produces. In some ways, therefore, the religion which has no dogma is greater and more religious than one which rests upon the belief that in the end our ideals are fulfilled in the outer world.

1. *Worship.*—Worship is not easily defined, because it grows and changes as the worshipper grows. In crude religions it may be inspired by fear alone, and given to whatever is powerful. This element lingers in the worship of God, which may consist largely of fear and be given largely from respect for power. But the element of fear tends more and more to be banished by love, and in all the best worship fear is wholly absent. As soon as the worship inspired by fear has been surpassed, worship brings joy in the contemplation of what is worshipped. But joy alone does not constitute worship: there must be also some reverence and sense of mystery not easy to define. These three things, contemplation with joy, reverence, and sense of mystery, seem essential to constitute any of the higher forms of worship.

Within worship in this very wide sense there are varieties which it is important to distinguish. There is a selective worship, which demands that its object shall be good, and admits an opposite attitude towards a bad object; and there is an impartial worship, which can be given to whatever exists, regardless of its goodness or badness. Besides this division, there is another, equally important. There is a worship which can only be given to an actually existing object, and another worship which can be given to what merely has its place in the world of ideals; these two kinds may be distinguished as worship of the actual and worship of the ideal. The two are combined in worship of God, since God is conceived as both actual and the complete embodiment of the ideal.

Worship of God is selective, since it depends upon God's goodness. So is all worship of great men or great deeds, and of everything of which the worship depends upon some pre-eminent quality which calls forth our admiration. Worship of this sort, though it can be given to much of what exists in the actual world, cannot be given unreservedly and so as to produce a religious attitude towards the universe as a whole, except by those who believe in an omnipotent Creator or in a pantheistic all-pervading spiritual unity. For those in whom there is no such belief, the selective worship finds its full object only in the ideal good which creative contemplation imagines. The ideal good forms an essential part of the religious life, since it supplies the motive to action by giving content to the desire for universal good which forms a part of universal love. Without the knowledge and worship of the ideal good, the love of man is blind, not knowing in what direction to seek the welfare of those whom it loves. Every embodiment of good in the actual world is imperfect, if only by its brevity. Only the ideal good can satisfy fully our hunger for perfection. Only the ideal good demands no surrender to power, no sacrifice of aspiration to possibility, and no slavery of thought to fact. Only the vision of the ideal good gives infinity to our pursuit, in action, of those fragments of good which the world permits us to create, but the worship of the ideal good, though it brings with it the joy that springs from the contemplation of what is perfect, brings with it also the pain that results from the imperfection of the actual world. When this worship stands alone, it produces a sense of exile in a world of shadows, of infinite solitude amid alien forces. Thus this worship, though necessary to all religious action, does not alone suffice, since it does not produce that sense of union with the actual world which compels us to descend from the world of contemplation and seek, with however little success, to realize what is possible of the good here on earth.

For this purpose we need the kind of worship which is only given to what exists. Such worship, where there is belief in God, can be selective, since God exists and is completely good. Where there is not belief in God, such worship may be selective in regard to great men and great deeds, but towards such objects selective worship is always hampered by their imperfection and their limitation of duration and extent. The worship which can be given to whatever exists must not be selective, it must not involve any judgement as to the goodness of what is worshipped, but must be a direct impartial emotion. Such a worship is given by the contemplative vision, which finds mystery and joy in all that exists, and brings with it love to all that has life. This impartial worship has been thought, wrongly, to require belief in God, since it has been thought to involve the judgement that whatever exists is good. In fact, however, it involves no judgement whatever; hence it cannot be intellectually mistaken, and cannot be in any way dependent upon dogma. Thus the combination of this worship with the ideal good gives a faith wholly independent of beliefs as to the nature of the actual world, and therefore not assailable by the arguments which have destroyed the tenets of traditional religion.

Religion, therefore, results from the combination of two different kinds of worship—the selective, which is given to the good on account of its goodness, and the impartial, which is given to everything that exists. The former is the source of the belief in theism, the latter of the belief in pantheism, but in neither case is such a belief necessary for the worship which gives rise to it. The object of the selective worship is the ideal good, which belongs to the world of universals. Owing to oblivion of the world of universals, men have supposed that the ideal good could not have being or be worshipped unless it formed part of the actual world; hence they have believed that without God this worship could not survive. But the study of the world of universals shows that this was an error: the object of this worship need not exist, though it will be an essential part of the worship to wish it to exist as fully as possible. The object of the impartial worship, on the other hand, is whatever exists; in this case, though the object is known to exist, it is not known to be good, but it is an essential part of the worship to wish that it may be as good as possible. Pantheism, from the contemplative joy of impartial worship, and from the unity of its outlook on the universe, infers, mistakenly, that such worship involves the belief that the universe is good and is one. This belief is no more necessary to the impartial worship than the belief in God is to the selective worship. The two worships subsist side by side, without any dogma: the one involving the goodness but not the existence of its object, the other involving the existence but not the goodness of its object. Religious action is a continual endeavour to bridge the gulf between the objects of these two worships, by making more good exist and more of existence good. Only in the complete union of the two could the soul find permanent rest.

2. *Acquiescence.*—Although, in a world where much evil exists and much good does not exist, no religion which is true can give permanent rest or free the soul from the need for action, yet religion can give acquiescence in evil which it is not within our power to cure. Christianity effects this by the belief that, since the apparent evil is in accordance with the will of God, it cannot really be evil. This view, however, demands a falsification of our standard of good and evil, since much that exists is evil to any unbiased consideration. Moreover, if pursued to a conclusion, it destroys all motive to action, since the reason given for acquiescence, namely, that whatever happens must be for the best, is a reason which renders our efforts after the best superfluous. If, to avoid this consequence, we limit either the omnipotence or the goodness of God, acquiescence can no longer be urged on the same ground, since what happens may be either not in accordance with the will of God, or not good in spite of being in accordance with His will. For these reasons, though Christianity is in fact often effective both in causing acquiescence and in providing a religious motive for action, yet this effectiveness is due to a confusion of thought, and tends to cease as men grow more clear-sighted.

The problem we have to deal with is more difficult than the Christian's problem. We have to learn to acquiesce in the inevitable without judging that the inevitable must be good, to keep the feeling which prompts Christians to say, 'Thy will be done', while yet admitting that what is done may be evil.

Acquiescence, whatever our religion may be, must always require a large element of moral discipline. But this discipline may be made easier, and more visibly worth the pain which it involves, by religious considerations. There are two different though closely related kinds of acquiescence, the one in our private griefs, the other in the fundamental evils of the world. Acquiescence in our private griefs comes in the moment of submission which brings about the birth of the impartial will. Our private life, when it absorbs our thoughts and wishes, becomes a prison, from which, in times of grief, there is no escape but by submission. By submission our thoughts are freed, and our will is led to new aims which, before, had been hidden by the personal goods which had been uselessly desired. A large contemplation, or the growth of universal love, will produce a certain shame of absorption in our own life; hence the will is led away from protest against the inevitable, towards the pursuit of more general goods which are not wholly unattainable. Thus acquiescence in private griefs is an essential element in the growth of universal love and the impartial will.

Acquiescence does not consist in judging that things are not bad when in fact they are so. It consists in freedom from anger and indignation and preoccupied regret. Anger and indignation against those who cause our griefs will not be felt if universal love is strong; preoccupied regret will be avoided where the desire of contemplative freedom exists. The man to whom a large contemplation has become habitual will not readily allow himself to be long turned aside from the thoughts which give breadth to his life: in the absence of such thoughts he will feel something small and unworthy, a bondage of the infinite to the finite. In this way both contemplation and universal love will promote asquiescence so far as our own sorrows are concerned.

It is possible, however, to emerge from private protest, not into complete acquiescence, but into a Promethean indignation against the universe. Contemplation may only universalize our griefs; it may show us all life as a tragedy, so full of pain as to make us wish that consciousness could vanish wholly from the world. The belief that this would be desirable if it were possible is one which cannot be refuted, though it also cannot be shown to be true. But even this belief is not incompatible with acquiescence. What is incompatible is indignation, and a preoccupation with evils which makes goods invisible or only partially visible. Indignation seems scarcely possible in regard to evils for which no one is responsible; those who feel indignation in regard to the fundamental evils of the universe feel it against God or the Devil or an imaginatively personified Fate. When it is realized that the fundamental evils are due to the blind empire of matter, and are the wholly necessary effects of forces which have no consciousness and are therefore neither good nor bad in themselves, indignation becomes absurd, like Xerxes chastising the Hellespont. Thus the realization of necessity is the liberation from indignation. This alone, however, will not prevent an undue preoccupation with evil. It is obvious that some things that exist are good, some bad, and we have no means of knowing whether the good or the bad preponderate. In action, it is essential to have knowledge of good and evil; thus in all the matters subject to our will, the question what is good and what bad must be borne in mind. But in matters which lie outside our power, the question of good or bad, though knowledge about it, like all knowledge, is worth acquiring, has not that fundamental religious importance which has been assigned to it in discussions of theism and optimism. The dualism of good and bad, when it is too strongly present to our minds, prevents impartial contemplation and interferes with universal love and worship. There is, in fact, something finite and unduly human about the practice of emphasizing good and bad in regard to matters with which action is not concerned. Thus acquiescence in fundamental evils, like acquiescence in personal griefs, is furthered by the impartiality of contemplation and universal love and worship, and must already exist to some extent before these become possible. Acquiescence is at once a cause and an effect of faith, in much the same way when faith dispenses with dogma as when it rests upon a belief in God. In so far as acquiescence is a cause of faith, it rests upon moral discipline, a suppression of self and its demands, which is necessary to any life in harmony with the universe, and to any emergence from the finite into the infinite. This discipline is more severe in the absence of all optimistic dogma, but in proportion as it is more severe its outcome is greater, more unshakable, more capable of so enlarging the bounds of self as to make it welcome with love whatever of good or evil may come before it.

3. *Love.*—Love is of two kinds, the selective earthly love, which is given to what is delightful, beautiful, or good, and the impartial heavenly love, which is given to all indifferently. The earthly love is balanced by an opposing hatred: to friends are opposed foes; to saints, sinners; to God, the Devil. Thus this love introduces disunion into the world, with hostile camps and a doubtful warfare. But the heavenly love does not demand that its object shall be delightful, beautiful, or good; it can be given to everything that has life, to the best and the worst, to the greatest and to the least. It is not merely compassion, since it does not merely wish to relieve misfortune, but finds joy in what it loves, and is given to the fortunate as well as to the unfortunate. Though it includes benevolence, it is greater than benevolence: it is contemplative as well as active, and can be given where there is no possibility of benefiting the object. It is love, contemplative in origin, but becoming active wherever action is possible; and it is a kind of love to which there is no opposing hatred.

To the divine love, the division of the world into good and bad, though it remains true, seems lacking in depth; it seems finite and limited in comparison with the boundlessness of love. The division into two hostile camps seems unreal; what is felt to be real is the oneness of the world in love.

It is in the birth of divine love that the life of feeling begins for the universal soul. What contemplation is to the intellect of the universal soul, divine love is to its emotions. More then anything else, divine love frees the soul from its prison and breaks down the walls of self that prevent its union with the world. Where it is strong, duties become easy, and all service is filled with joy. Sorrow, it is true, remains, perhaps deeper and wider than before, since the lives of most human beings are largely tragic. But the bitterness of personal defeat is avoided, and aims become so wide that no complete overthrow of all hopes is possible. The loves of the natural life survive, but harmonized with universal love, and no longer setting up walls of division between the loved and the unloved. And above all, through the bond of universal love the soul escapes from the separate loneliness in which it is born, and from which no permanent deliverance is possible while it remains within the walls of its prison.

Christianity enjoins love of God and love of man as the two great commandments. Love of God differs, however, from love of man, since we cannot benefit God, while we cannot regard man as wholly good. Thus love of God is more contemplative and full of worship, while love of man is more active and full of service. In a religion which is not theistic, love of God is replaced by worship of the ideal good. As in Christianity, this worship is quite as necessary as love of man, since without it love of man is left without guidance in its wish to create the good in human lives. The worship of good is indeed the greater of the two commandments, since it leads us to know that love of man is good, and this knowledge helps us to feel the love of man. Moreover, it makes us conscious of what human life might be, and of the gulf between what it might be and what it is; hence springs an infinite compassion, which is a large part of love of man, and is apt to cause the whole. Acquiescence, also, greatly furthers love of man, since in its absence anger and indignation and strife come between the soul and the world, preventing the union in which love of man has its birth. The three elements of religion, namely worship, acquiescence, and love, are intimately interconnected; each helps to produce the others, and all three together form a unity in which it is impossible to say which comes first, which last. All three can exist without dogma, in a form which is capable of dominating life and of giving infinity to action and thought and feeling; and life in the infinite, which is the combination of the three, contains all that is essential to religion, in spite of its absence of dogmatic beliefs.

Religion derives its power from the sense of union with the universe which it is able to give. Formerly, union was achieved by assimilating the universe to our own conception of the good; union with God was easy since God was love. But the decay of traditional belief has made this way of union no longer one which can be relied upon: we must find a mode of union which asks nothing of the world and depends only upon ourselves. Such a mode of union is possible through impartial worship and universal love, which ignore the difference of good and bad and are given to all alike. In order to free religion from all dependence upon dogma, it is necessary to abstain from any demand that the world shall conform to our standards. Every such demand is an endeavour to impose self upon the world. From this endeavour the religion which can survive the decay of dogma must be freed. And in being freed from this endeavour, religion is freed from an element extraneous to its spirit and not compatible with its unhampered development. Religion seeks union with the universe by subordination of the demands of self; but this subordination is not complete if it depends upon a belief that the universe satisfies some at least of the demands of self. Hence for the sake of religion itself, as well as because such a belief appears unfounded, it is important to discover a form of union with the universe which is independent of all beliefs as to the nature of the universe. By life in the infinite, such a form of union is rendered possible; and to those who achieve it, it gives nearly all, and in some ways more than all, that has been given by the religions of the past.

The essence of religion, then, lies in subordination of the finite part of our life to the infinite part. Of the two natures in man, the particular or animal being lives in instinct, and seeks the welfare of the body and its descendants, while the universal or divine being seeks union with the universe, and desires freedom from all that impedes its seeking. The animal being is neither good nor bad in itself; it is good or bad solely as it helps or hinders the divine being in its search for union with the world. In union with the world the soul finds its freedom. There are three kinds of union: union in thought, union in feeling, union in will. Union in thought is knowledge, union in feeling is love, union in will is service. There are three kinds of disunion: error, hatred, and strife. What promotes disunion is insistent instinct, which is of the animal part of man: what promotes union is the combination of knowledge, love, and consequent service which is wisdom, the supreme good of man.

The life of instinct views the world as a means for the ends of instinct; thus it makes the world of less account than self. It confines knowledge to what is useful, love to allies in conflict of rival instincts, service to those with whom there is some instinctive tie. The world in which it finds a home is a narrow world, surrounded by alien and probably hostile forces; it is prisoned in a beleaguered fortress, knowing that ultimate surrender is inevitable.

The life of wisdom seeks an impartial end, in which there is no rivalry, no essential enmity. The union which it seeks has no boundaries: it wishes to know all, to love all, and to serve all. Thus it finds its home everywhere: no lines of circumvallation bar its progress. In knowledge it makes no division of useful and useless, in love it makes no division of friend and foe, in service it makes no division of deserving and undeserving.

The animal part of man, knowing that the individual life is brief and impotent, is appalled by the fact of death, and, unwilling to admit the hopelessness of the struggle, it postulates a prolongation in which its failures shall be turned into triumphs. The divine part of man, feeling the individual to be but of small account, thinks little of death, and finds its hopes independent of personal continuance.

The animal part of man, being filled with the importance of its own desires, finds it intolerable to suppose that the universe is less aware of this importance; a blank indifference to its hopes and fears is too painful to contemplate, and is therefore not regarded as admissible. The divine part of man does not demand that the world shall conform to a pattern: it accepts the world, and finds in wisdom a union which demands nothing of the world. Its energy is not checked by what seems hostile, but inter-penetrates it and becomes one with it. It is not the strength of our ideals, but their weakness, that makes us dread the admission that they are ours, not the world's. We with our ideals must stand alone, and conquer, inwardly, the world's indifference. It is instinct, not wisdom, that finds this difficult and shivers at the solitude it seems to entail. Wisdom does not feel this solitude, because it can achieve union even with what seems most alien. The insistent demand that our ideals shall be already realized in the world is the last prison from which wisdom must be freed. Every demand is a prison, and wisdom is only free when it asks nothing.

(*The Hibbert Journal*, Vol. II, October 1912.)

62

WHAT IS AN AGNOSTIC?

A N Agnostic thinks it impossible to know the truth in matters such as God and the future life with which Christianity and other religions are concerned. Or, if not impossible, at least impossible at the present time.

ARE AGNOSTICS ATHEISTS?

No. An atheist, like a Christian, holds that we *can* know whether or not there is a God. The Christian holds that we can know there is a God; the atheist, that we can know there is not. The Agnostic suspends judgment, saying that there are not sufficient grounds either for affirmation or for denial. At the same time, an Agnostic may hold that the existence of God, though not impossible, is very improbable; he may even hold it so improbable that it is not worth considering in practice. In that case, he is not far removed from atheism. His attitude may be that which a careful philosopher would have towards the gods of ancient Greece. If I were asked to *prove* that Zeus and Poseidon and Hera and the rest of the Olympians do not exist, I should be at a loss to find conclusive arguments. An Agnostic may think the Christian God as improbable as the Olympians; in that case, he is, for practical purposes, at one with the atheists.

SINCE YOU DENY 'GOD'S LAW', WHAT AUTHORITY DO YOU ACCEPT AS A GUIDE TO CONDUCT?

An Agnostic does not accept any 'authority' in the sense in which religious people do. He holds that a man should think out questions of conduct for himself. Of course, he will seek to profit by the wisdom of others, but he will have to select for himself the people he is to consider wise, and he will not regard even what they say as unquestionable. He will observe that what passes as 'God's law' varies from time to time. The Bible says both that a woman must not marry her deceased husband's brother, and that, in certain circumstances, she must do so. If you have the misfortune to be a childless widow with an unmarried brother-in-law, it is logically impossible for you to avoid disobeying 'God's law'.

HOW DO YOU KNOW WHAT IS GOOD AND WHAT IS EVIL?
WHAT DOES AN AGNOSTIC CONSIDER A SIN?

The Agnostic is not quite so certain as some Christians are as to what is good and what is evil. He does not hold, as most Christians in the past held, that people who disagree with the government on abstruse points of theology ought to suffer a painful death. He is against persecution, and rather chary of moral condemnation.

As for 'sin', he thinks it not a useful notion. He admits, of course, that some kinds of conduct are desirable and some undesirable, but he holds that the punishment of undesirable kinds is only to be commended when it is deterrent or reformatory, not when it is inflicted because it is thought a good thing on its own account that the wicked should suffer. It was this belief in vindictive punishment that made men accept Hell. This is part of the harm done by the notion of 'sin'.

DOES AN AGNOSTIC DO WHATEVER HE PLEASES?

In one sense, no; in another sense, everyone does whatever he pleases. Suppose, for example, you hate someone so much that you would like to murder him. Why do you not do so? You may reply: 'Because religion tells me that murder is a sin.' But as a statistical fact, Agnostics are not more prone to murder than other people; in fact, rather less so. They have the same motives for abstaining from murder as other people have. Far and away the most powerful of these motives is the fear of punishment. In lawless conditions, such as a gold rush, all sorts of people will commit crimes, although in ordinary circumstances they would have been law-abiding. There is not only actual legal punishment; there is the discomfort of dreading discovery, and the loneliness of knowing that, to avoid being hated, you must wear a mask even with your closest intimates. And there is also what may be called 'conscience'. If you ever contemplated a murder, you would dread the horrible memory of your victim's last moments or lifeless corpse. All this, it is true, depends upon your living in a law-abiding community, but there are abundant secular reasons for creating and preserving such a community.

I said that there is another sense in which every man does as he pleases. No one but a fool indulges every impulse, but what holds a desire in check is always some other desire. A man's anti-social wishes may be restrained by a wish to please God, but they may also be restrained by a wish to please his friends, or to win the respect of his community, or to be able to contemplate himself without disgust. But if he has no such wishes, the mere abstract precepts of morality will not keep him straight.

HOW DOES AN AGNOSTIC REGARD THE BIBLE?

An Agnostic regards the Bible exactly as enlightened clerics regard it. He does not think that it is divinely inspired; he thinks its early history legendary, and no more exactly true than that in Homer; he thinks its moral teaching sometimes good, but sometimes very bad. For example: Samuel ordered Saul, in a war, to kill not only every man, woman, and child of the enemy, but also all the sheep and cattle. Saul, however, let the sheep and cattle live, and for this we are told to condemn him. I have never been able to admire Elisha for cursing the children who laughed at him, or to believe (what the Bible asserts) that a benevolent Deity would send two she-bears to kill the children.

HOW DOES AN AGNOSTIC REGARD JESUS, THE VIRGIN BIRTH, AND THE HOLY TRINITY?

Since an Agnostic does not believe in God, he cannot think that Jesus was God. Most Agnostics admire the life and moral teachings of Jesus as told in the Gospels, but not necessarily more than those of certain other men. Some would place him on a level with Buddha, some with Socrates and some with Abraham Lincoln. Nor do they think that what He said is not open to question, since they do not accept any authority as absolute.

They regard the Virgin Birth as a doctrine taken over from pagan mythology, where such births were not uncommon. (Zoroaster was said to have been born of a virgin; Ishtar, the Babylonian goddess, is called the Holy Virgin.) They cannot give credence to it, or to the doctrine of the Trinity, since neither is possible without belief in God.

CAN AN AGNOSTIC BE A CHRISTIAN?

The word 'Christian' has had various different meanings at different times. Throughout most of the centuries since the time of Christ, it has meant a person who believed in God and immortality and held that Christ was God. But Unitarians call themselves Christians, although they do not believe in the divinity of Christ, and many people nowadays use the word God in a much less precise sense than that which it used to bear. Many people who say they believe in God no longer mean a person, or a trinity of persons, but only a vague tendency or power or purpose immanent in evolution. Others, going still further, mean by 'Christianity' merely a system of ethics which, since they are ignorant of history, they imagine to be characteristic of Christians only.

When, in a recent book, I said that what the world needs is 'love, Christian love, or compassion', many people thought this showed some change in my views, although, in fact, I might have said the same thing at any time. If you mean by a 'Christian' a man who loves his neighbour, who has wide sympathy with suffering and who ardently desires a world freed from the cruelties and abominations which at present disfigure it, then, certainly, you will be justified in calling me a Christian. And, in this sense, I think you will find more 'Christians' among Agnostics than among the orthodox. But, for my part, I cannot accept such a definition. Apart from other objections to it, it seems rude to Jews, Buddhists, Mohammedans, and other non-Christians, who, so far as history shows, have been at least as apt as Christians to practise the virtues which some modern Christians arrogantly claim as distinctive of their own religion.

I think also that all who called themselves Christians in an earlier time, and a great majority of those who do so at the present day, would consider that belief in God and immortality is essential to a Christian. On these grounds, I should not call myself a Christian, and I should say that an Agnostic cannot be a Christian. But, if the word 'Christianity' comes to be generally used to mean merely a kind of morality, then it will certainly be possible for an Agnostic to be a Christian.

DOES AN AGNOSTIC DENY THAT MAN HAS A SOUL?

This question has no precise meaning unless we are given a definition of the word 'soul'. I suppose what is meant is, roughly, something non-material which persists throughout a person's life and even, for those who believe in immortality, throughout all future time. If this is what is meant, an Agnostic is not likely to believe that man has a soul. But I must hasten to add that this does not mean that an Agnostic must be a materialist. Many Agnostics (including myself) are quite as doubtful of the body as they are of the soul, but this is a long story taking one into difficult metaphysics. Mind and matter alike, I should say, are only convenient symbols in discourse, not actually existing things.

DOES AN AGNOSTIC BELIEVE IN A HEREAFTER, IN HEAVEN OR HELL?

The question whether people survive death is one as to which evidence is possible. Psychical research and spiritualism are thought by many to supply such evidence. An Agnostic, as such, does not take a view about survival unless he thinks that there is evidence one way or the other. For my part, I do not think there is any good reason to believe that we survive death, but I am open to conviction if adequate evidence should appear.

Heaven and hell are a different matter. Belief in hell is bound up with the belief that the vindictive punishment of sin is a good thing, quite independently of any reformative or deterrent effect that it may have.

Hardly any Agnostic believes this. As for heaven, there might conceivably someday be evidence of its existence through spiritualism, but most Agnostics do not think that there is such evidence, and therefore do not believe in heaven.

ARE YOU NEVER AFRAID OF GOD'S JUDGMENT IN DENYING HIM?

Most certainly not. I also deny Zeus and Jupiter and Odin and Brahma, but this causes me no qualms. I observe that a very large portion of the human race does not believe in God and suffers no visible punishment in consequence. And if there were a God, I think it very unlikely that He would have such an uneasy vanity as to be offended by those who doubt His existence.

HOW DO AGNOSTICS EXPLAIN THE BEAUTY AND HARMONY OF NATURE?

I do not understand where this 'beauty' and 'harmony' are supposed to be found. Throughout the animal kingdom, animals ruthlessly prey upon each other. Most of them are either cruelly killed by other animals or slowly die of hunger. For my part, I am unable to see any very great beauty or harmony in the tapeworm. Let it not be said that this creature is sent as a punishment for our sins, for it is more prevalent among animals than among humans. I suppose the questioner is thinking of such things as the beauty of the starry heavens. But one should remember that stars every now and again explode and reduce everything in their neighbourhood to a vague mist. Beauty, in any case, is subjective and exists only in the eye of the beholder.

HOW DO AGNOSTICS EXPLAIN MIRACLES AND OTHER REVELATIONS OF GOD'S OMNIPOTENCE?

Agnostics do not think that there is any evidence of 'miracles' in the sense of happenings contrary to natural law. We know that faith healing occurs and is in no sense miraculous. At Lourdes, certain diseases can be cured and others cannot. Those that can be cured at Lourdes can probably be cured by any doctor in whom the patient has faith. As for the records of other miracles, such as Joshua commanding the sun to stand still, the Agnostic dismisses them as legends and points to the fact that all religions are plentifully supplied with such legends. There is just as much miraculous evidence for the Greek gods in Homer as for the Christian God in the Bible.

THERE HAVE BEEN BASE AND CRUEL PASSIONS, WHICH RELIGION OPPOSES. IF YOU ABANDON RELIGIOUS PRINCIPLES, COULD MANKIND EXIST?

The existence of base and cruel passions is undeniable, but I find no evidence in history that religion has opposed these passions. On the contrary, it has sanctified them, and enabled people to indulge them without remorse. Cruel persecutions have been commoner in Christendom than anywhere else. What appears to justify persecution is dogmatic belief. Kindliness and tolerance only prevail in proportion as dogmatic belief decays. In our day, a new dogmatic religion, namely, Communism, has arisen. To this, as to other systems of dogma, the Agnostic is opposed. The persecuting character of present-day Communism is exactly like the persecuting character of Christianity in earlier centuries. In so far as Christianity has become less persecuting, this is mainly due to the work of free-thinkers who have made dogmatists rather less dogmatic. If they were as dogmatic now as in former times, they would still think it right to burn heretics at the stake. The spirit of tolerance which some modern Christians regard as essentially Christian is, in fact, a product of the temper which allows doubt and is suspicious of absolute certainties. I think that anybody who surveys past history in an impartial manner will be driven to the conclusion that religion has caused more suffering than it has prevented.

WHAT IS THE MEANING OF LIFE TO THE AGNOSTIC?

I feel inclined to answer by another question: What is the meaning of 'the meaning of life'? I suppose what is intended is some general purpose. I do not think that life in general has any purpose. It just happened. But individual human beings have purposes, and there is nothing in agnosticism to cause them to abandon these purposes. They cannot, of course, be certain of achieving the results at which they aim; but you would think ill of a soldier who refused to fight unless victory was certain. The person who needs religion to bolster up his own purposes is a timorous person, and I cannot think as well of him as of the man who takes his chances, while admitting that defeat is not impossible.

DOES NOT THE DENIAL OF RELIGION MEAN THE DENIAL OF MARRIAGE AND CHASTITY?

Here again, one must reply by another question: Does the man who asks this question believe that marriage and chastity contribute to earthly happiness here below, or does he think that, while they cause misery here below, they are to be advocated as means of getting to heaven? The man who takes the latter view will no doubt expect agnosticism to lead to a decay of what he calls virtue, but he will have to admit that what he calls virtue is not what ministers to the happiness of the human race while on earth. If, on the other hand, he takes the former view, namely, that there are terrestrial arguments in favour of marriage and chastity, he must also hold that these arguments are such as should appeal to an Agnostic. Agnostics, as such, have no distinctive views about sexual morality. But most of them would admit that there are valid arguments against the unbridled indulgence of sexual desires. They would derive these arguments, however, from terrestrial sources and not from supposed divine commands.

IS NOT FAITH IN REASON ALONE A DANGEROUS CREED? IS NOT REASON IMPERFECT AND INADEQUATE WITHOUT SPIRITUAL AND MORAL LAW?

No sensible man, however Agnostic, has 'faith in reason alone'. Reason is concerned with matters of fact, some observed, some inferred. The question whether there is a future life and the question whether there is a God concern matters of fact, and the Agnostic will hold that they should be investigated in the same way as the question, 'Will there be an eclipse of the moon tomorrow?' But matters of fact alone are not sufficient to determine action, since they do not tell us what ends we ought to pursue. In the realm of ends, we need something other than reason. The Agnostic will find his ends in his own heart and not in an external command. Let us take an illustration: Suppose you wish to travel by train from New York to Chicago; you will use reason to discover when the trains run, and a person who thought that there was some faculty of insight or intuition enabling him to dispense with the timetable would be thought rather silly. But no timetable will tell him that it is wise to travel to Chicago. No doubt, in deciding that it is wise, he will have to take account of further matters of fact; but behind all the matters of fact, there will be the ends that he thinks fitting to pursue, and these, for an Agnostic as for other men, belong to a realm which is not that of reason, though it should be in no degree contrary to it. The realm I mean is that of emotion and feeling and desire.

DO YOU REGARD ALL RELIGIONS AS FORMS OF SUPERSTITION OR DOGMA? WHICH OF THE EXISTING RELIGIONS DO YOU MOST RESPECT, AND WHY?

All the great organized religions that have dominated large populations have involved a greater or less amount of dogma, but 'religion' is a word of which the meaning is not very definite. Confucianism, for instance, might be called a religion, although it involves no dogma. And in some forms of liberal Christianity, the element of dogma is reduced to a minimum.

Of the great religions of history, I prefer Buddhism, especially in its earliest forms, because it has had the smallest element of persecution.

COMMUNISM LIKE AGNOSTICISM OPPOSES RELIGION. ARE AGNOSTICS COMMUNISTS?

Communism does not oppose religion. It merely opposes the Christian religion, just as Mohammedanism does. Communism, at least in the form advocated by the Soviet Government and the Communist Party, is a new system of dogma of a peculiarly virulent and persecuting sort. Every genuine Agnostic must therefore be opposed to it.

DO AGNOSTICS THINK THAT SCIENCE AND RELIGION ARE IMPOSSIBLE TO RECONCILE?

The answer turns upon what is meant by 'religion'. If it means merely a system of ethics, it can be reconciled with science. If it means a system of dogma, regarded as unquestionably true, it is incompatible with the scientific spirit, which refuses to accept matters of fact without evidence, and also holds that complete certainty is hardly ever attainable.

WHAT KIND OF EVIDENCE COULD CONVINCE YOU THAT GOD EXISTS?

I think that if I heard a voice from the sky predicting all that was going to happen to me during the next twenty-four hours, including events that would have seemed highly improbable, and if all these events then proceeded to happen, I might perhaps be convinced at least of the existence of some superhuman intelligence. I can imagine other evidence of the same sort which might convince me, but so far as I know, no such evidence exists.

(*Look* Magazine, Copyright © 1953 Cowles Magazine, Inc., subsequently reprinted in *The Religions of America*, ed. Leo Rosten, London: Heinemann.)

63

WHY I AM NOT A CHRISTIAN

This lecture was delivered on March 6, 1927, at Battersea Town Hall, under the auspices of the South London Branch of the National Secular Society.

As your chairman has told you, the subject about which I am going to speak to you tonight is 'Why I am not a Christian'. Perhaps it would be as well, first of all, to try to make out what one means by the word 'Christian'. It is used these days in a very loose sense by a great many people. Some people mean no more by it than a person who attempts to live a good life. In that sense I suppose there would be Christians in all sects and creeds; but I do not think that that is the proper sense of the word, if only because it would imply that all the people who are not Christians—all the Buddhists, Confucians, Mohammedans, and so on—are not trying to live a good life. I do not mean by a Christian any person who tries to live decently according to his lights. I think that you must have a certain amount of definite belief before you have a right to call yourself a Christian. The word does not have quite such a full-blooded meaning now as it had in the times of St Augustine and St Thomas Aquinas. In those days, if a man said that he was a Christian it was known what he meant. You accepted a whole collection of creeds which were set out with great precision, and every single syllable of those creeds you believed with the whole strength of your convictions.

WHAT IS A CHRISTIAN?

Nowadays it is not quite that. We have to be a little more vague in our meaning of Christianity. I think, however, that there are two different items which are quite essential to anybody calling himself a Christian. The first is one of a dogmatic nature—namely, that you must believe in God and immortality. If you do not believe in those two things, I do not think that you can properly call yourself a Christian. Then, further than that, as the name implies, you must have some kind of belief about Christ. The Mohammedans, for instance, also believe in God and in immortality, and yet they would not call themselves Christians. I think you must have at the very lowest the belief that Christ was, if not divine, at least the best and wisest of men. If you are not going to believe that much about Christ, I do not think you have any right to call yourself a Christian. Of course there is another sense which you find in *Whitaker's Almanack* and in geography books, where the population of the world is said to be divided into Christians, Mohammedans, Buddhists, fetish worshippers, and so on; and in that sense we are all Christians. The geography books count us all in, but that is a purely geographical sense, which I suppose we can ignore. Therefore I take it that when I tell you why I am not a Christian I have to tell you two different things; first, why I do not believe in God and in immortality; and, secondly, why I do not think that Christ was the best and wisest of men, although I grant Him a very high degree of moral goodness.

But for the successful efforts of unbelievers in the past, I could not take so elastic a definition of Christianity as that. As I said before, in olden days it had a much more full-blooded sense. For instance, it included the belief in hell. Belief in eternal hell fire was an essential item of Christian belief until pretty recent times. In this country, as you know, it ceased to be an essential item because of a decision of the Privy Council, and from that decision the Archbishop of Canterbury and the Archbishop of York dissented; but in this country our religion is settled by Act of Parliament, and therefore the Privy Council was able to override Their Graces and hell was no longer necessary to a Christian. Consequently I shall not insist that a Christian must believe in hell.

THE EXISTENCE OF GOD

To come to this question of the existence of God, it is a large and serious question, and if I were to attempt to deal with it in any adequate manner I should have to keep you here until Kingdom Come, so that you will have to excuse me if I deal with it in a somewhat summary fashion. You know, of course, that the Catholic Church has laid it down as a dogma that the existence of God can be proved by the unaided reason. That is a somewhat curious dogma, but it is one of their dogmas. They had to introduce it because at one time the free-thinkers adopted the habit of saying that there were such and such arguments which mere reason might urge against the existence of God, but of course they knew as a matter of faith that God did exist. The arguments and the reasons were set out at great length, and the Catholic Church felt that they must stop it. Therefore they laid it down that the existence of God can be proved by the unaided reason, and they had to set up what they considered were arguments to prove it. There are, of course, a number of them, but I shall take only a few.

THE FIRST CAUSE ARGUMENT

Perhaps the simplest and easiest to understand is the argument of the First Cause. (It is maintained that everything we see in this world has a cause, and as you go back in the chain of causes further and further you must come to a First Cause, and to that First Cause you give the name of God.) That argument, I suppose, does not carry very much weight nowadays, because, in the first place, cause is not quite what it used to be. The philosophers and the men of science have got going on cause, and it has not anything like the vitality it used to have; but, apart from that, you can see that the argument that there must be a First Cause is one that cannot have any validity. I may say that when I was a young man and was debating these questions very seriously in my mind, I for a long time accepted the argument of the First Cause, until one day, at the age of eighteen, I read John Stuart Mill's Autobiography, and I there found this sentence: 'My father taught me that the question, "Who made me?" cannot be answered, since it immediately suggests the further question, "Who made God?"' That very simple sentence showed me, as I still think, the fallacy in the argument of the First Cause. If everything must have a cause, then God must have a cause. If there can be anything without a cause, it may just as well be the world as God, so that there cannot be any validity in that argument. It is exactly of the same nature as the Hindu's view, that the world rested upon an elephant and the elephant rested upon a tortoise; and when they said, 'How about the tortoise?' the Indian said, 'Suppose we change the subject'. The argument is really no better than that. There is no reason why the world could not have come into being without a cause; nor, on the other hand, is there any reason why it should not have always existed. There is no reason to suppose that the world had a beginning at all. The idea that things must have a beginning is really due to the poverty of our imagination. Therefore, perhaps, I need not waste any more time upon the argument about the First Cause.

THE NATURAL LAW ARGUMENT

Then there is a very common argument from natural law. That was a favourite argument all through the eighteenth century, especially under the influence of Sir Isaac Newton and his cosmogony. People observed the planets going round the sun according to the law of gravitation, and they thought that God had given a behest to these planets to move in that particular fashion, and that was why they did so. That was, of course, a convenient and simple explanation that saved them the trouble of looking any further for explanations of the law of gravitation. Nowadays we explain the law of gravitation in a somewhat complicated fashion that

Einstein has introduced. I do not propose to give you a lecture on the law of gravitation as interpreted by Einstein, because that again would take some time; at any rate, you no longer have the sort of natural law that you had in the Newtonian system, where, for some reason that nobody could understand, nature behaved in a uniform fashion. We now find that a great many things we thought were natural laws are really human conventions. You know that even in the remotest depths of stellar space there are still three feet to a yard. That is, no doubt, a very remarkable fact, but you would hardly call it a law of nature. And a great many things that have been regarded as laws of nature are of that kind. On the other hand, where you can get down to any knowledge of what atoms actually do, you will find they are much less subject to law than people thought, and that the laws at which you arrive are statistical averages of just the sort that would emerge from chance. There is, as we all know, a law that if you throw dice you will get double sixes only about once in thirty-six times, and we do not regard that as evidence that the fall of the dice is regulated by design; on the contrary, if the double sixes came every time we should think that there was design. The laws of nature are of that sort as regards a great many of them. They are statistical averages such as would emerge from the laws of chance; and that makes this whole business of natural law much less impressive than it formerly was. Quite apart from that, which represents the momentary state of science that may change tomorrow, the whole idea that natural laws imply a law-giver is due to a confusion between natural and human laws. Human laws are behests commanding you to behave a certain way, in which way you may choose to behave, or you may choose not to behave; but natural laws are a description of how things do in fact behave, and being a mere description of what they in fact do, you cannot argue that there must be somebody who told them to do that, because even supposing that there were you are then faced with the question, 'Why did God issue just those natural laws and no others?' If you say that He did it simply from His own good pleasure, and without any reason, you then find that there is something which is not subject to law, and so your train of natural law is interrupted. If you say, as more orthodox theologians do, that in all the laws which God issues He had a reason for giving those laws rather than others—the reason, of course, being to create the best universe, although you would never think it to look at it—if there was a reason for the laws which God gave, then God Himself was subject to law, and therefore you do not get any advantage by introducing God as an intermediary. You have really a law outside and anterior to the divine edicts, and God does not serve your purpose, because He is not the ultimate law-giver. In short, this whole argument about natural law no longer has anything like the strength that it used to have. I am travelling on in time in my review of the arguments. The arguments that are used for the existence of God change their character as time goes on. They were at first hard, intellectual arguments embodying certain quite definite fallacies. As we come to modern times they become less respectable intellectually and more and more affected by a kind of moralizing vagueness.

THE ARGUMENT FROM DESIGN

The next step in this process brings us to the argument from design. You all know the argument from design: everything in the world is made just so that we can manage to live in the world, and if the world was ever so little different we could not manage to live in it. That is the argument from design. It sometimes takes a rather curious form; for instance, it is argued that rabbits have white tails in order to be easy to shoot. I do not know how rabbits would view that application. It is an easy argument to parody. You all know Voltaire's remark, that obviously the nose was designed to be such as to fit spectacles. That sort of parody has turned out to be not nearly so wide of the mark as it might have seemed in the eighteenth century, because since the time of Darwin we understand much better why living creatures are adapted to their environment. It is not that their environment was made to be suitable to them, but that they grew to be suitable to it, and that is the basis of adaptation. There is no evidence of design about it.

When you come to look into this argument from design, it is a most astonishing thing that people can believe that this world, with all the things that are in it, with all its defects, should be the best that omnipotence has been able to produce in millions of years. I really cannot believe it. Do you think that, if you were granted omnipotence and omniscience and millions of years in which to perfect your world, you could produce nothing better than the Ku-Klux-Klan or the Fascists? Moreover, if you accept the ordinary laws of science, you have to suppose that human life and life in general on this planet will die out in due course: it is a stage in the decay of the solar system; at a certain stage of decay you get the sort of conditions of temperature and so forth which are suitable to protoplasm, and there is life for a short time in the life of the whole solar system. You see in the moon the sort of thing to which the earth is tending—something dead, cold, and lifeless.

I am told that that sort of view is depressing, and people will sometimes tell you that if they believed that they would not be able to go on living. Do not believe it; it is all nonsense. Nobody really worries much about what is going to happen millions of years hence. Even if they think they are worrying much about that, they are really deceiving themselves. They are worried about something much more mundane, or it may merely be a bad digestion; but nobody is really seriously rendered unhappy by the thought of something that is going to happen to this world millions and millions of years hence. Therefore, although it is of course a gloomy view to suppose that life will die out—at least I suppose we may say so, although sometimes when I contemplate the things that people do with their lives I think it is almost a consolation—it is not such as to render life miserable. It merely makes you turn your attention to other things.

THE MORAL ARGUMENTS FOR DEITY

Now we reach one stage further in what I shall call the intellectual descent that the theists have made in their argumentations, and we come to what are called the moral arguments for the existence of God. You all know, of course, that there used to be in the old days three intellectual arguments for the existence of God, all of which were disposed of by Immanuel Kant in the *Critique of Pure Reason*; but no sooner had he disposed of those arguments than he invented a new one, a moral argument, and that quite convinced him. He was like many people: in intellectual matters he was sceptical, but in moral matters he believed implicitly in the maxims that he had imbibed at his mother's knee. That illustrates what the psychoanalysts so much emphasize—the immensely stronger hold upon us that our very early associations have than those of later times.

Kant, as I say, invented a new moral argument for the existence of God, and that in varying forms was extremely popular during the nineteenth century. It has all sorts of forms. One form is to say that there would be no right or wrong unless God existed. I am not for the moment concerned with whether there is a difference between right and wrong, or whether there is not: that is another question. The point I am concerned with is that, if you are quite sure there is a difference between right and wrong, you are then in this situation: is that difference due to God's fiat or is it not? If it is due to God's fiat, then for God Himself there is no difference between right and wrong, and it is no longer a significant statement to say that God is good. If you are going to say, as theologians do, that God is good, you must then say that right and wrong have some meaning which is independent of God's fiat, because God's fiats are good and not bad independently of the mere fact that He made them. If you are going to say that, you will then have to say that it is not only through God that right and wrong came into being, but that they are in their essence logically anterior to God. You could, of course, if you liked, say that there was a superior deity who gave orders to the God who made this world, or could take up the line that some of the gnostics took up— a line which I often thought was a very plausible one—that as a matter of fact this world that we know was made by the devil at a moment when God was not looking. There is a good deal to be said for that, and I am not concerned to refute it.

THE ARGUMENT FOR THE REMEDYING OF INJUSTICE

Then there is another very curious form of moral argument, which is this: they say that the existence of God is required in order to bring justice into the world. In the part of this universe that we know there is great injustice, and often the good suffer, and often the wicked prosper, and one hardly knows which of those is the more annoying; but if you are going to have justice in the universe as a whole you have to suppose a future life to redress the balance of life here on earth. So they say that there must be a God, and there must be heaven and hell in order that in the long run there may be justice. That is a very curious argument. If you looked at the matter from a scientific point of view, you would say: 'After all, I know only this world. I do not know about the rest of the universe, but so far as one can argue at all on probabilities one would say that probably this world is a fair sample, and if there is injustice here the odds are that there is injustice elsewhere also.' Supposing you got a crate of oranges that you opened, and you found all the top layer of oranges bad, you would not argue: 'The underneath ones must be good, so as to redress the balance.' You would say: 'Probably the whole lot is a bad consignment'; and that is really what a scientific person would argue about the universe. He would say: 'Here we find in this world a great deal of injustice and so far as that goes that is a reason for supposing that justice does not rule in the world; and therefore so far as it goes it affords a moral argument against deity and not in favour of one.' Of course I know that the sort of intellectual arguments that I have been talking to you about are not what really moves people. What really moves people to believe in God is not any intellectual argument at all. Most people believe in God because they have been taught from early infancy to do it, and that is the main reason.

Then I think that the next most powerful reason is the wish for safety, a sort of feeling that there is a big brother who will look after you. That plays a very profound part in influencing people's desire for a belief in God.

THE CHARACTER OF CHRIST

I now want to say a few words upon a topic which I often think is not quite sufficiently dealt with by Rationalists, and that is the question whether Christ was the best and the wisest of men. It is generally taken for granted that we should all agree that that was so. I do not myself. I think that there are a good many points upon which I agree with Christ a great deal more than the professing Christians do. I do not know that I could go with Him all the way, but I could go with Him much farther than most professing Christians can. You will remember that He said: 'Resist not evil, but whosoever shall smite thee on thy right cheek, turn to him the other also.' That is not a new precept or a new principle. It was used by Lao-Tze and Buddha some five or six hundred years before Christ, but it is not a principle which as a matter of fact Christians accept. I have no doubt that the present Prime Minister,[1] for instance, is a most sincere Christian, but I should not advise any of you to go and smite him on one cheek. I think you might find that he thought this text was intended in a figurative sense.

Then there is another point which I consider is excellent. You will remember that Christ said: 'Judge not lest ye be judged.' That principle I do not think you would find was popular in the law courts of Christian countries. I have known in my time quite a number of judges who were very earnest Christians, and they none of them felt that they were acting contrary to Christian principles in what they did. Then Christ says: 'Give to him that asketh thee, and from him that would borrow of thee turn not thou away.' That is a very good principle.

Your Chairman has reminded you that we are not here to talk politics, but I cannot help observing that the last general election was fought on the question of how desirable it was to turn away from him that would borrow of thee, so that one must assume that the Liberals and Conservatives of this country are composed of people who do not agree with the teaching of Christ, because they certainly did very emphatically turn away on that occasion.

Then there is one other maxim of Christ which I think has a great deal in it, but I do not find that it is very popular among some of our Christian friends. He says: 'If thou wilt be perfect, go and sell that thou hast, and give to the poor.' That is a very excellent maxim, but, as I say, it is not much practised. All these, I think, are good maxims, although they are a little difficult to live up to. I do not profess to live up to them myself; but then, after all, it is not quite the same thing as for a Christian.

DEFECTS IN CHRIST'S TEACHING

Having granted the excellence of these maxims, I come to certain points in which I do not believe that one can grant either the superlative wisdom or the superlative goodness of Christ as depicted in the Gospels; and here I may say that one is not concerned with the historical question. Historically it is quite doubtful whether Christ ever existed at all, and if He did we do not know anything about Him, so that I am not concerned with the historical question, which is a very difficult one. I am concerned with Christ as He appears in the Gospels, taking the Gospel narrative as it stands, and there one does find some things that do not seem to be very wise. For one thing, He certainly thought that His second coming would

[1] Stanley Baldwin.

occur in clouds of glory before the death of all the people who were living at that time. There are a great many texts that prove that. He says, for instance: 'Ye shall not have gone over the cities of Israel, till the Son of Man be come.' Then He says: 'There are some standing here which shall not taste death till the Son of Man comes into His kingdom'; and there are a lot of places where it is quite clear that He believed that His second coming would happen during the lifetime of many then living. That was the belief of His earlier followers, and it was the basis of a good deal of His moral teaching. When He said, 'Take no thought for the morrow', and things of that sort, it was very largely because He thought that the second coming was going to be very soon, and that all ordinary mundane affairs did not count. I have, as a matter of fact, known some Christians who did believe that the second coming was imminent. I knew a parson who frightened his congregation terribly by telling them that the second coming was very imminent indeed, but they were much consoled when they found that he was planting trees in his garden. The early Christians did really believe it, and they did abstain from such things as planting trees in their gardens, because they did accept from Christ the belief that the second coming was imminent. In that respect clearly He was not so wise as some other people have been, and He was certainly not superlatively wise.

THE MORAL PROBLEM

Then you come to moral questions. There is one very serious defect to my mind in Christ's moral character, and that is that He believed in hell. I do not myself feel that any person who is really profoundly humane can believe in everlasting punishment. Christ certainly as depicted in the Gospels did believe in everlasting punishment, and one does find repeatedly a vindictive fury against those people who would not listen to His preaching—an attitude which is not uncommon with preachers, but which does somewhat detract from superlative excellence. You do not, for instance, find that attitude in Socrates. You find him quite bland and urbane towards the people who would not listen to him; and it is, to my mind, far more worthy of a sage to take that line than to take the line of indignation. You probably all remember the sort of things that Socrates was saying when he was dying, and the sort of things that he generally did say to people who did not agree with him.

You will find that in the Gospels Christ said: 'Ye serpents, ye generation of vipers, how can ye escape the damnation of hell?' That was said to people who did not like His preaching. It is not really to my mind quite the best tone, and there are a great many of these things about hell. There is, of course, the familiar text about the sin against the Holy Ghost: 'Whosoever speaketh against the Holy Ghost it shall not be forgiven him neither in this world nor in the world to come.' That text has caused an unspeakable amount of misery in the world, for all sorts of people have imagined that they have committed the sin against the Holy Ghost, and thought that it would not be forgiven them either in this world or in the world to come. I really do not think that a person with a proper degree of kindliness in his nature would have put fears and terrors of that sort into the world.

Then Christ says: 'The Son of Man shall send forth His angels, and they shall gather out of His kingdom all things that offend, and them which do iniquity, and shall cast them into a furnace of fire; there shall be wailing and gnashing of teeth'; and He goes on about the wailing and gnashing of teeth. It comes in one verse after another, and it is quite manifest to the reader that there is a certain pleasure in contemplating wailing and gnashing of teeth, or else it would not occur so often. Then you all, of course, remember about the sheep and the goats; how at the second coming to divide the sheep and the goats He is going to say to the goats: 'Depart from me, ye cursed, into everlasting fire.' He continues: 'And these shall go away into everlasting fire.' Then He says again: 'If thy hand offend thee, cut it off; it is better for thee to enter into life maimed, than having two hands to go into hell, into the fire that never shall be quenched; where the worm dieth not and the fire is not quenched.' He repeats that again and again also. I must say that I think all this doctrine, that hell-fire is a punishment for sin, is a doctrine of cruelty. It is a doctrine that put cruelty into the world and gave the world genera-tions of cruel torture; and the Christ of the Gospels, if you could take Him as His chroniclers represent Him, would certainly have to be con-sidered partly responsible for that.

There are other things of less importance. There is the instance of the Gadarene swine where it certainly was not very kind to the pigs to put the devils into them and make them rush down the hill to the sea. You must remember that He was omnipotent, and He could have made the devils simply go away; but He chooses to send them into the pigs. Then there is the curious story of the fig-tree, which always rather puzzled me. You remember what happened about the fig-tree. 'He was hungry; and seeing a fig-tree afar off having leaves, He came if haply He might find anything thereon; and when He came to it He found nothing but leaves, for the time of figs was not yet. And Jesus answered and said unto it: "No man eat fruit of thee hereafter for ever", . . . and Peter . . . saith unto Him: "Master, behold the fig-tree which thou cursedst is withered away." ' This is a very curious story, because it was not the right time of year for figs, and you really could not blame the tree. I cannot myself feel that either in the matter of wisdom or in the matter of virtue Christ stands quite as high as some other people known to history. I think I should put Buddha and Socrates above Him in those respects.

THE EMOTIONAL FACTOR

As I said before, I do not think that the real reason why people accept religion has anything to do with argumentation. They accept religion on emotional grounds. One is often told that it is a very wrong thing to attack religion, because religion makes men virtuous. So I am told; I have not noticed it. You know, of course, the parody of that argument in Samuel Butler's book, *Erewhon Revisited*. You will remember that in *Erewhon* there is a certain Higgs who arrives in a remote country, and after spending some time there he escapes from that country in a balloon. Twenty years later he comes back to that country and finds a new religion, in which he is worshipped under the name of the 'Sun Child', and it is said that he ascended into heaven. He finds that the Feast of the Ascension is about to be celebrated, and he hears Professors Hanky and Panky say to each other that they never set eyes on the man Higgs, and they hope they never will; but they are the high priests of the religion of the Sun Child. He is very indignant, and he comes up to them, and he says: 'I am going to expose all this humbug and tell the people of Erewhon that it was only I, the man Higgs, and I went up in a balloon.' He was told: 'You must not do that, because all the morals of this country are bound round this myth, and if they once know that you did not ascend into heaven they will all become wicked'; and so he is persuaded of that and he goes quietly away.

That is the idea—that we should all be wicked if we did not hold to the Christian religion. It seems to me that the people who have held to it have been for the most part extremely wicked. You find this curious fact, that the more intense has been the religion of any period and the more profound has been the dogmatic belief, the greater has been the cruelty and the worse has been the state of affairs. In the so-called ages of faith, when men did really believe the Christian religion in all its completeness, there was the Inquisition, with its tortures; there were millions of unfortunate women burnt as witches; and there was every kind of cruelty practised upon all sorts of people in the name of religion.

You find as you look around the world that every single bit of progress in humane feeling, every improvement in the criminal law, every step towards the diminution of war, every step towards better treatment of the coloured races or every mitigation of slavery, every moral progress that there has been in the world, has been consistently opposed by the organized Churches of the world. I say quite deliberately that the Christian religion, as organized in its churches, has been and still is the principal enemy of moral progress in the world.

HOW THE CHURCHES HAVE RETARDED PROGRESS

You may think that I am going too far when I say that that is still so. I do not think that I am. Take one fact. You will bear with me if I mention it. It is not a pleasant fact, but the Churches compel one to mention facts that are not pleasant. Supposing that in this world that we live in today an inexperienced girl is married to a syphilitic man, in that case the Catholic Church says: 'This is an indissoluble sacrament. You must stay together for life.' And no steps of any sort must be taken by that woman to prevent herself from giving birth to syphilitic children. That is what the Catholic Church says. I say that that is fiendish cruelty, and nobody whose natural sympathies have not been warped by dogma, or whose moral nature was not absolutely dead to all sense of suffering, could maintain that it is right and proper that that state of things should continue.

That is only an example. There are a great many ways in which at the present moment the Church, by its insistence upon what it chooses to call morality, inflicts upon all sorts of people undeserved and unnecessary suffering. And of course, as we know, it is in its major part an opponent still of progress and of improvement in all the ways that diminish suffering in the world, because it has chosen to label as morality a certain narrow set of rules of conduct which have nothing to do with human happiness; and when you say that this or that ought to be done because it would make for human happiness, they think that has nothing to do with the matter at all. 'What has human happiness to do with morals? The object of morals is not to make people happy.'

FEAR THE FOUNDATION OF RELIGION

Religion is based, I think, primarily and mainly upon fear. It is partly the terror of the unknown, and partly, as I have said, the wish to feel that you have a kind of elder brother who will stand by you in all your troubles and disputes. Fear is the basis of the whole thing—fear of the mysterious, fear of defeat, fear of death. Fear is the parent of cruelty, and therefore it is no wonder if cruelty and religion have gone hand in hand. It is because fear is at the basis of those two things. In this world we can now begin a little to understand things, and a little to master them by help of science, which has forced its way step by step against the Christian religion, against the Churches, and against the opposition of all the old precepts. Science can help us to get over this craven fear in which mankind has lived for so many generations. Science can teach us, and I think our own hearts can teach us, no longer to look round for imaginary supports, no longer to invent allies in the sky, but rather to look to our own efforts here below to make this world a fit place to live in, instead of the sort of place that the churches in all these centuries have made it.

WHAT WE MUST DO

We want to stand upon our own feet and look fair and square at the world—its good facts, its bad facts, its beauties, and its ugliness; see the world as it is, and be not afraid of it. Conquer the world by intelligence and not merely by being slavishly subdued by the terror that comes from it. The whole conception of God is a conception derived from the ancient Oriental despotisms. It is a conception quite unworthy of free men. When you hear people in church debasing themselves and saying that they are miserable sinners, and all the rest of it, it seems contemptible and not worthy of self-respecting human beings. We ought to stand up and look the world frankly in the face. We ought to make the best we can of the world, and if it is not so good as we wish, after all it will still be better than what these others have made of it in all these ages. A good world needs knowledge, kindliness, and courage; it does not need a regretful hankering after the past, or a fettering of the free intelligence by the words uttered long ago by ignorant men. It needs a fearless outlook and a free intelligence. It needs hope for the future, not looking back all the time towards a past that is dead, which we trust will be far surpassed by the future that our intelligence can create.

> (Monograph published by C. A. Watts & Co., 1927 and subsequently reprinted in *Why I am not a Christian*, ed. by Paul Edwards, London: Allen & Unwin; New York: Simon & Schuster, 1957.)

64

CAN RELIGION CURE OUR TROUBLES?[1]

I

MANKIND is in mortal peril, and fear now, as in the past, is inclining men to seek refuge in God. Throughout the West there is a very general revival of religion. Nazis and Communists dismissed Christianity and did things which we deplore. It is easy to conclude that the repudiation of Christianity by Hitler and the Soviet Government is at least in part the cause of our troubles and that if the world returned to Christianity, our international problems would be solved. I believe this to be a complete delusion born of terror. And I think it is a dangerous delusion because it misleads men whose thinking might otherwise be fruitful and thus stands in the way of a valid solution.

The question involved is not concerned only with the present state of the world. It is a much more general question, and one which has been debated for many centuries. It is the question whether societies can practise a sufficient modicum of morality if they are not helped by dogmatic religion. I do not myself think that the dependence of morals upon religion is nearly as close as religious people believe it to be. I even think that some very important virtues are more likely to be found among those who reject religious dogmas than among those who accept them. I think this applies especially to the virtue of truthfulness or intellectual integrity. I mean by intellectual integrity the habit of deciding vexed questions in accordance with the evidence, or of leaving them undecided where the evidence is inconclusive. This virtue, though it is underestimated by almost all adherents of any system of dogma, is to my mind of the very greatest social importance and far more likely to benefit the world than Christianity or any other system of organized beliefs.

Let us consider for a moment how moral rules have come to be accepted. Moral rules are broadly of two kinds: there are those which have no basis except in a religious creed; and there are those which have an obvious basis in social utility. In the Greek Orthodox Church, two godparents of the same child must not marry. For this rule, clearly, there is only a

[1] The two parts of this essay originally appeared as articles in the Stockholm newspaper, *Dagens Nyheter*, on November 9 and 11, 1954.

theological basis; and, if you think the rule important, you will be quite right in saying that the decay of religion is to be deprecated because it will lead to the rule being infringed. But it is not this kind of moral rule that is in question. The moral rules that are in question are those for which there is a social justification independently of theology.

Let us take theft, for example. A community in which everybody steals is inconvenient for everybody, and it is obvious that most people can get more of the sort of life they desire if they live in a community where theft is rare. But in the absence of laws and morals and religion a difficulty arises: for each individual, the ideal community would be one in which everybody else is honest and he alone is a thief. It follows that a social institution is necessary if the interest of the individual is to be reconciled with that of the community. This is effected more or less successfully by the criminal law and the police. But criminals are not always caught, and the police may be unduly lenient to the powerful. If people can be persuaded that there is a God who will punish theft, even when the police fail, it would seem likely that this belief would promote honesty. Given a population that already believes in God, it will readily believe that God has prohibited theft. The usefulness of religion in this respect is illustrated by the story of Naboth's vineyard where the thief is the king, who is above earthly justice.

I will not deny that among semi-civilized communities in the past such considerations may have helped to promote socially desirable conduct. But in the present day such good as may be done by imputing a theological origin to morals is inextricably bound up with such grave evils that the good becomes insignificant in comparison. As civilization progresses, the earthly sanctions become more secure and the divine sanctions less so. People see more and more reason to think that if they steal they will be caught and less and less reason to think that if they are not caught God will nevertheless punish them. Even highly religious people in the present day hardly expect to go to hell for stealing. They reflect that they can repent in time, and that in any case hell is neither so certain nor so hot as it used to be. Most people in civilized communities do not steal, and I think the usual motive is the great likelihood of punishment here on earth. This is borne out by the fact that in a mining camp during a gold rush, or in any such disorderly community, almost everybody does steal.

But, you may say, although the theological prohibition of theft may no longer be very necessary, it at any rate does no harm since we all wish people not to steal. The trouble is, however, that as soon as men incline to doubt received theology it comes to be supported by odious and harmful means. If a theology is thought necessary to virtue and if candid inquirers see no reason to think the theology true, the authorities will set to work to discourage candid inquiry. In former centuries, they did so by burning the inquirers at the stake. In Russia they still have methods which are little better; but in Western countries the authorities have perfected somewhat milder forms of persuasion. Of these, schools are perhaps the most important: the young must be preserved from hearing the arguments in favour of the opinions which the authorities dislike, and those who nevertheless persist in showing an inquiring disposition will incur social displeasure and, if possible, be made to feel morally reprehensible. In this way, any system of morals which has a theological basis becomes one of the tools by which the holders of power preserve their authority and impair the intellectual vigour of the young.

I find among many people at the present day an indifference to truth which I cannot but think extremely dangerous. When people argue, for example, in defence of Christianity, they do not, like Thomas Aquinas, give reasons for supposing that there is a God and that He has expressed His will in the Scriptures. They argue instead that, if people think this, they will act better than if they do not. We ought not therefore—so these people contend—to permit ourselves to speculate as to whether God exists. If, in an unguarded moment, doubt rears its head, we must suppress it vigorously. If candid thought is a cause of doubt we must eschew candid thought. If the official exponents of orthodoxy tell you that it is wicked to marry your deceased wife's sister, you must believe them lest morals collapse. If they tell you that birth control is sin, you must accept their dictum however obvious it may be to you that without birth control disaster is certain. As soon as it is held that any belief, no matter what, is important for some other reason than that it is true, a whole host of evils is ready to spring up. Discouragement of inquiry, which I spoke of before, is the first of these, but others are pretty sure to follow. Positions of authority will be open to the orthodox. Historical records must be falsified if they throw doubt on received opinions. Sooner or later unorthodoxy will come to be considered a crime to be dealt with by the stake, the purge, or the concentration camp. I can respect the men who argue that religion is true and therefore ought to be believed, but I can only feel profound moral reprobation for those who say that religion ought to be believed because it is useful, and that to ask whether it is true is a waste of time.

It is customary among Christian apologists to regard Communism as something very different from Christianity and to contrast its evils with the supposed blessings enjoyed by Christian nations. This seems to me a profound mistake. The evils of Communism are the same as those that existed in Christianity during the Ages of Faith. The Ogpu differs only quantitatively from the Inquisition. Its cruelties are of the same sort, and the damage that it does to the intellectual and moral life of Russians is of the same sort as that which was done by the Inquisitors wherever they prevailed. The Communists falsify history, and the Church did the same until the Renaissance. If the Church is not now as bad as the Soviet Government, that is due to the influence of those who attacked the Church;

from the Council of Trent to the present day whatever improvements it has effected have been due to its enemies. There are many who object to the Soviet Government because they dislike the Communist economic doctrine, but this the Kremlin shares with the early Christians, the Franciscans, and the majority of medieval Christian heretics. Nor was the Communist doctrine confined to heretics: Sir Thomas More, an orthodox martyr, speaks of Christianity as Communistic and says that this was the only aspect of the Christian religion which commended it to the Utopians. It is not Soviet doctrine in itself that can be justly regarded as a danger. It is the way in which the doctrine is held. It is held as sacred and inviolable truth, to doubt which is sin and deserving of the severest punishment. The Communist, like the Christian, believes that his doctrine is essential to salvation, and it is this belief which makes salvation possible for him. It is the similarities between Christianity and Communism that make them incompatible with each other. When two men of science disagree, they do not invoke the secular arm; they wait for further evidence to decide the issue, because as men of science, they know that neither is infallible. But when two theologians differ, since there are no criteria to which either can appeal, there is nothing for it but mutual hatred and an open or covert appeal to force. Christianity, I will admit, does less harm than it used to do; but that is because it is less fervently believed. Perhaps, in time, the same change will come over Communism; and, if it does, that creed will lose much of what now makes it obnoxious. But if in the West the view prevails that Christianity is essential to virtue and social stability, Christianity will once again acquire the vices which it had in the Middle Ages; and, in becoming more and more like Communism, will become more and more difficult to reconcile with it. It is not along this road that the world can be saved from disaster.

II

In my first article I was concerned with the evils resulting from any system of dogmas presented for acceptance, not on the ground of truth, but on the ground of social utility. What I had to say applies equally to Christianity, Communism, Islam, Buddhism, Hinduism and all theological systems, except in so far as they rely upon grounds making a universal appeal of the sort that is made by men of science. There are, however, special arguments which are advanced in favour of Christianity on account of its supposed special merits. These have been set forth eloquently and with a show of erudition by Herbert Butterfield, Professor of Modern History in the University of Cambridge,[1] and I shall take him as spokesman of the large body of opinion to which he adheres.

Professor Butterfield seeks to secure certain controversial advantages

[1] *Christianity and History* (London, 1950.)

by concessions that make him seem more open-minded than in fact he is. He admits that the Christian Church has relied upon persecution and that it is pressure from without that has led it to abandon this practice in so far as it has been abandoned. He admits that the present tension between Russia and the West is a result of power politics such as might have been expected even if the Government of Russia had continued to adhere to the Greek Orthodox Church. He admits that some of the virtues which he regards as distinctively Christian have been displayed by some free-thinkers and have been absent in the behaviour of many Christians. But, in spite of these concessions, he still holds that the evils from which the world is suffering are to be cured by adherence to Christian dogma, and he includes in the necessary minimum of Christian dogma not only belief in God and immortality, but also belief in the Incarnation. He emphasizes the connection of Christianity with certain historical events, and he accepts these events as historical on evidence which would certainly not convince him if it were not connected with his religion. I do not think the evidence for the Virgin Birth is such as would convince any impartial inquirer if it were presented outside the circle of theological beliefs he was accustomed to. There are innumerable such stories in Pagan myth-ology, but no one dreams of taking them seriously. Professor Butterfield, however, in spite of being an historian, appears to be quite uninterested in questions of historicity wherever the origins of Christianity are con-cerned. His argument, robbed of his urbanity and his deceptive air of broad-mindedness, may be stated crudely but accurately as follows: 'It is not worth while to inquire whether Christ really was born of a Virgin and conceived of the Holy Ghost because, whether or not this was the case, the belief that it was the case offers the best hope of escape from the present troubles of the world.' Nowhere in Professor Butterfield's work is there the faintest attempt to prove the truth of any Christian dogma. There is only the pragmatic argument that belief in Christian dogma is useful. There are many steps in Professor Butterfield's contention which are not stated with as much clarity and precision as one could desire, and I fear the reason is that clarity and precision make them implausible. I think the contention, stripped of inessentials, is as follows: it would be a good thing if people loved their neighbours, but they do not show much inclination to do so; Christ said they ought to, and if they believe that Christ was God, they are more likely to pay attention to His teachings on this point than if they do not; therefore, men who wish people to love their neighbours will try to persuade them that Christ was God.

The objections to this kind of argumentation are so many that it is difficult to know where to begin. In the first place, Professor Butterfield and all who think as he does are persuaded that it is a good thing to love your neighbour, and their reasons for holding this view are not derived from Christ's teaching. On the contrary, it is because they already hold this view that they regard Christ's teaching as evidence of His divinity. They have, that is to say, not an ethic based on theology, but a theology based upon their ethic. They apparently hold, however, that the non-theological grounds which make them think it a good thing to love your neighbour are not likely to make a wide appeal, and they therefore proceed to invent other arguments which they hope will be more effective. This is a very dangerous procedure. Many Protestants used to think it as wicked to break the Sabbath as to commit murder. If you persuaded them it was not wicked to break the Sabbath, they might infer that it was not wicked to commit murder. Every theological ethic is in part such as can be defended rationally, and in part a mere embodiment of superstitious taboos. The part which can be defended rationally should be so defended, since otherwise those who discover the irrationality of the other part may rashly reject the whole.

But has Christianity, in fact, stood for a better morality than that of its rivals and opponents? I do not see how any honest student of history can maintain that this is the case. Christianity has been distinguished from other religions by its greater readiness for persecution. Buddhism has never been a persecuting religion. The Empire of the Caliphs was much kinder to Jews and Christians than Christian States were to Jews and Mohammedans. It left Jews and Christians unmolested, provided they paid tribute. Anti-Semitism was promoted by Christianity from the moment when the Roman Empire became Christian. The religious fervour of the Crusades led to pogroms in Western Europe. It was Christians who unjustly accused Dreyfus, and free-thinkers who secured his final rehabilitation. Abominations have in modern times been defended by Christians not only when Jews were the victims, but also in other connections. The abominations of King Leopold's government of the Congo were concealed or minimized by the Church and were ended only by an agitation conducted mainly by free-thinkers. The whole contention that Christianity has had an elevating moral influence can only be maintained by wholesale ignoring or falsification of the historical evidence.

The habitual answer is that the Christians who did things which we deplore were not *true* Christians in the sense that they did not follow the teachings of Christ. One might of course equally well argue that the Soviet Government does not consist of true Marxists, for Marx taught that Slavs are inferior to Germans and this doctrine is not accepted in the Kremlin. The followers of a teacher always depart in some respects from the doctrine of the master. Those who aim at founding a Church ought to remember this. Every Church develops an instinct of self-preservation and minimizes those parts of the founder's doctrine which do not minister to that end. But in any case what modern apologists call 'true' Christianity is something depending upon a very selective process. It ignores much that is to be found in the Gospels: for example, the parable of the sheep and the goats, and the doctrine that the wicked will suffer eternal torment in hell-fire. It picks out certain parts of the Sermon on the Mount, though even these it often rejects in practice. It leaves the doctrine of non-resistance, for example, to be practised only by non-Christians such as Gandhi. The precepts that it particularly favours are held to embody such a lofty morality that they must have had a divine origin. And yet Professor Butterfield must know that these precepts were all uttered by Jews before the time of Christ. They are to be found, for example, in the teaching of Hillel and in the 'Testaments of the Twelve Patriarchs', concerning which the Rev. Dr R. H. Charles, a leading authority in this matter, says: 'The Sermon on the Mount reflects in several instances the spirit and even reproduces the very phrases of our text: many passages in the Gospels exhibit traces of the same, and St Paul seems to have used the book as a *vade-mecum*.' Dr Charles is of the opinion that Christ must have been acquainted with this work. If, as we are sometimes told, the loftiness of the ethical teaching proves the divinity of its author, it is the unknown writer of these Testaments who must have been divine.

That the world is in a bad way is undeniable, but there is not the faintest reason in history to suppose that Christianity offers a way out. Our troubles have sprung, with the inexorability of Greek tragedy, from the First World War, of which the Communists and the Nazis were products. The First World War was wholly Christian in origin. The three Emperors were devout, and so were the more warlike of the British Cabinet. Opposition to the war came, in Germany and Russia, from the Socialists, who were anti-Christian; in France, from Jaurès, whose assassin was applauded by earnest Christians; in England, from John Morley, a noted atheist. The most dangerous features of Communism are reminiscent of the medieval Church. They consist of fanatical acceptance of doctrines embodied in a Sacred Book, unwillingness to examine these doctrines critically, and savage persecution of those who reject them. It is not to a revival of fanaticism and bigotry in the West that we must look for a happy issue. Such a revival, if it occurs, will only mean that the hateful features of the Communist régime have become universal. What the world needs is reasonableness, tolerance, and a realization of the interdependence of the parts of the human family. This interdependence has been enormously increased by modern inventions, and the purely mundane arguments for a kindly attitude to one's neighbour are very much stronger than they were at any earlier time. It is to such considerations that we must look, and not to a return to obscurantist myths. Intelligence, it might be said, has caused our troubles; but it is not unintelligence that will cure them. Only more and wiser intelligence can make a happier world.

(*Why I am not a Christian*, London: Allen & Unwin; New York: Simon & Schuster, 1957.)

PART XVI

The Philosopher and Expositor of Science

Philosophers in our time are no longer concerned with inventing vast systems of philosophy from crude imagination. Since the seventeenth century science has gradually whittled away the mortar between the bricks of the foundations erected by the dogmatic philosophers. Perhaps philosophic progress will always lag behind scientific achievements because of the kind of problems with which philosophy is concerned. But one thing now seems clear: advance in philosophy will probably be based upon the same kind of evidence that has made science so successful. In the beginning philosophy prodded science, now science prods philosophy.

Russell, as the selections that follow indicate, has ever been conscious of this relationship between science and philosophy, but he also has ever been mindful of the limitations of science and the ethical import of its application. He is one of our most lucid expositors of the far reaches of contemporary scientific theory.

65

PHYSICS AND NEUTRAL MONISM

I N this chapter, I wish to define the outcome of our analysis in regard to the old controversy between materialism and idealism, and to make it clear wherein our theory differs from both. So long as the views set forth in previous chapters are supposed to be either materialistic or idealistic, they will seem to involve inconsistencies, since some seem to tend in the one direction, some in the other. For example, when I say that my percepts are in my head, I shall be thought materialistic; when I say that my head consists of my percepts and other similar events, I shall be thought idealistic. Yet the former statement is a logical consequence of the latter.

Both materialism and idealism have been guilty, unconsciously and in spite of explicit disavowals, of a confusion in their imaginative picture of matter. They have thought of the matter in the external world as being represented by their percepts when they see and touch, whereas these percepts are really part of the matter of the percipient's brain. By examining our percepts it is possible—so I have contended—to infer certain formal mathematical properties of external matter, though the inference is not demonstrative or certain. But by examining our percepts we obtain knowledge which is not purely formal as to the matter of our brains. This knowledge, it is true, is fragmentary, but so far as it goes it has merits surpassing those of the knowledge given by physics.

The usual view would be that by psychology we acquire knowledge of our 'minds', but that the only way to acquire knowledge of our brains is to have them examined by a physiologist, usually after we are dead, which seems somewhat unsatisfactory. I should say that what the physiologist sees when he looks at a brain is part of his own brain, not part of the brain he is examining. The feeling of paradox about this view comes, I should say, from wrong views of space. It is true that what we see is not located where our percept of our brain would be located if we could see our own brain; but this is a question of perpetual space, not of the space of physics. The space of physics is connected with causation in a manner which compels us to hold that our percepts are in our brains, if we accept the causal theory of perception, as I think we are bound to do. To say that two events have no spatio-temporal separation is to say that they are compresent; to say that they have a small separation is to say that they are connected by causal chains all of which are short. The percept must therefore be nearer to the sense-organ than to the physical object, nearer to the nerve than to the sense-organ, and nearer to the cerebral end of the nerve than to the other end. This is inevitable, unless we are going to say that the percept is not in space-time at all. It is usual to hold that 'mental' events are in time but not in space; let us ask ourselves whether there is any ground for this view as regards percepts.

The question whether percepts are located in physical space is the same as the question of their causal connection with physical events. If they can be effects and causes of physical events, we are bound to give them a position in physical space-time in so far as interval is concerned, since interval was defined in causal terms. But the real question is as to 'compresence' in the sense of Chapter XXVIII. Can a mental event be compresent with a physical event? If yes, then a mental event has a position in the space-time order; if no, then it has no such position. This, therefore, is the crucial question.

When I maintain that a percept and physical event can be compresent, I am not maintaining that a percept can have to a piece of matter the sort of relation which another piece of matter would have. The relation of compresence is between a percept and a physical *event*, and physical events are not to be confounded with pieces of matter. A piece of matter is a logical structure composed of events; the causal laws of the events concerned, and the abstract logical properties of their spatio-temporal relations, are more or less known, but their intrinsic character is not known. Percepts fit into the same causal scheme as physical events, and are not known to have any intrinsic character which physical events cannot have, since we do not know of any intrinsic character which could be incompatible with the logical properties that physics assigns to physical events. There is therefore no ground for the view that percepts cannot be physical events, or for supposing that they are never compresent with other physical events.

The fact that mental events admittedly have temporal relations has much force, now that time and space are so much less distinct than they were. It has become difficult to hold that mental events, though in time, are not in space. The fact that their relations to each other can be viewed as only temporal is a fact which they share with any set of events forming the biography of one piece of matter. Relatively to axes moving with the percipient's brain, the interval between two percepts of his which are not compresent should always be temporal, if his percepts are in his head. But the interval between simultaneous percepts of different percipients is of a different kind; and their whole causal environment is such as to make us call this interval space-like. I conclude, then, that there is no good ground for excluding percepts from the physical world, but several strong reasons for including them. The difficulties that have been supposed to stand in the way seem to me to be entirely due to wrong views as to the physical world, and more particularly as to physical space. The wrong views as to physical space have been encouraged by the notion that the primary qualities are objective, which has been held imaginatively by many men who would have emphatically repudiated it so far as their explicit thought was concerned.

I hold, therefore, that two simultaneous percepts of one percipient have the relation of compresence out of which spatio-temporal order arises. It is almost irresistible to go a step further, and say that any two simultaneous perceived contents of a mind are compresent, so that all our conscious mental states are in our heads. I see as little reason against this extension as against the view that percepts can be compresent. A percept differs from another mental state, I should say, only in the nature of its causal relation to an external stimulus. Some relation of this kind no doubt always exists, but with other mental states the relation may be more indirect, or may be only to some state of the body, more particularly the brain. 'Unconscious' mental states will be events compresent with certain other mental states, but not having those effects which constitute what is called awareness of a mental state. However, I have no wish to go further into psychology than is necessary, and I will pursue this topic no longer, but return to matters of more concern to physics.

The point which concerns the philosophy of matter is that the events out of which we have been constructing the physical world are very different from matter as traditionally conceived. Matter was expected to be impenetrable and indestructible. The matter that we construct is impenetrable as a result of definition: the matter in a place is all the events that are there, and consequently no other event or piece of matter can be there. This is a tautology, not a physical fact; one might as well argue that London is impenetrable because nobody can live in it except one of its inhabitants. Indestructibility, on the other hand, is an empirical property, believed to be approximately but not exactly possessed by matter. I mean by indestructibility, not conservation of mass, which is known to be only approximate, but conservation of electrons and protons. At present it is not known whether an electron and a proton sometimes enter into a suicide pact or not,[1] but there is certainly no known reason why electrons and protons should be indestructible.

Electrons and protons, however, are not the stuff of the physical world: they are elaborate logical structures composed of events, and ultimately of particulars, in the sense of Chapter XXVII. As to what the events are that compose the physical world, they are, in the first place, percepts, and

[1] It is thought highly probable that they do. See Dr Jeans, 'Recent Developments of Cosmical Physics', *Nature*, December 4, 1926.

then whatever can be inferred from percepts by the methods considered in Part II. But on various inferential grounds we are led to the view that a percept in which we cannot perceive a structure nevertheless often has a structure, i.e. that the apparently simple is often complex. We cannot therefore treat the *minimum visible* as a particular, for both physical and psychological facts may lead us to attribute a structure to it—not merely a structure in general, but such and such a structure.

Events are neither impenetrable nor indestructible. Space-time is constructed by means of co-punctuality, which is the same thing as spatio-temporal interpenetration. Perhaps it is not unnecessary to explain that spatio-temporal interpenetration is quite a different thing from logical interpenetration, though it may be suspected that some philosophers have been led to favour the latter as a result of the arguments for the former. We are accustomed to imagining that numerical diversity involves spatio-temporal separation; hence we tend to think that, if two diverse entities are in one place, they cannot be wholly diverse, but must be also in some sense one. It is this combination that is supposed to constitute logical interpenetration. For my part, I do not think that logical interpenetration can be defined without obvious self-contradiction; Bergson, who advocates it, does not define it. The only author I know of who has dealt seriously with its difficulties is Bradley, in whom, quite consistently, it led to a thorough-going monism, combined with the avowal that, in the end, all truth is self-contradictory. I should myself regard this latter result as a refutation of the logic from which it follows. Therefore, while I respect Bradley more than any other advocate of interpenetration, he seems to me, in virtue of his ability, to have done more than any other philosopher to disprove the kind of system which he advocated. However that may be, the spatio-temporal interpenetration which is used in constructing space-time order is quite different from logical interpenetration. Philosophers have been slaves of space and time in the imaginative application of their logic. This is partly due to Euler's diagrams and the notion that the traditional *A, E, I, O* were elementary forms of propositions and the confounding of 'x is a β' with 'all α's are β's'. All this led to a confusion between classes and individuals, and to the inference that individuals can interpenetrate because classes can overlap. I do not suggest explicit confusions of this sort, but only that traditional elementary logic, taught in youth, is an almost fatal barrier to clear thinking in later years, unless much time is spent in acquiring a new technique.

On the question of the material out of which the physical world is constructed, the views advocated in this volume have, perhaps, more affinity with idealism than with materialism. What are called 'mental' events, if we have been right, are part of the material of the physical world, and what is in our heads is the mind (with additions) rather than what the physiologist sees through his microscope. It is true that we have not suggested that all reality is mental. The positive arguments in favour of such a view, whether Berkeleian or German, appear to me fallacious. The sceptical argument of the phenomenalists, that, whatever else there may be, we cannot know it, is much more worthy of respect. There are, in fact, if we have been right, three grades of certainty. The highest grade belongs to my own percepts; the second grade to the percepts of other people; the third to events which are not percepts of anybody. It is to be observed, however, that the second grade belongs only to the percepts of those who can communicate with me, directly or indirectly, and of those who are known to be closely analogous to people who can communicate with me. The percepts of minds, if such there be, which are not related to mine by communication—e.g. minds in other planets—can have, at best, only the third grade of certainty, that, namely, which belongs to the apparently lifeless physical world.

The events which are not perceived by any person who can communicate with me, supposing they have been rightly inferred, have a causal connection with percepts, and are inferred by means of this connection. Much is known about their structure, but nothing about their quality.

While, on the question of the stuff of the world, the theory of the foregoing pages has certain affinities with idealism—namely, that mental events are part of that stuff, and that the rest of the stuff resembles them more than it resembles traditional billiard-balls—the position advocated as regards scientific laws has more affinity with materialism than with idealism. Inference from one event to another, where possible, seems only to acquire exactness when it can be stated in terms of the laws of physics. There are psychological laws, physiological laws, and chemical laws, which cannot at present be reduced to physical laws. But none of them is exact and without exceptions; they state tendencies and averages rather than mathematical laws governing minimum events. Take, for example, the psychological laws of memory. We cannot say: At 12.55 G.M.T. on such and such a day, A will remember the event e—unless, indeed, we are in a position to remind him of it at that moment. The known laws of memory belong to an early stage of science—earlier than Kepler's laws or Boyle's law. We can say that, if A and B have been experienced together, the recurrence of A *tends* to cause a recollection of B, but we cannot say that it is sure to do so, or that it will do so in one assignable class of cases and not in another. One supposes that, to obtain an exact causal theory of memory, it would be necessary to know more about the structure of the brain. The ideal to be aimed at would be something like the physical explanation of fluorescence, which is a phenomenon in many ways analogous to memory. So far as causal laws go, therefore, physics seems to be supreme among the sciences, not only as against other sciences of matter, but also as against the sciences that deal with life and mind.

There is, however, one important limitation to this. We need to know in what physical circumstances such and such a percept will arise, and we must not neglect the more intimate qualitative knowledge which we possess concerning mental events. There will thus remain a certain sphere which will be outside physics. To take a simple instance: physics might, ideally, be able to predict that at such a time my eye would receive a stimulus of a certain sort; it might be able to trace the physical properties of the resulting events in the eye and the brain, one of which is, in fact, a visual percept; but it could not itself give us the knowledge that one of them is a visual percept. It is obvious that a man who can see knows things which a blind man cannot know; but a blind man can know the whole of physics. Thus the knowledge which other men have and he has not is not part of physics.

Although there is thus a sphere excluded from physics, yet physics, together with a 'dictionary', gives, apparently, all causal knowledge. One supposes that, given the physical characteristics of the events in my head, the 'dictionary' gives the 'mental' events in my head. This is by no means a matter of course. The whole of the foregoing theory of physics might be true without entailing this consequence. So far as physics can show, it might be possible for different groups of events having the same structure to have the same part in causal series. That is to say, given the physical causal laws, and given enough knowledge of an initial group of events to determine the purely physical properties of their effects, it might never-theless be the case that these effects could be qualitatively of different sorts. If that were so, physical determinism would not entail psychological determinism, since, given two percepts of identical structure but diverse quality, we could not tell which would result from a stimulus known only as to its physical, i.e. structural, properties, This is an unavoidable consequence of the abstractness of physics. If physics is concerned only with structure, it cannot, *per se*, warrant inferences to any but the structural properties of events. Now it may be a fact that (e.g.) the structure of visual percepts is very different from that of tactual percepts; but I do not think such differences could be established with sufficient strictness and generality to enable us to say that such and such a stimulus must produce a visual percept, while such another must produce a tactual percept.

On this matter, we must, I think, appeal to evidence which is partly psychological. We do know, as a matter of fact, that we can, in normal circumstances, more or less infer the percept from the stimulus. If this were not the case, speaking and writing would be useless. When the lessons are read, the congregation can follow the words in their own Bibles. The differences in their 'thoughts' meanwhile can be connected causally, at least in part, with differences in their past experience, and these are supposed to make themselves effective by causing differences in the structure of brains. All this seems sufficiently probable to be worth taking seriously; but it lies ouside physics, and does not follow from the causal autonomy of physics, supposing this to be established even for human bodies. It will be observed that what we are now considering is the converse of what is required for the inference from perception to physics. What is wanted there is that, given the percept, we should be able to infer, at least partially, the structure of the stimulus—or at any rate that this should be possible when a sufficient number of percepts are given. What we want now is that, given the *structure* of the stimulus (which is all that physics can give), we should be able to infer the *quality* of the percept—with the same limitations as before. Whether this is the case or not is a question lying outside physics; but there is reason to think that it is the case.

The aim of physics, consciously or unconsciously, has always been to discover what we may call the causal skeleton of the world. It is perhaps surprising that there should be such a skeleton, but physics seems to prove that there is, particularly when taken in conjunction with the evidence that percepts are determined by the physical character of their stimuli. There is reason—though not quite conclusive reason—for regarding physics as causally dominant, in the sense that, given the physical structure of the world, the qualities of its events, in so far as we are acquainted with them, can be inferred by means of correlations. We have thus in effect a psycho-cerebral parallelism, although the interpretation to be put upon it is not the usual one. We suppose that, given sufficient knowledge, we could infer the qualities of the events in our heads from their physical properties. This is what is really meant when it is said, loosely, that the state of the mind can be inferred from the state of the brain. Although I think that this is probably true, I am less anxious to assert it than to assert, what seems to me much more certain, that its truth does not follow from the causal autonomy of physics or from physical determinism as applied to all matter, including that of living bodies. This latter result flows from the abstractness of physics, and belongs to the philosophy of physics. The other proposition, if true, cannot be established by considering physics alone, but only by a study of percepts for their own sakes, which belongs to psychology. Physics studies percepts only in their cognitive aspect; their other aspects lie outside its purview.

Even if we reject the view that the quality of events in our heads can be inferred from their structure, the view that physical determinism applies to human bodies brings us very near to what is most disliked in materialism. Physics may be unable to tell us what we shall hear or see or 'think', but it can, on the view advocated in these pages, tell us what we shall say or write, where we shall go, whether we shall commit murder or theft, and so on. For all these are bodily movements, and thus come within the scope of physical laws. We are often asked to concede that the beauties of poetry or music cannot result from physical laws. I should concede that the beauty does not result from physics, since beauty depends in part upon intrinsic quality; if it were, as some writers on aesthetics contend, solely a matter of form, it would come within the scope of physics, but I think these writers do not realize what an abstract affair form really is. I should concede also that the *thoughts* of Shakespeare or Bach do not come within the scope of physics. But their thoughts are of no importance to us: their whole social efficacy depended upon certain black marks which they made on white paper. Now there seems no reason to suppose that physics does not apply to the making of these marks, which was a movement of matter just as truly as the revolution of the earth in its orbit. In any case, it is undeniable that the socially important part of their thought had a one-one relation to certain purely physical events, namely the occurrence of the black marks on the white paper. And no one can doubt that the causes of our emotions when we read Shakespeare or hear Bach are purely physical. Thus we cannot escape from the universality of physical causation.

This, however, is perhaps not quite the last word on the subject. We have seen that, on the basis of physics itself, there may be limits to physical determinism. We know of no laws as to when a quantum transaction will take place or a radio-active atom will break down. We know fairly well what will happen *if* anything happens, and we know statistical averages, which suffice to determine macroscopic phenomena. But if mind and brain are causally interconnected, very small cerebral differences must be correlated with noticeable mental differences. Thus we are perhaps forced to descend into the region of quantum transactions, and to desert the macroscopic level where statistical averages obtain. Perhaps the electron jumps when it likes; perhaps the minute phenomena in the brain which make all the difference to mental phenomena belong to the region where physical laws no longer determine definitely what must happen. This, of course, is merely a speculative possibility; but it interposes a veto upon materialistic dogmatism. It may be that the progress of physics will decide the matter one way or other; for the present, as in so many other matters, the philosopher must be content to await the progress of science.

(*The Analysis of Matter*, reprinted with a new Introduction by Lester E. Denonn, London: Allen & Unwin; New York: Dover Publications, Inc., 1955.)

66

SCIENCE AND EDUCATION

EDUCATION in the past has been a haphazard and traditional affair, supposed not to begin until the child was at least six years old, and to be concerned almost exclusively with the acquisition of knowledge. It has gradually come to be realized that the earlier years have an enormous importance for the whole of the rest of life, and that the traditional methods developed by uneducated nurses and mothers are by no means the best.

It cannot be said that we know as yet what are the best methods for dealing with very young children. Dr John B. Watson has pointed out the curious fact that, while men of science have studied with great care the behaviour of nearly everything in the world, they have abstained almost with one accord from a scientific study of human infants. For this there have been several reasons: in the first place, most men consider it *infra dig.* to notice an infant, which, it is thought, should be left to the exclusive care of women; in the second place, hardly any man of science had time to observe his own infants. He can get a grant from a university or other learned body to study the Papuans or the Andaman Islanders, but if he said he wanted to study his own child, he would be laughed at. The observations of nurses and mothers are rendered unreliable by partiality and by the fact that they are seldom trained observers.

Babies are regarded by some as darlings, by others as nuisances, but by practically no one as facts to be impartially studied. Anything that may be said about them at present is, therefore, tentative and provisional. But I think we may expect that in the near future scientific studies, such as those initiated by Dr Watson, will become more frequent. We cannot, however, hope for really valuable results until it has been possible to follow the development of large numbers of young people from birth to the age of twenty, and to obtain such data as will enable us to trace separately the effects of heredity and environment. One could wish that some wealthy scientist would offer a benefaction consisting in giving, in a large number of cases, expensive education in a well-to-do environment to one of two twins born of indigent parents, the twins to be separated as soon as weaned. In this way we might gradually get some data as to heredity, for the similarities between such twins when adult might be fairly regarded as mainly congenital.

Whatever may be thought of psycho-analysis, there is one point in which it is unquestionably in the right, and that is in the enormous stress which it lays upon the emotional life. Given the right emotional development, both character and intelligence ought to develop spontaneously. It is, therefore, to the emotions above all that the scientific educator should direct his attention.

In regard to the emotional life, there are two elements to be considered: on the one hand, the nature of the emotions; on the other hand, the objects toward which they are directed. Take, for example, curiosity; this may take the form of peeping or prying, in which case it must be regarded as undesirable, or it may take the form of a desire for scientific knowledge, in which case it is in the highest degree useful. Or again, take hatred; a man may hate the Government, in which case he is a subversive revolutionary, or he may hate the Reds, in which case he is a pillar of society. The quality of the emotions is the same, but the object is different. The scientific educator has two things to think about: in the first place, he must produce emotions in the right proportions; and in the second place, he must attach them to the right objects. The first is probably, in the last analysis, a matter of chemistry; the second is a matter of 'conditioning' in the sense of Pavlov and Watson. But, although the first may be a matter of chemistry when it comes to be adequately understood, it is at the moment much more easily dealt with along the lines studied by psycho-analysis. Moreover, the two departments overlap. A wrong object for an emotion may cause the emotion to increase or decrease unduly, while a new emotion may be cultivated by providing it with a suitable object.

Let us take first the question of the quality of the emotions. One may in a sense divide emotional attitudes into positive and negative; the emotions of hate, rage, and fear are negative, while emotions of affection, pleasure, and experimentation are positive. Speaking broadly, it is a good thing to have much of the positive emotions and little of the negative. There are, of course, exceptions. It is useful to be afraid of snakes, tigers, precipices, and interviewers. But often in such cases fear is not the ideally best reaction; the ideally best reaction is prudence, that is to say, a rational apprehension of danger without the emotion of terror. The more intelligent and rational people become, the less need they have for negative attitudes. A pre-scientific community can, for example, do nothing with criminals except hate, fear, and punish them, whereas a scientific community can study the sources of their criminality, and so attempt reform or prevention of criminal impulses. Or, again, take lightning; fear alone would never have led to the construction of lightning conductors, which depended upon the positive attitude of curiosity.

Science has made life less dangerous than it used to be, and has thus greatly diminished the need of fear as a motive. Education ought from the start to take account of this fact, and to aim at producing the kind of attitude that leads to lightning conductors rather than the kind that leads to cowering terror during a thunderstorm. I am not at the moment concerned with specific fears; these will come under our second heading; I am concerned at the moment with timidity, that is to say, the habit of being frightened easily and by many things.

Timidity depends partly upon physical health: a given child is more timid on a day when his digestion is out of order than on a day when it is functioning properly. But timidity also depends upon various mental causes: a child who is frequently punished or frequently threatened with punishment will become timid; so will, conversely, a child who is always carefully guarded against minor dangers. Muscular activities, as unimpeded as possible, are the best method of producing physical fearlessness in children, while mental fearlessness is the product of unhampered curiosity. Indeed, curiosity is to the mind exactly what muscular activity is to the body. It will be found that mind and body interact in these respects, and that the unimpeded activity which promotes courage also promotes a good digestion, except, of course, in such cases as eating poisonous berries to see whether they are poisonous. (All educational principles have to be applied with common sense.)

Dr Cameron, author of *The Nervous Child*, has lately written a paper[1] in which, although he has hitherto chiefly stressed the psychological causes and cures of nervousness, he points out that the nervous child generally suffers from excessive acidity and can often be greatly helped by the administration of alkalis. This is a good example of the importance of keeping the psychological and chemical aspects of child-welfare equally prominent in our thoughts.

Then again, take rage: both rage and fear, as we know from the work of Cannon, are due to secretion of adrenalin in the blood. Presumably, anything that makes the adrenal gland more active will make people more prone to these emotions, of which the one or the other is felt according to the nature of the external situation. Perhaps we shall learn in time to eliminate both emotions by regulating the action of the adrenal gland or by administering an antidote. But in the case of rage also, the psychological causes are for the present easier to ascertain and control than the chemical causes.

The primitive stimulus to rage, as Dr Watson has shown, consists in impediment to the free movement of the limbs. And the habit of rage in later life is generated as a rule by the existence of some irritating obstacle to free activity which is considered to be insurmountable, and,

[1] An address on Children in General Practice: A Study Both of Temperament and of Disease. *The Lancet*, January 7, 1928.

therefore, produces feelings of anger which vent themselves upon other objects. Therefore, so far as is compatible with social good behaviour, it is desirable, if men are to be free from the habit of rage, that they should not have the sense of being impeded in activities toward which they feel powerful impulses. One of the really difficult problems of education is to secure in the young the necessary minimum of good behaviour without producing this attitude of anger at the existence of insurmountable obstacles, but this is a problem of conditioning.

Affectionateness is an emotional habit which is good in moderation, but can easily be carried too far. When carried too far, it involves a lack of self-dependence, which may have very undesirable effects upon character. Some people who are moralists rather than psychologists confound affection with benevolence, and imagine that it consists in a desire for the happiness of the beloved object. This is only very partially the case; in fact, affection in its instinctive manifestations is bound up with jealousy, and is not in all its forms a desirable emotion. A good deal of psychological discrimination is necessary in this matter; no child or adult can develop adequately without affection, but at the same time affection should not play too large a part in life, and great care should be taken to free it from jealousy and from undue dependence upon others. This is a problem which is often very unwisely handled in the home, largely from the mistaken notion that it is impossible for children to be too fond of their parents.

I come now to the question of the object toward which emotions are directed. This is the question of 'conditioning' which has been stressed by the behaviourists. It is undoubtedly very important, but I do not agree with them in thinking that it constitutes practically the whole of education. There are not only good and bad objects for emotions, there are also, speaking broadly, good and bad emotions. The cultivation of good emotions and the elimination of bad ones is not in the main a question of conditioning, which is concerned with the objects to which the emotions are attached. The great work of Pavlov on *Conditioned Reflexes* has provided a wealth of material on this subject, so far as dogs are concerned, but where human beings are concerned experimentation is much more difficult, although Dr Watson made some valuable investigations on infants in hospitals. Nevertheless, observation affords considerable material which becomes easier to interpret in the light of the experimental data concerning dogs.

The hatred of knowledge, which is general among civilized mankind, has been produced by a procedure which was entirely correct from a scientific point of view, namely, the creation of an association between lessons and punishment. The modern educationalist aims at an entirely opposite kind of conditioning. He aims at providing the children with comparatively easy tasks, which can be surmounted with a moderate degree of effort and which appear interesting from the first. By this method learning is associated with the pleasure derived from success, and the efforts which it involves come to be met as cheerfully as the muscular efforts involved in football. In sexual education, to take another matter, the difference between wisdom and unwisdom is almost wholly a question of conditioning.

One of the characteristics of the scientific method is that it is quantitative and aims at discovering the just balance of the different ingredients required to produce a good result, whereas pre-scientific methods consider some things good and some bad without regard to quantity. Take, for example, the question of the quantity of adult attention that is best for a child. In old days most children got less of this than they should have had; nowadays, most children of the well-to-do get more. When such children first come to school they cling to the adults and find it difficult to mix with their contemporaries, toward whom their first reaction is one of hatred and fear. Many of them have been rendered nervous in a greater or less degree by the constant anxiety of parents, and by the effort to understand grown-up conversation.

The modern careful parent has been alarmed by all the dangers to which children are exposed, and has tended to convey to them a certain timidity through the contagion of the unconscious. At the same time, the child has become accustomed to thinking of himself as the centre of the universe and to expecting from the world at large a degree of solicitude which only parents are likely to feel. This is a bad preparation for the world and is best remedied by association with contemporaries. A child is, on the whole, better fighting with other children than being coddled by grown-up people, but the fighting must be kept within limits, and adult supervision is necessary to see that the less vigorous, physically, are not made to suffer.

The spontaneous development of community feeling in a group of children is an interesting study, but it is impossible where adults intervene constantly to promote what they consider social behaviour. A good many years of study and experiment will be necessary before anything very definite can be said on this subject.

(Fiftieth Anniversary Number, *St Louis Post Dispatch*, subsequently reprinted in *The Drift of Civilization*, New York: Simon & Schuster, 1929.)

67

LIMITATIONS OF SCIENTIFIC METHOD

WHATEVER knowledge we possess is either knowledge of particular facts or scientific knowledge. The details of history and geography lie outside science in a sense; that is to say, they are presupposed by science, and form the basis upon which it is a superstructure. The sort of things that are demanded on a passport, such as name, date of birth, colour of grandfather's eyes, etc., are brute facts; the past existence of Caesar and Napoleon, the present existence of the earth and the sun and the other heavenly bodies, may also be regarded as brute facts. That is to say, most of us accept them as such, but strictly speaking they involve inferences which may, or may not, be correct. If a boy learning history were to refuse to believe in the existence of Napoleon, he would probably be punished, which might, for a pragmatist, constitute sufficient proof that there was such a man; but if the boy were not a pragmatist, he might reflect that if his teacher had had any reason to believe in Napoleon, the reason might have been disclosed. Very few teachers of history, I believe, would be able to produce any good argument to show that Napoleon was not a myth. I am not saying that such arguments do not exist; I am only saying that most people do not know what they are. Clearly, if you are going to believe anything outside your own experience, you should have some reason for believing it. Usually the reason is authority. When it was first proposed to establish laboratories at Cambridge, Todhunter, the mathematician, objected that it was unnecessary for students to see experiments performed, since the results could be vouched for by their teachers, all of them men of the highest character, and many of them clergymen of the Church of England. Todhunter considered that the argument from authority should suffice, but we all know how often authority has been proved mistaken. It is true that most of us must inevitably depend upon it for most of our knowledge. I accept on authority the existence of Cape Horn, and it is clearly impossible that each of us should verify all the facts of geography; but it is important that the opportunity for verification should exist, and that its occasional necessity should be recognized.

To revert to history: as we proceed into the past there is a gradually increasing doubt. Did Pythagoras exist? Probably. Did Romulus exist? Probably not. Did Remus exist? Almost certainly not. But the difference between the evidence for Napoleon and the evidence for Romulus is only one of degree. Strictly speaking, neither the one nor the other can be accepted as mere matter of fact, since neither comes within our direct experience.

Does the sun exist? Most people would say that the sun does come within our direct experience in a sense in which Napoleon does not, but in thinking this they would be mistaken. The sun is removed from us in space as Napoleon is removed from us in time. The sun, like Napoleon, is known to us only through its effects. People say they see the sun; but that only means that something has travelled through the intervening ninety-three million miles, and produced an effect upon the retina, the optic nerve, and the brain. This effect, which happens where we are, is certainly not identical with the sun as understood by astronomers. Indeed, the same effect might be produced by other means: in theory, a hot globe of molten metal could be hung up in such a position that, to a given observer, it would seem just like the sun. The effect upon the observer might be made indistinguishable from the effect which the sun produces. The sun, therefore, is an inference from what we see, and is not the actual patch of brightness of which we are immediately aware.

It is characteristic of the advance of science that less and less is found to be datum, and more and more is found to be inference. The inference is, of course, quite unconscious, except in those who have trained themselves to philosophical scepticism; but it must not be supposed that an unconscious inference is necessarily valid. Babies think that there is another baby on the other side of the looking-glass, and although they have not arrived at this conclusion by a logical process, it is nevertheless mistaken. Many of our unconscious inferences, which are, in fact, conditioned reflexes acquired in early infancy, are highly dubious as soon as they are subjected to logical scrutiny. Physics has been compelled by its own necessities to take account of some of these unwarrantable prejudices. The plain man thinks that matter is solid, but the physicist thinks that it is a wave of probability undulating in nothingness. To put it briefly, the matter in a place is defined as the likelihood of your seeing a ghost there. For the moment, however, I am not yet concerned with these metaphysical speculations, but with the features of scientific method which have given rise to them. The limitations of scientific method have become much more evident in recent years than they ever were before. They have become most evident in physics, which is the most advanced of the sciences, and so far these limitations have had little effect upon the other sciences. Nevertheless, since it is the theoretical goal of every science to be absorbed in physics, we are not likely to go astray if we apply to science in general the doubts and difficulties which have become obvious in the sphere of physics.

The limitations of scientific method may be collected under three heads: (1) the doubt as to the validity of induction; (2) the difficulty of drawing inferences from what is experienced to what is not experienced; and (3) even allowing that there can be inference to what is not experienced, the fact that such inference must be of an extermely abstract character, and gives, therefore, less information than it appears to do when ordinary language is employed.

(1) *Induction.*—All inductive arguments in the last resort reduce themselves to the following form: 'If this is true, that is true: now that is true, therefore this is true.' This argument is, of course, formally fallacious. Suppose I were to say: 'If bread is a stone and stones are nourishing, then this bread will nourish me; now this bread does nourish me; therefore it is a stone, and stones are nourishing.' If I were to advance such an argument, I should certainly be thought foolish, yet it would not be fundamentally different from the argument upon which all scientific laws are based. In science, we always argue that since the observed facts obey certain laws, therefore other facts in the same region will obey the same laws. We may verify this subsequently over a greater or smaller region, but its practical importance is always in regard to those regions where it has not yet been verified. We have verified the laws of statics, for example, in countless cases, and we employ them in building a bridge; in regard to the bridge, they are not verified until we find that the bridge stays up, but their importance lies in enabling us to predict beforehand that the bridge will stay up. It is easy to see why we *think* it will; this is merely an example of Pavlov's conditioned reflexes, which cause us to expect whatever combinations we have frequently experienced in the past. But if you have to cross a bridge in a train, it is no comfort to you to know why the engineer thought it was a good bridge: the important thing is that it should *be* a good bridge, and this requires that his induction from the laws of statics in observed cases to the same laws in unobserved cases should be a valid one.

Now, unfortunately, no one has hitherto shown any good reason for supposing that this sort of inference is sound. Hume, nearly two hundred years ago, threw doubt upon induction, as, indeed, upon most other things. The philosophers were indignant, and invented refutations of Hume which passed muster on account of their extreme obscurity. Indeed, for a long time philosophers took care to be unintelligible, since otherwise everybody would have perceived that they had been unsuccessful in answering Hume. It is easy to invent a metaphysic which will have as a consequence that induction is valid, and many men have done so; but they have not shown any reason to believe in their metaphysic except that it was pleasant. The metaphysic of Bergson, for example, is undoubtedly pleasant: like cocktails, it enables us to see the world as a unity without sharp distinctions, and all of it vaguely agreeable, but it has no better claim than cocktails have to be included in the technique for the pursuit of knowledge. There may be valid grounds for believing in induction, and, in fact, none of us can help believing in it, but it must be admitted that, in theory, induction remains an unsolved problem of logic. As this doubt, however, affects practically the whole of our knowledge, we may pass it by, and assume pragmatically that inductive procedure, with proper safeguards, is admissible.

(2) *Inferences to what is not Experienced.*—As we observed above, what is actually experienced is much less than one would naturally suppose. You may say, for example, that you see your friend, Mr Jones, walking along the street; but this is to go far beyond what you have any right to say. You see a succession of coloured patches, traversing a stationary background. These patches, by means of a Pavlov conditioned reflex, bring into your mind the word 'Jones', and so you say you see Jones; but other people, looking out of their windows from different angles, will see something different, owing to the laws of perspective: therefore, if they are all seeing Jones, there must be as many different Joneses as there are spectators, and if there is only one true Jones, the sight of him is not vouchsafed to anybody. If we assume for a moment the truth of the account which physics gives, we shall explain what you call 'seeing Jones' in some such terms as the following. Little packets of light, called 'light quanta', shoot out from the sun, and some of these reach a region where there are atoms of a certain kind, composing Jones's face, and hands, and clothes. These atoms do not themselves exist, but are merely a compendious way of alluding to possible occurrences. Some of the light quanta, when they reach Jones's atoms, upset their internal economy. This causes him to become sunburnt, and to manufacture vitamin D. Others are reflected, and of those that are reflected, some enter your eye. They there cause a complicated disturbance of the rods and cones, which, in turn, send a current along the optic nerve. When this current reaches the brain, it produces an event. The event which it produces is that which you call 'seeing Jones'. As is evident from this account, the connection of 'seeing Jones' with Jones is a remote, roundabout causal connection. Jones himself, meanwhile, remains wrapped in mystery. He may be thinking about his dinner, or about how his investments have gone to pieces, or about that umbrella he lost; these thoughts are Jones, but these are not what you see. To say that you see Jones is no more correct than it would be, if a ball bounced off a wall in your garden and hit you, to say that the wall had hit you. Indeed, the two cases are closely analogous.

We do not, therefore, ever see what we think we see. Is there any reason to think that what we think we see exists, although we do not see it? Science has always prided itself on being empirical and believing only what could be verified. Now you can verify the occurrences in yourself which you call 'seeing Jones', but you cannot verify Jones himself. You may hear sounds which you call Jones speaking to you; you may feel sensations of touch which you call Jones bumping into you. If he has not lately had a bath, you may also have olfactory sensations of which you suppose him to be the source. If you have been impressed by this argument, you may address him as if we were at the other end of the telephone, and say, 'Are you there?' And you may subsequently hear the words: 'Yes, you idiot, can't you see me?' But if you regard these as affording evidence that he is there, you have missed the point of the argument. The point is that Jones is a convenient hypothesis by means of which certain of your own sensations can be collected into a bundle; but what really makes them belong together is not their common hypothetical origin, but certain resemblances and causal affinities which they have to each other. These remain, even if their common origin is mythical. When you see a man in the cinema, you know that he does not exist when he is off the stage, though you suppose that there was an original who did exist continuously. But why should you make this supposition? Why should not Jones be like the man you see at the cinema? He may get annoyed with you if you suggest such an idea, but he will be powerless to disprove it, since he cannot give you any experience of what he is doing when you do not experience him.

Is there any way of proving that there are occurrences other than those that you yourself experience? This is a question of some emotional interest, but the theoretical physicist of the present day would consider it unimportant. 'My formulae', he would say, 'are concerned to provide causal laws connecting my sensations. In the statement of these causal laws I may employ hypothetical entities; but the question whether these entities are more than hypothetical is otiose, since it lies outside the sphere of possible verification.' At a pinch, he may admit that other physicists exist, since he wishes to use their results; and, having admitted physicists, he may be led by politeness to admit students of other sciences. He may, in fact, form an argument by analogy to prove that, just as his body is connected with his thoughts, so bodies closely resembling his own are probably also connected with thoughts. It may be questioned how much strength there is in this argument; but, even if it be admitted, it does not allow us to conclude that the sun and stars exist, or, indeed, any lifeless matter. We are, in fact, led to the position of Berkeley, according to which only thoughts exist. Berkeley saved the universe and the permanence of bodies by regarding them as God's thoughts, but this was only a wish-fulfilment, not logical thinking. However, as he was at once a bishop and an Irishman, we ought not to be too hard on him. The fact is that science started with a large amount of what Santayana calls 'animal faith', which is, in fact, thought dominated by the principle of the conditioned reflex. It was this animal faith that enabled physicists to believe in a world of matter. Gradually they have turned traitor, like men who, from studying the history of kings, have become republicans. The physicists of our day no longer believe in matter. That in itself, however, would be no great loss, provided we could still have a large and varied external world, but unfortunately they have not supplied us with any reason for believing in a non-material external world.

The problem is not essentially one for the physicist, but for the logician. It is, in essence, a simple one, namely: are circumstances ever such as to enable us, from a set of known events, to infer that some other event has occurred, is occurring, or will occur? Or, if we cannot make such an inference with certainty, can we ever make it with any high degree of probability, or at any rate with a probability greater than a half? If the answer to this question is in the affirmative, we may be justified in believing, as we all do in fact believe, in the occurrence of events which we have not personally experienced. If the answer is in the negative, we can never be justified in our belief. Logicians have hardly ever considered this question in its naked simplicity, and I do not know of any clear answer to it. Until an answer is forthcoming, one way or another, the question must remain an open one, and our faith in the external world must be merely animal faith.

(3) *The Abstractness of Physics.*—Even allowing that the sun, the stars, and the material world generally, are not a figment of our imagination, or a set of convenient coefficients in our equations, what can be said about them is extraordinarily abstract, much more so than appears from the language employed by physicists when they attempt to be intelligible. The space and time that they deal with are not the space and time of our experience. The orbits of the planets do not resemble the pictorial ellipses which we see drawn in charts of the solar system, except in certain quite abstract properties. It is possible that the relation of contiguity which occurs in our experience may be extended to the bodies of the physical world, but other relations known in experience are not themselves known to exist in the physical world. The most that can be known, and that only on the most hopeful view, is that there are certain relations in the physical world which share certain abstract logical characteristics with the relations that we know. The characteristics which they share are those that can be expressed mathematically, not those that distinguish them imaginatively from other relations. Take, for example, what there is in common between a gramophone record and the music that it plays; the two share certain structural properties which can be expressed in abstract terms, but they do not share any properties that are obvious to the senses. In virtue of their structural similarity, the one can cause the other. Similarly, a physical world sharing the structure of our sensible world can cause it, even though it may resemble it in nothing except structure. At best, therefore, we

can only know concerning the physical world such properties as the gramophone record and the music have in common, not such as distinguish them one from the other. Ordinary language is totally unsuited for expressing what physics really asserts, since the words of everyday life are not sufficiently abstract. Only mathematics and mathematical logic can say as little as the physicist means to say. As soon as he translates his symbols into words, he inevitably says something much too concrete, and gives his readers a cheerful impression of something imaginable and intelligible, which is much more pleasant and everyday than what he is trying to convey.

Many people have a passionate hatred of abstraction, chiefly, I think, because of its intellectual difficulty; but as they do not wish to give this reason, they invent all sorts of others that sound grand. They say that all reality is concrete, and that in making abstractions we are leaving out the essential. They say that all abstraction is falsification, and that as soon as you have left out any aspect of something actual you have exposed yourself to the risk of fallacy in arguing from its remaining aspects alone. Those who argue in this way are, in fact, concerned with matters quite other than those that concern science. From the aesthetic point of view, for example, abstraction is likely to be wholly misleading. The music may be beautiful, while the gramophone record is aesthetically null; from the point of view of imaginative vision, such as an epic poet may desire in writing the history of the creation, the abstract knowledge offered by physics is not satisfying. He wants to know what God saw when He looked upon the world and saw that it was good; he cannot be satisfied with formulae giving the abstract logical properties of the relations among the different parts of what God saw. But scientific thought is different from this. It is essentially power-thought—the sort of thought, that is to say, whose purpose, conscious or unconscious, is to give power to its possessor. Now power is a causal concept, and to obtain power over any given material one need only understand the causal laws to which it is subject. This is an essentially abstract matter, and the more irrelevant details we can omit from our purview, the more powerful our thoughts will become. The same sort of thing can be illustrated in the economic sphere. The cultivator, who knows every corner of his farm, has a concrete knowledge of wheat, and makes very little money; the railway which carries his wheat views it in a slightly more abstract way, and makes rather more money; the stock exchange manipulator, who knows it only in its purely abstract aspect of something which may go up or down, is, in his way, as remote from concrete reality as the physicist, and he, of all those concerned in the economic sphere, makes the most money and has the most power. So it is with science, though the power which the man of science seeks is more remote and impersonal than that which is sought on the stock exchange.

The extreme abstractness of modern physics makes it difficult to understand, but gives to those who can understand it a grasp of the world as a whole, a sense of its structure and mechanism, which no less abstract apparatus could possibly supply. The power of using abstractions is the essence of intellect, and with every increase in abstraction the intellectual triumphs of science are enhanced.

(*The Scientific Outlook*, London: Allen & Unwin; New York: W. W. Norton, 1931.)

68

THE NEW PHYSICS AND RELATIVITY

THE theory of quanta and the theory of relativity have been derived from very different classes of phenomena. The theory of quanta is concerned with the smallest quantities known to science, the theory of relativity with the largest. Distances too small for the microscope are concerned in the theory of quanta; distances too large for the telescope are concerned in the theory of relativity. Relativity came, in the first instance, from astronomy and the study of the propagation of light in astronomical spaces, and its most noteworthy triumphs have been in regard to astronomical phenomena—the motion of the perihelion of Mercury, and the bending of light from the stars when it passes near the sun. The material of the quantum theory, on the contrary, is mainly derived from small quantities of very rarefied gases in laboratories, and from tiny particles running about in a vacuum as nearly perfect as we can make it. In the theory of relativity, 300,000 kilometres counts as a small distance; in the theory of quanta, a thousandth of a centimetre counts as infinitely great. The result of this divergence is that two theories have been pursued by different investigators, because they required different apparatus and different methods. In this final chapter, we shall consider what bearing the two theories have on each other, and, in particular, whether there is anything in relativity that makes the theory of quanta seem less odd and irrational.

The theory of relativity, as everyone knows, was discovered by Einstein in two stages, of which the first is called the special theory and the second the general theory. The first dates from 1905, the second from 1915. The first is not superseded by the second, but absorbed into it as a part. We shall not attempt to explain the theory of relativity, which has been done popularly (so far as is possible) in a multitude of books and scientifically in two books which should be read by all who have sufficient mathematical equipment: Hermann Weyl's *Space, Time, Matter*, and Eddington's *Mathematical Theory of Relativity*. We are only concerned with the points where this theory touches the problem of atomic structure.

The special theory of relativity, as we have already seen, is relevant to the problems we have been considering at several points. It is relevant through its doctrine that mass, as measured by our instruments, varies with velocity, and is, in fact, merely a part of the energy of a body. It is part of the theory of relativity to show that the results of measurement, in a great many cases, do not yield physical facts about the quantities intended to be measured, but are dependent upon the relative motion of the observer and what is observed. Since motion is a purely relative thing, we cannot say that the observer is standing still while the object observed is moving; we can only say that the two are moving relatively to each other. It follows that any quantity which depends upon the motion of a body relatively to the observer cannot be regarded as an intrinsic property of the body. Mass, as commonly measured, is such a property; if the body is moving with a velocity which approaches that of light, its measured mass increases, and as the velocity gets nearer to that of light, the measured mass increases without limit. But this increase of mass is only apparent; it would not exist for an observer moving with the body whose mass is being measured. The mass as measured by an observer moving with the body is what counts as the true mass, and it is easily inferred from the measured mass when we know how the body concerned is moving relatively to ourselves. When we say that any two electrons have the same mass, or that any two hydrogen nuclei have the same mass, we are speaking of the true mass. The apparent mass of an electron which is shot out in the form of a β-ray may be several times as great as the true mass.

There are two other points where the variability of apparent mass is relevant in the theory of atoms. One concerns the 'fine structure' and the analogy between the electron in a hydrogen atom and the planet Mercury; this was considered in Chapter VII. The other is the explanation of the fact that the helium nucleus is less than four times as heavy as the hydrogen nucleus, which concerned us in Chapter XI. On both these points, as we have seen, the theory of relativity provides admirably satisfactory explanations of facts which would otherwise remain obscure. Both, however, raise the question of the relativity of energy, which might be thought awkward for the quantum theory, because this theory uses the conservation of energy, and something merely relative to the observer cannot be expected to be conserved.

In elementary dynamics, as everyone knows, energy consists of two parts, kinetic and potential. Ignoring the latter, let us consider the former. The kinetic energy depends upon the mass and the velocity, but the velocity depends upon the observer, and is not an intrinsic property of a body. The result is that energy has to be defined in the theory of relativity. It turns out that we can identify the energy of a body with its mass as measured by the observer (or, in ordinary units, with this mass multiplied by the square of the velocity of light). Although, for a particular body this mass varies with the observer, its sum throughout the universe will be constant for a given observer, however he may be moving.[1]

In the theory of relativity, there are two kinds of variation of mass to be distinguished, of which so far we have only considered one.

We have considered the change of measured mass (as we have called it) which is brought about by a change in the relative motion of the observer and the body whose mass is being measured. This is not a change in the body itself, but merely in its relation to the observer. It is this change which has to be allowed for in deducing from experimental data that all electrons have the same mass. We allow for it by means of a formula, which enables us to infer what we may call the 'proper mass' of the body. This is the mass which it will be found to have by an observer who shares its motion. In all ordinary cases, in which we determine mass (or weight) by means of a balance, we and the body which we are weighing share the same motion, namely that of the earth in its rotation and revolution; thus weighing with a balance gives the 'proper mass'. But in the case of swiftly moving electrons and α-particles we have to adopt other ways of measuring their mass, because we cannot make ourselves move as fast as they do; thus in these cases we only arrive at the 'proper mass' by a calculation. The 'proper mass' is a genuine property of a body, not relative to the observer. As a rule, the proper mass is constant, or very nearly so, but it is not always strictly constant. When a body absorbs radiant energy, its proper mass is increased; when it radiates out energy, its proper mass is diminished. When four hydrogen nuclei and two electrons combine to form a helium nucleus, they radiate out energy. The loss of mass involved is loss of proper mass, and is quite a different kind of phenomenon from the variation of measured mass when an electron changes its velocity.

There is another point, not easy to explain clearly, and as yet amounting to no more than a suggestion, but capable of proving very important in the future. We saw that Planck's quantum h is not a certain amount of energy, but a certain amount of what is called 'action'. Now the theory of relativity would lead us to expect that action would be more important than energy. The reason for this is derived from the fact that relativity diminishes the gulf between space and time which exists in popular thought and in traditional physics. How this affects our question we must now try to understand.

Consider two events, one of which happens at noon on one day in London, while the other happens at noon the next day in Edinburgh. Common sense would say that there are two kinds of intervals between these two events, an interval of twenty-four hours in time, and an interval of 400 miles in space. The theory of relativity says that this is a mistake, and that there is only one kind of interval between them, which may be analysed

[1] Eddington, op. cit., pp. 30–2.

into a space-part and a time-part in a number of different ways. One way will be adopted by a person who is not moving relatively to the events concerned, while other ways will be adopted by persons moving in various ways. If a comet were passing near the earth when our two events happened, and were moving very fast relatively to the earth, an observer on the comet would divide the interval of our two events differently between space and time, although, if he knew the theory of relativity, he would arrive at the same estimate of the total interval as would be made by our relativity physicists. Thus the division of the interval into a space-portion and a time-portion does not belong to the physical relation of the two events, but is something subjective, contributed by the observer. It cannot, therefore, enter into the correct statement of any law of the physical world.

The importance of this principle (which is supported by a multitude of empirical facts) is impossible to exaggerate. It means, in the first place, that the ultimate facts in physics must be events, rather than bodies in motion. A body is supposed to persist through a certain length of time, and its motion is only definite when we have fixed upon one way of dividing intervals between space and time. Therefore any physical statement in terms of the motions of bodies is in part conventional and subjective, and must contain an element not belonging to the physical occurrence. We have therefore to deal with events, whose relative positions, in the conventional space-time system that we have adopted, are fixed by four quantities, three giving their relations in space (e.g. east-and-west, north-and-south, up-and-down), while the fourth gives their relation in time. The true interval between them can be calculated from these, and is the same whatever conventional system we adopt; just as the time-interval between two historical events would be the same whether we dated both by the Christian era or by the Mohammedan, only that the calculation is not so simple.

It follows from these considerations that, when we wish to consider what is happening in some very small region (as we have to do whenever we apply the differential or integral calculus), we must not take merely a small region of space, but a small region of space-time, i.e. in conventional language, what is happening in a small volume of space during a very short time. This leads us to consider, not merely the energy at an instant, but the effect of energy operating for a very short time; and this, as we saw, is of the nature of action (in the technical sense). A quotation from Eddington[1] will help to make the point clear:

'After mass and energy there is one physical quantity which plays a very fundamental part in modern physics, known as *Action*. *Action* here is a very technical term, and is not to be confused with Newton's "Action and Reaction". In the relativity theory in particular this seems in many

[1] *Space, Time and Gravitation*, p. 147.

respects to be the most fundamental thing of all. The reason is not difficult to see. If we wish to speak of the continuous matter present *at* any particular point of space and time, we must use the term *density*. Density multiplied by volume in space gives us *mass* or, what appears to be the same thing, *energy*. But from our space-time point of view, a far more important thing is density multiplied by a four-dimensional volume of space and time; this is *action*. The multiplication by three dimensions gives mass or energy; and the fourth multiplication gives mass or energy multiplied by time. Action is thus mass multiplied by time, or energy multiplied by time, and is more fundamental than either.'

It is a fact which must be significant that action thus turns out to be fundamental both in relativity theory and in the theory of quanta. But as yet it is impossible to say what is the interpretation to be put upon this fact; we shall probably have to wait for some new and more fundamental way of stating the quantum theory.

There is one other respect in which some of the later developments of relativity suggest the possibility of answers to questions which have hitherto seemed quite unanswerable. Our theory, so far, leads us to brute facts which have to be merely accepted. We do not know why there are two kinds of electricity, or why opposite kinds attract each other while similar kinds repel each other. This dualism is one of the things which is intellectually unsatisfying about the present condition of physics. Another thing is the conflict between the discontinuous process by which energy is radiated from the atom into the surrounding medium, and the continuous process by which it is transmitted through the surrounding medium. Relativity throws very little light on these points, but there is another point upon which it throws at least a glimmer. We find it hard to rest content with the existence of unrelated absolute constants, such as Planck's quantum and the size of an electron, which, so far as we can see, might just as easily have had any different magnitude. To the scientific mind, such facts are a challenge, leading to a search for some way of inter-relating them and making them seem less accidental. As regards the quantum, no plausible suggestion has yet been made. But as regards the size of an electron, Eddington makes some suggestive observations, which, however, require some preliminary explanations.

We saw that, according to the theory of relativity, the interval between two events may be separated into a time-part and a space-part in various ways, all of which are equally legitimate, and each of which will seem natural to an observer who is moving suitably. The first effect of this is to diminish the sharpness of the distinction between space and time. But the distinction comes back in a new form. It is found that the interval between two events can, in some cases, be regarded as merely a space-interval; this will happen if an observer who is moving suitably would regard them as simultaneous. Whenever this does not happen, the interval can be regarded as merely a time-interval; this will be the case when an observer could travel so as to be present at both events. It takes eight minutes for light to travel from the sun to the earth, and nothing can travel faster than light; therefore if we consider some event which happens on the earth at 12 noon, any event which happens on the sun between 11.52 a.m. and 12.8 p.m. could not have happened in the presence of anything which was present at the event on earth at 12 noon. Events happening on the sun during these 16 minutes have an interval from the event on earth which will, for a suitable observer, seem to be a spatial separation between simultaneous events; such intervals are called space-like. Events happening earlier or later than these 16 minutes will be separated from the event on earth at noon by an interval which would appear to be purely temporal to an observer who had spent the interval in travelling from the sun to the earth, or vice versa as the case may be; such intervals are called time-like. Two parts of one light-ray are on the borderland between time-like and space-like intervals, and in fact the interval between them is zero. But in all other cases there is a separation which is either time-like or space-like, and in this way we find that there is still a distinction between what is to be called temporal and what is to be called spatial, though the distinction is different from that of everyday life.

For reasons which we cannot go into, Einstein and others have suggested that the universe has a 'curvature', so that we could theoretically go all round it and come back to our starting-point, in the sort of way in which we go round the earth. All the way round the universe, in that case, must be a certain length, fixed in nature. Eddington suggests that some relation will probably be found between this, the greatest length in nature, and the radius of the electron, which is the least length in nature. As he humorously puts it: 'An electron could never decide how large it ought to be unless there existed some length independent of itself for it to compare itself with.'

He goes on to make another application of this principle, which is suggestive, though perhaps not intended to be treated too solemnly. The curvature of the universe, if it exists, is only in space, not in time. This leads him to say:[1]

'By consideration of extension in time-like directions we obtain a confirmation of these views which is, I think, not entirely fantastic. We have said that an electron would not know how large it ought to be unless there existed independent lengths in space for it to measure itself against. Similarly it would not know how long it ought to exist unless there existed a length in time for it to measure itself against. But there is not radius of curvature in a time-like direction; so the electron does *not* know how long it ought to exist. Therefore it just goes on existing indefinitely.'

[1] *The Mathematical Theory of Relativity*, p. 155.

But even if the size of an electron should ultimately prove, in this way, to be related to the size of the universe, that would leave a number of unexplained brute facts, notably the quantum itself, which has so far defied all attempts to make it seem anything but accidental. It is *possible* that the desire for rational explanation may be carried too far. This is suggested by some remarks, also by Eddington, in his book, *Space, Time and Gravitation* (p. 200). The theory of relativity has shown that most of traditional dynamics, which was supposed to contain scientific laws, really consisted of conventions as to measurement, and was strictly analogous to the 'great law' that there are always three feet to a yard. In particular, this applies to the conservation of energy. This makes it plausible to suppose that every apparent law of nature which strikes us as reasonable is not really a law of nature, but a concealed convention, plastered on to nature by our love of what we, in our arrogance, choose to consider rational. Eddington hints that a real law of nature is likely to stand out by the fact that it appears to us irrational, since in that case it is less likely that we have invented it to satisfy our intellectual taste. And from this point of view he inclines to the belief that the quantum-principle is the first real law of nature that has been discovered in physics.

This raises a somewhat important question: Is the world 'rational', i.e. such as to conform to our intellectual habits? Or is it 'irrational', i.e. not such as we should have made it if we had been in the position of the Creator? I do not propose to suggest an answer to this question.

(*The ABC of Atoms*, London: Routledge & Kegan Paul; New York: E. P. Dutton & Co., 1923.)

69

SCIENCE AND VALUES

THE philosophy which has seemed appropriate to science has varied from time to time. To Newton and most of his English contemporaries science seemed to afford proof of the existence of God as the Almighty Lawgiver: He had decreed the law of gravitation and whatever other natural laws had been discovered by Englishmen. In spite of Copernicus, Man was still the *moral* centre of the universe, and God's purposes were mainly concerned with the human race. The more radical among the French *philosophes*, being politically in conflict with the Church, took a different view. They did not admit that laws imply a lawgiver; on the other hand, they thought that physical laws could explain human behaviour. This led them to materialism and denial of free will. In their view, the universe has no purpose and man is an insignificant episode. The vastness of the universe impressed them and inspired in them a new form of humility to replace that which atheism had made obsolete. This point of view is well expressed in a little poem by Leopardi and expresses, more nearly than any other known to me, my own feeling about the universe and human passions:

THE INFINITE[1]

Dear to me always was this lonely hill
And this hedge that excludes so large a part
Of the ultimate horizon from my view.
But as I sit and gaze, my thought conceives
Interminable vastnesses of space
Beyond it, and unearthly silences,
And profoundest calm; whereat my heart almost
Becomes dismayed. And as I hear the wind
Blustering through these branches, I find myself
Comparing with this sound that infinite silence;

[1] Translation by R. C. Trevelyan from *Translations from Leopardi*: Cambridge University Press, 1941.

And then I call to mind eternity,
And the ages that are dead, and this that now
Is living, and the noise of it. And so
In this immensity my thought sinks drowned:
And sweet it seems to shipwreck in this sea.

But this has become an old-fashioned way of feeling. Science used to be valued as a means of getting to *know* the world; now, owing to the triumph of technique, it is conceived as showing how to *change* the world. The new point of view, which is adopted in practice throughout America and Russia, and in theory by many modern philosophers, was first proclaimed by Marx in 1845, in his *Theses on Feuerbach*. He says:

The question whether objective truth belongs to human thinking is not a question of theory, but a practical question. The truth, i.e. the reality and power, of thought must be demonstrated in practice. The contest as to the reality or non-reality of a thought which is isolated from practice, is a purely scholastic question. . . . Philosophers have only *interpreted* the world in various ways, but the real task is to alter it.

From the point of view of technical philosophy, this theory has been best developed by John Dewey, who is universally acknowledged as America's most eminent philosopher.

This philosophy has two aspects, one theoretical and the other ethical. On the theoretical side, it analyses away the concept 'truth', for which it substitutes 'utility'. It used to be thought that, if you believed Caesar crossed the Rubicon, you believed truly, because Caesar did cross the Rubicon. Not so, say the philosophers we are considering: to say that your belief is 'true' is another way of saying that you will find it more profitable than the opposite belief. I might object that there have been cases of historical beliefs which, after being generally accepted for a long time, have in the end been admitted to be mistaken. In the case of such beliefs, every examinee would find the accepted falsehood of his time more profitable than the as yet unacknowledged truth. But this kind of objection is swept aside by the contention that a belief may be 'true' at one time and 'false' at another. In 1920 it was 'true' that Trotsky had a great part in the Russian Revolution; in 1930 it was 'false'. The results of this view have been admirably worked out in George Orwell's '1984'.

This philosophy derives its inspiration from science in several different ways. Take first its best aspect, as developed by Dewey. He points out that scientific theories change from time to time, and that what recommends a theory is that it 'works'. When new phenomena are discovered, for which it no longer 'works', it is discarded. A theory—so Dewey concludes—is a tool like another; it enables us to manipulate raw material.

Like any other tool, it is judged good or bad by its efficiency in this manipulation, and like any other tool, it is good at one time and bad at another. While it is good it may be called 'true', but this word must not be allowed its usual connotations. Dewey prefers the phrase 'warranted assertibility' to the word 'truth'.

The second source of the theory is technique. What do we want to know about electricity? Only how to make it work for us. To want to know more is to plunge into useless metaphysics. Science is to be admired because it gives us power over nature, and the power comes wholly from technique. Therefore an interpretation which reduces science to technique keeps all the useful part, and dismisses only a dead weight of medieval lumber. If technique is all that interests you, you are likely to find this argument very convincing.

The third attraction of pragmatism—which cannot be wholly separated from the second—is love of power. Most men's desires are of various kinds. There are the pleasures of sense; there are aesthetic pleasures and pleasures of contemplation; there are private affections; and there is power. In an individual, any one of these may acquire predominance over the others. If love of power dominates, you arrive at Marx's view that what is important is not to understand the world, but to change it. Traditional theories of knowledge were invented by men who loved contemplation—a monkish taste, according to modern devotees of mechanism. Mechanism augments human power to an enormous degree. It is therefore this aspect of science that attracts the lovers of power. And if power is all you want from science, the pragmatist theory gives you just what you want, without accretions that to you seem irrelevant. It gives you even more than you could have expected, for if you control the police it gives you the god-like power of *making truth*. You cannot make the sun cold, but you can confer pragmatic 'truth' on the proposition 'the sun is cold' if you can insure that everyone who denies it is liquidated. I doubt whether Zeus could do more.

This engineer's philosophy, as it may be called, is distinguished from common sense and from most other philosophies by its rejection of 'fact' as a fundamental concept in defining 'truth'. If you say, for example, 'the South Pole is cold', you say something which, according to traditional views, is 'true' in virtue of a 'fact', namely that the South Pole is cold. And this is a fact, not because people believe it, or because it pays to believe it; it just *is* a fact. Facts, when they are not about human beings and their doings, represent the limitations of human power. We find ourselves in a universe of a certain sort, and we find out what sort of a universe it is by observation, not by self-assertion. It is true that we can make changes on or near the surface of the earth, but not elsewhere. Practical men have no wish to make changes elsewhere, and can therefore accept a philosophy which treats the surface of the earth as if it were the whole universe. But even on the surface of the earth our power is limited. To forget that we are hemmed in by facts which are for the most part independent of our desires is a form of insane megalomania. This kind of insanity has grown up as a result of the triumph of scientific technique. Its latest manifestation is Stalin's refusal to believe that heredity can have the temerity to ignore Soviet decrees, which is like Xerxes whipping the Hellespont to teach Poseidon a lesson.

'The pragmatic theory of truth [I wrote in 1907] is inherently connected with the appeal to force. If there is a non-human truth, which one man may know while another does not, there is a standard outside the disputants, to which, we may urge, the dispute ought to be submitted; hence a pacific and judicial settlement of disputes is at least theoretically possible. If, on the contrary, the only way of discovering which of the disputants is in the right is to wait and see which of them is successful, there is no longer any principle except force by which the issue can be decided. . . . In international matters, owing to the fact that the disputants are often strong enough to be independent of outside control, these considerations become more important. The hopes of international peace, like the achievement of internal peace, depend upon the creation of an effective force of public opinion formed upon an estimate of the rights and wrongs of disputes. Thus it would be misleading to say that the dispute is decided by force, without adding that force is dependent upon justice. But the possibility of such a public opinion depends upon the possibility of a standard of justice which is a cause, not an effect, of the wishes of the community; and such a standard of justice seems incompatible with the pragmatist philosophy. This philosophy, therefore, although it begins with liberty and toleration, develops, by inherent necessity, into the appeal to force and the arbitrament of the big battalions. By this development it becomes equally adapted to democracy at home and to imperialism abroad. Thus here again it is more delicately adjusted to the requirements of the time than any other philosophy which has hitherto been invented.

'To sum up: Pragmatism appeals to the temper of mind which finds on the surface of this planet the whole of its imaginative material; which feels confident of progress, and unaware of non-human limitations to human power; which loves battle, with all the attendant risks, because it has no real doubt that it will achieve victory; which desires religion, as it desires railways and electric light, as a comfort and a help in the affairs of this world, not as providing non-human objects to satisfy the hunger for perfection. But for those who feel that life on this planet would be a life in prison if it were not for the windows into a greater world beyond; for those to whom a belief in man's omnipotence seems arrogant; who desire rather the stoic freedom that comes of mastery over the passions than the Napoleonic domination that sees the kingdoms of this world at its feet—in a word, to men who do not find man an adequate object of their worship, the pragmatist's world will seem narrow and petty, robbing life of all that gives it value, and making man himself smaller by depriving the universe which he contemplates of all its splendour.'

Let us now try to sum up what increases in human happiness science has rendered possible, and what ancient evils it is in danger of intensifying.

I do not pretend that there is any way of arriving at the millennium. Whatever our social institutions, there will be death and illness (though in a diminishing quantity); there will be old age and insanity; there will be either danger or boredom. So long as the present family survives, there will be unrequited love and parents' tyranny and children's ingratitude; and if something new were substituted for the family, it would bring new evils, probably worse. Human life cannot be made a matter of unalloyed bliss, and to allow oneself excessive hopes is to court disappointment. Nevertheless what can be soberly hoped is very considerable. In what follows, I am not prophesying what *will* happen, but pointing out the best that *may* happen, and the further fact that this best will happen if it is widely desired.

There are two ancient evils that science, unwisely used, may intensify: they are tyranny and war. But I am concerned now rather with pleasant possibilities than with unpleasant ones.

Science can confer two kinds of benefits: it can diminish bad things, and it can increase good things. Let us begin with the former.

Science can abolish poverty and excessive hours of labour. In the earliest human communities, before agriculture, each human individual required two or more square miles to sustain life. Subsistence was precarious and death from starvation must have been frequent. At that stage, men had the same mixture of misery and carefree enjoyment as still makes up the lives of other animals.

Agriculture was a technical advance of the same kind of importance as attaches to modern machine industry. The way that agriculture was used is an awful warning to our age. It introduced slavery and serfdom, human sacrifice, absolute monarchy and large wars. Instead of raising the standard of life, except for a tiny governing minority, it merely increased the population. On the whole, it probably increased the sum of human misery. It is not impossible that industrialism may take the same course.

Fortunately, however, the growth of industrialism has coincided in the West with the growth of democracy. It is possible now, if the population of the world does not increase too fast, for one man's labour to produce much more than is needed to provide a bare subsistence for himself and his family. Given an intelligent democracy not misled by some dogmatic creed this possibility will be used to raise the standard of life. It has been so used, to a limited extent, in Britain and America, and would have been so used more effectively but for war. Its use in raising the standard of life has depended mainly upon three things: democracy, trade unionism, and birth control. All three, of course, have incurred hostility from the rich. If these three things can be extended to the rest of the world as it becomes industrialized, and if the danger of great wars can be eliminated, poverty can be abolished throughout the whole world and excessive hours of labour will no longer be necessary anywhere. But without these three things, industrialism will create a régime like that in which the Pharaohs built the pyramids. In particular, if world population continues to increase at the present rate, the abolition of poverty and excessive work will be totally impossible.

Science has already conferred an immense boon on mankind by the growth of medicine. In the eighteenth century people expected most of their children to die before they were grown up. Improvement began at the beginning of the nineteenth century, chiefly owing to vaccination. It has continued ever since and is still continuing. In 1920 the infant mortality in England and Wales was 80 per thousand, in 1948 it was 34 per thousand. The general death rate in 1948 (10·8) was the lowest ever recorded up to that date. There is no obvious limit to the improvement of health that can be brought about by medicine. The sum of human suffering has also been much diminished by the discovery of anaesthetics.

The general diminution of lawlessness and crimes of violence would not have been possible without science. If you read eighteenth-century novels, you get a strange impression of London: unlighted streets, footpads and highwaymen, nothing that we should count as a police force, but, in a futile attempt to compensate for all this, an abominably savage and ferocious criminal law. Street lighting, telephones, finger-printing, and the psychology of crime and punishment are scientific advances which have made it possible for the police to reduce crime below anything that the most Utopian philosopher of the 'Age of Reason' would have imagined possible.

Coming now to positive goods, there is, to begin with, an immense increase of education which has been rendered possible by the increased productivity of labour. As regards general education, this is most marked in America, where even university education is free. If I took a taxi in New York, I would often find that the driver was a Ph.D., who would start arguing about philosophy at imminent risk to himself and me. But in England as well as in America the improvement at the highest level is equally remarkable. Read, for instance, Gibbon's account of Oxford.

With this goes an increase of opportunity. It is much easier than it used to be for an able young man without what are called 'natural' advantages (i.e. inherited wealth) to rise to a position in which he can make the best use of his talents. In this respect there is still much to be done, but there is every reason to expect that in England and in America it will be done. The waste of talent in former times must have been appalling; I shudder to think how many 'mute inglorious Miltons' there must have been. Our modern Miltons, alas, remain for the most part inglorious, though not mute. But ours is not a poetic age.

Finally, there is more diffused happiness than ever before, and if the fear of war were removed this improvement would be very much greater than it is.

Let us consider for a moment the kind of disposition that must be widely diffused if a good world is to be created and sustained.

I will begin with the intellectual temper that is required. There must be in many a desire to know the important facts, and in most an unwillingness to give assent to pleasant illusions. There are in the world at the present day two great opposing systems of dogma: Catholicism and Communism. If you believe either with such intensity that you are prepared to face martyrdom, you can live a happy life, and even enjoy a happy death if it comes quickly. You can inspire converts, you can create an army, you can stir up hatred of the opposite dogma and its adherents, and generally you can *seem* immensely effective. I am constantly asked: What can you, with your cold rationalism, offer to the seeker after salvation that is comparable to the cosy home-like comfort of a fenced-in dogmatic creed?

To this the answer is many-sided. In the first place, I do not say that I can offer as much happiness as is to be obtained by the abdication of reason. I do not say that I can offer as much happiness as is to be obtained from drink or drugs or amassing great wealth by swindling widows and orphans. It is not the happiness of the individual convert that concerns me; it is the happiness of mankind. If you genuinely desire the happiness of mankind, certain forms of ignoble personal happiness are not open to you. If your child is ill, and you are a conscientious parent, you accept medical diagnosis, however doubtful and discouraging; if you accept the cheerful opinion of a quack and your child consequently dies, you are not excused by the pleasantness of belief in the quack while it lasted. If people loved humanity as genuinely as they love their children, they would be as unwilling in politics as in the home to let themselves be deceived by comfortable fairy tales.

The next point is that all fanatical creeds do harm. This is obvious when they have to compete with other fanaticisms, since in that case they promote hatred and strife. But it is true even when only one fanatical creed is in the field. It cannot allow free inquiry, since this might shake its hold. It must oppose intellectual progress. If, as is usually the case, it involves a priesthood, it gives great power to a caste professionally devoted to maintenance of the intellectual status quo, and to a pretence of certainty where in fact there is no certainty.

Every fanatical creed essentially involves hatred. I knew once a fanatical advocate of an international language, but he preferred Ido to Esperanto. Listening to his conversation, I was appalled by the depravity of the

Esperantists, who, it seemed, had sunk to hitherto unimaginable depths of wickedness. Luckily my friend failed to convince any government, and so the Esperantists survived. But if he had been at the head of a state of two hundred million inhabitants, I shudder to think what would have happened to them.

Very often the element of hatred in a fanatical doctrine becomes predominant. People who tell you they love the proletariat often in fact only hate the rich. Some people who believe that you should love your neighbour as yourself think it right to hate those who do not do so. As these are the vast majority, no notable increase of loving kindness results from their creed.

Apart from such specific evils, the whole attitude of accepting a belief unquestioningly on a basis of authority is contrary to the scientific spirit, and, if widespread, scarcely compatible with the progress of science. Not only the Bible, but even the works of Marx and Engels, contain demonstrably false statements. The Bible says the hare chews the cud, and Engels said that the Austrians would win the war of 1866. These are only arguments against fundamentalists. But when a Sacred Book is retained while fundamentalism is rejected, the authority of The Book becomes vested in the priesthood. The meaning of 'dialectical material-ism' changes every decade, and the penalty for a belated interpretation is death or the concentration camp.

The triumphs of science are due to the substitution of observation and inference for authority. Every attempt to revive authority in intellectual matters is a retrograde step. And it is part of the scientific attitude that the pronouncements of science do not claim to be certain, but only to be the most probable on present evidence. One of the greatest benefits that science confers upon those who understand its spirit is that it enables them to live without the delusive support of subjective certainty. That is why science cannot favour persecution.

The desire for a fanatical creed is one of the great evils of our time. There have been other ages with the same disease: the late Roman Empire and the sixteenth century are the most obvious examples. When Rome began to decay, and when, in the third century, barbarian irruptions produced fear and impoverishment, men began to look for safety in another world. Plotinus found it in Plato's eternal world, the followers of Mithra in a solar Paradise, and the Christians in heaven. The Christians won, largely because their dogmatic certainty was the greatest. Having won, they started persecuting each other for small deviations, and hardly had leisure to notice the barbarian invaders except to observe that they were Arians—the ancient equivalent of Trotskyites. The religious fervour of that time was a product of fear and despair; so is the religious fervour—Christian or Communist—of our age. It is an irrational reaction to danger, tending to bring about what it fears. Dread of the hydrogen bomb promotes fanaticism, and fanaticism is more likely than anything else to lead to actual use of the hydrogen bomb. Heavenly salvation perhaps, if the fanatics are right, but earthly salvation is not to be found along that road.

I will say a few words about the connection of love with intellectual honesty. There are several different attitudes that may be adopted towards the spectacle of intolerable suffering. If you are a sadist, you may find pleasure in it; if you are completely detached, you may ignore it; if you are a sentimentalist, you may persuade yourself that it is not as bad as it seems; but if you feel genuine compassion you will try to apprehend the evil truly in order to be able to cure it. The sentimentalist will say that you are coldly intellectual, and that, if you really minded the sufferings of others, you could not be so scientific about them. The sentimentalist will claim to have a tenderer heart than yours, and will show it by letting the suffering continue rather than suffer himself.

There is a tender-hearted lady in Gilbert and Sullivan who remarks:

I heard one day	A gentleman say
That criminals who	Are sawn in two
Do not much feel	The fatal steel
But come in twain	Without much pain.
If this be true	How lucky for you.

Similarly, the men who made the Munich surrender would pretend, (a) that the Nazis didn't go in for pogroms, (b) that Jews enjoy being massacred. And fellow-travellers maintain, (a) that there is no forced labour in Russia, (b) that there is nothing Russians find more delectable than being worked to death in an Arctic winter. Such men are not 'coldly intellectual'.

The most disquieting psychological feature of our time, and the one which affords the best argument for the necessity of some creed, however irrational, is the death wish. Everyone knows how some primitive communities, brought suddenly into contact with white men, become listless, and finally die from mere absence of the will to live. In Western Europe, the new conditions of danger which exist are having something of the same effect. Facing facts is painful, and the way out is not clear. Nostalgia takes the place of energy directed towards the future. There is a tendency to shrug the shoulders and say 'Oh well, if we are exterminated by hydrogen bombs, it will save a lot of trouble'. This is a tired and feeble reaction, like that of the late Romans to the barbarians. It can only be met by courage, hope, and a reasoned optimism. Let us see what basis there is for hope.

First: I have no doubt that, leaving on one side, for the moment, the danger of war, the average level of happiness, in Britain as well as in America, is higher than in any previous community at any time. Moreover improvement continues whenever there is not war. We have therefore something important to conserve.

There are certain things that our age needs, and certain things that it should avoid. It needs compassion and a wish that mankind should be happy; it needs the desire for knowledge and the determination to eschew pleasant myths; it needs, above all, courageous hope and the impulse to creativeness. The things that it must avoid, and that have brought it to the brink of catastrophe, are cruelty, envy, greed, competitiveness, search for irrational subjective certainty, and what Freudians call the death wish.

The root of the matter is a very simple and old-fashioned thing, a thing so simple that I am almost ashamed to mention it, for fear of the derisive smile with which wise cynics will greet my words. The thing I mean—please forgive me for mentioning it—is love, Christian love, or compassion. If you feel this, you have a motive for existence, a guide in action, a reason for courage, an imperative necessity for intellectual honesty. If you feel this, you have all that anybody should need in the way of religion. Although you may not find happiness, you will never know the deep despair of those whose life is aimless and void of purpose; for there is always something that you can do to diminish the awful sum of human misery.

What I do want to stress is that the kind of lethargic despair which is now not uncommon, is irrational. Mankind is in the position of a man climbing a difficult and dangerous precipice, at the summit of which there is a plateau of delicious mountain meadows. With every step that he climbs, his fall, if he does fall, becomes more terrible; with every step his weariness increases and the ascent grows more difficult. At last there is only one more step to be taken, but the climber does not know this, because he cannot see beyond the jutting rocks at his head. His exhaustion is so complete that he wants nothing but rest. If he lets go he will find rest in death. Hope calls: 'One more effort—perhaps it will be the last effort needed.' Irony retorts: 'Silly fellow! Haven't you been listening to hope all this time, and see where it has landed you.' Optimism says: 'While there is life there is hope.' Pessimism growls: 'While there is life there is pain.' Does the exhausted climber make one more effort, or does he let himself sink into the abyss? In a few years those of us who are still alive will know the answer.

Dropping metaphor, the present situation is as follows: science offers the possibility of far greater well-being for the human race than has ever been known before. It offers this on certain conditions: abolition of war, even distribution of ultimate power, and limitation of the growth of population. All these are much nearer to being possible than they ever were before. In Western industrial countries, the growth of population is almost nil; the same causes will have the same effect in other countries as they become modernized, unless dictators and missionaries interfere. The even distribution of ultimate power, economic as well as political, has been nearly achieved in Britain, and other democratic countries are rapidly moving towards it. The prevention of war? It may seem a paradox to say that we are nearer to achieving this than ever before, but I am persuaded that it is true. I will explain why I think so.

In the past, there were many sovereign States, any two of which might at any moment quarrel. Attempts on the lines of the League of Nations were bound to fail, because, when a dispute arose, the disputants were too proud to accept outside arbitration, and the neutrals were too lazy to enforce it. Now there are only two sovereign States: Russia (with satellites) and the United States (with satellites). If either becomes preponderant, either by victory in war or by an obvious military superiority, the preponderant Power can establish a single Authority over the whole world, and thus make future wars impossible. At first this Authority will, in certain regions, be based on force, but if the Western nations are in control, force will as soon as possible give way to consent. When that has been achieved, the most difficult of world problems will have been solved, and science can become wholly beneficent.

I do not think there is reason to fear that such a régime, once established, would be unstable. The chief causes of large-scale violence are: love of power, competition, hate, and fear. Love of power will have no national outlet when all serious military force is concentrated in the international army. Competition will be effectively regulated by law, and mitigated by governmental controls. Fear—in the acute form in which we know it— will disappear when war is no longer to be expected. There remains hate and malevolence. This has a deep hold on human nature. We all believe at once any gossip discreditable to our neighbours, however slender the evidence may be. After the first world war many people hated Germany so much that they could not believe in injury to themselves as a necessary result of extreme severity to the Germans. One sees in Congress a widespread reluctance to admit that self-preservation requires help to Western Europe. America wishes to sell without buying, but finds that this often involves giving rather than selling; the benefit to the recipients is felt by many to be almost unendurable. This wide diffusion of malevolence is one of the most unfortunate things in human nature, and it must be lessened if a world State is to be stable.

I am persuaded that it can be lessened, and very quickly. If peace becomes secure there will be a very rapid increase of material prosperity, and this tends more than anything else to provide a mood of kindly feeling. Consider the immense diminution of cruelty in Britain during the Victorian age; this was mainly due to rapidly increasing wealth in all classes. I think we may confidently expect a similar effect throughout the world owing to the increased wealth that will result from the elimination of war. A great deal, also, is to be hoped from a change in propaganda. Nationalist propaganda, in any violent form, will have to be illegal, and children in schools will not be taught to hate and despise foreign nations. Active instruction in the evils of the old times and the advantages of the new system would do the rest. I am convinced that only a few psychopaths would wish to return to the daily dread of radio-active disintegration.

What stands in the way? Not physical or technical obstacles, but only the evil passions in human minds: suspicion, fear, lust for power, hatred, intolerance. I will not deny that these evil passions are more dominant in the East than in the West, but they certainly exist in the West as well. The human race could, here and now, begin a rapid approach to a vastly better world, given one single condition: the removal of mutual distrust between East and West. I do not know what can be done to fulfil this condition. Most of the suggestions that I have seen have struck me as silly. Meanwhile the only thing to do is to prevent an explosion somehow, and to hope that time may bring wisdom. The near future must either be much better or much worse than the past; which it is to be will be decided within the next few years.

> (*The Impact of Science on Society*, London: Allen & Unwin, 1952; New York: Columbia University Press, 1951 and Simon & Schuster, 1953.)

70

NON-DEMONSTRATIVE INFERENCE

I RETURNED to England in June 1944, after three weeks on the Atlantic. Trinity had awarded me a five-years lectureship and I chose as the subject of my annual course, 'Non-Demonstrative Inference', or N-D.I. for short. I had become increasingly aware of the very limited scope of deductive inference as practised in logic and pure mathematics. I realized that all the inferences used both in common sense and in science are of a different sort from those in deductive logic, and are such that, when the premisses are true and the reasoning correct, the conclusion is only probable. During the first six months after my return from America I had rooms in College and enjoyed a feeling of peacefulness in spite of V1's and V2's. I set to work to investigate probability and the kind of inference which confers probability. I found the subject at first somewhat bewildering as there was a tangle of different problems and each thread had to be separated from every other. The positive outcome appeared in *Human Knowledge*, but I did not, in that book, mention the various perplexities and tentative hypotheses through which I had arrived at my final conclusions. I now think this was a mistake, as it made the conclusions appear more slap-dash and less solid than, in fact, they were.

I found the subject of non-demonstrative inference much larger and much more interesting than I had expected. I found that it had in most discussions been unduly confined to the investigation of induction. I came to the conclusion that inductive arguments, unless they are confined within the limits of common sense, will lead to false conclusions much more often than to true ones. The limitations imposed by common sense are easy to feel but very difficult to formulate. In the end, I came to the conclusion that, although scientific inference needs indemonstrable extra-logical principles, induction is not one of them. It has a part to play, but not as a premiss. I shall return to this subject presently.

Another conclusion which was forced upon me was that not only science, but a great deal that no one sincerely doubts to be knowledge, is impossible if we only know what can be experienced and verified. I felt that much too much emphasis had been laid upon experience, and that, there-fore, empiricism as a philosophy must be subjected to important limitations.

I was at first bewildered by the vastness and multiplicity of the problems involved. Seeing that it is of the essence of non-demonstrative inference to confer only probability upon its conclusions, I thought it prudent to begin with an investigation of probability, especially as, on this subject, there existed a body of positive knowledge floating like a raft upon the great ocean of uncertainty. For some months, I studied the calculus of probability and its applications. There are two kinds of probability, of which one is exemplified by statistics, and the other by doubtfulness. Some theorists have thought that they could do with only one of these, and some have thought that they could do with only the other. The mathematical calculus, as usually interpreted, is concerned with the statistical kind of probability. There are fifty-two cards in a pack, and therefore, if you draw a card at random, the chance that it will be the seven of diamonds is one in fifty-two. It is generally assumed, without conclusive evidence, that if you drew cards at random a great many times, the seven of diamonds would appear about once in every fifty-two times. The subject of probability owed its origin to the interest of aristocrats in games of chance. They hired mathematicians to work out systems which should make gambling lucrative rather than expensive. The mathematicians produced a lot of interesting work, but it does not appear to have enriched their employers.

The theory which considers that all probability is of this statistical kind is called the 'frequency' theory. What, for example, is the probability that a person chosen at random from the population of England will be called 'Smith'? You find out how many people there are in England and how many of them are called 'Smith'. You then *define* the probability that a person chosen at random will be called 'Smith' as the ratio of the number of Smiths to the number of the total population. This is a perfectly precise mathematical conception, having nothing whatever to do with uncertainty. Uncertainty only comes in when you *apply* the conception as, for example, if you see a stranger across the street and you bet a hundred to one that he is not called 'Smith'. But so long as you do not apply the calculus of probability to empirical material, it is a perfectly straightforward branch of mathematics with all the exactness and certainty characteristic of mathematics.

There is, however, another, quite different, theory which was adopted by Keynes in his *Treatise on Probability*. He held that there can be a relation between two propositions consisting in the fact that one of them makes the other probable in a greater or less degree. He held that this relation is indefinable and capable of varying degrees, the extreme degrees being when the one proposition makes the truth of the other certain, and when it makes its falsehood certain. He did not believe that all probabilities are numerically measureable or reducible, even in theory, to frequencies.

I came to the conclusion that, wherever probability is definite, the frequency theory is applicable, but that there is another conception misleadingly called by the same name, to which something more like Keynes's theory is applicable. This other conception I called 'degree of credibility' or 'degree of doubtfulness'. It is obvious that we are much more certain about some things than we are about others, and that our uncertainty often has no statistical aspect. It is true that the statistical aspect can sometimes be discovered where it is not obvious at first sight. I read a book about the Saxon invasion of England which led me to think that Hengist was indubitable but Horsa was perhaps a legend. It would perhaps be possible to put the evidence for Horsa alongside of evidence for other historical characters, and discover in what proportion of cases such evidence had been found to lead aright or to lead astray. But, although this sort of thing is sometimes possible, it certainly does not cover the ground, and leaves degrees of doubtfulness as a necessary conception in the investigation of what passes for knowledge.

It seemed to me that, in the problems with which I was concerned, doubtfulness was much more important than mathematical probability. It was not only that, in the inferences with which I was concerned, the premisses, even if true, do not make the conclusion certain. What was much more important was that the premisses themselves are uncertain. This led me to the conclusion that the mathematical aspects of probability have less to do than might be thought with the problems of scientific inference.

I next devoted myself to a collection of instances where we make inferences that we feel to be quite solid although the inferences in question can only be validated by extra-logical principles. In collecting such instances, I accepted whatever would only be doubted by a philosopher in defence of a theory. Broadly speaking, I did not reject common sense, except where there was some very cogent scientific argument against it. Take a very simple example: suppose you are walking out of doors on a sunny day; your shadow walks with you; if you wave your arms, your shadow waves its arms; if you jump, your shadow jumps; for such reasons, you unhesitatingly call it *your* shadow and you have no doubt whatever that it has a causal connection with your body. But, although the inference is one which no sane man would question, it is not logically demonstrative. It is not logically impossible that there should be a dark patch going through movements not unlike the movements of your body, but having an independent existence of its own. I attempted, by collecting as many instances as I could think of in which non-demonstrative inferences seem to us unquestionable, to discover by analysis what extra-logical principles must be true if we are not mistaken in such cases. The evidence in favour of the principles is derived from the instances and not vice versa. There seemed to me to be several such principles, but I came to the conclusion that induction is not one of them.

I found that, for lack of analysis, people had admitted blocks of non-demonstrative inference because they had a subjective prejudice in favour of certain kinds of knowledge, and had rejected other blocks on account of a contrary prejudice. It appeared to me that, in any particular case of an inference which seemed unquestionable, one should discover the principle upon which it depended and accept other inferences depending upon the same principle. I found that almost all philosophers had been mistaken as to what can and what cannot be inferred from experience alone. I divided the problem of empirical knowledge into three stages: (1) knowledge about myself; (2) knowledge about other minds—which includes the acceptance of testimony; and (3) knowledge about the physical world. Beginning with knowledge about myself, I found that solipsism as commonly expounded admits a great deal that is incompatible with the caution by which such a system is inspired. I do not remember anything that happened to me before I was two years old, but I do not think it plausible to maintain that I began to exist at the age of two. And in later life, I am quite convinced that many things happened to me which I do not remember. Even what I remember may have never happened. I have sometimes had dreams in which there were dream-memories that were wholly imaginary. I once dreamt that I was in terror of the police because I 'remembered' that, a month ago, Whitehead and I together had murdered Lloyd George. It follows that my recollecting something is not, *per se*, conclusive evidence that the something really happened. The solipsist, therefore, if he is to attain the logical safety of which he is in search, will be confined to what I call 'solipsism of the moment'. He will say not only 'I do not know whether the physical world exists or whether there are minds other than my own', but he will have to go further and say, 'I do not know whether I had a past or shall have a future, for these things are just as doubtful as the existence of other people or of the physical world'. No solipsist has ever gone as far as this, and therefore every solipsist has been inconsistent in accepting inferences about himself which have no better warrant than inferences about other people and things.

A very great deal of what we all unquestioningly accept as knowledge depends upon testimony, and testimony, in turn, depends upon the belief that there are other minds besides our own. To common sense, the existence of other minds does not appear open to doubt, and I do not myself see any reason to disagree with common sense on this point. But, undoubtedly, it is through experiences of my own that I am led to believe in the minds of others; and, undoubtedly, as a matter of pure logic, it would be possible for me to have these experiences even if other minds did not exist. Part of our reason for believing in other minds is derived from analogy, but part is derived from another source which has a wider application. Suppose you compare two copies of the same book and find that they agree word for word, you cannot resist the conclusion that they have a common cause, and you can trace this common cause backward through compositors and publishers to the author. You do not find it credible that the author's body went through the motions of writing the book without his having any thoughts meanwhile. Such grounds for admitting other minds are not demonstrative in the logical sense. You might have experiences in a dream which would be equally convincing while you still slept, but which you would regard as misleading when you woke. Such facts warrant a certain degree of doubtfulness, but usually only a very small degree. In the immense majority of cases, they justify you in accepting testimony if there is no evidence to the contrary.

I come next to purely physical occurrences. Take, for example, our reason for believing in sound-waves. If a loud explosion occurs at some point, the time when different people hear it depends upon their distance from that point. We find it incredible that these different people, at different times, should all experience a loud noise, unless something had been happening in the intervening spaces. A system of events at places where there were ears, combined with a total absence of connected events elsewhere, strikes us as altogether too staccato to be credible. An even simpler example is the persistence of material objects. We cannot believe that Mount Everest ceases to exist when no one is seeing it, or that our room goes out with a pop when we leave it. There is no reason why we should believe such absurdities. The principles which lead us to reject them are essentially the same as those which lead us to believe that things have happened to us which we have now forgotten.

Not only science, but a great deal of common sense, is concerned, not with individual occurrences, but with general laws. Our knowledge of general laws, however, when it is empirical, is inferred, validly or invalidly, from our knowledge of a number of particular occurrences. 'Dogs bark' is a general law, but it could not be known if people had not heard particular dogs barking on particular occasions. I found that our knowledge of such particular occurrences raises problems which some philosophers, notably the logical positivists, have not sufficiently considered. These problems, however, are not those involved in non-demonstrative inference, since the inferences with which we are concerned can only be justifiable in virtue of some general law such as you employ when, hearing a bark, you infer a dog. The laws that science seeks are, for the most part, in some sense causal. And this brings me to the question: 'What do we mean by causal laws, and what evidence is there of their occurrence?'

It used to be the custom among philosophers to think that causal laws can be stated in the form 'A causes B', interpreted as meaning that whenever an event of a certain kind A occurs, it is followed by an event of another specified kind, B. It was held by many that a causal sequence involves something more than invariability and must have some character that can be called 'necessity'. Many empiricists, however, denied this and thought that nothing was involved except invariable sequence. This whole point of view, however, could never have persisted among philosophers if they had had any acquaintance with science. Causal laws must be either not invariable or such as state only tendencies. In classical dynamics they take the form of differential equations, stating acceleration, not actual occurrences. In modern physics the laws have become statistical: they do not state what will happen in any particular case, but only different things, each of which will happen in an assigned proportion of cases. For such reasons, causation is no longer what it used to be in the books of old-fashioned philosophers. Nevertheless, it still retains an essential place. Take, for example, what we mean by a single 'thing' which is more or less persistent. This 'thing' must really consist of a series of sets of occurrences, each set characterizing what we may call a momentary state of the 'thing'. The states of the 'thing' at different times are often, though not always, connected by means of laws which can be stated without mentioning other 'things'. If this were not the case, scientific knowledge could never get a start. Unless we can know something without knowing everything, it is obvious that we can never know something. And this applies, not only to particular events, but also to the laws connecting events. In physics, atoms and molecules persist for a time, and, if they did not, the conception of motion would become meaningless. A human body persists for a time, although the atoms and molecules of which it is composed are not always the same. A photon which travels from a star to a human eye persists throughout its journey, and if it did not, we should not be able to state what we mean by seeing a star. But all these kinds of persistence are only usual, not invariable, and the causal laws with which science begins must state only an approximation to what usually happens. Whether, in the end, something more exact is attainable, we do not know. What I think we can say is something like this: given any event, there is usually, at any neighbouring time and in some neighbouring place, an event very like the given event; and, as a rule, it is possible to discover some law approximately determining its small difference from the given event. Some such principle is necessary to explain the approximate persistence of many 'things', and also to explain the difference between perceiving A and perceiving B—for example, if A and B are stars, both of which we are seeing.

I give the name of 'causal line' to a series of events having the property that from any one of them something can be inferred as to neighbouring events in the series. It is the fact that such causal lines exist which has made the conception of 'things' useful to common sense, and the conception of 'matter' useful to physics. It is the fact that such causal lines are approximate, impermanent, and not universal which has caused modern physics to regard the conception of 'matter' as unsatisfactory.

There is another conception which seemed to me of great utility in non-demonstrative inference, namely that of 'structure'. It seems reasonable to suppose that, if you see red in one direction and blue in another, there is some difference between what is happening in the one direction and what is happening in the other. It follows that, though we may be compelled to admit that the external causes for our sensations of colour are not themselves coloured in the same sense in which our sensations are, nevertheless, when you see a pattern of colours, there must be a similar pattern in the causes of your sensations of colour. The conception of space-time structure as something which often remains constant, or approximately constant, throughout a series of causally connected events, is very important and very fruitful. Suppose, to take a very simple example, A reads aloud from a book and B takes down what he hears from dictation, and what A saw in the book is verbally identical with what B has written, it would be quite absurd to deny a causal connection between four sets of events—viz. (1) what is printed in the book, (2) the noises made by A in reading aloud, (3) the noises heard by B, and (4) the words written by B. The same sort of thing applies to the relation between a gramophone record and the music that it produces. Or, again, consider broadcasting, where sounds are transformed into electro-magnetic waves, and the electro-magnetic waves are transformed back into sound. It would be impossible for the spoken sounds and the heard sounds to resemble each other as closely as they do unless the intervening electro-magnetic waves had had a space-time structure very closely similar to that of the words, spoken and heard. There are, in nature, innumerable examples of complex structures transmitted causally throughout changes of intrinsic quality, such as those between sound and electro-magnetic waves in broadcasting. In fact, all visual and auditory perceptions have this character of transmitting structure but not intrinsic quality.

People unaccustomed to modern logic find it difficult to suppose that we can know about a space-time structure without knowing the qualities that compose it. This is part of a larger aspect of knowledge. Unless we are to land ourselves in preposterous paradoxes, we shall find it necessary to admit that we may know such propositions as 'all A is B' or 'some A is B', without being able to give any instance of A—e.g. 'all the numbers that I have never thought of and never shall think of are greater than a thousand'. Although this proposition is undeniable, I should contradict myself if I attempted to give an instance. The same sort of thing applies to space-time structure in the purely physical world, where there is no reason to suppose that the qualities composing the structure bear any intrinsic resemblance to the qualities that I know in sensible experience.

The general principles necessary to validate scientific inferences are not susceptible of proof in any ordinary sense. They are distilled out by analysis from particular cases which seem totally obvious, like the one that I gave a moment ago in which A dictates to B. There is a gradual development from what I call 'animal expectation' up to the most refined laws of quantum physics. The whole process starts from experiencing A and expecting B. An animal experiences a certain smell and expects the food to be good to eat. If its expectations were usually mistaken, it would die. Evolution and adaptation to environment cause expectations to be more often right than wrong, although the expectations go beyond anything logically demonstrable. Nature, we may say, has certain habits. The habits of animals must have a certain adaptation to the habits of nature if the animals are to survive.

This would be a poor argument if employed against Cartesian scepticism. But I do not think it is possible to get anywhere if we start from scepticism. We must start from a broad acceptance of whatever seems to be knowledge and is not rejected for some specific reason. Hypothetical scepticism is useful in logical dissection. It enables us to see how far we can get without this or that premiss—as, for example, we can inquire how much of geometry is possible without the axiom of parallels. But it is only for such purposes that hypothetical scepticism is useful.

Before explaining the exact epistemological function of the indemonstrable premisses of non-demonstrative inference something further must be said about induction.

Induction, as I said above, is not among the premisses of non-demonstrative inference. But this is not because it is not used; it is because in the form in which it is used it is not indemonstrable. Keynes, in his *Treatise on Probability*, made an extremely able investigation of the possibility of deriving induction from the mathematical theory of probability. The question that he had to investigate was this: given a number of instances of As which are Bs and no contrary instances, in what circumstances does the probability of the generalization 'all A is B' approach certainty as a limit when the number of As that are Bs is continually increased? The conclusion that he arrives at is that two conditions must be fulfiled if this is to happen. The first and more important of these conditions is that, before we know any instances of As that are Bs, the generalization 'all A is B' should have a finite probability on the basis of the remainder of our knowledge. The second condition is that the probability of our observing only favourable instances, if the generalization is false, should tend to zero as a limit when the number of inferences is sufficiently increased. This condition is found by Keynes to be satisfied if there is some probability short of certainty, say P, such that, given that the generalization is false and that $n - 1$ As have been found to be Bs, the chance that the nth A will be found to be a B is always less than P provided n is sufficiently great.

The second of these two conditions is less important than the first and is also much less inconvenient. I shall concentrate attention upon the first of the two conditions.

How are we to know that some suggested generalization has a finite probability in its favour before we have examined any of the evidence for or against it? It is this that we must know if Keynes's argument is to give any high degree of probability to a generalization when we know a great many instances in its favour and none against it. The postulates at which I arrived by an analysis of instances of non-demonstrative inference were intended to be such as would confer this finite *a priori* probability upon certain generalizations and not upon others. It will be observed that, in order that the postulates in question should fulfil their function, it is not necessary that they should be certain; it is only necessary that they should have a finite probability. In this respect they differ very profoundly from the kind of *a priori* principles that idealistic philosophers have sought, for such principles have been supposed by their advocates to possess a certainty greater than that of most empirical knowledge.

The postulates at which I finally arrived were five. I do not lay any stress upon their exact formulation. I think it highly probable that their number could be reduced and that they could be stated with more precision. But, while I am not persuaded that they are all *necessary*, I do think they are *sufficient*. It should be noted that all of them state only probabilities, not certainties, and are designed only to confer that finite antecedent probability which Keynes needs to validate his inductions. I have already said something in a preliminary way about these postulates, but I will now repeat them more exactly and more explicitly.

The first of these I call 'the postulate of quasi-permanence', which may be regarded, in a sense, as replacing Newton's first law of motion. It is in virtue of this postulate that common sense is able to operate more or less successfully with the concept of 'persons' and the concept of 'things'. It is also in virtue of this postulate that science and philosophy were able, for a long time, to make use of the concept of 'substance'. What the postulate states is as follows:

Given any event A, it happens very frequently that, at any neighbouring time, there is at some neighbouring place an event very similar to A.

This very similar event will be regarded by common sense as part of the history of the person or thing to whom the event A happened.

The second postulate is that of separable causal lines. This is perhaps the most important of all the five. It enables us, from partial knowledge, to make a partial probable inference. We believe that everything in the universe has, or may have, *some* effect upon everything else, and since we do not know everything in the universe, we cannot tell exactly and certainly what will happen to anything; but we can tell approximately and with probability; and if we could not, knowledge and scientific laws could never get started. The postulate is as follows:

It is frequently possible to form a series of events such that, from one or two members of the series, something can be inferred as to all the other members.

The most obvious examples are such things as sound waves and light waves. It is owing to the permanence of such waves that hearing and sight can give us information about more or less distant occurrences.

The third postulate is that of spatio-temporal continuity, which is mainly concerned to deny action at a distance. It maintains that, when there is a causal connection between two events that are not contiguous, there must be intermediate links in the causal chain. For example, if A hears what B says, we think that some process must have intervened between A and B. I do not feel sure, however, that this postulate could not be reduced to a tautology, since physical space-time is entirely inferential and the ordering of space-time events is dependent upon causality.

The fourth postulate, which I call 'the structural postulate', is very important and very fruitful. It is concerned with such cases as a number of people hearing the same speech or seeing the same performance in a theatre or, to take an example with wider scope, seeing the same stars in the sky. What the postulate says is as follows:

When a number of structurally similar complex events are ranged about a centre in regions not widely separated, it is usually the case that all belong to causal lines having their origin in an event of the same structure at the centre.

The importance of space-time structure, which I first emphasized in *The Analysis of Matter*, is very great. It explains how one complex event can be causally connected with another complex event, although they are not in any way qualitatively similar. They need only resemble each other in the abstract properties of their space-time structure. It is obvious that the electro-magnetic waves used in broadcasting cause the sensations of the hearers, but do not resemble them except in structural respects. It is because of the importance of structure that theoretical physics is able to content itself with formulae that are about unexperienced occurrences which need not, except in structure, resemble any of the occurrences that we experience.

The last postulate is that of analogy, the most important function of which is to justify the belief in other minds. The postulate is as follows:

Given two classes of events A and B, and given that, whenever both A and B can be observed, there is reason to believe that A causes B, then if, in a given case, A is observed, but there is no way of observing whether B occurs or not, it is probable that B occurs; and similarly if B is observed, but the presence or absence of A cannot be observed.

The above postulates, I repeat, are justified by the fact that they are implied in inferences which we all accept as valid, and that, although they cannot be proved in any formal sense, the whole system of science and everyday knowledge, out of which they have been distilled, is, within limits, self-confirmatory. I do not accept the coherence theory of *truth*, but there is a coherence theory of *probability* which is important and I think valid. Suppose you have two facts and a causal principle which connects them, the probability of all three may be greater than the probability of any one, and the more numerous and complex the inter-connected facts and principles become, the greater is the increase of probability derived from their mutual coherence. It is to be observed that, without the introduction of principles, no suggested collection of facts, or supposed facts, is either coherent or inconsistent, since no two facts can either imply or contradict each other except in virtue of some extra-logical principle. I believe that the above five principles, or something analogous to them, can form the basis for the kind of coherence which gives rise to the increased probability with which we have been concerned. Something vaguely called 'causality' or 'the uniformity of nature' appears in many discussions of scientific method. The purpose of my postulates is to substitute something more precise and more effective in place of such rather vague principles. I feel no great confidence in the precise postulates above enumerated, but I feel considerable confidence that something of the same sort is necessary if we are to justify the non-demonstrative inferences concerning which none of us, in fact, can feel any doubt.

Ever since I was engaged on *Principia Mathematica*, I have had a certain method of which at first I was scarcely conscious, but which has gradually become more explicit in my thinking. The method consists in an attempt to build a bridge between the world of sense and the world of science. I accept both as, in broad outline, not to be questioned. As in making a tunnel through an Alpine mountain, work must proceed from both ends in the hope that at last the labour will be crowned by a meeting in the middle.

Let us begin with the analysis of some body of scientific knowledge. All scientific knowledge uses artificially manufactured entities of which the purpose is to be easily manipulated by the methods of some calculus. The more advanced the science, the more true this is. Among empirical sciences, it is most completely true in physics. In an advanced science, such as physics, there is, for the philosopher, a preliminary labour of exhibiting the science as a deductive system starting with certain principles from which the rest follows logically and with certain real or supposed entities in terms of which everything dealt with by the science in question can, at least theoretically, be defined. If this labour has been adequately performed, the principles and entities, which remain as the residue after analysis, can be taken as hostages for the whole science in question, and the philosopher need no longer concern himself with the rest of the complicated knowledge which constitutes that science.

But no empirical science is intended merely as a coherent fairy-tale. It is intended to consist of statements having application to the real world and believed because of their relation to that world. Even the most abstract parts of science, such, for instance, as the general theory of relativity, are accepted because of observed facts. The philosopher is thus compelled to investigate the relation between observed facts and scientific abstractions. This is a long and arduous task. One of the reasons for its difficulty is that common sense, which is our starting-point, is already infected with theory, though of a crude and primitive kind. What we think that we observe is more than what we in fact observe, the 'more' being added by common-sense metaphysics and science. I am not suggesting that we should wholly reject the metaphysics and science of common sense, but only that it is part of what we have to examine. It does not belong to either of the two poles of formulated science, on the one hand, or unmixed observation, on the other.

I have been much criticized for applying the methods of mathematical logic to the interpretation of physics, but, in this matter, I am wholly unrepentant. It was Whitehead who first showed me what was possible in this field. Mathematical physics works with a space composed of points, a time composed of instants, and a matter composed of punctual particles. No modern mathematical physicist supposes that there are such things in nature. But it is possible, given a higgledy-piggledy collection of things destitute of the smooth properties that mathematicians like, to make structures composed of these things and having the properties which are convenient to the mathematician. It is because this is possible that mathematical physics is more than an idle amusement. And it is mathematical logic which shows how such structures are to be made. For this reason, mathematical logic is an essential tool in constructing the bridge between sense and science of which I spoke above.

The method of Cartesian doubt, which appealed to me when I was young and may still serve as a tool in the work of logical dissection, no longer seems to me to have fundamental validity. Universal scepticism cannot be refuted, but also cannot be accepted. I have come to accept the facts of sense and the broad truth of science as things which the philosopher should take as data, since, though their truth is not quite certain, it has a higher degree of probability than anything likely to be achieved in philosophical speculation.

In the transition from crude fact to science, we need forms of inference additional to those of deductive logic. Traditionally, it was supposed that induction would serve this purpose, but this was an error, since it can be shown that the conclusions of inductive inferences from true premises are more often false than true. The principles of inference required for the transition from sense to science are to be attained by analysis. The analysis involved is that of the kinds of inference which nobody, in fact, questions: as, for example, that if, at one moment, you see your cat on the hearth-rug and, at another, you see it in a doorway, it has passed over intermediate positions although you did not see it doing so. If the work of analysing scientific inference has been properly performed, it will appear that concrete instances of such inferences are (*a*) such as no one honestly doubts, and (*b*) such as are essential if, on the basis of sensible facts, we are to believe things which go beyond this basis.

The outcome of such work is to be regarded rather as science than as philosophy. That is to say, the reasons for accepting it are the ordinary reasons applied in scientific work, not remote reasons derived from some metaphysical theory. More especially, there is no such claim to certainty as has, too often and too uselessly, been made by rash philosophers.

(*My Philosophical Development*, London: Allen & Unwin; New York: Simon & Schuster, 1959.)

PART XVII

The Analyst of International Affairs

Any cursory attempt to assess international affairs is, of course, only indulged in by the uneducated. The analyst of world problems in the second half of the twentieth century is faced with a peculiar dilemma. The turbulence of the period and the unpredictability of human behaviour make even the most exhaustive attempt exceedingly uncertain. Mistakes in science and business are both costly and deplorable but continued mistakes in international affairs today could result in the destruction of civilization as we know it.

Russell has, perhaps more than other thinkers in our time, successfully seen through the maze of conflicting fanaticisms, and with his characteristic sobriety pointed out fallacies in the arguments of proposed saviours. He was among the earliest of severe critics of Marxism and of its Soviet manifestations, but not without a recognition of the realities which require a world perspective for the solution of the problems confronting us in this nuclear age.

71

THE TAMING OF POWER

'IN passing by the side of Mount Thai, Confucius came on a woman who was weeping bitterly by a grave. The Master pressed forward and drove quickly to her; then he sent Tze-lu to question her. "Your wailing", said he, "is that of one who has suffered sorrow on sorrow." She replied, "that is so. Once my husband's father was killed here by a tiger. My husband was also killed, and now my son has died in the same way." The Master said, "why do you not leave the place?" The answer was, "there is no oppressive government here". The Master then said, "Remember this, my children: oppressive government is more terrible than tigers". '

The subject of the present chapter is the problem of ensuring that government shall be *less* terrible than tigers.

The problem of the taming of power is, as the above quotation shows, a very ancient one. The Taoists thought it insoluble, and advocated anarchism; the Confucians trusted to a certain ethical and governmental training which should turn the holders of power into sages endowed with moderation and benevolence. At the same period, in Greece, democracy, oligarchy, and tyranny were contending for mastery; democracy was intended to check abuses of power, but was perpetually defeating itself by falling a victim to the temporary popularity of some demagogue. Plato, like Confucius, sought the solution in a government of men trained to wisdom. This view has been revived by Mr and Mrs Sidney Webb, who admire an oligarchy in which power is confined to those who have the 'vocation of leadership'. In the interval between Plato and the Webbs, the world has tried military autocracy, theocracy, hereditary monarchy, oligarchy, democracy, and the Rule of the Saints—the last of these, after the failure of Cromwell's experiment, having been revived in our day by Lenin and Hitler. All this suggests that our problem has not yet been solved.

To anyone who studies history or human nature, it must be evident that democracy, while not a complete solution, is an essential part of the solution. The complete solution is not to be found by confining ourselves to political conditions; we must take account also of economics, of propaganda, and of psychology as affected by circumstances and education.

Our subject thus divides itself into four parts: (I) political conditions, (II) economic conditions, (III) propaganda conditions, and (IV) psychological and educational conditions. Let us take these in succession.

I

The merits of democracy are negative: it does not ensure good government, but it prevents certain evils. Until women began to take part in political affairs, married women had no control over their own property, or even over their own earnings; a charwoman with a drunken husband had no redress if he prevented her from using her wages for support of her children. The oligarchical Parliament of the eighteenth and early nineteenth centuries used its legislative power to increase the wealth of the rich by depressing the condition of both rural and urban labour. Only democracy has prevented the law from making trade unionism impossible. But for democracy, Western America, Australia, and New Zealand would be inhabited by a semi-servile yellow population governed by a small white aristocracy. The evils of slavery and serfdom are familiar, and wherever a minority has a secure monopoly of political power, the majority is likely to sink, sooner or later, into either slavery or serfdom. All history shows that, as might be expected, minorities cannot be trusted to care for the interests of majorities.

There is a tendency, as strong now as at any former time, to suppose that an oligarchy is admirable if it consists of 'good' men. The government of the Roman Empire was 'bad' until Constantine, and then it became 'good'. In the Book of Kings, there were those who did right in the sight of the Lord, and those who did evil. In English history as taught to children, there are 'good' kings and 'bad' kings. An oligarchy of Jews is 'bad', but one of Nazis is 'good'. The oligarchy of Tsarist aristocrats was 'bad', but that of the Communist Party is 'good'.

This attitude is unworthy of grown-up people. A child is 'good' when it obeys orders, and 'naughty' when it does not. When it grows up and becomes a political leader, it retains the ideas of the nursery, and defines the 'good' as those who obey its orders and the 'bad' as those who defy it. Consequently our own political party consists of 'good' men, and the opposite party consists of 'bad' men. 'Good' government is government by our group, 'bad' government that by the other group. The Montagues are 'good', the Capulets 'bad', or vice versa.

Such a point of view, if taken seriously, makes social life impossible. Only force can decide which group is 'good' and which 'bad', and the decision, when made, may at any moment be upset by an insurrection. Neither group, if it attains power, will care for the interests of the other, except in so far as it is controlled by the fear of rousing rebellion. Social life, if it is to be anything better than tyranny, demands a certain impartiality. But since, in many matters, collective action is necessary, the only practicable form of impartiality, in such matters, is the rule of the majority.

Democracy, however, though necessary, is by no means the only political condition required for the taming of power. It is possible, in a democracy, for the majority to exercise a brutal and wholly unnecessary tyranny over a minority. In the period from 1885 to 1922, the government of the United Kingdom was (except for the exclusion of women) democratic, but that did not prevent the oppression of Ireland. Not only a national, but a religious or political minority may be persecuted. The safeguarding of minorities, so far as is compatible with orderly government, is an essential part of the taming of power.

This requires a consideration of the matters as to which the community must act as a whole, and those as to which uniformity is unnecessary. The most obvious questions as to which a collective decision is imperative are those that are essentially geographical. Roads, railways, sewers, gas mains, and so on, must take one course and not another. Sanitary precautions, say against plague or rabies, are geographical: it would not do for Christian Scientists to announce that they will take no precautions against infection, because they might infect others. War is a geographical phenomenon, unless it is civil war, and even then it soon happens that one area is dominated by one side, and another by the other.

Where there is a geographically concentrated minority, such as the Irish before 1922, it is possible to solve a great many problems by devolution. But when the minority is distributed throughout the area concerned, this method is largely inapplicable. Where Christian and Mohammedan populations live side by side, they have, it is true, different marriage laws, but except where religion is concerned they all have to submit to one government. It has been gradually discovered that theological uniformity is not necessary to a State, and that Protestants and Catholics can live peaceably together under one government. But this was not the case during the first 130 years after the Reformation.

The question of the degree of liberty that is compatible with order is one that cannot be settled in the abstract. The only thing that can be said in the abstract is that, where there is no technical reason for a collective decision, there should be some strong reason connected with public order if freedom is to be interfered with. In the reign of Elizabeth, when Roman Catholics wished to deprive her of the throne, it is not surprising that the government viewed them with disfavour. Similarly in the Low Countries, where Protestants were in revolt against Spain, it was to be expected that the Spaniards would persecute them. Nowadays theological questions have not the same political importance. Even political differences, if they do not go too deep, are no reason for persecution. Conservatives,

Liberals, and Labour people can all live peaceably side by side, because they do not wish to alter the Constitution by force; but Fascists and Communists are more difficult to assimilate. Where there is democracy, attempts of a minority to seize power by force, and incitements to such attempts, may reasonably be forbidden, on the ground that a law-abiding majority has a right to a quiet life if it can secure it. But there should be toleration of all propaganda not involving incitement to break the law, and the law should be as tolerant as is compatible with technical efficiency and the maintenance of order. I shall return to this subject under the head of psychology.

From the point of view of the taming of power, very difficult questions arise as to the best size of a governmental unit. In a great modern State, even when it is a democracy, the ordinary citizen has very little sense of political power; he does not decide what are to be the issues in an election, they probably concern matters remote from his daily life and almost wholly outside his experience, and his vote makes so small a contribution to the total as to seem to himself negligible. In the ancient City State these evils were much less; so they are, at present, in local government. It might have been expected that the public would take more interest in local than in national questions, but this is not the case; on the contrary, the larger the area concerned, the greater is the percentage of the electorate that takes the trouble to vote. This is partly because more money is spent on propaganda in important elections, partly because the issues are in themselves more exciting. The most exciting issues are those involving war and relations to possible enemies. I remember an old yokel in January 1910, who told me he was going to vote Conservative (which was against his economic interests), because he had been persuaded that if the Liberals were victorious the Germans would be in the country within a week. It is not to be supposed that he ever voted in Parish Council elections, though in them he might have had some understanding of the issues; these issues failed to move him because they were not such as to generate mass hysteria or the myths upon which it feeds.

There is thus a dilemma: democracy gives a man a feeling that he has an effective share in political power when the group concerned is small, but not when it is large; on the other hand, the issue is likely to strike him as important when the group concerned is large, but not when it is small.

To some extent this difficulty is avoided when a constituency is vocational, not geographical; a really effective democracy is possible, for example, in a trade union. Each branch can meet to discuss a vexed question of policy; the members have a similarity of interest and experience, and this makes fruitful discussion possible. The final decision of the whole union may, therefore, be one in which a large percentage of members feel that they have had a part.

This method, however, has obvious limitations. Many questions are so essentially geographical that a geographical constituency is unavoidable. Public bodies affect our lives at so many points that a busy man who is not a politician cannot take action about most of the local or national issues that concern him. The best solution would probably be an extension of the method of the trade union official, who is elected to represent a certain interest. At present, many interests have no such representative. Democracy, if it is to exist psychologically as well as politically, demands organization of the various interests, and their representation, in political bargaining, by men who enjoy whatever influence is justified by the numbers and enthusiasm of their constituents. I do not mean that these representatives should be a substitute for Parliament, but that they should be the channel by which Parliament is made aware of the wishes of various groups of citizens.

A federal system is desirable whenever the local interests and sentiments of the constituent units are stronger than the interests and sentiments connected with the federation. If there were ever an international government, it would obviously have to be a federation of national governments, with strictly defined powers. There are already international authorities for certain purposes, e.g. postage, but these are purposes which do not interest the public so much as do those dealt with by national governments. Where this condition is absent, the federal government tends to encroach upon the governments of the several units. In the United States, the federal government has gained at the expense of the States ever since the Constitution was first enacted. The same tendency existed in Germany from 1871 to 1918. Even a federal government of the world, if it found itself involved in a civil war on the question of secession, as might well happen, would, if victorious, be immeasurably strengthened as against the various national governments. Thus the efficacy of federation, as a method, has very definite limits; but within these limits it is desirable and important.

Very large governmental areas are, it would seem, quite unavoidable in the modern world; indeed, for some of the most important purposes, especially peace and war, the whole world is the only adequate area. The psychological disadvantage of large areas—especially the sense of impotence in the average voter, and his ignorance as to most of the issues—must be admitted, and minimized as far as possible, partly, as suggested above, by the organization of separate interests, and partly by federation or devolution. Some subjection of the individual is an inevitable consequence of increasing social organization. But if the danger of war were eliminated, local questions would again come to the fore, and men's political interests would be much more concerned than at present with questions as to which they could have both knowledge and an effective voice. For it is the fear of war, more than anything else, which compels men to direct their attention to distant countries and to the external activities of their own government.

Where democracy exists, there is still need to safeguard individuals and minorities against tyranny, both because tryanny is undesirable in itself, and because it is likely to lead to breaches of order. Montesquieu's advocacy of the separation of legislative, executive, and judiciary, the traditional English belief in checks and balances, Bentham's political doctrines, and the whole of nineteenth-century liberalism, were designed to prevent the arbitrary exercise of power. But such methods have come to be considered incompatible with efficiency. No doubt the separation of the War Office and the Horse Guards was a safeguard against military dictatorship, but it had disastrous results in the Crimean War. When, in former times, the legislature and the executive disagreed, the result was a highly inconvenient deadlock; now in England, efficiency is secured by uniting both powers, to all intents and purposes, in the Cabinet. The eighteenth- and nineteenth-century methods of preventing arbitrary power no longer suit our circumstances, and such new methods as exist are not yet very effective. There is need of associations to safeguard this or that form of liberty, and to bring swift criticism to bear upon officials, police, magistrates and judges who exceed their powers. There is need also of a certain political balance in every important branch of the public service. For example, there is danger to democracy in the fact that average opinion in the police and the air force is far more reactionary than in the country at large.

In every democracy, individuals and organizations which are intended to have only certain well-defined executive functions are likely, if unchecked, to acquire a very undesirable independent power. This is especially true of the police. The evils resulting from an insufficiently supervised police force are very forcibly set forth, as regards the United States, in *Our Lawless Police*, by Ernest Jerome Hopkins. The gist of the matter is that a policeman is promoted for action leading to the conviction of a criminal, that the Courts accept confession as evidence of guilt, and that, in consequence, it is to the interest of individual officers to torture arrested persons until they confess. This evil exists in all countries in a greater or less degree. In India it is rampant. The desire to obtain a confession was the basis of the tortures of the Inquisition. In Old China, torture of suspected persons was habitual, because a humanitarian Emperor had decreed that no man should be condemned except on his own confession. For the taming of the power of the police, one essential is that a confession shall never, in any circumstances, be accepted as evidence.

This reform, however, though necessary, is by no means sufficient. The police system of all countries is based upon the assumption that the collection of evidence against a suspected criminal is a matter of public interest, but that the collection of evidence in his favour is his private concern. It is often said to be more important that the innocent should be acquitted than that the guilty should be condemned, but everywhere it is the duty of the police to seek evidence of guilt, not of innocence. Suppose you are unjustly accused of murder, and there is a good *prima facie* case against you. The whole of the resources of the State are set in motion to seek out possible witnesses against you, and the ablest lawyers are employed by the State to create prejudice against you in the minds of the jury. You, meanwhile, must spend your private fortune collecting evidence of your innocence, with no public organization to help you. If you plead poverty, you will be allotted Counsel, but probably not so able a man as the public prosecutor. If you succeed in securing an acquittal, you can only escape bankruptcy by means of the cinemas and the Sunday Press. But it is only too likely that you will be unjustly convicted.

If law-abiding citizens are to be protected against unjust persecution by the police, there must be two police forces and two Scotland Yards, one designed, as at present, to prove guilt, the other to prove innocence; and in addition to the public prosecutor there must be a public defender, of equal legal eminence. This is obvious as soon as it is admitted that the acquittal of the innocent is no less a public interest than the condemnation of the guilty. The defending police force should, moreover, become the prosecuting police force where one class of crime is concerned, namely crimes committed by the prosecuting police in the execution of their 'duty'. By this means, but by no other (so far as I can see), the present oppressive power of the police could be mitigated.

II

I come now to the economic conditions required in order to minimize arbitrary power. This subject is of great importance, both on its own account, and because there has been a very great deal of confusion of thought in relation to it.

Political democracy, while it solves a part of our problems, does not by any means solve the whole. Marx pointed out that there could be no real equalization of power through politics alone, while economic power remained monarchical or oligarchic. It followed that economic power must be in the hands of the State, and that the State must be democratic. Those who profess, at the present day, to be Marx's followers, have kept only the half of his doctrine, and have thrown over the demand that the State should be democratic. They have thus concentrated both economic and political power in the hands of an oligarchy, which has become, in consequence, more powerful and more able to exercise tryanny than any oligarchy of former times.

Both old-fashioned democracy and new-fashioned Marxism have aimed at the taming of power. The former failed because it was only political, the latter because it was only economic. Without a combination of both, nothing approaching to a solution of the problem is possible.

The arguments in favour of State ownership of land and the large economic organizations are partly technical, partly political. The technical arguments have not been much stressed except by the Fabian Society, and to some extent in America in connection with such matters as the Tennessee Valley Authority. Nevertheless they are very strong, especially in connection with electricity and water power, and cause even Conservative governments to introduce measures which, from a technical point of view, are socialistic. We have seen how, as a result of modern technique, organizations tend to grow and to coalesce and to increase their scope; the inevitable consequence is that the political State must either increasingly take over economic functions, or partially abdicate in favour of vast private enterprises which are sufficiently powerful to defy or control it. If the State does not acquire supremacy over such enterprises, it becomes their puppet, and they become the real State. In one way or another, wherever modern technique exists, economic and political power must become unified. This movement towards unification has the irresistible impersonal character which Marx attributed to the development that he prophesied. But it has nothing to do with the class war or the wrongs of the proletariat.

Socialism as a political movement has aimed at furthering the interests of industrial wage-earners; its technical advantages have been kept comparatively in the background. The belief is that the economic power of the private capitalist enables him to oppress the wage-earner, and that, since the wage-earner cannot, like the handicraftsman of former times, individually own his means of production, the only way of emancipating him is collective ownership by the whole body of workers. It is argued that, if the private capitalist were expropriated, the whole body of the workers would constitute the State; and that, consequently, the problem of economic power can be solved completely by State ownership of land and capital, and in no other way. This is a proposal for the taming of economic power, and therefore comes within the purview of our present discussion.

Before examining the argument, I wish to say unequivocally that I consider it valid, provided it is adequately safeguarded and amplified. *Per contra*, in the absence of such safeguarding and amplifying I consider it very dangerous, and likely to mislead those who seek liberation from economic tyranny so completely that they will find they have inadvertently established a new tyranny at once economic and political, more drastic and more terrible than any previously known.

In the first place, 'ownership' is not the same thing as 'control'. If (say) a railway is owned by the State, and the State is considered to be the whole body of the citizens, that does not ensure, of itself, that the average citizen will have any power over the railway. Let us revert, for a moment, to what Messrs Berle and Means say about ownership and control in large American corporations. They point out that, in the majority of such corporations, all the directors together usually own only about one or two per cent of the stock, and yet, in effect, have complete control:

'In the election of the board the stock holder ordinarily has three alternatives. He can refrain from voting, he can attend the annual meeting and personally vote his stock, or he can sign a proxy transferring his voting power to certain individuals selected by the management of the corporation, the proxy committee. As his personal vote will count for little or nothing at the meeting unless he has a very large block of stock, the stock holder is practically reduced to the alternative of not voting at all or else of *handing over his vote to individuals over whom he has no control and in whose selection he did not participate.* In neither case will he be able to exercise any measure of control. Rather, control will tend to be in the hands of those who select the proxy committee. . . . Since the proxy committee is appointed by the existing management, the latter can virtually dictate their own successors.'[1]

The helpless individuals described in the above passage are, it should be noted, not proletarians, but capitalists. They are part owners of the corporation concerned, in the sense that they have legal rights which may, with luck, bring them in a certain income; but owing to their lack of control, the income is very precarious. When I first visited the United States in 1896, I was struck by the enormous number of railways that were bankrupt; on inquiry, I found that this was not due to incompetence on the part of the directors, but to skill: the investments of ordinary shareholders had been transferred, by one device or another, to other companies in which the directors had a large interest. This was a crude method, and nowadays matters are usually managed in a more decorous fashion, but the principle remains the same. In any large corporation, power is necessarily less diffused than ownership, and carries with it advantages which, though at first political, can be made sources of wealth to an indefinite extent. The humble investor can be politely and legally robbed; the only limit is that he must not have such bitter experiences as to lead him to keep his future savings in a stocking.

The situation is in no way essentially different when the State takes the place of a corporation; indeed, since it is the size of the corporation that causes the helplessness of the average shareholder, the average citizen is likely to be still more helpless as against the State. A battleship is public property, but if, on this ground, you try to exercise rights of ownership, you will be soon put in your place. You have a remedy, it is

[1] Op. cit., pp. 86–7.

true: at the next General Election, you can vote for a candidate who favours a reduction in the Navy Estimates, if you can find one; or you can write to the papers to urge that sailors should be more polite to sightseers. But more than this you cannot do.

But, it is said, the battleship belongs to a capitalist State, and when it belongs to a workers' State everything will be different. This view seems to me to show a failure to grasp the fact that economic power is now a matter of government rather than ownership. If the United States Steel Corporation, say, were taken over by the United States Government, it would still need men to manage it; they would either be the same men who now manage it, or men with similar abilities and a similar outlook. The attitude which they now have towards the shareholders they would then have towards the citizens. True, they would be subject to the government, but unless it was democratic and responsive to public opinion, it would have a point of view closely similar to that of the officials.

Marxists, having retained, as a result of the authority of Marx and Engels, many ways of thinking that belong to the forties of last century, still conceive of businesses as if they belonged to individual capitalists, and have not learnt the lessons to be derived from the separation of ownership and control. The important person is the man who has control of economic power, not the man who has a fraction of the nominal ownership. The Prime Minister does not own No. 10 Downing Street, and Bishops do not own their palaces; but it would be absurd to pretend, on this account, that they are no better off as regards housing than the average wage-earner. Under any form of Socialism which is not democratic, those who control economic power can, without 'owning' anything, have palatial official residences, the use of the best cars, a princely entertainment allowance, holidays at the public expense in official holiday resorts, and so on and so on. And why should they have any more concern for the ordinary worker than those in control have now? There can be no reason why they should have, unless the ordinary worker has power to deprive them of their positions. Moreover the subordination of the small investor in existing large corporations shows how easy it is for the official to overpower the democracy, even when the 'democracy' consists of capitalists.

Not only, therefore, is democracy essential if State ownership and control of economic enterprises is to be in any degree advantageous to the average citizen, but it will have to be an effective democracy, and this will be more difficult to secure than it is at present, since the official class will, unless very carefully supervised, combine the powers at present possessed by the government and the men in control of industry and finance, and since the means of agitating against the government will have to be supplied by the government itself, as the sole owner of halls, paper, and all the other essentials of propaganda.

While, therefore, public ownership and control of all large-scale industry and finance is a *necessary* condition for the taming of power, it is far from being a *sufficient* condition. It needs to be supplemented by a democracy more thorough-going, more carefully safeguarded against official tyranny, and with more deliberate provision for freedom of propaganda, than any purely political democracy that has ever existed.

The dangers of State Socialism divorced from democracy have been illustrated by the course of events in the USSR. There are those whose attitude to Russia is one of religious faith; to them, it is impious even to examine the evidence that all is not well in that country. But the testimony of former enthusiasts is becoming more and more convincing to those whose minds are open to reason on the subject. The arguments from history and psychology have shown how rash it is to expect irresponsible power to be benevolent. What actually happens, as regards power, is summed up by Eugene Lyons in the following words:

'Absolutism at the top implies hundreds of thousands, even millions, of large and small autocrats in a state that monopolizes all means of life and expression, work and pleasure, rewards and punishments. A centralized autocratic rule must function through a human machine of delegated authority, a pyramid of graded officialdom, each layer subservient to those above and overbearing to those below. Unless there are brakes of genuinely democratic control and the corrective of a hard and fast legality to which everyone, even the anointed of the Lord, is subjected, the machine of power becomes an engine of oppression. Where there is only one employer, namely, the State, meekness is the first law of economic survival. Where the same group of officials wields the terrible power of secret arrests and punishments, disfranchisement, hiring and firing, assignment of ration categories and living space—only an imbecile or someone with a perverted taste for martydom will fail to kow-tow to them.'[1]

If concentration of power in a single organization—the State—is not to produce the evils of despotism in an extreme form, it is essential that power within that organization should be widely distributed, and that subordinate groups should have a large measure of autonomy. Without democracy, devolution, and immunity from extra-legal punishment, the coalescence of economic and political power is nothing but a new and appalling instrument of tyranny. In Russia, a peasant on a collective farm who takes any portion of the grain that he has himself grown is liable to the death penalty. This law was made at a time when millions of peasants were dying of hunger and attendant diseases, owing to the famine which the government deliberately refrained from alleviating.[2]

[1] *Assignment in Utopia*, p. 195.   [2] Ibid., p. 492.

III

I come now to the propaganda conditions for the taming of power. It is obvious that publicity for grievances must be possible; agitation must be free provided it does not incite to breaches of the law; there must be ways of impeaching officials who exceed or abuse their powers. The government of the day must not be in a position to secure its own permanence by intimidation, falsification of the register of electors, or any similar method. There must be no penalty, official or unofficial, for any well-grounded criticism of prominent men. Much of this, at present, is secured by party government in democratic countries, which causes the politicians in power to be objects of hostile criticism by nearly half the nation. This makes it impossible for them to commit many crimes to which they might otherwise be prone.

All this is more important when the State has a monopoly of economic power than it is under capitalism, since the power of the State will be vastly augmented. Take a concrete case: that of women employed in the public service. At present they have a grievance, because their rates of pay are lower than those of men; they have legitimate ways of making their grievance known, and it would not be safe to penalize them for making use of these ways. There is no reason whatever for supposing that the present inequality would necessarily cease with the adoption of Socialism, but the means of agitating about it would cease, unless express provision were made for just such cases. Newspapers and printing presses would all belong to the government, and would print only what the government ordered. Can it be assumed as certain that the government would print attacks on its own policy? If not, there would be no means of political agitation by means of print. Public meetings would be just as difficult, since the halls would all belong to the government. Consequently, unless careful provision were made for the express purpose of safeguarding political liberty, no method would exist of making grievances known, and the government, when once elected, would be as omnipotent as Hitler, and could easily arrange for its own re-election to the end of time. Democracy might survive as a form, but would have no more reality than the forms of popular government that lingered on under the Roman Empire.

To suppose that irresponsible power, just because it is called Socialist or Communist, will be freed miraculously from the bad qualities of all arbitrary power in the past, is mere childish nursery psychology: the wicked prince is ousted by the good prince, and all is well. If a prince is to be trusted, it must be not because he is 'good', but because it is against his interest to be 'bad'. To insure that this shall be the case is to make power innocuous; but it cannot be rendered innocuous by transforming men whom we believe to be 'good' into irresponsible despots.

The BBC is a State institution which shows what is possible in the way of combining freedom of propaganda with government monopoly. At such a time as that of the General Strike, it must be admitted, it ceases to be impartial; but at ordinary times it represents different points of view, as nearly as may be, in proportion to their numerical strength. In a Socialist State, similar arrangements for impartiality would have to be made in regard to the hiring of halls for meetings and the printing of controversial literature. It might be found desirable instead of having different newspapers representing different points of view, to have only one, with different pages allocated to different parties. This would have the advantage that readers would see all opinions, and would tend to be less one-sided than those who, at present, never see in a newspaper anything with which they disagree.

There are certain regions, such as art and science, and (so far as public order allows) party politics, where uniformity is not necessary or even desirable. These are the legitimate sphere of competition, and it is important that public feeling should be such as to bear differences on such matters without exasperation. Democracy, if it is to succeed and endure, demands a tolerant spirit, not too much hate, and not too much love of violence. But this brings us to the psychological conditions for the taming of power.

IV

The psychological conditions for the taming of power are in some ways the most difficult. In connection with the psychology of power, we saw that fear, rage, and all kinds of violent collective excitement, tend to make men blindly follow a leader, who, in most cases, takes advantage of their trust to establish himself as a tyrant. It is therefore important, if democracy is to be preserved, both to avoid the circumstances that produce general excitement, and to educate in such a way that the population shall be little prone to moods of this sort. Where a spirit of ferocious dogmatism prevails, any opinion with which men disagree is liable to provoke a breach of the peace. Schoolboys are apt to ill-treat a boy whose opinions are in any way odd, and many grown men have not got beyond the mental age of schoolboys. A diffused liberal sentiment, tinged with scepticism, makes social co-operation much less difficult, and liberty correspondingly more possible.

Revivalist enthusiasm, such as that of the Nazis, rouses admiration in many through the energy and apparent self-abnegation that it generates. Collective excitement, involving indifference to pain and even to death, is historically not uncommon. Where it exists, liberty is impossible. The enthusiasts can only be restrained by force, and if they are not restrained they will use force against others. I remember a Bolshevik whom I met in Peking in 1920, who marched up and down the room exclaiming with complete truth: 'If vee do not keel zem, zay vill keel us'! The existence of this mood on one side of course generates the same mood on the other side: the consequence is a fight to a finish, in which everything is subordinated to victory. During the fight, the government acquires despotic power for military reasons; at the end, if victorious, it uses its power first to crush what remains of the enemy, and then to secure the continuance of its dictatorship over its own supporters. The result is something quite different from what was fought for by the enthusiasts. Enthusiasm, while it can achieve certain results, can hardly ever achieve those that it desires. To admire collective enthusiasm is reckless and irresponsible, for its fruits are fierceness, war, death, and slavery.

War is the chief promoter of despotism, and the greatest obstacle to the establishment of a system in which irresponsible power is avoided, as far as possible. The prevention of war is therefore an essential part of our problem—I should say, the most essential. I believe that, if once the world were freed from the fear of war, under no matter what form of government or what economic system, it would in time find ways of curbing the ferocity of its rulers. On the other hand, all war, but especially modern war, promotes dictatorship by causing the timid to seek a leader and by converting the bolder spirits from a society into a pack.

The risk of war causes a certain kind of mass psychology, and reciprocally this kind, where it exists, increases the risk of war, as well as the likelihood of despotism. We have therefore to consider the kind of education which will make societies least prone to collective hysteria, and most capable of successfully practising democracy.

Democracy, if it is to succeed, needs a wide diffusion of two qualities which seem, at first sight, to tend in opposite directions. On the one hand, men must have a certain degree of self-reliance and a certain willingness to back their own judgement; there must be political propaganda in opposite directions, in which many people take part. But on the other hand men must be willing to submit to the decision of the majority when it goes against them. Either of these conditions may fail: the population may be too submissive, and may follow a vigorous leader into dictatorship; or each party may be too self-assertive, with the result that the nation falls into anarchy.

What education has to do in this matter may be considered under two heads: first, in relation to character and the emotions; secondly, in relation to instruction. Let us begin with the former.

If democracy is to be workable, the population must be as far as possible free from hatred and destructiveness, and also from fear and subservience. These feelings may be caused by political or economic circumstances, but what I want to consider is the part that education plays in making men more or less prone to them.

Some parents and some schools begin with the attempt to teach children complete obedience, an attempt which is almost bound to produce either a slave or a rebel, neither of which is what is wanted in a democracy. As to the effects of a severely disciplinary education, the view that I hold is held by all the dictators of Europe. After the war, almost all the countries of Europe had a number of free schools, without too much discipline or too much show of respect for the teachers; but one by one, the military autocracies, including the Soviet Republic, have suppressed all freedom in schools and have gone back to the old drill, and to the practice of treating the teacher as a miniature Führer or Duce. The dictators, we may infer, all regard a certain degree of freedom in school as the proper training for democracy, and autocracy in school as the natural prelude to autocracy in the State.

Every man and woman in a democracy should be neither a slave nor a rebel, but a citizen, that is, a person who has, and allows to others, a due proportion, but no more, of the governmental mentality. Where democracy does not exist, the governmental mentality is that of masters towards dependants; but where there is democracy it is that of equal co-operation, which involves the assertion of one's own opinion up to a certain point, but no further.

This brings us to a source of trouble to many democrats, namely what is called 'principle'. Most talk about principle, self-sacrifice, heroic devotion to a cause, and so on, should be scanned somewhat sceptically. A little psycho-analysis will often show that what goes by these fine names is really something quite different, such as pride, or hatred, or desire for revenge, that has become idealized and collectivized and personified as a noble form of idealism. The warlike patriot, who is willing and even anxious to fight for his country, may reasonably be suspected of a certain pleasure in killing. A kindly population, a population who in their childhood had received kindness and been made happy, and who in youth had found the world a friendly place, would not develop that particular sort of idealism called patriotism, or class-war, or what not, which consists in joining together to kill people in large numbers. I think the tendency to cruel forms of idealism is increased by unhappiness in childhood, and would be lessened if early education were emotionally what it ought to be. Fanaticism is a defect which is partly emotional, partly intellectual; it needs to be combated by the kind of happiness that makes men kindly, and the kind of intelligence that produces a scientific habit of mind.

The temper required to make a success of democracy is, in the practical life, exactly what the scientific temper is in the intellectual life; it is a half-way house between scepticism and dogmatism. Truth, it holds, is neither completely attainable nor completely unattainable; it is attainable to a certain degree, and that only with difficulty.

Autocracy, in its modern forms, is always combined with a creed: that of Hitler, that of Mussolini, or that of Stalin. Wherever there is autocracy, a set of beliefs is instilled into the minds of the young before they are capable of thinking, and these beliefs are taught so constantly and so persistently that it is hoped the pupils will never afterwards be able to escape from the hypnotic effect of their early lessons. The beliefs are instilled, not by giving any reason for supposing them true, but by parrot-like repetition, by mass hysteria and mass suggestion. When two opposite creeds have been taught in this fashion, they produce two armies which clash, not two parties that can discuss. Each hypnotized automaton feels that everything most sacred is bound up with the victory of his side, everything most horrible exemplified by the other side. Such fanatical factions cannot meet in Parliament and say 'let us see which side has the majority'; that would be altogether too pedestrian, since each side stands for a sacred cause. This sort of dogmatism must be prevented if dictatorships are to be avoided, and measures for preventing it ought to form an essential part of education.

If I had control of education, I should expose children to the most vehement and eloquent advocates on all sides of every topical question, who should speak to the schools from the BBC. The teacher should afterwards invite the children to summarize the arguments used, and should gently insinuate the view that eloquence is inversely proportional to solid reason. To acquire immunity to eloquence is of the utmost importance to the citizens of a democracy.

Modern propagandists have learnt from advertisers, who led the way in the technique of producing irrational belief. Education should be designed to counteract the natural credulity and the natural incredulity of the uneducated: the habit of believing an emphatic statement without reasons, and of disbelieving an unemphatic statement even when accompanied by the best of reasons. I should begin in the infant school, with two classes of sweets between which the children should choose: one very nice, recommended by a coldly accurate statement as to its ingredients; the other very nasty, recommended by the utmost skill of the best advertisers. A little later I should give them a choice of two places for a country holiday: a nice place recommended by a contour map, and an ugly place recommended by magnificent posters.

The teaching of history ought to be conducted in a similar spirit. There have been in the past eminent orators and writers who defended with an appearance of great wisdom positions which no one now holds: the reality of witchcraft, the beneficence of slavery, and so on. I should cause the young to know such masters of eloquence, and to appreciate at once their rhetoric and their wrong-headedness. Gradually I should pass on to current questions. As a sort of *bonne bouche* to their history, I should read to them what is said about Spain (or whatever at the moment is most controversial) first by the *Daily Mail*, and then by the *Daily Worker*; and I should then ask them to infer what really happened. For undoubtedly few things are more useful to a citizen of a democracy than skill in detecting, by reading newspapers, what it was that took place. For this purpose, it would be instructive to compare the newspapers at crucial moments during the Great War with what subsequently appeared in the official history. And when the madness of war hysteria, as shown in the newspapers of the time, strikes your pupils as incredible, you should warn them that all of them, unless they are very careful to cultivate a balanced and cautious judgement, may fall overnight into a similar madness at the first touch of government incitement to terror and blood lust.

I do not wish, however, to preach a purely negative emotional attitude; I am not suggesting that all strong feeling should be subjected to destructive analysis. I am advocating this attitude only in relation to those emotions which are the basis of collective hysteria, for it is collective hysteria that facilitates wars and dictatorships. But wisdom is not *merely* intellectual: intellect may guide and direct, but does not generate the force that leads to action. The force must be derived from the emotions. Emotions that have desirable social consequences are not so easily generated as hate and rage and fear. In their creation, much depends upon early childhood; much, also, upon economic circumstances. Something, however, can be done, in the course of ordinary education, to provide the nourishment upon which the better emotions can grow, and to bring about the realization of what may give value to human life.

This has been, in the past, one of the purposes of religion. The Churches, however, have also had other purposes, and their dogmatic basis causes difficulties. For those to whom traditional religion is no longer possible, there are other ways. Some find what they need in music, some in poetry. For some others, astronomy serves the same purpose. When we reflect upon the size and antiquity of the stellar universe, the controversies on this rather insignificant planet lose some of their importance, and the acerbity of our disputes seems a trifle ridiculous. And when we are liberated by this negative emotion, we are able to realize more fully, through music or poetry, through history or science, through beauty or through pain, that the really valuable things in human life are individual, not such things as happen on a battlefield or in the clash of politics or in the regimented march of masses of men towards an externally imposed goal. The organized life of the community is necessary, but it is necessary as mechanism, not something to be valued on its own account. What is of most value in human life is more analogous to what all the great religious teachers have spoken of. Those who believe in the Corporate State maintain that our highest activities are collective, whereas I should maintain that we all reach our best in different ways, and that the emotional unity of a crowd can only be achieved on a lower level.

This is the essential difference between the liberal outlook and that of the totalitarian State, that the former regards the welfare of the State as residing ultimately in the welfare of the individual, while the latter regards the State as the end and individuals merely as indispensable ingredients, whose welfare must be subordinated to a mystical totality which is a cloak for the interest of the rulers. Ancient Rome had something of the doctrine of State-worship, but Christianity fought the emperors and ultimately won. Liberalism, in valuing the individual, is carrying on the Christian tradition; its opponents are reviving certain pre-Christian doctrines. From the first, the idolators of the State have regarded education as the key to success. This appears, for example, in Fichte's *Addresses to the German Nation*, which deal at length with education. What Fichte desires is set forth in the following passage:

'If anyone were to say: "how could anyone demand more of education than that it should show the pupil the right and strongly recommend it to him; whether he follows these recommendations is his own affair, and if he does not do it, his own fault; he has free will, which no education can take from him": I should answer, in order to characterize more sharply the education I contemplate, that just in this recognition of and counting on the free will of the pupil lies the first error of education hitherto and the distinct acknowledgement of its impotence and emptiness. For inasmuch as it admits that, after all its strongest operation, the will remains free, that is oscillating undecidedly between good and bad, it admits that it neither can nor wishes to mould the will, or, since will is the essential root of man, man himself; and that it holds this to be altogether impossible. The new education, on the contrary, would have to consist in a complete annihilation of the freedom of the will in the territory that it undertook to deal with.'

His reason for desiring to create 'good' men is not that they are in themselves better than 'bad' men; his reason is that 'only in such (good men) can the German nation persist, but through bad men it will necessarily coalesce with foreign countries'.

All this may be taken as expressing the exact antithesis of what the liberal educator will wish to achieve. So far from 'annihilating the freedom of the will', he will aim at strengthening individual judgment; he will instil what he can of the scientific attitude towards the pursuit of knowledge; he will try to make beliefs tentative and responsive to evidence; he will not pose before his pupils as omniscient, nor will he yield to the love of power on the pretence that he is pursuing some absolute good. Love of power is the chief danger of the educator, as of the politician; the man who can be trusted in education must care for his pupils on their own account, not merely as potential soldiers in an army of propagandists for a cause. Fichte and the powerful men who have inherited his ideals, when they see children, think: 'Here is material that I can manipulate, that I can teach to behave like a machine in furtherance of my purposes; for the moment I may be impeded by joy of life, spontaneity, the impulse to play, the desire to live for purposes springing from within, not imposed from without; but all this, after the years of schooling that I shall impose, will be dead; fancy, imagination, art, and the power of thought shall have been destroyed by obedience; the joy of death will have bred receptiveness to fanaticism; and in the end I shall find my human material as passive as stone from a quarry or coal from a mine. In the battles to which I shall lead them, some will die, some will live; those who die will die exultantly, as heroes, those who live will live on as my slaves, with that deep mental slavery to which my schools will have accustomed them.' All this, to any person with natural affection for the young, is horrible; just as we teach children to avoid being destroyed by motor cars if they can, so we should teach them to avoid being destroyed by cruel fanatics, and to this end we should seek to produce independence of mind, somewhat sceptical and wholly scientific, and to preserve, as far as possible, the instinctive joy of life that is natural to healthy children. This is the task of a liberal education: to give a sense of the value of things other than domination, to help to create wise citizens of a free community, and through the combination of citizenship with liberty in individual creativeness to enable men to give to human life that splendour which some few have shown that it can achieve.

(*Power: A New Social Analysis*, London: Allen & Unwin; New York: W. W. Norton, 1938.)

72

IF WE ARE TO SURVIVE THIS DARK TIME—

THERE is only too much reason to fear that Western civilization, if not the whole world, is likely in the near future to go through a period of immense sorrow and suffering and pain—a period during which, if we are not careful to remember them, the things that we are attempting to preserve may be forgotten in bitterness and poverty and disorder. Courage, hope, and unshakable conviction will be necessary if we are to emerge from the dark time spiritually undamaged. It is worth while, before the actual danger is upon us, to collect our thoughts, to marshal our hopes, and to plant in our hearts a firm belief in our ideasl.

It is not the first time that such disasters have threatened the Western World. The fall of Rome was another such time, and in that time, as now, varying moods of despair, escape, and robust faith were exemplified in the writings of leading men. What emerged and became the kernal of the new civilization was the Christian Church. Many pagans were noble in their thoughts and admirable in their aspirations, but they lacked dynamic force.

Plotinus, the founder of neo-Platonism, was the most remarkable of the pagans of that time. In his youth he hoped to play some part in world affairs and accompanied the emperor in a campaign against Persia, but the Roman soldiers murdered the emperor and decided to go home. Plotinus found his way home as best he could, and decided to have done with practical affairs.

He then retired into meditation and wrote books full of beauty, extolling the eternal world and the inactive contemplation of it. Such philosophy, however admirable in itself, offered no cure for the ills from which the empire was suffering.

I think Plotinus was right in urging contemplation of eternal things, but he was wrong in thinking of this as enough to constitute a good life. Contemplation, if it is to be wholesome and valuable, must be married to practice; it must inspire action and ennoble the aims of practical states-manship. While it remains secluded in the cloister it is only a means of escape.

Boethius, who represents the very last blossoming of Roman civilization, was a figure of more use to our age. After a lifetime spent in public administration and in trying to civilize a Gothic king, he fell into disfavour and was condemned to death. In prison he composed his great book, *The Consolations of Philosophy*, in which, with a combination of majestic calm and sweet reasonableness, he sets forth, as imperturbably as though he were still a powerful minister, the joys of contemplation, the delight in the beauty of the world and the hopes for mankind, which, even in that situation, did not desert him. Throughout the Dark Ages his book was studied and it transmitted to happier times the last purified legacy of the ancient world.

The sages of our time have a similar duty to perform. It is their duty to posterity to crystallize the achievements, the hopes, and the ideals which have made our time great—to study them with monumental simplicity, so they may shine like a beacon light through the coming darkness.

Two very different conceptions of human life are struggling for mastery of the world. In the West we see man's greatness in the individual life. A great society for us is one which is composed of individuals who, as far as is humanly possible, are happy, free, and creative. We do not think that individuals should be alike. We conceive society as like an orchestra, in which the different performers have different parts to play and different instruments upon which to perform, and in which co-operation results from a conscious common purpose. We believe that each individual should have his proper pride. He should have his personal conscience and his personal aims, which he should be free to develop except where they can be shown to cause injury to others. We attach importance to the diminution of suffering and poverty, to the increase of knowledge, and the production of beauty and art. The State for us is a convenience, not an object of worship.

The Russian Government has a different conception of the ends of life. The individual is thought of no importance: he is expendable. What is important is the State, which is regarded as something almost divine and having a welfare of its own not consisting in the welfare of citizens. This view, which Marx took over from Hegel, is fundamentally opposed to the Christian ethic, which in the West is accepted by free-thinkers as much as by Christians. In the Soviet world human dignity counts for nothing.

It is thought right and proper that men should be grovelling slaves, bowing down before the semi-divine beings who embody the greatness of the State. When a man betrays his dearest friend and causes him, as a penalty for a moment's peevish indiscretion, to vanish into the mysterious horror of a Siberian labour camp; when a schoolchild, as the result of indoctrination by his teacher, causes his parents to be condemned to death; when a man of exceptional courage, after struggling against evils, is tried, convicted, and abjectly confesses that he has sinned in opposing the Moloch power of the authorities, neither the betrayal nor the confession brings any sense of shame to the perpetrator, for has he not been engaged in the service of his divinity?

It is this conception that we have to fight, a conception which, to my mind and to that of most men who appreciate what the Western world stands for, would, if it prevailed, take everything out of life that gives it value, leaving nothing but a regimented collection of grovelling animals. I cannot imagine a greater or more profound cause for which to fight. But if we are to win a victory—not only on the battlefield but in the hearts of men and in the institutions that they support—we must be clear in our own minds as to what it is that we value, and we must, like Boethius, fortify our courage against the threat of adversity.

While Russia underestimates the individual, there are those in the West who unduly magnify the separateness of separate persons. No man's ego should be enclosed in granite walls; its boundaries should be translucent. The first step in wisdom, as well as in morality, is to open the windows of the ego as wide as possible. Most people find little difficulty in including their children within the compass of their desires. In slightly lesser degree they include their friends, and in time of danger their country. Very many men feel that what hurts their country hurts them. In 1940 I knew Frenchmen living prosperously in America who suffered from the fall of France almost as they would have suffered from the loss of a leg. But it is not enough to enlarge our sympathies to embrace our own country. If the world is ever to have peace it will be necessary to learn to embrace the whole human race in the same kind of sympathy which we now feel toward our compatriots. And if we are to retain calm and sanity in difficult times, it is a great help if the furniture of our minds contains past and future ages.

Few things are more purifying to our conception of values than to contemplate the gradual rise of man from his obscure and difficult beginnings to his present eminence. Man, when he first emerged, was a rare and hunted species, not so fleet as the deer, not so nimble as the monkey, unable to defend himself against wild beasts, without the protection of warm fur against rain and cold, living precariously upon the food that he could gather, without weapons, without domestic animals, without agriculture.

The one advantage that he possessed—intelligence—gave him security. He learned the use of fire, of bows and arrows, of language, of domestic animals and, at last, of agriculture. He learned to co-operate in communities, to build great palaces and pyramids, to explore the world in all directions and, at last, to cope with disease and poverty. He studied the stars, he invented geometry, and he learned to substitute machines for muscles in necessary labour. Some of the most important of these advances are very recent and are as yet confined to Western nations.

In former days most children died in infancy, mortality in adult life was very high, and in every country the great majority of the population endured abject poverty. Now certain nations have succeeded in preserving the lives of the overwhelming majority of infants, in lowering enormously the adult death rate, and in nearly eliminating abject poverty. Other nations, where disease and abject poverty are still the rule, could achieve the same level of well-being by adopting the same methods. There is, therefore, a new hope for mankind.

The hope cannot be realized unless the causes of present evils are understood. But it is the hope that needs to be emphasized. Modern man is master of his fate. What he suffers he suffers because he is stupid or wicked, not because it is nature's decree. Happiness is his if he will adopt the means that lie ready to his hands.

We of the Western world, faced with Communism's hostile criticism, have been too modest and too defensive in our attitude. Throughout the long ages since life began the mechanism of evolution has involved cruel suffering, endless struggle for bare subsistence, and in the end, in most cases, death by starvation. This is the law in the animal kingdom, and it remained, until the present century, the law among human beings also. Now, at last, certain nations have discovered how to prevent abject poverty, how to prevent the pain and sorrow and waste of useless births condemned to premature death, and how to substitute intelligence and care for the blind ruthlessness of nature.

The nations that have made this discovery are trustees for the future of mankind. They must have the courage of their new way of life and not allow themselves to be bemused or bewildered by the slogans of the semi-civilized. We have a right to hopes that are rational, that can be itemized and set forth in statistics. If we allow ourselves to be robbed of these hopes for the sake of irrational dreams, we shall be traitors to the human race.

If bad times lie ahead of us, we should remember while they last the slow march of man, chequered in the past by devastations and retrogressions, but always resuming the movement towards progress. Spinoza, who was one of the wisest of men and who lived consistently in accordance with his own wisdom, advised men to view passing events 'under the aspect of eternity'. Those who can learn to do this will find a painful present much more bearable than it would otherwise be. They can see it as a passing moment—a discord to be resolved, a tunnel to be traversed. The small child who has hurt himself weeps as if the world contained nothing but sorrow, because his mind is confined to the present. A man who has learned wisdom from Spinoza can see even a lifetime of suffering as a passing moment in the life of humanity. And the human race itself, from its obscure beginning to its unknown end, is only a minute episode in the life of the universe.

What may be happening elsewhere we do not know, but it is improbable that the universe contains nothing better than ourselves. With increase of wisdom our thoughts acquire a wider scope both in space and in time. The child lives in the minute, the boy in the day, the instinctive man in the year. The man imbued with history lives in the epoch. Spinoza would have us live not in the minute, the day, the year or the epoch but in eternity. Those who learn to do this will find that it takes away the frantic quality of misfortune and prevents the trend towards madness that comes with overwhelming disaster. He spent the last day of his life telling cheerful anecdotes to his host. He had written: 'The wise man thinks less about death than about anything else', and he carried out this precept when it came to his own death.

I do not mean that the wise man will be destitute of emotion—on the contrary, he will feel friendship, benevolence, and compassion in a higher degree than the man who has not emancipated himself from personal anxieties. His ego will not be a wall between him and the rest of mankind. He will feel, like Buddha, that he cannot be completely happy while anybody is miserable. He will feel pain—a wider and more diffused pain than that of the egoist—but he will not find the pain unendurable. He will not be driven by it to invent comfortable fairy-tales which assure him that the sufferings of others are illusory. He will not lose poise and self-control. Like Milton's Satan, he will say:

> The mind is its own place, and in itself
> Can make a Heav'n of Hell, a Hell of Heav'n.

Above all, he will remember that each generation is trustee to future generations of the mental and moral treasure that man has accumulated through the ages. It is easy to forget the glory of man. When King Lear is going mad he meets Edgar, who pretends to be mad and wears only a blanket. King Lear moralizes: 'Unaccommodated, man is no more but such a poor, bare, forked animal as thou art.'

This is half of the truth. The other half is uttered by Hamlet:

'What a piece of work is a man! how noble in reason! how infinite in faculty! In form and moving how express and admirable! in action how like an angel! in apprehension how like a god!'

Soviet man, crawling on his knees to betray his friends and family to slow butchery, is hardly worthy of Hamlet's words, but it is possible to be worthy of them. It is possible for every one of us. Every one of us can enlarge his mind, release his imagination, and spread wide his affection and benevolence. And it is those who do this whom ultimately mankind reveres. The East reveres Buddha, the West reveres Christ. Both taught love as the secret of wisdom. The earthly life of Christ was contemporary with that of the Emperor Tiberius, who spent his life in cruelty and disgusting debauchery. Tiberius had pomp and power; in his day millions trembled at his nod. But he is forgotten by historians.

Those who live nobly, even if in their day they live obscurely, need not fear that they will have lived in vain. Something radiates from their lives, some light that shows the way to their friends, their neighbours—perhaps to long future ages. I find many men nowadays oppressed with a sense of impotence, with the feeling that in the vastness of modern societies there is nothing of importance that the individual can do. This is a mistake. The individual, if he is filled with love of mankind, with breadth of vision, with courage and with endurance, can do a great deal.

As geological time goes, it is but a moment since the human race began and only the twinkling of an eye since the arts of civilization were first invented. In spite of some alarmists, it is hardly likely that our species will completely exterminate itself. And so long as man continues to exist, we may be pretty sure that, whatever he may suffer for a time, and whatever brightness may be eclipsed, he will emerge sooner or later, perhaps strengthened and reinvigorated by a period of mental sleep. The universe is vast and men are but tiny specks on an insignificant planet. But the more we realize our minuteness and our impotence in the face of cosmic forces, the more astonishing becomes what human beings have achieved.

It is to the possible achievements of man that our ultimate loyalty is due, and in that thought the brief troubles of our unquiet epoch become endurable. Much wisdom remains to be learned, and if it is only to be learned through adversity, we must endeavour to endure adversity with what fortitude we can command. But if we can acquire wisdom soon enough, adversity may not be necessary and the future of man may be happier than any part of his past.

(*The New York Times Magazine*, September 3, 1950.)

73

WHAT WOULD HELP MANKIND MOST?

EVER since 1914, everybody conscious of trends in the world has been deeply troubled by what has seemed like a fated and predetermined march towards ever greater disaster. Many serious people have come to feel that nothing can be done to avert the plunge towards ruin. They see the human race, like the hero of a Greek tragedy, driven on by angry gods and no longer the master of fate. I think this view is at once lazy and superstitious. Misfortunes can be imagined for which men, individually and collectively, would be not responsible: if the sun were to explode, we could not blame the government. But the misfortunes of the human race since 1914, and those much greater misfortunes with which it is threatened, are not of this order. They are brought on by human volition, by the passions of the many and the decisions of the few.

It is the custom nowadays to underestimate the importance of the decisions of the few, and to attribute all great events to the passions of the many. This is a partial analysis designed, as a rule subconsciously, to make the course of history seem less irrational than it is. It is true that great events depend upon passions felt by many. But, in most cases, there are opposite passions which might have prevailed, and often the decisive factor in determining which shall prevail is some very small force supplied by an individual. So it has been since 1914. Unfortunately, the small fortuitous force has, by a run of bad luck, always been applied in the wrong direction.

I will give a few illustrations out of many. The Serbian Prime Minister informed his Cabinet that he had reason to expect the Sarajevo murders. If he had also informed the Austro-Hungarian Government, the murders would not have taken place, and the First World War would at least have been postponed. Rasputin always maintained that, if he had not been in hospital during the crucial day, war would have been averted. I think this is probably true, for, though a scoundrel, he favoured peace. He could probably have prevented one of the decisive steps leading to war, which was the Russian mobilization order by the War Minister without the knowledge of the Czar. And, if the war had been postponed, it would probably have never taken place, since the German Social Democrats were very close to obtaining a majority in the Reichstag, and, if they had obtained a majority, German policy would have been completely changed.

There is no end to the small events that have great effects. If a certain subordinate German official had not decided to let Lenin go to Russia in 1917, Russia would not have become Communist. If one or two Republican Senators had voted to ratify the Treaty of Versailles, the United States would have been a member of the League of Nations and might have preserved the peace of the world. I will not pursue further this catalogue of petty mistakes leading to great misfortunes. My motive in making the catalogue is to show that hope is not irrational. If small decisions can do great harm, they can also do great good, and it is therefore irrational to let our hopes be smothered by a sense of impotence.

In the world of today there are two enormous popular forces: one is the hostility between Communists and non-Communists; the other is the wish to avoid another world war. Each of these forces is immensely strong. They work in opposite directions, and have kept each other in an uneasy balance throughout recent years. This is exactly the sort of situation in which something small and apparently trivial may give the victory to one force or the other. It is easy to imagine small events that would unleash war. If a Russian were to assassinate the President, or if an American lunatic were to blow up the Kremlin, it is very likely that the resulting fury would be impossible to curb. It is not quite so easy to imagine events giving added strength to the desire for peace, but I think it is possible, and I think that, if it is possible, to do so would be at the present time the greatest benefit that could be conferred upon mankind.

How can this be done? It is no use to advocate something that certainly will not happen. Some people pin their hopes to a universal change of heart. Certainly this would prevent war, if it happened, but I do not see the rulers of the USSR adopting the principles of the Sermon on the Mount in any near future. Nor is one-sided appeasement a road to peace, since it encourages the other side to continually more outrageous demands, until at last a point is reached where resistance is felt to be imperative. Nor is there much hope in argument designed to convince the other side of the righteousness of our own. However convincing such argument may appear on one side of the Iron Curtain, it loses persuasiveness in passing to the other side. If the danger of war is to be lessened, it must be by emphasis upon something about which both sides are agreed.

I know of only one thing about which, so far as can be judged, there is general agreement on both sides, and that is that a great war would be disastrous to the victors as well as to the vanquished. There have been a number of occasions during recent years when either side might have precipitated war; but neither has done so. If I were an influential statesman, I should advocate a conference of *all* the great powers to consider one single matter: namely, the destruction to be expected in a new world war.

This conference should be bound by certain rigid rules. No one at the conference should be allowed to suggest that one side was better than the other, or that in a war one side was more likely to achieve a victory than the other. No one should be allowed to suggest any concessions by the other side which might seem to make negotiation easier. The sole and exclusive business of the conference should be to draw up an authoritative statement of the sufferings to be expected among all the belligerents.

If, for example, the hydrogen bomb is mentioned, it must be mentioned not as an engine of victory but as an engine of destruction solely. No good can come of the schoolboy wrangles in which, at present, both sides indulge. 'We have the hydrogen bomb', says one side. 'So have we', says the other. 'But we have more', says the one. 'But you present more convenient targets', says the other. This sort of thing can be kept up indefinitely, but there is a danger—a very grave danger—that sooner or later the wrangling will exasperate people to the point where they say: 'Oh, well, let us be done with bragging and put it to the test.'

Any such procedure is suicidal on both sides. What I suggest is a conference in which weapons of war are considered strictly as leading to universal and utter defeat on both sides equally. This is the only matter in which the interests of the two sides are identical; and it is, therefore, the only matter which can be considered by a conference without exacerbating hostile feeling in both parties.

I would have such a conference composed of men who would abstain from boasting of any supposed technical superiority against the potential enemy. It should be assumed—which I am afraid is the fact—that whatever one side can achieve in a technical way, the other can also achieve. If the Pentagon knows of ways (which it imagines to be secret) by which it can blow up the Kremlin, it is safe to assume that Moscow knows of ways by which it can blow up Washington. This should be taken for granted at the conference, and all competitive boasting should be strictly forbidden.

I think it possible that such a conference might, in the course of its deliberations, generate on each side a belief that the other side is aware of the inevitable evils of a world war, and that it is not likely to indulge in such a war unless compelled to do so. If once this belief existed on both sides, a general *détente* would become very much easier. At present we of the West are persuaded—rightly, I am sure—that we shall never engage in a great war except in resistance to attacks from the other side; but we are not persuaded that such attacks are unlikely.

I think—though this is partly a guess—that an exactly correlative attitude exists in the Soviet Government. I think that it is determined not to engage in aggressive war, but is not by any means certain that we can be trusted not to do so. It is this mutual distrust which causes the difficulty, and it is this mutual distrust which I should seek to dispel by emphatic statements of the arguments of self-interest which should deter either side from aggressive action.

The belief that man is a rational animal has always been difficult to sustain, and has especially received many nasty knocks during the last forty years. But the question as to the extent of man's irrationality is still debatable. Very few people will imitate the irrationality of Empedocles, who leapt into the crater of a volcano in eruption. Anyone who, in the present state of the world, contemplates inaugurating a world war is equally irrational, and on a much vaster scale.

I believe that both sides could be got to state this fact with emphasis and to make it clear that they will only fight in defence. I believe they could be got to admit that neither the Governments of the West nor the Governments of the USSR and its satellites could survive the shock of total war. I believe they could be got to admit that peoples and governments alike would suffer disaster in such a contest. I believe they could be induced to admit that the hope of victory has become illusory, even if (which is unlikely) the war should end in something that fanatical militarists could welcome as total defeat of the enemy.

I do not wish to see such a view prevailing on one side only, for then it becomes defeatist, and, terrible as a new war would be, I still for my part should prefer it to a universal Communist empire. What I wish is to see the point of view that I am advocating recognized on both sides equally.

I think the preliminary steps ought to be taken by neutrals. They should combine to draw up a document setting forth in a wholly neutral spirit what seemed to them the likely results of war, and they should invite comments upon this document from both camps. This is, to my mind, the most useful function that neutrals can perform in the present state of the world. If they do their work in the right spirit, it ought to be possible to get both camps to admit the justice of what they say. And if they have admitted this to the neutrals, it is no very great step to go on to admit it to each other.

It would, of course, be essential that the report reached by such an inquiry should receive the widest publicity on both sides of the Iron Curtain. It would have to emphasize, not only the probable overthrow of governments, but the inevitable harm to practically every inhabitant of a belligerent country. I am not thinking only of such spectacular disasters as the obliteration of large cities. I am thinking also of such things as the destruction of crops, and the failure of agriculture for lack of fertilizers, and the inevitable spread of disease.

As far as is compatible with the claims of impartiality, the misfortunes to be expected should not be left general and vague, but should be such as to be vivid to each individual. It should be clear what will happen to industrial workers, what will happen to those in agriculture, what will happen to professional men, and what will happen to children.

All this should be worked out in some detail so as to be brought home to each individual. So long as it remains a vast vague horror, it has for many people a certain morbid fascination. But they will not like it so much if they are led to reflect: 'Even if I do survive, it will be on a diet of acorns and mangel-wurzels.' It is necessary to emphasize aspects which are not grand and heroic, for, though heroism has its legitimate place, it should not be indulged at the expense of the whole human race.

I believe that some investigation, promoted in the first instance by neutrals, might turn men aside from collective madness. I believe that both sides could be persuaded that nothing is to be gained by war, and that there is no harm in saying so. It would then become possible for both sides to have confidence that disputes would be settled by negotiation. Mankind would gradually awake from the nightmare in which we have all been living, and the downward trend of the last forty years might again give place to ordered progress.

(*The New York Times Magazine*, September 27, 1953.)

74

CURRENT PERPLEXITIES

THE present time is one in which the prevailing mood is a feeling of impotent perplexity. We see ourselves drifting towards a war that hardly anyone desires—a war that, as we all know, must bring disaster to the great majority of mankind. But like a rabbit fascinated by a snake, we stare at the peril without knowing what to do to avert it. We tell each other horror stories of atom bombs and hydrogen bombs, of cities exterminated, of Russian hordes, of famine and ferocity everywhere. But although our reason tells us we ought to shudder at such a prospect, there is another part of us that enjoys it, and so we have no firm will to avert misfortune, and there is a deep division in our souls between the sane and the insane parts. In quiet times the insane parts can slumber throughout the day and wake only at night. But in times like ours they invade our waking time as well, and all rational thinking becomes pale and divorced from the will. Our lives become balanced on a sharp edge of hypothesis—if there is to be a war one way of life is reasonable; if not, another. To the great majority of mankind such a hypothetical existence is intolerably uncomfortable, and in practice they adopt one hypothesis or the other, but without complete conviction. A youth who finds scholastic education boring will say to himself: 'Why bother? I shall be killed in battle before long.' A young woman who might live constructively thinks to herself that she had better have a good time while she can since presently she will be raped by Russian soldiery until she dies. Parents wonder whether the sacrifices called for by their children's upbringing are worth while since they are likely to prove futile. Those who are lucky enough to possess capital are apt to spend it on riotous living, since they foresee a catastrophic depreciation in which it would become worthless. In this way uncertainty balks the impulse to every irksome effort, and generates a tone of frivolous misery mistakenly thought to be pleasure, which turns outward and becomes hatred of those who are felt to be its cause. Through this hatred it brings daily nearer the catastrophe which it dreads. The nations seem caught in a tragic fate, as though, like characters in a Greek drama, they were blinded by some offended god. Bewildered by mental fog, they march towards the precipice while they imagine that they are marching away from it.

It must be said that the purely intellectual problems presented by the world of our day are exceedingly difficult. There is not only the great problem: can we defend our Western world without actual war? There are also problems in Asia and problems in Africa and problems in tropical America which cannot be solved within the framework of the traditional political ideas. There are those, it is true, who are quite certain that they can solve these problems by ancient methods. Consider MacArthur and his Republican supporters. So limited is his intelligence and his imagination that he is never puzzled for one moment. All we have to do is to go back to the days of the Opium War. After we have killed a sufficient number of millions of Chinese, the survivors among them will perceive our moral superiority and hail MacArthur as a saviour. But let us not be one-sided. Stalin, I should say, is equally simple-minded and equally out of date. He, too, believes that if his armies could occupy Britain and reduce us all to the economic level of Soviet peasants and the political level of convicts, we should hail him as a great deliverer and bless the day when we were freed from the shackles of democracy. One of the painful things about our time is that those who feel certainty are stupid, and those with any imagination and understanding are filled with doubt and indecision. I do not think this is necessary. I think there is a view of man and his destiny and his present troubles which can give certainty and hope together with the completest understanding of the moods, the despairs, and the maddening doubts that beset modern men. It is my hope to set forth such an outlook in the following pages in a way that shall be convincing and overwhelmingly encouraging, that shall enable men of goodwill to work with the same vigour which of late has been the monopoly of cruel bigots; to take away from our Western mentality the reproach that we have nothing to offer inspiring the same firm conviction and the same solid body of belief as is offered by the disciples of the Kremlin. But I anticipate. And after this digression into hope I must return to the causes of its opposite, which have all too much sway in the reflections of thoughtful men. If we forget MacArthur and his simplicities, what are we to think about Asia? From the time of Vasco da Gama until the Russo-Japanese war, the Western world did not think seriously about Asia. No doubt it was a picturesque continent, and amid our progressive schemes we enjoyed talking about the unchanging East. Philosophers with kindly contempt, and missionaries with reforming zeal, studied what we were pleased to call their superstitions. We enjoyed their military incompetence, and their incapacity to extract high wages. For all these reasons we rather liked them. We realized, of course, that the inhabitants of Asia did not all form one community. There were Mohammedans and Hindus and Buddhists, and it was our hope that they would continue to hate each other for ever. And on this ground the more enlightened among administrators deprecated the work of missionaries for fear lest it should diminish the virulence of 'superstition'.

The first country of Asia to cause misgivings in Europeans was Japan. At first, after Commodore Perry had opened the country to our curiosity, we admired the cherry blossom, Bushido, and the chivalrous virtues of the Samurai. We liked the temples and the art, and our aesthetes imagined the Japanese to be kindred souls. But gradually a change came over the spirit of our dream. It may be seen in the works of Lafcadio Hearn. At first he was enthusiastic about the Japanese, but his last book, *Japan, an Interpretation*, has begun to be aware of things slightly more serious than cherry blossom. The Japanese refused to stay put. They set to work to imitate the West, and in the measure in which they succeeded they inspired hatred in Western minds.

The Japanese for the moment encountered disaster; they mastered our brutalities, but not our suppleness. But they left to the rest of Asia a legacy of war-like rebellion against Western insolence. Western men of liberal outlook cannot but sympathize with the wish of Asia to be independent, but it would be a pity if this sympathy were to blind Western thought to certain matters of the gravest import. The Western world has achieved, not completely but to a considerable extent, a way of life having certain merits that are new in human history. It has nearly eliminated poverty. It has cut down illness and death to a degree that a hundred years ago would have seemed fantastic. It has spread education throughout the population, and it has achieved a quite new degree of harmony between freedom and order. These are not things which Asia, if it becomes quickly independent, can hope to achieve. We, in the West, aware of the appalling poverty of South-East Asia, and convinced that this poverty is a propaganda weapon in the hands of the Russians, have begun to think for the first time that something ought to be done to raise the standard of life in these regions. But their habits and our beliefs between them make the task, for the present, a hopeless one. Every increase of production, instead of raising the standard of life, is quickly swallowed up by an increase in population. Eastern populations do not know how to prevent this, and Western bigots prevent those who understand the problem from spreading the necessary information. What is bad in the West is easily spread: our restlessness, our militarism, our fanaticism, and our ruthless belief in mechanism. But what is best in the West—the spirit of free inquiry, the understanding of the conditions of general prosperity, and emancipation from superstition—these things powerful forces in the West prevent the East from acquiring. So long as this continues, Eastern populations will remain on the verge of destitution, and in proportion as they become powerful, they will become destructive through envy. In this they will, of course, have the help of Russia, unless and until Russia is either defeated or liberalized. For these reasons, a wise policy towards Asia is still to seek.

In Africa the same problems exist, though for the present they are less menacing. Everything done by European administrators to improve the lot of Africans is, at present, totally and utterly futile because of the growth of population. The Africans, not unnaturally, though now mistakenly, attribute their destitution to their exploitation by the white man. If they achieve freedom suddenly before they have men trained in administration and a habit of responsibility, such civilization as white men have brought to Africa will quickly disappear. It is no use for doctrinaire liberals to deny this; there is a standing proof in the Island of Haiti.

It must not be supposed that there is any essential stability in a civilized way of life. Consider the regions overrun by the Turks and contrast their condition under the Turks with what they were in Roman days. Over great parts of the earth's surface, similar misfortunes are not impossible in the near future. On the other hand it must be admitted that until we include birth-control in our African policies every increase in efficiency and honesty and scientific skill on the part of European administrators will only increase the sum of human misery.

The population problem is similar in Central and South America, but it does not there have the same political importance.

I have been speaking hitherto of public perplexities, but it is not these alone which trouble the Western mind. Traditional systems of dogma and traditional codes of conduct have not the hold that they formerly had. Men and women are often in genuine doubt as to what is right and what is wrong, and even as to whether right and wrong are anything more than ancient superstitions. When they try to decide such questions for themselves they find them too difficult. They cannot discover any clear purpose that they ought to pursue or any clear principle by which they should be guided. Stable societies may have principles that, to the outsider, seem absurd. But so long as the societies remain stable their principles are subjectively adequate. That is to say they are accepted by almost everybody unquestioningly, and they make the rules of conduct as clear and precise as those of the minuet or the heroic couplet. Modern life, in the West, is not at all like a minuet or a heroic couplet. It is like free verse which only the poet can distinguish from prose. Two great systems of dogma lie in wait for the modern man when his spirit is weary: I mean the system of Rome and the system of Moscow. Neither of these gives scope for the free mind, which is at once the glory and the torment of Western man. It is the torment only because of growing pains. The free man, full grown, shall be full of joy and vigour and mental health, but in the meantime he suffers.

Not only publicly, but privately also, the world has need of ways of thinking and feeling which are adapted to what we know, to what we can believe, and what we feel ourselves compelled to disbelieve. There are ways of feeling that are traditional and that have all the prestige of the past and weighty authority, and that yet are not adapted to the world in which we live, where new techniques have made some new virtues necessary and some old virtues unnecessary. The Hebrew prophets, surrounded by hostile nations, and determined that their race should not be assimilated by Gentile conquerors, developed a fierce doctrine in which the leading conception was sin. The Gentiles sinned always and in all their ways, but the Jews, alas, were only too apt to fall into sin themselves. When they did so they were defeated in battle and had to weep by the waters of Babylon. It is this pattern which has inspired moralists ever since. The virtuous man has been conceived as one who, though continually surrounded by temptation, though passionately prompted to sin, nevertheless, by almost superhuman strength of will, succeeds in walking along the straight and narrow path, looking meanwhile disdainfully to the right and left at those inferior beings who have loitered to pluck flowers by the way. In this conception, virtue is difficult, negative, and arid. It is constrictive and suspicious of happiness. It is persuaded that our natural impulses are bad and that society can only be held together by means of rigid prohibitions. I do not wish to pretend that society can hold together if people murder and steal. What I do say is that the kind of man whom I should wish to see in the world is one who will have no impulse to murder, who will abstain from murder not because it is prohibited but because his thoughts and feelings carry him away from impulses of destruction. The whole conception of sin has, as it were, gone dead, so far, at least, as conscious thought and feeling are concerned. Most people have not thought out any other system of ethics, and have not, perhaps, theoretically rejected the old system. But it has lost its hold on them. They do not murder or steal as a rule, because it would not be to their interest to do so, but one cannot say as much for their obedience to the Seventh Commandment. They have, in fact, no wish to conform to the ancient pattern. The Publican thanks God that he is not as this Pharisee, and imagines that in so doing he has caught the point of the parable. It does not occur to him that feeling superior is what is reprehended, and that whether it is the Publican or the Pharisee who feels superior is an unimportant detail.

I should wish to persuade those to whom traditional morals have gone dead, and who yet feel the need of some serious purpose over and above momentary pleasure, that there is a way of thinking and feeling which is not difficult for those who have not been trained in its opposite, and which is not one of self-restraint, negation, and condemnation. The good life, as I conceive it, is a happy life. I do not mean that if you are good you will be happy; I mean that if you are happy you will be good. Unhappiness is deeply implanted in the souls of most of us. How many people we all know who go through life apparently gay, and who yet are perpetually in search of intoxication whether of the Bacchic kind or some other. The happy man does not desire intoxication. Nor does he envy his neighbour and therefore hate him. He can live the life of impulse like a child, because happiness makes his impulses fruitful and not destructive. There are many men and women who imagine themselves emancipated from the shackles of ancient codes but who, in fact, are emancipated only in the upper layers of their minds. Below these layers lies the sense of guilt crouching like a wild beast waiting for moments of weakness or inattention, and growling venomous angers which rise to the surface in strange distorted forms. Such people have the worst of both worlds. The feeling of guilt makes real happiness impossible for them, but the conscious rejection of old codes of behaviour makes them act perpetually in ways that feed the maw of the ancient beast beneath. A way of life cannot be successful so long as it is a mere intellectual conviction. It must be deeply felt, deeply believed, dominant even in dreams. I do not think that the best kind of life is possible in our day for those who, below the level of consciousness, are still obsessed by the load of sin. It is obvious that there are things that had better not be done, but I do not think the best way to avoid the doing of such things is to label them sin and represent them as almost irresistibly attractive. And so I should wish to offer to the world something scarcely to be called an ethic, at any rate in the old acceptation of that word, but something which, nonetheless, will save men from moral perplexity and from remorse and from condemnation of others. What I should put in the place of an ethic in the old sense is encouragement and opportunity for all the impulses that are creative and expansive. I should do everything possible to liberate men from fear, not only conscious fears, but the old imprisoned primeval terrors that we brought with us out of the jungle. I should make it clear, not merely as an intellectual proposition, but as something that the heart spontaneously believes, that it is not by making others suffer that we shall achieve our own happiness, but that happiness and the means to happiness depend upon harmony with other men. When all this is not only understood but deeply felt, it will be easy to live in a way that brings happiness equally to ourselves and to others. If men could think and feel in this way, not only their personal problems, but all the problems of world politics, even the most abstruse and difficult, would melt away. Suddenly, as when the mist dissolves from a mountain top, the landscape would be visible and the way would be clear. It is only necessary to open the doors of our hearts and minds to let the imprisoned demons escape and the beauty of the world take possession.

(*New Hopes for a Changing World*, London: Allen
& Unwin; New York: Simon & Schuster, 1951.)

75

WORLD GOVERNMENT

F OR technical reasons it becomes advantageous that social units should increase in size as technique becomes more elaborate. Marx made the world familiar with this thesis in economics, though even there it has applications which he did not think of. Commerce, so far as it still exists, has tended to become an affair of trade between nations, in which the part of merchants is taken by Governments. The economic links between an industrial and an agricultural country, for example between Britain and Argentina, are important; and the fact that both countries are sovereign States makes trade between them a prickly matter, tending to cause hatred between Governments and peoples. This, of course, is absurd. A butcher needs bread and a baker needs meat. There is, therefore, every reason why the butcher and the baker should love one another, since each is useful to the other. But if the butcher is one sovereign State and the baker is another, if the number of loaves that the butcher can exchange for his joints depends upon his skill with the revolver, it is possible that the baker may cease to regard him with ardent affection. This is precisely the situation in international trade at the present day; and if it did not occur we should say that mankind could not be capable of anything so ridiculous. Economic interdependence is very much greater than at any former time, but owing partly to the fact that our economic system has developed from one of private profit, and partly to separate national sovereignties, interdependence, instead of producing friendliness, tends to be a cause of hostility. As economics everywhere has come to be more and more intimately connected with the State, it has become more and more subordinate to politics. Marx held that politics is determined by economics, but that was because he was still under the influence of eighteenth-century rationalism, and imagined that what people most desire is to grow rich. Experience since his time has shown that there is something which people desire even more strongly, and that is to keep others poor. This is a matter in which military power necessarily plays a great part as soon as trade has come to be mainly between nations rather than between individuals. That is why politics has more and more come to predominate over economics.

The advantages of increasing the size of a social unit are nowhere so obvious as in war. In fact, war has been the main cause of the growth of units from families to tribes, from tribes to nations, and from nations to alliances of nations. But it is beginning to dawn upon some people that although large units are a great help towards victory, there is something which is even better than victory, and that is avoidance of war. In the past, war was often a profitable enterprise. The Seven Years War certainly brought the English a good return on the capital expended, and the profitableness of earlier wars to the victors is even more evident. But modern war is an altogether different matter. This is due in the main to two causes: one, that weapons have become enormously expensive; and the other, that the social groups concerned in modern wars are very large. It is a mistake to think that modern war is more destructive of life than the simpler wars of former times. The actual casualties in the past were often quite as high a percentage of the forces engaged as they are now; and apart from casualties in battle, the deaths from disease were usually enormous. Over and over again in ancient and medieval history, you find whole armies practically exterminated by the plague. The atom bomb is, of course, more spectacular, but the actual mortality rate among combatant populations, even where the atom bomb is employed, is not as great as in many former wars. The population of Japan increased by about five millions during the Second World War, whereas it is estimated that during the Thirty Years War the population of Germany was halved. Broadly speaking, it is not in general the case that as weapons become technically more efficient, the mortality in war is increased.

There is, however, in the use of the atom bomb and the hydrogen bomb a new danger, a danger which is not only new in kind but greater in degree than any that has existed in previous wars. We do not quite know what may be the effects of letting loose great floods of radio-activity. There are those—among them Einstein—who think that the result may be the extinction of all life on our planet. Short of that, it may easily happen that large fertile regions become infertile and uninhabitable, and that the populations of considerable areas are wiped out. I do not say that this will happen if atomic energy is employed in war; no one knows yet whether it will happen or not. But there is a risk that it may happen, and if it does repentance will come too late.

There is an oscillation in warfare between the strength of the attack and the strength of the defence. The happy ages are those in which the defence is strong; the unhappy, those in which the attack has the advantage. There is always a danger in our scientific age that at some moment the attack may acquire a really disastrous advantage. Bacteriological warfare, for example, may exterminate the enemy, but would be very likely to exterminate at the same time those who had inaugurated it. On the whole, increase of scientific skill makes war more dangerous, even if at any given moment it does not make it more deadly.

Apart from mortality, there are other respects in which modern war is worse than most wars of former times. Owing to the increased productivity of labour, it is possible to set aside a greater part of the population for the business of mutual slaughter, and the dislocation of daily life is greater in a modern world war than in most of the wars of former times. Fear of atomic bombs has made it irrational for populations to live in great cities. Americans, who have room to expand, are seriously contemplating spreading the population of New York over a large area. In England no such possibilities exist, short of large-scale emigration. In the pleasant and comfortable wars of the eighteenth and nineteenth centuries, it was chiefly the combatants who suffered; now the suffering falls increasingly upon civilians. I am an old man, and I can remember a time when it was not thought quite the thing to make war on women and children; but that happy age is past.

For all these reasons, war is a greater menace now than it was formerly. The prevention of war has become necessary if civilized life is to continue, perhaps if any kind of life is to continue. This matter is so imperative that we must not shrink from new forms of political thought or from the realization of new problems which could formerly be ignored, if not with impunity, at any rate without ultimate disaster.

War may be avoided by makeshifts and expedients and subtle diplomacy for a time, but precariously; and so long as our present political system continues, it must be taken as nearly certain that great wars will occur from time to time. This will inevitably happen so long as there are different sovereign States, each with its own armed forces, and each the unfettered judge of its own rights in any dispute. There is only one way in which the world can be made safe from war, and that is the creation of a single world-wide authority, possessing a monopoly of all the more serious weapons.

If a world Government is to prevent serious wars, there are certain minimum powers that it must possess. First and foremost, it must have a monopoly of all the major weapons of war, and adequate armed forces for their employment. Whatever steps may be necessary must be taken to ensure that the armed forces will in all circumstances be loyal to the central Government. The world Government should proclaim certain rules for the employment of its armed forces. The most important of these should be that, in any dispute between two States, each must submit to the decision of the world Government. Any employment of force by any State against any other shall constitute it a public enemy, and shall bring punishment by the armed forces of the world Government. These are the essential powers if the preservation of peace is to be possible. Given these, others will follow. There will be need of bodies to perform legislative and judicial functions. These will develop naturally if the military conditions are fulfilled; the difficult and vital point is the placing of irresistible force in the hands of the central authority.

The central Government may be democratic or totalitarian; it may owe its origin to consent or to conquest; it may be the national Government of a State which has achieved world conquest, or it may be an authority in which each State, or alternatively, each human being, has equal rights. For my part I believe that, if it is constituted, it will be on a basis of consent in some regions and conquest in others. In a world war between two groups of nations, it may be that the victorious group will disarm the defeated group and proceed to govern the world by means of unifying institutions developed during the war. Gradually the defeated nations could be admitted to partnership as war hostility cooled. I do not believe that the human race has sufficient statesmanship or capacity for mutual forbearance to establish a world Government on a basis of consent alone. That is why I think that an element of force will be needed in its establishment and in its preservation through the early years of its existence.

But although force may be necessary at first in some parts of the world, there will be no stability and no possibility of a liberal and democratic system unless certain great causes of conflict cease to be operative. I am not thinking of the day-to-day conflicts that at present characterize the cold war, nor of the see-saw of power politics. What I am thinking of are matters in which, as things stand, there is a genuine clash between the interests of one part of the world and the interests of another. I am thinking of matters regarded as so important that each side would sooner fight then yield. For instance: shall South-East Asia continue to be overcrowded, or shall Australia and South America cease to be white men's countries? Such really difficult causes of conflict centre round three problems: population, race, and creed.

I have already spoken of the population problem, but a few words must be added about its political aspects. Until it is solved it will be impossible to bring the poorer parts of the world to anything like the same level of prosperity as is now enjoyed by the richer parts, and until there is a certain economic equalization throughout the world, there will be causes of envy and hatred such as will make any world Government dependent upon continual exercise of force by the stronger nations. Such a state of affairs will be unstable and dangerous and harsh. It will be impossible to feel that the world is in a satisfactory state until there is a certain degree of equality, and a certain acquiescence everywhere in the power of the world Government, and this will not be possible until the poorer nations of the world have become educated, modernized in their technique, and more or less stationary in population. This, you may think, is a distant prospect, but it need not be so. Vital statistics in the West during the last half-century have shown what is possible, and certainly hardly anybody in the West would have thought anything of the kind possible in the year 1800.

The conclusion to which we are driven by the facts that we have been considering is that, while great wars cannot be avoided until there is a world Government, a world Government cannot be stable until every important country has a nearly stationary population. As this is very far from being the case at present, our conclusion may seem depressing. But there is another side to it which is by no means depressing. In former days most children died in infancy, mortality in adult life was very high, and in every country the great majority of the population endured abject poverty. Now certain nations have succeeded in preserving the lives of the overwhelming majority of infants, in enormously lowering the adult death rate, and in nearly eliminating abject poverty. All this would have been impossible but for the fall in the birth rate. Other nations, where disease and abject poverty are still the rule, could achieve the same level of well-being by adopting the same methods. There is therefore a new hope for mankind. The hope cannot be realized unless the causes of present evils are understood. But it is the hope that needs to be emphasized. Modern man is master of his fate. What he suffers, he suffers because he is stupid or wicked, not because it is nature's decree. Happiness is his if he will adopt the means that lie ready to his hands.

(*New Hopes for a Changing World*, London: Allen & Unwin; New York: Simon & Schuster, 1951.)

76

THE NEXT HALF-CENTURY

THE twentieth century so far has not been a credit to the human race. True, a number of emperors have disappeared, which from the point of view of 1793 would be adjudged a gain. But the results have not always been happy. There are those who may doubt whether Stalin is much better for the world than Nicholas II, whether Hitler was a great improvement on Kaiser Wilhelm, and even (greatly daring) whether Hirohito was much worse than MacArthur. In any case, these tranfers were somewhat expensive. Each of them cost many millions of human lives, many billions of dollars, much abasement of the currency of civilization. There were also special horrors, such as the extermination of Jews, the deliberate starvation of Russian peasants, and the invention of the terror of atomic death. These, so far, are the achievements of the twentieth century. There is a risk, a very imminent risk that, glorious as these achievements are, they will sink into insignificance beside those of the next few years. As I write, I do not know—no one knows—whether London and New York will still exist six months hence. I do not know—no one else of my age in Western Europe knows—whether the children and the grandchildren upon whom care has been lavished will survive another twelve months. I do not know, and no one else knows what, if anything, will be left of the structure of Western civilization which has been slowly built up from the time of Homer. All this is in doubt. All this depends upon the degree of hysteria in the United States, on the courage of Truman, the independence of Western Europe, and the good or bad temper of the Politbureau. I will not venture to prophesy; I will consider only what, if the immediate crisis can be successfully passed, can and should be done to make the future less precarious.

The first and most important thing concerning which I shall have much to say is a change of outlook on the part of Western statesmen and the Western public. We have allowed ourselves to be hypnotized by fear. When I say 'fear', I do not mean a rational apprehension of danger. Undoubtedly there is danger; undoubtedly the danger is imminent and terrible. But dangers are not averted by terror; they are averted by calm thought. A captain who finds his ship in danger of sinking is expected to avoid hysteria, but an American statesman in the same situation is thought to be a fellow-traveller if he remains calm.

What the present situation demands is evident. It demands first and foremost sufficient armaments to make Western Europe secure. When this has been achieved, Western Germany and France and Italy will revive spiritually, since they will no longer live under the imminent threat of obliteration. And when the West feels secure against invasion, there will no longer be any risk of a third world war, unless from the truculence of America. If America can be induced to be less truculent, the whole world will be able to breathe freely once more. When there is security, there will no longer be need for a hostile demeanour in dealings with the Russians. They will in time perceive that the hope of world dominion is vain, and that the best they can expect is to hold their present territories. It will then become necessary to persuade them that we do not wish or intend to conquer them. They are full of suspicion, a suspicion for which it must be said they have grounds, both in the allied intervention at the end of the First World War, and in the present attitude of the most vocal section of American opinion. It will take time to overcome this suspicion, but when once the West has obviously superior strength, and yet does not go to war, it will become year by year easier to make Russia believe that conquest forms no part of our purposes. I believe that when once they are persuaded of this, the harshness of their régime will rapidly grow less, and by slow stages friendly co-operation will become possible. This is not a dramatic policy, but in fact drama is dangerous and should be carefully avoided. If and when Russia becomes less illiberal, international control of atomic energy will become possible, and one of the horrors that darken our imaginations and fill our sleep with nightmares will be dissipated. Then at last the way will be open for the creation of a world Government by agreement. I see no reason why this should not be achieved before the end of the present century.

Meanwhile there are problems in Asia and problems in Africa which, unless wise statesmanship is used, will become daily more threatening and more insoluble. Even if no motive were involved except self-preservation, it would be urgently necessary for the West to find ways of raising Asia and Africa to the economic level of Western Europe, if not of America. So long as this is not done, Asia and Africa will inevitably feel envy, and the envy will turn to destructiveness. While destructive passions dominate half the human race, the other half cannot be safe. Europe and America therefore, even if very considerable immediate sacrifices are involved, will, if they are wise, devote themselves to the economic welfare of populations that are not white. Even a very considerable expenditure in this direction will bring an actual cash reward to the nations that make it, because prosperity in one place tends to produce prosperity in another, and conversely, poverty in one place tends to impoverish another.

For the reasons which I have given in earlier chapters, it will not be enough to invest capital in Asia and Africa, to modernize their agriculture and develop their industry. These things must be done, but whatever improvement they may produce will be very short-lived unless the populations concerned learn to practise the limitation of population. It is common in the West to suppose that there are insuperable psychological and theological obstacles to limitation of population in countries that are now backward. This is an entire mistake. Anyone who will look back to the pronouncement by Nehru will see that so far as this matter is concerned there is less superstition in the East than in Massachusetts or Connecticut. I do not think any reasonable person can doubt that in India, China and Japan, if the knowledge of birth-control existed, the birth-rate would fall very rapidly. In Africa the process might take longer, but there also it could be fairly easily achieved if negro doctors, trained in the West, were given the funds to establish medical clinics in which every kind of medical information would be given. I do not suppose that America would contribute to this beneficent work, because if either party favoured it, that party would lose the Catholic vote in New York State, and therefore the Presidency. This obviously would be a greater disaster than the extermination of the human race by atomic war. But we need not think that surplus funds will always continue to come only from America. The British and the French have much larger interests in Africa than the Americans have, and given economic recovery, the British and the French will be able to carry out policies in that continent even if America does not actively favour them.

In all suggestions for work by white men in either Asia or Africa, we are met by the difficulty that past history has made white imperialism suspect. For some reason—certainly a very bad one—Asia and Africa do not regard the Russians as imperialists, even when they see a great country like China reduced to the position of a satellite. But when the Americans, the French, or the British attempt any work, however beneficial and however humanitarian, in either Asia or Africa, they are at once suspected of territorial designs. It will take time and patience and honesty to overcome this suspicion; but if European influence were withdrawn suddenly, the result might easily be anarchy and chaos. The problem of preserving European influence where it is fruitful but not where it is imperialistic is a very delicate one. I do not think it can be solved except by people imbued with something like a missionary spirit, not in favour of any Church, but of a rational and productive way of life. There will need to be a large body of men in the West who understand, as few men now understand, what it is that the West has to offer, in its ways of life, its conquest of poverty, its high standard of education and its diminution of disease. These are things depending upon a certain technique. That technique, since it has been a white man's technique, has been intimately associated with white man's imperialism. I met once a Mexican Marxist and I asked him what he considered the message of Marx to Mexico. The message was, he said, that the Maya civilization was superior to that of Spain. This, of course, was because the descendants of the Maya are poor and the descendants of the Spaniards tend to be rich. I do not wish to say a word against Maya civilization, since I know very little about it; still less do I wish to say anything in favour of the civilization of Spain. Nevertheless, in a country full of oil and next door to the United States, I do not think a return to pre-Columbian civilization is a very practical policy. The same kind of problem will arise in other parts of the world. It will be very regrettable if the cessation of Western imperialism prevents the spread of what is good in Western ways of life. If this is to be prevented it will only be by a very considerable expenditure of disinterested zeal on the part of Western technicians and men of science and those who support them.

One of the great dangers of our time is nationalist and theological fanaticism. When one observes that the high idealism of the Indian Government in international matters breaks down completely when confronted with the question of Kashmir, it is difficult to avoid a feeling of despair. Quarrels of Jews and Arabs produce similar emotions, especially when one observes that whichever side is not favoured by the State Department feels inclined to call in the Communists, in spite of the steam-roller characteristics of their régime. Another example of the same sort of thing is Ireland. I will not take sides on the Ulster question; I will only observe that both sides apparently consider it more important than the preservation of Western civilization, or even of the human race, a view which to my mind is slightly exaggerated. Then there are premature aspirations. Iran wishes to be independent and has every right to be so, but until the conflict between Russia and the West has been decided, neither party is likely to concede independence to Iran, and certainly Iran is not in a position to exact it at present. There is need everywhere of a much greater knowledge of international affairs and of the place of one's own country in relation to the whole. Until this kind of knowledge is widely disseminated, many fragments will aim at a degree of isolation which is no longer possible. For good or ill, the human race has become one family. It can bring itself to disaster in a family quarrel or to happiness by means of harmony, but no member of the family can effectively cut itself off from the rest—not even Tibet or Chicago, the last refuges of isolationism.

This brings me to the subject of education. If there is to be effective international co-operation, such as was hoped for by the creators of the League of Nations and the United Nations, there will have to be very widespread education of an internationalist character. Schools will have to teach not only the narrow and biased nationalistic history which has hitherto been often thought sufficient, but world history from an impartial point of view. The books to be used in teaching world history will have to be books free from national bias, as far as this is humanly possible. There would have to be devices to secure impartiality. I should have the parts dealing with South America written by Norwegians, but the parts dealing with the Vikings should be written by Italians, and the parts dealing with medieval Italy by Americans. I should try to get all the books of history that would be used in schools written by men imbued with a feeling for man as man, and for human progress as opposed to the progress of this or that particular nation. And a great deal more should be taught about the world of the present day. It is all very well to know about Marathon, but it is not much help in dealing with the troubles of the Anglo-Iranian Oil Company, whose employees should not regard themselves as descendants of the army of Miltiades. Children should from an early age be made aware of the modern interdependence of different groups of men, and the importance of co-operation and the folly of conflict. They should have a new morality of growth and mutual adaptation, with consequent possibilities of freedom, in place of the older morality of prohibitions, conflicts, victories and defeats. In a word, they should be brought up to be citizens of the world in which they will have to live, not of the world of those bygone centuries among which academic culture loves to dwell. I do not mean that they should be ignorant of the past but I do mean that they should know that it is past, and that our world has need of different beliefs, different desires and different aptitudes from those that were required in technically simpler ages.

No teacher should be tolerated who teaches hostility to some group, whether Jews or negroes or plutocrats. For it is not by hostility that good things are achieved. I believe myself that the existence of plutocrats is regrettable, but I think the heat and fury generated by a class war is even more regrettable. There is almost always a way, though sometimes a much slower way, of doing things without violence. The French Revolution and the Russian Revolution, in spite of rivers of blood, did not achieve nearly so much towards economic equality as has been achieved in Britain in recent years, without any violence whatever. The teaching of hatred, however socially harmful may be the class against which the hatred is directed, always injects poison into the social system. When the immediate purpose of the hatred has been achieved, the emotion survives as a habit and looks for new victims. All advocacy of social change should be positive and not negative. It should emphasize the good things in a possible future more than the bad things in the present. I do not mean this as an absolute principle. When, for example, it is found that many lunatic asylums practise atrocious cruelties on the patients, it is necessary to concentrate in the first place upon the evil to be abolished. But this is not enough, and if it is thought to be enough, the evil will soon reappear, perhaps in a new form. It is necessary to probe deeper, to discover the causes of the evil, and the sources of malevolence in those who ill-treat their victims. In all such cases there will be found to be some distortion, some impediment to growth, something causing a deep inner discord in those who take pleasure in cruelty. And no reformer should be satisfied until he has arrived at the sources of these psychological misfortunes, and has discovered how to create for the young a world in which such things will not occur. This is a vast task, but it is not beyond the possibilities of economics and psychology combined. The world could within a couple of generations be made to consist of men and women who would be happy and sane, and because they were happy and sane, would be kindly in their impulses towards others, since they would have no impulse to regard others as their enemies in the absence of positive evidence. What we know about the formation of character is, as yet, very insufficiently utilized knowledge. It must be utilized to the full if we are to create a world where men are more prone to like each other than to feel mutual hatred.

I have spoken in this chapter on the assumption that a third world war will be avoided, but this is a very doubtful assumption. Any day a third world war may be upon us. If it happens, it will be far more terrible than the two that have preceded it, and will postpone for an indefinite period of time the realization of such hopes as I am dealing with in this book. But it will not postpone them for ever. Those among us who wish to see the sort of world that men could now create must not lose faith and hope if a third world war descends upon them. It will not be the end of the world; it will be a long illness, but not death, and it will be our duty, through whatever darkness and whatever sorrow, to keep hope alive and to bend our thoughts, in spite of present misery, upon the future of which that misery is perhaps only the labour pangs. Men are slow to learn, even when all that is to be learned is the road to happiness. Perhaps they can only learn by even more bitter experience than they have already had of the opposite road. But if they are to learn, if torture is to bring them sanity rather than madness, it will only be because some men have pre-served sanity and hope throughout. And the more such men there are, the more chance there is that experience will bring wisdom. Each separate one of us can do something to increase this chance, by steadfastness and courage throughout the days of darkness.

(*New Hopes for a Changing World*, London: Allen & Unwin; New York: Simon & Schuster, 1951.)

77

LIFE WITHOUT FEAR

THE thing that above all others I have been concerned to say is that because of fears that once had a rational basis mankind has failed to profit by the new techniques that, if wisely used, could make him happy. Fear makes man unwise in the three great departments of human conduct: his dealings with nature, his dealings with other men, and his dealings with himself. I wish in this chapter to consider the ways in which the world would be better if we were exempt from the tyranny of ancient fears.

It is necessary first of all to distinguish between fear as an emotion and rational apprehension of danger as a piece of knowledge. It would be foolish to be unaware of dangers when they exist, but it is very seldom that a danger can be dealt with as adequately by fear as by rational apprehension. Fear is a reaction which we share with the animals. It is crude and slapdash. Sometimes it serves the purposes of self-preservation, but sometimes it does quite the opposite. The man who is not mastered by fear is much better able to think out what kind of action will minimize the danger. Fear frequently prevents people from admitting the danger which in fact they are fearing, and therefore causes them not to take precautions that wisdom would advise. Sometimes this takes very absurd forms, as, for example, when fear of death prevents a man from making a will. It is important to make this point clear, since otherwise it might be thought that in speaking against fear one is speaking against a clear view of real perils.

Different kinds of dangers need different kinds of treatment. There are limitations to which human beings are subject owing to the physical facts of nature. These limitations are to a certain degree unavoidable, and to that degree must be accepted. On the other hand, the obstacles to well-being which arise from our relations to other people or to ourselves are to a very great extent unnecessary. There is nothing unavoidable about the misery that people cause each other through hatred or ill-will, nor about the misery that they cause themselves from a sense of guilt. Methods of dealing with the different kinds of evils are for this reason very different.

The limitations imposed by nature have to do with food and raw materials and with the physiological fact of death. These are not absolute; by more labour it is possible to produce more food, and by better technique it is possible to economize raw materials or make use of new substances that were previously thought worthless. Death can be postponed by medicine and wise living. But in all these three respects, although we cannot place an exact limit at one precise point, limits do exist. No amount of medicine will make a man immortal, and no amount of science could provide food if there were only standing room for the population. These limitations that are imposed by nature must be considered scientifically, in order that they may be met in the manner that will involve the smallest amount of suffering. In regard to food, the solution lies in birth-control; as regards raw materials, the solution will lie partly in a more scientific technique and partly in international control to prevent waste and secure just distribution; the postponement of death is a medical matter, but willing submission to it is a matter of psychology to which I shall return later.

In the past, the limitations imposed by nature have been dealt with superstitiously. There were gods or demons, or witches capable of invoking evil spirits, and if they were not placated, they caused bad weather. To this day, archbishops think that drought or excessive rain should be dealt with by prayer. Very often the methods demanded by superstition aggravate the evil. In the Middle Ages when there was a plague the population were encouraged to assemble in churches to pray; this, of course, provided an ideal method of spreading infection. Such evils, so far as they can be eradicated, can be eradicated only by science. The scientific attitude has the two-fold merit of causing willingness to admit the evil and intelligence in the search for means of mitigating it. There are still many evils in the world, of which over-population is perhaps the most menacing, in regard to which a large proportion of even the most civilized nations are wholly unscientific.

Fear of other human beings in the world as we have known it is often well founded, in the sense that there are those who will injure us if they can. But even when this is the case, it is not by fear, as a rule, that those who wish us ill can be best prevented from injuring us. If you have ever owned a dog that had a propensity to pursue sheep, you will have noticed that although he may remain well behaved so long as the sheep are stationary, he cannot resist temptation if they begin to run away. In this respect many of us are like the dog and many of us like the sheep. I once observed a purely psychological encounter between a Great Dane and a kitten three weeks old. The kitten stayed its ground, and spat and bristled and hissed. What went on in the mind of the Great Dane I do not know, but he behaved as if he thought the kitten had supernatural protection. After staring for a while, he put his tail between his legs and slunk away. If you have as much courage as this kitten, you will find it capable of protecting you against a great deal of aggression from which you might otherwise suffer. But this sort of behaviour is all within the capacity of animals, and I am more concerned with the sort of behaviour of which only human beings are capable. A great deal of the aggressiveness in the world is inspired by fear. We bark at our neighbour for fear that he will attack us, and he barks at us for the same reason. It happens not infrequently that you can cure aggressiveness by a display of friendliness. This is the element of truth in the doctrine of non-resistance, a doctrine which in its theoretical and absolute form I cannot accept, but which certainly contains a larger proportion of practical wisdom than most people would suppose. I think that every individual who does not display aggressive impulses does something to diminish some of such impulses in others. Even a mere external code of manners has its good effect in this respect, but when the non-aggressiveness is deeply rooted in character its effect is very much greater than it can ever be when it springs from a mere conventional rule.

Whenever a fear is well grounded in the sense that the danger apprehended is real, there are two different things that need to be done: one is to create in the individual that kind of fortitude that makes him able to face possible misfortunes calmly, and the other is to ameliorate the social system in such a way as to cause the danger to disappear. This applies, for example, to the fear of destitution, which is very widespread and very deep seated in all competitive countries. A very great many people who seem otherwise sane are quite irrational about money. There are men who, though they are willing to write large cheques, cannot bear to part with loose cash, and rather than do so will face black looks from untipped waiters. Arnold Bennett's Clayhanger, throughout a completely successful business career, continues to be haunted by fear of the workhouse. To prevent such fears there are three different sorts of things to be done. There is first the purely Stoic method of persuading a man that he should face misfortune calmly, and not let himself mind too much even when misfortunes occur. The supreme example of this is Milton's Satan. Then there is the method of persuading him that he is not very likely to become destitute; in mild cases this may be done by economic arguments, but in extreme cases it is a matter for the psychiatrist. Lastly there is the political method of coping with the whole problem of destitution, and making it no longer one of the things that befall the unfortunate. All these methods should be pursued in all such cases. The Stoic method is admirable when nothing better is possible, but although a man may face misfortune bravely, it would still be better if he did not have to face it. And it is clear that fear, when it exists to a morbid degree, is a product of a society in which real misfortunes are not unusual. Methods which deal only with the individual, therefore, useful as they may be, can never be substitutes for methods that remove the evil wholly by political means. It is important to realize this, for there are those who have so passionate an admiration for courage that they rejoice in opportunities for its exercise. This is absurd. You may admire a man who endures a long and painful illness without repining, but clearly it would be better if he enjoyed good health. You may admire a soldier who dies nobly in battle, but it would be much better if he did not die. In this respect the Stoics were to blame, since they praised endurance so much as to make cruelty seem almost a good thing, for cruelty was a necessary means to what they considered the highest good. It used to be a custom to praise the patient endurance of the poor, but that was before they had the vote.

Social dealings in private life are filled with fear, especially in Britain. People take pains not to wear their heart on their sleeves for daws to peck at. As far as they can, they keep their emotions to themselves. They will behave in exactly the same way to you whether they like you or dislike you, provided they have no motive of self-interest for making up to you. They are stiff and shy and unspontaneous. They wear an armour designed to conceal the frightened child within. The result is that social intercourse becomes boring, that friendships have little life in them, and that love is only a pale shadow of what it might be. People quote with approval Browning's remark:

> God be thanked, the meanest of his creatures
> Boasts two soul-sides, one to face the world with,
> One to show a woman when he loves her.

I am not a psycho-analyst, but I think that if I were I could find something to say about Browning's thankfulness on this point. The side that he faces the world with is the one that he feels he can exploit without the fear of being hurt, the one that gives no handle for ridicule and no knowledge that may be used to inflict pain; the other 'soul-side', the one that he shows a woman when he loves her, contains all the vanity and conceit and bombast that he dare not show to the men at his club. It is almost as much a product of fear as the other, because the other prevents him from letting fresh air into the inner chambers of his ego, and no one can be admitted to these inner chambers except in a relation of mutual adulation. The outer world is bleak, the inner world is stuffy. This is not how human relations should be. They should be free and spontaneous. Vanity should be less touchy and envy less widespread. The habit of reserve not only makes it easy for self-deception to flourish secretly, but also, owing to the energy spent in the purely negative occupation of preventing self-expression, greatly diminishes the fruitful outflow of energy in useful ways. It has the further defect that men are particularly anxious to conceal friendly impulses, since these especially, if known, make them feel that they are vulnerable. Hours of tedium and years of ossification result from this reign of social terror.

I do not imagine a world without fear as an anarchic world. There will be freedom in certain directions in which now freedom is much restricted, but in other directions where now there is freedom there will instead be law. There will be laws regulating the food supply and the distribution of raw materials. Above all, there will have to be laws for the prevention of war. I think, also, that it is impossible to have a world in which there is much freedom without excessive anarchy unless certain things are taught in the process of education. Where man's relation to physical nature is concerned, there is to be scientific discipline, that is to say, a habit of trying to ascertain the facts and admitting them when they have been ascertained. The world at present is full of sentimentalists who, when they find a fact unpleasant, merely refuse to admit that it is a fact. This habit of mind is capable of doing untold harm, because the unpleasant facts will have their unpleasant effects all the more fully for having been not recognized. Intellectual discipline, in the sense of willingness to admit facts, should result from education. It is merely stupid not to acknowledge the power of nature in so far as this power exists. Any attempt at self-assertion in this sphere is a failure of sanity.

Owing to the power of physical nature, certain habits, which only education is likely to create, are very useful for survival. I do not believe that any child brought up without discipline will brush its teeth. Indeed it is unlikely that the child will be sufficiently cleanly in its habits to be free from vermin. The preservation of health demands physical discipline which it is not likely that children will acquire through mere exhortations addressed to self-interest in later years. I think a certain amount of discipline in education is necessary, not only for reasons of health, but also to produce those habits of social behaviour which make perpetual quarrelling unnecessary. We do not at meal-times snatch the food from our neighbour, but the reason that we do not is that we were taught not to at a very early age. Long before we are grown up, the habit has become so engrained that we have ceased to be conscious of it. Punctuality at meals, though it is a tedious virtue, is important, since it miminizes the amount of service required. For such reasons, I think that habit-formation must be an important part of early education. Some modern educators have perhaps carried freedom in education somewhat too far in this respect. There is, however, a kind of freedom which education should preserve, though it seldom does so. I am thinking of emotional freedom. The reasons in favour of emotional freedom are various: on the one hand, too much control over the emotions is deadening, and causes loss of vitality; on the other hand, emotions which are not allowed an outlet turn bad, and find other outlets much more harmful than those that have been forbidden. There is also a third reason, which is that wherever a society is much bound by conventional rules, many emotions will be considered undesirable which in fact are harmless. I think, therefore, that while discipline is necessary in regard to scientific fact and in regard to certain habits without which social life becomes difficult, there should in education be as little as possible of discipline over the emotions. Above all, there must never be any attempt to cause the expression of emotions which are likely to be insincere.

Educators in the past tended too much to believe in original sin, and to think that the child ought to be made into something quite different from what nature would make it. The extreme example of this occurs in St Augustine's account of his learning Latin and Greek. Latin, he says, he learned without difficulty at his mother's knee, and, of course, in the end he knew it well; Greek he learned from a cruel schoolmaster with many beatings and much harshness, and with the result, so he tells us, that he never knew it well. Nevertheless, he thinks better of the method by which he was taught Greek, for this, he says, cured him of 'pernicious blithe-someness'. This is the exact antithesis of what an educator ought to feel. An educator should think of a child as a gardener thinks of a plant, as something to be made to grow by having the right soil and the right amount of water. If your roses fail to bloom, it does not occur to you to whip them, but you try to find out what has been amiss in your treatment of them. If your children fail to bloom, you should treat them as you would the roses. With few exceptions, what is wanted is positive, not negative. The important thing is what the children do, not what they do not do. And what they do, if it is to have value, must be a spontaneous expression of their own vital energy. You can, if you think fit, prepare children for a military life by teaching them all to do the same thing at the same moment when they hear the word of command. If you do, they will grow up thwarted and stunted and full of a deep-seated anger against the world— no doubt useful emotions if they are to be soldiers employed in killing, but not if they are to be happy citizens of a world at peace.

(*New Hopes for a Changing World*, London: Allen & Unwin; New York: Simon & Schuster, 1951.)

78

SCIENCE AND HUMAN LIFE

SCIENCE and the techniques to which it has given rise have changed human life during the last hundred and fifty years more than it had been changed since men took to agriculture, and the changes that are being wrought by science continue at an increasing speed. There is no sign of any new stability to be attained on some scientific plateau. On the contrary, there is every reason to think that the revolutionary possibilities of science extend immeasurably beyond what has so far been realized. Can the human race adjust itself quickly enough to these vertiginous transformations, or will it, as innumerable former species have done, perish from lack of adaptability? The dinosaurs were, in their day, the lords of creation, and if there had been philosophers among them not one would have foreseen that the whole race might perish. But they became extinct because they could not adapt themselves to a world without swamps. In the case of man and science, there is a wholly new factor, namely that man himself is creating the changes of environment to which he will have to adjust himself with unprecedented rapidity. But, although man through his scientific skill is the cause of the changes of environment, most of these changes are not willed by human beings. Although they come about through human agencies, they have, or at any rate have had so far, something of the inexorable inevitability of natural forces. Whether nature dried up the swamps or men deliberately drained them, makes little difference as regards the ultimate result. Whether men will be able to survive the changes of environment that their own skill has brought about is an open question. If the answer is in the affirmative, it will be known some day; if not, not. If the answer is to be in the affirmative, men will have to apply scientific ways of thinking to themselves and their institutions. They cannot continue to hope, as all politicians hitherto have, that in a world where everything has changed, the political and social habits of the eighteenth century can remain inviolate. Not only will men of science have to grapple with the sciences that deal with man, but—and this is a far more difficult matter—they will have to persuade the world to listen to what they have discovered. If they cannot succeed in this difficult enterprise, man will destroy himself by his halfway cleverness. I am told that, if he were out of the way, the future would lie with rats. I hope they will find it a pleasant world, but I am glad I shall not be there.

But let us pass from these generalities to more specific questions.

One of the most obvious problems raised by a scientific technique is that of the exhaustion of the soil and of raw materials. This subject has been much discussed, and some governments have actually taken some steps to prevent the denudation of the soil. But I doubt whether, as yet, the good done by these measures is outweighing the harm done in less careful regions. Food, however, is such an obvious necessity that the problem is bound to receive increasing attention as population pressure makes it more urgent. Whether this increased attention will do good or harm in the long run is, I fear, questionable. By a spendthrift use of fertilizers, food production in the present can be increased at the cost of food production in the future. Can you imagine a politician going to his constituents and saying: 'Ladies and gentlemen, it is in your power to have abundance of food for the next thirty years, but the measures that will give you this abundance will cause scarcity for your grandchildren. I am therefore proposing measures to ensure frugality in the present in order to avoid famine in the somewhat distant future.' Is it possible to believe that a politician who said this would win elections against one less addicted to foresight? I hardly think so, unless the general level of political intelligence and virtue can be very considerably increased.

The question of raw materials is more difficult and complex than the question of food. The raw materials required at one stage of technique are different from those required at another. It may be that by the time the world's supply of oil is exhausted, atomic power will have taken its place. But to this sort of process there is a limit, though not an easily assignable one. At present there is a race for uranium, and it would seem likely that before very long there will be no easily accessible source of uranium. If, when that happens, the world has come to depend upon nuclear energy as its main source of power, the result may be devastating. All such speculations are of course very questionable, since new techniques may always make it possible to dispense with formerly necessary raw materials. But we cannot get away from the broad fact that we are living upon the world's capital of stored energy and are transforming the energy at a continually increasing rate into forms in which it cannot be utilized. Such a manner of life can hardly be stable, but must sooner or later bring the penalty that lies in wait for those who live on capital.

In primitive times, when the human population of the globe was small, such problems did not arise. Agriculture, it is true, was practised in ways that exhausted the soil for a time, but there were usually new vacant lands available; and if there were not, the corpses of enemies sufficed as fertilizers. The system was 'conservative' in the physicist's sense. That is to say, energy on the whole accumulated as fast as it was used. Now, this is not the case; and, so far as one can see, it will never be the case while scientific technique continues.

All this, however, you may say, is distant and doubtful: we have more pressing matters to consider. This is true, and I will proceed to consider some of them.

The problem which most preoccupies the public mind at the present moment is that of scientific warfare. It has become evident that, if scientific skill is allowed free scope, the human race will be exterminated, if not in the next war, then in the next but one or the next but two—at any rate at no very distant date. To this problem there are two possible reactions: there are those who say: 'Let us create social institutions which will make large-scale war impossible'; there are others who say: 'Let us not allow war to become *too* scientific. We cannot perhaps go back to bows and arrows, but let us at any rate agree with our enemies that, if we fight them, both sides will fight inefficiently.' For my part, I favour the former answer, since I cannot see that either side could be expected to observe an agreement not to use modern weapons if once war had broken out. It is on this ground that I do not think that there will long continue to be human beings unless methods are found of permanently preventing large-scale wars. But this is a serious question as to which I will say no more at the moment. I shall return to it presently.

The substitution of machines for human labour raises problems which are likely to become acute in the not very distant future. These problems are not new. They began with the Industrial Revolution, which ruined large numbers of skilled and industrious handicraftsmen, inflicting upon them hardships that they had in no way deserved and that they bitterly resented. But their troubles were transitory: they died; and such of their children as survived sought other occupations. The sufferers had no political power and were not able to offer any effective resistance to 'progress'. Nowadays, in democratic countries, the political situation is different and wage-earners cannot be expected to submit tamely to starvation. But if we are to believe Norbert Wiener's book on cybernetics—and I see no reason why we should not—it should soon be possible to keep up the existing level of production with a very much smaller number of workers. The more economical methods, one may suppose, would be introduced during a war while the workers were at the front, if such a war were not quickly ended by H-bomb extermination, and when the survivors returned their former jobs would no longer be available. The social discontent resulting from such a situation would be very grave. It could be dealt with in a totalitarian country, but a democracy could only deal with it by radical changes in its social philosophy and even in its ethics. Work has been thought to be a duty, but in such a situation there would be little work to do and duty would have to take new forms.

Changes in political philosophy are necessary for several reasons. One of the most important is that modern techniques make society more organic in the sense that its parts are more interdependent and an injury to one individual or group is more likely than it formerly was to cause injury to other individuals or groups. It is easier to kill a man than to kill a sponge because he is more highly organized and more centralized. In like manner it is easier to inflict vital damage upon a scientific community than upon a community of nomads or scattered peasants. This increase of interdependence makes it necessary to limit freedom in various ways which liberals in the past considered undesirable. There are two spheres in which such limitation is especially necessary: the one is in economics; and the other in the relations between States.

Take economics first. Suppose, as is not improbable, that most of the power used in industry comes to be distributed from a fairly small number of atomic power-stations, and suppose that the men working in these stations retained the right to strike. They could completely paralyse the industrial life of a nation and could levy almost unlimited blackmail in the form of demands for higher wages. No community would tolerate such a state of affairs. The workers in power-stations would have to have understudies like actors in a theatre, and the forces of the State would have to be employed if necessary to enable the understudies to replace workers on strike. Another example, which war has already brought to the fore, is the supply and use of raw materials. Whenever raw materials are scarce their distribution has to be controlled and not left to the free play of unfettered economic forces. Scarcity of this sort has hitherto been thought of as a transitory phenomenon due to the needs and ravages of war. But it is likely to remain, in regard to many essentials, a normal condition of highly developed industry. Some central authority for the allocation of raw materials must therefore be expected as a necessary limitation of economic freedom. Another unavoidable limitation comes from the vastness of some obviously desirable enterprises. To bring fertility to the interior of Australia and to parts of Siberia is almost certainly possible, but only by an expenditure far beyond the capacity of private enterprise. One may expect that the progress of science will increase the number of such possible enterprises. Perhaps it will be possible in time to make the Sahara rainy, or even to make northern Canada warm. But, if such things become possible, they will be possible only for whole communities and not for private corporations.

Even more important than the limitations of economic liberty are the limitations on the liberty of States. The liberal doctrine of nationality, which was preached by liberals before 1848 and embodied in the Treaty of Versailles by President Wilson, had its justification as a protest against alien domination. But to allow *complete* liberty to any national State is just as anarchic as it would be to allow complete liberty to an individual. There are things which an individual must not do because the criminal law forbids them. The law and the police are in most cases strong enough to prevent such things from being done: murderers are a very small percentage of the population of any civilized country. But the relations between States are not governed by law and cannot be until there is a supranational armed force strong enough to enforce the decisions of a supranational authority. In the past, although the wars resulting from international anarchy caused much suffering and destruction, mankind was able to survive them, and, on the whole, the risks of war were thought less irksome than the controls that would be necessary to prevent it. This is ceasing to be true. The risks of war have become so great that the continued existence of our species either has become or soon will become incompatible with the new methods of scientific destruction.

The new dangers resulting from our more organic society call for certain changes in the kind of character that is admired. The bold buccaneer, or the great conqueror such as Alexander or Napoleon, has been admired and is still admired although the world can no longer afford this type of character. We come here upon a difficulty. It is a good thing that people should be adventurous and that there should be scope for individual enterprise; but the adventure and enterprise, if they are not to bring total disaster, must steer clear of certain fields in which they were formerly possible. You may still, without harm to your fellow men, wish to be the first man to reach the moon. You may wish to be a great poet or a great composer or a man who advances the boundaries of scientific knowledge. Such adventure injures no one. But if Napoleon is your ideal, you must be restrained. Certain kinds of anarchic self-assertion, which are splendid in the literature of tragedy, have come to involve too much risk. A motorist alone on an empty road may drive as he pleases, but in crowded traffic he must obey the rules. More and more the lives of individuals come to resemble the motorist in traffic rather than the lonely driver in an empty desert.

I come at last to a question which is causing considerable concern and perplexity to many men of science, namely: what is their social duty towards this new world that they have been creating? I do not think this question is easy or simple. The pure man of science, as such, is concerned with the advancement of knowledge, and in his professional moments he takes it for granted that the advancement of knowledge is desirable. But inevitably he finds himself casting his pearls before swine. Men who do not understand his scientific work can utilize the knowledge that he provides. The new techniques to which it gives rise often have totally unexpected effects. The men who decide what use shall be made of the new techniques are not necessarily possessed of any exceptional degree of wisdom. They are mainly politicians whose professional skill consists in knowing how to play upon the emotions of masses of men. The emotions which easily sway masses are very seldom the best of which the individuals composing the masses are capable. And so the scientist finds that he has unintentionally placed new powers in the hands of reckless men. He may easily come to doubt, in moments of depression or overwork, whether the world would not be a happier place if science did not exist. He knows that science gives power and that the power which it gives could be used to increase human welfare; but he knows also that very often it is used, not so, but in the very opposite direction. Is he on this account to view himself as an unintentional malefactor?

I do not think so. I think we must retain the belief that scientific knowledge is one of the glories of man. I will not maintain that knowledge can never do harm. I think such general propositions can almost always be refuted by well-chosen examples. What I will maintain—and maintain vigorously—is that knowledge is very much more often useful than harmful and that fear of knowledge is very much more often harmful than useful. Suppose you are a scientific pioneer and you make some discovery of great scientific importance, and suppose you say to yourself: 'I am afraid this discovery will do harm': you know that other people are likely to make the same discovery if they are allowed suitable opportunities for research; you must therefore, if you do not wish the discovery to become public, either discourage your sort of research or control publication by a board of censors. Nine times out of ten, the board of censors will object to knowledge that is in fact useful—e.g. knowledge concerning contraceptives—rather than to knowledge that would in fact be harmful. It is very difficult to foresee the social effects of new knowledge, and it is very easy from the sheer force of habit to shrink from new knowledge such as might promote new kinds of behaviour.

Apart from the more general duties of scientists towards society, they have a quite special and exceptional duty in the present critical condition of the world. All men of science who have studied thermonuclear warfare are aware of two superlatively important facts: first, that whatever agreements may have been reached to the contrary, thermonuclear weapons will certainly be employed by both sides in a world war; second, that if such weapons are employed there can be no hope of victory for either side, but only of universal destruction involving, quite possibly, the end of all human and animal life and almost certainly, failing that, a complete reversion to barbarism. A great war with thermonuclear weapons will not produce a universal victory of Communism. It will also not produce the sort of world desired by the Western Powers. Nor will it give opportunity for the independent flourishing of South-East Asia or Africa. Radio-active clouds, borne by the wind, will not respect frontiers and will ignore the legal rights of neutrals. In view of this prospect, there is one matter upon which the interests of the whole world coincide. Whether you are a Communist or an anti-Communist, an inhabitant of Asia or Europe or America, a white, brown, yellow, or black man, your interests are exactly the same as those of the rest of the human race. Your paramount interest, if you are aware of the situation, must be to preserve the existence of mankind by preventing a great war. It is clearly the duty of men of science to bring the facts home, as far as lies in their power, to the governments and peoples of both East and West. This is no easy task. The governments of both East and West, whether from ignorance or from motives of prestige, are engaged in trying to persuade their populations that thermonuclear weapons will destroy the enemy but not themselves. *The Red Star*, the official military organ of the Soviet Government, published several articles on methods of defence against thermonuclear weapons. These articles were so absurd that one could hardly believe their authors to be sincere. It seemed obvious that the purpose of the articles was to deceive people in Russia as to the perils to which they would be exposed. I am afraid that the schemes for civil defence put forward in America and Britain are equally misleading. I hope that this is because the authorities are ignorant and not because they are dishonest.

Clearly, scientists both of the East and of the West have an imperative duty: namely, the duty of bringing home to the protagonists the fact that the time is past for swashbuckling and boasting and campaigns of bluff which, if the bluff is called, can end only in utter disaster. I have been glad to see a lead given by a small number of men of science of the highest eminence, representing many countries and all creeds, Americans, Western Europeans, Poles, and Japanese. I have rejoiced to see these men issue a clear statement as to what is likely to happen in a great war; and I should wish them to invite all other men of science, in all countries, to subscribe to this statement.

I am aware that this will involve a certain degree of heroism and self-sacrifice. But there will be a reward which brave men should find sufficient: the reward of preserving uprightness and self-respect in the face of danger. These virtues are common in battle, and men of science should be able to show them also in a conflict with ignorance and ferocity. Science has fought great fights in former centuries against the embattled forces of obscurantism. In the nineteenth century it seemed as though science were victorious, but the victory is in danger of proving illusory. If science is to do its duty by mankind, men of science must once again face martydom and obloquy and the accusation of indifference to moral values. Perhaps their prestige may suffice to save them from the worst penalties for their courage, but of this we cannot be confident. What we can say with confidence is that it is not worth while to prolong a slavish and cowardly existence for a few miserable years while those who know the magnitude of the impending catastrophe wait for that radio-active death that is in store for them as well as for others.

A difficult readjustment in the scientists' conception of duty is imperatively necessary. As Lord Adrian said in his address to the British Association: 'Unless we are ready to give up some of our old loyalties, we may be forced into a fight which might end the human race.' This matter of loyalty is the crux. Hitherto, in the East and in the West alike, most scientists, like most other people, have felt that loyalty to their own State is paramount. They have no longer a right to feel this. Loyalty to the human race must take its place. Everyone in the West will at once admit this as regards Soviet scientists. We are shocked that Kapitza, who was Rutherford's favourite pupil, was willing, when the Soviet Government refused him permission to return to Cambridge, to place his scientific skill at the disposal of those who wished to spread Communism by means of H-bombs. We do not so readily apprehend a similar failure of duty on our own side. I do not wish to be thought to suggest treachery, since that is only a transference of loyalty to another national State; I am suggesting a very different thing: that scientists the world over should join in enlightening mankind as to the perils of a great war and in devising methods for its prevention. I urge with all the emphasis at my disposal that this is the duty of scientists in East and West alike. It is a difficult duty, and one likely to entail penalties for those who perform it. But, after all, it is the labours of scientists which have caused the danger and on this account, if on no other, scientists must do everything in their power to save mankind from the madness which they have made possible.

Science from the dawn of history, and probably longer, has been intimately associated with war. I imagine that when our ancestors descended from the trees they were victorious over the arboreal conservatives because flints were sharper than coconuts. To come to more recent times, Archimedes was respected for his scientific defence of Syracuse against the Romans; Leonardo obtained employment under the Duke of Milan because of his skill in fortification, though he did mention in a postscript that he could also paint a bit; Galileo similarly derived an income from the Grand Duke of Tuscany because of his skill in calculating the trajectories of projectiles. In the French Revolution, those scientists who were not guillotined devoted themselves to making new explosives. There is therefore no departure from tradition in the present-day scientists' manufacture of A-bombs and H-bombs. All that is new is the extent of their destructive skill.

I do not think that men of science can cease to regard the disinterested pursuit of knowledge as their primary duty. It is true that new knowledge and new skills are sometimes harmful in their effects, but scientists cannot profitably take account of this fact since the effects are impossible to foresee. We cannot blame Columbus because the discovery of the Western Hemisphere spread throughout the Eastern Hemisphere an appallingly devastating plague. Nor can we blame James Watt for the Dust Bowl, although if there had been no steam engines and no railways the West would not have been so carelessly or so quickly cultivated. To see that knowledge is wisely used is primarily the duty of statesmen, not of men of science; but it is part of the duty of men of science to see that important knowledge is widely disseminated and is not falsified in the interests of this or that propaganda.

Scientific knowledge has its dangers; but so has every great thing. And over and beyond the dangers with which it threatens the present, it opens up as nothing else can the vision of a possible happy world, a world without poverty, without war, with little illness. And, what is perhaps more than all, when science has mastered the forces which mould human character, it will be able to produce populations in which few suffer from destructive fierceness and in which the great majority regard other people, not as competitors to be feared, but as helpers in a common task. Science has only recently begun to apply itself to human beings except in their purely physical aspect. Such science as exists in psychology and anthropology has hardly begun to affect political behaviour or private ethics. The minds of men remain attuned to a world that is fast disappearing. The changes in our physical environment require, if they are to bring well-being, correlative changes in our beliefs and habits. If we cannot effect these changes, we shall suffer the fate of the dinosaurs who could not live on dry land. I think it is the duty of science—I do not say of every individual man of science—to study the means by which we can adapt ourselves to the new world. There are certain things that the world quite obviously needs: tentativeness, as opposed to dogmatism, in our beliefs; an expectation of co-operation, rather than competition, in social relations; a lessening of envy and collective hatred. These are things which education could produce without much difficulty. They are not things adequately sought in the education of the present day.

It is to progress in the human sciences that we must look to undo the evils which have resulted from a knowledge of the physical world hastily and superficially acquired by populations unconscious of the changes in themselves that the new knowledge has made imperative. The road to a happier world than any known in the past lies open before us if atavistic destructive passions can be kept in leash while the necessary adaptations are made. Fears are inevitable in our time, but hopes are equally rational and far more likely to bear good fruit. We must learn to think rather less of the dangers to be avoided than of the good that will lie within our grasp if we can believe in it and let it dominate our thoughts. Science, whatever unpleasant consequences it may have by the way, is in its very nature a liberator, a liberator of bondage to physical nature and, in time to come, a liberator from the weight of destructive passions. We are on the threshold of utter disaster or unprecedentedly glorious achievements. No previous age has been fraught with problems so momentous; and it is to science that we must look for a happy issue.

> (*What is Science?* edited by James R. Newman,
> New York: Simon & Schuster, 1955.)

79

OPEN LETTER TO EISENHOWER
AND KHRUSHCHEV

I AM addressing you as the respective heads of the two most powerful countries in the world. Those who direct the policies of these countries have a power for good or evil exceeding anything ever possessed before by any man or group of men. Public opinion in your respective countries has been focused upon the points in which your national interests are thought to diverge, but I am convinced that you, as far-seeing and intelligent men, must be aware that the matters in which the interests of Russia and America coincide are much more important than the matters in which they are thought to diverge. I believe that if you two eminent men were jointly to proclaim this fact and to bend the policies of your great countries to agreement with such a proclamation, there would be throughout the world, and not least in your own countries, a shout of joyful agreement which would raise you both to a pinnacle of fame surpassing anything achieved by other statesmen of the past or present. Although, of course, you are both well aware of the points in which the interests of Russia and America are identical, I will, for the sake of explicitness, enumerate some of them.

1. The supreme concern of men of all ways of thought at the present time must be to ensure the continued existence of the human race. This is already in jeopardy from the hostility between East and West and will, if many minor nations acquire nuclear weapons, be in very much greater jeopardy within a few years from the possibility of irresponsible action by thoughtless fanatics.

Some ignorant militarists, both in the East and in the West, have apparently thought that the danger could be averted by a world war giving victory to their own side. The progress of science and technology has made this an idle dream. A world war would result, not in the victory of either side, but in the extermination of both. Neither side can desire such a cataclysm.

The hope of world dominion, either military or ideological, is one which has hovered before many men in the past and has led invariably to disaster. Philip II of Spain made the attempt and reduced his country to the status of a minor power. Louis XIV of France made the attempt and, by exhausting his country, led the way to the French Revolution, which he would have profoundly deplored. Hitler, in our own day, fought for the world-wide supremacy of the Nazi philosophy, and perished miserably. Two great men propounded ideologies which have not yet run their course: I mean the authors of the Declaration of Independence and the Communist Manifesto. There is no reason to expect that either of these ideologies will be more successful in conquering the world than their predecessors, Buddhist, Christian, Moslem—or the Nazis. What is new in the present situation is not the impossibility of success, but the magnitude of the disaster which must result from the attempt. We must, therefore, hope that each side will abandon the futile strife and agree to allow to each a sphere proportionate to its present power.

2. The international anarchy which will inevitably result from the unrestricted diffusion of nuclear weapons is not to the interest of either Russia or America. There was a time when only America had nuclear weapons. This was followed by a time when only Russia and America had such weapons. And now only Russia, America and Britain possess them. It is obvious that, unless steps are taken, France and Germany will shortly manufacture these weapons. It is not likely that China will lag far behind.

We must expect that, during the next few years, the manufacture of engines of mass destruction will become cheaper and easier. No doubt Egypt and Israel will then be able to follow the example set by the great powers. So will the states of South America. There is no end to this process until every sovereign State is in a position to say to the whole world: 'You must yield to my demands or you shall die.'

If all sovereign States were governed by rulers possessed of even the rudiments of sanity, they would be restrained from such blackmail by the fear that their citizens also would perish. But experience shows that, from time to time, power in this or that country falls into the hands of rulers who are not sane. Can anyone doubt that Hitler, if he had been able to do so, would have chosen to involve all mankind in his own ruin?

For such reasons, it is imperative to put a stop to the diffusion of nuclear weapons. This can easily be done by agreement between Russia and America, since they can jointly refuse military or economic assistance to any country other than themselves which persists in the manufacture of such weapons. But it cannot be achieved without agreement between the two dominant powers, for, without such agreement, each new force of nuclear weapons will be welcomed by one side or the other as an increase to its own strength. This helter-skelter race towards ruin must be stopped if anything that anybody could desire is to be effected.

3. So long as the fear of world war dominates policy and the only deterrent is the threat of universal death, so long can there be no limit to

the diversion of expenditure of funds and human energy into channels of destruction. It is clear that both Russia and America could save nine-tenths of their present expenditure if they concluded an alliance and devoted themselves jointly to the preservation of peace throughout the world. If they do not find means of lessening their present hostility, reciprocal fear will drive them further and further, until, apart from immense armaments, nothing beyond a bare subsistence will be left to their populations.

In order to promote efficiency in the preparation of death, education will have to be distorted and stunted. Everything in human achievement that is not inspired by hatred and fear will be squeezed out of the curriculum in schools and universities. Any attempt to preserve the vision of man as the triumph—so far—of the long ages of evolution will come to be viewed as treachery, since it will be thought not to minister to the victory of this group or that. Such a prospect is death to the hopes of all who share the aspirations which have inspired human progress.

4. I cannot but think that you would both rejoice if a way could be found to disperse the pall of fear which at present dims the hopes of mankind. Never before, since our remote ancestors descended from the trees, has there been valid reason for such fear. Never before has such a sense of futility blighted the visions of youth. Never before has there been reason to feel that the human race was travelling along a road ending only in a bottomless precipice. Individual death we must all face, but collective death has never, hitherto, been a grim possibility.

And all this fear, all this despair, all this waste is utterly unnecessary. One thing only is required to dispel the darkness and enable the world to live again in a noonday brightness of hope. The one thing necessary is that East and West should recognize their respective rights, admit that each must learn to live with the other and substitute argument for force in the attempt to spread their respective ideologies. It is not necessary that either side should abandon belief in its own creed. It is only necessary that it should abandon the attempt to spread its own creed by force of arms.

I suggest, Sirs, that you should meet in a frank discussion of the conditions of co-existence, endeavouring no longer to secure this or that more or less surreptitious advantage for your own side, but seeking rather such agreements and such adjustments in the world as will diminish future occasions of strife. I believe that if you were to do this, the world would acclaim your action, and the forces of sanity, released from their long bondage, would ensure for the years to come a life of vigour and achievement and joy surpassing anything known in even the happiest eras of the past.

(*New Statesman*, Nov. 7, 1957 and *Look* magazine, Jan. 21, 1958, subsequently reprinted in *The Vital Letters of Russell, Khrushchev and Dulles*, London: Macgibbon & Kee.)

80

MAN'S PERIL

I AM speaking on this occasion not as a Briton, not as a European, not as a member of a Western democracy, but as a human being, a member of the species Man, whose continued existence is in doubt. The world is full of conflicts: Jews and Arabs; Indians and Pakistanis; white men and negroes in Africa; and, overshadowing all minor conflicts, the titanic struggle between Communism and anti-Communism.

Almost everybody who is politically conscious has strong feelings about one or more of these issues; but I want you, if you can, to set aside such feelings for the moment and consider yourself only as a member of a biological species which has had a remarkable history and whose disappearance none of us can desire. I shall try to say no single word which should appeal to one group rather than to another. All, equally, are in peril and, if the peril is understood, there is hope that they may collectively avert it. We have to learn to think in a new way. We have to learn to ask ourselves not what steps can be taken to give military victory to whatever group we prefer, for there no longer are such steps. The question we have to ask ourselves is: What steps can be taken to prevent a military contest of which the issue must be disastrous to all sides?

The general public, and even many men in positions of authority, have not realized what would be involved in a war with hydrogen bombs. The general public still thinks in terms of the obliteration of cities. It is understood that the new bombs are more powerful than the old and that, while one atomic bomb could obliterate Hiroshima, one hydrogen bomb could obliterate the largest cities such as London, New York, and Moscow. No doubt in a hydrogen-bomb war great cities would be obliterated. But this is one of the minor disasters that would have to be faced. If everybody in London, New York, and Moscow were exterminated, the world might, in the course of a few centuries, recover from the blow. But we now know, especially since the Bikini test, that hydrogen bombs can gradually spread destruction over a much wider area than had been supposed. It is stated on very good authority that a bomb can now be manufactured which will be 25,000 times as powerful as that which destroyed Hiroshima. Such a bomb, if exploded near the ground or under water, sends radio-active particles into the upper air. They sink gradually and reach the surface of the earth in the form of a deadly dust or rain. It was this dust which infected the Japanese fishermen and their catch of fish although they were outside what American experts believed to be the danger zone. No one knows how widely such lethal radio-active particles might be diffused, but the best authorities are unanimous in saying that a war with hydrogen bombs is quite likely to put an end to the human race. It is feared that if many hydrogen bombs are used there will be universal death—sudden only for a fortunate minority, but for the majority a slow torture of disease and disintegration.

I will give a few instances out of many. Sir John Slessor, who can speak with unrivalled authority from his experiences of air warfare, has said: 'A world war in this day and age would be general suicide'; and has gone on to state: 'It never has and never will make any sense trying to abolish any particular *weapon* of war. What we have got to abolish is *war*.' Lord Adrian, who is the leading English authority on nerve physiology, recently emphasized the same point in his address as President of the British Association. He said: 'We must face the possibility that repeated atomic explosions will lead to a degree of general radio-activity which no one can tolerate or escape'; and he added: 'Unless we are ready to give up some of our old loyalties, we may be forced into a fight which might end the human race.' Air Chief Marshal Sir Philip Joubert says: 'With the advent of the hydrogen bomb, it would appear that the human race has arrived at a point where it must abandon war as a continuation of policy or accept the possibility of total destruction.' I could prolong such quotations indefinitely.

Many warnings have been uttered by eminent men of science and by authorities in military strategy. None of them will say that the worst results are certain. What they do say is that these results are possible and no one can be sure that they will not be realized. I have not found that the views of experts on this question depend in any degree upon their politics or prejudices. They depend only, so far as my researches have revealed, upon the extent of the particular expert's knowledge. I have found that the men who know most are most gloomy.

STARK, INESCAPABLE PROBLEM

Here, then, is the problem which I present to you, stark and dreadful and inescapable: Shall we put an end to the human race; or shall mankind renounce war? People will not face this alternative because it is so difficult to abolish war. The abolition of war will demand distasteful limitations of national sovereignty. But what perhaps impedes understanding of the situation more than anything else is that the term 'mankind' feels vague and abstract. People scarcely realize in imagination that the danger is to themselves and their children and their grandchildren, and not only to a dimly apprehended humanity. And so they hope that perhaps war may be allowed to continue provided modern weapons are prohibited. I am afraid this hope is illusory. Whatever agreements not to use hydrogen bombs had been reached in time of peace, they would no longer be considered binding in time of war, and both sides would set to work to manufacture hydrogen bombs as soon as war broke out, for if one side manufactured the bombs and the other did not, the side that manufactured them would inevitably be victorious.

On both sides of the Iron Curtain there are political obstacles to emphasis on the destructive character of future war. If either side were to announce that it would on no account resort to war, it would be diplomatically at the mercy of the other side. Each side, for the sake of self-preservation, must continue to say that there are provocations that it will not endure. Each side may long for an accommodation, but neither side dare express this longing convincingly. The position is analogous to that of duellists in former times. No doubt it frequently happened that each of the duellists feared death and desired an accommodation, but neither could say so, since, if he did, he would be thought a coward. The only hope in such cases was intervention by friends of both parties suggesting an accommodation to which both could agree at the same moment. This is an exact analogy to the present position of the protagonists on either side of the Iron Curtain. If an agreement making war improbable is to be reached, it will have to be by the friendly offices of neutrals, who can speak of the disastrousness of war without being accused of advocating a policy of 'appeasement'. The neutrals have every right, even from the narrowest consideration of self-interest, to do whatever lies in their power to prevent the outbreak of a world war, for if such a war does break out, it is highly probable that all the inhabitants of neutral countries, along with the rest of mankind, will perish. If I were in control of a neutral government, I should certainly consider it my paramount duty to see to it that my country would continue to have inhabitants, and the only way by which I could make this probable would be to promote some kind of accommodation between the powers on opposite sides of the Iron Curtain.

I, personally, am of course not neutral in my feeling and I should not wish to see the danger of war averted by an abject submission of the West. But, as a human being, I have to remember that, if the issues between East and West are to be decided in any manner that can give any possible satisfaction to anybody, whether Communist or anti-Communist, whether Asian or European or American, whether white or black, then these issues must not be decided by war. I should wish this to be understood on both sides of the Iron Curtain. It is emphatically not enough to have it understood on one side only. I think the neutrals, since they are not caught in our tragic dilemma, can, if they will, bring about this realization on both sides. I should like to see one or more neutral powers appoint a commission of experts, who should all be neutrals, to draw up a report on the destructive effects to be expected in a war with hydrogen bombs, not only among the belligerents but also among neutrals. I should wish this report presented to the Governments of all the Great Powers with an invitation to express their agreement or disagreement with its findings. I think it possible that in this way all the Great Powers could be led to agree that a world war can no longer serve the purposes of any of them, since it is likely to exterminate friend and foe equally and neutrals likewise.

As geological time is reckoned, man has so far existed only for a very short period—1,000,000 years at the most. What he has achieved, especially during the last 6,000 years, is something utterly new in the history of the cosmos, so far at least as we are acquainted with it. For countless ages the sun rose and set, the moon waxed and waned, the stars shone in the night, but it was only with the coming of man that these things were understood. In the great world of astronomy and in the little world of the atom, man has unveiled secrets which might have been thought undiscoverable. In art and literature and religion, some men have shown a sublimity of feeling which makes the species worth preserving. Is all this to end in trivial horror because so few are able to think of man rather than of this or that group of men? Is our race so destitute of wisdom, so incapable of impartial love, so blind even to the simplest dictates of self-preservation, that the last proof of its silly cleverness is to be the extermination of all life on our planet?—for it will be not only men who will perish, but also the animals, whom no one can accuse of Communism or anti-Communism.

I cannot believe that this is to be the end. I would have men forget their quarrels for a moment and reflect that, if they will allow themselves to survive, there is every reason to expect the triumphs of the future to exceed immeasurably the triumphs of the past. There lies before us, if we choose, continual progress in happiness, knowledge, and wisdom. Shall we, instead, choose death, because we cannot forget our quarrels? I appeal as a human being to human beings: remember your humanity, and forget the rest. If you can do so, the way lies open to a new Paradise; if you cannot, nothing lies before you but universal death.

(*Portraits from Memory*, London: Allen & Unwin; New York: Simon & Schuster, 1956.)

METHODS OF SETTLING DISPUTES
IN THE NUCLEAR AGE

I SHALL assume the following three propositions conceded:

(1) A large-scale nuclear war would be an utter disaster, not only to the belligerents, but to mankind, and would achieve no result that any sane man could desire.

(2) When a small war occurs, there is a considerable risk that it may turn into a great war; and in the course of many small wars the risk would ultimately become almost a certainty.

(3) If all existing nuclear weapons had been destroyed and there were an agreement that no new ones should be manufactured, any serious war would, nevertheless, become a nuclear war as soon as the belligerents had time to manufacture the forbidden weapons.

From these three theses, it follows that, if we are to escape unimaginable catastrophes, we must find a way of avoiding all wars, whether great or small and whether intentionally nuclear or not.

I think that, in a more or less undecided fashion, this conclusion is admitted by most of those who have studied the subject. But statesmen, both in the East and the West, have not arrived at any possible programme for implementing the prevention of war. Since the nuclear stalemate became apparent, the Governments of East and West have adopted the policy which Mr Dulles calls 'brinkmanship'. This is a policy adapted from a sport which, I am told, is practised by the sons of very rich Americans. This sport is called 'Chicken!' It is played by choosing a long straight road with a white line down the middle and starting two very fast cars towards each other from opposite ends. Each car is expected to keep the wheels of one side on the white line. As they approach each other, mutual destruction becomes more and more imminent. If one of them swerves from the white line before the other, the other, as he passes, shouts 'Chicken!', and the one who has swerved becomes an object of contempt. As played by youthful plutocrats, this game is considered decadent and immoral, though only the lives of the players are risked. But when the game is played by eminent statesmen, who risk not only their own lives but those of many hundreds of millions of human beings, it is thought on both sides that the statesmen on one side are displaying a high degree of wisdom and courage, and only the statesmen on the other side are reprehensible. This, of course, is absurd. Both are to blame for playing such an incredibly dangerous game. The game may be played without misfortune a few times, but sooner or later it will come to be felt that loss of face is more dreadful than nuclear annihilation. The moment will come when neither side can face the derisive cry of 'Chicken!' from the other side. When that moment is come, the statesmen of both sides will plunge the world into destruction.

Practical politicians may admit all this, but they argue that there is no alternative. If one side is unwilling to risk global war, while the other side is willing to risk it, the side which is willing to run the risk will be victorious in all negotiations and will ultimately reduce the other side to complete impotence. 'Perhaps'—so the practical politician will argue—'it might be ideally wise for the sane party to yield to the insane party in view of the dreadful nature of the alternative, but, whether wise or not, no proud nation will long acquiesce in such an ignominious role. We are, therefore, faced, quite inevitably, with the choice between brinkmanship and surrender.'

This view has governed policy on both sides in recent years. I cannot admit that brinkmanship and surrender are the only alternatives. What the situation requires is a quite different line of conduct, no longer governed by the motives of the contest for power, but by motives appealing to the common welfare and the common interests of the rival parties. What needs to be done is, first of all, psychological. There must be a change of mood and a change of aim, and this must occur on both sides if it is to achieve its purpose. Possibly the initiative, in so far as it is governmental, may have to come from uncommitted nations; but the general attitude to be desired is one which, in the committed nations of East and West, will have to be first advocated by individuals and groups capable of commanding respect.

The argument to be addressed to East and West alike will have to be something on the following lines. Each side has vital interests which it is not prepared to sacrifice. Neither side can defeat the other except by defeating itself at the same time. The interests in which the two sides conflict are immeasurably less important than those in which they are at one. The first and most important of their common interests is survival. This has become a *common* interest owing to the nature of nuclear weapons.

It might be possible for Americans, or some of them, to desire a world containing no Russians; and it might be possible for Russians, or some of them, to desire a world containing no Americans; but neither Americans nor Russians would desire a world in which both nations had been wiped out. Since it must be assumed that a war between Russia and America would exterminate both, the two countries have a common interest in the preservation of peace. Their common survival should, therefore, be the supreme aim of policy on both sides.

A second motive for agreement is the need to escape from the burdens of the arms race. If present policies continue, this burden will grow greater and greater as time goes on. More and more expensive weapons will be invented, more and more labour will be diverted from the production of consumable commodities to the production of lethal weapons. Before very long, the population in each group will be reduced to subsistence level. New inventions, which in other circumstances might be beneficent, will no longer be so, since every increase in productivity will release more labour for warlike purposes. If one side rebels sooner than the other against the burden of this insanity, it will incur a risk of defeat and, in the bitter atmosphere produced by the dreadful danger, this risk will appear one to be avoided at almost any sacrifice.

It is not only prevention of evils, but the securing of immense goods, that can result from a cessation of tension between the two groups. Scientific technique has become capable of raising the standard of life in every part of the world, and more especially in the poorer parts. There is no reason except human folly for the perpetuation of a lower standard of life in Asia and Africa than that which now prevails in America. But if the arms race continues, the standard of life in America must gradually decline towards the level now prevailing in the poorest parts of the world, and, instead of the universal material well-being which has become technically possible, we shall have a universal poverty as dire as mutual hatreds can cause rival nations to endure.

Nor is it only in material ways that the present hostility of East and West is harmful. It is even more harmful in the sphere of morality and emotion. We have been told on the highest governmental authority that, if Britain became involved in a nuclear war, no serious attempt would be made to defend the civilian population, but those in charge of missiles and bombs to be fired against Russia would be kept alive a little longer than the civilians and could in their last moments cause some hundreds of millions of deaths in Russia. These last survivors would die knowing that their own nation no longer existed, but enjoying (or so one must suppose) the sweet thought of a useless revenge. I am not saying this as a special criticism of British policy. A very similar policy is advocated throughout the two hostile groups. Even religion is often enlisted in its support, and many people sincerely though mistakenly believe that it can be justified by idealistic motives. The mentality which makes such an outlook possible, however sincere it may be, is morally dreadful and poisons all wholesome thought and feeling in those who allow themselves to be dominated by it.

For all these reasons, not only idealistic motives, but the plainest and most insistent motives of self-interest make it imperative that East and West should no longer seek to settle their differences by war or the threat of war. If East and West, alike, can admit the force of the very plain and simple arguments in favour of this conclusion, it will no longer seem impossible to find other methods by which agreements as to disputed matters can be reached. Hitherto, agreements have been difficult because they were not genuinely desired by either side unless they constituted diplomatic victories. But, if it comes to be realized by both sides that it is more important to reach agreements than to win diplomatic victories, it will soon be found that impartial agreements are not nearly so difficult as was thought.

It should be made clear by those who advocate the point of view that I have been trying to recommend that it is a view put forward, not in the special interests of the West or in the special interests of the East, and that it does not aim at giving to either side any advantage not balanced by an equal advantage to the other side. The essential points which both sides must realize are that the continuation of conflict is disastrous to both, and that the gain to both to be derived from concord is one of quite immeasurable magnitude.

(*Common Sense and Nuclear Warfare*, London: Allen & Unwin; New York: Simon & Schuster, 1959.)

THE END